market new to this edition

 Canadian market

 international market

 award-winning market

 indicates a change in address, contact name, phone number, e-mail address, or website from last year's edition

 market places music in film/TV

 market open to beginners' submissions, regardless of past success

 market mostly interested in previously published songwriters/well-established acts, but will consider beginners

 market not interested in submissions from beginners, only from previously published song writers/well-established acts

only accepts material referred to them by a reputable industry source

● comment from the editor of *Writer's Market*

SASE self-addressed, stamped envelope

SAE self-addressed envelope

IRC International Reply Coupon, for use in countries other than your own

(For definitions of words and expressions relating specifically to the music industry, see the Glossary in the back of this book.)

Thank you for purchasing **Songwriter's Market**. Visit SongwritersMarket.com for updates and access to other useful features.

TEAR ALONG PERFORATION

SWM09

2009

SONGWRITER'S MARKET®

Greg Hatfield, Editor

WRITER'S DIGEST BOOKS
CINCINNATI, OH

If you would like to be considered for a listing in the next edition of *Songwriter's Market*, send a SASE (or SAE and IRC) with your request for a questionnaire to *Songwriter's Market*—QR, 4700 East Galbraith Road, Cincinnati, Ohio 45236. Please indicate which section would like to be included.

Editorial Director, Writer's Digest Books: Jane Friedman
Managing Editor, Writer's Digest Market Books: Alice Pope

Songwriter's Market Web page: www.songwritersmarket.com
Writer's Market Web site: www.writersmarket.com
Writer's Digest Web site: www.writersdigest.com
F+W Media Bookstore: http://fwmedia.com

Distributed in Canada by Fraser Direct
100 Armstrong Ave.
Georgetown, ON, Canada L7G 5S4
Tel: (905) 877-4411

Distributed in the U.K. and Europe by David & Charles
Brunel House, Newton Abbot, Devon, TQ12 4PU, England
Tel: (+44) 1626 323200, Fax: (+44) 1626 323319
E-mail: postmaster@davidandcharles.co.uk

Distributed in Australia by Capricorn Link
P.O. Box 704, Windsor, NSW 2756, Australia
Tel: (02) 4577-3555

Distributed in New Zealand by David Bateman Ltd.
P.O. Box 100-242, N.S.M.C., Auckland 1330, New Zealand
Tel: (09) 415-7664, Fax: (09) 415-8892

Distributed in South Africa by Real Books
P.O. Box 1040, Auckland Park 2006, Johannesburg, South Africa
Tel: (011) 837-0643, Fax: (011) 837-0645
E-mail: realbook@global.co.za

ISSN: 0897-9790
ISBN-13: 978-1-58297-547-4
ISBN-10: 1-58297-547-7

Cover design by Claudean Wheeler
Interior design by Clare Finney
Production coordinated by Greg Nock

fw
F+W PUBLICATIONS, INC.

Contents

MARKETS

RESOURCES

INDEXES

From the Editor

"Music writers don't keep no hours—they work when they're inspired. And it ain't just writing the songs that takes time. You have to go around places, and keep in contact with the other boys, so you get new notions. You got to keep getting new notions in this game."

From the play, *June Moon* by Ring Lardner and George S. Kaufman

Mention songwriters and many images are conjured up in the mind. There's the sleeves-rolled-up Broadway composer and lyricist, sweating in a hot New York hotel room, hammering out the next big show tune. There's the youthful exuberance of Lennon and McCartney, huddling in the corner, frantically writing a 2 minute 30 pop masterpiece. Tom Waits wrote that he always thought "songwriters sat alone at upright pianos in cramped smoky little rooms with a bottle and an ashtray." Joan Baez says that when she and Bob Dylan were living in Greenwich Village, Bob would type out his lyrics meticulously on a manual typewriter, usually single spaced, and rarely making any changes afterwards. And entering the phrase "Songwriting is like giving birth" in Google brings more than 104,000 returns from songwriters all over the world who make that statement.

No matter what kind of songwriter you are, you need information at your fingertips on the best way to present your music to producers, publishers, record companies, and other industry professionals. The music business is ever-changing. The delivery format for music is constantly evolving, with the more traditional ways of how we get music (CDs, radio) rapidly being replaced by newer delivery systems (online, video games). Today's successful songwriter has to be cognizant of every opportunity available to him or her and be able to deliver to any market that uses music.

I used the word "conjure" purposefully in my first sentence above. For me, listening to a well-crafted song is like watching a magic trick skillfully done. When completed, it both gives the audience a sense of awe and, for a moment, can transport them to another place in their mind where the imagery takes over.

I hope you succeed in your songwriting and I hope this edition of *Songwriter's Market* gives you the inspiration and the tools you need to help you achieve your goals.

Greg Hatfield
songmarket@fwpubs.com

How To Use *Songwriter's Market*

by Greg Hatfield

Before you dive into the *Songwriter's Market* listings and start submitting songs willy-nilly, it's a good idea to take the time to read the following information. By educating yourself on how to best use this book, you'll be better prepared when you actually do send off your tape or CD.

Let's take a look at what is actually inside *Songwriter's Market*, why these articles were put into the book in the first place and why they can actually help you in your career.

THE ARTICLES

Songwriting, as in every profession, has its own culture. If you're serious about your career, then you're reading everything you can about it. There are magazines, such as *American Songwriter* and *Performing Songwriter* that are published for the songwriter, and other trade publications, such as *Billboard*, that cover news and trends.

This year's *Songwriter's Market* features articles written by both established professionals and new voices. I think it's one of the most balanced group of articles we've published in some time, all designed to help give you an overview of the industry.

We're kicking off the book with "Taking Control of Your Career" (page 35), by Julie Frost. Frost has been in the business for some time now and has done everything from working as an A&R rep (someone who scouts artists and helps with their development) to launching her own label. Her article gives you the inside scoop on how to begin to just think about your career and avoid the mistakes others have made.

Next up is "Web Power: Marketing Yourself Through Social Networking Sites" (page 43), by David McPherson. You don't have to be a genius to know that the Internet has changed everything we know about delivering music to the people. My 14-year-old son can post a YouTube video faster than I can type this sentence. Undoubtedly, you can't expect to have any kind of musical career without knowing how to use the Internet to promote yourself, whether it's through MySpace, Facebook, or your own Web site. McPherson's article will guide you through the World Wide Haze and make things crystal clear.

When you're ready to record that all important first demo, you'll want to check in with Stuart Griffin's article "Top Five Tips for a Successful First Demo" (page 49). Stuart has

---

GREG HATFIELD has been involved in music since his college days, when he produced music for coffeehouses and concerts. He eventually produced concerts on a larger scale featuring all types of musical acts and worked behind the scenes for other music.

boiled down the essential points to the five most important ones and if you follow those tips, then you'll most certainly be ahead of the game.

Let's never forget that songwriting is a business. Many, many songwriters will wish that they had the information you are getting in "Songwriting 101: What Every Songwriter Should (and Probably Doesn't) Know about Music Publishing" (page 52), by Hank Bordowitz. Bordowitz has written several books on music and has been a university professor of music business. His article is a terrific piece to start you on your music business education.

Of course you might be inclined to go to Nashville, where there's still a traditional music industry that is thriving in spite of all the problems plaguing music in all other places. You might be inclined to read "The Real Secret to Success: And Why Nashville Still Matters" (page 57), by Michael Kosser. Michael is a senior editor at *American Songwriter* and he has written over a hundred songs, several of which have been hits. Oh, and he really knows the Nashville scene. Lucky for you.

Outside of Nashville, there is another place where the music scene is hot and that's Miami. Fueled by a new generation of Latin American performers whose influences come from Cuba, Venezuela, Mexico, and Columbia, Florida music beat writer John Anderson writes all about it in his article, "The Latin Music Scene: It's Hot, Hot, Hot in Miami, Baby!" (page 63).

And from a local scene with international flavor we move to a look "Across the Pond: International Opportunities for Songwriters" (page 68), by Maureen O'Donnell. O'Donnell has worked in the business on both sides of the Atlantic and her article offers yet another way for songwriter's to get their work noticed.

Two great interviews round out this edition of *Songwriter's Market*. First you'll hear from experienced producer Adam Moseley in "Adam Moseley: Producer/Engineer Is Best Collaborator a Songwriter Can Have" (page 74), by Shelley Marie Marks. Marks details exactly what happens when noted producer and arranger Moseley (Rush, The Cure, Blow Monkeys) hears a song for the first time and how he works with the songwriter to get the most out of a song. It's the next best thing to having an established producer take a listen to your work.

Finally, it wouldn't be *Songwriter's Market* without an exclusive interview with some of the greats of the business. Ken Sharp, who writes for *Goldmine*, among other publications, and has written 10 books on music, gives us "Kenny Gamble & Leon Huff: Hall of Famers on Their Remarkable Career" (page 79). Known as being the creators of the "Philly Sound," Gamble and Huff are truly geniuses in the world of songwriting.

THE LISTINGS

Beyond the articles, there are 11 sections in the book, from Music Publishers and Record Companies to Contests & Awards. Each section begins with an introduction detailing how the different types of companies function—what part of the music industry they work in, how they make money, and what you need to think about when approaching them with your music.

These listings are the heart of *Songwriter's Market*. They are the names, addresses and contact information of music biz companies looking for songs and artists, as well as descriptions of the types of music they are looking for.

So how do I use *Songwriter's Market*?

The quick answer is that you should use the indexes to find companies who are interested in your type of music, then read the listings for details on how they want the music submitted. For support and help of all sorts, join a songwriting or other music industry association. Read everything you can about songwriting. Talk to other songwriters. That's a good start.

How does *Songwriter's Market* 'work'?

The listings in *Songwriter's Market* are packed with a lot of information. It can be intimidating at first, but they are put together in a structured way to make them easy to work with. Take a few minutes to get used to how the listings are organized, and you'll have it down in no time. For more detailed information about how the listings are put together, skip ahead to "Where Should I Send My Songs?" on page 6.

The following are general rules about how to use the listings:

1. **Read the entire listing** to decide whether to submit your music. Please do not use this book as a mass mailing list. If you blindly mail out demos by the hundreds, you'll waste a lot of money on postage, annoy a lot of people, and your demos will wind up in the trash anyway.
2. **Pay close attention to the "Music" section in each listing.** This will tell you what kind of music the company is looking for. If they want rockabilly only and you write heavy metal, don't submit to that company. That's just common sense.
3. **Pay close attention to submission instructions** shown under "How to Contact" and follow them to the letter. A lot of listings are very particular about how they want submissions packaged. Pay close attention. If you do not follow their instructions, they will probably throw your submission in the garbage. If you are confused about their directions, contact the company for clarification.
4. **If in doubt, contact the company for permission to submit.** This is a good general rule. Many companies don't mind if you send an unsolicited submission, but some will want you to get special prior permission from them. Contacting a company first is also a good way to find out their latest music needs. This is also a chance to briefly make contact on a personal level.
5. **Be courteous, be efficient and always have a purpose** to your personal contact. Do not waste their time. If you call, always have a reason for making contact— permission to submit, checking on guidelines, following up on a demo, etc. These are solid reasons to make personal contact, but once you have their attention, do not wear out your welcome. Always be polite.
6. **Check for a preferred contact.** A lot of listings have a designated contact person shown after a bolded "Contact" in the heading. This is the person you should contact with questions or to whom you should address your submission.
7. **Read the "Tips" section.** This part of the listing provides extra information on how to submit or what it might be like to work with the company. This is just the beginning. For more detailed information about the listings, see "Where Should I Send My Songs?" on page 6 and the sidebar with the sample listing called "A Sample Listing Decoded" on page 8.

FREQUENTLY ASKED QUESTIONS

How do these companies get listed in the book anyway?

No company pays to be included—all listings are free. The listings come from a combination of research the editor does on the music industry and questionnaires requested by companies who want to be listed (many of them contact us to be included). All questionnaires are screened for known sharks and to make sure they meet our requirements.

Why aren't other companies I know about listed in the book?

We may have sent them a questionnaire, but they did not return it, were removed for complaints, went out of business, specifically asked not to be listed, could not be contacted for an update, etc.

What's the deal with companies that don't take unsolicited submissions?

In the interest of completeness, the editor will sometimes include listings of crucial music companies and major labels he thinks you should be aware of. We want you to at least have some idea of what their policies are.

A company said in their listing they take unsolicited submissions. My demo came back unopened. What happened?

Some companies' needs change rapidly and may have changed since we contacted them for this edition of the book. This is another reason why it's often a good idea to contact a company before submitting.

So that's it. You now have the power in your fingertips to go out and become the professional songwriter you always wanted to be. Let us know how you're doing. Drop us a line at info@songwritersmarket.com and tell us about any successes you have had because you used the materials found in this book.

Getting Started

Where Should I Send My Songs?

I t depends a lot on whether you write mainly for yourself as a performer, or if you only write and want someone else to pick up your song for their recording (usually the case in country music, for example). *Are you mainly a performing songwriter or a non-performing songwriter?* This is important for figuring out what kind of companies to contact, as well as how you contact them. (For more detail, skip to Submission Strategies on page 20.)

What if I'm a non-performing songwriter?

Many well-known songwriters are not performers in their own right. Some are not skilled instrumentalists or singers, but they understand melody, lyrics and harmony and how they go together. They can write great songs, but they need someone else to bring it to life through skilled musicianship. A non-performing songwriter will usually approach music publishers first for access to artists looking for songs, as well as artists' managers, their producers and their record companies. On the flip side, many incredibly talented musicians can't write to save their lives and need someone else to provide them with good songs to perform. (For more details on the different types of companies and the roles they play for performing songwriters, see the section introductions for Music Publishers on page 88, Record Companies on page 133, Record Producers on page 180, and Managers & Booking Agents on page 203. Also see Submission Strategies on page 20.)

What if I am a performing songwriter?

Many famous songwriters are also famous as performers. They are skilled interpreters of their own material, and they also know how to write to suit their own particular talents as musicians. In this case, their intention is also usually to sell themselves as a performer in hopes of recording and releasing an album, or they have an album and want to find gigs and people who can help guide their careers. They will usually approach record companies or record producers first, on the basis of recording an album. For gigs and career guidance, they talk to booking agents and managers.

A smaller number also approach publishers in hopes of getting others to perform their songs, much like non-performing songwriters. Some music publishers in recent years have also taken on the role of developing artists as both songwriters and performers, or are connected to a major record label, so performing songwriters might go to them for these reasons. (For more details on the different types of companies and the roles they play for performing songwriters, see the section introductions for Music Publishers on page 88, Record Companies on page 133, Record Producers on page 180, and Managers & Booking Agents on page 203. Also see Submission Strategies on page 20.)

How do I use *Songwriter's Market* to narrow my search?

Once you've identified whether you are primarily interested in getting others to perform your songs (non-performing songwriter) or you perform your own songs and want a record deal, etc., there are several steps you can then take:

1. **Identify what kind of music company you wish to approach.** Based on whether you're a performing or non-performing songwriter, do you want to approach a music publisher for a publishing deal? Do you want to approach a record producer because you need somone to help you record an album in the studio? Maybe you want to approach a producer in hopes that an act he's producing needs songs to complete their album. Also see "Submission Strategies" on page 20 and the Section Introductions for Music Publishers on page 88, Record Companies on page 133, Record Producers on page 180, and Managers & Booking Agents on page 203.

2. **Check for companies based on location.** Maybe you need a manager located close by. Maybe you need to find as many Nashville-based companies as you can because you write country and most country publishers are in Nashville. In this case start with the Geographic Index on page 390. You can also tell Canadian and Foreign listings by the icons in the listing (see "A Sample Listing Decoded" on page 8).

3. **Look for companies based on the type of music they want.** Some companies want country. Some record labels want only punk rock. Check the Category Indexes on page 359 for a list of music companies broken down by the type of music they are interested in.

4. **Look for companies based on how open they are to beginners.** Some companies are more open than others to beginning artists and songwriters. Maybe you are a beginner and it would help to approach these companies first. Some music publishers are hoping to find that wild card hit song and don't care if it comes from an unknown writer. Maybe you are just starting out looking for gigs or record deals, and you need a manager willing to help build your band's career from the ground up. Check the Openness to Submissions Index on page 382.

For more information on how to read the listings, see "A Sample Listing Decoded" on page 8.

Types of Music Companies

- **Music Publishers**—evaluate songs for commercial potential, find artists to record them, finds other uses for the songs such as film or TV, collects income from songs, protects copyrights from infringement

- **Record Companies**—sign artists to their labels, finance recordings, promotion and touring, releases songs/albums to radio and TV

- **Record Producers**—works in the studio and records songs (independently or for a record company), may be affiliated with a particular artist, sometimes develop artists for record labels, locates or co-writes songs if an artist does not write their own

- **Managers & Booking Agents**—works with artists to manage their careers, finds gigs, locates songs to record if the artist does not write their own

A SAMPLE LISTING DECODED
What do the little symbols at the beginning of the listing mean?

Those are called "icons," and they give you quick information about a listing with one glance. Here is a list of the icons and what they mean:

Openness to submissions

◻   means the company is open to beginners' submissions, regardless of past success

◪   means the company is mostly interested in previously published songwriters/well-established acts*, but will consider beginners

◖   these companies do not want submissions from beginners, only from previously published songwriters/well-established acts*

◉   companies with this icon only accept material referred by a reputable industry source**

*   Well-established acts are those with a following, permanent gigs or previous record deal

**   Reputable industry sources include managers, entertainment attorneys, performing rights organizations, etc.

Other icons

❖   means the listing is Canadian

⊕   means the listing is based overseas (Europe, Britain, Australia, etc.)

Ⓝ   indicates a listing is new to this edition

☑   means there has been a change in the contact information: contact name, phone number, fax, e-mail or Web site

$ is for companies who have won an industry award of some sort

▨   shows a company places songs in films or television shows (excluding commercials)

EASY-TO-USE REFERENCE ICONS

DETAILED SUBMISSION GUIDELINES

INSIDER ADVICE

TERMS OF AGREEMENT

WHAT THEY'RE LOOKING FOR

Ⓝ◪▨☑ **METAL BLADE RECORDS** 2828 Cochran St., Suite 302, Simi Valley CA 93065. (805)522-9111. Fax: (805)522-9380. E-mail: metalblade@metalblade.com. Website: www.metalblade.com. Record company. Estab. 1982. Releases 20 LPs, 2 EPs and 20 CDs/year. Pays negotiable royalty to artists on contract.

How to Contact Submit demo CD by mail. Unsolicited submissions are OK. CD with 3 songs. Does not return material. Responds in 3 months.

Music Mostly **heavy metal** and **industrial;** also **hardcore, gothic** and **noise.** Released "Gallery of Suicide," recorded by Cannibal Corpse; "Voo Doo," recorded by King Diamond; and "A Pleasant Shade of Gray," recorded by Fates Warning, all on Metal Blade Records. Other artists include As I Lay Dying, The Red Chord, The Black Dahlia Murder, and Unearth.

Tips "Metal Blade is known throughout the underground for quality metal-oriented acts."

Additional Resources

For More Info

Songwriter's Market lists music publishers, record companies, producers and managers (as well as advertising firms, play producers and classical performing arts organizations) along with specifications on how to submit your material to each. If you can't find a certain person or company you're interested in, there are other sources of information you can try.

The Recording Industry Sourcebook, an annual directory published by Norris-Whitney Communications, lists record companies, music publishers, producers and managers, as well as attorneys, publicity firms, media, manufacturers, distributors and recording studios around the U.S. Trade publications such as *Billboard* or *Variety*, available at most local libraries and bookstores, are great sources for up-to-date information. These periodicals list new companies as well as the artists, labels, producers and publishers for each song on the charts.

CD booklets can also be valuable sources of information, providing the name of the record company, publisher, producer and usually the manager of an artist or group. Use your imagination in your research and be creative—any contacts you make in the industry can only help your career as a songwriter. See Publications of Interest on page 339.

Getting Started

Demo Recordings

What Should I Know?

What is a "demo"?

The demo, shorthand for *demonstration recording*, is the most important part of your submission package. They are meant to give music industry professionals a way to hear all the elements of your song as clearly as possible so they can decide if it has commercial potential.

Should I send a cassette or a CD?

More and more music industry people want CDs, although the cassette is still commonly accepted. A few companies want demos sent on CD only. It's getting cheaper and easier all the time to burn recordings onto CDR ("CD-Recordable"), so it is worth the investment to buy a burner or borrow one. Other formats such as DAT ("Digital Audio Tape") are rarely requested.

What should I send if I'm seeking management?

Some companies want a video of an act performing their songs. Check with the companies for specific requirements.

How many songs should I send, and in what order and length?

Most music industry people agree that three songs is enough. Most music professionals are short on time, and if you can't catch their attention in three songs, your songs probably don't have hit potential. Also, put three *complete songs* on your demo, not just snippets. Make sure to put your best, most commercial song first. An up-tempo number is usually best. If you send a cassette, *put all the songs on one side of the cassette and cue the tape to the beginning of the first song so no time is wasted fast-forwarding or rewinding.*

Should I sing my own songs on my demo?

If you can't sing well, you may want to find someone who can. There are many places to check for singers and musicians, including songwriters organizations, music stores, and songwriting magazines. Some aspiring professional singers will sing on demos in exchange for a copy they can use as a demo to showcase their singing.

Should I use a professional demo service?

Many songwriters find professional demo services convenient if they don't have time or the resources to put together musicians on their own. For a fee, a demo service will produce your songs in their studio using in-house singers and musicians (this is pretty common in Nashville). Many of these advertise in music magazines, songwriting newsletters and bulletin boards at music stores. Make sure to hear samples of work they've done in the past. Some are mail-order businesses—you send a rough tape of your song or the sheet music, and they produce and record a demo within a month or two. Be sure you find a service that will let you have some control over how the demo is produced, and tell them exactly how you want your song to sound. As with studios, look around for a service that fits your needs and budget. (Some will charge as low as $300 for three songs, while others may go as high as $3,000 and boast a high-quality sound—*shop around and use your best judgment!*)

Should I buy equipment and record demos myself?

If you have the drive and focus to learn good recording technique, yes. If not, it might be easier to have someone else do it. Digital multi-track recorders are now easily available and within reasonable financial reach of many people. For performing songwriters in search of record deals, the actual sound of their recordings can often be an important part of their artistic concept. Having the "means of production" within their grasp can be crucial to artists pursuing the independent route. But, if you don't know how to use the equipment, it may be better to go into a professional studio.

How elaborate and full should the demo production be if I'm a non-performing songwriter?

Many companies in *Songwriter's Market* tell you what they prefer. If in doubt, contact them and ask. In general, country songs and pop ballads can often be demoed with just a vocal plus guitar or piano, although many songwriters in those genres still prefer to get a more complete recording with drums, guitars and other backing instruments. Up-tempo pop, rock and dance demos usually need a more full production.

What kind of production do I need if I'm a performing songwriter?

If you are a band or artist looking for a record deal, you will need a demo that is as fully produced as possible. Many singer/songwriters record their demos as if they were going to be released as an album. That way, if they don't get a deal, they can still release it on their own. Professionally pressed CDs are also now easily within reach of performing songwriters, and many companies offer graphic design services for a professional-looking product.

How Do I Submit My Demo?

You have three basic options for submitting your songs: submitting by mail, submitting in person and submitting over the Internet (the newest and least widely accepted option at this time).

SUBMITTING BY MAIL

Should I call, write or e-mail first to ask for permission or submission requirements?

This is always a good idea, and many companies ask you to contact them first. If you call, be polite, brief and specific. If you send a letter, make sure it is typed and to the point. Include a typed SASE they can use to reply. If you send an e-mail, again be professional and to the point. Proofread your message before you send it, and then be patient. Give them some time to reply. Do not send out mass e-mails or otherwise spam their e-mail account.

What do I send with my demo?

Most companies have specific requirements, but here are some general pointers:

- Read the listing carefully and submit *exactly* what they ask for, in the exact way they describe. It's also a good idea to call first, just in case they've changed their submission policies.
- Listen to each demo to make sure they sound right and are in the right order (see Demo Recordings: What Should I Know? on page 10).
- If you use cassettes, make sure they are cued up to the beginning of the first song.
- Enclose a *brief*, typed cover letter to introduce yourself. Tell them what songs you are sending and why you are sending them. If you are pitching your songs to a particular artist, say so in the letter. If you are an artist/songwriter looking for a record deal, you should say so. Be specific.
- Include *typed* lyric sheets or lead sheets, if requested. Make sure your name, address and phone number are on each sheet.
- Neatly label each tape or CD with your name, address, e-mail and phone number, along with the names of the songs in the order they appear on the recording.
- Include a SASE with sufficient postage and large enough to return all your materials. **Warning: Many companies do not return materials, so read each listing carefully!**
- If you submit to companies in other countries, include a self-addressed envelope (SAE) and International Reply Coupon (IRC), available at most post offices. Make sure the envelope is large enough to return all of your materials.
- Pack everything neatly. Neatly type or write the company's address and your return

Submission Mailing Pointers

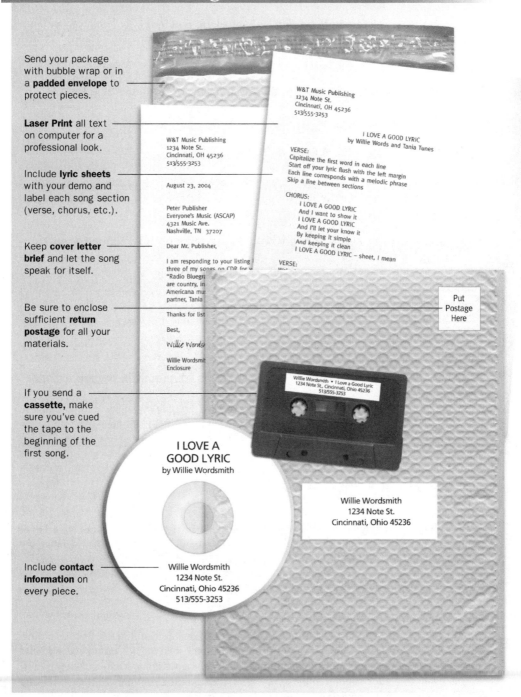

Send your package with bubble wrap or in a **padded envelope** to protect pieces.

Laser Print all text on computer for a professional look.

Include **lyric sheets** with your demo and label each song section (verse, chorus, etc.).

Keep **cover letter brief** and let the song speak for itself.

Be sure to enclose sufficient **return postage** for all your materials.

If you send a **cassette,** make sure you've cued the tape to the beginning of the first song.

Include **contact information** on every piece.

W&T Music Publishing
1234 Note St.
Cincinnati, OH 45236
513/555-3253

I LOVE A GOOD LYRIC
by Willie Words and Tania Tunes

VERSE:
Capitalize the first word in each line
Start off your lyric flush with the left margin
Each line corresponds with a melodic phrase
Skip a line between sections

CHORUS:
I LOVE A GOOD LYRIC
And I want to show it
I LOVE A GOOD LYRIC
And I'll let your know it
By keeping it simple
And keeping it clean
I LOVE A GOOD LYRIC – sheet, I mean

VERSE:

W&T Music Publishing
1234 Note St.
Cincinnati, OH 45236
513/555-3253

August 23, 2004

Peter Publisher
Everyone's Music (ASCAP)
4321 Music Ave.
Nashville, TN 37207

Dear Mr. Publisher,

I am responding to your listing
three of my songs on CDR for
"Radio Bluegr
are country, in
Americana mu
partner, Tania

Thanks for list

Best,

Willie Words

Willie Wordsmit
Enclosure

Put Postage Here

Willie Wordsmith • I Love a Good Lyric
1234 Note St., Cincinnati, Ohio 45236
513/555-3253

Willie Wordsmith
1234 Note St.
Cincinnati, Ohio 45236

I LOVE A
GOOD LYRIC
by Willie Wordsmith

Willie Wordsmith
1234 Note St.
Cincinnati, Ohio 45236
513/555-3253

address so they are clearly visible. Your package is the first impression a company has of you and your songs, so neatness counts!

- Mail first class. Stamp or write "First Class Mail" on the package and the SASE you enclose.
- **Do not use registered or certified mail unless requested!** Most companies will not accept or open demos sent by registered or certified mail for fear of lawsuits.
- Keep records of the dates, songs and companies you submit to.

Is it OK to send demos to more than one person or company at a time?

It is usually acceptable to make simultaneous submissions. One exception is when a publisher, artist or other industry professional asks to put your song "on hold."

What does it mean when a song is "on hold"?

This means they intend to record the song and don't want you to give the song to anyone else. This is not a guarantee, though. Your song may eventually be returned to you, even if it's been on hold for months. Or it may be recorded and included on the album. If either of these happens, you are free to pitch your song to other people again.

How can I protect myself from my song being put "on hold" indefinitely?

You can, and should, protect yourself. Establish a deadline for the person who asks for the hold (for example, "You can put my song on hold for [number of] months."), or modify the hold to specify you will still pitch the song to others but won't sign another deal without allowing the person with the song on hold to make you an offer. Once you sign a contract with a publisher, they have exclusive rights to your song and you may not pitch it to other would-be publishers.

SUBMITTING IN PERSON

Is a visit to New York, Nashville or Los Angeles to submit in person a good idea?

A trip to one of the major music hubs can be valuable if you are organized and prepared to make the most of it. You should have specific goals and set up appointments before you go. Some industry professionals are difficult to see and may not feel meeting out-of-town writers is a high priority. Others are more open and even encourage face-to-face meetings. By taking the time to travel, organize and schedule meetings, you can appear more professional than songwriters who submit blindly through the mail.

What should I take?

Take several copies of your demo and typed lyric sheets of each of your songs. More than one company you visit may ask you to leave a copy for them to review. You can expect occasionally to find a person has cancelled an appointment, but want you to leave a copy of your songs so they may listen and contact you later. (Never give someone the only or last copy of your demo if you absolutely want it returned, though.)

Where should I network while visiting?

Coordinate your trip with a music conference or make plans to visit ASCAP, BMI, or SESAC offices while you are there. For example, the South by Southwest Music Conference in Austin and the NSAI Spring Symposium often feature demo listening sessions, where industry professionals listen to demos submitted by songwriters attending the seminar. ASCAP, BMI, and SESAC also sometimes sponsor seminars or allow aspiring songwriters to make appointments with counselors who can give them solid advice.

How do I deal with rejection?

Many good songs have been rejected simply because they were not what the publisher or record company was looking for at that particular point. Do not take it personally. If few people like your songs, it does not mean they are not good. On the other hand, if you have a clear vision for what your particular songs are trying to get across, specific comments can also teach you a lot about whether your concept is coming across as you intended. If you hear the same criticisms of your songs over and over—for instance, the feel of the melody isn't right or the lyrics need work—give the advice serious thought. Listen carefully and use what the reviewers say constructively to improve your songs.

SUBMITTING OVER THE INTERNET
Is it OK to submit over the Internet?

It can be done, but it's not yet widely accepted. There can still be problems with audio file formats. Although e-mail is more common now if you look through the listings in *Songwriter's Market*, not all music companies are necessarily equipped with computers or Internet access sufficient to make the process easy. But it shows a lot of promise for the future. Web-based companies like Tonos.com or TAXI, among many others are making an effort to connect songwriters and industry professionals over the Internet. The Internet is proving important for networking. Garageband.com has extensive bulletin boards and allow members to post audio files of songs for critique. Stay tuned for future developments.

If I want to try submitting over the Internet, what should I do?

First, send an e-mail to confirm whether a music company is equipped to stream or download audio files properly (whether mp3 or real audio, etc.). If they do accept demos online, one strategy becoming common is build a Web site with audio files that can be streamed or downloaded. Then, when you have permission, send an e-mail with links to that Web site or to particular songs. All they have to do is click on the link and it launches their Web browser to the appropriate page. Do not try to send mp3s or other files as attachments. They are often too large for the free online e-mail accounts people commonly use, and they may be mistakenly erased as potential viruses.

How Do I Avoid the Rip-Offs?

The music industry has its share of dishonest, greedy people who will try to rip you off by appealing to your ambition, by stroking your ego, or by claiming special powers to make you successful—for a price, of course. Most of them use similar methods, and you can prevent a lot of heartbreak by learning to spot them and stay away.

What is a "song shark"?

"Song sharks," as they're called, prey on beginners—songwriters unfamiliar with how the music industry works and what the ethical standards are. Two general signs of a song shark are:

- Song sharks will take *any* songs—quality doesn't count.
- They're not concerned with future royalties, since they get their money up front from songwriters who think they're getting a great deal.

What are some of the more blatant rip-offs?

A request for money up front is the most common element. Song sharks may ask for money in the form of submission fees, an outright offer to publish your song for a fee or an offer to re-record your demo for a sometimes hefty price (with the implication that they will make your song wildly successful if you only pay to have it re-demoed in *their studio*). There are many variations on this theme.

If You Write Lyrics, But Not Music

- **You must find a collaborator.** The music business is looking for the complete package: music plus lyrics. If you don't write music, find a collaborator who does. The best way to find a collaborator is through songwriting organizations. Check the Organizations section (page 291) for songwriting groups near you.

- **Don't get ripped-off.** "Music mills" advertise in the back of magazines or solicit you through the mail. For a fee they will set your lyrics or poems to music. The rip-off is that they may use the same melody for hundreds of lyrics and poems, whether it sounds good or not. Publishers recognize one of these melodies as soon as they hear it.

Here is a list of rules that can help you avoid a lot of scams:

- **DO NOT SELL YOUR SONGS OUTRIGHT!** It's unethical for anyone to offer such a proposition. If your song becomes successful after you've sold it outright, you will never get royalties for it.
- **Never pay any sort of "submission fees," "review fees," "service fees," "filing fees," etc.** Reputable companies review material free of charge. If you encounter a company in this book who charges to submit, report them to the editor. If a company charges "only" $15 to submit your song, consider this: *if "only" 100 songwriters pay the $15, this company has made an extra $1,500 just for opening the mail!*
- **Never pay to have your songs published.** A reputable company interested in your songs assumes the responsibility and cost of promoting them, in hopes of realizing a profit once the songs are recorded and released. If they truly believe in your song, they will accept the costs involved.
- **Do not pay a company to pair you with a collaborator.** It's much better to contact a songwriting organization that offers collaboration services to their members.
- **Never pay to have your lyrics or poems set to music.** This is a classic rip-off. "Music mills"—for a price—may use the same melody for hundreds of lyrics and poems, whether it sounds good or not. Publishers recognize one of these melodies as soon as they hear it.
- **Avoid "pay-to-play" CD compilation deals.** It's totally unrealistic to expect this will open doors for you. These are mainly a money-maker for the music company. CDs are cheap to manufacture, so a company that charges $100 to include your recording on a CD is making a killing. They claim they send these CDs to radio stations, producers, etc., but they usually wind up in the trash or as drink coasters. Music industry professionals have no incentive to listen to them. Everybody on the CD paid to be included, so it's not like they were carefully screened for quality.
- **Avoid "songpluggers" who offer to "shop" your song for an upfront fee or retainer.** This practice is not appropriate for *Songwriter's Market* readers, many of whom are beginners and live away from major music centers like Nashville. Professional, established songwriters in Nashville are sometimes known to work on a fee basis with songpluggers they have gotten to know over many years, *but the practice is controversial even for professionals.* Also, the songpluggers used by established professionals are very selective about their clients and have their own reputation to uphold. Companies who offer you these services but barely know you or your work are to be avoided. Also, contracting a songplugger by long distance offers little or no accountability—you have no direct way of knowing what they're doing on your behalf.
- **Avoid paying a fee up front to have a publisher make a demo of your song.** Some publishers may take demo expenses out of your future royalties (a negotiable contract point usually meant to avoid endless demo sessions), but avoid paying up front for demo costs. Avoid situations where it is implied or expressed that a company will publish your song in return for you paying up front to use their demo services.
- **No record company should ask you to pay them or an associated company to make a demo.** The job of a record company is to make records and decide which artists to sign *after* listening to demo submissions.
- **Read all contracts carefully before signing.** And don't sign any contract you're unsure about or that you don't fully understand. It is well worth paying an attorney for the time it takes him to review a contract if you can avoid a bad situation that may cost you thousands of dollars.
- **Before entering a songwriting contest, read the rules carefully.** Be sure what you're

giving up in the way of entry fees, etc., is not more than what you stand to gain by winning the contest. See the Contests & Awards section on page 276.

- **Verify any situation about an individual or company if you have any doubts at all.** Contact the company's Performing Rights Society—ASCAP, BMI, SESAC, or SOCAN (in Canada). Check with the Better Business Bureau in the company's town, or contact the state attorney general's office. Contact professional organizations you're a member of and inquire about the reputation of the company.

- **If a record company or other company asks you to pay expenses up front, be careful.** Record producers commonly charge up front to produce an artist's album. Small indie labels sometimes ask a band to help with recording costs (but seek less control than a major label might). It's up to you to decide whether or not it is a good idea. Talk to other artists who have signed similar contracts before you sign one yourself. Research companies to find out if they can deliver on their claims, and what kind of distribution they have. Visit their Web site, if they have one. Beware of any company that won't let you know what it has done in the past. If a company has had successes and good working relationships with artists, it should be happy to brag about them.

I noticed record producers charge to produce albums. Is this bad?

Not automatically. Just remember what your goals are. If you write songs, but do not sing or perform, you are looking for publishing opportunities with the producer instead of someone who can help you record an album or CD. If you are a performing artist or band, then you might be in the market to hire a producer, in which case you will most likely pay them up front (and possibly give them a share in royalties or publishing, depending on the specific deal you negotiate). For more information see the Record Producers section introduction on page 180 and Royalties: Where Does the Money Come From? on page 23.

Will it help me avoid rip-offs if I join a songwriting organization?

Yes. You will have access to a lot of good advice from a lot of experienced people. You will be able to research and compare notes, which will help you avoid a lot of pitfalls.

What should I know about contracts?

Negotiating a fair contract is important. You must protect yourself, and there are specific things you should look for in a contract (see What About Contracts? on page 31).

How Do I File a Complaint?

Write to the *Songwriter's Market* editor at: 4700 E. Galbraith Rd., Cincinnati OH 45236. Include:

- A complete description of the situation, as best you can describe it.

- Copies of any materials a company may have sent you that we may keep on file.

If you encounter situations similar to any of the "song shark" scenarios described above, let us know about it.

Are companies that offer demo services automatically bad?

No, but you are not obligated to make use of their services. Many music companies have their own or related recording studios, and with good recording equipment becoming so cheap and easy to use in recent years, a lot of them are struggling to stay afloat. This doesn't mean a company is necessarily trying to rip you off, but use your best judgment. In some cases, a company will submit a listing to *Songwriter's Market* for the wrong reasons—to pitch their demo services instead of finding songs to sign—in which case you should report them to the *Songwriter's Market* editor.

Submission Strategies

NON-PERFORMING SONGWRITERS

Here's a short list of avenues non-performing songwriters can pursue when submitting songs:

1. Submit to a music publisher. This is the obvious one. Look at the information under "**Music**" in the listing to see examples of a publisher's songs and the artists they've found cuts with. Do you recognize the songs? Have you heard of the artists? Who are the writers? Do they have cuts with artists you would like to get a song to?

2. Submit to a record company. Are the bands and artists on the record company's roster familiar? Do they tend to use outside songs on their albums? When pursuing this angle, it often helps to contact the record company first. Ask if they have a group or artist in development who needs material.

3. Submit to a record producer. Do the producer's credits in the listings show songs written by songwriters other than the artist? Does he produce name artists known for using outside material? Be aware that producers themselves often write with the artists, so your song might also be competing against the producer's songwriting.

4. Submit to an artist's manager. If an artist needs songs, their manager is a prime gateway for your song. Contact the manager and ask if he has an act in need of material.

5. Join a songwriting organization. Songwriting organizations are a good way to make contacts. You'll discover opportunities through the contacts you make that others might not hear about. Some organizations can put you in direct contact with publishers for song critique sessions. You can increase your chances of a hit by co-writing with other songwriters. Your songs will get better because of the feedback from other members.

6. Approach Performing Rights Organizations (PROs). PROs like ASCAP and BMI have writer relations representatives who can sometimes (if they think you're ready) give you a reference to a music company. This is one of the favored routes to success in the Nashville music scene.

PERFORMING SONGWRITERS

This is a bit more complicated, because there are a lot of different avenues available.

Finding a record deal.

This is often a performing songwriter's primary goal—to get a record deal and release an album. Here are some possible ways to approach it:

1. Approach a record company for a record deal. This is another obvious one. Independent labels will be a lot more approachable than major labels, who are usually deluged with demos. Independent labels give you more artistic freedom, while major labels will demand more compromise, especially if you do not have a previous track record. A compromise between the two is to approach one of the "fake indie" labels owned by a major. You'll get more of the benefits of an indie, but with more of the resources and connections of a major label.

2. Approach a record producer for a development deal. Some producers sign artists, produce their album and develop them like a record company, and then approach major labels for distribution deals. This has advantages and drawbacks. For example, the producer gives you guidance and connections, but it can also be harder to get paid because you are signed to the producer and not the label.

3. Get a manager with connections. The right manager with the right connections can make all the difference in getting a record deal.

4. Ask a music publisher. Publishers are taking on more and more of a role of developing performing songwriters as artists. Many major publishers are sister companies to record labels and can shop you for a deal when they think you're ready. They do this in hopes of participating in the mechanical royalties from an album release, and these monies can be substantial when it's a major label release.

5. Approach an entertainment attorney. Entertainment attorneys are a must when it comes to negotiating record contracts, and some moonlight by helping artists make connections for record deals (they will get their cut, of course).

6. Approach PROs. ASCAP and BMI can counsel you on your career and possibly make a referral. They also commonly put on performance showcases where A&R ("artist and repertoire") people from record labels attend to check out new artists.

Finding a producer to help with your album

Independently minded performing songwriters often find they need help navigating the studio when it comes time to produce their own album. In this case, the producer often works for an upfront fee from the artist, for a percentage of the royalty when the album is released and sold (referred to as "points," as in "percentage points"), or a combination of both.

Things to keep in mind when submitting a demo to a producer on this basis:

1. Is the producer known for a particular genre or "sound"? Many producers have a signature sound to their studio productions and are often connected to specific genres. Phil Spector had the "Wall of Sound." Bob Rock pioneered a glossy metal sound for Metallica and The Cult. Daniel Lanois and Brian Eno are famous for the atmospheres they created on albums by U2. Look at your favorite CDs to see who produced. Use these as touchstones when approaching producers to see if they are on your wavelength.

2. What role does a particular producer like to take in the studio? The "Tips" section of *Songwriter's Market* Record Producers listings often have notes from the producer about how they like to work with performing songwriters in the studio. Some work closely as a partner with the artist on developing arrangements and coaching performances. Some prefer final authority on creative decisions. Think carefully about what kind of working relationship you want.

Finding a manager

Many performing songwriters eventually find it necessary to find a manager to help with developing their careers and finding gigs. Some things to keep in mind when looking:

1. Does the manager work with artists in my genre of music? A manager who typically works with punk rock bands may not have as many connections useful to an aspiring country singer-songwriter. A manager who mainly works with gospel artists might not know what to do with a hedonistic rock band.

2. How big is the manager's agency? If a manager is working with multiple acts, but has a small (or no) staff, you might not get the attention you want. Some of the listings have information in the heading about the agency's staff size.

3. Does the manager work with acts from my region? You can check the Geographic Index on page 390 to check for management agencies located near your area. Many of the listings also have information in their headings provided by the companies describing whether they work with regional acts only or artists from any region.

4. Does the manager work with name acts? A manager with famous clients could work wonders for your career. Or you could get lost in the shuffle. Use your best judgment when sizing up a potential manager and be clear with yourself about the kind of relationship you would like to have and the level of attention you want for your career.

5. If I'm a beginner, will the manager work with me? Look in the Openness to Submissions Index on page 382 to find companies open to beginners. Some may suggest extensive changes to your music or image. On the other hand, you may have a strong vision of what you want to do and need a manager who will work with you to achieve that vision instead of changing you around. Decide for yourself how much you are willing to compromise in good faith.

Remember that a relationship between you and a manager is a two-way street. You will have to earn each other's trust and be clear about your goals for mutual success.

Royalties

Where Does the Money Come From?

NON-PERFORMING SONGWRITERS

How do songwriters make money?

The quick answer is that songwriters make money through rights available to them through the copyright laws. For more details, keep reading and see the article "What About Copyright?" on page 27.

What specific rights make money for songwriters?

There are two primary ways songwriters earn money on their songs: Performance Royalties and Mechanical Royalties.

What is a performance royalty?

When you hear a song on the radio, on television, in the elevator, in a restaurant, etc. the songwriter receives royalties, called "Performance Royalties." Performing Rights Organizations (ASCAP, BMI and SESAC in the U.S.A.) collect payment from radio stations, television, etc. and distribute those payments to songwriters (see below).

What is a mechanical royalty?

When a record company puts a song onto a CD, cassette, etc. and distributes copies for sale, they owe a royalty payment to the songwriter for each copy they press of the album. It is called a "mechanical royalty" because of the mechanical process used to mass produce a copy of a CD, cassette or sheet music. The payment is small per song (see the "Royalty Provisions" subhead of the Basic Song Contract Pointers sidebar on page 33), but the earnings can add up and reach massive proportions for songs appearing on successful major label albums. ****Note: This royalty is totally different from the artist royalty on the retail price of the album.****

Who collects the money for performance and mechanical royalties?

Performing Rights Organizations collect performance royalties. There are three organizations that collect performance royalties: ASCAP, BMI and SESAC. These organizations arose many years ago when songwriters and music publishers gathered together to press for their rights and improve their ability to collect fees for the use of their songs. ASCAP, BMI and SESAC collect fees for the use of songs and then pass along the money to their member songwriters and music publishers.

Mechanical rights organizations collect mechanical royalties. There are three organizations that collect mechanical royalties: The Harry Fox Agency (HFA), The American Mechanical Rights Agency (AMRA) and The Songwriters Guild of America (SGA). These three organizations collect mechanical royalties from record companies of all sizes—major labels, mid-size and independents—and pass the royalties along to member music publishers and songwriters.

Music Publishing Royalties

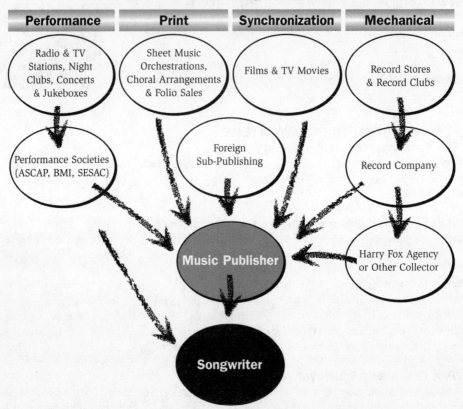

How do songwriters hook up with this system to earn royalties?

For **Performance Royalties**, individual songwriters **affiliate** with a Performing Rights Organization of their choice, and register their songs in the PRO database. Each PRO has a slightly different method of calculating payment, different ownership, and different membership structure, so choosing a PRO is an individual choice. Once a songwriter is affiliated and has registered their songs, the PROs then collect fees as described above and issue a check to the songwriter.

For **Mechanical Royalties**, three different things can happen:

1. The songwriter is signed to a publisher that is affiliated with The Harry Fox Agency. The Harry Fox Agency collects the mechanical royalties and passes them along to the publisher. The publisher then passes these along to the songwriter within 30 days. This case usually happens when a songwriter is signed to a major publisher and has a song on a major label album release.

2. The songwriter is not signed to a publisher and owns exclusive rights to his songs, and so works with AMRA or The Songwriters Guild of America, who cut a check directly to the songwriter instead of passing them to the publisher first.

3. They are signed to a publisher, but the songs are being released on albums by independent labels. In this case, the songwriter often works with AMRA since they have a focus on the independent music publishing market.

PERFORMING SONGWRITERS/ARTISTS
How do performing songwriters make money?
Performing songwriters and artists (if they write their own songs) make money just like non-performing songwriters, as described above, but they also make money through royalties made on the retail price of an album when it is sold online, in a store, etc.

What about all the stories of performing songwriters getting into bad deals?
The stories are generally true, but if they're smart, performing songwriters usually can hold on to the money they would be owed as songwriters (performing and mechanical royalties). But when it comes to retail sale royalties, all they will usually see is an ''advance''—essentially a loan—which must then be paid off from record sales. You will not see a royalty check on retail sales until you're advance is paid off. If you are given a $600,000 advance, you will have to pay back the record company $600,000 out of your sales royalties before you see any more money.

Do performing songwriters and artists get to keep the advance?
Not really. If you have a manager who has gotten you a record deal, he will take his cut. You will probably be required in the contract to pay for the producer and studio time to make the album. Often the producer will take a percentage of subsequent royalties from album sales, which comes out of your pocket. Then there are also music video costs, promotion to radio stations, tour support, paying sidemen, etc. Just about anything you can think of is eventually paid for out of your advance or out of sales royalties. There are also deductions to royalties usually built in to record company contracts that make it harder to earn out an advance.

What should a performing songwriter wanting to sign with a major label do?
Their best option is to negotiate a fair contract, get as big of an advance as possible, and then manage that advance money the best they can. A good contract will keep the songwriting royalties described above completely separate from the flow of sales royalties, and will also cut down on the number of royalty deductions the record company builds into the contract. And because of the difficulty in earning out any size advance or auditing the record company, it makes sense to get as much cash up front as you can, then to manage that as best you can. You will need a good lawyer.

RECORD COMPANIES, PRODUCERS AND MANAGERS & BOOKING AGENTS
How do music publishers make money?
A publisher works as a songwriter's agent, looks for profitable commercial uses for the songs he represents, and then takes a percentage of the profits. This is typically 50% of all earning from a particular song—often referred to as the *publisher's share*. A successful publisher stays in contact with several A&R reps, finding out what upcoming projects are in need of new material, and whether any songs he represents will be appropriate.

How do record companies make money?
Record companies primarily make their money from profits made selling CDs, cassettes, DVDs, etc. Record companies keep most of the profit after subtracting manufacturing costs,

royalties to recording artists, distribution fees and the costs of promoting songs to radio (which for major labels can reach up to $300,000 per song). Record companies also usually have music publishing divisions that make money performing all the functions of publishers.

How do record producers make money?

Producers mostly make their money by charging a flat fee up front to helm a recording project, by sharing in the royalties from album sales, or both. A small independent producer might charge $10,000 (or sometimes less) up front to produce a small indie band, while a "name" producer such as Bob Rock, who regularly works with major label bands, might charge $300,000. Either of these might also take a share in sales royalties, referred to as "points"— as in "percentage points." A producer might say, "I'll produce you for $10,000 and 2 points." If an artist is getting a 15% royalty an album sales, then two of those percentage points will go to the producer instead. Producers also make money by co-writing with the artists to get publishing royalties, or they may ask for part of the publishing from songs written by outside songwriters.

How do managers make money?

Most managers make money by taking a percentage commission of their clients' income, usually 10-25%. If a touring band finishes a show and makes a $2,000 profit, a manager on 15% commission would get $300. If an artist gets a $40,000 advance from a mid-size label, the manager would get $6,000. Whether an artist's songwriting income is included in the manager's commission comes down to negotiation. *The commission should give the manager incentive to make things happen for your career, so avoid paying flat fees up front.*

What About Copyright?

How am I protected by the copyright laws?

Copyright protection applies to your songs the instant you put them down in fixed form—a recording, sheet music, lead sheet, etc. This protection lasts for your lifetime plus 70 years (or the lifetime of the last surviving writer, if you co-wrote the song with somebody else). When you prepare demos, place notification of copyright on all copies of your song—the lyric sheets, lead sheets and labels for cassettes, CDs, etc. The notice is simply the word "copyright" or the symbol © followed by the year the song was created (or published) and your name: © 2005 by John Q. Songwriter.

What parts of a song are protected by copyright?

Traditionally, only the melody line and the lyrics are eligible for copyright. Period. Chords and rhythm are virtually never protected. An incredibly original arrangement can sometimes qualify. Sound recordings can also be copyrighted, but this applies strictly to the actual sounds on the recording, not the song itself (this copyright is usually owned by record companies).

What songs are not protected?

Song titles or mere ideas for music and lyrics cannot be copyrighted. Very old songs in the "public domain" are not protected. You could quote a melody from a Bach piece, but you could not then stop someone else from quoting the same melody in their song.

When would I lose or have to share the copyright?

If you *collaborate* with other writers, they are assumed to have equal interests unless you state some other arrangement, in writing. If you write under a *work-for-hire* arrangement, the company or person who hired you to write the song then owns the copyright. Sometimes your spouse may automatically be granted an interest in your copyright as part of their *spousal rights*, which might then become important if you got divorced.

Should I register my copyright?

Registering you copyright with the Library of Congress gives the best possible protection. Registration establishes a public record of your copyright—even though a song is legally protected whether or not it is registered—and could prove useful in any future court cases involving the song. Registration also entitles you to a potentially greater settlement in a copyright infringement lawsuit.

How do I register my song?

To register your song, request government form PA from the Copyright Office. Call the 24-hour hotline at (202)707-9100 and leave your name and address on the messaging system. Once you receive the PA form, you must return it, along with a registration fee and a CD (or tape) and lead sheet of your song. Send these to the Register of Copyrights, Copyright Office, Library of Congress, Washington DC 20559. It may take several months to receive your certificate of registration from the Copyright Office, but your songs are protected from the date of creation (the date of registration will reflect the date you applied). For more information, call the Copyright Office's Public Information Office at (202)707-3000 or visit their Web site at www.copyright.gov.

Government Resources

For More Info

The Library of Congress's copyright Web site is your best source for current, complete information on the subject of copyright. Not only can you learn all you could possibly wish to know about intellectual property rights and U.S. copyright law (the section of the U.S. Code dealing with copyright is reprinted there in its entirety), but you can also download copyright forms directly from the site. The site also includes links to other copyright-related web pages, many of which will be of interest to songwriters, including ASCAP, BMI, SESAC, and the Harry Fox Agency. Check it out at **www.copyright.gov.**

How likely is it that someone will try to steal my song?

Copyright infringement is very rare. But, if you ever feel that one of your songs has been stolen—that someone has unlawfully infringed on your copyright—you must prove that you created the work and that the person you are suing had access to your song. Copyright registration is the best proof of a date of creation. You *must* have your copyright registered in order to file a lawsuit. Also, it's helpful if you keep your rough drafts and revisions of songs, either on paper or on tape.

Why did song sharks begin soliciting me after I registered my song?

This is one potential, unintended consequence of registering your song with the Library of Congress. The copyright indexes are a public record of your songwriting, and song sharks often search the copyright indexes and mail solicitations to songwriters who live out away from major music centers such as Nashville. They figure these songwriters don't know any better and are easy prey. *Do not allow this possibility to stop you from registering your songs!* Just be aware, educate yourself, and then throw the song sharks' mailings in the trash.

What if I mail a tape to myself to get a postmark date on a sealed envelope?

The "poor man's copyright" has not stood up in court, and is not an acceptable substitute for registering your song. If you feel it's important to shore up your copyright, register it with the Library of Congress.

Career Songwriting

What Should I Know?

What career options are open to songwriters who do not perform?

The possibilities range from a beginning songwriter living away from a music center like Nashville who lands an occasional single-song publishing deal, to a staff songwriter signed to a major publishing company. And then there are songwriters like Desmond Child who operate independently, have developed a lot of connections, work with numerous artists, and have set up their own independent publishing operations.

What is "single-song" songwriting about?

In this case, a songwriter submits songs to many different companies. One or two songs gain interest from different publishers, and the songwriter signs separate contracts for each song with each publisher. The songwriter can then pitch other songs to other publishers. In Nashville, for instance, a single-song contract is usually the first taste of success for an aspiring songwriter on his way up the ladder. Success of this sort can induce a songwriter to move to a music center like Nashville (if they haven't already), and is a big boost for a struggling songwriter already living there. A series of single-song contracts often signals a songwriter's maturing skill and marketability.

What is a "staff songwriter"?

A staff songwriter usually works for a major publisher and receives a monthly stipend as an advance against the royalties he is likely to earn for the publisher. The music publisher has exclusive rights to everything the songwriter writes while signed to the company. The publisher also works actively on the writer's behalf to hook him or her up with co-writers and other opportunities. A staff songwriting position is highly treasured by many because it offers a steady income, and in Nashville is a sign the songwriter has "arrived."

What comes after the staff songwriting position?

Songwriters who go to the next level have a significant reputation for their ability to write hit songs. Famous artists seek them out, and they often write actively in several markets at once. They often write on assignment for film and television, and commonly keep their own publishing companies to maximize their income.

As my career grows what should I do about keeping track of expenses, etc.?

You should keep a ledger or notebook with records on all financial transactions related to your songwriting—royalty checks, demo costs, office supplies, postage, travel expenses, dues to organizations, class and workshop fees, plus any publications you purchase pertaining to songwriting. You may also want a separate checking account devoted to your songwriting activities. This will make record keeping easier and help to establish your identity as a business for tax purposes.

What should I know about taxes related to songwriting income?

Any royalties you receive will not reflect taxes or any other mandatory deductions. It is your responsibility to keep track of income and file the correct tax forms. For specific information, contact the IRS or talk to an accountant who serves music industry clients.

What About Contracts?

CO-WRITING

What kind of agreements do I need with co-writers?

You may need to sign a legal agreement between you and a co-writer to establish percentages you will each receive of the writer's royalties. You will also have to iron out what you will do if another person, such as an artist, wants to change your song and receive credit as a cowriter. For example, in the event a major artist wants to cut your song for her album—but also wants to rewrite some lyrics and take a share of the publishing—you and your co-writer need to agree whether it is better to get a song on an album that might sell millions (and make a lot of money) or pass on it because you don't want to give up credit. The situation could be uncomfortable if you are not in sync on the issue.

When do I need a lawyer to look over agreements?

When it comes to doing business with a publisher, producer, or record company, you should always have the contract reviewed by a knowledgeable entertainment attorney. As long as the issues at stake are simple, the co-writers respect each other, and they discuss their business philosophies before writing a song together, they can probably write up an agreement without the aid of a lawyer.

SINGLE-SONG CONTRACTS

What is a single-song contract?

A music publisher offers a single-song contract when he wants to sign one or more of your songs, but doesn't want to hire you as a staff songwriter. You assign your rights to a particular song to the publisher for an agreed-upon number of years, so that he may represent the song and find uses profitable for both of you. This is a common contract and will probably be the first you encounter in your songwriting career.

What basic elements should every single-song contract contain?

Every contract should have the publisher's name, the writer's name, the song's title, the date, and the purpose of the agreement. The songwriter also declares the song is a original work and he is creator of the work. The contract *must* specify the royalties the songwriter will earn from various uses of the song, including performance, mechanical, print and synchronization royalties.

How should the royalties usually be divided in the contract?

The songwriter should receive no less than 50% of the income his song generates. That means the songwriter and publisher split the total royalties 50/50. The songwriter's half is

When Does 50% Equal 100%?

Tip

NOTE: the publisher's and songwriter's share of the income are sometimes referred to as each being 100%—for 200% total! You might hear someone say, "I'll take 100% of the publisher's share." **Do not be needlessly confused!** If the numbers confuse you, ask for the terms to be clarified.

called the "writer's share" and the publisher's half is called the "publisher's share." If there is more than one songwriter, the songwriters split the writer's share. Sometimes, successful songwriters will bargain for a percentage of the publisher's share, negotiating what is basically a co-publishing agreement. For a visual explanation of how royalties are collected and flow to the songwriter, see the chart called Music Publishing Royalties on page 29.

What should the contract say about a "reversion clause"?

Songwriters should always negotiate for a "reversion clause," which returns all rights back to the songwriter if some provision of the contract is not met. Most reversion clauses give a publisher a set amount of time (usually one or two years) to work the song and make money with it. If the publisher can't get the song recorded and released during the agreed-upon time period, the songwriter can then take his song to another publisher. The danger of *not* getting some sort of reversion clause is that you could wind up with a publisher sitting on your song for the entire life-plus-70-years term of the copyright—which may as well be forever.

Is a reversion clause difficult to get?

Some publishers agree to it, and figure if they can't get any action with the song in the first year or two, they're not likely to ever have much luck with it. Other publishers may be reluctant to agree to a reversion clause. They may invest a lot of time and money in demoing and pitching a song to artists and want to keep working at it for a longer period of time. Or, for example, a producer might put a song on hold for a while and then go into a lengthy recording project. A year can easily go by before the artist or producer decides which songs to release as singles. This means you may have to agree to a longer time period, be flexible and trust the publisher has your best mutual interests in mind. Use your best judgment.

What other basic issues should be covered by a single-song contract?

The contract should also address these issues:

- will an advance be paid, and if so, how much will the advance be?
- when will royalties be paid (annually or semiannually)?
- who will pay for demos—the publisher, songwriter or both?
- how will lawsuits against copyright infringement be handled, including the cost of lawsuits?
- will the publisher have the right to sell its interest in the song to another publisher without the songwriter's consent?
- does the publisher have the right to make changes in a song, or approve changes by someone else, without the songwriter's consent?
- the songwriter should have the right to audit the publisher's books if he feels it is necessary and gives the publisher reasonable notice.

Basic Song Contract Pointers

Tips

The following list, taken from a Songwriters Guild of America publication, enumerates the basic features of an acceptable songwriting contract:

1 **Work for Hire.** When you receive a contract covering just one composition, you should make sure the phrases "employment for hire" and "exclusive writer agreement" are *not* included. Also, there should be no options for future songs.

2 **Performing Rights Affiliation.** If you previously signed publishing contracts, you should be affiliated with either ASCAP, BMI, or SESAC. All performance royalties must be received directly by you from your performing rights organization and this should be written into your contract.

3 **Reversion Clause.** The contract should include a provision that if the publisher does not secure a release of a commercial sound recording within a specified time (one year, two years, etc.), the contract can be terminated by you.

4 **Changes in the Composition.** If the contract includes a provision that the publisher can change the title, lyrics or music, this should be amended so that only with your consent can such changes be made.

5 **Royalty Provisions.** You should receive fifty percent (50%) of all publisher's income on all licenses issued. If the publisher prints and sells his own sheet music, your royalty should be ten percent (10%) of the wholesale selling price. The royalty should not be stated in the contract as a flat rate ($.05, $.07, etc.).

6 **Negotiable Deductions.** Ideally, demos and all other expenses of publication should be paid 100% by the publisher. The only allowable fee is for the Harry Fox Agency collection fee, whereby the writer pays one half of the amount charged to the publisher for mechanical rights. The current mechanical royalty collected by the Harry Fox Agency is 9.1 cents per cut for songs under 5 minutes; and 1.75 cents per minute for songs over 5 minutes.

7 **Royalty Statements and Audit Provision.** Once the song is recorded, you are entitled to receive royalty statements at least once every six months. In addition, an audit provision with no time restriction should be included in every contract.

8 **Writer's Credit.** The publisher should make sure that you receive proper credit on all uses of the composition.

9 **Arbitration.** In order to avoid large legal fees in case of a dispute with your publisher, the contract should include an arbitration clause.

10 **Future Uses.** Any use not specifically covered by the contract should be retained by the writer to be negotiated as it comes up.

Music Biz Basics

Music Biz Basics

Where else can I go for advice on contracts?

The Songwriters Guild of America has drawn up a Popular Songwriter's Contract which it believes to be the best minimum songwriter contract available (see the Ten Basic Points Your Contract Should Include sidebar above). The Guild will send a copy of the contract at no charge to any interested songwriter upon request (see the Songwriters Guild of America listing in the Organizations section on page 291). SGA will also review—free of charge—any contract offered to its members, and will check it for fairness and completeness. Also see these two books published by Writer's Digest Books: *The Craft and Business of Songwriting, 3rd Edition*, by John Braheny and *The New Songwriter's Guide to Music Publishing, 3rd Edition*, by Randy Poe.

Taking Control of Your Career

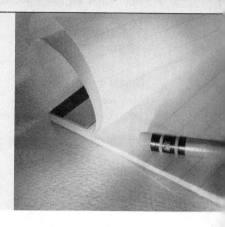

by Julie Frost

Trying to transform musical talent into monetary means is not easy. There is no set formula for it, but there are some fundamental issues that apply to everyone that should be considered.

In my years working either for a music company or representing independent artists, I have witnessed the same common mistakes by artists in their efforts to achieve success. These mistakes not only cripple chances to succeed but also waste time, money, and energy. Here I'll discuss how to avoid these mistakes, take control of your career, and maximize your efforts in the business.

CREATE A PLAN OF ACTION

When setting out for (or maintaining) a career in the music industry, whether as a songwriter or a recording artist, you must have a plan of action. If you were pursuing any other profession, you would go through the process of educating yourself, putting in time learning from experienced mentors, building an impressive résumé, and researching the best jobs that suit your specific profession. As an artist, if you want to be taken seriously and do well in the business, you must approach your career in the same manner. Take some time to step back, look at the big picture, pinpoint where you fit in best, and make a plan of how you can get there.

EDUCATE YOURSELF

Whether you are a DIY artist or you have a team to assist you, it is essential that you have a clear understanding and overall awareness of how the business works. It can seem daunting and a bit complicated because there are so many ways to go about it, but at the same time, it is not rocket science. Just learning some basic elements could make all the difference in major decision-making that could change the course of your career. Knowledge is power and it will keep you from making simple yet critical mistakes throughout your journey.

There is so much accessible information available these days (in books, online, etc.) and absolutely no reason for not taking advantage of it. I hear of too many artists finding them-

JULIE FROST has worked at Antone's Record Label (Warner Bros.) as A&R and Assistant International Rep, launched Dialtone Records with two partners, served as Marketing Coordinator and A&R Rep at Louisiana Red Hot Records, and has assisted on projects with local producers and artists, often acting as advocate in helping artists advance their careers. She's represented various independent artists taking on development, solicitation, promotion, booking, and contract negotiation, and continues to work as a freelance writer, publicist, booking agent, and artist and industry development consultant. She studied Journalism at the University of Oklahoma.

selves in bad contracts they can't get out of or not understanding why they aren't making more money, etc. If only they taken the time to educate themselves before making a move. Even if you are hiring council, you should still acquire a working knowledge of the things you care about most. If you are aware of how the machine works, you can use it more to your advantage. You, in the end, are solely in charge of your destiny, and there no one else will be accountable for the decisions that you make in your career.

MAINTAIN BUSINESS SENSE

Whether you like it or not, you also have to learn to treat your talent as a business as well. Finding a balance between art and commerce is key. You are your own boss and the proprietor of your art, so in a sense, you are also your own salesman. Your product needs to be marketed and sold just like in any other business. Most successful businesses secure funds to produce a quality product, study their market, target their audience, advance on latest trends, and provide customer support. The music business really isn't much different. You will encounter plenty of monetary obstacles along the way—it takes money to cover administrative costs, recording, production, promotion, and touring, so make sure you budget for these things. Any effort you make in this process is an investment in yourself.

It is no secret that songwriting/publishing is one of the last viable sources of income streams for artists these days. Too many artists are quick to sign deals or give up publishing rights unaware of what that may mean for them down the line. There are so many options to generate royalties for your music, so make sure you are in control of them. Always remember that when signing contracts, everything is negotiable. Don't think that you have to take the first offer or cannot ask for more.

PREPARE FOR SUCCESS

This is something I see happening all the time: An artist makes all this noise to try and get noticed, and when the moment comes, they are not truly prepared for it. That moment rarely will come to you twice in a lifetime, so if you fail to move on it during that window of opportunity, it may be gone forever. Then you may find yourself wasting time trying to backtrack, get your ducks in a row, and then catch back up to where you were before. To avoid that, there are a few basic steps that you should have covered before soliciting or promoting your music.

Register copyrights

A very important step (that would seem a no-brainer yet too many artists fail to do) is to copyright your song(s) before sending them out, whether they are published or unpublished. Yes, technically once you have written a song you automatically become the owner of the copyright, but I wouldn't rely on that. If you find yourself in a legal battle, the only thing that stands up in a court of law is an official registration through the U.S. Copyright Office (www.copyright.gov). Plus, you will need to legally own the copyright of your songs before registering with a performing rights organization or signing any publishing or licensing deals. It is a simple procedure and is really not that costly. You can register a collection of songs (if by the same author) or a published, commercial recording in one application. Keep in mind that the process of registration can take anywhere from six to eight weeks, but your copyright will take effect the date of receipt (or will retroactively cover the date you wrote the song) so it is wise to mail it certified.

Register songs with a PRO

If you intend on your songs to be recorded, published, and played, it's absolutely necessary to affiliate yourself with a performing rights organization (PRO). If you ever want to see any income from your music, you must join a PRO and register your songs according to how your publishing will be set-up. If you don't understand how publishing works, then it is critical you read up and educate yourself. Publishing is by far the most important basis of your future in songwriting.

Sign necessary agreements

Before writing, recording, publishing, or soliciting your songs, it is always a good idea to draft agreements between any entities who will be working together—that goes for collaborators, producers, managers, publishers—everybody. It happens way too often that, after the fact, something comes up that someone misunderstood or disagrees with. If you don't have it in writing, there's not much you can do about it.

Register name/trademark logo

Make sure before you come up with the most brilliant name for a band or its logo that there isn't someone else out there just as brilliant. You don't want to be in a situation where you have gone to the trouble of establishing a name and an image, only to find that you're going to have to change it because it's already in use. This can be a little costly to do but it's worth it to avoid the time and expense of starting over with a new name.

Incorporate/set-up financial base

If you are a band who shares in the writing, work, cost, and/or profits, it is wise to incorporate your band and establish a financial basis for tax purposes. Setting up a bank account to keep tabs on what is going in and out is so important. If you are the sole proprietor of your songs, record sales, touring, etc., then make sure you choose a way that works best for you since you will be responsible for self-employment taxes and 1099s.

Prepare/update Web site(s) and PR materials

One of the easiest and most valuable promotional tools you will ever need in this business is to have information available at people's fingertips—not just available, but very accessible and updated. There is nothing more frustrating than to discover an artist or be solicited by an artist that either doesn't have enough information available, or does, but it is out-dated. No one wants to or has time to wait or wade through the Internet looking for basic information about you, your songs, your tour dates, and your status. Again, it is a simple procedure, not too costly—and is a must. Have it ready before soliciting yourself.

Ready product

Do not send out a demo of something that you are not proud of or you feel does not represent you well. If you are soliciting a song or demo that you do not feel 100% confident about but think you can just explain to whomever is listening that you can do better, think again. You have not only wasted your time, but the listener's time. They will most likely not consider it or wait for you to come up with something "better." Just make sure that your music is where you want it, and is ready and waiting. Cutting demos should be your best effort and your work should sound professional. When you have material ready, make sure your tunes are also accessible online, available in an audio file to e-mail or download, or you have plenty of product to send out.

Keep producing material

Once you do have product ready, don't just sit on it as your prize egg—keep writing, recording, and putting stuff out there. When pitching songs or demos, someone may not want one particular song or sound at the moment, but may think another song of yours is perfect.

Sometimes it only takes that one song to reel someone in to hear others. Keep adding to your own catalog. It not only helps you grow as an artist but also raises your chances of having the right song at the right time.

SPECIFY & TARGET YOUR AUDIENCE & MARKET

We live in an extremely specialized day and age that offers everything for everybody. This is good news and bad news for artists. It does help in finding your niche and targeting a specific audience quicker, but if you have a crossover sound, it may mean more work on your part to cover more ground. It can be more effective to streamline your sound, whatever that may be, and work in that particular genre. Sometimes the crossover factor can be a huge success and reach a greater audience, but sometimes it can work against you, spreading you too thin. There are a few things to keep in mind when considering your audience or niche.

Research

The biggest waste of time when soliciting songs, demos, or an album is not doing research before sending out your music. There are more labels, publishers, and producers than ever before. If you try to blanket the whole bunch of them thinking your chances are greater, you will most likely be throwing away quite a bit of time and money. It can be a bit painstaking, but make the time to piece through what particular sound, artists, songs, and style they have worked with in the past or may be soliciting in the future. There are plenty of resources available that offer up-to-date listings of this information, and it doesn't hurt to make your own contacts with whom to inquire and confirm information about companies themselves. Everyone has their own particular guidelines of how they look for music and what they expect when being solicited. The same goes for when you are promoting your music—media, booking, building a fan-base—it is all the same game.

Streamline sound

I often notice that in artists' demos or debut albums that they usually cover too many different sounds, and this is usually because their first attempt is an accumulation of many years' worth of work. There's a difference in having a crossover sound and just having too many sounds that don't have a common denominator. It may be impressive that you have the talent and ability to write or perform a variety of things, but when approaching it from a sales market perspective, it will hurt you. Most artists I know don't feel that they should be pigeonholed into one specific genre because they believe it is limiting, but in reality, it can be more limiting if you don't. I'm not saying that every song has to sound alike; it just helps to have an overall singular vibe and feel. Then if you do decide to try another sound down the line or on another project, it has more appeal and creates more of a curiosity and an interest from the listener.

Find, build, and keep your audience

Discovering and targeting an appropriate audience is not always as simple as it would seem. Again, researching who has listened to or supported similar music or which lifestyles relate to that specific sound is helpful. Use every means to reach out to anyone who takes an interest and build on that. When developing a fan-base, seek out listeners of like-minded music, or inquire how they discovered your music and ask what else they are interested in, etc. and continue directing your energy towards that. Once you build an audience, communicate with them, involve them, and listen to them—they are your greatest asset and something your career cannot thrive without.

DECIDING ON REPRESENTATION

Why, you ask, might you need representation? Well, there are a few reasons and a few different roads to go down. It is certainly attainable to get where you want on your own, but having representation can be a very beneficial. For one, if you hire someone, they will possess the experience, knowledge, manpower, and leverage that you don't. Having representation shows that you have some sort of validation in your work from others who may be investing in you on some level. Another reason to consider it may be that you just don't have the time or the interest in dealing with all the ins and outs of the industry. Whatever the case, it is a good idea not only for these reasons but because most companies prefer to have a professional buffer between you and them. Of course, any rep you choose will get a piece of the pie, but that is because their time, advice, and influence can be a very valuable resource. Some suggested methods of representation are:

- **Manager/Agent.** When taking on a manager or agent, make sure you go with someone you trust wholeheartedly and who is committed. They are usually responsible for all areas of advancing your career and in return take a percentage of your gross sales. Most companies prefer this so they always have a point person with whom they can build a long-lasting relationship.
- **Entertainment Attorney.** Most artists hire an attorney to shop their songs or demo for a fee. If you don't feel comfortable maintaining your legal paperwork for your music, they may offer that service as well, but that can be expensive. Eventually you will need to hire an attorney when landing a deal to review contracts before signing (or after you encounter a problem).
- **Producer.** Some artists choose to work with a producer that takes on their project and shops it to labels, publishers, or other connected artists and in return gets points on the album or a cut of the publishing. It can be worth their investment if they believe you are going to be big because it puts their name out there as well.

USING YOUR RESOURCES

There are many national, regional, and statewide resources and organizations that are present solely to support musicians and songwriters in their careers. Some are membership based and some are non-profit, state, or federally funded. They can help in every aspect of the trade, from advocating rights of artists to showcasing. Reach out, connect, and use these resources to your advantage. That's what they are there for. Some examples are:

- unions (American Federation of Musicians)
- performing rights organizations
- songwriters groups
- associations, societies, coalitions and alliances
- guilds and foundations
- state arts/music commissions or offices

APPEALING TO A&R REPS

It should go without saying that the most important thing that A&R reps look for first in an artist is great songwriting or a distinguished sound. When it comes down to it, if you are talented enough and right for the job, a lot of the other formalities may not seem to matter as much, or sometimes they may make an effort to help develop you if they think it worth their while. To increase your overall chances of success, it is wise to have the whole package already in place. Most companies these days want to see that you have already done a lot of the work developing yourself because it means less risk to them. Below are a few qualities (other than talent and good songs) that will always be important to A&R.

Create a buzz/strong following

First, become that big fish in a small pond. Create a buzz locally then start expanding regionally, nationally, and internationally if you can. You want to show that you have a dedicated audience that wants your music and that there is a strong connection. As a band, one of the biggest mistakes you can make is to move to a big city where music is overly abundant and try to stake your claim—you may be overshadowed by too much competition. Although it's not a bad idea if you are a songwriter trying to network with other musicians, hone your craft, or be in close proximity to those looking for songs to be in the hub of things.

Standout from the crowd

Most artists believe that they are special and should automatically be recognized. What you have to keep in mind is that there are thousands of talented artists right behind you going for the same prize, and if you can't prove you are special and exceptional someone else will quickly take your place. Most A&R reps look for what sets you apart from the next guy. If you offer a unique or distinguished sound that is fresh, you automatically are a step-up above the rest. There are companies that do sometimes want a certain sound, but they still want to hear it done in a way that may be edgier or distinctive. Discover what is original about your work and go with it.

Show dedication

If you do not have a proven track record of putting in time writing, recording, and touring, you might not look as serious as the next guy. Companies want to see that you are dedicated to your craft and willing and able to move on it 100%. It is an extremely hard thing to juggle keeping a day job with trying to be available (and having the energy) to work as an artist. There has to be a crossroads that you reach to eventually jump in and take the risk of making music your priority. Sometimes it just takes that leap forward to change your fate.

Be professional, always put your best foot forward

When approaching A&R reps with material for consideration, be aware and considerate of their time and guidelines. When sending packages or e-mail, keep things brief, direct, and to the point. Do let them know what you offer and what your status is, but most important, your music should do the talking. Honestly, when I used to screen solicited songs or demos, I always listened to the music first and then read the correspondence that went with it later. Keep in mind that most reps may only have the time to give your song 30 seconds before deciding if they want to hear more. Make sure your best is what they hear first. When you are playing live, whether you have 5 or 500 people listening, make sure you are at your best game. You never know who may be in that audience—your big shot may be listening when you don't realize it.

GETTING NOTICED BY A&R

This is usually the toughest part for artists. Getting your music to A&R is half the battle. The other half takes just the right combination of following-up, networking/building relationships, keeping a profile (and position yourself/be available to showcase), and being productive and persistent. These steps should set you on the right path to get some attention and consideration:

- **Follow-up.** Once you send something out, don't just assume it got into the right person's hands. Call or e-mail very politely asking if they received it, and let them know how to find you. Make friends with receptionists, assistants, and interns—they may be the ones screening your music, or at least the middleman to the person you are trying to reach. Also remember that these folks may eventually move up to a position that will be the deciding figure, so get to know them and listen to them.

Industry Insights from A&R

Scott Billington is vice president of A&R at Rounder Records which was founded in 1970 and has since become one of the top Independent labels producing everything from American roots to World music. They have released over 3,000 titles including work from artists such as Allison Krauss, Irma Thomas, Joe Ely, and Sam Bush. Billington has been with Rounder for 30 years and is a Grammy-winning producer. He has produced Johnny Adams, Irma Thomas, Ruth Brown, Buckwheat Zydeco, and many other roots music artists, and is half of the remix duo called Tangle Eye. Here he offers insights and advice from an A&R point of view.

How do you normally go about assisting your artists search for songs to record (i.e. do you solicit songwriters, outside publishers, or producers, referrals from BMI/ASCAP or services like TAXI, work with in-house writers, etc.)?

There can be a number of approaches, but I'll usually go to writers or publishers that I know would have appropriate material and ask. I'll sometimes tell writers what we're looking for and ask them to write specifically for a project. On occasion, the artist and I will write together, or I'll introduce the artist to a co-writer that I think he or she would hit it off with. I've never had any luck with requests made through tip sheets—I've never found one song that way that I've ever recorded.

What do you look for most when considering songs for your artists?

First and foremost, a compelling melody, then lyrics that tell a story I feel the artist will relate to. Melody and harmony have often taken a back seat to attitude in many new songs I hear, but it's melody that makes a song stick, or at least that gives it a long life.

When looking for new talent to sign, what usually catches your attention and what is an immediate turn-off?

Well, lack of melody is a turn-off! Seriously, I want someone with a distinctive voice who truly has something to say. I'm drawn to artists who have found a way to bring roots sensibilities forward. I'm also drawn to great singers who are open to letting me work with them on recording concepts. Over the years, I've been fortunate to have produced singers such as Irma Thomas, Johnny Adams and Charlie Rich, and they've set high standards for me. Great singers don't come along all that often.

It's also critical to know that the artist has developed a local following. I can make a record, but if the bond between audience and performer is not there, it's impossible to manufacture, at least for a label like Rounder. That's what it comes down to: if an artist can build a growing following on his or her own, the record and the record company can help take them to a higher level. If the audience doesn't come away from a show inspired by the artist, the artist needs to look at what's not happening. It's that basic. You can't sell music to an audience if the audience hears it and doesn't want it.

How often do you listen to and /or work with artists that send you demos? Do you have any advice for them?

I listen to just about everything I get, but if I'm turned off after the first 30 seconds or so, I stop. There just isn't enough time in the day. I'd prefer to get one song to start the artist's very best effort.

- **Network/relationship building.** Every person you meet in this business or related to it is useful on some level. You never know who may be connected to whom, or will be down the line. Don't burn bridges. Keep in touch. Reach out. Spread the word. If you do make contact with A&R, build a relationship with them. They are human and it helps to show that you are too. Some artists choose to bank on membership-based listings or tip-sheets as a means to get music to A&R. In my dealings and the majority of A&R reps that I know do not find songs/artists that way. It is your best bet to establish that connection yourself.

- **Keep a profile, position yourself, and be available.** Continue to keep a profile by sending notice out of your progress to anyone that may take an interest. Send tour dates, accolades, media coverage, etc. to show that you are on the radar. They will take notice if others do. Showcase at industry conferences and festivals and research who will be attending or sitting on a panel and invite them to see you. When you're touring, let them know when you will be in their town next and invite them, or try and set up a personal showcase. If they say that they will help arrange a showcase, be available to them. It's rare these days that they will come to you.

- **Keep productive and be persistent.** Again, it is important to companies that you remain productive and progressive on your own. They want to see that you are a creative well that they can draw from. Don't let one or two turndowns stop you. Remember that this is very much like auditioning for a specific part in a movie or play; you may not fit that specific character for that role, but that doesn't mean you wouldn't for another. Try and try again. Most successful artists out there will tell you that they heard quite a few ''no's'' before they heard a ''yes.'' Perseverance will always be your friend.

Most artists I know write, sing, or play because it is their calling—regardless of what measured success comes with it. There is a way to make the most of that talent and make it your livelihood, but it takes work and know-how. Luck does play a big part in it, but you have to be ready to take luck up when it comes your way. This is a fickle, competitive, and discriminating business, and as cliché as it may sound, it is so true that talent will only get you so far (and even if it gets you somewhere, that doesn't guarantee it will keep you there). It is a constant struggle to keep in the game, and even more challenging to find some sort of stability or longevity in it. Hopefully these words of advice will get you somewhere, and keep you there.

Web Power

Marketing Yourself Through
Social Networking Sites

by David McPherson

Thanks to the power of the Web 2.0, it's truly a new wide wide world for songwriters in the twenty-first century. Through the Internet and its myriad free Web sites for musicians, the opportunities to gain exposure, sell songs, post gigs, and reach out to new fans has never been easier. Whether it's popular social media sites such as MySpace, Sonicbids (where musicians can create their own electronic press kits) or Facebook, the online tools for songwriters to market their music is endless.

"The Net is the very best thing that has ever happened to everybody," wrote Bob Lefsetz in one of his famed *The Lefsetz Letter*—one of the most popular blogs about the music industry (www.lefsetz.com). "Everything you build comes back to you," he writes later in the same blog post. "Every effort you make enhances your career. Choices may not be as obvious, effects might not be measured instantly, but get in the game for the long haul and watch as dividends get paid. First and foremost, for the very first time in history, you can know who your audience is. You can collect the e-mail address of everybody who likes your music. Maybe give a track away for free for an e-mail address. Maybe not all of the addresses will be valid, but if they're truly fans, they'd love it if you contacted them in the future—you have to harvest e-mail addresses. So, when you go on tour, when you've got something to sell, you can alert your fans."

REACHING YOUR AUDIENCE

Access to fans from every corner of the globe is one of the biggest advantages social media sites such as Facebook and MySpace offer. "As an artist you're pretty much expected to have a MySpace, Facebook and Sonicbids presence," says Astrid Young, Neil Young's half-sister and a seasoned songwriter. "That's something that might have been merely a bonus in earlier years, but is now taken for granted. It's a shame some songwriters and artists have not embraced this particular media since not embracing it can significantly reduce the people who have access to your work."

As Young indicates, these social media Web sites are all about networking, marketing and reaching out to a wider audience. On Facebook, for example, musicians can post songs,

DAVID MCPHERSON is a Toronto-based freelance writer with more than 15 years experience. A graduate of the University of Western Ontario, with a Masters in Journalism, David has published thousands of articles in daily newspapers, consumer magazines, and Web sites across North America, including the *National Post*, *Golf Canada*, *ScoreGolf*, *Penguin Eggs*, and *Paste* magazine. His Web site is www.davidmcpherson.ca.

link to videos, and also create posters for their next gig. It creates immediate awareness and free publicity.

"I remember when I became aware of MySpace in 2004. I was playing in the U.S., and people in Brooklyn and Long-Island were hip to it and I didn't understand how it could be useful," recalls Rob Szabo, a Toronto-based artist who plays more than 100 gigs per year. "It's funny to think about a time when not everyone was using MySpace, but it wasn't that long ago.

"At the time, I was like, 'I don't have time for this; I don't want to screw around on the Internet that much.' Then, the next thing you know, I'm booking gigs and making connections with other songwriters through MySpace in a way I wasn't doing over e-mail and I started seeing how it could be useful."

Romi Mayes, a songwriter from Winnipeg, Manitoba, Canada, raves about this wide new world of online promotion, agreeing with Szabo, Young and Lefsetz as to its power and usefulness.

"As an independent musician who is attempting to literally reach the world via my laptop I find every outlet possible on the Internet a valuable tool for promotion," she says. "When I have a show or tour coming up that I want to promote, I don't bother getting posters made, printed, and put up in the city anymore. Instead, I do a mass mail out using Facebook, MySpace, my Web site, and area-based e-mail lists that I have acquired over years at shows and online.

"Because I'm aware of how regularly people are on their computers, I think it's wise to hit such a large audience in such a short time and at absolutely no cost to me. Anyone will tell you that free marketing is the most ideal marketing."

NETWORKING ONLINE

Beyond marketing, Mayes also uses the Internet and social media sites to network. "I have booked many tours, sent out digital copy posters to venues, sent out press releases and promo photos to media, and advanced details of the shows on tour all from my laptop. It's like a one-stop shop. Due to the highly accessible and commonality of groups like Facebook, MySpace, Youtube, etc., it is very easy to reach everyone from a promoter to a radio DJ to a band and hear back within days.

"With little capital to work with, I have to try to keep up with the masses and bust my butt to use all the resources I can that don't cost me thousands of dollars," she adds. "While groups like Facebook, MySpace, Youtube and others continue to grow in popularity, I will definitely be taking its offerings and see how far I can take it until it no longer proves effective or free."

Shannon Lyon, a soulful songwriter, originally from Kitchener, Ontario, Canada, who currently lives in Berlin, Germany, (www.shannonlyon.net) says MySpace and similar social media platforms have also allowed artists to eliminate record companies from the musical equation, which he believes is a good thing since it gives musicians more control over their music.

"This has inspired songwriters to create and control their own musical microcosms," he says. "Hopefully with such freedoms this allows the artist to be as true to their craft as possible . . . getting back to the important stuff without having to deal with record executives, moulding and marketing techniques and also finding networks of like-minded artists and fans, which has certainly helped artists develop large numbers of fans without leaving the comforts of their homes."

That said, Lyon cautions, that it's not all positive: "In Warholian 15-minutes-of-fame fashion, these platforms have also allowed room for much mediocrity, not to mention the allowance of five-star rating systems equipped with comment infiltration that has seemingly helped spawn a mass overload of negative opinion polls and all out verbal wars within and among these societies of computer-world dwellers, music lovers and freaks."

Still the positives outweigh the negatives; Lefsetz urges more musicians to embrace these new popular online tools that are user-friendly and offer free cost-efficient distribution. "You're living in the best era for music creation and distribution in the history of mankind," he says. "Knowing how to play is not enough just like you can't survive in today's world without knowing how to type. Don't cling tighter to history and complain, take a typing lesson, do some research, take a chance!"

MYSPACE

Nat Jay is a Vancouver-based folk artist who took a chance on the power of the Web 2.0 and continues to reap the rewards. She says "the Net and technology rules." After her single, "Love When I Can" was featured on ABC's *Men in Trees* in 2008, her MySpace plays skyrocketed.

"I received over 10,000 plays on MySpace in the weeks following the show," she wrote to Lefsetz after reading his blog. "I was able to interact directly with each and every fan who contacted me on the Web and was able to post personal messages on fansites. I had all my songs available for free download and as a result, my music is now all over North America and my fanbase is growing exponentially. Thanks to the Net, I know I have fans who will buy my music, come to my shows and buy my T-shirts. "Ten years ago, this option was simply not available for an unknown, unsigned artist who made a demo in a storage room in eight hours and had her unmastered song featured in the last three minutes of a network television drama."

Asked to offer advice for other songwriters on new marketing tools, Jon Brooks, a Toronto-based folk singer, is not short on opinions. While he thinks Facebook is a waste of time, he likes MySpace. "For the most part, MySpace has helped my career," he says. "How? Getting gigs mainly. I've met many connections through it and reached a lot of people in some small way. I doubt I've sold a ton of CDs through it, but I've sold some. Recently I sold 35 CDs to the Toronto Public Library, in part, thanks to MySpace—but only in part, since the first reason they contacted me was because a few people walked into the Toronto public libraries asking if they carried my CDs.

"I make a living now fulltime as a songwriter and yet I still fight the problem of obscurity," he adds. "A great book is called *The Long Tail*. Essentially, it argues that yes fewer companies and businesses are making obscene amounts of money; however, more companies are making a respectable amount of money. In music this translates into the '1,000 fans' idea: the idea that we're all basically collecting enough fans to survive. If and when we find 1,000 fans, we will forever be successful. A 'fan' is someone who will buy every new CD I release, someone who will drive two hours to a gig when they find out I'm in their province and someone who will actually share my music with others. MySpace gives witness to this new world."

SONGRAMP, CDBABY, LAST.FM

Contacted through Facebook, Larry Killam is a beginning songwriter, but he's found yet another Web marketing tool to help advance his career. The site is SongRamp—a music community focused on the creative aspects of music and songwriting.

"They have a Writer's Room where I do 97 percent of my writing," he says. "Before I had no songs, but since I found SongRamp I have almost 20 songs. Before, no one heard my songs and now people from England, Australia and all around the world have listened to them . . . that didn't happen 20 years ago."

What also didn't happen two decades ago is the ability for artists to sell songs and gain mass distribution with such ease, without having to rely on a major record label. When it comes to selling songs on the Net, songwriters can sell them directly from their Web sites, creating their own online record stores and podcasts. But, if you're not ready to go the full

DIY route, online sites such as CDBaby.com and Last.fm will sell and distribute your music for a fair price.

CD Baby is an online record store based in Portland, Oregon that sells albums by independent musicians and pays them directly. Unlike a regular record distribution deal where musicians often make only $1-2 per album, when selling through CD Baby, musicians make $6-12 per album, and get paid weekly. CD Baby has been in business since 1998 and to date has paid more than $50 million directly to independent musicians around the world.

Jonathon Coulton, a New York based independent musician, has nothing but praise for CD Baby. "Anyone can put a CD in their store," he says. "You set the price, send them 10 records to start, if those sell, then send 20, then 40, etc. They also do digital distribution and have made deals with entire catalogues on iTunes, Amazon and Rhapsody . . . they care about artists in a way a lot of other companies don't." That's basically how Coulton's Net songwriting success story started.

EXPERIMENT GOING VIRAL

An independent musician with the heart of a geek, Coulton is a Yale graduate who left his day-job as a computer programmer to stay home and write songs. Between 2005 and 2006 he wrote, recorded, and published a new song every week as a free podcast project called "Thing a Week." This year-long experiment produced 52 consistently well-written and solidly produced songs, and he soon became an Internet sensation. Coulton's songs cover unusual topics not often heard in music and tend to make even the most jaded listeners excited about music again.

"I always intended to become a musician, but never got around to doing it professionally," he says. "I accidentally got a fulltime job at a company that wasn't awful, paid me well; I got comfortable and wasn't thinking about music very much. Around that time, a friend of mine started doing this reading series in Brooklyn once a month . . . a bunch of writer friends would get together and read stuff on a theme and he asked me if I would play a song at every show. I started writing a song for every show and it got me back into music and put me in front of an audience.

"Doing that is what woke me up and reminded me I like writing things and performing in front of people. I made a CD on my PC in my home studio and put it up on CD Baby. I sold 25 quickly to my friends, by no means a living, and all this while I was still working the day job. Then, in 2005, when I was 34-years-old, I quit that job to do music fulltime. For me to become successful as a musician lots of people needed to hear me and until that happened there was nothing else to think about.

"So, I started doing this Thing a Week. Every Friday I would post a new song that I had recorded that week, tried as often as possible to have it one I had written that week—there were some covers, a couple of recordings of half-finished songs I finished off, but 90 per cent were new songs. By this time, my Web site had become a blog; every Friday I would post saying here is what the song is about and here is a link to the MP3. I also published it as a podcast, so people could subscribe to it for free and get these songs pushed to their iPods or whatever software they used to listen to podcasts.

Coulton says a couple of these songs became viral hits. "People would e-mail me about them and blog about them or play them on their own podcasts," he says. "When that happens traffic would spike and lots of new people would come to my Web site. Over the course of that year, I set up a store, so the day I published a song for free, I would also add it to the store for one dollar. So, people could get it for free if they wanted, but I made it clear I was trying to make a living doing this. It was a very small percentage of the people who came who paid for it, but when the traffic numbers went up, good things would happen—by end of that year I was profitable—I was making enough money to pay for the nanny that was taking care of my daughter for the day. At the end of each week, I would put out all of the songs in their original order on a bunch of CDs.''

For Coulton, the most amazing part of his Net success is that it didn't feel like a lot of work. ''I just put my music out there and it found its way to an audience that was willing to support it.''

While Coulton admits to having a Facebook and MySpace page, he doesn't have an active presence in any of those sites. ''They really are just signposts . . . a trail of breadcrumbs back to where I live—my Web site.''

MORE ON MARKETING

Returning to Astrid Young, she says that while having a Web site and a presence on these social media sites is essential for songwriters, she believes you still need to market yourself in the traditional way. She likens these tools to the popularity of the expensively-produced rock video of the '80s and '90s.

''It's not going to increase your sales, but it's something that both your people and the industry at large expect you to have,'' she says. ''It's something that impacts one's ability to do business as opposed to being something that edifies your business in a financial way. There are lots of people who won't give you the time of day if you don't have these things in place. Just like artists, they are swamped with work, songs, other artists, projects, etc. It's next to impossible to get some people to do business on the phone anymore, or even in person—especially if you are trying to break into a market or niche.

''So if they can't dial up your various Web sites, you're out of luck. The networking sites, especially MySpace, has made it a lot easier for most of the world to have a viable site together, by putting together an easy plug and play package that anyone can use. And who knows, maybe you get lucky and someone happens along that really can do something for you. I have got a few gigs, a commissioned piece of art for another artists' album cover and some sessions . . . odd things here and there.''

According to Young, at the end of the day, you still have to market directly to the people who have an interest in you, which means gigging, selling your CDs to your audience at your live shows and getting a leg up on other ways of accessing commercial venues to promote yourself, such as radio and music videos.

THE MODERN MUSIC AGE

Daniel Lanois, 10-time Grammy Award winning producer and songwriter, who has worked with everyone from U2 and Bob Dylan to Emmylou Harris and Willie Nelson, released his sixth solo record *Here Is What Is* digitally on his own Red House Records—another advantage that the World Wide Web provides in these modern musical times.

''We tried this out as a way of bypassing the myriad of complexities associated with record releases in modern times,'' explains Lanois. ''If you want to put out a record through a record company these days, six months will go by before something even comes close to being on the stand for purchasing.

''I own the rights to this lovely collection of music, so I said, 'Why not put it up on the Web site immediately?' So there you have it: Lanois' corner store . . . we've harvested a nice batch of apples and here they are on the stand . . . they have not been on a truck ripening, and we did not have to clear them through customs or anything. That is what is special about the technology. Spontaneity can be our friend in these modern times.''

Songwriter Nancy Josephson agrees with Lanois that spontaneity is one of the biggest benefits of the modern music age. Josephson has a long and varied musical pedigree. As a vocalist and bass player she did stints with the Buffalo Gals, David Bromberg Band, Arlo Guthrie, Peter Rowan and Fiddle Fever. Nancy was also a vocalist with the legendary Chicago

Gospel Choir, The Annettes. Currently, she is a member of the trio Angel Band.

''When I wrote the words to 'We Are Shepherds' I didn't know how to get the song out in a larger way,'' she explains. ''It's a stinging anti-war song inspired by 'the surge' called for by President Bush. We put the song on our Web site (www.angelband.net) and invited folks to download it for free and pass it along. I don't know if it has had the ripple effect we were hoping for, but it felt really good to use what is arguably the largest way to get music to a broader audience.''

From reaching more fans to distributing your songs, songwriters need to harness the power of the Web 2.0 to help advance their musical careers. ''These social networking sites are indispensable to what I do as an independent artist,'' says Szabo. ''I couldn't do what I do, the way that I do, without them.''

Top Five Tips for a Successful First Demo

by Stuart Griffin

As a musician or songwriter, your demo CD acts as the primary part of your portfolio. Demos sell our talent and music to both fans and potential record labels, and they are the lifeblood of all unsigned bands and songwriters. While recording for the first time can be daunting, these tips will help you through the process and ensure your demo stands out from all the rest.

Tip 1: Attention to detail & preparation

Bands and songwriters often pay too little attention to their songs before recording them. A track can sound great in the rehearsal room, but you must evaluate your material from every angle before recording. Write out your song in a score program like Guitar Pro or Sibelius so you know exactly what everyone plays and when. Work with click-tracks at rehearsals and at home until everyone can play the songs from start to finish using *just the click*. Accuracy counts in a recording, and shoddy timing or playing from any musician will damage it.

Make sure you've fully written and rehearsed any extra sections prior to recording; for example, vocal harmonies or extra guitar parts. Musicians often waste too much studio time trying to hit a solo just right or a harmony exactly in tune. If you spend time in advance making sure you can hit the right note or play the solo just right, you won't waste hours in the studio. Preparation is the most important part of recording. If you want your demo to sound amazing, you have to sound amazing too—and that means putting in the hours before you get there!

Tip 2: Recording & the studio

Studio recording contrasts greatly with the rehearsal room. First, you will work with an engineer whose primary function, apart from running all the recording equipment, involves drawing the best out of musicians. Develop a thick skin if you find constructive criticism difficult! The engineer will tell the truth if you sang a note a little out, or hit a guitar note or drum out of time. He works to make your recording (and his studio) sound as good as possible, and that sometimes requires multiple takes. Your preparation before the recording will pay off here. Don't lose your cool when asked to sing the same section of song for the tenth time—trust your engineer to get the best out of you.

Take regular short breaks while recording. Hearing the same sound clip repeatedly dam-

---

STUART GRIFFIN is a freelance writer with seven years experience in the music industry, and has worked as a recording artist and promoter at both local and national level. He shares his time between writing and music.

ages critical appraisal; if you're losing the ability to tell the difference between take one and take two, take a break for five minutes. Head outside or into the studio lounge to "refresh your ears."

Finally, always allow enough time for your recording, including instrument and microphone set-up. Divide recording time into sections for each instrument. Add an extra hour's "grace time" between each instrument in case of problems.

Tip 3: Recording at home

Home recording provides an excellent way to make a demo. Programs like the free, open-source Audacity (Mac/Windows/Linux) and Garage Band (part of Apple's iLifepackage) make simple home recording accessible to anyone with a computer. DigiDesign's MBOX family (complete with Pro Tools) starts at under $500 and contains everything you need to get started.

The key to home recording is experimentation. Spend some time before recording your demo learning how to use your software and equipment. Run test recordings of individual instruments before attempting your main project to get comfortable with the process. Acquire essential equipment like quality recording microphones and cables to avoid sound degradation.

Explore different effects, sound plug-ins and EQ settings to find the ones that suit you. Experiment with different microphone placement to get the best guitar and drum tones, or try out different vocal mics for your singer. Fine-tune each aspect of your sound before you cut your demo.

Remember, if you try home recording and work with other musicians, *you are the engineer*. That means not settling for second best and encouraging your musicians or band-mates to push themselves to get the best take, just like a studio engineer. The most important word here is "encourage"—good engineers don't bark orders or belittle their musicians. Be friendly and professional and your musicians will follow suit.

Home recording may seem more intimidating than a studio recording, but if you spend time learning how to use the programs and equipment, you can have a professional sounding recording without ever setting foot in a studio.

Tip 4: Producing & mixing your demo

Once the instruments are finalized, it is time to mix your demo. If you can, familiarize your engineer with your sound and style of music in advance. Send him earlier demos if you have them (and a list of things you'd like to sound different this time around), or invite him to a live show or rehearsal. Bring along CDs of bands whose recordings you really admire so you can show him the drum sound you want, or a particular effect you like. Show the engineer examples of your vision to help him bring it to life.

Always leave enough time to mix the finished product. Mixing often takes longer than planned, so make sure you have enough studio time to finalize the mix. If you can, allow for more than one mixing session after the first. Take your first mix home, play it on as many different sound systems as possible and take notes to improve the second mix.

Mastering (also known as Post Production) unifies the tracks on your demo by equalizing volume levels, EQ adjustment and compressing the overall tracks. This gives a warmer, more rounded and louder sound than the basic mix and is essential for all demos. Most studios offer mastering at reasonable prices, or as part of your overall studio package.

Poor quality mastering leads to the downfall of many demos, especially those recorded at home. Mastering requires expensive hardware out of reach for the average musician and is difficult to replicate with home software. If mastering with home recording software, be careful not to over-process your demo and play it on as many sound systems as possible to ensure you have a fully rounded sound.

Tip 5: Packaging & press packs

Unprofessional packaging is just as damaging as poor quality mastering. Remember that your demo is your most focused, intensive selling tool; it must look as good as it sounds. A&R representatives receive hundreds of demos *every day*—yours must stand out. Spend extra money to have your CD professionally pressed and printed; it will give your demo a much better chance of being heard. If you cannot afford or have no access to a duplication company, make sure the CD has a good quality printed label and inlay card, and a proper case.

Most A&R representatives who listen to demos will only play them for a short time before moving on to the next one. Make sure your demo's first track has instant impact on their ears—edit out any long intro sections and choose your best track for the opener. Keep the overall length of your demo to three or four tracks maximum. Successful demos make an impression in the first 30 seconds of listening.

When you send demos to record labels or agents you must include a press pack, which acts like the blurb on the back of a novel. It sells the band or songwriter to the reader, and it should include a short biography, a good quality photograph of the band or songwriter, a description of the music, a list of any noteworthy forthcoming live shows, and complete contact details. Present your press pack concisely and cleanly on good quality paper (no photocopies), and limit it to one page, if possible. In addition, include any up-to-date supporting information (band Web sites, etc.) in the press pack.

Follow up your demo with a phone call two weeks after sending. A&R representatives are busy people; you may have to call several times. Be patient, polite and professional. Send your demo to as many labels and agents as possible to maximize your chances, and make use of any feedback offered to improve future demos.

KEY POINTS TO REMEMBER

- Preparation makes all the difference.
- Your demo is an offer to engage in business—be professional.
- Good quality mastering is essential.
- If unsuccessful on the first go, keep trying!

The music industry is incredibly competitive, so don't be downhearted if you receive rejections. Millions of songwriters and musicians struggle to "make it." Don't give up.

Articles & Interviews

Songwriting 101

What Every Songwriter Should (and Probably Doesn't) Know about Music Publishing

by Hank Bordowitz

S o, you've written a song. Now what? How do you make money from your creation? One of the key, well-established ways—in fact, the main way—of making money with your creation is publishing it.

Which leads us to, what exactly is "music publishing"? A complicated question, actually, but I'll try to explain.

While at one time—say, around the 15th Century—music publishing was all about the printing press, paper and sheet music (or "folios"), over the last 150 years it has come to be less about that, and more about the other ways people use music. This is a key thing to understand—any time music gets used publicly, that music has been published. So, once we get our heads around that, the question becomes how do we best exploit that?

The first order of business is to protect your work. Once you set your song down in a fixed medium—on a piece of paper, on tape, in a digital format of any kind—that song is copyrighted. When you fill out the form PA and send in that form, a check, and your song, in its fixed medium, to the Copyright Office (you can find the form at www.copyright.gov/forms/) they send you a receipt with the date and time they received the song and the number of the storage box they put it in, in case they have to retrieve it at some later date to prove your copyright. Now all this says is that at the time and date stamped on the paper, the Library of Congress acknowledges that you owned that particular piece of intellectual property. Very basic, but it puts the integrity of the US Government behind your claim of ownership. Once you send this off, you can move on to the next step, but be aware: The copyright office gets around 25,000 new applications every day. It might take four months until you hear from them.

If the song is a collaboration, you should also create a split sheet, which lays out just how much of the song you own and how much your collaborator owns. This becomes important when you start to collect royalties, as if the organizations paying the royalties don't know how to split them, they won't. There are some huge escrow accounts at music publishing houses for collaborative efforts where the songwriters couldn't (or wouldn't) do this paperwork. Make sure you do it first thing.

HANK BORDOWITZ has taught about music and the music business at Western Illinois University, City University of New York, Colorado State University and several other noted schools. He has written eight critically acclaimed books, including *Bad Moon Rising, The Unauthorized History of Creedence Clearwater Revival; Dirty Little Secrets of the Record Business: Why So Much Music You Hear Sucks*, and *Every Little Thing Gonna Be Alright: The Bob Marley Reader.*

"Royalties?!" I hear you ask. "Did you say royalties? As in money? Now, what about these royalties?"

Royalties are the heart of making money in songwriting. Since the days when people discovered that movable type could be used for music as well as words, composers and publishers—the people who created the work and the people with the means to produce, exploit, and disseminate the work—have had an interesting symbiotic relationship. They split proceeds from the work 50/50. The monetary nature of the relationship hasn't changed a great deal, even if the actual job that the publisher does has. The writer and publisher still split the royalties, but now publishing is mostly about the exploiting of the songwriter's work, knowing and tapping into as many of these royalty streams as the work allows. For the early part of your career, however, chances are you will want to assume both the roles of the songwriter and the role of the publisher.

This means you need to form your publishing company. This will involve going to your county courthouse and getting a DBA for your company. A DBA turns your company into a legal, recognized entity, allowing you to take the tax breaks of a company, open a bank account, and do all the things a sanctioned business can. Choose an original name, as when you get to the next step, if your company name is already in use, you will have to get a new DBA (not really expensive—the price ranges from around $5 to as high as $75—but do you really want to be running around doing paperwork at the county courthouse when you could be writing songs?).

Next order of business, you need to register as both a publisher and a songwriter with a performing rights organization or PRO. In the U.S., these organizations are the American Society of Composers, Authors and Publishers (ASCAP), Broadcast Music Incorporated (BMI), and the Society of European Stage Authors and Composers (SESAC). These companies monitor and pay for performances of songs in their catalog. We will go much deeper into that process momentarily, but first be warned: There is a Catch-22 involved in joining a PRO. In order to discourage everyone who picks up a guitar and thinks they're the new Dylan, sits down at a piano and thinks they're the new Dianne Warren or blows a sax and thinks they're Coltrane, you have to demonstrate that your songs have a chance of being performed, that, although you don't have an actual publishing company (because you have to register it through the PRO), your song is going to be published imminently. After all, BMI already represents over 375,000 songwriters, with millions and millions of songs, ASCAP somewhat more, SESAC less. As we will see, this number of songs is hard enough to administer without what the PROs see as dead weight on their books. So, your song will need demonstrated performances on stage, release on a commercial sound recording, radio play, commercial internet downloading, or some other use in a commercial and professional way.

The PRO will ask you several questions. The first is whether you are contracted to either of the other two PROs. You can only belong to one at a time. They will want to know if you have belonged to any of the other PROs, and what works are registered with which. They will ask you to fill out a W9 form for the IRS. This is, after all, about money, and Uncle Sam demands his pound of flesh. They will tell you that you need to register your songs. ASCAP, in fact, has a membership check sheet (https://members.ascap.com/ma/EwaWeb/pub/validateWriterApplication.do) that asks these questions, as well as questions about citizenship status, age, whether you have a credit card (there's a membership fee for publishers at all of the PROs), and whether you have e-mail.

OK, now that you belong to a PRO, just what have you accomplished, aside from joining the ranks of a third to half a million other songwriters? Just what do the PROs do? Simply, the PROs are one of the major sources of money for the successful songwriter. They issue licenses to the users of music performances and keep some of the money for operating expenses. Then, using incredibly Byzantine formulas that take into account the number of performances, the location of those performances, and the nature of those performances to determine what each song is worth during that particular time period in terms of cold, hard cash, they pass the rest of the money on to songwriters and publishers. In your case, you get both checks, one made out to your company, one made out to you. Not that the songwriter's share cannot go to an it, or a company. It must go to a who, or a person.

So, what constitutes a performance and gets plugged into those aforementioned incredibly Byzantine formulas? Just what do the PROs pay you for?

- Radio Play—any time the song gets played on the radio, particularly commercial radio, that's a performance.
- Television play—a song that is played on a television show is a performance. Prime time TV is worth more than daytime, network is worth more than local. When Kid Creole and the Coconuts played the Miss Teen Universe contest several years ago, they performed a dozen songs by the band's leader, August Darnell. "Now, the great thing about that is BMI pays enormous money for the use on TV when it's national and prime time," Darnell said. "So the fact that they used twelve August Darnell compositions was great money."
- Live performances of the song—these are harder to document and generally harder to get paid for, but theoretically, every time a song is played live, the songwriter and publisher get performance royalties. Certainly, everyone who puts on concerts pays for the license—it's a line item in the budget of every concert.
- If the song is played on a restaurant sound system, that's a performance.
- If a song is played at a football stadium, that's a performance.
- If a band plays it at a wedding, that's a performance.

Performance Royalties are just one income stream however. If your song is recorded and released—on CD, on the web, in a movie, in a video game, as a piano roll—that is called a mechanical duplication and makes you eligible for another kind of royalty, Mechanical Royalties. These royalties are generally administered by the Harry Fox Agency, and so you need to register your publishing company there, as well.

Harry Fox payments are very specific. For every recording pressed, the government mandates a Statutory Rate. As this is being written, the Statutory Rate is 9.1 cents for every song pressed on a CD, etc. However, the Copyright Royalty Board—the branch of the government (a part of the Library of Congress to be specific) that administers this rate has yet to decide on whether the rate will remain the same, go up, or go down over the course of the next decade. The decision is about half a year overdue already.

Unlike the PROs, once Harry Fox takes out their 6% operating fee, they pay the publisher 100% of the Mechanical Royalties. The publisher (in this case, your business entity) then pays the writer his or her half.

One type of Mechanical Royalty Harry Fox no longer administers is Synchronization (or Synch) Rights or Licenses. This is because most publishers, especially the large companies, prefer to negotiate these deals themselves. Any time music is matched up (or synchronized) with a moving image, the person doing the synchronizing has to get the rights from the person (or company) that owns or controls the music. These permissions can range from a letter of permission with no money changing hands to deals worth millions of dollars. The Rolling Stones, for example, licensed the song "Start Me Up" to Microsoft for the introduction of Windows 95 (the first with the "START" button). While synch rights were only part of the deal, the entire deal netted them a cool $15 million.

So, how does this all work? Well, let's walk through a hypothetical example. One morning, you wake up, put your robe on over your jammies, slip on your bunny slippers, and walk on down to the piano with an idea that's been jangling around in your head. So attired, you sit down and compose a song you are sure is going to be a massive hit. You switch on your MIDI composer, play the song into it, print a few copies out, and send one off, with check and paperwork, to the copyright office. You send another one, with appropriate paperwork, to your PRO.

With all the legalities out of the way, the song protected and now part of your body of licensable work, you bring it to a friend in a band that's rising fast on the record label radar (we all have friends like that, right?). The band loves the song and adds it to their set. It becomes a crowd favorite. Now, theoretically, this should earn you some performance royalties, but don't hold your breath waiting for them to come. For one thing, the processing time between when the song gets played by the band at whatever venues they play, until the time the checks get cut can run from nine to 18 months, depending on the PRO you choose. Secondly, the PROs don't have a great method for tracking play of songs in venues, so these "performances" often don't get credited.

However, in addition to rocking the crowds, your song also becomes the favorite of a talent scout who's followed the band around and made reports to the record company for which she works. Your song becomes the third viable hit she hears. She asks the band for a demo of those three viable hits, sends it to her employers at the record company, and sooner than you can get paid by a PRO, the band has a recording contract.

During the course of making the album, the band or their producer goes to Songfile, the Harry Fox Licensing Web site, and gets a license to record your song, thus registering the album title and record company and linking their recording financially with your intellectual property. So, when the record company presses up the first run of 25,000 CDs, they pay 9.1¢ per to Harry Fox, or $2,275 (those pennies add up!). Harry Fox deducts 6% for operating expenses, leaving you with $2,138.50. They send this check to you as your business entity, the publishing company. You put the check into your business account, then pay $1,069.25 into your personal account, i.e.; paying yourself as the songwriter.

The song also gets aggregated for digital distribution. Every time someone pays to download it, you get another 9.1¢. If 1,000 people download it, you get $91, minus the 6%, or $85.54, with $42.77 staying in your publishing company account, and $42.77 going into your songwriter's "pocket."

The record company releases two of those tracks that the talent scout thought could be smashes, and they do okay. The band begins to build a following in a few areas that add the records at radio, cover the band when they play there. The third emphasis track is your song. Several things happen:

The record company presses up 50,000 more CDs

- This puts another $4,277 in your publisher's pocket.
- $2,138.50 gets put into your songwriter's pocket.

They make a video of the song

- This means they have to obtain synch rights.
- Since Harry Fox no longer handles these rights, the video producer comes directly to you (wearing your publisher's hat) and offers you $3,000 for the rights.
- You accept it, without having to deal with the 10% that Harry Fox used to take off the top.
- The full $3,000 goes into the publishing company account.
- $1,500 goes into your songwriter "pocket."

The record company also presses up 10,000 CD singles with three different versions of the song.

- You get 9.1¢ for each version, or 27.3¢ for each CD single they press up, or $2,730.

- Harry Fox sends your publishing company $2,566.20 after they take out their 6%.
- You pay yourself as the songwriter $1,283.10.

As the emphasis track, digital sales increase as well.

As the song begins to get played on radio, and the video on TV, the performance royalties start to accrue. You'll see these in a year or so, but you know that they're there.

The song starts to climb the charts and people start to take notice. You begin to get calls from larger publishing companies offering you sub-publishing deals. While you have been doing okay as an independent, don't take these lightly. An established, "professional" publishing company can offer a lot:

- They know how to collect foreign royalties, for example. Some European countries will not pay royalties, for example, unless you specifically ask them. An established publisher knows how to deal with these foreign rights organizations.
- They can take care of administering the songs in other ways, making sure they get exploited to the fullest (if they do the job well).
- They know the players who use music.
- These players know the publishers.

Some of these potential sub-publishers will want to take over your publishing totally, telling you that it will make you more as a songwriter, you won't have to worry about the business end of things, and it will give you more time to create. You might want to resist that. A more typical sub-publishing deal will do all the scut work for 50% of your publishing. It is often (though not always) a case of giving up something to get more. Decide carefully.

In this case, you decide to sign up with a medium-sized publishing company for 50% of your publishing money to let them administer your work. Your songwriter's share remains totally yours.

Your new partners get busy. They start collecting foreign royalties. As the song climbs the charts, others begin to express interest in your song, as well. Production companies and music supervisors want to use it for the "ending" song for episodes of TV series. Other music supervisors want to put it into films. Your sub-publisher calls you up one afternoon and asks, "So, how would you like $100,000 for synch rights in the new Jet Li film?"

Now, in this case the royalty split is a bit more complicated. The $100,000 has been negotiated directly by the sub-publishing company. They take $25,000, or half of the publisher's share, right off the top. They send $75,000 on to your publishing company. You put it into your publishing account and then pay $50,000 of that to yourself as the songwriter.

Add this all up, and you've made $87,145, and that's not counting print rights, digital rights or those performance royalties. Not too shabby for something you whipped up one morning in your PJs, robe, and bunny slippers!

Of course, it doesn't always work out this way, even for successful songwriters. While not a "best case" scenario, it's a pretty good one and not a common one. It does illustrate how the money from publishing can flow in, with a bit of hard work and luck, a pair that often go together. As Thomas Jefferson once said, "I'm a strong believer in luck. I find the harder I work, the more of it I have."

On the other hand, things like this can and do happen. "When I sold my first song," said the late Tommy Boyce, who wrote many memorable tunes like "Last Train to Clarksville," for the Monkees, among many others, "I gave my mother a box of candy. After things got better I gave her a box of candy and some roses. When the Monkees started to happen, I gave her a box of candy, roses and a car. Finally, I gave her a box of candy, roses and I drove my parents in the car to the new building I bought for them."

It just takes one song to get a career rolling in a big way.

The Real Secret to Success

And Why Nashville Still Matters

by Michael Kosser

bout 45 years ago I read an article about becoming a songwriter. I think it was in *Writer's Market*—*Songwriter's Market* didn't existed then. I read the article again and again because it had to do with being a professional songwriter, and I had never even thought of such a thing. I didn't think it had anything to do with me. *I* was going to be an *author*.

Not that I was really, though I was going to be the published novelist I wanted to be. Books or songs, I was fairly certain that the people who actually saw their books in stores and heard their songs on the radio were people who had *something* I didn't have. Maybe it was contacts who could guide them into the business. Maybe it was the sheer nerve necessary to talk their way past the gatekeepers. Maybe it was even talent. Whatever it was, I didn't have it and they did.

What a fool I was to think such nonsense—and how smart I was to ignore my own stupidity. I love writing songs and I love writing books and I've written a lot of each. Yet I know that it's natural to have misgivings. The odds are against us all.

Who with any sense wants to buck big odds when an important life decision is hanging in the balance? Answer: We are capable of making all sorts of wrong life decisions.

People graduate from law school and fail at law. People go to medical school and fail at medicine. Or even worse, they go to law or medical school and succeed, only to find that they hate what they're doing every working day of their lives. So if you've found that you love writing songs, and you think you'd like to make it your life's work, then why not give it a try? Only there's no reason to give it a try unless you intend to put your heart and soul into it. That means you have to stop worrying about other people and what they'll think of you if you fail. In other words, take yourself seriously.

If you want to be a successful songwriter, you have to learn two disciplines. First, you have to learn the craft of songwriting. Second, you have to learn the business of songwriting. Now, here is the most important part of all this. If you have not experienced much of the process of becoming a songwriter, your goals feel very far away. And as you lie in bed at

MICHAEL KOSSER is a songwriter, author and editor with approximately 100 cuts to his credit, including recordings by country stars George Jones, Charlie Rich, Conway Twitty, Ray Price, Tammy Wynette, Barbara Mandrell and many others. His hit songs have earned him two ASCAP awards and two BMI Awards. His music career also includes experience in music publishing and the record industry. His most recent book is *How Nashville became Music City, U.S.A: Fifty Years of Music Row* (Hal Leonard, 2006). He is a senior editor at *American Songwriter Magazine*, where he has written a column on songwriting called "Street Smarts" for the past 20 years and has written extensively for news media and music publications, national and local. He and his wife live in Kingston Springs, Tennessee.

night thinking about how far away these goals are, you get this lonesome, helpless feeling in the pit of your stomach saying, *Why try, it's too hard, it's too far? I haven't got the connections, I haven't got the knowledge. I don't know where to start. I'm gonna work in fast food the rest of my life!*

I know the feeling. Forty years have passed but I can still remember what it felt like. So let's examine the steps that took me to Nashville, and while we're at it, I'll explain why Nashville is so important to nonperforming songwriters.

A SONGWRITER'S EARLY DAYS

In my early twenties I went off to Fort Sill, Oklahoma, to serve two years in the army. While I was there I learned to play guitar well enough to write songs. Nobody taught me; I taught me—not very well, but it was a start. If you're smart enough to find someone to teach you, you'll learn faster. I also started writing songs. Revisiting them today, they weren't very good, but they, too, were a start.

I returned to my hometown, Mt. Vernon, N.Y., just north of New York City, and played a little music in the area. I also wrote more songs. They were a bit better than the first batch.

Next I moved to Chicago (never mind why). I fronted a country band for 25 dollars a night on weekends and the eight-hour gigs reminded me that I didn't want to be a singer. I also met a man who ran a recording studio, who knew just enough about Nashville to make me believe I ought to move down there and strive to be a successful songwriter. Notice I make no mention about trying to be a professional songwriter in either Chicago or New York. Although both cities have a strong music community, I could not find a song industry in either with which I felt comfortable.

In early 1971, five years after I left the army, I spent two weeks in Nashville. I knew nobody, and didn't get to play songs for anyone, yet I met enough people to make me believe I could move there and make a go of it. So I moved here, got a teeny apartment, and began to play songs for publishers. In those days it was easier to walk into publishers' offices and play songs than today. But it's still possible.

Eventually I found Green Grass Music, a small publishing company run by a man named Curly Putman, writer of "Green Green Grass of Home" and co-writer of "He Stopped Loving Her Today" and a hundred more hits, country and otherwise. My songs still weren't all that good but he could see the hungry look and he let me hang around.

Within two years, I was beginning to get songs recorded, by people like George Jones, Barbara Mandrell and Tammy Wynette.

Putnam's company was then absorbed by Tree International, a major Nashville company that 15 years later would be bought by Sony. Tree put me out on the street a year or two later for lack of hits. A few years later some of those early cuts and a few others turned into hits. For awhile I rode in style. I felt connected. I felt appreciated. I even felt talented. For awhile. Then suddenly it all stopped—and stayed stopped for year after year after year. I felt abandoned. Unappreciated. Untalented. So I started writing books, had a little success, and that made me feel better. But I still missed the music more than I cared to admit. Then, a few years ago I was asked to run a small music publishing company, which got me back into the business, and my songs began to get recorded again.

SURVIVAL TIPS

During the last 20 years of this up and down period, I have been writing a column for *American Songwriter Magazine*, a good magazine that became considerably better a couple of years ago when two young go-getters acquired it and converted it from a small, country-based publication into a 100-page product that covers the entire American songwriting scene.

I have had a chance to study the industry from a songwriter's point of view and write extensively about it.

I don't write much about the craft of songwriting. Mostly I write about survival. I have seen hundreds of songwriters come to Nashville from nowhere with nobody to smooth the way for them. Most of them are good songwriters. Few of them are great. The determined ones often climb the mountain, have a year or three of hits, think the success will last forever, fail to take care of business, then slide down the mountain and never reclaim the determination to make that hard climb one more time.

I'd like to make a couple of blanket statements about becoming a successful songwriter.

- A lot of determination and a little talent can get you through the door and even to the top of the charts—once or twice. These days a number one country hit can make you so much money that if you really know how to take care of that money, it'll take care of you for four or five years.
- At the beginning, the songwriting business can be an enormous amount of fun. The first time you sit in a studio watching and listening to a group of session players turn your raw tune into a demo that sounds like a record, you'll think you died and went to heaven. And when you actually hear your song playing on the radio every day, your self-respect will border on self-worship—for awhile.
- As the years pass and the novelty wears off, you may soon find yourself writing songs strictly for the money, knowing that nine out of 10 of the songs you sweat over will never get recorded—or is it 19 out of 20? Then it will stop being glamorous or fun.
- And then when you find that your time has passed, you'll kick yourself for letting it slip away, and you'll remember how much fun it all really was when you dressed up in formalwear and headed for the ASCAP and BMI award dinners to get recognized for your most recent hit. And you'll long to get the feeling back again, that precious feeling of being a part of the Nashville hit machine.

I know the Internet has changed the business, the labels are dying and all that, but there is still terrestrial radio and mega-hits and in Nashville not all artists write all their own songs. How can *you* be a part of that?

I'll start by saying nobody is going to "discover" you. I'm sure you've read stories written by journalists who love to write about people who were discovered by some big-hearted, fatherly "talent scout" who found this guy basking in the park or that guy playing at The Bluebird or that girl singing her songs at her girlfriend's pajama party. I'm sure these stories are all true—but waiting to be discovered is like waiting for the Second Coming. Don't wait, *live*! In the case of being a songwriter, you must find a way to get a door opened for you, and when you do, have the goods to make the guy behind the big desk believe that you can make him some money. It's simple but complicated, difficult but doable. But so help me, people find a way to get through that door every day.

TIN PAN ALLEY

There is a wonderful songwriting tradition that flows from New York's Tin Pan Alley, uptown to the Brill Building and then to Nashville's Music Row. Each of these places knew an era when songwriters stumbled from their homes in the morning and made their way to their publishing companies, where they convened with other songwriters and wrote songs for their industry. Tin Pan Alley and the Brill Building are from a bygone era, while Music Row survives. In spite of consolidated radio's determination to kill musical creativity, the songwriting industry goes on and even thrives today on Nashville's Music Row. Music Row keeps the faith. It continues to believe that if you marry a great lyric to a great melody you can get a great song. It believes that if you write enough great songs, or at least enough competitive songs, then every so often the right song will meet the right artist and everybody will be happy.

From where you sit, you might imagine a happy band of merry tunesmiths writing songs, playing them for their genial, understanding publishers, smiling while their publishers tell them what a wonderful song they just wrote, and kicking back as these publishers turn these songs into radio music, and money. Well, it's true, sometimes . . . rarely. Most professional songwriters I know go through little streaks of success but are generally anxiety-ridden, wondering where their next hit was coming from, hoping their option will be renewed, glad for their newest cut but wondering if it's even going to make the album. If it makes the album, will it turn into a single? Getting a single may be the difference between making a few thousand dollars or a quarter million on the cut. It's mostly a struggle. It's mostly frustration. But then, so is the average rush hour commute, and many jobs.

I remember, my first year in Nashville, talking to my publisher about how nice it would be just having the "B" side of a hit single so I had something to root for on the charts. It's lovely having a couple of shelves full of LPs and/or CDs, each one containing at least one song of yours so when your old high school classmates come visiting you can assure them that, yes indeed, you have been successful in this difficult business, even though they never saw you singing your song on TV.

But let's face it, what you are truly striving for is the good fortune of making a living writing songs, so you can kiss your day job goodbye and spend a few hours a day in a Music Row office creating wonderful songs.

I can feel you tapping your foot impatiently. *Hey*, you say, *I'm reading this to find out how to get into the songwriting business. If you know, give me a hint, please!* Let me begin by assuring you that every week people come from Sioux Falls or White Plains or Toledo or West Yennumville or anyplace one can imagine filled with hopes and fears. They arrive in Nashville with no idea who to see or how to get started. Some go home quickly, but some of them stay and succeed.

LEARN THE CRAFT

Before you consider making such a journey, I'll assume you've learned something about writing songs. If you haven't, you're just dreaming, just pretending. There are colleges and night schools all over the country that have songwriting courses, and some of them may be good, but I'm not demanding that you take formal schooling. I assume you have listened to a lot of music over the years. I am suggesting that you have learned to play enough on a piano or guitar to understand something about rhythms, chords and melodies. In the old days of Tin Pan Alley and the Brill Building, this guy was a lyricist and that guy was the composer.

In Nashville, writers collaborate on both words and music. There are exceptions like pure lyricists, but they are exceptions. I assume that you have written quite a few songs and that you have decided that some of your songs are a lot better than the others. I assume you have put some of these songs on a tape or CD, and I hope you have been confident enough to play them for friends and relatives, because you'll have to do an awful lot of that on Music Row. If you've played out a lot, in clubs and bars, you're ahead of the game because playing in front of audiences gives you the kind of professional confidence that makes music publishers comfortable with you, and you want that working for you.

Arriving in Nashville is just like arriving in many other mid-sized U.S. cities. Music Row is just a part of what Nashville is so don't expect the population to be walking around in ten-gallon cowboy hats and don't expect most folks' lives to revolve around the music industry. Music Row is about half a dozen blocks long mostly on 16th, 17th and 18th Avenues South. The Nashville music business was, and still is, largely built on music publishing companies and independent recording studios. As a songwriter, the publishing companies are your targets because they are the middlemen between your songs and the recording artists you want to record your songs. Today a significant number of veteran songwriters are their own publishers, but being your own successful publisher takes time and experience. I suggest you leave the self-publishing for much later, after you've learned something about the business.

OPEN DOORS

Thirty-seven years ago when I arrived in Nashville, most publishers had an open door to new songwriters. Today the doors are closed tightly. Many publishers (especially the big ones) simply don't listen to newcomers. They work the catalogues of their staff writers and are not really interested in picking up single songs from newcomers or anybody else, unless they happen to be very promising young singers they can convert into singer/songwriters.

And yet there are ways and means to pry open those doors. You might start with the Nashville Songwriters Association International (NSAI), a strong pro-songwriter organization. Then there are the performing rights organizations, ASCAP, BMI and SESAC. From time to time these organizations present seminars for songwriters. You can get your songs critiqued at these seminars, but more important, you can meet peers, and you can meet established songwriters who are participating in these seminars. The performing rights organizations (PROs) have staff employees whose job is to spot talented songwriters and get them signed to their PRO instead of the competition. Or you can find out which clubs have writers nights. Sometimes established or semi-established songwriters play these writers' nights. The point is, performing rights organization staffers, veteran songwriters, and other folks you can meet all have something you don't: access. You could make cold calls to publisher after publisher and not gain access to a legitimate one. But there are literally hundreds of people you can meet who can make a phone call and get you through that door.

Now comes the challenge. When you meet an established songwriter or music business person, how do you charm that person into hearing what you've got and then somehow make him or her care enough to get you past the gatekeepers? After all, most of them are struggling for *their* next cuts. Why should they care about you?

And yet that's how it often works. So you appear at the front door of Ajax Publishing Company. It's locked. You ring the buzzer and do your best to look harmless. The receptionist lets you in. You explain that you would like someone to listen to your songs. She explains that they don't accept unsolicited material. You ask her where a new songwriter in town can get a hearing. She says she doesn't know. But meanwhile maybe there's a staff writer hanging around the lobby who is in a tender mood and drags you into a writer's room to listen to your song. Pure chance? Sure. But if you appear in enough lobbies, at enough seminars, maybe sing your songs at a few open mic nights yourself, wait tables in the right places ("Here's your check. I couldn't help but overhear that you work for Ajax Music. Do you have a card?"), then you really improve your chances to find a way through that door. And guess what—your early songs might not be good enough. But if you act professional—I mean this—if you act unanxious, interested in what the person has to say to you, and undemanding, you might make a friend or two who can help you. And believe me, this is one business where you need all the friends you can get.

Also, over the past three decades the Nashville songwriting business has largely become a co-writing business. Your co-writer may be strong where you are weak and weak where you are strong. Your co-writer is your best critic. Find co-writers with great talent, get better because you're writing with them, and never *never* assume that your line is better than his or hers simply because it's yours. When your co-writer comes up with a great line, praise him or her to the skies. And if you find a co-writer you really like, both personally and professionally, that's a cause for celebration.

YOUR JOB: WRITING SONGS

Now, this is *very* important. The word *no* is no big deal. Your job is not getting that one meeting with a publisher and hoping that lightning will strike. Your job is writing songs, getting meetings, writing more songs, getting more meetings and oh, by the way, doing the best you can to learn not just what's good, but what is good for radio and records. And if you spend your nights imagining that tomorrow's meeting will utterly change your life, you're setting yourself up for disappointment. It's the journey, not the destination, that matters most.

The way I'm describing the songwriting business, it seems hard—and it is. (If you are a really good singer/songwriter, it's a whole lot easier to get people interested in you. That's another whole story, however.) The trick, simply put, is to believe in yourself, not because you're the greatest writer who ever lived, but because you have the character to work hard, year after year, and keep learning, year after year, and not expect success overnight but expect success eventually. In other words, respect your abilities, and take your self seriously without taking yourself *too* seriously.

As we all know, the industry is changing rapidly and nobody knows what it'll be like ten years—heck, five years from now. Maybe we're living at the very end of the old era of publishers, record labels and radio hits. Who knows?

If you ask a hit songwriter how he or she found his or her way inside the business, he or she might have trouble explaining. I don't want to discourage anybody. But I know that there are those of you who think that writing country songs is an easy, pleasant way to spend your days if only they'll let you in. Well, it may be pleasant, but it's not easy.

Can you do it? I've known dozens of eager beavers who started by reading an article like this, journeying alone to town full of strangers, working at it, working at it, and finally enjoying real success. Don't you be one of those sourpusses who spends his lunches complaining to his friends that there's no sense trying to become a songwriter because they won't let you in. That's a copout that leads to a life of dreams but no substance. On the other hand, I'm not going to guarantee you that having hits on the radio will bring you a happy life. Still, it's fair to say that if you really, *really* want to do something with your life, you need to go out and at least try to do it. The dream may be better than the reality, but it's still not real, and in life it's real that counts.

The Latin Music Scene

It's Hot, Hot, Hot in Miami, Baby!

by John Anderson

t's a story of success, typical or not, but made to seem all too easy in the telling: Aspiring singer/songwriter shows up at a family party and meets a guest who so happens to be a professional music producer. Songs are sung, producer is duly impressed, studio time is arranged and a demo is produced, later released independently as an album. And to make a long story short, this eventually leads to a recording and publishing deal.

But when the setting is Miami—the de facto cultural capital of Latin America—such a story will almost always have a Latin inflection, switching between Spanish and English like the Spanglish speakers that populate the city. In this case, the singer/songwriter, Carlos Bertonatti, is originally from Venezuela, moved to Miami with his family as a young teen, and began pursuing music in earnest during a brief return to Venezuela and college there.

Back in South Florida, he began playing around town, and through a mutual MySpace connection was heard by Jorge Mejia, VP of publishing at Sony/ATV Latin, which is head-quartered in Miami. Mejia was impressed enough to offer Bertonatti a publishing deal. But there was one catch.

At this point, one would assume Bertonatti sings boleros, or rock-en-Español, or some such style consistent with his native tongue. But Bertonatti is most definitely an English-language singer/songwriter, citing influences like Nirvana, Guns N' Roses and other '80s and '90s rock groups, and with a sound as American as Jack Johnson, an artist he compares closely to. Mejia asked him for some songs in Spanish, but Bertonatti's affections, and talents, were with writing and singing in English. Even Mejia, a transplant originally from Colombia, sings and writes primarily in English with his rock band The Green Room.

BLURRING LINES

It defies conventional wisdom. No genre or market would seem as solidly in its own camp as Latin music and Latin publishing. Salsa, merengue, reggaeton and other styles under the Latin banner have strongly distinct beats and sound, and if nothing else, the language difference would seem to be an almost insurmountable barrier. And while that holds mostly true, the lines are beginning to blur, especially with prominent crossover artists like Gloria Estefan, Ricky Martin, Shakira, Marc Anthony, and Paulina Rubio, who have had success in both the Latin and domestic markets, and in some cases have even been on the leading edge of pop music.

JOHN ANDERSON is a Miami-based writer who has written extensively on the South Florida music scene, from soca to salsa to sacred steel, for a variety of publications including *Miami New Times* and the *Miami Herald's Street Weekly*.

For songwriters, this genre crossing is a little more difficult, requiring a certain poetic mastery in both English and Spanish. But it's growing, especially with first and second generation transplants to the U.S. from Latin America who are equally adept at both languages. And it's also reflected in the way labels and publishers do business, mainly with larger companies that have their hands in multiple markets.

In Bertonatti's case, the fluidity between Sony/ATV's branch offices, in New York, Los Angeles, Nashville and Miami, allowed Mejia to easily facilitate a deal between Bertonatti and their domestic division in New York. While the producer of Bertonatti's independently-released album, Chris Rodriguez, who's worked with both Latin and Anglo artists, was able to set up a meeting between Bertonatti and Charlie Walk, the president of Epic Records.

"As far as Sony's concerned, we're a big team. We're constantly talking, we're constantly doing things together," says Mejia of the collaboration between divisions and offices. For instance he says, "We're sending one of our songwriters to write with the (Sony/ATV) Nashville writers. I was in L.A. a few weeks ago talking up some of my writers that they need to sell to the TV department. As far as Sony is concerned, we're like a big family."

This reach is one advantage a company the size of Universal, Warner/Chappell or Sony/ATV, which operates separately from its record label division Sony BMG, has over it's smaller rivals. "Small labels work the same way we do, through relationships. But because we have a relationship with our sister company (Sony BMG), sometimes we have information that smaller publishers wouldn't have," says Mejia, who oversees offices in Argentina, Brazil, Chile, Colombia, and Mexico. "And because we have bonds with other big companies, because of our songwriters who write for their artists, then smaller publishers would most likely not have as much information as we do. That ultimately makes a difference."

CREATING A CIRCLE

One such songwriter who has benefited from relationships, and another product of the Miami music scene, is David Cabrera, a second-generation Cuban-American born in New York. Contributing to a diversity of genres, from pop, rock, hip-hop, jazz, Christian music and of course Latin, and in a variety of roles (guitarist, producer, songwriter), Cabrera's long path to a publishing deal began years earlier as a teenage guitar prodigy. He started as an apprentice at a Miami recording studio, and formed a band, The Front, that eventually signed a recording contract with Geffen Records. When rock stardom proved elusive, he went back to school, studying music at Florida International University in Miami, and followed, as he says, "a gradual progression of paying dues, teaching, playing clubs," before landing a gig playing with South Florida-based KC and the Sunshine Band.

"I became their musical director, and from there the circle kind of seemed to get bigger," says Cabrera of his professional contacts. He met people while working at studios who were under contract with different record companies, and soon began to do session work as a guitar player, as well as being musical director for anyone who needed it, since he says, "I could do that kind of stuff." Things began to snowball, and before he knew it he had performed or recorded with the likes of Christina Aguilera, Lauren Hill, Lenny Kravitz, Carlos Santana, Jose Feliciano, P. Diddy, Quincy Jones and Jimmy Buffet, to name a few. But he's probably best known for his work for the past 10 years with Latin pop-star Ricky Martin, first as guitarist and musical director, and recently as producer and songwriter.

But Cabrera had also been writing songs, lots of them, English and Spanish, stretching back to his days in the mid-'80s with The Front. He says he has amassed a library of nearly 200 songs that he can use, either in full or in part, to fit a variety of situations that might come up in his role as producer or musical director. For him, professional songwriting was a process that arose out of his other work in the industry, and the possibilities were a revelation of sorts. It started with a salsa song he penned and produced for a friend and publisher based in France, a song that took off there.

"It was like the gift that kept on giving. As much as I knew about music, I didn't realize the whole publishing game—that one could write a bunch of songs and strike a deal that way," says Cabrera. "It wasn't until I got involved with people I knew who were writing and had those sorts of deals, like Soraya, that I realized this was another avenue. I was like, 'This is definitely where I should be,' because I can still be myself and do what it is that I want to do, without worrying about the next gig or the next big tour."

The success of the salsa single spurred Cabrera to increase his writing and producing, but he didn't feel the need to pursue a publishing deal, doing well enough on his own through his connections as a session worker. But after Ricky Martin won several Grammys (music Cabrera worked closely on), he felt he now had a substantial body of work and a track record that people could take seriously. As an established producer, he was able to set up meetings with several music publishers. "When they heard the stuff that I had and saw the pedigree, I think they decided to make a move," he says of his deal with Sony/ATV Latin.

As a producer working with Latin artists like Soraya and Paulina Rubio, he has the influence, and the temptation, to push his own songs into the mix. But his goals as a producer mostly trump his aspirations as a songwriter. "Yeah, I could be a big fish and all my songs will appear. But that's not realistic and that's not really best for the record," says Cabrera. "My goal as a producer, even if only one or none of my songs appear on the record, is to achieve the best possible record and picture of that artist's wants and soul at that moment in life, and I think that is paramount." At the same time, if one of his tunes or melodies fits in a certain situation, and the artist likes it, then they both win.

Cabrera was fortunate. Because he was already established and known in the music industry, he was able to get in the door with many record labels. Unlike smaller companies, most major music publishers don't accept unsolicited material, out of legal and copyright issues. Instead they rely on referrals from known sources and established relationships, which for Sony/ATV Latin also includes demos arriving from their five Latin American offices. Songs come to them in various forms, from basic 4-track demos of just voice and guitar or piano, to full professional productions with the intended recording artist on vocals.

What someone like Mejia looks for in new material is its commercial viability, along with that ineffable quality that makes it stand out as a great song. He often prefers bare bones demos of voice and guitar/piano, to get an idea of the different ways it could be produced. But he insists there's really no set way, that there are many paths to successful music publishing. "As long as they've got songs that can do something commercially," he says. "We're looking for that magic, that indefinable quality that makes a song something that you love. But you can't really ever know exactly what it is. You kind of know it when you hear it, and you hope to be right, and you hope for things to be aligned to allow you to be right."

SINGER TURNED SONGWRITER

A songwriter who seems to have that magic in spades is Latin Grammy winner Fernando Osorio, who moved to Miami in 1996 after years of success in Venezuela. For Osorio, a songwriting profession was something that happened during the pursuit of his own singing career. He had formed a duet with singing partner Juan Carlos Perez-Solon in the early 1980s, and made the rounds to the record labels in Venezuela in the hopes of a securing a recording contract. But while nothing materialized initially, the producers were impressed with Osorio's songs and a number of them ended up on the albums of Latin music and Venezuelan superstars like Ricardo Montaner and Guillermo Davila. With success in songwriting, the label eventually rewarded Osorio and his partner with a record deal, and Fernando y Juan Carlos released two albums and enjoyed tremendous popularity throughout Venezuela.

After the duo split, Osorio began to pursue another record deal, sending demos to record labels, including to Miami-based A&R rep Ellen Moraskie, whom he had met on a previous trip to South Florida. "She loved my songs, and she wanted to offer me some kind of writing deal. But I didn't want to do that, I wanted to keep on singing my songs, and I was really looking for a record deal more than a songwriter deal," says Osorio. "I didn't get it at that time. I had no idea of what was a songwriter deal, because in Venezuela they don't use that very much there. She (Moraskie) went to Warner/Chappell, and opened the first Warner/Chappell office in Miami, and she signed me, I was her first sign. That was 1995. Then I moved here (the next year)."

Osorio, who likes to stay with the main idea when presenting newly minted songs—usually just voice and guitar—emphasizes the importance of a good publisher when talking about Moraskie and their working relationship. "She had this artistic vision when she heard a song, she knew exactly to whom it would work, and she would right away send it to the producer or the artist or the manager. So she understood everything you could show her," says Osorio. "She had a lot of believers inside the industry. It helped me so much, it was like going to college for me."

And while Osorio continues to release his own albums, his mainstay these days is as a songwriter. Nominated on several occasions for a Latin Grammy, he finally won for Best Tropical Song in 2004 for "Ríe y Llora," a song co-written with Sergio George and performed by Celia Cruz. It was the sequel to their smash hit "La Negra Tiene Tumbao" written and released several years earlier. "It became a huge song for her, and for us of course. And after that song, that album, Sergio was again in charge of Celia Cruz's album and they wanted a new 'La Negra Tiene Tumbao'," says Osorio. "Which is funny, because you want to write a huge song every time you sit down, but it doesn't happen all the time. So we just sat down and tried to write a good song, and that's when we wrote 'Ríe y Llora' which became a huge song again."

CROSSING GENRES

For a prime example of the modern genre-jumping songwriter, one need look no further than the prolific and highly sought-after Claudia Brant. From Pop and Rock to Merengue and Cumbia, English and Spanish, writing for Josh Groban and Danny Elfman to Mark Anthony and La Ley, Brant seems to have no limits to what she can write. Starting her career as a singer/songwriter in Argentina in the late 1980s, Brant released several albums while at the same time writing songs for a number of prominent Latin artists. When her label (Warner) began to go through wholesale changes, they parted ways and her focus turned to writing. "I said, 'Well, I might as well keep working on what's really going very well,' which was writing songs for other people," says Brant. "So I continued writing songs for more and more people and continued getting more cuts, so that's why I took the chance to come to the big U.S. To see if there was something else I could do over here."

With 20 Latin hit songs to her writing credit, along with awards from songwriting contests in Mexico and Chile, Brant was already a prominent songwriter when she moved to the U.S. in 1998. Not surprisingly, she fielded offers from all the major music publishers and signed with peermusic, before leaving after three years to open her own publishing company.

As far as the challenge of adapting songs from one language to the other, Brant tries to keep the exact music and the same sound and rhythm of the words. For Cabrera, he tends to think in English and has the most trouble translating idioms that make no sense in the other language. It's all about finding a new poetic way to say something, and still keep the gist of the song.

"It's a very difficult process to adapt a song from one market to the next," says Mejia, who often calls on writers with a proven track record in adaptations. "You need to make sure that each song makes sense in each market independently of what it did in the other market. Unless you're a singer/songwriter like Shakira, then it's the artist you're buying. But if it's a hit song in English, to put it in Spanish, the song needs to makes sense in the new language. Sometimes it needs to be an entirely different song as far as the lyrics are concerned. You can't just translate it, and you can come up with a totally different song.''

Adaptations may become more common as the lines between genres continue to blur. There's a generation of Latin songwriters and artists coming on the scene who have been as influenced by the Beatles and Pearl Jam as they have Celia Cruz and Tito Puente. A look across the border in Mexico and further south, and you'll see the rise of emo kids, hard rockers and punks.

''It evokes a lot of the classic (American) stuff we grew up and loved and listened to, and I think the Latin music scene has gotten better exponentially,'' says Cabrera. ''Even watching the American MTV awards, and Watching the Latin MTV awards. I'm watching Brittany and Rihanna over here, but on the Latin MTV awards I'm watching The Cure. The heritage side is such a big part of our (Latin) culture. And when that gets infused with some mix of The Cure, infused with the funk like the Stax sound of old, it really begins a fusion of other cultures mixed together. And I really see it progressing even more, now with the internet, and now with all the equipment that's available. The musicians can really create and really use all these different things that weren't available even 10 years ago. I think the sky's the limit.''

Across the Pond

*International Opportunities
for Songwriters*

by Maureen O'Donnell

What links Jimi Hendrix, Blondie, The Strokes, The White Stripes, Orson, and Scissor Sisters? They are all U.S. artists who had their first success in the U.K.

The artistic exchange between the U.S. and the U.K. has been going on for decades and is as healthy today as it's ever been.

British Radio deejay Steve Lamacq believes that U.S. tastemakers now consider the U.K. as a type of buzz barometer for U.S. artists and gives the example of The Strokes who played small venues in New York's Lower East Side without success for two years. They packed their bags and came to the U.K. for six months where they collected glowing music press reviews, loyal fans and a string of chart albums, picking up several U.K. and Irish music industry awards along the way.

The Scissor Sisters recorded a disco paced version of "Comfortably Numb," an old Pink Floyd track, as a B side for their first U.S. single. British club deejay's picked up on the track and it was subsequently released in the U.K. as an A side, reaching number 10 in the U.K. charts. The band went from strength to strength releasing chart singles and albums in the U.K. and winning three International awards at the 2005 Brits (the U.K. version of the Grammy's)—the first time in the Awards' history that any act had won in all three International categories.

On the back of the success of their initial venture into the U.K. market, both bands achieved chart singles and albums in the rest of Europe as well as Australia, New Zealand and China.

Music has no boundaries, so why create a self-imposed boundary on *your* music by limiting your submissions to only the U.S. music industry? In the dim and distant past sending your music overseas meant making copies of a cassette in real time, photocopying your biography and favorable press reviews, buying padded envelopes and lugging it all down to the post office where you paid a small fortune to air mail all these packages. Now you can e-mail MP3s, burn CDs quickly or send a link to your MySpace site where any record label or publisher in the world can listen to your music and explore the information that you've uploaded. There's no longer an excuse to exclude the rest of the world when you're looking for a home for your music.

MAUREEN O'DONNELL has worked in the music industry in New York and London. During her career, she has worked in the A&R Department at Chrysalis, Phonogram and United Artists, both as an A&R coordinator and A&R manager. She has also worked in music publishing and at BBC Radio. In 2000 she went freelance, working with record labels, recording studios, mastering rooms, artists and producer management and new media. She now lives in London.

Twenty-seven European countries currently make up the membership of the EU/EEC (European Union/European Economic Community) with another six countries awaiting membership approval. It's the biggest single developed market in the world with over 450 million consumers.

As the two examples of U.S. acts The Strokes and Scissor Sisters demonstrate, it can be beneficial to pay attention to the music industry outside of the U.S.A. What follows is information on several U.K.-based companies to consider.

EVANGELINE RECORDED WORKS

Based in North London, **Evangeline Recorded Works** has been releasing music by American bands and singer-songwriters for the last 12 years and is a well-established and respected label among devotees of Americana in the U.K. and Europe. The label covers genres you wouldn't expect to find outside the U.S. such as Zydeco, Southern Boogie, Texan blues and Cajun. Evangeline has championed American singer-songwriters such as New Yorker Ed Hamell (Hamell on Trial) and Austin-based blues composer-musician Tom Ovans, both of whom tour extensively in the U.K. and Europe in support of album releases. The label has a genuine soft spot for Americana and Roots music and also releases contemporary albums by heritage acts (Tracy Nelson, Loudon Wainwright III, John Prine, Ian McLagan).

Evangeline's sister label **Acadia** release re-issues, the majority being American '60s and '70s Psychedelic Rock (Spirit, Lothar and the Hand People, The Loading Zone, John Cipollina) West Coast rock (Hot Tuna, Sons of Champlin) as well as landmark Folk, Roots, Country, Bluegrass, Blues and Soul albums (Sir Douglas Quintet, Pure Prairie League, Link Wray, Brewer & Shipley, Screaming Jay Hawkins, The Fabulous Thunderbirds, Lee Clayton, Dr. John). Acadia is definitely worth approaching for European licensing if you are the copyright owner of back catalogue.

Both labels are widely distributed in Europe (Spain, Portugal, Italy, Germany, Holland, Belgium and France among others) as well as Japan, Canada, South Africa, and the U.S.

Evangeline will accept unsolicited material and prefers to receive CDs rather than audio files. They will also consider self-released albums for licensing and, as mentioned, interesting back catalogue for its Acadia label. Evangeline's Director, Pete Macklin, is down to earth and realistic. "It may not be a pot of gold on this side of the pond, but we try!" he says.

Send your material to: Pete Macklin, Evangeline Recorded Works, Executive Suite, Northway House, 1379 High Road, London N. 20 9LP, U.K. Visit their Web site, www.evangeline.co.uk, to get an idea of the eclectic mix of the music they like.

INDEPENDENT RECORDS LTD.

Another London-based label worthy of consideration is **Independent Records Ltd. (IRL)**. The label was started in 2003 initially as an outlet for new and established Irish artists (Sinead O'Connor, Sharon Shannon, Damien Dempsey), but it quickly expanded its repertoire to include home grown artists (Miles Hunt, We Start Fires) as well as artists from as far away as Mali (Tinariwen), Canada (Madviolet, Priya Thomas) and the U.S. (astroPuppees). The label has distribution and licensing deals in place in various European countries including Ireland, France, Spain, Portugal and Italy as well as Australia, Japan and the U.S. IRL is actively looking to license music in the roots, folk, world music, rock and pop genres from anywhere in the world. They will accept demos only as an MP3 sent via yousendit (www.yousendit.com) a free, secure ftp site, with a follow up e-mail to info@spiritmm.com containing your contact details. An alternative is to send them a link to your Web site where samples of your music can be heard. If you're looking to license a finished album and need to send a finished CD, contact them by e-mail giving them information about the album and request their mailing address.

IRL's sister company, **Spirit Music and Media**, manages several producers including John Reynolds (produced Sinead O'Connor, Belinda Carlisle, Indigo Girls, Madviolet) and would be interested in listening to projects in need of a producer. Spirit also manages artists and songwriters such as Jonny Male, ex-member of Republica and composer of their worldwide hit "Ready to Go" and is open to co-writes. *Contact them by e-mai:* info@spiritmm.com.

DOME RECORDS

Soul and R&B specialist label **Dome Records** (www.domerecords.co.uk) is the brainchild of former RCA and Chrysalis Records A&R Director, Peter Robinson. Based in the southern coastal town of East Preston, England, the label recently celebrated its 16th anniversary.

Branded as "The Home of Soul and R&B in the UK," Dome's current roster of U.S. acts includes New York singer-songwriter-producer Angela Johnson, Cleveland based singer-song-writer Conya Doss, Atlanta singers Anthony David and Donnie, Chicago native Donald McCollum and New Jersey's Eric Roberson, among many others. U.K. acts signed to the label include Incognito and Carleen Anderson. The label periodically releases "Soul Lounge," an album compilation series of soul and R&B tracks including a few tracks licensed in from third party labels. These compilation albums have consistently topped the iTunes R&B/Soul category download charts in a number of European countries. Dome has a network of European distributors, including Rough Trade in Germany, Belgium and Holland and Family Affair in Italy. The label is also making headway in South Africa, where its distributor is Essential Distribution.

Peter Robinson has a life-long love affair with soul and R&B music. "Although I have a wide taste in music, my first love has always been soul and R&B, ever since I saw Ray Charles and his band live in London in 1961 in my early teens," he says. "Soon after that I heard amazing records like 'Fingertips' by Little Stevie Wonder, Marvin Gaye's 'Stubborn Kind of Fella' and 'Don't Make Me Over' by Dionne Warwick, and I was hooked on this music.

"As I progressed in the music business, working in A&R for major labels, I was heavily involved with U.S. R&B and disco records in the late '70s and early '80s, and then signed my own U.K. R&B group, Five Star, who went on to top the Billboard R&B charts and appeared on Soul Train in the mid-'80s. When I started Dome in 1992, two of our first three artists were R&B acts, Sinclair and Beverley Knight, both of whom charted, and after that we were on our way."

Dome's pro-active approach includes press and radio & TV promotion to specialist radio stations and print media where they have an excellent relationship with the leading Urban Music magazines. The label services the two specialized urban music radio outlets in the U.K.: BBC 1Xtra and London's Choice FM, as well as Kiss, Galaxy, BBC6 Music and BBC Manchester that broadcasts dedicated soul/R&B programs. Dome also targets the increasingly popular London-based Internet and cable station Solar FM which airs adult soul and R&B to the U.K. and the world. Dome artists also feature from time to time on the more mainstream stations, national BBC Radio 2 and BBC London. Some of the label's artists, like Anthony David, have appeared on the BBC network TV show *Later with Jools Holland*.

Dome accepts demos as well as finished tracks and albums for licensing, and tends to focus on the more adult soul/R&B. Many of the label's artists have formerly been signed to major labels and retain strong followings. Material can be sent to Dome either by mail or e-mail and they will look at your Web site if you send them the link.

Submit CD's by mail to: Dome Records, P.O. Box 3274, East Preston West Sussex BN16 9BD, U.K. If you prefer to e-mail an MP3, send it to info@domerecords.co.uk. Dome will accept a maximum of three MP3 submissions (sent as one MP3 per e-mail).

JUST MUSIC

Founded in 2001 by former China Records Managing Director John Benedict and his partner Serena, **Just Music** is a fiercely independent label with admirable green credentials (all CD packaging is made from recycled material and paper from sustainable managed forests) the label specializes in cutting edge electronica, acoustic, ambient, down-tempo laid back grooves and chill music.

The label strongly believes the way forward is digital distribution, as John Benedict observes that most record shops are now devoting less floor space to CDs and increasing stock of DVDs and games in its place. Just Music has set up excellent digital distribution deals around the world and its music is regularly featured on iTunes' Electro and New Age pages as well as on Tune Tribe, 7digital and specialist Nu Groove site Click Groove. As a result, digital sales have steadily increased, nearly overtaking sales of physical CDs.

Just Music constantly strives to market its artists in alternative ways. The label regularly promotes its own club nights (Absolute Zero) and Serena is launching a series of Just Music compilation albums entitled *Just Music Café* which both she and John believe will be attractive to both consumers and business. Consumers will get a taste of the label's output and businesses will have an ongoing catalogue of music from the label available for synchs. Serena handles the label's synch licensing and, because of the type of music it releases, she is regularly contacted by TV production companies and ad agencies looking for atmospheric music. She advises artists not to write off outtakes from recording sessions. "I keep a library of session outtakes by our artists, snippets of music of a minute to a minute and a half, and have successfully placed them with ad agencies and on US TV shows" she says.

Just Music is especially interested in instrumental music and neo-classical musicians. Serena recommends that anyone who is thinking of submitting music to Just Music first looks at the label's Web site (www.justmusic.co.uk) to familiarize themselves with the genres that most interest Just Music. The label is very niche and there is no point in sending them music outside those genres.

Just Music is happy to take on representation of artists as well as license music for the world including the U.S. and would be interested in label partnerships. They prefer receiving CDRs when possible but are equally happy to receive a link to an artist's MySpace site where they can hear samples of music.

Submit CDs to: Just Music, P.O. Box 19780, London SW 15 1WU, UK. Contact them by e-mail at justmusic@justmusic.co.uk.

BUG MUSIC LTD.

Moving on to the world of music publishing, **Bug Music Ltd.** is the European arm of independent U.S. publisher **Bug Music/Windswept**. Based in West London, the company has signed U.S. songwriters and acts (Midlake, Chip Taylor, Deadstring Brothers, Madeleine Peyroux, Nina Nastasia) as well as U.S. publisher catalogues (Doormat Publishing the publishing arm of Matador Records, Coinfish Publishing the offshoot of Vagrant Records) independently of its U.S. office.

Bug can offer administration deals as well as standard publishing agreements. This means that after the term of your administration deal has expired, all your songs revert to your ownership; a significant yet often overlooked alternative when you're seeking to place your songs.

Bug's catalogue is gloriously diverse—Willie Dixon to Ryan Adams, Iggy Pop to Roseanne Cash, Calexico to Sir George Martin, members of Wilco to members of the Foo Fighters.

"For a publisher to do its job it needs a wide variety of music, especially when approached by ad agencies and film and TV researchers looking for a specific style of music. Bug's catalogue is incredibly varied which enables us to submit music to a precise brief," says Bug's International President Mark Anders.

Bug Music Ltd. is responsible for the rest of the world outside the U.S. and Canada—meaning all of Europe, all of Asia, Australia, New Zealand, The Baltic States, etc. They will sign worldwide deals to include the States as well.

Bug Ltd. welcomes co-writes with their local songwriters whether their writers are visiting the States or U.S. writers are visiting the U.K.

Submissions accepted via e-mail: (two MP3's maximum per e-mail) to: info@bugmusic.co.uk.

LONDON CALLING

Tracie London-Rowell is the former Director of TV, Film and Advertising at Universal Music in the U.K. and left in 2007 to form her own company **London Calling** which specializes in placing music in TV, films and ads. During her time at Universal London-Rowell successfully placed artist's music in various ad campaigns, such as Madeleine Peyroux for Simple (a range of skincare products) and the much praised use of Leftfield's "Phat Planet" in the Guinness "surfer" ad (which you can find on YouTube).

Unlike some synch agents, London-Rowell does not believe that London Calling should own or share in the ownership of an artist's compositions as a condition for successfully placing music. "Song-writing is an under-appreciated art form and I feel that it's unfair for anyone else to claim ownership of an unpublished song in exchange for synch licensing," she says. Instead, for a small monthly retainer and a percentage of the fee she negotiates for a successful synch, she regularly supplies samplers to the broad list of contacts with whom she has established long-term relationships including Working Title Films, Saatchi and Saatchi, JWT and Hothouse (TV) Productions. London Calling is on the "must call" list of all the top U.K. ad agencies, film Music Supervisors and TV Music Researchers when they are looking for the right kind of music to enhance a project.

The company has recently taken on U.S. singer-songwriters, John Mraz and Robert Francis for representation as well as the catalogue of New York based publishers, Shapiro Bernstein.

London-Rowell prefers to receive CDs but will accept MP3s attached to an e-mail (one MP3 per e-mail). She will also check your Web site to listen to samples of your music if you send her a link.

CD submissions should be sent to: Tracie London-Rowell, London Calling, 178 Doyle Gardens, Kensal Rise, London NW 10 3SU, UK. *MP3 submissions to:* tracie@londoncallinguk.net.

ADDITIONAL OPPORTUNITIES

The above are a small selection of the traditional routes available to U.S. songwriters and acts in Europe via the U.K.—but it pays to think outside of the box too.

It is not unheard of for an act to gain some radio play simply by sending a track directly to the radio station. The late John Peel, a revered BBC Radio deejay, specialized in playing unknown acts just because he liked what he heard.

An excellent Web site called **Radio-Locator** (www.radio-locator.com) lists just about every terrestrial and Internet radio station in the world, with links to those who broadcast live or stream online. It's a good way to research the stations in the U.K. and Europe that are playing your genre of music. For example, **Sing Sing Radio** based in Northern France (www.sing-sing.org) plays an extraordinary mix of music genres in an effortless blend and apart from a newsfeed every couple of hours, there are no ads and no deejays. Music by total unknowns is played alongside the good and the great. Someone at the station has a good ear!

Music press in the U.K. has always played an important part in introducing new acts. Often they champion an artist long before a record label or publisher takes interest. The prestigious weekly publication **New Music Express** (NME, www.nme.com) embraced the emerging genres of the '70s, '80s, and '90s like Punk, New Wave, New Romantics, and BritPop and was instrumental in introducing The Strokes and White Stripes to the British market. NME holds annual awards ceremonies and in 2008 held its first NME USA Awards at the Elray Theatre in Los Angeles which was co-hosted by American singer Har Mar Superstar who is relatively unknown in the States but well-known in the U.K. indie rock/dance scene. The publication recently launched a TV Channel (NME TV) which transmits weekly on the U.K.'s number one satellite TV provider, Sky TV. In addition, the publication has been promoting live shows around the U.K. since 2004 under the brand *Club NME*. In 2007, it initiated *Club NME (ITC)* nights in Los Angeles and New York City (at The Annex on Orchard Street) and is looking to expand into other U.S. cities.

The annual **In the City Music Conference** began in 1992 in Manchester, England and prides itself on being the premier unsigned music event. Over the years, ITC has held conferences in Liverpool, Dublin, and Glasgow and twice brought the event to New York in 2003 and 2007.

The British ITC accepts submissions for showcases from overseas acts. In 2005, Los Angeles band Orson appeared at ITC in Manchester where they were snapped up by a U.K. publisher and label. Their debut album reached number one on the U.K. charts and achieved Platinum sales.

The ITC event is heavily attended by the U.K. music industry. Daily panels, seminars, and master classes feature participants such as musicians (Billy Bragg, Brian Eno), music industry legends (Chris Blackwell founder of Island Records, The Rolling Stones' first manager Andrew Loog Oldham, rock photographer Mick Rock, Sire Records founder Seymour Stein), artist's managers (Ed Bicknell, former Dire Straits manager; Red Hot Chilli Peppers' manager Peter Mensch), record producers, and presidents of publishing companies and record labels from the U.K, Europe and the U.S. Attending these panels is a great way to network.

The U.K. ITC is held in the autumn, usually in October and demo submissions for a showcase are accepted from mid-May either online or by mail. Visit the ITC Web site, www.inthecity.co.uk, for information about submitting a demo. ITC has also released a compilation album of the best of the unsigned acts.

Originally held in Cologne and now Berlin, Germany's annual music industry event, **Popkomm**, is a threefold concept—a congress where music industry moguls discuss local and global issues affecting the industry, a trade show featuring panels and keynote speakers, and a festival. The festival presents more than 400 artists from around the world and applications to submit material for a showcase spot can be downloaded from Popkomm's Web site: www.popkomm.com.

London holds its annual **City Showcase** in the summer. Submissions are invited to perform at daytime or evening shows. During the four-day event some 500 acts covering all genres of music (including classical) appear at leading London venues such as The Borderline, The Barfly and The Metro Club in the evenings and during the daytime at participating City Showcase stores such as The Apple Store and Zavvi Record shops. Applications for U.S. acts can be downloaded from Sonicbids, www.sonicbids.com. Chosen artists from the U.S. will receive funds to help cover travel costs.

There are ample opportunities for U.S. songwriters and acts in Europe; all it takes is a little thought, a little time and a little effort. It's also about being in the right place at the right time; you may just find that those 450 million European consumers have been waiting for you.

Articles & Interviews

Adam Moseley

*Producer/Engineer Is Best Collaborator
a Songwriter Can Have*

by Shelley Marie Marks

The first listen—when from silence comes a melody and vocal so incredible that it rushes through every cell—is a one-chance opportunity that can launch a songwriter's career. Is your song ready for first listen? How good could it get if you had a veteran producer/engineer known for developing and recording platinum artists by your side, one who has the knowledge and the capacity learned to capture the greatest version of your song?

For veteran British producer and recording engineer Adam Moseley the art of song development, engineering and arranging is a bankable, time-honored legacy. Regarded worldwide for his song arrangement and instrumentation skill, Moseley has a proven ability to nurture, identify, direct and achieve exceptional performances from artists. Moseley chooses to take that first listen privately in order to make detailed notes based upon the first impression of the song. He often notes ideas for possible changes to structure or for additional parts to be written, such as a bridge.

During the first listen, Moseley says that sometimes the song is heading towards that first chorus and you have no idea what is coming next. "It may drop an amazing chorus on me, or not, or the song may take a twist and go somewhere else, or the pre-chorus may start to set up the chorus, but then fail to deliver. I will be listening, hopefully drawn in by the song, and suddenly wonder why the writer went to a certain part of the song at that time—or didn't. Sometimes a verse may ramble on too long, and fail to develop the melody into the pre-chorus. The most interesting part of a song can be the bridge, if there is one; often, it is the telling part of a songwriter's ability," Moseley says, then sites one of the most amazing song structures as "Weather With You" by Crowded House. "Just follow the journey that the songs take you on—remarkable writing, melodic development and structure."

Now is not the time to go it alone, especially as the music industry treads the digital sea. Top artists are relying even more on the visionary talents of producers and engineers to supercharge their songs and careers. When asked by *Rolling Stone* what musicians he sees leading us into the future, Coldplay's Chris Martin said, "Producers are like gold dust nowadays . . . they are the ones to watch." The producers seem to be the extra boost helping to lift the songs off the mostly mediocre, flooded playing fields. They can bring an edge to expand a song's vibe.

For songwriters from the U.K. to the Americas, Moseley brings an inborn talent and years

SHELLEY MARIE MARKS is a media content specialist and feature writer in the worlds of music, entertainment, visual effects, innovation, business, health, education and sport. She is partner/CMO of WAKENfx and is a creative online producer. Her Web site is www.shelleymariemarks.com.

of accomplishment at discovering the essence of artistry. He is renowned for brilliantly wrapping arrangements around the melody and vocals and is a natural leader when it comes to creating music, envisioning and capturing textures of lyric and melody while bringing out the best in someone. These traits have been of significant value for Moseley over the years as he engineered and produced at the famed Trident Studios in London, launch pad to some of the greatest songs, artists, records, engineers and producers on the planet, and onto legendary The Boat Studio in Los Angeles. Moseley is always about capturing the best version of a song at that moment in time. The process starts at first listen.

STARTING THE PROCESS

"When a song first comes to me, I am always aware of the legacy passed from my forefathers at Trident, my family and my musical education. The privilege of being given a first listen, and the ideas I may get, is a process often influenced by the great songs I have heard throughout my life. For every artist, every song, I take proper time. I only take that first listen when I can give undivided, calm, focused attention to listen properly. If I am in the midst of making a record, it could be a wait of days or weeks before I can give my full attention," he says.

"Every artist deserves that. Every song deserves that. For me too, it is essential that when I take that first listen, I can be open to the songs and allow my gut instincts to react to the initial impression. Usually I will review a minimum of three quality artist tracks. I know right away, even if it comes to me in a very rough form, whether the song has potential or not. Every time I finish a song, or even create a drum sound in the recording, I always ask myself if this is worthy of this legacy passed to me from Trident where some of the greatest songs were recorded, often through the keys of the Trident piano—from Elton John, David Bowie, Genesis, Peter Gabriel, Queen, Lou Reed, T Rex, Carly Simon to the Beatles."

Once there is a decision to work together, the process begins with Moseley sitting down with the artist/band members. He invests a lot of time to get to know the artist—where he grew up, his interests, influences and passions, his life situations. When creating an album and choosing the right balance of songs that will make up that record, Moseley also likes to hear some of the earlier songs written by the artists that have been discarded or not played for him. "Many times, songs are left behind because they were written at an earlier stage in the artist's life under different influences or circumstance. A good song will shine through—it may just be a case of reworking it to make it fit into the character, sound or treatment of the new songs."

EXPLORING THE SONG

Next, Moseley learns about the song—what the artist wrote and why, from every angle—what was going on when the melody was made in the artist's head, and when the lyric went on paper. The background work builds rapport and helps define the direction to be taken with the song, the textures that will carry and convey the sentiment and purpose of the song. Moseley then reviews his song notes with the artist discussing where the song is or is not working and why. They talk about song structure and instrument patterns—the details. It all gets mapped out.

Moseley gives input and the artist is encouraged to explore it and return with their next level of work. He declares, "It is the point where I find out the depth and potential of the artist; how they take the suggested ideas and stretch or adapt those ideas; who they become in the process is all very telling."

The filtering system of song and artist development is a proving ground built on mutual trust, respect, and understanding.

Most important to Moseley is the artist feeling completely that it is their record and understanding that he is merely bringing his experience to help them make a better record. He is careful to co-direct the song without physically writing it. Together, they evaluate segments of a song be it the pre-chorus or bridge, or release after the chorus before a bridge or middle section or the song's resolution, looking to ensure the mood is fully represented and that all the emotional points of the song are being achieved before recording. It may be an arrangement or structure issue that is simply changed or slightly modified and the next moment, the song is feeling more honest to heart.

"It is the best use of time, creative energy and money. Being prepared by really working the song to its absolute potential—these are not issues to be worked out in the studio. The trust must be built prior with everyone clearly aimed toward the same direction for the version of the song before we are anywhere near the studio."

Pre-production can take days or weeks. Moseley will constantly bounce ideas around with the artist for structure changes, performance style and approach, all within the experimental freedom of the rehearsal room environment. To try an idea or quick change in rehearsal takes only minutes—and it is usually pretty clear to everyone whether an idea works or can be taken further. There is rarely any resistance to at least trying an idea. If there is reluctance, it reflects a lack of trust, which does not bode well for the relationship and upcoming studio phase. That must be addressed. Everyone must be clear about the song's direction and on the same page.

The amount of preparation time and attention Moseley dedicates to finding a pure, honest, simple rendition of the song could be daunting for some. After three decades in the studio with multi-platinum artists, he knows the fundamental physical, mental and musical discipline necessary to making a great song. "Many artists are naïve to the mental and musical focus that is required," says Moseley. "It takes massive preparation to be musically conditioned and capable of handling the emotional and physical pressure while aligning everyone to the best version of a song. It takes willingness to receive input and awareness to apply it correctly."

SONG DEVELOPMENT

The development phase helps to sift through the ideas that don't work so that all the creative energy can be spent on improving the song. The intense work ahead of studio time clarifies the heart and purpose of a song and reveals the most honest expression of an artist. Knowing that something may change once in session, Moseley always works to capture the best possible version of that song at that time. He taps into his vast range of experience from tracking with classic Neve and Trident boards, to utilizing the latest ProTools HD3 technology and recording/mixing systems. Drawing from his culturally diverse project history, Moseley helps the artist to reach a scope of sound not thought possible. "The techniques and tools change, but the captured sound is unmistakable whether old-school or modern technology. For my work it comes down to awareness and proper use of the equipment to help us achieve one end goal. We utilize whatever is appropriate and best suits the recording, to achieve the goal we set for the song," says Moseley. "If it feels good, then probably it's right."

The pre-production time developing the song shows through in the studio when an artist really opens up. Moseley relishes those amazing moments with a songwriter when the textures and colors of the song start to fit and lay in perfectly. "To get the vocal delivered honestly is a key. I strive to really place the performer in the midst of the inspiration that led to the creation of the song. The vocal must absolutely reflect the purpose and emotion of the song and lyric, be that humility, frailty, love, anger—or being really pissed off!" Moseley questions the artist, "Why did you write this song in the first place? What's it about and what are you saying in the lyric? Now go and perform that so I can capture it! Each song is unique, each artist is different and the whole process is a truly personal and subjective experience. A great song is a great song, and you can't cheat that."

From Moseley's producer/engineer/arranger perspective, a knockout song starts with an amazing melody and a great vocal. "Great artists just sing the song—there is purity in the delivery—a pure presentation where the vibe and melody shine forth and the arrangement unifies around the vocal. The greatest songs have a commonality; they are believable and earnest. The achievement is to capture and represent the essence and purpose of the song and deliver that emotion."

If the level of quality, honesty and timelessness makes a song, what holds a song back? Moseley talks about the irony of arrogance and ignorance. The arrogance can manifest in an unwillingness to try something different, or a laziness not to want to work a little bit harder shaping or developing the song if necessary. The ignorance can simply be the inexperience of not knowing how. In either case, Moseley feels his role and responsibility is to be the catalyst, the mirror image to the songwriter—and push, encourage, motivate or help them make a better song. For Moseley, there is no justification or excuse for not trying.

Ultimately the songwriter must find and build internal encouragement. The purpose of the learning is to tap the quiet, honest brilliance in the artist and bring it out so it freely reflects where you want to go with the song. Some artists who are not songwriters may fail to properly interpret or understand the essence or purpose of a song. They may end up projecting something quite different from what was intended by the writer and the motivation that created the song. It comes across shallow and cold in their performance. Moseley says, "Don't show off and sing scales—just sing the bloody song—it's all there in the melody!"

Honest, clear reflection is what Moseley listens for and that sometimes is raw, bold and in your face. Turmoil and angst can move people when it is expressed responsibly from smart introspection. Moseley says it takes a huge amount of awareness to focus the energy properly and not get blindsided by it.

"Sometimes the artist is unaware of what can actually be achieved—the capacity. It can hold back the song. Other times an artist is not willing to put the work in to better it—the song suffers. This is the double edge with arrogance . . . being single minded and determined to do things your own way can also be the factor that sets you apart and has often led to some of the greatest success stories. Consider U2, Coldplay, Muse, Alanis Morrisett, Radiohead, Björk . . . and my favorite band, Elbow. Not following the trend, or predictably being safe and following the trend, either has set artists apart to win worldwide audiences. It is so subjective, and who is anyone to judge? There are artists who I want to be self-indulgent—direct about who they are and what they are saying. It is a delicate balance."

WORKING AS A TEAM

Developing songs and working with renowned artists of this broad scope is not about taking over. It is a team effort. From first listen when a song catches his attention, Moseley looks to work with two kinds of artists—one who has really found his center and one who has raw talent, fresh and eager, who can be really helped. He looks for professionalism and willingness. It is clear to him in the way someone cares for himself, his health, practice habits, and application and focus. Inspiring characteristics in songwriters are often organic. There are so many factors to look for in commitment and how well one knows oneself. It seems to always be about the honesty and purity of the musical presence. "Is the artist real, believable—do they mean what they are singing—are they captivating and holding my attention—are they saying something with their music?" asks Moseley.

He enjoys working with diverse artists who bring an awareness of a larger vision for themselves and their passions. "It fires me up to hear the energy of a song come through from deep passions and life experiences. Today's marketplace for an artist is as probable in Asia or Europe as America. We work to build that into the record—the cross-cultural timelessness of a song can only be honestly presented from an artist willing to express the fullness of their character and life knowledge," says Moseley. "It is inspiring to others hearing the vulnerability, the discovery and the mood so fully represented—no matter where you were born or what language you speak. The mood and vibe is universal. Whether mature and worldly, naïve and inexperienced—the purity of the song lies in the performance, which must be honest to the essence of the message."

Discussing Moseley's client roster and review of favorite songwriters is like playing global Twister crossing so many planes of music from so many countries. After years between Europe and the U.S., Moseley resides in Los Angeles bringing his experience and skills to the development of new artists while he continues to work with established artists.

Recent artists include Lucybell, Los PinGuos, John Cale, Airpushers, Building a Better Spaceship, Four Fifty One, Johnnie Burton, Michelle Aragon and Ryan Hanifl. His current favorite songwriters are Elbow, Travis, Muse and Damian Rice. Adam's all-time favorites are Elbow, Lennon, McCartney, Stevie Wonder and Joni Mitchell.

Moseley talks about Bonnie Raitt's "I Can't Make You Love Me," produced by Don Was/ piano by Herbie Hancock, as another perfect example of just sing the song—the purity of delivery, the artist reliving and presenting the lyric and melody simply, unpretentiously, with the most sublime arrangement to encompass the song and respect the moment and the sentiment that created the song. "But then again," he says, "Trent Reznor is pretty convincing with his Nine Inch Nails vocal performance on 'Closer.' Just be honest to the song, create a believable vibe and capture the performance."

A PRODUCER'S LEGACY

Thirty years ago, Moseley was involved in different roles on some of the great songs of time: in 1979, Rush's "Spirit of Radio"; in the '80s, The Cure's "Close to Me," Blow Monkeys "Dig'n Your Scene," Bugles "Video Killed the Radio Star," Richard Marx's "Endless Summer Nights," Maxi Priest's "Ease the Pain," and Wet, Wet, Wet's "Broke Away," plus work by other artists including Roxette.

In 1994, one of Moseley's favorite songs ever, "Born to Grow" by Misty Oldland, was a song that was started at an upright piano in her living room and ended up with the most beautiful arrangement with strings. The creation and production of this song encompasses all that Moseley talks about in his approach. The process is still the same, if not even more important to be aware and awake to what is most honest for the artist and the song.

"It has been a long time since I was first allowed in the Trident mix room—in 1979 when they were aligning the main monitors by measuring the frequencies and 'passing white and pink noise' through the monitors. Once the monitors were technically adjusted to spec, they would bring forth the 'reference reel'—a compilation of some of the great songs recorded and mixed at the studio—Elton John's 'Rocket Man,' David Bowie's 'Soul Love,' Genesis' 'Follow Me, Follow You,' and Queen's 'Killer Queen.' It was so overwhelming to feel the power of such outstanding songs blasting through the speakers—traveling through me with the melody, vocals, arrangements and engineering—the mood completely reflected. That single moment has lived in me throughout my career.

"The legacy and standards instilled in me by my peers has driven and pushed me to do my very best to achieve the maximum potential and purpose when working with a songwriter and recording a song. It has been amazing to come full circle to work with the Blow Monkeys again on a new record after three albums and 23 years later. Hearing a Maxi Priest song I recorded and produced playing on a bus in Barbados or my son's friends playing as their ring tone a song made 10 years before they were born—this is the priceless privilege of my life working with music."

Articles & Interviews

Kenny Gamble & Leon Huff

Hall of Famers on Their Remarkable Career

© Whitney Thomas

by Ken Sharp

Songwriting legends, hit producers, and label founders of Philly International, Kenny Gamble and Leon Huff are known as "Architects of the Philly Sound."

Through such timeless self-penned songs as "Love Train," "For the Love of Money," "If You Don't Know Me By Now," "Me and Mrs. Jones," "Only the Strong Survive," "TSOP (The Sound of Philadelphia)," "The Love I Lost," and countless other smash hits, Gamble & Huff surrounded themselves with a talented roster including the O'Jays, Harold Melvin & the Blue Notes, Archie Bell and the Drells, Lou Rawls, Teddy Pendergrass, the Three Degrees and others.

Quickly, they built a towering musical dynasty, fashioning impeccably crafted message songs, awash in strings, horns, violins, and cellos, all driven by the passionate musicality of the MFSB ("Mother Father Sister Brother") band.

Inducted into the Rock and Roll Hall of Fame in March of 2008, Gamble & Huff are living testament to the enduring appeal of their wonderful body of work.

Here they talk about the Philly Sound, the inspiration and collaboration behind some of their enduring hits, and the R&B royalty who recorded them.

Characterize what each of you brings to the table as a creative team.

Leon Huff: I'm the musician and Gamble's the lyric writer. It's a pure collaboration but sometimes Gamble will come up with something musically. For instance, I think Gamble was the one who came up with the "Me and Mrs. Jones" chords that he showed me. It's a pure collaboration. Whatever needs to be done we can do it.

Kenny Gamble: Huff said it pretty much. Huff's a master keyboard player. We feed off of each other. He might play a chord—and it's hard to explain—but that chord resonates in my brain into words. Then another word will come and then another chord and before you know it we're rollin'. Huff is banging on that piano and the groove is being set. It's destiny. It's magic. Some things are just meant to be and you have no explanation for it. It just works.

KEN SHARP is a music writer who's authored more than 10 music books including *Elvis Presley: Writing for The King*; *KISS: Behind the Mask*; *Overnight Sensation: The Story of the Raspberries*; *Rick Springfield: A Year in The Life of a Working Class Dog*; *Eric Carmen: Marathon Man*; *Reputation Is a Fragile Thing: The Story of Cheap Trick*; and others. He's also a singer-songwriter with three CDs to his credit including his latest release, *Sonic Crayons*. Visit www.myspace.com/kensharpmusic.

What's the quickest song you ever wrote, a song that came almost like a gift?

Gamble: A lot of songs came like that but the one that pops in my head is "Family Reunion" by the O'Jays. That came quick. That was a great inspiration because that song has now become a classic for family reunions.

Can you define the Philly Sound?

Huff: When Gamble & Huff came up on the scene I think that's the first time I started hearing that phrase, the "Philly Sound." We had a style of writing that people took notice of. After we started our production company and began working with Wilson Pickett and Nancy Wilson, Archie Bell and the Drells, Dusty Springfield, people started noticing a certain style that was coming out of Philadelphia. We basically were using the same musicians, the same arrangers, and the same studio (Sigma Sound), and the same engineer (Joe Tarsia). Sooner or later you develop a signature sound that people start noticing.

What were some of the musical trademarks of that sound?

Huff: I'd say the orchestration. I played in bands and Gamble was always into orchestration. We started using tympani, vibes, French horns in our music. We loved strings. Cellos and violas. We incorporated all of that into our orchestration.

There's a classical overtone to much of your music.

Huff: Most of the string players were classical players that played in the Philadelphia Symphony Orchestra, some were retired players. So you can imagine those musicians playing Mozart and then coming over to our studio and playing funk. It was amazing.

Gamble: They loved it though.

Huff: We see some of those players today. They're just thankful that they experienced that.

The core band on all the Philly International records was spectacular.

Huff: Gamble had a band called Kenny Gamble and the Romeos and I was his keyboard player. Thommy (Bell) was the original keyboard player and I took his place when he changed careers and became an arranger. I became the keyboard player. That band evolved into the MFSB orchestra. The first players were myself on keyboards—I was playing electric Wurlitzer. Then you had Roland Chambers on guitar, his brother Carl on drums. Then we had Winnie Wilford on bass. That was the beginning. Then when we started making records it changed into Earl Young on drums, Ronnie Baker on bass, and Norman Harris on guitar. We had Barry Washington on congas. Then we had Jimmy Williams on bass and Charles Collins on drums. We also had Bobby Eli on guitar. In fact, Bobby Eli was the one who brought us the wah-wah 'cause Bobby used to come in the studio with all these contraptions. I'd say, "Let's listen to what that sounds like." We were amazed with his wah-wah sound. We used it on Wilson Pickett's productions, "Engine Number Nine." It just kept evolving and building. I think we had the best musicians in Philly at that time.

Discuss how Gamble & Huff's songs reflected the outside world, the social and political tumult in the culture.

Gamble: Say for example, "Love Train." That song came around '72, '73 when the Vietnam War was still happening. It was just unbelievable. The sentiment in the country and around the world, people were just so hostile to each other. Huff and I were talking, we were saying, people all over this world need to be together. "Love Train" was a way to say that without it being dogmatic or like you were beating somebody over the head with a message. But it was fun, it was light and it was happy. We were talking about people sharing and caring about each other and that's a good thing. That message is still out there today. I think that characteristic of humans where he treats his fellow man with so much oppression is sadly not going away any time soon. So this song gives hope. We tried to mention many countries in the song. All of those countries are still in the spotlight—Russia, China, Israel, Egypt, Africa, India, Japan, the United States of America. We got them all in there. (*laughs*)

That's the kind of song that comes out of that kind of climate and environment that you live in. Plus you gotta remember that Philadelphia is the birthplace of America. The spirit that created America, the Constitution and the Declaration of Independence, and this whole great democracy that we have was in Philadelphia. It's the first capital of the United States. The first flag is in Philadelphia too. You've got some tremendous events in history that happened in Philadelphia. When you walk the streets of Philadelphia you're walking around history and that's reflected in our music. So it's still there. We're living with that and that's still in that vicinity. Our songs are in different categories. Some of the songs would be political and social. Some of them would be great love songs like "Me and Mrs. Jones," "Close the Door" by Teddy Pendergrass, the O'Jays' "Darling Darling Baby" and then the other category were songs that make you dance and make you have a good time like "For the Love of Money."

But that song still carries a strong message.

Gamble: Yeah, it's got a message. The whole theme of our music was, "a message in the music." In fact, we wrote a song for the O'Jays called "Message in the Music." And on all the liner notes featured on the back of our albums we would mention "a message in the music." That's what we were trying to convey. One of the lyrics in the song, "Message in the Music" was "understand while you dance . . ." In other words, don't just dance but listen to the music and the words too.

Huff: The best thing about our message songs is none were written with anger. We were just talking about how we were feeling and the reality of it all. Gamble is such a freestyle writer; those words in songs like "For the Love of Money" were just automatically flying off his brain.

Daryl Hall, another Philly boy, has lauded "Me and Mrs. Jones" as the greatest song ever written.

Huff: "Me and Mrs. Jones" was a scene that came before our eyes. Every morning I used to come from Camden, New Jersey, to meet Gamble and we'd eat breakfast together in this restaurant. We kept seeing this couple come in every day. They used to sit at the same table. When they'd get up to go, she'd go her way and he'd go his way. The next day at the same time, same place, same table, the same thing would happen all over again. Me and Gamble saw that scene develop and worked that out in a story. It wasn't Jones at first. We had some other names, Smith, Johnson.

Gamble: "Me and Mrs. Johnson." (*laughs*)

Huff: But Jones worked out to be the one that sounded the best. That was a real scene that developed before our eyes.

"Backstabbbers" could be directed towards quite a few folks in the music business.

Huff: McFadden and Whitehead brought that story to us. Me and Gamble were starting to get busy. I happened to go to an area in my studio where we had a candy machine and a water fountain. They kept saying to me, "Huff, we got something that we want you to read." They didn't have any music, just words written on a piece of paper. I took it and showed it to Gamble because the story was so real. What are they doing? Smiling in your face. . . . I'm not sure where they got their idea but "Back Stabbers" is so universal. You've got more back stabbers today than you had in the '70s. I think that story is gonna be around forever. Me and Gamble went into the studio and cut that track. I thought something had to be dramatic in the song because the story was so dramatic so I came up with that piano roll up in the front. That roll says, Uh oh, something's comin'.

Many of the themes in your songs are still timeless—"Love Train," "For the Love of Money," "Only the Strong Survive."

Gamble: Let's take "For the Love of Money." I think it hits you more today because you're learning more. It hit me when we first did it and today it still stands up. Where that song came from is there's a verse in the Bible that says, "The love of money is the root of all evil." It's not money itself. We were talking about how people will do anything for money. Just listen to the lyrics. For the love of money you can do good things but you can do bad things with it, it all depends on who you are. We talked about how for the love of money (*recites lyrics*) "people will steal from their mother, for the love of money people will rob their own brother. For the love of money, people can't even walk the street because they never know who in the world they're gonna beat, for that lean, mean, mean green Almighty dollar. A woman will sell her precious body and a small piece of paper has got so much weight. Money means so much to people."

That song characterizes people who are in it just for the money. You don't have much substance when you're just in it for the money. You've got to be in it for the excellence and in it for the greatness of things. Money is something that everybody needs but it's best not to even talk about it. It's better just to be conservative and to be respectful. In today's society that's all that they're thinking about, the "bling bling" and the money. So you wind up living in a shallow world.

We wanted to make great records and great songs. We wanted to make a living too. Don't misunderstand me, we wanted to get that paper, just like everybody else. (*laughs*) But we also had good judgments. We always would confer with each other, What's the best thing for us to do? We decided to be conservative. We decided to invest our dollars into ourselves and into other people and into our community. So our lives are fulfilled because it's got substance to it.

"If You Don't Know Me by Now" by Harold Melvin & the Blue Notes has had an amazing life, and was resurrected in 1989 by Simply Red.

Gamble: "If You Don't Know Me by Now" is a song about relationships. Just imagine yourself in a relationship, you come home from work and she says, "Where you been at?" You say, "I've been working?" Then she says, "Why you out so late?" It's like somebody's trying to smell you to see if you have perfume on you. It's suspicion. They don't trust you. That's the kind of thing that song is about. People who have been together 10 or 15 years and still don't know each other and still don't trust each other. (*Recites lyrics*) "If you don't know me by now you'll never ever know me . . ." That was the key to that song. (*Recites more lyrics*) "What good is a love affair when you can't see eye to eye?" It don't mean nothin'; you're just fooling yourself.

"I'm Gonna Make You Love Me" was an early hit.

Huff: Gamble and a gentleman named Jerry Ross started writing that song and I came in as a third writer. That song didn't take that long to write. It was one of the fast ones. We recorded that song first with by Dee Dee Warwick, Dionne Warwick's sister. She was the first one to record that song. Then an artist from London named Madeline Bell recorded that song. But for me, the best version of that song is the one done as a duet by the Temptations and the Supremes. That version knocked me out. I wasn't aware that they recorded it until I heard it on the radio one day and I just loved it. Thanks to Nick Ashford, who produced it. That song is one of my favorite ones. Here I am listening to David Ruffin and Paul (Williams) and Melvin (Franklin) and Diana Ross singing that song. I was on cloud nine, much the same way I felt when I heard Elvis Presley sing "Only the Strong Survive." I'm still on cloud nine with that one.

How did you come to write "Only the Strong Survive?"

Gamble: I wrote "Only the Strong Survive" with Jerry Butler and Leon Huff. Jerry Butler is an unbelievable artist. He's a traditional superstar in the R&B world. Me and Huff wrote a lot of songs with Jerry and I learned so much from that experience. We wrote songs like "Never Gonna Give You Up," "Moody Woman," and "Hey, Western Union Man." We were sitting around one day writing and we came up with the title "Only the Strong Survive." We were talking about people who survive. Once we came up with the title, the music started happening. It didn't take long to write the song—it took longer to come up with the idea. Once we came up with the idea the song just flowed out. Then as usual we sat around a piano and came up with a story and that groove came together. Jerry's a great lyricist, I'm a lyricist and Huff is a great keyboard player and lyricist. We all got together and made that concept happen.

The song really had a great story to it and a great message. We tried to write songs with good messages that would uplift people. Most of the songs we wrote were songs meant to uplift people of all races. You take a song like "Love Train"—we're talkin' people all over the world. There's only one humanity, you've gotta love everybody. One love, like Bob Marley used to say. "Only the Strong Survive" carried the message that if you endure to the end you will survive, you just gotta keep goin'. "You gotta be strong, you gotta hold on, only the strong survive." That's the lyrics. We made it into a love song, of course, but in any given situation no matter how hard it may seem if you hold on you're gonna survive. That's what we were talkin' about. Even in the music business it's hard to get ahead, it's hard to get your records played and only the strong will survive. In the late sixties "Only the Strong Survive" went number one on the R&B charts and went top five on the pop charts.

Huff: When I heard that Elvis recorded a song we wrote I thought, I've arrived! (*laughs*)

Gamble: Hey man, it was like having Frank Sinatra sing one of your songs! That was such a great thing. It was unbelievable. Elvis Presley is the King of Rock and Roll—just to be included in his life in some small way is a great honor for us. Just the fact that he would pick up on of our songs is amazing. Elvis Presley, the Beatles, Ray Charles, Frank Sinatra, and Aretha Franklin—those artists are in a class of their own. When I listened to Elvis' version of "Only the Strong Survive" it seemed to be the same arrangement as ours. Elvis kind of followed the way Jerry sang it but he put his own little twist to it. To have Elvis Presley record one of your songs was no easy feat in the first place because he had a lot of people trying to give him songs. He must have really liked that song in order for him to have recorded it.

Huff: Gamble met Lisa Marie (Presley) and she told him that her father would be singing "Only the Strong Survive" every day.

Gamble: Before he recorded it he used to play Jerry Butler's versions of that song over and over at Graceland. That song was inspirational to him. If anybody should have recorded that song it's Elvis Presley. He's been dead for over 30 years and he's bigger now than he ever was.

"The Love I Lost" is another classic Gamble & Huff song.

Gamble: "The Love I Lost" is one of those songs where you need to just close your eyes and think about some of the relationships you had or somebody else had and you go, "Wow, that was a sweet girl but I lost her." That's a great love song and it started out as a ballad. When we got into the studio, we decided to put a groove up underneath of it. As soon as we put the groove on, it took off. We always said when we were writing songs—we would do this from time to time—if you've got a great song that song should be able to be performed slow. It should be able to be performed as a cha-cha, and it should be able to be performed fast. It should be able to fit all formats. So we took that one from being a ballad to an up-tempo song.

Huff: When the musicians got into the groove of that song we didn't stop playing. That was one of the long cuts. Our engineer, Joe Tarsia, just kept the tape running and we just kept playing. How long did we play that song?

Gamble: The tape ran off.

Huff: *(Laughs)* Yeah, we were just so hypnotized with the groove. I remember it like it was yesterday. We kept playing it until the tape just ran off the reel.

Gamble: We put it out as part one and part two.

Tell me about the Three Degrees smash, "When Will I See You Again."

Gamble: I saw this girl one day and we were talking and all of a sudden I said, "When will I see you again?" That was it. Just like that and we had the idea. We tried to use phrases that people say all the time. How many times do you say "When will I see you again?" or "I'll see you when I get there." *(laughs)* That was another Lou Rawls song. I put that title on a pad and when me and Huff came together the music made the words come together.

Huff: That song won the Japanese song festival that year. In our studio we've got a picture of the Three Degrees with Prince Charles. That was his favorite song and his favorite group.

Gamble: That song opened up our relationship with the European market because it was huge.

While the Philly International label had tons of hits in America, the music of Gamble & Huff and the Philly International label is still so revered in England. Why?

Gamble: I think the people overseas are just a little bit more respectful to rhythm and blues artists. You take for example, the Beatles and the Rolling Stones. Any interview with them you hear them saying "We learned from Chuck Berry and Little Richard." They'd give the credit to the African American artists. It just seems that the European culture is just a little bit more adult than American culture because for some reason it's hard for America to give the credit to a lot of these people that really started the music.

The first time we went to Europe I was amazed. They knew the drummers on our records, they knew the engineers. Their research was just so thorough. The fans and the media were very knowledgeable. They seemed to appreciate the art more. About a year and a half ago we went to London and they gave us the Ivor Novello Award, which is a big award over there. The day we got the award, the Bee Gees got one too. The standing ovation that we got over there was beautiful.

You gave Lou Rawls one of the defining hits of his career with "You'll Never Find Another Love like Mine."

Gamble: That song is a love story. A relationship is getting ready to break up and a guy's telling a girl that she'll never find another love like mine. You're gonna miss me. He wasn't bragging but he said *(recites lyrics)* "You're gonna miss my lovin'." I think there's a lot of people that have been in that situation and they can relate to it. I think that the chords and the music that Huff put to that was different for me and him. We were like Rodgers and Hart on that one. I was singing and Huff was playing the melody back at me *(sings)* "You'll never find . . ." *(imitates piano notes)* I said, "Wow, we're really writing now!" *(laughs)* That song is a classic.

It seems you have a creative ESP together.

Huff: Sometimes when we'll be writing and we'll be moving so fast that Gamble would say, "Second verse," and I'd be right there without even stopping.

Gamble: At a moment's notice.

Huff: Bang! I was right there. Kind of like when James Brown hollers, "To the bridge, to the bridge!" (*laughs*) We never had to work at that, it was just there.

Gamble: Sometimes I'd say, "Let's modulate, let's modulate!"

Huff: And I'd immediately go into another key. Let me tell you about a little trick that I used. The upright piano that was in Gamble's office, the keys weren't bouncing fast enough. So I went to the drug store and bought four boxes of thumbtacks. You know the hammers that bounce off the piano strings? I put the thumbtacks on the hammers that bounced off the keys so it created a sound like a harpsichord. I played drums in elementary school in a marching band. I used the pedal as a back beat because you had to feel that back beat. The action on the piano keys was so fast. That was something that I experimented with and it worked.

Gamble: Those tacks took a dull sound and made it much brighter.

Let's talk about one of your most recognizable tracks, "TSOP (The Sound of Philadelphia)."

Huff: Don Cornelius, the host of the TV show, *Soul Train*, contacted Gamble. He was getting ready to launch that show and he was desperate for a theme song. Gamble told Don, "Come on to Philadelphia and we'll see what we can come up with." So it was a Saturday night and we called the musicians and went into Sigma Sound but we didn't come up with anything that night. One thing Gamble and I do is we don't force creativity. Don got a little frustrated and wanted to fly back home. Gamble convinced him to come back the next day. Me and Gamble went back to our offices and we came up with that (*sings melody line of "TSOP"*). We called the musicians back into the studio and it came together just like that. Don was very happy. Gamble took the Three Degrees into the studio and put the vocals on the track.

"I Love Music" typifies how you feel about what you do.

Gamble: One day we were in the studio and we were enjoying all this great success. We just said, "I love music" and boom, it was like a light just came on. Then Huff started playing and I came up with "I love music, any kind of music." See, I do love all kinds of music. I like jazz, I like it all. (*recites lyrics*) "As long as it's swinging all the joy that it's bringing . . ."

You have that great skill to pick up on a common phrase and turn it into a great song.

Huff: Yeah, you gotta watch what you say around us because we might pick up on something. (*laughs*) But we're always listening. Somebody might say something that is catchy and we'll go back to the studio and write it.

You've enjoyed more than 70 #1 Pop and R&B singles, and millions and millions in sales around the world. What does your induction into the Rock and Roll Hall of Fame mean to both of you?

Huff: It's wonderful. It's a thrill of a lifetime to be inducted into the Rock and Roll Hall of Fame. What makes it so significant is it's the Ahmet Ertegun Award. We're the first recipients of that award. We had the opportunity to be in Ahmet's company when we were doing independent production for Atlantic Records plus Ahmet is a pioneer with the Rhythm and

Blues Foundation and The Rock and Roll Hall of Fame. To be in the company of Madonna and John Mellencamp and the Ventures and the Dave Clark Five, is amazing.

What's the latest with the Philly International reissue program?

Gamble: We just signed a new licensing agreement with Sony/BMG. Most of our catalog is being repackaged and we're repackaging even more. We're bringing out some product featuring material that's never been released. There's some lost gems that are coming out, which is really exciting because some of the songs I'd forgotten about. They have this package out now called *Conquer the World*. Leo Sacks and Steve Berkowitz were the guys who helped put it together and they found all this old stuff in our archives. This is volume one. These are masters that go back to the early '60s. Some of them have been released; maybe they were regional hits or local hits. The good part of it is that you're able to look at the body of work that we've done. You can listen to these songs and see how Gamble & Huff grew as songwriters, how the musicians grew, how the studio sound changed.

The Gamble & Huff roster of artists was spectacular. Characterize the talents of some of your brightest acts starting with the O'Jays.

Huff: Powerful. Just watching Eddie Levert put his voice on will amaze you. They liked to record at night. Eddie was stripped down with his shirt off. You could see all that sweat and all that grit. I used to sit there and watch him sing with amazement. Walter Williams had a powerful voice too.

Lou Rawls.

Huff: Lou Rawls? Class. Lou was always prepared, always loved to rehearse. He was very serious about his performances. Lou had one of the classiest voices that we ever worked with.

MFSB.

Gamble: MFSB is a great group of guys and girls. It was a diverse group of people. Young and old. Italians. Hispanics. African Americans. It was a melting pot and everybody got along because the music made everybody harmonize with each other. That's the healing thing in the world, music. Everybody wanted that music to be right. We didn't concentrate on how a person looked or whether they were young or old, dark or light. We were really concentrating on whether you were hitting the right note. I think MFSB was a symbol to me of real brotherhood. That's why we called them MFSB. Some people thought MFSB meant something else, people with dirty minds. But it means "Mother, Father, Sister, Brother," which represented a family. MFSB was a funky funky group.

Harold Melvin & the Blue Notes.

Gamble: Harold Melvin & the Blue Notes was an evolving group. It started out as the Blue Notes and then Harold Melvin & the Blue Notes, and then Harold Melvin & the Blue Notes featuring Teddy Pendergrass, and then Harold Melvin & the Blue Notes featuring Teddy Pendergrass and Sharon Page. So they just kept growing and they were tremendous performers.

Archie Bell and the Drells.

Gamble: Archie Bell and the Drells were unique. You'd know Archie's voice anywhere. That's what we tried to do with all the acts we had on the label. We tried to get identifiable voices. Jerry Wexler called us and we talked to him about the group. They'd had a big hit with "Tighten Up" and they didn't have a follow-up. I told him, "Well, let me and Huff do something on them." Then sure enough, we came up to New York, went into Atlantic Studios and recorded "I Can't Stop Dancing." That was a big great happy record. After that we had "There's Gonna Be a Showdown" and "Girl You're Too Young." We had about four or five good records with Archie Bell.

Teddy Pendergrass.

Gamble: There'll never be another Teddy Pendergrass. To this day, no one has the magnetism that Teddy Pendergrass projected. It was just unbelievable.

Pick a Gamble & Huff song that wasn't a hit that deserves rediscovery.

Huff: When we were working with Michael Jackson and his brothers, the Jacksons, we did a song called "Find Me a Girl," and that's one of my favorites. There's a song that we did with the Sweet Inspirations with Cissy Houston, called "(Gotta Find) A Brand New Lover." That was a great one. Whenever Cissy couldn't find a baby sitter she'd bring her daughter (Whitney Houston) to our studio in Philly. The Sweet Inspirations went on the road with Elvis soon after we finished working with them.

Is there an inherent message in your work?

Gamble: I think that if somebody listened to all of our music they'd see that our songs weren't just regular songs. These songs had a purpose and a meaning. No matter how many groups we had on our label, none of them sounded alike. The O'Jays didn't sound like Harold Melvin & the Blue Notes. Teddy Pendergrass didn't sound like Lou Rawls. The Jones Girls didn't sound like the Three Degrees. Patti LaBelle didn't sound like Phyllis Hyman. It's easy to say now but back then it was hard to do, to stay on top of that and be consistent, album after album, year after year. That's just unheard of to maintain that kind of consistency in a business that's changing so fast. And then today to have these young artists sampling our music and keeping us current in the industry is just phenomenal. Recently, Kanye West had a song called "Stronger." It's got a sample from the *Edwin Birdsong* album on a song called "Cola Bottle Baby." Edwin Birdsong was an artist signed to Philly International. A group in Europe called Daft Punk had a big hit with a song called "Harder, Better, Faster, Stronger," which sampled "Cola Bottle Baby" and then Kanye West sampled Daft Punk's song. So we're all in the mix there.

Music Publishers

Music publishers find songs and then get them recorded. In return for a share of the money made from your songs, they work as an agent for you by plugging your songs to recording artists, taking care of paperwork and accounting, setting you up with co-writers (recording artists or other songwriters), and so on.

HOW DO MUSIC PUBLISHERS MAKE MONEY FROM SONGS?

Music publishers make money by getting songs recorded onto albums, Film and TV sound-tracks, commericals, etc. and other areas. While this is their primary function, music publish-ers also handle administrative tasks such as copyrighting songs; collecting royalties for the songwriter; negotiating and issuing synchronization licenses for use of music in films, televi-sion programs and commercials; arranging and administering foreign rights; auditing record companies and other music users; suing infringers; and producing new demos of new songs. In a small, independent publishing company, one or two people may handle all these jobs. Larger publishing companies are more likely to be divided into the following departments: creative (or professional), copyright, licensing, legal affairs, business affairs, royalty, account-ing and foreign.

HOW DO MUSIC PUBLISHERS FIND SONGS?

The *creative department* is responsible for finding talented writers and signing them to the company. Once a writer is signed, it is up to the creative department to develop and nurture the writer so he will write songs that create income for the company. Staff members often put writers together to form collaborative teams. And, perhaps most important, the creative department is responsible for securing commercial recordings of songs and pitching them for use in film and other media. The head of the creative department—usually called the "professional manager"—is charged with locating talented writers for the company.

HOW DO MUSIC PUBLISHERS GET SONGS RECORDED?

Once a writer is signed, the professional manager arranges for a demo to be made of the writer's songs. Even though a writer may already have recorded his own demo, the publisher will often re-demo the songs using established studio musicians in an effort to produce the highest-quality demo possible.

Once a demo is produced, the professional manager begins shopping the song to various outlets. He may try to get the song recorded by a top artist on his or her next album or get the song used in an upcoming film. The professional manager uses all the contacts and leads he has to get the writer's songs recorded by as many artists as possible. Therefore, he must be able to deal efficiently and effectively with people in other segments of the music industry, including A&R personnel, recording artists, producers, distributors, managers and lawyers. Through these contacts, he can find out what artists are looking for new material, and who may be interested in recording one of the writer's songs.

HOW IS A PUBLISHING COMPANY ORGANIZED?

After a writer's songs are recorded, the other departments at the publishing company come into play.

- The *licensing and copyright departments* are responsible for issuing any licenses for use of the writer's songs in film or TV and for filing various forms with the copyright office.
- The *legal affairs department and business affairs department* works with the professional department in negotiating contracts with its writers.
- The *royalty and accounting departments* are responsible for making sure that users of music are paying correct royalties to the publisher and ensuring the writer is receiving the proper royalty rate as specified in the contract and that statements are mailed to the writer promptly.
- Finally, the *foreign department*'s role is to oversee any publishing activities outside of the United States, to notify sub-publishers of the proper writer and ownership information of songs in the catalogue and update all activity and new releases, and to make sure a writer is being paid for any uses of his material in foreign countries.

LOCATING A MUSIC PUBLISHER

How do you go about finding a music publisher that will work well for you? First, you must find a publisher suited to the type of music you write. If a particular publisher works mostly with alternative music and you're a country songwriter, the contacts he has within the industry will hardly be beneficial to you.

Each listing in this section details, in order of importance, the type of music that publisher is most interested in; the music types appear in **boldface** to make them easier to locate. It's also very important to submit only to companies interested in your level of experience (see A Sample Listing Decoded on page 8). You will also want to refer to the Category Indexes on page 359, which list companies by the type of music they work with. Publishers placing music in film or TV will be proceded by a ◩ (see the Film & TV Index on page 388 for a complete list of these companies).

Do your research!

It's important to study the market and do research to identify which companies to submit to.

- Many record producers have publishing companies or have joint ventures with major publishers who fund the signing of songwriters and who provide administration services. Since producers have an influence over what is recorded in a session, targeting the producer/publisher can be a useful avenue.
- Since most publishers don't open unsolicited material, try to meet the publishing representative in person (at conferences, speaking engagements, etc.) or try to have an intermediary intercede on your behalf (for example, an entertainment attorney; a manager, an agent, etc.).
- As to demos, submit no more than 3 songs.
- As to publishing deals, co-publishing deals (where a writer owns part of the publishing share through his or her own company) are relatively common if the writer has a well-established track record.

- Are you targeting a specific artist to sing your songs? If so, find out if that artist even considers outside material. Get a copy of the artist's latest album, and see who wrote most of the songs. If they were all written by the artist, he's probably not interested in hearing material from outside writers. If the songs were written by a variety of different writers, however, he may be open to hearing new songs.
- Check the album liner notes, which will list the names of the publishers of each writer. These publishers obviously have had luck pitching songs to the artist, and they may be able to get your songs to that artist as well.
- If the artist you're interested in has a recent hit on the *Billboard* charts, the publisher of that song will be listed in the "Hot 100 A-Z" index. Carefully choosing which publishers will work best for the material you write may take time, but it will only increase your chances of getting your songs heard. "Shotgunning" your demo packages (sending out many packages without regard for music preference or submission policy) is a waste of time and money and will hurt, rather than help, your songwriting career.

Once you've found some companies that may be interested in your work, learn what songs have been successfully handled by those publishers. Most publishers are happy to provide you with this information in order to attract high-quality material. As you're researching music publishers, keep in mind how you get along with them personally. If you can't work with a publisher on a personal level, chances are your material won't be represented as you would like it to be. A publisher can become your most valuable connection to all other segments of the music industry, so it's important to find someone you can trust and feel comfortable with.

Independent or major company?
Also consider the size of the publishing company. The publishing affiliates of the major music conglomerates are huge, handling catalogs of thousands of songs by hundreds of songwriters. Unless you are an established songwriter, your songs probably won't receive enough attention from such large companies. Smaller, independent publishers offer several advantages. First, independent music publishers are located all over the country, making it easier for you to work face-to-face rather than by mail or phone. Smaller companies usually aren't affiliated with a particular record company and are therefore able to pitch your songs to many different labels and acts. Independent music publishers are usually interested in a smaller range of music, allowing you to target your submissions more accurately. The most obvious advantage to working with a smaller publisher is the personal attention they can bring to you and your songs. With a smaller roster of artists to work with, the independent music publisher is able to concentrate more time and effort on each particular project.

SUBMITTING MATERIAL TO PUBLISHERS
When submitting material to a publisher, always keep in mind that a professional, courteous manner goes a long way in making a good impression. When you submit a demo through the mail, make sure your package is neat and meets the particular needs of the publisher. Review each publisher's submission policy carefully, and follow it to the letter. Disregarding this information will only make you look like an amateur in the eyes of the company you're submitting to.

Listings of companies in Canada are preceded by a ◼, and international markets are designated with a ⊕. You will find an alphabetical list of these companies at the back of the book, along with an index of publishers by state in the Geographic Index (see page 390).

Icons

For More Info

For more instructional information on the listings in this book, including explanations of symbols (N ✓ 🍸 📷 🍁 🌐 ◯ ◑ ◐ ◒), read the article *How To Use Songwriter's Market* on page 2.

PUBLISHING CONTRACTS

Once you've located a publisher you like and he's interested in shopping your work, it's time to consider the publishing contract—an agreement in which a songwriter grants certain rights to a publisher for one or more songs. The contract specifies any advances offered to the writer, the rights that will be transferred to the publisher, the royalties a songwriter is to receive and the length of time the contract is valid.

- When a contract is signed, a publisher will ask for a 50-50 split with the writer. *This is standard industry practice*; the publisher is taking that 50% to cover the overhead costs of running his business and for the work he's doing to get your songs recorded.
- It is always a good idea to have a publishing contract (or any music business contract) reviewed by a competent entertainment lawyer.
- There is no "standard" publishing contract, and each company offers different provisions for their writers.

Make sure you ask questions about anything you don't understand, especially if you're new in the business. Songwriter organizations such as the Songwriters Guild of America (SGA) provide contract review services, and can help you learn about music business language and what constitutes a fair music publishing contract. Be sure to read What About Contracts? on page 31 for more information on contracts. See the Organizations section, beginning on page 291 of this book, for more information on the SGA and other songwriting groups.

When signing a contract, it's important to be aware of the music industry's unethical practitioners. The "song shark," as he's called, makes his living by asking a songwriter to pay to have a song published. The shark will ask for money to demo a song and promote it to radio stations; he may also ask for more than the standard 50% publisher's share or ask you to give up all rights to a song in order to have it published. Although none of these practices is illegal, it's certainly not ethical, and no successful publisher uses these methods. *Songwriter's Market* works to list only honest companies interested in hearing new material. (For more on "song sharks," see How Do I Avoid the Rip-Offs? on page 16.)

ADDITIONAL PUBLISHERS

There are **more publishers** located in other sections of the book! On page 131 use the list of Additional Publishers to find listings within other sections who are also music publishers.

◢ ABEAR PUBLISHING (BMI)/SONGTOWN PUBLISHING (ASCAP)

323 N. Walnut St., Murfreesboro TN 37130. (615)890-1878. Fax: (615)890-3771. E-mail: info@songtownpublishing.com. Web site: www.songtownpub.com. **Contact:** Ron Hebert, publisher. Estab. 2000. Pays standard royalty.

How to Contact Submit demo by mail. Unsolicited submissions are OK. Prefers CD of 5 songs with lyric sheets. "Finished demos only, please." Does not return material. Responds in 2 weeks if interested.

Music Mostly **country**, **country/pop**, **pop**, **dance**, and **Christian**.

◨ ◢ ACKEAN MUSIC PUBLISHING/PROMOTION/CRITIQUE (SOCAN)

5454 198th St., Suite 208, Langley BC V3A 1G2.(604)532-9203. E-mail: pamelaroyal47@shaw.ca. Web site: www.ackeanmusic.net. **Contact:** Pamela Royal, professional manager (country). Professional Managers: Kim McLeod (traditional country); Cristine Royal (instrumental country). Music publisher and Promotion/Critique. Estab. 2005. Publishes 6 songs/year. Publishes 3 new songwriters/year. Staff size: 2. Pays standard royalty of 50%.

Affiliate(s) Crowe Entertainment. "Crowe Entertainment is our co-publisher in Nashville"

How to Contact *Write first and obtain permission to submit a demo.* Prefers CD with 3 songs with lyric sheets and cover letter. Include SASE or SAE and IRC for outside United States. "Please include SASE, cover letter, and clean typed lyric sheets." Responds in 2 months.

Film & TV Places 2 songs/year in film. Music Supervisor: Joe Lenders (Minnot Lenters Music, Florida). Recently selected "Someone Like You" and "Heart on the Line" (singles by Angie Bull), recorded by Marie Willson, in *Terror Within* (film).

Music Mostly **country**, **traditional country**, and **instrumental country**; also **instrumental music for film**. Published "Someone Like You" and "The Cheater's Out of Town" (single by Angie Bull) from *Rock Hard Lovin'* (album), recorded by Marie Willson (traditional country), released independently in 2006; "Where My Truck Stops" (single) from *Where My Truck Stops* (album), written and recorded by Wolfe Milestone(country), released in 1999.

Tips "Professional demos only, best one to three songs, great voice. Keep the hook exciting. First impression is important. Serious writers only, please. We also pitch songs to TV/film/movie companies, so music should be broadcast quality. Interested also in instrumental music for film productions. Please have songs registered and copyrighted. Ackean Music is a new company and will work hard for the songwriters and artists we publish and promote. We also offer a critique service."

◻ ALIAS JOHN HENRY TUNES (BMI)

11 Music Square E., Suite 607, Nashville TN 37203. (615)582-1782. E-mail: bobbyjohnhenry@gmail.com. **Contact:** Bobby John Henry, owner. Music publisher and record producer. Publishes 3 songs/year; publishes 1 new songwriter/year. Staff size: 3. Pays standard royalty.

How to Contact Send by mail. Prefers cassette or CD with 3 songs and lyric sheet. Does not return material. Responds in 6 months only if interested.

Music Mostly **country**, **rock** and **alternative**; also **inspirational**, **gospel**, **Christian** and **jazz**. Does not want rap. Published *Mr. Right Now* (album by Kari Jorgensen), recorded by "Hieke" on Warner Bros. (rock); and *Nothing to Me* (album by B.J. Henry), recorded by Millie Jackson on Spring.

Tips "Focus and rewrite, rewrite, rewrite. We are looking into inspirational material, any style, also gospel and Christian music, any style. I like when the story is so good you don't even realize it's a spiritual or inspirational song. I'm not crazy about the 'glory be, glory be' type of song. I'm all gloried out! I'm also interested in hearing jazz standard types of songs that might be done with a big band. I don't know what I'll do with them, but if you have them, let me hear them. I don't know if anyone knows what to do with them, but I know some great singers that are singing new material in the Cole Porter/Johnny Mercer tradition. What have ya got?"

N ⊕ ☐ ALL ROCK MUSIC

(31)186-604266. Fax: (32)0186-604366. Web site: www.collectorrecords.nl. **Contact:** Cees Klop, president. Music publisher, record company (Collector Records) and record producer. Estab. 1967. Publishes 40 songs/year; publishes several new songwriters/year. Staff size: 3. Pays standard royalty.

Affiliate(s) All Rock Music (United Kingdom).

• Also see the listings for Collector Records in the Record Companies and Record Producers sections of this book.

How to Contact Submit demo package by mail. Unsolicited submissions are OK. Prefers cassette. SAE and IRC. Responds in 2 months.

Music Mostly **'50s rock**, **rockabilly** and **country rock**; also **piano boogie woogie**. Published *Rock Crazy Baby* (album), written and recorded by Art Adams (1950s rockabilly), released 2004; *Marvin Jackson* (album), by Marvin Jackson (1950s rockers), released 2005; *Western Australian Snake Pit R&R* (album), recorded by various (1950s rockers), released 2005, all on Collector Records.

Tips "Send only the kind of material we issue/produce as listed."

☒ ☑ ALPHA MUSIC INC. (BMI)

Dept. SM, One International Blvd Ste. 212, Mahwah, NJ 07495. (201)335-0005. Fax: (201)335-0004. E-mail: alpha@trfmusic.com. Web site: www.trfmusic.com. **Contact:** Michael Nurko. Music publisher. Estab. 1931. Pays standard royalty.

Affiliate(s) Dorian Music Publishers, Inc. (ASCAP) and TRF Music Inc.

• Also see listing for TRF Production Music Libraries in the Advertising, Audiovisual & Commercial Music Firms section of this book.

How to Contact "We accept submissions of new compositions. Submissions are not returnable."

Music All categories, mainly **instrumental** and **acoustic** suitable for use as **production music**, including **theme and background music for television and film**. "Have published over 50,000 titles since 1931."

AVI 39563 MUSIC (ASCAP)

P.O. Box 5537, Kreole Station, Moss Point MS 39563-1537. (601)914-9413 or (228)235-8092 (cell). "No collect calls, please." **Contact:** Jemiah F. Mitchell, president/owner. Estab. 2003. Music publisher and record company (Avitor Music International Records).Releases 10 singles and 5 LPs/year. Pays negotiable royalty to artists on contract; statutory rate to publisher per song on record. "Avitor Music has National and International distribution."

- Also see the listing for Avitor Music International in the Record Companies section of this book.

Affiliate(s) AVI 39563 Music (ASCAP).

How to Contact *Write or call first for submission instructions. "* We will review traditional country. Always whenever you write, be sure you include a #10 business-size envelope addressed back to yourself with a first-class USA postage stamp on the envelope. A reply will come back to you using the SASE you include in your mailing when you write. *Absolutely no reply postcards—only SASE.* If you only write lyrics, do not submit; only complete songs reviewed, so you must find a collaborator. Not interested in reviewing homemade recordings." Prefers CD (first choice) or cassette with 3-10 songs along with lyrics to songs submitted. Responds in 2 months.

Music Mostly **country, modern country today, mainstream, rock, Americana, hip-hop, rap, R&B, bluegrass, hot AC, adult AC, urban, jazz, blues, teen, gospel, top 40, Spanish, Spanish R&B, Spanish pop, Spanish hip-hop**, and **world music**. "If there is a convincing market for you music, then we are basically open to all genres." Released "6 O'Clock," "Cowboy Mix," and "Second Chance" (singles) from Aron Dees (album), written and recorded by Aron Dees (modern country), released on Avitor. "On July 4, 2007, Aron Dees played as opening for Universal Records recording artist Keith Anderson before a crowd of 6,500 people at the University of Wyoming. Aron Dees' Web site is: www.arondees.com."

Tips "We work with artists on trying to get financial support through creative means. Artists submitting material that is accepted must be ready and willing to work together with us to create a buzz. We are looking for serious-minded artists who are talented and want to make a career for themselves. If you are a team player and know what you want to accomplish, then by all means, give us a call or write us today. You matter to us and we will respond ASAP."

N ⊕ BEARSONGS (PRS)

Box 944, Birmingham B16 8UT United Kingdom. 44-121-454-7020. E-mail: jim@bigbearmusic.com. Web site: www.bigbearmusic.com. Managing Director: Jim Simpson. Professional Manager: Russell Fletcher. Music publisher and record company (Big Bear Records). Member PRS, MCPS. Publishes 25 songs/year; publishes 15-20 new songwriters/year. Pays standard royalty.

- Also see the listings for Big Bear Records in the Record Companies section and Big Bear in the Record Producers section of this book.

How to Contact Submit demo by mail. Unsolicited submissions are OK. Prefers CD. Does not return material. Responds in 3 months.

Music Mostly **blues, swing** and **jazz**. Published *Blowing With Bruce* and *Cool Heights* (by Alan Barnes), recorded by Bruce Adams/Alan Barnes Quintet; and *Blues For My Baby* (by

Charles Brown), recorded by King Pleasure & The Biscuit Boys, all on Big Bear Records.
Tips "Have a real interest in jazz, blues, swing."

⬛ ☑ BIG FISH MUSIC PUBLISHING GROUP (ASCAP, BMI)

11927 Magnolia Blvd., Suite 3, N. Hollywood CA 91607. (818)984-0377. President, CEO and Music Publisher: Chuck Tennin. Producer: Gary Black (country, pop, adult contemporary, rock, crossover songs, other styles). Professional Music Manager: Lora Sprague (jazz, New Age, instrumental, pop rock, R&B). Professional Music Manager: B.J. (pop, TV, film and special projects). Professional Music & Vocal Consultant: Zell Black (country, pop, gospel, rock, blues). Producer Independent Artists: Darryl Harrelson—Major Label Entertainment (country, pop and other genres). Nashville Music Associate: Ron Hebert (Abear/Songtown Publishing). Songwriter/Consultant: Jerry Zanandrea (Z Best Muzic). Music publisher, record company (California Sun Records) and production company. Estab. 1971. Publishes 10-20 songs/year; publishes 5-10 new songwriters/year. Staff size: 7. Pays standard royalty. "We also license songs and music copyrights to users of music, especially TV and film."

Affiliate(s) Big Fish Music (BMI) and California Sun Music (ASCAP).

How to Contact *Write first and obtain permission to submit.* Include SASE for reply. *"Please do not call.* After permission to submit is confirmed, we will assign and forward to you a submission code number allowing you to submit up to 4 songs maximum, preferably on CD or cassette. Include a properly addressed cover letter, signed and dated, with your source of referral (*Songwriter's Market*) with your assigned submission code number and SASE for reply and/or return of material. Include lyrics. *Unsolicited material will not be accepted.* That is our Submission Policy to review outside and new material." Responds in 2 weeks.

Film & TV Places 6 songs in TV/year. Recently published "Even the Angels Knew" (by Cathy Carlson/Craig Lackey/Marty Axelrod); "Stop Before We Start" (by J.D. Grieco); "Oh Santa" (by Christine Bridges/John Deaver), all recorded by The Black River Girls in *Passions* (NBC); licensed "A Christmas Wish" (by Ed Fry/Eddie Max), used in *Passions* (NBC); "Girls Will Be Girls" (by Cathy Carlson/John LeGrande), recorded by The Black River Girls, used in *All My Children* (ABC); "The Way You're Drivin' Me" and "Ain't No Love 'Round Here" (by Jerry Zanandrea), both recorded by The Black River Girls, used in *Passions* (NBC); "Since You Stole My Heart" (by Rick Coimbra/Jamey Whiting), used in *Passions* (NBC); "Good Time to Fly," "All I Need Is a Highway," and "Eyes of the Children" (by Wendy Martin), used in *Passions* (NBC); "It's An Almost Perfect Christmas" (by Michael Martin), used in *Passions* (NBC).

Music Country, including **country pop**, **country A/C** and **country crossover** with a cutting edge; also **pop**, **pop ballads**, **adult contemporary**, **uplifting**, **praise**, **worship**, **spiritual**, and **inspirational adult contemporary gospel** with a powerful message, **instrumental background and theme music** for TV & films, **New Age/instrumental jazz** and **novelty**, **orchestral classical**, **R&B** and **Children's music** for all kinds of commercial use. Published "If Wishes Were Horses" (single by Billy O'Hara); "Purple Bunny Honey" (single by Robert Lloyd/Jim Love); "Leavin' You for Me" (single by J.D. Grieco); "Move That Train" (single by Robert Porter); "Happy Landing" (by T. Brawley/B. Woodrich); "Girls Will Be Girls" (single by Cathy Carlson/John LeGrande); "You Should Be Here With Me" (single by Ken McMeans); "Stop Before We Start" (single by J.D. Grieco); "The Way You're Drivin' Me" and "Ain't No Love 'Round Here" (singles by Jerry Zanandrea), all recorded by Black River Girls on California Sun Records; "Let Go and Let God" and "There's a Power in Prayer" (singles by Corinne Porter/Molly Finkle), recorded by Molly Pasutti, released on California Sun Records; "Good Time to Fly," "All I Need Is a Highway," and "Eyes of the Children" (singles by Wendy Martin); "Don't Give Up," "Sinner's Prayer," and "I'm Living a Brand New Life" (singles) from *Now Is The Time For Living A Brand New Life* (album), written and recorded by Zell Black.

Tips "Demo should be professional, high quality, clean, simple, dynamic, and must get the song across on the first listen. Good clear vocals, a nice melody, a good musical feel, good musical arrangement, strong lyrics and chorus—a unique, catchy, clever song that sticks with you. Looking for unique country and pop songs with a different edge that can crossover to the mainstream market for ongoing Nashville music projects and songs for a hot female country trio that crosses over to adult contemporary and pop with great lush, warm harmonies that reach out to middle America and baby boomers and their grown up children (25 to 65). Also, catchy up-tempo songs with an attitude, meaningful lyrics (Shania Twain style), and unique pop songs (Celine Dion style) for upcoming album projects and song pitches. Also, soundtrack music of all types (melodic, uplifting, moody, mystique, orchestral, mind soothing, pretty, action packed, etc.) for new film production company and upcoming film and TV projects. Demo should be broadcast quality."

▣ ▣ ⊘ BIXIO MUSIC GROUP & ASSOCIATES/IDM MUSIC (ASCAP)

111 E. 14th St., Suite 140, New York NY 10003. (212)695-3911. Fax: (212)967-6284. E-mail: dusl@idmusic.com. Web site: www.bixio.com and www.idmmusic.com. **General Manager**: Johannes in der Muhlen. Administrator: Miriam Westercappel (all styles). A&R Director: Office Manager: Courtney Stack-Slutsky. Administrative Assistant: Karlene Evans (soundtracks). Creative Director: Robert Draghi (all styles). Senior Creative Director/Producer: Tomo. A&R: Claudene Neysmith (world/New Age). Music publisher, record company and rights clearances. Estab. 1985. Publishes a few hundred songs/year; publishes 2 new songwriters/year. Staff size: 6. Pays standard royalty.

How to Contact *Does not accept unsolicited material.*

Music Mostly **soundtracks**. Published "La Strada Nel Bosco," included in the TV show *Ed* (NBC); "La Beguine Du Mac," included in the TV show *The Chris Isaac Show* (Showtime); and "Alfonsina Delle Camelie," included in the TV show *UC: Undercover* (NBC).

⊘ BMG MUSIC PUBLISHING (ASCAP)

245 5th Ave. 8th Floor, New York NY 10016. (212)287-1300. Fax: (212)930-4263. Web site: www.bmgmusicsearch.com. **Contact:** Adam Epstein (pop/rock). **Beverly Hills office:** 8750 Wilshire Blvd., Beverly Hills CA 90211. (310)358-4700. Fax: (310)358-4727. **Contact:** Monti Olson (pop/rock), Brad Aarons (pop/rock), or Derrick Thompson (urban). **Nashville office:** 1600 Division St. Suite 225, Nashville TN 37203. (615)687-5800. Fax: (615)687-5839. Music publisher.

How to Contact *BMG Music Publishing does not accept unsolicited submissions.*
Music Published works by Maroon 5, Christina Aguilera, Coldplay, Nelly, Britney Spears, Keane, R. Kelly, Ne-Yo, and The All-American Rejects.

◻ BRANDON HILLS MUSIC, LLC (BMI)/HEATH BROWN MUSIC (ASCAP)/STEVEN LYNN MUSIC (SESAC)

N. 3425 Searle County Line Rd., Brandon WI 53919. (920)398-3279 or (cell) (920)570-1076. E-mail: marta@dotnet.com. **Contact:** Marsha Brown, president. Music publishers. Estab. 2005. Publishes 4 new songwriters/year. Staff size: 2. Pays standard royalty of 50%.
How to Contact Submit demo package by mail. Unsolicited submissions are OK. Prefers CD with 1-4 songs and cover letter. Does not return submissions. Responds only if interested.
Music Mostly **country (traditional, modern, country rock)**, **contemporary Christian**, **blues**; also **children's** and **bluegrass**. Does not want rap or hip-hop.
Tips "We prefer studio-produced CDs. The lyrics and the CD must match. Cover letter, lyrics, and CD should have a professional look. Demos should have vocals up front and every word should be distinguishable. Please make sure your lyrics match your song. Submit only your best. The better the demo, the better of chance of getting your music published and recorded."

◙ BUG MUSIC, INC. (ASCAP, BMI)

7750 Sunset Blvd., Los Angeles CA 90046. (323)969-0988. Fax: (323)969-0968. E-mail: buginfo@bugmusic.com. Web site: www.bugmusic.com. Vice President of Creative: Eddie Gomez. Creative Manager: Mara Schwartz. Creative Assistant: Nissa Pedraza. **Nashville:** 1910 Acklen Ave., Nashville TN 37212. (615)279-0180. Fax: (615)279-0184. Creative Director: John Allen; Creative Manager: Drew Hale. **New York:** 347 W. 36th St., Suite 1203, New York NY 10018. (212)643-0925. Fax: (212)643-0897. Senior Vice President: Garry Valletri. Music publisher. Estab. 1975. "We handle administration."
Affiliate(s) Bughouse (ASCAP).
How to Contact *Does not accept unsolicited submissions.*
Music All genres. Published "You Were Mine" (by E. Erwin/M. Seidel), recorded by Dixie Chicks on Monument.

Ⓝ ◻ BURNSONGS (ASCAP)

1110 17th Ave. S. #4, Nashville TN 37212-2221. E-mail: e@burnsongs.com. Web site: www. burnsongs.com. **Contact:** Ernie Petrangelo. Music publisher, record company (Da'ville Records, and record producer (Ernie Petrangelo). Estab. 1986. Publishes 13 songs/year; publishes 3 new songwriters/year. Staff size: 1. Pays standard royalty.
Affiliate(s) Raproductions.com (BMI).
How to Contact Submit CDs and links to e-mail address. Unsolicited submissions are OK. Prefers cassette or CD/CDR with 3 songs, lyric sheet and cover letter. Include SASE. Responds in 2-3 weeks only if interested.
Film and TV Places 2 songs in film/year. Music supervisor: Ernie Petrangelo. Recently published "Instruments of Destruction" and "Aw S#!t What Are We Gonna Do Now!" (by

Burns/Serpa/Ward), recorded by NRG2 in *Transformers—The Movie* (released to DVD).
Music Mostly **hip-hop**, **rap** and **r&b**; also **urban pop**, **rock/rap** and **pop/rock/alternative**.
Does not want country, "unless it's very different, edgy and hip." Recently published
"Instruments of Destruction," "Aw S#!t What Are We Gonna Do Now!" (singles by Burns/
Serpa/Ward) and "Come and Get It" (single by Burns/Ward) from *Transformed* (album),
recorded by NRG2 (heavy metal), released 2001 on Da'Ville Records.
Tips "Please submit the best quality demo you can afford. We are interested in hit quality
material with great hooks. Raps must be interesting & have meaning. No thugged-out
material please. No excessive profanity. If you are an artist, please send a photo and bio
with your package."

☐ CALIFORNIA COUNTRY MUSIC (BMI)

112 Widmar Pl., Clayton CA 94517. (925)833-4680. **Contact:** Edgar J. Brincat, owner. Music
publisher and record company (Roll On Records). Estab. 1985. Staff size: 1. Pays standard
royalty.
Affiliate(s) Sweet Inspirations Music (ASCAP).
  • Also see the listing for Roll On Records in the Record Companies section of this book.
How to Contact Submit demo by mail. Unsolicited submissions are OK. "Do not call or
write. Any calls will be returned collect to caller." Send CD with 3 songs and lyric sheet.
Include SASE. Responds in 6 weeks.
Music Mostly **MOR**, **contemporary country** and **pop**. Does not want rap, metal or rock.
Published *For Realities Sake* (album by F.L. Pittman/R. Barretta) and *Maddy* (album by
F.L. Pittman/M. Weeks), both recorded by Ron Banks & L.J. Reynolds on Life & Bellmark
Records; and *Quarter Past Love* (album by Irwin Rubinsky/Janet Fisher), recorded by Darcy
Dawson on NNP Records.

☒ ☑ CHRISTMAS & HOLIDAY MUSIC (BMI)

26642 Via Noveno, Mission Viejo CA 92961. (949)859-1615. E-mail: justinwilde@christmas
songs.com. Web site: www.christmassongs.com. **Contact:** Justin Wilde, president. Music
publisher. Estab. 1980. Publishes 8-12 songs/year; publishes 8-12 new songwriters/year.
Staff size: 1. "All submissions must be complete songs (i.e., music and lyrics)." Pays
standard royalty.
Affiliate(s) Songcastle Music (ASCAP).
How to Contact Submit demo CD or cassette by mail. Unsolicited submissions are OK. *Do
not call. Do not send unsolicited MP3s or links to Web sites.* See Web site for submission
guidelines. "First class mail only. Registered or certified mail not accepted." Prefers CD or
cassette with no more than 3 songs with lyric sheets. Do not send lead sheets or promotional
material, bios, etc." Include SASE but does not return material out of the US. Responds
only if interested.
Film & TV Places 4-5 songs in TV/year. Published "Mr. Santa Claus" in *Casper's Haunted
Christmas*.
Music Strictly **Christmas**, **Halloween**, **Hanukkah**, **Mother's Day**, **Thanksgiving**, **Father's
Day** and **New Year's Eve music** in every style imaginable: easy listening, rock, R&B, pop,

blues, jazz, country, reggae, rap, children's secular or religious. *Please do not send anything that isn't a holiday song.* Published "It Must Have Been the Mistletoe" (single by Justin Wilde/Doug Konecky) from *Christmas Memories* (album), recorded by Barbra Streisand (pop Christmas), released 2001 by Columbia; "What Made the Baby Cry?" (single by Toby Keith) and "You've Just Missed Christmas" (single by Penny Lea/Buzz Smith/Bonnie Miller) from *The Vikki Carr Christmas Album* (album), recorded by Vikki Carr (holiday/Christmas), released 2000 on Delta; and "Mr. Santa Claus" (single by James Golseth) from *Casper's Haunted Christmas* soundtrack (album), recorded by Scotty Blevins (Christmas), released 2000 on Koch International.

Tips "We only sign one out of every 200 submissions. Please be selective. If a stranger can hum your melody back to you after hearing it twice, it has 'standard' potential. Couple that with a lyric filled with unique, inventive imagery, that stands on its own, even without music. Combine the two elements, and workshop the finished result thoroughly to identify weak points. Submit to us only when the song is polished to perfection. Submit positive lyrics only. Avoid negative themes like 'Blue Christmas'."

☑ CHRYSALIS MUSIC GROUP (ASCAP, BMI)

8500 Melrose Ave., Suite 207, Los Angeles CA 90069. (310)652-0066. Fax: (310)652-5428. E-mail: enquiries@chrysalis.com. Web site: www.chrysalis.com. **Contact:** Mark Friedman, vice president of A&R. Music publisher. Estab. 1968.

How to Contact *Chrysalis Music does not accept any submissions.*

Music Published "Sum 41" (single), written and recorded by OutKast; "Light Ladder" (single), written and recorded by David Gray. Administer, David Lee Roth, Andrea Boccelli, Velvet Revolver, and Johnta Austin.

☑ COME ALIVE COMMUNICATIONS, INC. (ASCAP)

348 Valley Rd., Suite A, P.O. Box 436, West Grove PA 19390-0436. (610)869-3660. Fax: (610)869-3660. E-mail: info@comealivemusic.com. Web site: www.comealivemusic.com. Professional Managers: Joseph L. Hooker (pop, rock, jazz); Bridget G. Hylak (spiritual, country, classical). Music publisher, record producer and record company. Estab. 1985. Publishes 4 singles/year. Staff: 7. Pays standard royalty of 50%.

• Come Alive Communications received a IHS Ministries Award in 1996, John Lennon Songwriting Contest winnter, 2003.

How to Contact *Call first to obtain permission to submit a demo.* For song publishing submissions, prefers CD with 3 songs, lyric sheet, and cover letter. Does not return submissions. Responds only if interested.

Music Mostly **pop**, **easy listening**, **contemporary Christian**, and **patriotic**; also **country** and **spiritual**. Does not want obscene, suggestive, violent, or morally offensive lyrics. Produced "In Search of America" (single) from *Long Road to Freedom* (album), written and recorded by J. Hooker (patriotic), released 2003 on ComeAliveMusic.com.

☑ COPPERFIELD MUSIC GROUP/PENNY ANNIE MUSIC (BMI)/TOP BRASS MUSIC (ASCAP)/BIDDY BABY MUSIC (SESAC)

1400 South St., Nashville TN 37212. (615)726-3100. E-mail: ken@copperfieldmusic.com. Web site: www.copperfieldmusic.com. **Contact**: Ken Biddy, president/CEO.

How to Contact Contact first and obtain permission to submit a demo. Does not return submissions. Responds only if interested.

Music Mostly **country**; also **pop**, and **modern bluegrass**. Does not want rap or heavy/metal/rock. Recently published "Daddy Won't Sell the Farm" from *Tattoos and Scars* (album), recorded by Montgomery Gentry (country).

▢ CORELLI MUSIC GROUP (BMI/ASCAP)

P.O. Box 2314, Tacoma WA 98401-2314. (253)536-6751. E-mail: JerryCorelli@CorelliMusic Group.com. Web site: www.CorelliMusicGroup.com. **Contact:** Jerry Corelli, owner. Music publisher, record company (Omega III Records), record producer (Jerry Corelli/Angels Dance Recording Studio) and booking agency (Tone Deaf Booking). Estab. 1996. Publishes 12 songs/year; publishes 6 new songwriters/year. Staff size: 3. Pays standard royalty.

Affiliate(s) My Angel's Songs (ASCAP); Corelli's Music Box (BMI).

How to Contact Submit demo by mail. Unsolicited submissions are OK. "No phone calls, e-mails, or letters asking to submit." Prefers CD with 3 songs, lyric sheet and cover letter. "*We DO NOT accept MP3s vie e-mail.* We want love songs with a message and overtly Christian songs. Make sure all material is copyrighted. *You MUST include SASE or we DO NOT respond!*" Responds in 2 months

Music Mostly **contemporary Christian**, **Christian soft rock** and **Christmas**; also **love songs**, **ballads** and **new country**. Does not want songs without lyrics or lyrics without music. Published "I Can't Believe I'm Yours (by Jerry Corelli), "Grandfather Moon" (by Kevin Mannarino & Jerry Corelli), and "What'd I Even Came Here For" (by Rich Green), all from *Grandfather Moon* (album), released 2008 on Omega III Records.

Tips "Success is obtained when opportunity meets preparation! If a SASE is not sent with demo, we don't even listen to the demo. Be willing to do a rewrite. Don't send material expecting us to place it with a Top Ten artist. Be practical. Do your songs say what's always been said, except differently? Don't take rejection personally. Always send a #10 self-adhesive envelope for your SASE."

▢ THE CORNELIUS COMPANIES/GATEWAY ENTERTAINMENT, INC. (BMI, ASCAP, SESAC)

Dept. SM, 1710 Grand Ave., Nashville TN 37212. (615)321-5333. E-mail: corneliuscomps@ bellsouth.net. Web site: www.gatewayentertainment.com. **Contact:** Ron Cornelius, owner/president. Music publisher and record producer (Ron Cornelius). Estab. 1986. Publishes 60-80 songs/year; publishes 2-3 new songwriters/year. Occasionally hires staff writers. Pays standard royalty.

Affiliate(s) RobinSparrow Music (BMI), Strummin' Bird Music (ASCAP) and Bridgeway Music (SESAC).

How to Contact *Contact by e-mail or call for permission to submit material.* Submit demo package by mail. Unsolicited submissions are OK. "Send demo on CD format only with 2-3 songs." Include SASE. Responds in 2 months.

Music Mostly **country** and **pop**; also **positive country**, **gospel** and **alternative**. Published songs by Confederate Railroad, Faith Hill, David Allen Coe, Alabama and over 50 radio singles in the positive Christian/country format.

Tips "Looking for material suitable for film."

ℕ ⊕ CRINGE MUSIC (PRS, MCPS)

The Cedars, Elvington Lane, Folkestone Kent CT18 7AD United Kingdom. (01)(303)893-472. Fax: (01)(303)893-833. E-mail: info@cringemusic.co.uk. Web site: www.cringemusic.co.uk. **Contact:** Christopher Ashman. Music publisher and record company (Red Admiral Records). Estab. 1979. Staff size: 2.

How to Contact Submit demo package by mail. Unsolicited submissions are OK. CD only with unlimited number of songs and lyric sheet, lead sheet. Submission materials are not returned. Responds if interested.

Music All styles.

ℕ ◙ THE CROSSWIND CORPORATION

(formerly The Magnet), P.O. Box 120816, Nashville TN 37212. (615)467-3860. Fax: (615)467-3859. E-mail: tdchoate@aol.com. **Contact:** Terry Choate.

ⓥ ◯ CUPIT MUSIC GROUP (ASCAP, BMI)

P.O. Box 121904, Nashville TN 37212. (615)731-0100. Fax: (615)731-3005. E-mail: dan@cupitmusic.com. Web site: www.cupitmusic.com. **Contact:** Publishing Division. Music publisher, record producer, record company, entertainment division and recording studio. Estab. 1986. Staff size: 8. Pays standard royalty.

Affiliate(s) Cupit Memaries (ASCAP) and Cupit Music (BMI).

• Also see the listing for Jerry Cupit Productions in the Record Producers section. Cupit Music's "Jukebox Junkie" won BMI Millionair Award.

How to Contact *Please visit cupitmusic.com for our submission policy.* Prefers CD with lyric sheet. "We will return a response card." Include SASE. Usually responds in 2 months.

Music Mostly **country**, **bluegrass**, **blues**, **pop**, **gospel** and **instrumental**. Does not want rap, hard rock or metal. Published "He'll Never Be A Lawyer Cause He Can't Pass the Bar" (single), recorded by Mustang Creek (country), released 2007 on Cupit Records; "Your Love Reaches Me" (single), recorded by Kevin Sharp (country), released 2007 on Cupit Records; "I Bought the Shoes (That Just Walked Out On Me)" (single) from *Dierks Bentley* (album), recorded by Dierks Bentley (country), released 2005 on Cupit Records; and "I Know What You Got Up Your Sleeve" (single) from *Maverick* (album), recorded by Hank Williams, Jr. (country), released 2001 on Curb Records.

◪ ◙ THE EDWARD DE MILES MUSIC COMPANY (BMI)

10573 W. Pico Blvd., #352, Los Angeles CA 90064-2348. Phone: (310)948-9652. Fax: (310)474-7705. E-mail: info@edmsahara.com. Web site: www.edmsahara.com. **Contact:** Professional Manager. Music publisher, record company (Sahara Records), record producer, management, bookings and promotions. Estab. 1984. Publishes 50-75 songs/year; publishes 5 new songwriters/year. Hires staff songwriters. Pays standard royalty.

● Also see the listings for Edward De Miles in the Record Producers and Managers & Booking Agents sections, and Sahara Records And Filmworks Entertainment in the Record Companies section of this book.

How to Contact *Write first and obtain permission to submit.* Prefers CD with 1-3 songs and lyric sheet. Does not return material. Reponds in 1 month.

Music Mostly **top 40 pop/rock**, **R&B/dance** and **country**; also **musical scores for TV, radio, films** and **jingles**. Published "Dance Wit Me" and "Moments" (singles), written and recorded by Steve Lynn; "Games" (single), written and recorded by D'von Edwards (jazz), all on Sahara Records. Other artists include Multiple Choice.

Tips "Copyright all materials before submitting. Equipment and showmanship a must."

⚏ DEFINE SOMETHING IN NOTHING MUSIC (ASCAP)

11213 W. Baden Street, Avondale AZ 85323.(623)215-8376. E-mail: jkrprozack@gmail.c om. **Contact**: Jaime Reynolds, president. Estab. 2008. Music Publisher. Staff Size: 5. Pays standard royalty of 50%.

How to Contact Contact first and obtain permission to submit a demo. Prefers MP3s sent to e-mail only and/or link to band Web site with 4 songs and cover letter. Does not return submissions. Responds in 1 week.

Music Interested in all styles. "We welcome everything all over the world."

Tips "Please e-mail a short cover letter with a link to your band or 4 of your strongest MP3s. No phone calls or mail, no CDs or cassettes."

⊘ DELEV MUSIC COMPANY (ASCAP, BMI)

7231 Mansfield Ave., Philadelphia PA 19138-1620. (215)276-8861. Fax: (215)276-4509. E-mail: delevmusic@msn.com. President/CEO: William L. Lucas. A&R: Darryl Lucas. Music publisher. Publishes 6-10 songs/year; publishes 6-10 new songwriters/year. Pays standard royalty.

Affiliate(s) Sign of the Ram Music (ASCAP) and Delev Music (BMI).

How to Contact *Does not accept unsolicited material. Write or call first to obtain permission to submit.* Prefers CD format only—no cassettes—with 1-4 songs and lyric sheet. "We will not accept certified mail or SASE." Does not return material. Responds in 1-2 months.

Music Mostly **R&B ballads** and **dance-oriented**; also **pop ballads**, **christian/gospel**, **crossover** and **country/western**. We do not accept rap song material. Published "Angel Love" (single by Barbara Heston/Geraldine Fernandez) from *The Silky Sounds of Debbie G* (album), recorded by Debbie G (light R&B/easy listening), released 2000 on Blizzard Records; *Variety* (album), produced by Barbara Heston and Carment Lindsay, released on Luvya Records; and "Ever Again" by Bernie Williams, released 2003 on SunDazed Records.

Tips "Persevere regardless if it is sent to our company or any other company. Most of all, no matter what happens, believe in yourself."

⚏ ⊞ ⊘ DEMI MONDE RECORDS & PUBLISHING LTD.

Foel Studio, Llanfair, Caereinion Wales POWYS United Kingdom. E-mail: demi-monde@dia l.pipex.com. Web site: www.demi.monde.co.uk/demimonde. **Contact:** Dave Anderson, managing director. Music publisher, record company (Demi Monde Records & Publishing

Ltd.), record producer (Dave Anderson). Member MCPS. Estab. 1983. Publishes 50-70 songs/year; publishes 10-15 new songwriters/year. Pays standard royalty.

How to Contact Submit demo tape by mail. Unsolicited submissions are OK. Prefers cassette or VHS videocassette with 3-4 songs. Does not return material. Responds in 6 weeks.

Music Mostly **rock**, **R&B** and **pop**. Published "I Feel So Lazy" (by D. Allen), recorded by Gong (rock); "Phalarn Dawn" (by E. Wynne), recorded by Ozric Tentacles (rock); and "Pioneer" (by D. Anderson), recorded by Amon Dual (rock), all on Demi Monde Records.

☑ DISNEY MUSIC PUBLISHING, (ASCAP, BMI)

500 S. Buena Vista St., Burbank CA 91521-6182. (818)567-5069. Web site: http://home.disney.go.com/music/. **Contact:** Ashley Saunig, DMP creative department.

Affiliate(s) Seven Peaks Music and Seven Summits Music.

• Part of the Buena Vista Music Group.

How to Contact *"We cannot accept any unsolicited material."*

☑ EARTHSCREAM MUSIC PUBLISHING CO., (BMI)

8377 Westview Dr., Houston TX 77055. (713)464-GOLD. E-mail: sarsjef@aol.com. Web site: www.soundartsrecording.com. **Contact:** Jeff Wells; Peter Verkerk. Music publisher, record company and record producer. Estab. 1975. Publishes 12 songs/year; publishes 4 new songwriters/year. Pays standard royalty.

• Also see the listings for Surface Records in the Record Companies section and Sound Arts Recording Studio in the Record Producers section of this book.

Affiliate(s) Reach For The Sky Music Publishing (ASCAP).

How to Contact Submit demo by mail. Unsolicited submissions are OK. Prefers CD or videocassette with 2-5 songs and lyric sheet. Does not return material. Responds in 6 weeks.

Music Mostly **new rock**, **country**, **blues** and **top 40/pop**. Published "Baby Never Cries" (single by Carlos DeLeon), recorded by Jinkies on Surface Records (pop); "Telephone Road" (single), written and recorded by Mark May(blues) on Icehouse Records; "Do You Remember" (single by Barbara Pennington), recorded by Perfect Strangers on Earth Records (rock), and "Sheryl Crow" (single), recorded by Dr. Jeff and the Painkillers (pop); "Going Backwards" (single), written and recorded by Tony Vega (Gulf swamp blues), released on Red Onion Records.

EAST MADISON MUSIC PUBLISHING (ASCAP)

9 Music Square South, #143, Nashville TN 37203.(615)838-4171. E-mail: eastmadisonmusic @charter.net. Web site: www.emmrecords.net. **Contact:** Dean Holmen, publisher. Music publisher, record company (East Madison Music Records), and record producer (Dean Holmen). Estab. 2003 Published 6 songs/year; publishes 3 new songwriters/year. Staff size: 2. Pays standard royalty.

• East Madison Music Publishing received a First Place Award in 2005 for "If Teardrops Played the Juke Box" and First Place in 2006 for "I Should Get 30 Years" from Songwriters of Wisconsin.

Affiliate(s) Ricki Lynn Publishing (BMI).

How to Contact Submit demo by mail. Unsolicited submissions are OK. Prefers CD with 1-3 songs with lyric sheet and cover letter. Does not return submissions. Responds only if interested.

Music Mostly **traditional country** and **gospel**; does not want rock or hip-hop. Published "Weekend Willie Nelson," "I Gave My Heart Away," and "Don't Ever Leave Me" (singles by Tim Schweeberger) from *Heartaches & Honky Tonks*, recorded by Dean Holmen (traditional country), released 2006 on EMM Records.

Tips "Please follow submission guidelines. If you follow our guidelines, your song will be reviewed. If not, it will be disregarded. Don't overlook the independent artist. Most songs cut today are cut by them."

EMF PRODUCTIONS (ASCAP)

1000 E. Prien Lake Rd., Suite D, Lake Charles LA 70601. E-mail: emfprod@aol.com. Web site: www.emfproductions.com. President: Ed Fruge. Music publisher and record producer. Estab. 1984. Pays standard royalty.

How to Contact Submit demo package by mail. Unsolicited submissions are OK. Prefers CD or DVDs with 3 of your best songs and lyric sheets. Does not return material. Responds in 6 weeks.

Music Mostly **R&B**, **pop** and **rock**; also **country** and **gospel**.

EMI MUSIC PUBLISHING

1290 Avenue of the Americas, 42nd Floor, New York NY 10104. (212)492-1200. Web site: www.emimusicpub.com. Music publisher.

How to Contact *EMI does not accept unsolicited material.*

Music Published "All Night Long" (by F. Evans/R. Lawrence/S. Combs), recorded by Faith Evans featuring Puff Daddy on Bad Boy; "You" (by C. Roland/J. Powell), recorded by Jesse Powell on Silas; and "I Was" (by C. Black/P. Vassar), recorded by Neal McCoy on Atlantic.

Tips "Don't bury your songs. Less is more—we will ask for more if we need it. Put your strongest song first."

EMSTONE MUSIC PUBLISHING (BMI)

Box 398, Hallandale FL 33008. (305)936-0412. E-mail: webmaster@emstonemusicpublishing.com. **Contact:** Michael Gary, creative director. President: Mitchell Stone. Vice President: Madeline Stone. Music publisher. Estab. 1997. Pays standard royalty.

How to Contact Submit demo CD by mail with any number of songs. Unsolicited submissions are OK. Does not return material. Responds only if interested.

Music Everything except classical and opera. Published "www.history" (written by Tim Eatman) and "Gonna Recall My Heart" (written by Dan Jury) from *No Tears* (album), recorded by Cole Seaver and Tammie Darlene, released on CountryStock Records; and "I Love What I've Got" (single by Heather and Paul Turner) from *The Best of Talented Kids* (compilation album) recorded by Gypsy.

Tips "We only offer publishing contracts to writers whose songs exhibit a spark of genius. Anything less can't compete in the music industry."

N ENCORE PERFORMANCE PUBLISHING

P.O. Box 14367, Tallahassee FL 32317. (850)385-2463. E-mail: editor@encoreplay.com. Web site: www.encoreplay.com. **Contact**: Meredith Edward, senior editor. Drama publisher. "We publish complete musicals, not single songs." Estab. 1978. Publishes 1-2 musicals/year. Pays standard royalty.

How to Contact *E-mail first and obtain permission to submit a demo.* Materials should include complete musical including libretto, lyrics, lead sheets, and demo CD. Responds in 2 months.

Musical Theater "We are especially interested in musicals for schools (from grade school through high school)."

Publications *Elephants*, music by Larrance Fingerhut, books and lyrics by Jeff Goode; *Anne With an "e": The Green Gables Musical*, books and lyrics by Neil K. Newell and C. Michael Perry.

☐ FIFTH AVENUE MEDIA, LTD. (ASCAP)

1208 W. Broadway, Hewlett NY 11557. (212)691-5630. Fax: (212)645-5038. E-mail: thefirm @thefirm.com. Web site: www.thefirm.com. Professional Managers: Bruce E. Colfin(rootsy bluesy rock/reggae, Jam Bands/alternative rock/heavy metal); Jeffrey E. Jacobson (hip-hop/R&B/dance). Music publisher and record company (Fifth Avenue Media, Ltd.). Estab. 1995. Publishes 2 songs/year. Staff size: 4. Pays standard royalty.

Music Published "Analog" (single by Paul Byrne) from *Paul Byrne & the Bleeders* (album), recorded by Paul Byrne (pop rock), released 2001 on Independent.

⊕ 🖼 ☐ FIRST TIME MUSIC (PUBLISHING) U.K. (PRS, MCPS)

Sovereign House, 12 Trewartha Road, Praa Sands, Penzance, Cornwall TR20 9ST United Kingdom. (01736)762826. Fax: (01736)763328. E-mail: panamus@aol.com. Web site: www .panamamusic.co.uk. **Contact:** Roderick G. Jones, managing director. Music publisher, record company (Digimax Records Ltd www.digimaxrecords.com, Rainy Day Records, Mohock Records, Pure Gold Records). Estab. 1986. Publishes 500-750 songs/year; 20-50 new songwriters/year. Staff size: 6. Hires staff writers. Pays standard royalty; "50-60% to established and up-and-coming writers with the right attitude."

Affiliate(s) Scamp Music Publishing, Panama Music Library, Musik Image Library, Caribbean Music Library, Psi Music Library, ADN Creation Music Library, Promo Sonor International, Eventide Music, Melody First Music Library, Piano Bar Music Library, Corelia Music Library, Panama Music Ltd, Panama Music Productions, Digimax Worldwide Digital Distribution Services.

How to Contact Submit demo package by mail. Unsolicited submissions are OK. Submit on CD only, "of professional quality" with unlimited number of songs and lyric or lead sheets. Responds in 1 month. SAE and IRC required for reply.

Film & TV Places 200 songs in film and TV/year. "Copyrights and phonographic rights of Panama Music Limited and its associated catalogue idents have been used and subsist in various productions broadcasts and adverts produced by major and independent production companies, television, film/video companies, radio broadcasters (not just in the UK, but in various countries world-wide) and by commercial record companies for general release and sale. In the UK & Republic of Ireland they include the BBC networks of national/regional television and radio, ITV network programs and promotions (Channel 4, Border TV, Granada TV, Tyne Tees TV, Scottish TV, Yorkshire TV, HTV, Central TV, Channel TV, LWT, Meridian TV, Grampian TV, GMTV, Ulster TV, Westcountry TV, Channel TV, Carlton TV, Anglia TV, TV3, RTE (Ireland), Planet TV, Rapido TV, VT4 TV, BBC Worldwide, etc.), independent radio stations, satellite Sky Television (BskyB), Discovery Channel, Learning Channel, National Geographic, Living Channel, Sony, Trouble TV, UK Style Channel, Hon Cyf, CSI, etc., and cable companies, GWR Creative, Premier, Spectrum FM, Local Radio Partnership, Fox, Manx, Swansea Sound, Mercury, 2CRFM, Broadland, BBC Radio Collection, etc. Some credits include copyrights in programs, films/videos, broadcasts, trailers and promotions such as *Desmond's*, *One Foot in the Grave*, *EastEnders*, *Hale* and *Pace*, *Holidays from Hell*, *A Touch of Frost*, *999 International*, and *Get Away*."

Music All styles. Published "Perfection" recorded by DJ Chaos Feat: Scarlet (hardcore dance) released by Nukleuz Records (album/single and digital downloads), released 2008 also released by Digimix Records Ltd (www.digimixrecords.com) on *Pure Hardcore* (a two pack 38 track album & singles mixed by AudioJunkie & Stylus) (album/single and digital downloads) released 2008; "Some Mothers Son" (from *Under Blue Skies* (album/single & digital downloads), recorded by Charlie Landsborough (country/MOR), released 2008 on Rosette Records; "Wii Go Crazy" (Hardcore/club) from *Clubland Extreme Hardcore 4* (album/single and digital downloads), recorded by DJ Dougal & Gammer released 2008 on Universal Records; "Remembrance Day" (folk) from *The Drums of Childhood Dreams* (album/single and digital downloads) recorded by Pete Arnold (folk), released 2007 on Digimix Records Ltd. (www.digimixrecords.com); "Rippin" (Hardcore/club) from *True Hardcore 2*, recorded by DJ Gammer released 2008 on Gut TV/Gut Records (album/single and digital downloads); "Big Sleep 2008" (Indie Brit rock/Pop) from the *Saturday Night Singles* (album/single and digital downloads) and every other track from the *Saturday Night Singles* (album/single and digital downloads) recorded by Toots Earl & Clown released on Digimix Records Ltd (www.digimixrecords.com); "Dancing DJ" (Hardcore/club) recorded by Dougal & Gammer (album track & single) released by Ministry of Sound (album/single and digital downloads), released 2008; "My Limerick Vales" recorded by Sean Wilson (album track & single—easy listening) released by H & H Music Ltd.(album/single and digital downloads), released 2008; "Blitz" recorded by Bram Stoker (album track & single—Progressive rock /gothic rock) released by Digimix Records Ltd (www.digimixrecords.com) (album/single and digital downloads), released 2008.

Tips "Have a professional approach—present well produced demos. First impressions are important and may be the only chance you get. Writers are advised to join the Guild of International Songwriters and Composers in the United Kingdom (www.songwriters-guild.co.uk)."

FRICON MUSIC COMPANY (BMI)

1050 S. Ogden Dr., Los Angeles CA 90019. (323)931-7323. Fax: (323)938-2030. E-mail: fricon@comcast.net. President: Terri Fricon. **Contact:** Madge Benson, professional manager. Music publisher. **Tennessee Office:** 134 Bluegrass Circle, Hendersonville TN 37075.

(615)826-2288. **Contact:** Jan Morales. Estab. 1981. Publishes 25 songs/year; publishes 1-2 new songwriters/year. Staff size: 6. Pays standard royalty.

Affiliate(s) Fricout Music Company (ASCAP) and Now and Forever Songs (SESAC).

How to Contact *Contact first and obtain permission to submit.* Prefers CD with 3-4 songs and lyric or lead sheet. "Prior permission must be obtained or packages will be returned." Include SASE. Responds in 2 months.

Music Mostly **country**.

✔ G MAJOR MUSIC (BMI)

P.O. Box 3331, Fort Smith AR 72913-3331. E-mail: JerryGlidewell@juno.com. Web site: www.GMajorPublishing.com. Owner: Jerry Glidewell. Professional Managers: Alex Hoover. Music publisher. Estab. 1992. Publishes 10 songs/year; publishes 2 new songwriters/year. Staff size: 2. Pays standard royalty.

How to Contact *No unsolicited submissions.* Submit inquiry by mail with SASE. Prefers CD or MP3. Submit up to 3 songs with lyrics. Include SASE. Responds in 4-6 weeks.

Music Mostly **country** and **contemporary Christian**. Published *Set The Captives Free* (album by Chad Little/Jeff Pitzer/Ben Storie), recorded by Sweeter Rain (contemporary Christian), for Cornerstone Television; "Hopes and Dreams" (single by Jerry Glidewell), recorded by Carrie Underwood (country), released on Star Rise; and "Be Still" (single by Chad Little/Dave Romero/Bryan Morse/Jerry Glidewell), recorded CO3 (contemporary Christian), released on Flagship Records.

Tips "We are looking for 'smash hits' to pitch to the Country and Christian markets."

☐ GLAD MUSIC CO. (ASCAP, BMI, SESAC)

14340 Torrey Chase, Suite 380, Houston TX 77014. (281)397-7300. Fax: (281)397-6206. E-mail: hwesdaily@gladmusicco.com. Web site: www.gladmusicco.com. **Contact:** Wes Daily, A&R Director (country). Music publisher, record company and record producer. Estab. 1958. Publishes 5 songs/year; publishes 2 new songwriters/year. Staff size: 4. Pays standard royalty.

Affiliate(s) Bud-Don (ASCAP) and Rayde (SESAC).

How to Contact *Write first and obtain permission to submit.* CDs only with 2 songs maximum, lyric sheet and cover letter. Does not return material. Responds in 6 weeks. SASE or e-mail address for reply.

Music Mostly **country**. Does not want weak songs. Published **Love Bug** (album by C. Wayne/W. Kemp), recorded by George Strait, released 1995 on MCA; *Walk Through This World With Me* (album), written and recorded by George Jones; and *Race Is On* (album by D. Rollins), recorded by George Jones, both released 1999 on Asylum.

☐ L.J. GOOD PUBLISHING (ASCAP)

P.O. Box 1696, Omak WA 98841.(509)422-1400. Fax: (509)267-8611. E-mail: lonnie@ljgood .com. Web site: www.wingstorchrist.com. **Contact:** Lonnie Good, president. Music publisher. Estab. 2006. Publishes 5 songs/year. Publishes 1 new songwriters/year. Staff size: 1. Pays standard royalty of 50%.

Affiliate(s) L.J. Good Publishing (ASCAP).

How to Contact Prefers CD or MP3 with 3 songs and lyric sheet, cover letter. Does not return submissions.

Music Mostly **country**, **blues**, **soft rock**, **contemporary Christian/Praise and Worship**.

☐ R L HAMMEL ASSOCIATES, INC. (ASCAP/BMI)

"Consultants to the Music, Recording & Entertainment Industries," P.O. Box 531, Alexandria IN 46001-0531. E-mail: info@rlhammel.com. Web site: www.rlhammel.com. **Contact:** A&R Department. President: Randal L. Hammel. Music publisher, record producer and consultant. Estab. 1974. Staff size: 3-5. Pays standard royalty.

Affiliate(s) LADNAR Music (ASCAP) and LEMMAH Music (BMI).

How to Contact Submit demo package and brief bio by mail. Unsolicited submissions are OK. Prefers CD, DAT or VHS/8mm videocassette with a maximum of 3 songs and typed lyric sheets. "Please notate three (3) best songs—no time to listen to a full project." Does not return material. Responds ASAP. "No fixed timeline."

Music Mostly **pop**, **R&B** and **Christian**; also **MOR**, **light rock**, **pop country** and **feature film title cuts**. Produced/arranged *The Wedding Collection Series* for WORD Records. Published *Lessons For Life* (album by Kelly Hubbell/Jim Boedicker) and *I Just Want Jesus* (album by Mark Condon), both recorded by Kelly Connor, released on iMPACT Records.

ℕ ⊕ ☐ HAPPY MELODY

VZW, Paul Gilsonstraat 31, St-Andries 8200 Belgium. 00 32 50-316380. Fax: 00 32 50-315235. E-mail: happymelody@skynet.be. **Contact:** Eddy Van Mouffaert, general manager. Music publisher, record company (Jump Records) and record producer (Jump Productions). Member SABAM S.V., Brussels. Publishes 100 songs/year; publishes 8 new songwriters/year. Staff size: 2. Pays standard royalty via SABAM S.V.

How to Contact Submit demo CD or tape by mail. Unsolicited submissions are OK. Prefers CD. Does not return material. Responds in 2 weeks.

Music Mostly **easy listening**, **disco** and **light pop**; also **instrumentals**. Published "Football Mania" (single by R. Mondes/J. Towers/D. Winters), recorded by Le Grand Julot (accordion), released 2005 on Scorpion; *Don't Give Up Your Dream* (album), written and recorded by Chris Clark (pop), released 2004 on 5 Stars; and *Instrumental Delight* (album), written and recorded by various artists (pop), released 2005 on Belstar.

Tips "Music wanted with easy, catchy melodies (very commercial songs)."

ℕ ⊘ HESFREE PRODUCTIONS & PUBLISHING COMPANY

P.O. Box 1214, Bryan TX 77806-1214. (979)268-3263. Fax: (979)589-2544. E-mail: hesfreeprodandpubco@yahoo.com. Web site: www.hesfreeproductions.com. President/CEO/Owner: Brenda M. Freeman-Heslip. Producer of songwriting: Jamie Heslip. Record producer, music publisher and management agency. Estab. 2001. Fee derived from sales royalty when song or artist is recorded, outright fee from recording artist and outright fee from record company.

How to Submit *Only accepts material referred to by a reputable industry source (manager,* *entertainment attorney, etc.).* Include CD/CDR. Does not return submissions. Responds in 6 weeks only if interested.

Music Gospel only. No other music will be accepted. "We will ensure that each project is complete with professionalism, with the highest technological strategies possible."

⊞ ⊕ ▣ ⊘ HEUPFERD MUSIKVERLAG GMBH

Ringwaldstr. 18, Dreieich 63303. Germany. E-mail: heupferd@t-online.de. Web site: http://www.heupferd-musik.de. **Contact:** Christian Winkelmann, general manager. Music publisher and record company (Viva La Difference). GEMA. Publishes 30 songs/year. Staff size: 3. Pays "royalties after GEMA distribution plan."

Affiliate(s) Song Bücherei (book series). "Vive La Difference!" (label).

How to Contact *Does not accept unsolicited submissions.*

Film & TV Places 1 song in film/year. Published "El Grito Y El Silencio" (by Thomas Hickstein), recorded by Tierra in *Frauen sind was Wunderbares* .

Music Mostly **folk**, **jazz** and **fusion**; also **New Age**, **rock** and **ethnic music**. Published "Mi Mundo" (single by Denise M'Baye/Matthias Furstenberg) from *Havana—Vamos A Ver* (album), recorded by Havana (Latin), released 2003 on Vive La Difference. Printed *Andy Irvine: Aiming For the Heart—Irish Song Affairs*, released in 2007.

⊕ ▣ ⊘ INTOXYGENE SARL

283 Fbg St. Antoine, Paris 75011 France. 011(33)1 43485151. Fax: 011(33)1 43485753. E-mail: infos@intoxygene.com. Web site: www.intoxygene.com or www.intoxygene.net. **Contact:** Patrick Jammes, managing director. Music publisher and record company. Estab. 1990. Staff size: 1. Publishes 30 songs/year. Pays 50% royalty.

How to Contact *Does not accept unsolicited submissions.*

Film & TV Places 3/5 songs in film and in TV/year.

Music Mostly **new industrial** and **metal**, **lounge**, **electronic**, and **ambient**. Publisher for Peeping Tom (trip-hop), Djaimin (house), Missa Furiosa by Thierry Zaboitzeff (progressive), and The Young Gods (alternative) amongst others.

⊕ ◻ ISLAND CULTURE MUSIC PUBLISHERS (BMI)

7005 Bordeaux, St. John 00830-9510. U.S. Virgin Islands. E-mail: L_monsanto@hotmail.com. Web site: www.IslandKingRecords.com. **Contact:** Liston Monsanto, Jr., president. Music publisher and record company (Island King Records). Estab. 1996. Publishes 10 songs/year; publishes 3 new songwriters/year. Hires staff songwriters. Staff size: 3. Pays standard royalty.

How to Contact Submit demo package by mail. Unsolicited submissions are OK. Prefers CD with 8 songs and lyric sheet. Send bio and 8×10 glossy. Does not return material. Responds in 1 month.

Music Mostly **reggae**, **calypso**, and **zouk**; also **house**. Published *De Paris a Bohicon* (album), recorded by Rasbawa (reggae), released 2006 on Island King Records; "Jah Give Me Life" (single by Chubby) from *Best of Island King* (album), recorded by Chubby (reggae), released 2003 on Island King Records; "When People Mix Up" (single by Lady Lex/L.

Monsanto/Chubby) and "I Am Real" (single by L. Monsanto) from *Best of Island King* (album), recorded by Lady Lex (reggae), released 2003 on Island King Records.

◻ IVORY PEN ENTERTAINMENT (ASCAP)

P.O. Box 1097, Laurel MD 20725. Fax: (240)786-6744. E-mail: ivorypen@comcast.net. Professional Managers: Steven Lewis (R&B, pop/rock, inspirational); Sonya Lewis (AC, dance) Wandaliz Colon (Latin, Ethic). Music publisher. Estab. 2003. Publishes 10 songs/year. Staff size: 4. Pays standard royalty.

How to Contact Submit demo package by mail. Unsolicited submissions are OK. Prefers CD with 3-5 songs and cover letter. Does not return material. Responds in 4 months. "Don't forget contact info with e-mail address for faster response! Always be professional when you submit your work to any company. Quality counts."

Music Mostly **R&B**, **dance**, **pop/rock**, **Latin**, **adult contemporary**, and **inspirational**. Published Ryan Vetter (single), writer recorded by Alan Johnson (/pop/rock), released on Ivory Pen Entertainment; and "Mirror" (single), by Angel Demone, on Vox Angel Inc./Ivory Pen Entertainment.

Tips "Learn your craft. Always deliver high quality demos. 'Remember, if you don't invest in yourself, don't expect others to invest in you. Ivory Pen Entertainment is a music publishing company that caters to the new songwriter, producer, and aspiring artist. We also place music tracks (no vocals) with artists for release."

◪ JANA JAE MUSIC (BMI)

P.O. Box 35726, Tulsa OK 74153. (918)786-8896. Fax: (918)786-8897. E-mail: janajae@janaj ae.com. Web site: www.janajae.com. **Contact:** Kathleen Pixley, secretary. Music publisher, record company (Lark Record Productions, Inc.) and record producer (Lark Talent and Advertising). Estab. 1980. Publishes 5-10 songs/year; publishes 1-2 new songwriters/year. Staff size: 8. Pays standard royalty.

How to Contact Submit demo by mail. Unsolicited submissions are OK. Prefers CD or VHS videocassette with 3-4 songs and typed lyric and lead sheet if possible. Does not return material. Responds only if accepted for use.

Music Mostly **country**, **bluegrass**, **jazz** and **instrumentals** (**classical** or **country**). Published *Mayonnaise* (album by Steve Upfold), recorded by Jana Jae; and *Let the Bible Be Your Roadmap* (album by Irene Elliot), recorded by Jana Jae, both on Lark Records.

▥ ◻ JERJOY MUSIC (BMI)

P.O. Box 1264, 6020 W. Pottstown Rd., Peoria IL 61654-1264. (309)673-5755. Fax: (309)673-7636. E-mail: uarltd@A5.com. Web site: www.unitedcyber.com and www.myspace.com/jerryhanlon. **Contact:** Jerry Hanlon, professional manager. Music publisher and record company (UAR Records). Estab. 1978. Publishes 6 songs/year; publishes 6 new songwriters/year. Staff size: 3. Pays standard royalty.

Affiliate(s) Kaysarah Music (ASCAP); Abilite Music (BMI).

• Also see the listing for Kaysarah Music in this section and UAR Records in the Record Companies section of this book.

How to Contact *Write first and obtain permission to submit. "WE DO NOT RESPOND TO TELEPHONE CALLS.* We are currently accepting only a limited number of submissions, *so please write for permission before sending.* Unsolicited submissions are OK, but be sure to send SASE and/or postage or mailing materials if you want a reply and/or a return of all your material. *WE DO NOT OFFER CRITIQUES OF YOUR WORK UNLESS SPECIFICALLY ASKED.* Simple demos—vocal plus guitar or keyboard—are acceptable. We DO NOT require a major demo production to interpret the value of a song." Prefers CD with 4-8 songs and lyric sheet. Responds in 2 weeks.

Music Mostly **Americancountry, Irish Country** and **religious**. Published "Philomena From Ireland," "I Wanted You for Mine," and "Lisa, Dance with Me" written by The Heggarty Twins of Northern Ireland (recorded by The Heggarty Twins and Jerry Hanlon, country), and "things My Daddy Used to Do" written by Mark Walton (recorded by Jerry Hanlon, country); "That Little Irish Church" written and recorded by Jerry Hanlon, country gospel Irish). "I'd Better Stand Up" written by Gene Gillen and Will Herring (recorded by The Heggarty Twins and Jerry Hanlon, country); "Rainbow" written by Dwight Howell (recorded by The Heggarty Twins and Jerry Hanlon, Irish country). "All Your Little Secrets" and "The Girl from Central High" written by Ron Czikall (recorded by Tracy Wells, country); all released on UAR Records.

Tips "Don't submit any song that you don't honestly feel is well constructed and strong in commercial value. Be critical of your writing efforts. Be sure you use each and every one of your lyrics to its best advantage. 'Think Big!' Make your songs tell a story and don't be repetitious in using the same or similar ideas or words in each of your verses. Would your musical creation stand up against the major hits that are making the charts today? Think of great hooks you can work into your song ideas."

☐ KAUPPS & ROBERT PUBLISHING CO. (BMI)

P.O. Box 5474, Stockton CA 95205. (209)948-8186. Fax: (209)942-2163. Web site: www.makingmusic4u.com. **Contact:** Melissa Glenn, A&R coordinator (all styles). Production Manager (country, pop, rock): Rick Webb. Professional Manager (country, pop, rock): Bruce Bolin. President: Nancy L. Merrihew. Music publisher, record company (Kaupp Records), manager and booking agent (Merri-Webb Productions and Most Wanted Bookings). Estab. 1990. Publishes 15-20 songs/year; publishes 5 new songwriters/year. Pays standard royalty.

How to Contact *Write first and obtain permission to submit.* Prefers cassette or VHS videocassette (if available) with 3 songs maximum and lyric sheet. "If artist, send PR package." Include SASE. Responds in 6 months.

Music Mostly **country, R&B** and **A/C rock**; also **pop, rock** and **gospel**. Published "Rushin' In" (singles by N. Merrihew/B. Bolin), recorded by Valerie; "Goin Postal" (singles by N. Merrihew/B. Bolin), recorded by Bruce Bolin (country/rock/pop); and "I Gotta Know" (single by N. Merrihew/B. Bolin), recorded by Cheryl (country/rock/pop), all released on Kaupp Records.

Tips "Know what you want, set a goal, focus in on your goals, be open to constructive criticism, polish tunes and keep polishing."

⬛ ❏ KAYSARAH MUSIC (ASCAP, BMI)

P.O. Box 1264, 6020 W. Pottstown Rd., Peoria IL 61654-1264. (309)673-5755. Fax: (309)673-7636. E-mail: uarltd@A5.com. Web site: www.unitedcyber.com and www.myspace.com/jerryhanlon. **Contact:** Jerry Hanlon, owner/producer. Music Publisher, record company (UAR Records), and record producer. Estab. 2000. Publishes 2 new songwriters/year. Staff size: 3. Pays standard royalty.

Affiliate(s) Jerjoy Music (BMI); Abilite Music (BMI).

- Also see the listing for Jerjoy Music in this section and UAR Records in the Record Companies section of this book.

How to Contact *Write first and obtain permission to submit. "WE DO NOT RESPOND TO TELEPHONE CALLS.* We are currently accepting only a limited number of submissions, *so please write for permission before sending.* Unsolicited submissions are OK, but be sure to send SASE and/or postage or mailing materials if you want a reply and/or a return of all your material. *WE DO NOT OFFER CRITIQUES OF YOUR WORK UNLESS SPECIFICALLY ASKED."* Prefers CD with 4 songs and lyric sheet and cover letter. Include SASE. Responds in 2 weeks.

Music Mostly **traditional country** and **country gospel**; also **Irish country**, **Irish ballads** and **Irish folk/traditional**.

Tips "Be honest and self-critical of your work. Make every word in a song count. Attempt to create work that is not over 2:50 minutes in length. Compare your work to the songs that seem to be what you hear on radio. A good A&R person or professional recording artist with a creative mind can determine the potential value of a song simply by hearing a melody line (guitar or keyboard) and the lyrics. DON'T convince yourself that your work is outstanding if you feel that it will not be able to compete with the tough competition of today 's market."

⬛ ⬛ ❏ LILLY MUSIC PUBLISHING (SOCAN)

61 Euphrasia Dr., Toronto ON M6B 3V8 Canada. (416)782-5768. Fax: (416)782-7170. E-mail: panfilo@sympatico.ca. **Contact:** Panfilo Di Matteo, president. Music publisher and record company (P. & N. Records). Estab. 1992. Publishes 20 songs/year; publishes 8 new songwriters/year. Staff size: 3. Pays standard royalty.

Affiliate(s) San Martino Music Publishing and Paglieta Music Publishing (CMRRA).

How to Contact Submit demo by mail. Unsolicited submissions are OK. Prefers CD (or videocassette if available) with 3 songs and lyric and lead sheets. "We will contact you only if we are interested in the material." Responds in 1 month.

Film & TV Places 12 songs in film/year.

Music Mostly **dance**, **ballads** and **rock**; also **country**. Published "I'd Give It All" (single by Glenna J. Sparkes), recorded by Suzanne Michelle (country crossover), released 2005 on Lilly Records.

❏ LITA MUSIC (ASCAP)

2831 Dogwood Place, Nashville TN 37204. (615)269-8682. Fax: (615)269-8929. Web site: http://songsfortheplanet.com. **Contact:** Justin Peters, president. Music publisher. Estab. 1980.

Affiliate(s) Justin Peters Music, Platinum Planet Music and Tourmaline (BMI).

How to Contact Submit demo package by mail. Unsolicited submissions are OK. Prefers CD with 5 songs and lyric sheet. Does not return material. "Place code '2009' on each envelope submission."

Music Mostly **Southern gospel/Christian**, **country**, **classic rock** and **worship songs**. Published "No Less Than Faithful" (single by Don Pardoe/Joel Lyndsey), recorded by Ann Downing on Daywind Records, Jim Bullard on Genesis Records and Melody Beizer (#1 song) on Covenant Records; "No Other Like You" (single by Mark Comden/Paula Carpenter), recorded by Twila Paris and Tony Melendez (#5 song) on Starsong Records; "Making A New Start" and "Invincible Faith" (singles by Gayle Cox), recorded by Kingdom Heirs on Sonlite Records; and "I Don't Want To Go Back" (single by Gayle Cox), recorded by Greater Vision on Benson Records; "Lost In The Shadow of the Cross" (single by James Elliott and Steven Curtis Chapman) recorded by Steven Curtis Chapman on Sparrow Records.

☐ M & T WALDOCH PUBLISHING, INC. (BMI)

4803 S. Seventh St., Milwaukee WI 53221. (414)482-2194. VP, Creative Management (rockabilly, pop, country): Timothy J. Waldoch. Professional Manager (country, top 40): Mark T. Waldoch. Music publisher. Estab. 1990. Publishes 2-3 songs/year; publishes 2-3 new songwriters/year. Staff size: 2. Pays standard royalty.

How to Contact Submit demo package by mail. Unsolicited submissions are OK. Prefers CD with 3-6 songs and lyric or lead sheet. "We will also accept a studio produced demo tape." Include SASE. Responds in 3 months.

Music Mostly **country/pop**, **rock**, **top 40 pop**; also **melodic metal**, **dance**, **R&B**. Does not want rap. Published "It's Only Me" and "Let Peace Rule the World" (by Kenny LePrix), recorded by Brigade on SBD Records (rock).

Tips "Study the classic pop songs from the 1950s through the present time. There is a reason why good songs stand the test of time. Today's hits will be tomorrow's classics. Send your best well-crafted, polished song material."

☑ MAKERS MARK GOLD PUBLISHING (ASCAP)

534 W. Queen Lane, Philadelphia PA 19144. E-mail: MakersMark@verizon.net. **Contact:** Paul Hopkins, producer/publisher. Music publisher and record producer. Estab. 1991. Pays standard royalty.

How to Contact Submit demo CD or tape by mail. Unsolicited submissions are OK. Prefers 2-4 songs. Does not return material. Responds in 6 weeks if interested.

Music "Our publishing and productions has changed to total **Christian/Inspirational. Gospel/ christian** only. All genres **contemporary, traditional, pop, dance, hip-hop gospel**." Historically mostly **R&B**, **hip-hop**, **gospel**, **pop** and **house**. Published "Silent Love," "Why You Want My Love" and "Something for Nothing," (singles), written and recorded by Elaine Monk, released on Black Sands Records/Metropolitan Records; "Get Funky" (single), written and recorded by Larry Larr, released on Columbia Records; and "He Made a Way" (single by Kenyatta Arrington), "We Give All Praises Unto God" (single by Jacqueline D. Pate), "I Believe He Will" (single by Pastor Alyn E. Waller), and "Psalms 146" (single by Rodney Roberson), all songs recorded by The Enon Tabernacle Mass Choir from *Pastor Alyn E. Waller Presents: The Enon Tabernacle Mass Choir*, released on ECDC Records (www.enontab.org). Also produces and publishes music for Bunim/Murray productions network television, MTV's *Real World*, *Road Rules*, *Rebel Billionaire*, *Simple Life*, and movie soundtracks worldwide. Also produced deep soul remixes for Brian McKnight, Musiq Souchild, Jagged Edge, John Legend, and Elaine Monk.

⚡ ✪ MANY LIVES MUSIC PUBLISHERS (SOCAN)

RR #1, Kensington PE C0B 1M0 Canada. (902)836-4571 (studio). E-mail: paul.milner@sum merside.ca. **Contact:** Paul C. Milner, publisher. Music publisher. Estab. 1997. "Owners of Shell Lane Studio www.shelllanestudio.com complete in-house production facility. Many Lives Music Publishers was also involved in the production and recording of all projects listed below." Pays standard royalty.

How to Contact Submit demo by mail. Unsolicited submissions are OK. Prefers CD and lyric sheet (lead sheet if available). Does not return material. Responds in 3 months if interested.

Music All styles. *Six Pack EP* and *Colour* (album), written and recorded by Chucky Danger (Pop/Rock), released 2005 on Landwash Entertainment. Chucky Danger's *Colour* album was named Winner Best Pop Recording at the East Coast Music Awards 2006, "Sweet Symphony" was nominated for Single of the Year, and Chucky Danger was nominated for Best New Group. Released *Temptation* (album by various writers), arrangement by Paul Milner, Patrizia, Dan Cutrona (rock/opera), released 2003 on United One Records; *The Edge Of Emotion* (album by various writers), arrangement by Paul Milner, Patrizia, Dan Cutrona (rock/opera), released 2006 on Nuff Entertainment/United One Records. The Single "Temptation" won a SOCAN #1 award. *Saddle River Stringband* (album) written and recorded by The Saddle River Stringband (Bluegrass) released on Panda Digital/Save As Music 2007. Winners of best Bluegrass recording East Coast Music Awards 2007. *Pat Deighan and the Orb Weavers* (album) "In A Fever In A Dream" (Alternative Rock) written by Pat Deighan, released on Sandbar Music April 2008.

MATERIAL WORTH PUBLISHING (ASCAP)

P.O. Box 162, Walden NY 12586-0162. (845)283-0795. E-mail: franksardella@materialwoth publishing.com. Web site: www.materialworthpublishing.com. **Contact:** Frank Sardella, owner. Music publisher. Estab. 2003. Staff size: 3. Pays standard royalty of 50%.

How to Contact *Visit Web site for how to obtain permission to submit. Do not call first.* Prefers CD, lyric sheet, and cover letter. Does not return submissions. Responds in 4-6 weeks.

Music Mostly **female pop**, **pop/country crossover**, **singer-songwriter**, **male pop alternative rock**.

✪ MAVERICK MUSIC (ASCAP)

3300 Warner Blvd., Burbank CA 91505. (310)385-7800. Web site: www.maverick.com. Music publisher and record company (Maverick).

How to Contact *Maverick Music does not accept unsolicited submissions.*

⚡ ◻ MAYFAIR MUSIC (BMI)

2600 John St., Unit 203, Markham ON L3R 3W3 Canada. (905)475-1848. Fax: (905)474-9870. **Contact:** John Loweth, A&R director. Music publisher, record company (MBD Records), music print publisher (Mayfairmusic), record producer and distributor. Member CMPA, CIRPA, CRIA. Estab. 1979. Pays standard royalty.

How to Contact Submit demo by mail. Unsolicited submissions are OK. Prefers CD/CDR with 2-5 songs. Does not return material. Responds in 3 weeks.

Music Mostly **instrumental**.

Tips "Strong melodic choruses and original-sounding music receive top consideration."

◻ MCCLURE & TROWBRIDGE PUBLISHING, LTD (ASCAP, BMI)

P.O. Box 70403, Nashville TN 37207. (615)902-0509. Web site: www.TrowbridgePlanetEarth.com. Contact: Miig Miniger, director of marketing. Music publisher, and record label (JIP Records) and production company (George McClure, producer). Estab. 1983. Publishes 35 songs/year. Publishes 5 new songwriters/year. Staff size: 8. Pays standard royalty of 50%.

How to Contact Do not email. *Follow directions ONLINE ONLY—obtain Control Number to submit a demo via US Mail.* Requires CD with 1-5 songs, lyric sheet, and cover letter. Does not return submissions. Responds in 3 weeks if interested.

Music Pop, **country**, **gospel**, **Latin** and **swing**. "We are very open-minded as far as genres. If it's good music, we like it!" Published "Playboy Swing," released 2008 on JIP Records; "You're One in a Million" (single), recorded by Layni Kooper (R&B/pop), released 2007 on JIP Records; "My Way or Hit the Highway" (single), written and recorded by Jacqui Watson (Americana), released 2005 on Artist Choice CD; and "I'm a Wild One" (single), recorded by Veronica Leigh, released 2006 on Artist Choice CD.

◻ JIM MCCOY MUSIC (BMI)

25 Troubadour Lane, Berkeley Springs WV 25411. (304)258-9381. E-mail: mccoytroubadour @aol.com. Web site: www.troubadourlounge.com. **Contact:** Bertha and Jim McCoy, owners. Music publisher, record company (Winchester Records) and record producer (Jim McCoy Productions). Estab. 1973. Publishes 20 songs/year; publishes 3-5 new songwriters/year. Pays standard royalty.

Affiliate(s) New Edition Music (BMI).

How to Contact Submit demo by mail with lyric sheet. Unsolicited submissions are OK. Prefers cassette or CD with 6 songs. Include SASE. Responds in 1 month.

Music Mostly **country**, **country/rock** and **rock**; also **bluegrass** and **gospel**. Published "She's the Best" recorded by Matt Hahn on Troubadour Records (written by Jim McCoy); "Shadows on My Mind" recorded by Sandy Utley (written by Jim McCoy), "Rock and Roll Hillbilly Redneck Girl" recorded by Elani Arthur (written by Jim McCoy), all released in 2007.

ⓝ ⊠ ⊘ MCJAMES MUSIC INC. (BMI)/37 SONGS (ASCAP)

1724 Stanford St., Suite B, Santa Monica CA 90404. (310)712-1916. Fax: (419)781-6644. E-mail: info@mcjamesmusic.com. Web site: www.mcjamesmusic.com and www.myspace.com/mcjamesmusic. Professional Managers: Tim James(country/pop); Steven McClintock (pop/country). Music publisher, record company (37 Songs) and record producer (Steven McClintock). Estab. 1977. Writers include: Pamela Phillips Oland, Stephen Petree, Jeremy Dawson, Chad Petree, Brian Stoner, Tom Templeman, Cathy-Anne McClintock, Tim James, Steven McClintock, Ryan Lawhon. Publishes 50 songs/year. Staff size: 4. Pays standard royalty. Does administration and collection for all foreign markets for publishers and writers.

Affiliate(s) 37 Songs (ASCAP) and McJames Music, Inc. (BMI).

How to Contact *Only accepts material referred by a reputable industry source.* Prefers CD with 2 songs and cover letter. Does not return material. Responds in 6 months.

Film & TV Places 2 songs in film and 3 songs in TV/year. Music Supervisor: Tim James/ Steven McClintock. Blood and Chocolate, 3 Day Weekend, Dirty Sexy Money, Brothers and Sisters, Dancing with the Stars, Dexter, Always Sunny in Philadelphia, America's Top Model. Commercials include Honda Australia, Scion California, Motorola Razr 2 worldwide.

Music Mostly **modern rock, country, pop, jazz** and **euro dance**; also **bluegrass** and **alternative**. Will accept some mainstream rap but no classical. Published ''Le Disko''; ''You are the One''; ''Rainy Monday'' (singles from Shiny Toy Guns on Universal), ''Be Sure''; ''What It Is'' (singles from Cris Barber), ''Keeps Bringing Me Back'' (from Victoria Shaw on Taffita), ''Christmas Needs Love to be Christmas'' (single by Andy Williams on Delta), recent cover by ATC on BMG/Universal with ''If Love is Blind''; single by new Warner Bros. act Sixwire called ''Look at me Now.''

Tips ''Write a song we don't have in our catalog or write an undeniable hit. We will know it when we hear it.''

⊠ ⊘ MIDI TRACK PUBLISHING (BMI)

P.O. Box 1545, Smithtown NY 11787. (718)767-8995. E-mail: allrsmusic@aol.com. Web site: www.geocities.com/allrsmusic. **Contact:** Renee Silvestri, president. F.John Silvestri, founder. Music publisher, record company (MIDI Track Records), music consultant, artist management, record producer. Voting member of NARAS (The Grammy Awards), Voting member of the Country Music Association (The CMA Awards), SGMA, Songwriters Guild of America (Diamond Member). Estab. 1994. Staff size: 5. Publishes 3 songs/year; publishes 2 new songwriters/year. Pays standard royalty.

Affiliate(s) Midi-Track Publishing Co. (BMI).

How to Contact ''Write or e-mail first to obtain permission to submit. We do not accept unsolicited submissions.'' Prefers CD or cassette with 3 songs, lyric sheet and cover letter. ''Make sure your CD or cassette tape is labeled with your name, mailing address, telephone number, and e-mail address. We do not return material.'' Responds via e-mail in 6 months.

Film & TV Places 1 song in film/year. Published ''Why Can't You Hear My Prayer'' (single by F. John Silvestri/Leslie Silvestri), recorded by Iliana Medina in a documentary by Silvermine Films.

Music Mostly **country**, **gospel**, **top 40**, **R&B**, **MOR** and **pop**. Does not want showtunes, jazz, classical or rap. Published "Why Can't You Hear My Prayer" (single by F. John Silvestri/Leslie Silvestri), recorded by eight-time Grammy nominee Huey Dunbar of the group DLG (Dark Latin Groove), released on Trend Records (other multiple releases, also recorded by Iliana Medina and released 2002 on MIDI Track Records); "Chasing Rainbows" (single by F. John Silvestri/Leslie Silvestri), recorded by Tommy Cash (country), released on MMT Records (including other multiple releases); "Because of You" (single by F. John Silvestri/Leslie Silvestri), recorded by Iliana Medina, released 2002 on MIDI Track Records, also recorded by three-time Grammy nominee Terri Williams, released on KMA Records; also recorded by Grand Ole Opry member Ernie Ashworth, released 2004 on KMA Records; "My Coney Island" (single by F. John Silvestri/Leslie Silvestri), recorded by eight-time Grammy nominee Huey Dunbar, released 2005 on MIDI Track Records.

Tips "Attend workshops, seminars, join songwriters organizations, and keep writing. You will achieve your goal."

⊠ ◪ MUST HAVE MUSIC (ASCAP, BMI)

P.O. Box 801181, Santa Clarita CA 91380-1181. (661)645-7618. Fax: (661)799-3732. E-mail: info@musthavemusic.com. Web site: www.musthavemusic.com. **Contact:** Kenneth R. Klar, managing director. Music publisher and music library. Estab. 1990. Pays standard royalty.

Affiliate(s) Must Have More Music (ASCAP); Must Have Music (BMI).

How to contact Submit demo by mail with your personal e-mail address included for directors response. Unsolicited submissions are OK. Prefers CD with lyric sheet and cover letter. Does not return submissions. Responds in 2 months.

Film & TV Music supervisor: Ken Klar, managing director.

Music Mostly **pop/R&B**, **pop/country** and **rock**; also **AAA**, **adult contemporary**, and **contemporary Christian/gospel**. Does not want instrumental music. "We only work with completed songs with lyric and vocal." Published "Come to the Table" (single by Ken Klar/Steve Massey) from *Worship Leader Magazine's Song Discovery, Vol. 26* (album), recorded by various artists, released 2002 on Worship Leader; "Fool" (single by Ken Klar) from *If You Want My Love* (album), recorded by Jennifer Young (pop/R&B), released 2002 on Independent; and "Blame It on My Heart" (single by Ken Klar/Steve Kirwan) from *Blame It on My Heart* (album), recorded by Steve Kirwan (adult contemporary), released 2001 on Independent.

Tips "Write what you know and what you believe. Then re-write it!"

⊠ ▦ ◯ NERVOUS PUBLISHING

5 Sussex Crescent, Northolt, Middlesex UB5 4DL United Kingdom. +44(020) 8423 7373. Fax: +44(020) 8423 7773. E-mail: info@nervous.co.uk. Web site: www.nervous.co.uk. **Contact:** Roy Williams, owner. Music publisher, record company (Nervous Records) and record producer. MCPS, PRS and Phonographic Performance Ltd. Estab. 1979. Publishes 100 songs/year; publishes 25 new songwriters/year. Pays standard royalty; royalties paid directly to US songwriters.

● Nervous Publishing's record label, Nervous Records, is listed in the Record Companies section.

How to Contact Submit demo by mail. Unsolicited submissions are OK. Prefers CD with 3-10 songs and lyric sheet. "Include letter giving your age and mentioning any previously published material." SAE and IRC. Responds in 3 weeks.

Music Mostly **psychobilly, rockabilly** and **rock** (impossibly fast music—e.g.: Stray Cats but twice as fast); also **blues, country**, **R&B** and **rock** ('50s style). Published *Trouble* (album), recorded by Dido Bonneville (rockabilly); *Rockabilly Comp* (album), recorded by various artists; and *Nervous Singles Collection* (album), recorded by various artists, all on Nervous Records.

Tips "Submit *no* rap, soul, funk—we want *rockabilly*."

☑ A NEW RAP JAM PUBLISHING (BMI)

P.O. Box 683, Lima OH 45802. E-mail: just_chilling_2002@yahoo.com. Professional Managers: William Roach (rap, clean); James Milligan (country, 70s music, pop). **Contact:** A&R Dept. Music publisher and record company (New Experience/Faze 4 Records, Pump It Up Records, and Rough Edge Records). Estab. 1989. Publishes 40 songs/year; publishes 2-3 new songwriters/year. Hires staff songwriters. Staff size: 6. Pays standard royalty.

Affiliate(s) Party House Publishing (BMI), Creative Star Management, and Rough Edge Records. Distribution through NER/SONY/BMG/SMD.

How to Contact *Write first to arrange personal interview or submit demo CD by mail.* Unsolicited submissions are OK. Prefers CD with 3-5 songs and lyric or lead sheet. Include SASE. Responds in 6-8 weeks weeks. "Visit www.NewExperienceRecords.com for more information."

Music Mostly **R&B**, **pop**, **blues** and **rock/rap** (clean); also **contemporary**, **gospel**, **country** and **soul**. Published "Lets Go Dancing" (single by Dion Mikel), recorded and released 2006 on Faze 4 Records/New Experience Records; "The Broken Hearted" (single) from *The Final Chapter* (album), recorded by T.M.C. the milligan conection (R&B/gospel), released 2003/2007 on New Experience/Pump It Up Records. Other artists include singer-songwriter James, Jr. on Faze 4 Records/Rough Edge Records/Sonic Wave/SONY/BMG.

Tips "We are seeking hit artists 70s, 80s, and 90s who would like to be signed, as well as new talent and female solo artists. Send any available information supporting the group or act. We are a label that does not promote violence, drugs or anything that we feel is a bad example for our youth. Establish music industry contacts, write and keep writing and most of all believe in yourself. Use a good recording studio but be very professional. Just take your time and produce the best music possible. Sometimes you only get one chance. Make sure you place your best song on your demo first. This will increase your chances greatly. If you're the owner of your own small label and have a finished product, please send it. And if there is interest we will contact you. Also be on the lookout for new artists on Rough Edge Records, now reviewing material. Please be aware of the new sampling laws and laws for digital downloading. It is against the law. People are being jailed and fined for this act. Do your homework. Read the new digital downloading contracts carefully or seek legal help if need be. Good luck and thanks for considering our company for your musical needs."

☑ NEWBRAUGH BROTHERS MUSIC (ASCAP, BMI)

228 Morgan Lane, Berkeley Springs WV 25411-3475. (304)261-0228. E-mail: Nbtoys@veriz on.net. **Contact:** John S. Newbraugh, owner. Music publisher, record company (NBT Re-

cords, BMI/ASCAP). Estab. 1967. Publishes 124 songs/year. Publishes 14 new songwriters/year. Staff size: 1. Pays standard royalty.

Affiliate(s) NBT Music (ASCAP) and Newbraugh Brothers Music (BMI).

How to Contact Submit demo by mail. Unsolicited submissions are OK. Prefers cassette or CD with any amount of songs, a lyric sheet and a cover letter. Include SASE. Responds in 6 weeks. 'Please don't call for permission to submit. Your materials are welcomed.''

Music Mostly **rockabilly, hillbilly, folk** and **bluegrass**; also **rock, country,** and **gospel**. ''We will accept all genres of music except songs with vulgar language.'' Published *''Ride the Train Series Vol. 24; Layin' It On the Line* by Night Drive (2008); *Country Like It Ought to Be* by Bobby ''Swampgrass'' Anderson (2008); and *The Gospel Songbird* Vol. 2 by Wanda Sue Watkins (2008).

Tips ''Find out if a publisher/record company has any special interest. NBT, for instance, is always hunting 'original' train songs. Our 'registered' trademark is a train and from time to time we release a compilation album of all train songs. We welcome all genres of music for this project.''

N ☐ NEWCREATURE MUSIC (BMI)

P.O. Box 1444, Hendersonville TN 37077-1444. (615)452-3234. E-mail: lmarkcom@bellsouth.net. Web site: www.landmarkcommunicationsgroup.com. **Contact:** Bill Anderson, Jr., president. Professional Manager: G.L. Score. Music publisher, record company, record producer (Landmark Communications Group) and radio and TV syndicator. Publishes 25 songs/year; publishes 2 new songwriters/year. Pays standard royalty.

Affiliate(s) Mary Megan Music (ASCAP).

How to Contact *Contact first and obtain permission to submit.* Prefers CD or videocassette with 4-10 songs and lyric sheet. Include SASE. Responds in 6 weeks.

Music Mostly **country, gospel, jazz, R&B, rock** and **top 40/pop**. Published *Let This Be the Day* by C.J. Hall; *When a Good Love Comes Along* by Gail Score; *The Wonder of Christmas* by Jack Mosley.

N ▦ ⊘ OLD SLOWPOKE MUSIC (BMI)

P.O. Box 52626, Tulsa OK 74152-0626. (918)742-8087. E-mail: ryoung@cherrystreetrecords.com. Web site: www.cherrystreetrecords.com. **Contact:** Steve Hickerson, professional manager. President: Rodney Young. Music publisher and record producer. Estab. 1977. Publishes 10- 20 songs/year; publishes 2 new songwriters/year. Staff size: 2. Pays standard royalty.

How to Contact CDs only, no cassettes.

Film & TV Places 1 song in film/year. Recently published ''Samantha,'' written and recorded by George W. Carroll in Samantha. Placed two songs for Tim Drummond in movies ''Hound Dog Man'' in *Loving Lu Lu* and ''Fur Slippers'' in a CBS movie *Shake, Rattle & Roll.*

Music Mostly **rock, country** and **R&B**; also **jazz**. Published *Promise Land* (album), written and recorded by Richard Neville on Cherry Street Records (rock).

Tips ''Write great songs. We sign only artists who play an instrument, sing and write songs.''

Ⓝ Ⓦ Ⓜ PEGASUS MUSIC

1 Derwent Street, Oamaru 9400, Otago, New Zealand. E-mail: peg.music@xtra.co.nz. Web site: www.pegasusmusic.biz. Professional Managers: Errol Peters (country, rock); Ginny Peters (gospel, pop). Music publisher and record company. Estab. 1981. Publishes 20-30 songs/year; publishes 5 new songwriters/year. Pays standard royalty.

How to Contact Submit demo package by mail. Unsolicited submissions are OK. Prefers CD with 3-5 songs and lyric sheet. SAE and IRC. Responds in 1 month.

Music Mostly **country**; also **bluegrass**, **easy listening** and **top 40/pop**. Published "I Can Climb Walls," written Ginny Peters, recorded Rhonda Lee, Australia; "Party All Night Long," written by Errol & Wendy Nicholson, recorded by Rhonda Lee, Australia; "If I Climbed Upon The Cross," written by Blake Hill & Carl Towns, recorded by Ginny Peters, NCM Records, England.

Tips "Get to the meat of the subject without too many words. Less is better."

Ⓜ PERLA MUSIC (ASCAP)

122 Oldwick Rd., Whitehouse Station NJ 08889-5014. (908)439-2336. Fax: (908)439-9119. E-mail: PM@PMRecords.Org. Web site: www.PMRecords.org. **Contact:** Gene Perla (jazz). Music publisher, record company (PMRecords.org), record producer (Perla.org), studio production (TheSystemMSP.com) and Internet Design (CCINYC.com). Estab. 1971. Publishes 5 songs/year. Staff size: 5. Pays 75%/25% royalty.

How to Contact *E-mail first and obtain permission to submit.*

Music Mostly **jazz** and **rock**.

Ⓜ JUSTIN PETERS MUSIC (BMI)

P.O. Box 40251, Nashville TN 37204. (615)269-8682. Fax: (615)269-8929. Web site: www.s ongsfortheplanet.com. **Contact:** Justin Peters, president. Music publisher. Estab. 1981.

Affiliate(s) Platinum Planet Music(BMI), Tourmaline (BMI) and LITA Music (ASCAP).

How to Contact Submit demo package by mail. Unsolicited submissions are OK. Prefers CD with 5 songs and lyric sheet. Does not return material. "Place code '2009' on each envelope submission."

Music Mostly **pop**, **reggae**, **country** and **comedy**. Published "Saved By Love" (single), recorded by Amy Grant on A&M Records; "Nothing Can Separate Us," recorded by Al Denson; "A Gift That She Don't Want" (single), recorded by Bill Engvall on Warner Brother Records; and "I Wanna Be That Man" (single), recorded by McKameys on Pamplin Records, all written by Justin Peters; "Heaven's Got to Help Me Shake These Blues" (single), written by Vizla Sharb and Justin Peters, recorded by B.J. Thomas; "It's Christmas Time Again" (single by Constance Peters/Justin Peters), recorded by Jimmy Fortune.

Ⓜ PIANO PRESS (ASCAP)

P.O. Box 85, Del Mar CA 92014-0085. (619)884-1401. Fax: (858)755-1104. E-mail: pianopres s@pianopress.com. Web site: www.pianopress.com. **Contact:** Elizabeth C. Axford, M.A., owner. Music publisher and distributor. Publishes songbooks & CD's for music students and teachers. Estab. 1998. Licenses 32-100 songs/year; publishes 1-24 new songwriters/

year. Staff size: 5. Pays standard print music and/or mechanical royalty; songwriter retains rights to songs.

How to Contact *E-mail first to obtain permission to submit.* Prefers CD with 1-3 songs, lyric and lead sheet, cover letter and sheet music/piano arrangements. "Looking for children's songs for young piano students and arrangements of public domain folk songs of any nationality." Currently accepting submissions for various projects. Include SASE. Responds in 2-3 months.

Music Mostly **children's songs**, **folk songs** and **holiday songs**; also **teaching pieces**, **piano arrangements**, **lead sheets with melody, chords and lyrics** and **songbooks**. Does not want commercial pop, R&B, etc. Published My Halloween Fun Songbook and CD and My Christmas Fun Songbook series. "I Can" (single by Tom Gardner) from *Kidtunes* (album), recorded by The Uncle Brothers (children's), released 2002 by Piano Press; "Rock & Roll Teachers" (single by Bob King) from *Kidtunes* (album), recorded by Bob King & Friends (children's), released 2002 by Piano Press; and "It Really Isn't Garbage" (single by Danny Einbender) from *Kidtunes* (album), recorded by Danny Eibende/Pete Seeger/et al. (children's), released 2002 by Piano Press.

Tips "Songs should be simple, melodic and memorable. Lyrics should be for a juvenile audience and well-crafted."

☑ POLLYBYRD PUBLICATIONS LIMITED (ASCAP, BMI, SESAC)

P.O. Box 261488, Encino CA 91426. (818)506-8533. Fax: (818)506-8534. E-mail: pplzmi@aol.com. Web site: www.pplzmi.com. Branch office: 468 N. Camden Drive Suite 200, Beverly Hills CA 90210. **Contact:** Dakota Hawk, vice president. Professional Managers: Cisco Blue (country, pop, rock); Tedford Steele (hip-hop, R&B). Music publisher, record company (PPL Entertainment) and Management firm (Sa'mall Management). Estab. 1979. Publishes 100 songs/year; publishes 25-40 new songwriters/year. Hires staff writers. Pays standard royalty.

Affiliate(s) Kellijai Music (ASCAP), Pollyann Music (ASCAP), Ja'Nikki Songs (BMI), Velma Songs International (BMI), Lonnvanness Songs (SESAC), PPL Music (ASCAP), Zettitalia Music, Butternut Music (BMI), Zett Two Music (ASCAP), Plus Publishing and Zett One Songs (BMI).

How to Contact *Write first and obtain permission to submit.* No phone calls. Prefers CD, cassette, or videocassette with 4 songs and lyric and lead sheet. Include SASE. Responds in 2 months.

Music Published "Return of the Players" (album) by Juz-Cuz 2004 on PPL; "Believe" (single by J. Jarrett/S. Cuseo) from *Time* (album), recorded by Lejenz (pop), released 2001 on PRL/Credence; *Rainbow Gypsy Child* (album), written and recorded by Riki Hendrix (rock), released 2001 on PRL/Sony; and "What's Up With That" (single by Brandon James/ Patrick Bouvier) from *Outcast* (album), recorded by Condottieré; (hip-hop), released 2001 on Bouvier.

Tips "Make those decisions—are you really a songwriter? Are you prepared to starve for your craft? Do you believe in delayed gratification? Are you commercial or do you write only for yourself? Can you take rejection? Do you want to be the best? If so, contact us— if not, keep your day job."

◨ ◻ QUARK, INC.

P.O. Box 452, Newtown, CT 06470. (917)687-9988. E-mail: quarkent@aol.com. **Contact:** Curtis Urbina, manager. Music publisher, record company (Quark Records) and record producer (Curtis Urbina). Estab. 1984. Publishes 12 songs/year; 2 new songwriters/year. Staff size: 4. Pays standard royalty.

Affiliate(s) Quarkette Music (BMI), Freedurb Music (ASCAP), and Quark Records.

How to Contact Prefers CD only with 2 songs. No cassettes. Include SASE. Responds in 2 months.

Film & TV Places 10 songs in film/year. Music Supervisor: Curtis Urbina.

Music Pop. Does not want anything short of a hit. Published [new credits in mid-July]

◨ ⊘ RAINBOW MUSIC CORP. (ASCAP)

45 E. 66 St., New York NY 10021. (212)988-4619. Fax: (212)861-9079. E-mail: fscam45@aol.com. **Contact:** Fred Stuart, vice president. Music publisher. Estab. 1990. Publishes 25 songs/year. Staff size: 2. Pays standard royalty.

Affiliate(s) Tri-Circle (ASCAP).

How to Contact *Only accepts material referred by a reputable industry source.* Prefers CD with 2 songs and lyric sheet. Include SASE. Responds in 1 week.

Film & TV Published "You Wouldn't Lie To An Angel, Would Ya?" (single by Diane Lampert/Paul Overstreet) from Lady of the Evening (album), recorded by Ben te Boe (country), released 2003 on Mega International Records; "Gonna Give Lovin' A Try" (single by Cannonball Adderley/Diane Lampert/Nat Adderley) from The Axelrod Chronicles (album), recorded by Randy Crawford (jazz), released 2003 on Fantasy Records; "Breaking Bread" (single by Diane Lampert/Paul Overstreet) from Unearthed (album), recorded by Johnny Cash (country), released 2003 on Lost Highway Records; "Gonna Give Lovin' a Try" (single by Cannonball Adderley/Diane Lampert/Nat Adderley) from *Day Dreamin'* (album), recorded by Laverne Butler (jazz), released 2002 on Chesky Records; "Nothin' Shakin' (But the Leaves on the Trees)" (single by Diane Lampert/John Gluck, Jr./Eddie Fontaine/Cirino Colcrai) recorded by the Beatles, from *Live at the BBC* (album).

Music Mostly **pop**, **R&B** and **country**; also **jazz**. Published "Break It to Me Gently" (single by Diane Lampert/Joe Seneca) from *TIME/LIFE* compilations *Queens of Country* (2004), *Classic Country* (2003), and *Glory Days of Rock 'N Roll* (2002), recorded by Brenda Lee.

◻ RED SUNDOWN MUSIC (BMI)

P.O. Box 609, Pleasant View TN 37146. (615)746-0844. E-mail: rsdr@bellsouth.net. Web site: www.redsundown.com. **Contact:** Ruby Perry.

How to Contact *Does not accept unsolicited submissions.* Submit CD and cover letter. Does not return submissions.

Music Country, **rock**, and **pop**. Does not want rap or hip-hop. Published "Take A Heart" (single by Kyle Pierce) from *Take Me With You* (album), recorded by Tammy Lee (country) released in 1998 on Red Sundown Records.

⚑ ⊘ REN ZONE MUSIC (ASCAP)

P.O. Box 3153, Huntington Beach CA 92605. (714)596-6582. Fax: (714)596-6577. E-mail: renzone@socal.rr.com. **Contact:** Renah Wolzinger, president. Music publisher. Estab. 1998. Publishes 14 songs/year; publishes 2 new songwriters/year. Staff size: 2. Pays standard royalty.

• This company won a Parents Choice 1998 Silver Honor Shield.

How to Contact *Does not accept unsolicited submissions.*

Music Mostly **world music** and **children's**. Published *Tumble-n-Tunes*, *Elementary My Friend*, *Songs from the Sea to the Shore*, *Pourings from the Heart*, *Classic American Klezmer*, *Klezmer Coast to Coast*, and *Yiddish America* (albums)

Tips "Submit well-written lyrics that convey important concepts to kids on good quality demos with easy to understand vocals."

ROCK SOLID ENTERTAINMENT (ASCAP)

P.O. Box 5537, Moss Point MS 39563. E-mail: jmitch7@student.mgccc.edu. Web site: www. solidasarock.net. **Contact:** Justin Mitchell, owner. Music Publisher, Record Company, Rock Solid: Engineers, Radio, Magazine & Solidasarock.net.

Affiliate(s) Force Tha Fitt Musik (ASCAP).

How to Contact We are looking for instrumentals. No request needed. Send instrumentals to address above.

Music Looking for instrumentals, which can be **Rap, R&B, Experimental, Techno, Bass, Jungle,** and **IDM**. Any questions please e-mail us.

Tips "Your sound quality has to be just as good as what you hear on the radio. Check for more tips on our site www.solidasarock.net. Maybe some people can do everything themselves. Stop at engineering. Please find a good engineer to shape, chisel, and smooth out your sound. Also, for those who have keyboards or any instrument, it is a must to have knowledge of tracking your instrument. Songs are done track for track, by midi or just by soloing your instrument. This contributes to 60% of the quality of your music."

◖ RUSTIC RECORDS, INC. PUBLISHING (ASCAP, BMI, SESAC)

6337 Murray Lane, Brentwood TN 37027. (615)371-0646. Fax: (615)370-0353. E-mail: info @countryalbums.com. Web site: www.countryalbums.com. **Contact:** Jack Schneider, president. Vice President: Claude Southall. Office Manager: Nell Tolson. Music publisher, record company (Rustic Records Inc.) and record producer. Estab. 1984. Publishes 20 songs/year. Pays standard royalty.

Affiliate(s) Covered Bridge Music (BMI), Town Square Music (SESAC), Iron Skillet Music (ASCAP).

How to Contact Submit demo by mail. Unsolicited submissions are OK. Prefers CD with 3-4 songs and lyric sheet. Include SASE. Responds in 3 months.

Music Mostly **country**. Published "In Their Eyes" (single by Jamie Champa); "Take Me As I Am" (single by Bambi Barrett/Paul Huffman); and "Yesterday's Memories" (single by Jack Schneider), recorded by Colte Bradley (country), released 2003.

Tips "Send three or four traditional country songs, novelty songs 'foot-tapping, hand-clapping' gospel songs with strong hook for male or female artist of duet. Enclose SASE (manilla envelope)."

⊠ ⃝ SABTECA MUSIC CO. (ASCAP)

P.O. Box 10286, Oakland CA 94610. (510)465-2805. Fax: (510)832-0464. Professional Managers: Sean Herring (pop, R&B, jazz); Lois Shayne (pop, R&B, soul, country). **Contact:** Duane Herring, president. Music publisher and record company (Sabteca Record Co., Andre Romare). Estab. 1980. Publishes 8-10 songs/year; 1-2 new songwriters/year. Pays standard royalty.

Affiliate(s) Toyiabe Publishing (BMI).

How to Contact *Write first and obtain permission to submit.* Prefers cassette with 2 songs and lyric sheet. Include SASE. Responds in 1 month.

Music Mostly **R&B**, **pop** and **country**. Published "Walking My Baby Home" (single by Reggie Walker) from *Reggie Walker* (album), recorded by Reggie Walker (pop), 2002 on Andre Romare Records/Sabteca; "Treat Me Like a Dog" (single by Duane Herring/Thomas Roller), recorded by John Butterworth (pop), released 2004 Sabteca Music Co.

Tips "Listen to music daily, if possible. Keep improving writing skills."

⃝ SANDALPHON MUSIC PUBLISHING (BMI)

P.O. Box 29110, Portland OR 97296. (503)957-3929. E-mail: jackrabbit01@sprintpcs.com. **Contact:** Ruth Otey, president. Music publisher, record company (Sandalphon Records), and management agency (Sandalphon Management). Estab. 2005. Staff size: 2. Pays standard royalty of 50%.

How to Contact Submit demo by mail. Unsolicited submissions are OK. Prefers cassette or CD with 1-5 songs, lyric sheet, and cover letter. Include SASE or SAE and IRC for outside United States. Responds in 1 month.

Music Mostly **rock**, **country**, and **alternative**; also **pop**, **blues**, and **gospel**.

⊘ SDB MUSIC GROUP

• *SDB Music Group only accepts music through reputable industry sources.*

Music Mostly **country**. SDB has had cuts with artists including John Michael Montgomery, Leann Rimes, Don Williams, Steve Holy, and Trace Adkins.

⊘ SHAWNEE PRESS, INC.

1107 17th Avenue S., Nashville TN 37212. (615)320-5300. Fax: (615)320-7306. E-mail: shawnee-info@shawneepress.com. Web site: www.ShawneePress.com. **Contact:** Director of Church Music Publications (sacred choral music): Joseph M. Martin. Director of School Music Publications (secular choral music): Greg Gilpin. Music publisher. Estab. 1939. Publishes 150 songs/year. Staff size: 12. Pays negotiable royalty.

Affiliate(s) GlorySound, Harold Flammer Music, Mark Foster Music, Wide World Music, Concert Works.

How to Contact Submit manuscript. Unsolicited submissions are OK. See Web site for guidelines. Prefers manuscript; recording required for instrumental submissions. Include SASE. Responds in 4 months. "No unsolicited musicals or cantatas."

Music Mostly **church/liturgical**, **educational choral** and **instrumental**.

Tips "Submission guidelines appear on our Web site."

SILVER BLUE MUSIC/OCEANS BLUE MUSIC (ASCAP, BMI)

3940 Laurel Canyon Blvd., Suite 441, Studio City CA 91604. (818)980-9588. E-mail: jdiamon d20@aol.com. **Contact:** Joel Diamond, president. Music publisher and record producer (Joel Diamond Entertainment). Estab. 1971. Publishes 50 songs/year. Pays standard royalty.

How to Contact *Does not accept unsolicited material.* "No tapes returned."

Film & TV Places 4 songs in film and 6 songs in TV/year.

Music Mostly **pop** and **R&B**; also **rap** and **classical**. Does not want country or jazz. Published "After the Lovin'" (by Bernstein/Adams), recorded by Engelbert Humperdinck; "This Moment in Time" (by Alan Bernstein/Ritchie Adams), recorded by Engelbert Humperdinck. Other artists include David Hasselhoff, Kaci (Curb Records), Ike Turner, Andrew Dice Clay, Gloria Gaynor, Tony Orlando, Katie Cassidy, and Vaneza.

SINUS MUSIK PRODUKTION, ULLI WEIGEL

Geitnerweg 30a, D-12209, Berlin Germany. +49-30-7159050. Fax: +49-30-71590522. E-mail: ulli.weigel@arcor.de. Web site: www.ulli-weigel.de. **Contact:** Ulli Weigel, owner. Music publisher, record producer and screenwriter. Wrote German lyrics for more than 500 records. Member: GEMA, GVL. Estab. 1976. Publishes 20 songs/year; publishes 6 new songwriters/year. Staff size: 3. Pays standard royalty.

Affiliate(s) Sinus Musikverlag H.U. Weigel GmbH.

How to Contact Submit demo package by mail. Unsolicited submissions are OK. Prefers CD or cassette with up to 10 songs and lyric sheets. Responds in 2 months by email. "If material should be returned, please send 2 International Reply Coupons (IRC) for cassettes and 3 for a CD. No stamps."

Music Mostly **rock**, **pop** and **New Age**; also **background music for movies**. Published "Simple Story" (single), recorded by MAANAM on RCA (Polish rock); *Die Musik Maschine* (album by Klaus Lage), recorded by CWN Productions on Hansa Records (pop/German), "Villa Woodstock" (film music/comedy) Gebrueder Blattschuss, Juergen Von Der Lippe, Hans Werner Olm (2005).

Tips "Take more time working on the melody than on the instrumentation. I am also looking for master-quality recordings for non-exclusive release on my label (and to use them as soundtracks for multimedia projects, TV and movie scripts I am working on)."

SME PUBLISHING GROUP (ASCAP, BMI)

P.O. Box 1150, Tuttle OK 73089. (405)381-3754. Fax: (405)381-3754. E-mail: smemusic@ju no.com. Web site: www.smepublishinggroup.com. Professional Managers: Cliff Shelder (southern gospel); Sharon Kinard (country gospel). Music publisher. Estab. 1994. Publishes 6 songs/year; publishes 2 new songwriters/year. Staff size: 2. Pays standard royalty.

Affiliates Touch of Heaven Music (ASCAP) and SME Music (BMI).

How to Contact Submit demo package by mail. Unsolicited submissions are OK. Prefers CD with 3 songs and lyric sheet. Make sure tapes and CDs are labeled and include song title, writer's name and phone number. Does not return material. Responds only if interested.

Music Mostly **Southern gospel**, **country gospel** and **Christian country**. Does not want Christian rap, rock and roll, and hard-core country. Released "Come See A Man" (single by Mike Spanhanks) from *God Writes Our Story* (album), recorded by The Jody Brown Indian Family (southern gospel) on Crossroads Records; "Look Who's in the Ship" (Single by Mike Spanhanks) from *How I Picture Me* (album), recorded by the Skyline Boys (Southern Gospel) on Journey Records; "What Kinda Car" (single by Quint Randle and Jeff Hinton) from *Heaven's Not that Far* (album) recorded by Joshua Creek (Christian country) on Covenant Records.

Tips "Always submit good quality demos. Never give up."

☑ SONY/ATV MUSIC PUBLISHING (ASCAP, BMI, SESAC)

8 Music Square W., Nashville TN 37203. (615)726-8300. Fax: (615)242-3441. E-mail: info@sonyatv.com. Web site: www.sonyatv.com. **Santa Monica**: 10635 Santa Monica Blvd., Suite 300, Los Angeles CA 90025. (310)441-1300. **New York**: 550 Madison Ave., 5th Floor, New York NY 10022. (212)833-7730.

How to Contact *Sony/ATV Music does not accept unsolicited submissions.*

☑ SOUND CELLAR MUSIC (BMI)

703 N. Brinton Ave., Dixon IL 61021. (815)288-2900. E-mail: president@cellarrecords.com. Web site: www.cellarrecords.com. **Contact:** Todd Joos (country, pop, Christian), president. Professional Managers: James Miller (folk, adult contemporary); Mike Thompson (metal, hard rock, alternative). Music publisher, record company (Sound Cellar Records), record producer and recording studio. Estab. 1987. Publishes 15-25 songs/year. Publishes 5 or 6 new songwriters/year. Staff size: 7. Pays standard royalty.

How to Contact Submit demo by mail. Unsolicited submissions are OK. Prefers CD with 3 or 4 songs and lyric sheet. Does not return material. "We contact by phone in 3-4 weeks only if we want to work with the artist."

Music Mostly **metal**, **country** and **rock**; also **pop** and **blues**. Published "Problem of Pain" (single by Shane Sowers) from *Before the Machine* (album), recorded by Junker Jorg (alternative metal/rock), released 2000; "Vaya Baby" (single by Joel Ramirez) from *It's About Time* (album), recorded by Joel Ramirez and the All-Stars (latin/R&B), released 2000; and "X" (single by Jon Pomplin) from *Project 814* (album), recorded by Project 814 (progressive rock), released 2001, all on Cellar Records. "Vist our Web site for up-to-date releases."

☑ SUPREME ENTERPRISES INT'L CORP. (ASCAP, BMI)

12304 Santa Monica Blvd., 3rd Floor, Los Angeles CA 90025. (818)707-3481. Fax: (818)707-3482. E-mail: supreme2@earthlink.net. **Contact:** Lisa Lew, general manager copyrights. Music publisher, record company and record producer. Estab. 1979. Publishes 20-30 songs/year; publishes 2-6 new songwriters/year. Pays standard royalty.

Affiliate(s) Fuerte Suerte Music (BMI), Bigh Daddy G. Music (ASCAP).
How to Contact *No phone calls.* Submit demo by mail. Unsolicited submissions are OK. Prefers CD. Does not return material and you must include an e-mail address for a response. **Mail Demos To:** P.O. Box 1373, Agoura Hills CA 91376. "Please copyright material before submitting and include e-mail." Responds in 12-16 weeks if interested.
Music Mostly **reggae**, **rap**, and **dance**. Published "Paso La Vida Pensando," recorded by Jose Feliciano on Universal Records; "Cucu Bam Bam" (single by David Choy), recorded by Kathy on Polydor Records (reggae/pop); "Volvere Alguna Vez" recorded by Matt Monro on EMI Records and "Mineaito" (single), recorded by Gaby on SEI Records.
Tips "A good melody is a hit in any language."

T.C. PRODUCTIONS/ETUDE PUBLISHING CO. (BMI)

121 Meadowbrook Dr., Hillsborough NJ 08844. (908)359-5110. Fax: (908)359-1962. E-mail: tcproductions@patmedia.net. Web site: www.tcproductions2005.com. President: Tony Camillo. Music publisher and record producer. Estab. 1992. Publishes 25-50 songs/year; publishes 3-6 new songwriters/year. Pays negotiable royalty.
Affiliate(s) We Iz It Music Publishing (ASCAP), Etude Publishing (BMI), and We B Records (BMI).
How to Contact *Write or call first and obtain permission to submit.* Prefers CD or cassette with 3-4 songs and lyric sheet. Include SASE. Responds in 1 month.
Music Mostly **R&B** and **dance**; also **country** and **outstanding pop ballads**. Published "I Just Want To Be Your Everything" (single) from *A Breath of Fresh Air* (album), recorded by Michelle Parto (spiritual), released 2006 on Chancellor Records; and New Jersey Jazz (album).
Tips "Michelle Parto will soon be appearing in the film musical Sing Out, directed by Nick Castle and written by Kent Berhard."

THISTLE HILL (BMI)

P.O. Box 707, Hermitage TN 37076. (615)320-6071. E-mail: acemusicgroup@hotmail.com. **Contact:** Arden Miller.
How to Contact Submit demo by mail. Unsolicited submissions OK. Prefers CD with 3-10 songs. *No* lyric sheets. Responds only if interested.
Music Country, **pop**, and **rock**; also **songs for film/TV**. Published "Angry Heart " (single) from *See What You Wanna See* (album), recorded by Radney Foster (Americana); and "I Wanna be Free" (single) from *I Wanna be Free* (album), recorded by Jordon MyCoskie (Americana), released 2003 on Ah! Records; "Que Vamos Hacer" (single) from *Rachel Rodriguez* (album), recorded by Rachel Rodriguez.

TOURMALINE MUSIC, INC. (BMI)

2831 Dogwood Place, Nashville TN 37204. (615)269-8682. Fax: (615)269-8929. Web site: www.songsfortheplanet.com. **Contact:** Justin Peters, president. Music publisher. Estab. 1980.
Affiliate(s) Justin Peters Music (BMI), LITA Music (ASCAP) and Platinum Planet Music (BMI).

How to Contact Submit demo package by mail. Unsolicited submissions are OK. Prefers CD with 5 songs and lyric sheet. Does not return material. "Place code '2009' on each envelope submissions."

Music Mostly **rock and roll**, **classy alternative**, **adult contemporary**, **classic rock**, **country**, **Spanish gospel**, and some **Christmas music**. Published "Santa Can You Bring My Daddy Home" (single by D. Mattarosa); "The Hurt Is Worth The Chance" (single by Justin Peters/Billy Simon), recorded by Gary Chapman on RCA/BMG Records; and "For So Long" (single by Monroe Jones/Chris McCollum), recorded by GLAD on Benson Records; "Love is Catching On" (single by Enoch Rich/Marcell Macarthy), recorded by Mighty Clouds of Joy, released on Word Entertainment.

TOWER MUSIC GROUP (ASCAP, BMI)

30 Music Square W., Suite 103, Nashville TN 37203. (615)401-7111. Fax: (615)401-7119. E-mail: castlerecords@castlerecords.com. Web site: www.castlerecords.com. **Contact:** Dave Sullivan, A&R Director. Professional Managers: Ed Russell; Eddie Bishop. Music publisher, record company (Castle Records) and record producer. Estab. 1969. Publishes 50 songs/year; publishes 10 new songwriters/year. Staff size: 15. Pays standard royalty.

Affiliate(s) Cat's Alley Music (ASCAP) and Alley Roads Music (BMI).

How to Contact See submission policy on Web site. Prefers CD with 3 songs and lyric sheet. Does not return material. "You may follow up via e-mail." Responds in 3 months only if interested.

Film & TV Places 2 songs in film and 26 songs in TV/year. Published "Run Little Girl" (by J.R. Jones/Eddie Ray), recorded by J.R. Jones in Roadside Prey.

Music Mostly **country** and **R&B**; also **blues**, **pop** and **gospel**. Published "If You Broke My Heart" (single by Condrone) from *If You Broke My Heart* (album), recorded by Kimberly Simon (country); "I Wonder Who's Holding My Angel Tonight" (single) from Up Above (album), recorded by Carl Butler (country); and "Psychedelic Fantasy" (single by Paul Sullivan/Priege) from *The Hip Hoods* (album), recorded by The Hip Hoods (power/metal/y2k), all released 2001 on Castle Records. "Visit our Web site for an up-to-date listing of published songs."

Tips "Please contact us via e-mail with any other demo submission questions."

TRANSAMERIKA MUSIKVERLAG KG

Wilhelmstrasse 10, Bad Schwartau 23611 Germany. (00) (49) 4512 1530. E-mail: transamerika@online.de. Web site: www.TRANSAMERIKAmusik.de. General Manager: Pia Kaminsky. **Hamburg:** Knauerstr 1, 20249 Hamburg, Germany. Phone: 0049-40-46 06 3394. E-mail: transamerika@t-online.de. License Manager: Kirsten Jung. Member: GEMA, KODA, NCB. Music publisher and administrator. Estab. 1978. Staff size: 3. Pays 50% royalty if releasing a record; 85% if only administrating.

Affiliate(s) Administrative agreements with: German Fried Music, MCI Ltd. (London), Origin Network PLC Australia Pty. Ltd. (Sydney), MCS Music America, Inc. (USA), Native Tongue Music Pty. (New Zealand), Pacific Electric Music Publishing (USA), Evolution Music Partners (USA).

How to Contact "We accept only released materials—no demos!" Submit CD or MP3. Does not return material. Responds only if interested.

Film & TV administration.

Music Mostly **pop**; also **rock**, **country**, **reggae,** and especially **film music**.

Tips "We are specializing in administering (filing, registering, licensing and finding un-claimed royalties, and dealing with counter-claims) publishers worldwide."

☐ TRANSITION MUSIC CORPORATION (ASCAP, BMI, SESAC)

P.O. Box 2586, Toluca Lake CA 91610. (323)860-7074. Fax: (323)860-7986. E-mail: onestop mus@aol.com. Web site: www.transitionmusic.com. Creative Director: Todd Johnson. Chief Administrator: Mike Dobson. Music publisher. Estab. 1988. Publishes 250 songs/year; publishes 20 new songwriters/year. Variable royalty based on song placement and writer.

Affiliate(s) Pushy Publishing (ASCAP), Creative Entertainment Music (BMI) and One Stop Shop Music (SESAC).

How to Contact Address submissions to: New Submissions Dept. Unsolicited submissions are accepted. Prefers CD with no more than 3 songs per. **Responses will not be given due to the high volume of submissions daily. Please do not call/e-mail to inquire about us receiving your submission. TMC will only contact who they intend on signing**. Include SASE. Responds in 5 weeks.

Film & TV "TMC provides music for all forms of visual media. Mainly Television."

Music All styles.

Tips "Supply master quality material with great songs."

☑ UNIVERSAL MUSIC PUBLISHING (ASCAP, BMI, SESAC)

2440 Sepulveda Blvd., Suite 100, Los Angeles CA 90064. (310)235-4700. New York: 1755 Broadway, 3rd Floor, New York NY 10019. (212)841-8000. **Tennessee:** 1904 Adelicia St., Nashville TN 37212. (615)340-5400. Web site: www.umusicpub.com or www.synchexpres s.com.

• In 1999, MCA Music Publishing and PolyGram Music Publishing merged into Universal Music Publishing.

How to Contact *Does not accept unsolicited submissions.*

ℕ ☑ UNKNOWN SOURCE MUSIC (ASCAP)

120-4d Carver Loop, Bronx NY 10475. E-mail: unknownsourcemusic@hotmail.com. **Contact:** James Johnson, A&R. Music publisher, record company (Smokin Ya Productions) and record producer. Estab. 1993. Publishes 5-10 songs/year; publishes 5-10 new songwriters/year. Hires staff songwriters. Staff size: 10. Pays standard royalty.

Affiliate(s) Sundance Records (ASCAP), Critique Records, WMI Records, and Cornell Entertainment.

How to Contact *Send e-mail first then mail.* Unsolicited submissions are OK. Prefers MP3s. Responds within 6 weeks.

Music Mostly **rap/hip-hop**, **R&B**, and **alternative**. Published "LAH" recorded by Force Dog; "Changed My World" recorded by Crysto.

Tips "Keep working with us, be patient, be willing to work hard. Send your very best work."

⦿ VAAM MUSIC GROUP (BMI)

P.O. Box 29550, Hollywood CA 90029-0550. E-mail: pmarti3636@aol.com. Web site: www. VaamMusic.com. **Contact:** Pete Martin, president. Music publisher and record producer (Pete Martin/Vaam Productions). Estab. 1967. Publishes 9-24 new songs/year. Pays standard royalty.

Affiliate(s) Pete Martin Music (ASCAP).

- Also see the listings for Blue Gem Records in the Record Companies section of this book and Pete Martin/Vaam Music Productions in the record Producers section of this book.

How to Contact Send CD or cassette with 2 songs and lyric sheet. Include SASE. Responds in 1 month. "Small packages only."

Music Mostly **top 40/pop**, **country**, and **R&B**. "Submitted material must have potential of reaching top 5 on charts."

Tips "Study the top 10 charts in the style you write. Stay current and up-to-date with today's market."

▢ WALKERBOUT MUSIC GROUP (ASCAP, BMI, SESAC)

(formerly The Goodland Music Group, Inc.), P.O. Box 24454, Nashville TN 37202. (615)269-7071. Fax: (615)269-0131. E-mail: info@walkerboutmusic.com. Web site: www.walkerbou tmusic.com. **Contact:** Matt Watkins, publishing coordinator. Estab. 1988. Publishes 50 songs/year; 5-10 new songwriters/year. Pays standard royalty.

Affiliate(s) Goodland Publishing Company (ASCAP), Marc Isle Music (BMI), Gulf Bay Publishing (SESAC), Con Brio Music (BMI), Wiljex Publishing (ASCAP), Concorde Publishing (SESAC).

How to Contact "Please see Web site for submission information."

Music Mostly **country/Christian** and **adult contemporary**.

🎵 ⦿ WARNER/CHAPPELL MUSIC, INC.

10585 Santa Monica Blvd., Third Floor, Los Angeles CA 90025. (310)441-8600. Fax: (310)470-3232. **New York**: 1290 Avenue of the Americas, 23rd floor, New York NY 10104. (212)707-2600. Fax: (212)405-5428. **Nashville**: 20 Music Square E., Nashville TN 37203. (615)733-1880. Fax: (615)733-1885. Web site: www.warnerchappell.com. Music publisher.

How to Contact *Warner/Chappell does not accept unsolicited material.*

ADDITIONAL MUSIC PUBLISHERS

The following companies are also music publishers, but their listings are found in other sections of the book. Read the listings for submission information.

Record Companies

R ecord companies release and distribute records, cassettes and CDs—the tangible products of the music industry. They sign artists to recording contracts, decide what songs those artists will record, and determine which songs to release. They are also responsible for providing recording facilities, securing producers and musicians, and overseeing the manufacture, distribution and promotion of new releases.

MAJOR LABELS & INDEPENDENT LABELS
Major labels and independent labels—what's the difference between the two?

The majors
As of this writing, there are four major record labels, commonly referred to as the "Big 4":

- **The EMI Group** (Capitol Music Group, Angel Music Group, Astralwerks, Chrysalis Records, etc.)
- **Sony BMG** (Columbia Records, Epic Records, RCA Records, Arista Records, J Records, Provident Label Group, etc.)
- **Universal Music Group** (Universal Records, Interscope/Geffen/A&M, Island/Def Jam, Dreamworks Records, MCA Nashville Records, Verve Music Group, etc.)
- **Warner Music Group** (Atlantic Records, Bad Boy, Asylum Records, Warner Bros. Records, Maverick Records, Sub Pop, etc.)

Each of the "Big 4" is a large publicly-traded corporation beholden to shareholders and quarterly profit expectations. This means the major labels have greater financial resources and promotional muscle than a smaller "indie" label, but it's also harder to get signed to a major. A big major label may also expect more contractual control over an artist or band's sound and image.

As shown in the above list, they also each act as umbrella organizations for numerous other well-known labels—former major labels in their own right, well-respected former independent/boutique labels, as well as subsidiary "vanity" labels fronted by successful major label recording artists. Each major label also has its own related worldwide product distribution system, and many independent labels will contract with the majors for distribution into stores.

If a label is distributed by one of these major companies, you can be assured any release coming out on that label has a large distribution network behind it. It will most likely be sent to most major retail stores in the United States.

The independents

Independent labels go through smaller distribution companies to distribute their product. They usually don't have the ability to deliver records in massive quantities as the major distributors do. However, that doesn't mean independent labels aren't able to have hit records just like their major counterparts. A record label's distributors are found in the listings after the **Distributed by** heading.

Which do I submit to?

Many of the companies listed in this section are independent labels. They are usually the most receptive to receiving material from new artists. Major labels spend more money than most other segments of the music industry; the music publisher, for instance, pays only for items such as salaries and the costs of making demos. Record companies, at great financial risk, pay for many more services, including production, manufacturing and promotion. Therefore, they must be very selective when signing new talent. Also, the continuing fear of copyright infringement suits has closed avenues to getting new material heard by the majors. Most don't listen to unsolicited submissions, period. Only songs recommended by attorneys, managers and producers who record company employees trust and respect are being heard by A&R people at major labels (companies with a referral policy have a ⊘ preceding their listing). But that doesn't mean all major labels are closed to new artists. With a combination of a strong local following, success on an independent label (or strong sales of an independently produced and released album) and the right connections, you could conceivably get an attentive audience at a major label.

But the competition is fierce at the majors, so you shouldn't overlook independent labels. Since they're located all over the country, indie labels are easier to contact and can be important in building a local base of support for your music (consult the Geographic Index at the back of the book to find out which companies are located near you). Independent labels usually concentrate on a specific type of music, which will help you target those companies your submissions should be sent to. And since the staff at an indie label is smaller, there are fewer channels to go through to get your music heard by the decision makers in the company.

HOW RECORD COMPANIES WORK

Independent record labels can run on a small staff, with only a handful of people running the day-to-day business. Major record labels are more likely to be divided into the following departments: A&R, sales, marketing, promotion, product management, artist development, production, finance, business/legal and international.

- The *A&R department* is staffed with A&R representatives who search out new talent. They go out and see new bands, listen to demo tapes, and decide which artists to sign. They also look for new material for already signed acts, match producers with artists and oversee recording projects. Once an artist is signed by an A&R rep and a record is recorded, the rest of the departments at the company come into play.
- The *sales department* is responsible for getting a record into stores. They make sure record stores and other outlets receive enough copies of a record to meet consumer demand.
- The *marketing department* is in charge of publicity, advertising in magazines and other media, promotional videos, album cover artwork, in-store displays, and any other means of getting the name and image of an artist to the public.
- The *promotion department*'s main objective is to get songs from a new album played on the radio. They work with radio programmers to make sure a product gets airplay.
- The *product management department* is the ringmaster of the sales, marketing and

The Case for Independents

Tip

If you're interested in getting a major label deal, it makes sense to look to independent record labels to get your start. Independent labels are seen by many as a stepping stone to a major recording contract. Very few artists are signed to a major label at the start of their careers; usually, they've had a few independent releases that helped build their reputation in the industry. Major labels watch independent labels closely to locate up-and-coming bands and new trends. In the current economic atmosphere at major labels—with extremely high overhead costs for developing new bands and the fact that only 10% of acts on major labels actually make any profit—they're not willing to risk everything on an unknown act. Most major labels won't even consider signing a new act that hasn't had some indie success.

But independents aren't just farming grounds for future major label acts; many bands have long term relationships with indies, and prefer it that way. While they may not be able to provide the extensive distribution and promotion that a major label can (though there are exceptions), indie labels can help an artist become a regional success, and may even help the performer to see a profit as well. With the lower overhead and smaller production costs an independent label operates on, it's much easier to "succeed" on an indie label than on a major.

promotion departments, assuring that they're all going in the same direction when promoting a new release.

- The *artist development department* is responsible for taking care of things while an artist is on tour, such as setting up promotional opportunities in cities where an act is performing.
- The *production department* handles the actual manufacturing and pressing of the record and makes sure it gets shipped to distributors in a timely manner.
- People in the *finance department* compute and distribute royalties, as well as keep track of expenses and income at the company.
- The *business/legal department* takes care of contracts, not only between the record company and artists but with foreign distributors, record clubs, etc.
- And finally, the *international department* is responsible for working with international companies for the release of records in other countries.

LOCATING A RECORD LABEL

With the abundance of record labels out there, how do you go about finding one that's right for the music you create? First, it helps to know exactly what kind of music a record label releases. Become familiar with the records a company has released, and see if they fit in with what you're doing. Each listing in this section details the type of music a particular record company is interested in releasing. You will want to refer to the Category Index on page 359 to help you find those companies most receptive to the type of music you write. You should only approach companies open to your level of experience (see A Sample Listing Decoded on page 8). Visiting a company's website can also provide valuable information about a company's philosophy, the artists on the label and the music they work with.

Networking

Recommendations by key music industry people are an important part of making contacts with record companies. Songwriters must remember that talent alone does not guarantee success in the music business. You must be recognized through contacts, and the only way to make contacts is through networking. Networking is the process of building an interconnecting web of acquaintances within the music business. The more industry people you meet, the larger your contact base becomes, and the better are your chances of meeting someone with the clout to get your demo into the hands of the right people. If you want to get your music heard by key A&R representatives, networking is imperative.

Networking opportunities can be found anywhere industry people gather. A good place to meet key industry people is at regional and national music conferences and workshops. There are many held all over the country for all types of music (see the Workshops and Conferences section for more information). You should try to attend at least one or two of these events each year; it's a great way to increase the number and quality of your music industry contacts.

Creating a buzz

Another good way to attract A&R people is to make a name for yourself as an artist. By starting your career on a local level and building it from there, you can start to cultivate a following and prove to labels that you can be a success. A&R people figure if an act can be successful locally, there's a good chance they could be successful nationally. Start getting booked at local clubs, and start a mailing list of fans and local media. Once you gain some success on a local level, branch out. All this attention you're slowly gathering, this "buzz" you're generating, will not only get to your fans but to influential people in the music industry as well.

SUBMITTING TO RECORD COMPANIES

When submitting to a record company, major or independent, a professional attitude is imperative. Be specific about what you are submitting and what your goals are. If you are strictly a songwriter and the label carries a band you believe would properly present your song, state that in your cover letter. If you are an artist looking for a contract, showcase your strong points as a performer. Whatever your goals are, follow submission guidelines closely, be as neat as possible and include a top-notch demo. If you need more information concerning a company's requirements, write or call for more details. (For more information on submitting your material, see the article Where Should I Send My Songs? on page 6 and Demo Recordings: What Should I Know? on page 10.)

Icons

For More Info

For more instructional information on the listings in this book, including explanations of symbols (N ✔ 🗹 ⬛ 🍁 🌐 ◯ ◒ ◎ ⊘), read the article *How To Use Songwriter's Market* on page 2.

RECORD COMPANY CONTRACTS

Once you've found a record company that is interested in your work, the next step is signing a contract. Independent label contracts are usually not as long and complicated as major label ones, but they are still binding, legal contracts. Make sure the terms are in the best interest of both you and the label. Avoid anything in your contract that you feel is too restrictive. It's important to have your contract reviewed by a competent entertainment lawyer. A basic recording contract can run from 40-100 pages, and you need a lawyer to help you understand it. A lawyer will also be essential in helping you negotiate a deal that is in your best interest.

Recording contracts cover many areas, and just a few of the things you will be asked to consider will be: What royalty rate is the record label willing to pay you? What kind of advance are they offering? How many records will the company commit to? Will they offer tour support? Will they provide a budget for video? What sort of a recording budget are they offering? Are they asking you to give up any publishing rights? Are they offering you a publishing advance? These are only a few of the complex issues raised by a recording contract, so it's vital to have an entertainment lawyer at your side as you negotiate.

ADDITIONAL RECORD COMPANIES

There are **more record companies** located in other sections of the book! On page 178 use the list of Additional Record Companies to find listings within other sections who are also record companies.

⚡ ◑ ALLIGATOR RECORDS

P.O. Box 60234, Chicago IL 60660.(773)973-7736. Fax: (773)973-2088. E-mail: info@allig.c om. Web site: www.alligator.com. **Contact:** A&R. Estab. 1971. Record Company.

• With a catalog of over 200 titles, Alligator Records is the largest independent blues label in the world. Its recordings have won more awards than any other contemporary blues label, including a total of 34 Grammy nominations (two wins), 18 Indie Awards from the Association For Independent Music (AFIM) and three Grand Prix du Disque awards. Alligator and its artists have won a total of 70 W.C. Handy Blues Awards, the blues community's highest honor.

How to Contact Submit demo package by mail. *"We do not visit artist Web sites or listen to e-mail submissions. DO NOT SEND DIGITAL FILES BY E-MAIL!"* Prefers CD with no more than 4 songs. "If we like what we hear, we will ask for more." Responds in 7 months. *"Alligator will NOT accept inquiries or phone calls regarding the receipt or status of submissions.* All submissions will be responded to by mail. If no legible address is on the demo material, there will be no response."

Music Mostly **blues**; also **roots rock**. Released *Old School* (album), recorded by Koko Taylor (blues); *Moment of Truth* (album), recorded by Tinsley Ellis (blues); *Black Cat Bone* (album), recorded by Lee Rocker (rockabilly); *Have A Little Faith* (album), recorded by Mavis Staples (gospel/soul). Other artists include Shemekia Copeland, Roomful of Blues, Guitar Shorty, and W.C. Clark.

◑ ALTERNATIVE TENTACLES

Attn: New Materials, P.O. Box 419092, San Francisco CA 94141.(510)596-8981. Fax: (510)596-8982. E-mail: jello@alternativetentacles.com. Web site: www.alternativetentacle s.com. **Contact:** Jello Biafra. Estab. 1979. Staff size: 4. Releases 15-20 albums/year.

Distributed by Lumberjack/Mordam Records.

How to Contact Unsolicited submissions OK. Prefers CD or cassette. Does not return material. Responds only if interested. *" We accept demos by postal mail ONLY! We do not accept MP3s sent to us.* We will not go out and listen to your MP3s on Web sites. If you are interested in having ATR hear your music, you need to send us a CD, tape or vinyl. We cannot return your demos either, so please don't send us your originals or ask us to send them back. Sometimes Jello replies to people submitting demos; sometimes he doesn't. There is no way for us to check on your 'status', so please don't ask us."

Music Mostly **punk rock**, **spoken word**, **Brazilian hardcore**, **bent pop**, **faux-country**, and **assorted rock & roll**. Released *It's Not the Eat, It's the Humidity* (album), recorded by the Eat (punk); *Fuck World Trade* (album), recorded by Leftover Crack (punk); *Live from the Armed Madhouse* (album), recorded by Greg Palast (spoken word); *Dash Rip Rock* (album), recorded by Hee Haw Hell (southern country punk); *Homem Inimigo Do Homem* (album), recorded by Ratos De Parao (Brazilian hardcore). Other artists include Jello Biafra, The (International) Noise Conspiracy, Subhumans, Butthole Surfers, Dead Kennedys, DOA, Pansy Division, and Melvins.

AMP RECORDS & MUSIC

Box BM F.A.M.E., London WC1N 3XX United Kingdom. E-mail: markjenkins@beeb.net. Web site: www.markjenkins.net or www.myspace.com/markjenkinsmusic. **Contact:** Mark Jenkins, A&R (New Age, instrumental, ambient, progressive rock). Record company. Estab. 1985. Staff size: 10. Releases 12 CDs/year. Pays negotiable royalty to artists on contract; negotiable rate to publisher per song on record.

Distributed by Shellshock (UK), Eurock/ZNR/NSA (USA), MP (Italy) and Crystal Lake (France).

How to Contact *"Your must be in the styles released by the label! You are strongly advised to e-mail us first, without any attachments. Singer-songwriter, R&B, soul, indie guitar rock, country, all go straight in the trash unplayed!"* Does not return material. Responds in 2 months.

Music Mostly **New Age**, **instrumental** and **ambient**; also **progressive rock**, **synthesizer** and **ambient dance**. Does not want ballads, country or AOR. Released *Changing States* (album), recorded by Keith Emerson (progressive rock); *Tyranny of Beauty* (album), written and recorded by Tangerine Dream (synthesizer); and *Spirit of Christmas* (album), written and recorded by various artists (instrumental compilation), all on AMP Records.

Tips "See what we're about from our Web site before wasting your money sending irrelevant styles of music."

ANGEL RECORDS

150 Fifth Ave., 6th Floor, New York NY 10011. (212)786-8600. Web site: www.angelrecords .com. Record company. Labels include EMI Classics, Manhattan Records, and Virgin Classics.

- Angel Records is a subsidiary of the EMI Group, one of the "Big 4" major labels. EMI is a British-based company.

Distributed by EMI Music Distribution.

How to Contact Angel/EMI Records does not accept unsolicited submissions.

Music Artists include Sarah Brightman, Paul McCartney, and Bernadette Peters.

ARIANA RECORDS

1312 S. Avenida Polar, Tucson AZ 85710. E-mail: jtiom@aol.com. Web site: www.cdbaby. com/all/myko. **Contact:** James M. Gasper, president. Vice President (pop, rock): Tom Dukes. Partners: Tom Privett (funk, experimental, rock); Scott Smith (pop, rock, AOR). Labels include Egg White Records. Record company, music publisher (Myko Music/BMI) and record producer. Estab. 1980. Staff size: 4. Releases 5 CDs a year and 1 compilation/ year. Pays negotiable royalty to artists on contract; negotiable rate to publisher per song on record.

Distributed by Impact Music Distributors and Care Free Music.

How to Contact "We are only interested in finished CD projects. *No tapes. No demos.*" Unsolicited submissions are OK. Include SASE. Responds in 6 months.

Music Mostly **rock**, **funk**, **jazz**, **anything weird**, **strange**, or **lo-fi** (must be mastered to CD). Released "Bloated Floater" (single by Mr. Jimi/Trece Broline/Larry's Fault) from

Bloated Floater (album), *PsychoPop* (Acidsoxx Musicks CD compilation), *Chuck & The Chair* (film soundtrack), recorded by Bloated Floater (space funk), released 2004 on Ariana Records; "Feel My Face" (single by James Gasper) from *Soledad* (album), recorded by Scuba Tails (electro rock), released 2004 on Ariana Records; and "Smak You Up" (single by Trece Broline/Mr. Jimi/Larry's Fault) from *Headphones Plez* (album), recorded by Beatnik Grip (trash euro funk), released 2004 on Ariana Records; *Just Arrived* (album), written and recorded by Gasper & Dukes (pop/rock), re-released 2005 on Ariana Records; *Songs From The Album* (album), written and recorded by The Rakeheads, released 2006 on Ariana Records. New artist GoofyBoyFemroid is currently working on a CD for 2007. Other artists include Tom P., Big White Teeth, J. Tiom, Slim Taco Explosion, and The Miller Boys.

Tips "We're a small company, but working your material is our job. If we like it, we'll sell it! It's a tough business. Keep trying."

ARISTA RECORDS

888 7th Ave., New York NY 10019. (212)489-7400. Fax: (212)977-9843. Web site: www.arist a.com. **Beverly Hills office:** 8750 Wilshire Blvd., 3rd Floor, Beverly Hills CA 90211. (310)358-4600. **Nashville office:** 7 Music Circle North, Nashville TN 37203. (615)846-9100. Fax: (615)846-9192. Labels include Bad Boy Records, Arista Nashville and Time Bomb Recordings. Record company.

- Arista Records is a subsidiary of Sony BMG, one of the "Big 4" major labels.

Distributed by BMG.

How to Contact Does not accept unsolicited material.

Music Artists include Outkast, Dido, Pink, Usher, Avril Lavigne, Babyface, and Sarah McLachlan.

ARKADIA ENTERTAINMENT CORP.

34 E. 23rd St., New York NY 10010. (212)674-5550. Fax: (212)979-0266. E-mail: info@arkad iarecords.com. Web site: www.arkadiarecords.com. **Contact:** A&R Song Submissions. Labels include Arkadia Jazz, Arkadia Classical, Arkadia Now and Arkadia Allworld. Record company, music publisher (Arkadia Music), record producer (Arkadia Productions) and Arkadia Video. Estab. 1995.

How to Contact *Write or call first and obtain permission to submit.*

Music Mostly **jazz**, **classical**, and **pop/R&B**; also **world**.

ASTRALWERKS

ATTN: A&R Dept. 101 Avenue of the Americas, 10th Floor, New York NY 10013. E-mail: A&R@astralwerks.net. Web site: www.astralwerks.com/demo.html. **Contact:** A&R. Record company. Estab. 1979. Releases 10-12 12" singles and 100 CDs/year. Pays varying royalty to artists on contract; statutory rate to publisher per song.

- Astralwerks is a subsidiary of the EMI Group, one of the "Big 4" major labels. EMI is a British-based company.

How to Contact Send submissions to: "A&R Dept." to address above. No unsolicited phone calls please. Prefers CD. "Please include any pertinent information, including your group name, track titles, names of members, bio background, successes, and any contact info. Do not send e-mail attachments."

Music Mostly **alternative/indie/electronic**. Artists include VHS or BETA, Badly Drawn boy, The Beta Band, Chemical Brothers, Turin Breaks, and Fatboy Slim.

Tips "We are open to artists of unique quality and enjoy developing artists from the ground up. We listen to all types of 'alternative' music regardless of genre. It's about the aesthetic and artistic quality first. We send out rejection letters so do not call to find out what's happening with your demo."

◻ ATLAN-DEC/GROOVELINE RECORDS

2529 Green Forest Court, Snellville GA 30078-4183. (770)985-1686. Fax: (877)751-5169. E-mail: atlandec@prodigy.net. Web site: www.ATLAN-DEC.com. President/Senior A&R Rep: James Hatcher. A&R Rep: Wiletta J. Hatcher. Record company, music publisher and record producer. Estab. 1994. Staff size: 2. Releases 3-4 singles, 3-4 LPs and 3-4 CDs/year. Pays 10-25% royalty to artists on contract; statutory rate to publisher per song on record.

Distributed by C.E.D. Entertainment Dist.

How to Contact Submit demo package by mail. Unsolicited submissions are OK. Prefers CD with lyric sheet. Does not return material. Responds in 3 months.

Music Mostly **R&B/urban**, **hip-hop/rap**, and **contemporary jazz**; also **soft rock**, **gospel**, **dance**, and **new country**. Released "Temptation" by Shawree, released 2004 on Atlan-Dec/Grooveline Records; *Enemy of the State* (album), recorded by Lowlife (rap/hip-hop); *I'm The Definition* (album), recorded by L.S. (rap/hip-hop), released 2007; "AHHW" (single), recorded by LeTebony Simmons (R&B), released 2007. Other artists include Furious D (rap/hip-hop), Mark Cocker (new country), and Looka, "From the Top" (rap/hip-hop) recorded in 2008.

▣ ⊘ ATLANTIC RECORDS

1290 Avenue of the Americas, New York NY 10104. (212)707-2000. Fax: (212)581-6414. Web site: www.atlanticrecords.com. **New York:** 1290 Avenue of the Americas, New York NY 10104. **Los Angeles:** 3400 W. Olive Ave., 3rd Floor, Burbank CA 91505. (818)238-6800 Fax: (310)205-7411. **Nashville:** 20 Music Square East, Nashville TN 37203. (615)272-7990. Labels include Big Beat Records, LAVA, Nonesuch Records, Atlantic Classics, and Rhino Records. Record company. Pays negotiable royalty to artists on contract; negotiable rate to publisher per song on record.

- Atlantic Records is a subsidiary of Warner Music Group, one of the "Big 4" major labels.

Distributed by WEA.

How to Contact *Does not accept unsolicited material.* "No phone calls please."

Music Artists include Missy Elliott, Simple Plan, Lupe Fiasco, Phil Collins, Gnarls Barkley, and Metallica.

⊘ AVITA RECORDS

P.O. Box 764, Hendersonville TN 37077-0764. (615)824-9313. Fax: (615)824-0797. E-mail: tachoir@bellsouth.net. Web site: www.tachoir.com. **Contact:** Robert Kayre, manager. Record company, music publisher (Riohcat Music, BMI) and record producer (Jerry Tachoir). Estab. 1976. Staff size: 8. Releases 2 LPs and 2 CDs/year. Pays negotiable royalty to artists on contract; statutory rate to publisher per song on record.

- Also see the listing for Riohcat Music in the Managers & Booking Agents section of this book.

How to Contact *Contact first and obtain permission to submit.* We only accept material referred to us by a reputable industry source. Prefers CD, cassette, or DAT. Does not return materials. Responds only if interested.

Music Mostly **jazz**. Released *Improvised Thoughts* (album by Marlene Tachoir/Jerry Tachoir/Van Manakas), recorded by Jerry Tachoir and Van Manakas (jazz), released 2001 on Avita Records. Other artists include Van Manakas.

⊘ AWARE RECORDS

624 Davis St., 2nd Floor, Evanston IL 60201. (874)424-2000. E-mail: info@awaremusic.com. Web site: www.awaremusic.com. A&R: Steve Smith. President: Gregg Latterman. Record company. Estab. 1993. Staff size: 7. Releases 5 LPs, 1 EP and 3 CDs/year. Pays negotiable royalty to artists on contract; statutory rate to publisher per song on record.

Distributed by Sony/Columbia.

How to Contact *Does not accept unsolicited submissions.*

Music Mostly **rock/pop**. Artists include John Mayer, Five for Fighting, Newton Faulkner, and Angel Taylor.

ℕ ⊕ BIG BEAR RECORDS

Box 944, Birmingham B16 8UT United Kingdom. 44-121-454-7020. Fax: 44-121-454-9996. E-mail: jim@bigbearmusic.com. Web site: www.bigbearmusic.com. A&R Director: Jim Simpson. Labels include Truckers Delight and Grandstand Records. Record company, record producer and music publisher (Bearsongs). Releases 6 LPs/year. Pays 8-10% royalty to artists on contract; $8\frac{1}{4}$% to publishers for each record sold. Royalties paid directly to songwriters and artists or through US publishing or recording affiliate.

- Big Bear's publishing affiliate, Bearsongs, is listed in the Music Publishers section, and Big Bear is listed in the Record Producers section of this book.

How to Contact Submit demo by mail. Unsolicited submissions are OK. Prefers CD. Does not return material. Responds in 3 weeks.

Music Blues and **jazz**. Released *I've Finished with the Blues* and *Blues for Pleasure* (by Skirving/Nicholls), both recorded by King Pleasure and the Biscuit Boys (jazz); and *Side-Steppin'* (by Barnes), recorded by Alan Barnes/Bruce Adams Quintet (jazz), all on Big Bear Records. Other artists include Lady Sings the Blues, Drummin' Man, Kenny Baker's Dozen, Tipitina, and Dr. Teeth Big Band.

⊘ BLACKHEART RECORDS

636 Broadway, Suite 1210, New York NY 10012.(212)353-9600. Fax: (212)353-8300. E-mail: blackheart@blackheart.com. Web site: www.blackheart.com. **Contact:** Zander Wolff, a&r. Record label. Estab. 1982.

How to Contact Unsolicited submissions are OK. Prefers CD with 1-3 songs and lyric sheets. Include SASE. Responds only if interested.

Music Mostly **rock**. Artists include Joan Jett & the Blackhearts, The Dollyrots, The Vacancies, Girl In A Coma, and The Eyeliners.

☐ BLUE GEM RECORDS

P.O. Box 29550, Hollywood CA 90029. (323)664-7765. E-mail: pmarti3636@aol.com. Web site: www.bluegemrecords.com. **Contact:** Pete Martin. Record company, music publisher (Vaam Music Group) and record producer (Pete Martin/Vaam Productions). Estab. 1981. Pays 6-15% royalty to artists on contract; statutory rate to publisher per song on record.

- Also see the listings for Vaam Music Group in the Music Publishers section of this book and Pete Martin/Vaam Music Productions in the Record Producers section of this book.

How to Contact Submit demo by mail. Unsolicited submissions are OK. Prefers CD or cassette with 2 songs. Include SASE. Responds in 3 weeks.

Music Mostly **country** and **R&B**; also **pop/top 40** and **rock**.

☑ CAMBRIA RECORDS & PUBLISHING

P.O. Box 374, Lomita CA 90717. (310)831-1322. Fax: (310)833-7442. E-mail: admin@cambriamus.com. **Contact:** Lance Bowling, director of recording operations. Labels include Charade Records. Record company and music publisher. Estab. 1979. Staff size: 3. Pays 5-8% royalty to artists on contract; statutory rate to publisher for each record sold.

Distributed by Albany Distribution.

How to Contact *Write first and obtain permission to submit.* Prefers cassette. Include SASE. Responds in 1 month.

Music Mostly *classical*. Released *Songs of Elinor Remick Warren* (album) on Cambria Records. Other artists include Marie Gibson (soprano), Leonard Pennario (piano), Thomas Hampson (voice), Mischa Leftkowitz (violin), Leigh Kaplan (piano), North Wind Quintet, and Sierra Wind Quintet.

Ⓝ ☑ CANDYSPITEFUL PRODUCTIONS

4204 County Rt 4, Oswego NY 13126. E-mail: mandrakerocks@yahoo.com. Web site: www.myspace.com/candyspiteful. President: William Ferraro. Professional Managers: Maxwell Frye (jazz, rock). Record company, music publisher (Candyspiteful Productions), record producer (William Ferraro). Estab. 2000. Staff size: 2. Produces 30 demo projects, 12 albums per year. Charges producer/engineer fee's, other fees are negotiable.

- Also see the listings for Candyspiteful Productions in the Record Producers section of this book.

How to Contact Submit demo package by mail. Unsolicited submissions are OK. Prefers CD with 3 songs, lyric sheet, and cover letter. "Please include a fact sheet, bio, current play dates, etc." Does not return material. Responds only if interested. Also digital promos MP3 format.

Music Mostly **hard rock**, **radio-friendly rock** and **hip-hop**.

Tips "Work hard before entering the studio to record."

◑ CANTILENA RECORDS

1925 5th Ave., Sacramento CA 95818. (916)600-2424. E-mail: llzz@aol.com. Web site: www.cantilenarecords.com. A&R: Laurel Zucker, owner. A&R: B. Houseman. Record company. Estab. 1993. Releases 5 CDs/year. Pays Harry Fox standard royalty to artists on contract; statutory rate to publishers per song on record.

How to Contact *Write first and obtain permission to submit or to arrange personal interview.* Prefers CD. Does not return material.

Music Classical, **jazz**, **world music**. Released "Caliente!" (single by Christopher Caliendo) from *Caliente! World Music for Flute & Guitar* (album), recorded by Laurel Zucker and Christopher Caliendo! (world crossover); *Suites No. 1 & 2 For Flute & Jazz Piano Trio* (album by Claude Bolling), recorded by Laurel Zucker, Joe Gilman, David Rokeach, Jeff Neighbor (jazz); and *HOPE! Music for Flute, Soprano, Guitar* (album by Daniel Akiva, Astor Piazzolla, Haim Permont, Villa-Lobos) (classical/world), recorded by Laurel Zucker, Ronit Widmann-Levy, Daniel Akiva, all released in 2004 by Cantilena Records. Other artists include Tim Gorman, Prairie Prince, Dave Margen, Israel Philharmonic, Erkel Chamber Orchestra, Samuel Magill, Renee Siebert, Robin Sutherland, and Gerald Ranch.

◎ CAPITOL RECORDS

1750 N. Vine St., Hollywood CA 90028-5274. (323)462-6252. Fax: (323)469-4542. Web site: www.hollywoodandvine.com. **Nashville:** 3322 West End Ave., 11th Floor, Nashville TN 37203. (615)269-2000. Labels include Blue Note Records, Grand Royal Records, Pangaea Records, The Right Stuff Records and Capitol Nashville Records. Record company.

• Capitol Records is a subsidiary of the EMI Group, one of the "Big 4" major labels.

Distributed by EMD.

How to Contact *Capitol Records does not accept unsolicited submissions.*

Music Artists include Coldplay, Beastie Boys, Liz Phair, Interpol, Lily Allen, and Auf der Maur.

◪ ◎ CAPP RECORDS

P.O. Box 150871, San Rafael CA 94915-0871. Phone/fax: (415)457-8617. E-mail: manus@capprecords.com. Web site: www.capprecords.com. CEO/International Manager: Dominique Toulon (pop, dance, New Age); Creative Manager/A&R: Manus Buchart (dance, techno). President: Rudolf Stember. Vice President/Publisher: Radi Tamimi (tamimi@capprecords.com); Public Relations/A&R: Michael Oliva (oliva@capprecords.com). Music publisher (Cappster music/ASCAP and CIDC Music/BMI) and record company. Member: NARAS, NCSA, Songwriter's Guild of America. Estab. 1993. Publishes 100 songs/year; publishes 25 new songwriters/year. Staff size: 8. Pays standard royalty.

Affiliate(s) Cary August Publishing Co./CAPP Company (Germany)/Capp Company (Japan).

How to Contact Submit demo package by mail. Unsolicited submissions are OK. Prefers CD or NTSC videocassette with 3 songs and cover letter. "E-mail us in advance for submissions, if possible." Include SASE. Only responds if interested.

Film & TV Places 20 songs in film and 7 songs in TV/year. Music Supervisors: Dominique Toulon (pop, dance, New Age). "Currently doing music placement for television—*MTV, VH1, Oprah, A&E Network*, and *Discovery Channel*."

Music Mostly **pop**, **dance**, and **techno**; also **New Age**. Does not want country. Released "It's Not a Dream" (single by Cary August/Andre Pessis), recorded by Cary August on CAPP Records (dance). "Visit our Web site for new releases."

☑ CELLAR RECORDS

703 N. Brinton Ave., Dixon IL 61021. (866)287-4997. E-mail: president@cellarrecords.com. Web site: www.cellarrecords.com. **Contact:** Todd Joos, president. A&R Department: Bob Brady, Albert Hurst, Jim Miller, Mark Summers, Jon Pomplin. Record company, music publisher (Sound Cellar Music/BMI) and record producer (Todd Joos). Estab. 1987. Staff size: 6. Releases 6-8 CDs/year. Pays 15-100% royalty to artists on contract; statutory rate to publisher per song on record. Charges in advance "if you use our studio to record."

Distributed by "We now service retail and online (Apple iTunes, etc. direct from Cellar Records."

How to Contact Submit demo package by mail. Unsolicited submissions are OK. Prefers CD with 3-4 songs and lyric sheet. Does not return material. Responds in 1 month only if interested. "If we like it we will call you."

Music Mostly **metal**, **country**, **rock**, **pop**, and **blues**. "No rap." Released "With Any Luck at All" (single by Tony Stampley/Randy Boudreaux/Joe Stampley) from *With Any Luck At All* (album), recorded by Cal Stage (pop/country); "Sleeping With a Smile" (single by Tony Stampley/Melissa Lyons/Tommy Barnes) from *With Any Luck At All* (album), recorded by Cal Stage (pop/country); and "Speed of My Life" (single by Jon Pomplin/Todd Joos) from *Declassified* (album), recorded by Project 814 (rock), all released 2001 on Cellar Records. "Visit our Web site for upcoming releases." Other artists include Eric Topper, Snap Judgment, Ballistic, Dago Red, Sea of Monsters, Rogue, Kings, James Miller, Vehement, Noopy Wilson, Dual Exhaust, Junker Jorg, The Unknown, Joel Ramirez & the Allstars, Tracylyn, Junk Poet, Cajun Anger, Roman, Flesh Pilgrims, LYZ, and Justice4.

Tips "Make sure that you understand your band is a business and you must be willing to self-invest time, effort and money just like any other new business. We can help you, but you must also be willing to help yourself."

☐ CHATTAHOOCHEE RECORDS

2544 Roscomare Rd., Los Angeles CA 90077. (818)788-6863. Fax: (310)471-2089. E-mail: cyardum@prodigy.net. **Contact:** Robyn Meyers, Music Director/A&R. Music Director: Chris Yardum. Record company and music publisher (Etnoc/Conte). Member NARAS. Releases 4 singles/year. Pays negotiable royalty to artists on contract.

How to Contact Submit demo by e-mail. Will respond only if interested.

Music Mostly **rock**. Released *Don't Touch It Let It Drip* (album), recorded by Cream House (hard rock), released 2000 on Chattahoochee Records. Artists include DNA, Noctrnl, and Vator.

N ☑ CHERRY STREET RECORDS

P.O. Box 52626, Tulsa OK 74152. (918)742-8087. Fax: (918)742-8003. E-mail: info@cherryst reetmusic.com. Web site: www.cherrystreetrecords.com. President: Rodney Young. Vice President: Steve Hickerson. Record company and music publisher. Estab. 1990. Staff size: 2. Releases 2 CD/year. Pays 50% royalty to artists on contract; statutory rate to publisher per song on record.

Distributed by Internet.

How to Contact *Write first and obtain permission to submit.* Prefers cassette or videocassette with 4 songs and lyric sheet. Include SASE. Responds in 4 months.

Music Rock, **country**, and **R&B**; also **jazz**. Released *Promised Land* (album), written and recorded by Richard Neville on Cherry Street (rock). Other artists include George W. Carroll and Chris Blevins.

Tips "We sign only artists who play an instrument, sing, and write songs. Send only your best 4 songs."

N ⊕ ◯ COLLECTOR RECORDS

P.O. Box 1200, 3260 AE oud beyerland Holland. (31)186 604266. Fax: (31)186 604366. E-mail: cees@collectorrec.com. Web site: www.collectorrecords.nl. **Contact:** Cees Klop, president. Manager: John Moore. Labels include All Rock, Downsouth, Unknown, Pro Forma and White Label Records. Record company, music publisher (All Rock Music Publishing) and record producer (Cees Klop). Estab. 1967. Staff size: 4. Release 25 LPs/year. Pays 10% royalty to artist on contract.

How to Contact Submit demo package by mail. Unsolicited submissions are OK. Prefers cassette. SAE and IRC. Responds in 2 months.

Music Mostly **'50s rock**, **rockabilly**, **hillbilly boogie** and **country/rock**; also **piano boogie woogie**. Released *Rock Crazy Baby* (album), by Art Adams (1950s rockabilly), released 2005; *Marvin Jackson* (album), by Marvin Jackson (1950s rockers), released 2005; *Western Australian Snake Pit R&R* (album), recorded by various (1950s rockers), released 2005, all on Collector Records. Other artists include Henk Pepping, Rob Hoeke, Eric-Jan Overbeek, and more. "See our Web site."

☑ COLUMBIA RECORDS

550 Madison Ave., 24th Floor, New York NY 10022. (212)833-4000. Fax: (212)833-4389. E-mail: sonymusiconline@sonymusic.com. Web site: www.columbiarecords.com. **Santa Monica:** 2100 Colorado Ave., Santa Monica CA 90404. (310)449-2100. Fax: (310)449-2743. **Nashville:** 34 Music Square E., Nashville TN 37203. (615)742-4321. Fax: (615)244-2549. Labels include So So Def Records and Ruffhouse Records. Record company.

● Columbia Records is a subsidiary of Sony BMG, one of the "Big 4" major labels.

Distributed by Sony.

How to Contact *Columbia Records does not accept unsolicited submissions.*

Music Artists include Aerosmith, Marc Anthony, Beyonce, Bob Dylan, and Patti Smith.

☑ COSMOTONE RECORDS

2951 Marina Bay Dr., Ste. 130, League City TX 77573-2733. E-mail: marianland@earthlink.net. Web site: www.cosmotonerecords.com. Record company, music publisher (Cosmotone Music, ASCAP) and record producer (Rafael Brom). Estab. 1984.

Distributed by marianland.com.

How to Contact "Sorry, we do not accept material at this time." Does not return materials.

Music Mostly **Christian pop/rock**. Released *Dance for Padre Pio, Peace of Heart, Music for Peace of Mind, The Sounds of Heaven, The Christmas Songs, Angelophany, The True Measure of Love, All My Love to You Jesus* (albums), and *Rafael Brom Unplugged* (live concert DVD), *Life is Good, Enjoy it While You Can* (album) by Rafael Brom.

☐ CREATIVE IMPROVISED MUSIC PROJECTS (CIMP) RECORDS

CIMP LTD, Cadence Building, Redwood NY 13679. (315)287-2852. Fax: (315)287-2860. E-mail: cimp@cadencebuilding.com. Web site: www.cimprecords.com. **Contact:** Bob Rusch, producer. Labels include Cadence Jazz Records. Record company and record producer (Robert D. Rusch). Estab. 1980. Releases 25-30 CDs/year. Pays negotiable royalty to artists on contract; pays statutory rate to publisher per song on record.

Distributed by North Country Distributors.

• CIMP specializes in jazz and creative improvised music.

How to Contact Submit demo by mail. Unsolicited submissions are OK. Prefers cassette or CD. "We are not looking for songwriters but recording artists." Include SASE. Responds in 1 week.

Music Mostly **jazz** and **creative improvised music**. Released *The Redwood Session* (album), recorded by Evan Parker, Barry Guy, Paul Lytton, and Joe McPhee; *Sarah's Theme* (album), recorded by the Ernie Krivda Trio, Bob Fraser, and Jeff Halsey; and *Human Flowers* (album), recorded by the Bobby Zankel Trio, Marily Crispell , and Newman Baker, all released on CIMP (improvised jazz). Other artists include Arthur Blythe, Joe McPhee, David Prentice, Anthony Braxton, Roswell Rudd, Paul Smoker, Khan Jamal, Odean Pope, etc.

Tips "CIMP Records are produced to provide music to reward repeated and in-depth listenings. They are recorded live to two-track which captures the full dynamic range one would experience in a live concert. There is no compression, homogenization, eq-ing, post-recording splicing, mixing, or electronic fiddling with the performance. Digital recording allows for a vanishingly low noise floor and tremendous dynamic range. This compression of the dynamic range is what limits the 'air' and life of many recordings. Our recordings capture the dynamic intended by the musicians. In this regard these recordings are demanding. Treat the recording as your private concert. Give it your undivided attention and it will reward you. CIMP Records are not intended to be background music. This method is demanding not only on the listener but on the performer as well. Musicians must be able to play together in real time. They must understand the dynamics of their instrument and how it relates to the others around them. There is no fix-it-in-the-mix safety; either it works or it doesn't. What you hear is exactly what was played. Our main concern is music not marketing."

⊘ CURB RECORDS

47 Music Square E., Nashville TN 37203. (615)321-5080. Fax: (615)327-1964. Web site: www.curb.com. **Contact:** John Ozler, A&R coordinator. Record company.

How to Contact Curb Records does not accept unsolicited submissions; accepts previously published material only. *Do not submit without permission.*

Music Released *Everywhere* (album), recorded by Tim McGraw; *Sittin' On Top of the World* (album), recorded by LeAnn Rimes; and *I'm Alright* (album), recorded by Jo Dee Messina, all on Curb Records. Other artists include Mary Black, Merle Haggard, Kal Ketchum, David Kersh, Lyle Lovett, Tim McGraw, Wynonna, and Sawyer Brown.

◖ DEEP SOUTH ENTERTAINMENT

P.O. Box 17737, Raleigh NC 27619-7737. (919)844-1515. Fax: (919)847-5922. E-mail: info@ deepsouthentertainment.com. Web site: www.deepsouthentertainment.com. Manager: Amy Cox. Record company and management company. Estab. 1996. Staff size: 10. Pays negotiable royalty to artists on contract; statutory rate to publisher per song on record.

Distributed by Redeye Distribution, Valley, Select-O-Hits, City Hall, AEC/Bassin, Northeast One Stop, Pollstar, and Koch International.

How to Contact Submit demo by mail. Unsolicited submissions are OK. Prefers cassette or CD with 3 songs, cover letter, and press clippings. Does not return material. Responds only if interested.

Music Mostly **pop, modern rock**, and **alternative**; also **swing**, **rockabilly**, and **heavy rock**. Does not want rap or R&B. Artists include Bruce Hornsby, Little Feat, Mike Daly, SR-71, Stretch Princess, Darden Smith, and Vienna Teng.

ℕ 🌐 ⊘ DEMI MONDE RECORDS AND PUBLISHING, LTD.

Foel Studio, Llanfair Caereinion, Powys, Wales, United Kingdom. (01938)810758. E-mail: demi.monde@dial.pipex.com. Web site: www.demimonde.co.uk/demimonde. Managing Director: Dave Anderson. Record company, music publisher (Demi Monde Records & Publishing, Ltd.) and record producer (Dave Anderson). Estab. 1983. Releases 5 12" singles, 10 LPs and 6 CDs/year. Pays 10% royalty to artists on contract; statutory rate to publisher per song on record.

Distributed by Pinnacle, Magnum and Shellshock.

How to Contact Submit demo tape by mail. Unsolicited submissions are OK. Prefers cassette with 3-4 songs. Does not return material. Responds in 6 weeks.

Music Mostly **rock**, **R&B** and **pop**. Released *Hawkwind*, *Amon Duul II & Gong* and *Groundhogs* (by T.S. McPhee), all on Demi Monde Records.

◖ DENTAL RECORDS

P.O. Box 20058, New York NY 10017. E-mail: info@dentalrecords.com. Web site: www.dentalrecords.com. **Contact:** Rick Sanford, owner. Record company. Estab. 1981. Staff size: 2. Releases 1-2 CDs/year. Pays negotiable royalty to artists on contract; statutory rate to publisher per song on record.

Distributed by Dutch East India Trading.

How to Contact *Not currently accepting unsolicited submissions.* Prefers CD with any number of songs, lyric sheet, and cover letter. "Check our Web site to see if your material is appropriate." Include SASE. Responds only if interested.

Music **Pop-derived structures**, **jazz-derived harmonies**, and **neo-classic-wannabee-pretenses**. Does not want urban, heavy metal, or hard core. Released *Perspectivism* (album), written and recorded by Rick Sanford (instrumental), released 2003 on Dental Records. Other artists include Les Izmor.

⚠ ⊘ DREAMWORKS RECORDS

2220 Colorado Ave., Santa Monica CA 90404. (310)865-1000. Fax: (310)865-8059. Web site: www.dreamworksrecords.com. **Nashville:** 60 Music Sq. E., Nashville TN 37203. (615)463-4600 Fax: (615)463-4601. Record company and music publisher (DreamWorks SKG Music Publishing). Labels include Interscope, Geffen, and A&M.

- Dreamworks Records is a subsidiary of Universal Music Group, one of the "Big 4" major labels.

How to Contact *Material must be submitted through an agent or attorney. Does not accept unsolicited submissions.*

⊘ ELEKTRA RECORDS

75 Rockefeller Plaza, 17th Floor, New York NY 10019. Web site: www.elektra.com. Labels include Elektra Records, Eastwest Records, and Asylum Records. Record company.

- Elektra Records is a subsidiary of Warner Music Group, one of the "Big 4" major labels.

Distributed by WEA.

How to Contact *Elektra does not accept unsolicited submissions.*

Music Mostly alternative/modern rock. Artists include Phish, Jason Mraz, Bjork, Busta Rhymes, and Metallica.

⊘ EPIC RECORDS

550 Madison Ave., 21st Floor, New York NY 10022. (212)833-8000. Fax: (212)833-4054. Web site: www.epicrecords.com. Senior Vice Presidents A&R: Ben Goldman, Rose Noone. **Santa Monica:** 2100 Colorado Ave., Santa Monica CA 90404. (310)449-2100 Fax: (310)449-2848. A&R: Pete Giberga, Mike Flynn. Labels include Epic Soundtrax, LV Records, Immortal Records, and Word Records. Record company.

- Epic Records is a subsidiary of Sony BMG, one of the "Big 4" major labels.

Distributed by Sony Music Distribution.

How to Contact *Write or call first and obtain permission to submit* (New York office only). Does not return material. Responds only if interested. *Santa Monica and Nashville offices do not accept unsolicited submissions.*

Music Artists include Celine Dion, Macy Gray, Modest Mouse, Alkaline Trio, Fuel, Jennifer Lopez, B2K, Incubus, Ben Folds.

Tips "Do an internship if you don't have experience or work as someone's assistant. Learn the business and work hard while you figure out what your talents are and where you fit in. Once you figure out which area of the record company you're suited for, focus on that, work hard at it and it shall be yours."

ℕ ◻ FLYING HEART RECORDS

Dept. SM, 4015 NE 12th Ave., Portland OR 97212. E-mail: flyheart@teleport.com. Web site: http://home.teleport.com/ ~ flyheart. **Contact:** Jan Celt, owner. Record company and record producer (Jan Celt). Estab. 1982. Releases 2 CDs/year. Pays variable royalty to artists on contract; negotiable rate to publisher per song on record.

Distributed by Burnside Distribution Co.

How to Contact Submit demo by mail. Unsolicited submissions are OK. Prefers cassette with 1-10 songs and lyric sheets. Does not return material. "SASE required for *any* response." Responds in 3 months.

Music Mostly **R&B**, **blues**, and **jazz**; also **rock**. Released *Vexatious Progr.* (album), written and recorded by Eddie Harris (jazz); *Juke Music* (album), written and recorded by Thara Memory (jazz); and *Lookie Tookie* (album), written and recorded by Jan Celt (blues), all on Flying Heart Records. Other artists include Janice Scroggins, Tom McFarland, Obo Addy, and Snow Bud & The Flower People.

ℕ ◰ MARTY GARRETT ENTERTAINMENT

320 West Utica Place, Broken Arrow OK 74011. (888)HE4-GAVE. E-mail: musicbusiness@te lepath.com. Web site: www.breakingintothemusicbiz.com and www.martygarrettentertain ment.com. **Contact:** Marty R. Garrett, president. Labels include MGE Records Lonesome Wind Records. Record company, record producer, music publisher, and entertainment consultant. Estab. 1988. Releases 1-2 EPs and 1 CD/year. Pays negotiable royalty to artists on contract; statutory rate to publisher per song on record.

How to Contact *Call or check Internet site first and obtain permission to submit.* Prefers CD or cassette with 4-5 songs and lyric or lead sheet with chord progressions listed. Does not return material. No press packs or bios, unless specifically requested. Responds in 4-6 weeks.

Music Mostly **honky tonk**, **progressive/traditional country**, or **scripturally-based gospel**. Released *Drinking the New Wine* (album) by Marty Garrett on MGE Records. Released singles include "He Brought Me Back Again," "My Father Made The Jailhouse Rock," "Drinking the New Wine," "Get Myself Off My Mind," "What Would God Say Then"; all singles released on MGE Records.

Tips "We help artists secure funding to record and release major label quality CD products to the public for sale through 1-800 television and radio advertising and on the Internet. Although we do submit finished products to major record companies for review, our main focus is to establish and surround the artist with their own long-term production, promotion and distribution organization. Professional studio demos are not required, but make sure vocals are distinct, up-front and up-to-date. I personally listen and respond to each submission received, so check Web site to see if we are reviewing for an upcoming project."

☐ GENERIC RECORDS, INC.

433 Limestone Rd., Ridgefield CT 06877. (203)438-9811. Fax: (203)431-3204. E-mail: hifiad d@aol.com. President (pop, alternative, rock): Gary Lefkowith. A&R (pop, dance, adult contemporary): Bill Jerome. Labels include Outback, GLYN. Record company, music publisher (Sotto Music/BMI) and record producer. Estab. 1976. Staff size: 2. Releases 6 singles and 2 CDs/year. Pays 15% royalty to artists on contract; statutory rate to publisher per song on record.

Distributed by Dutch East India.

How to Contact Submit demo package by mail. Unsolicited submissions are OK. Prefers CD or cassette with 2-3 songs. Include SASE. Responds in 2 weeks.

Music Mostly **alternative rock**, **rock**, and **pop**; also **country** and **rap**. Released "Young Girls" (by Eric Della Penna/Dean Sharenow), recorded by Henry Sugar (alternative/pop); "Rock It," written and recorded by David Ruskay (rock/pop); and Tyrus, written and recorded by Tyrus (alternative), all on Generic Records, Inc. Other artists include Hifi, Honest, Loose Change, and John Fantasia.

Tips "Love what you're doing. The music comes first."

☑ GIG RECORDS

520 Butler Ave., Point Pleasant NJ 08742. E-mail: lenny@gigrecords.com. Web site: www.gi grecords.com. **Contact:** Lenny Hip, A&R. Labels include AMPED. Record company and music publisher (Gig Music). Estab. 1998. Staff size: 8. Releases 2 singles, 2 EPs and 15 CDs/year. Pays negotiable royalty to artists on contract; statutory rate to publisher per song on record.

Distributed by Amazon, E-Music, CD Now, Nail, and Sumthing.

How to Contact Submit demo package by mail. Unsolicited submissions are OK. Prefers CD or DVD with lyric sheet and cover letter. Does not return materials, "but will respond if SASE is included." Responds ASAP if interested.

Music Mostly **rock** and **electronic**; also **drum & bass**, **trip-hop**, and **hip-hop**. Does not want country. Released *Hungry* (album), recorded by Gum Parker (electronico), released 2003 on Gig Records; *Waiting For You* (album), recorded by Nick Clemons Band (alternative rock/pop), released 2003 on Groove Entertainment; and a new release to come from Fight of Your Life. Other artists include Ned's Atomic Dustbin, Virginia, The Vibrators, Ground-swell UK, Nebula Nine, The Youth Ahead, Dryer, Red Engine Nine, Michael Ferentino, Amazing Meet Project, and Love in Reverse.

Tips "No egos."

☐ GOTHAM RECORDS

Attn: A&R, P.O. Box 7185, Santa Monica CA 90406. E-mail: info@gothamrecords.com. Web site: www.gothamrecords.com. Record company. Estab. 1994. Staff size: 3. Releases 8 LPs and 8 CDs/year. Pays negotiable royalty to artists on contract; statutory rate to publisher per song on record. "We now have a new division (Gotham Music Placement) that places songs with motion picture, TV, advertising, and video game companies."

Distributed by KOCH Distribution and Sony RED.

How to Contact Submit demo by mail "in a padded mailer or similar package." Unsolicited submissions are OK. Prefers cassette or CD and bios, pictures, and touring information. Does not return material. Responds in 6 weeks.

Music Mostly **rock**, **pop**, **alternative**, and **AAA**. New artists include SLANT, Red Horizon, The Day After . . ., The Vicious Martinis.

Tips "Send all submissions in regular packaging. Spend your money on production and basics, not on fancy packaging and gift wrap."

◻ HACIENDA RECORDS & RECORDING STUDIO

1236 S. Staple St., Corpus Christi TX 78404. (361)882-7066. E-mail: info@haciendarecords.com. Web site: www.haciendarecords.com. **Contact:** Rick Garcia, executive vice president. Founder/CEO: Roland Garcia. Record company, music publisher, and record producer. Estab. 1979. Staff size: 10. Releases 12 singles and 15 CDs/year. Pays negotiable royalty to artists on contract; negotiable rate to publisher per song on record.

How to Contact Submit demo package by mail. Unsolicited submissions are OK. Prefers CD with cover letter. Does not return material. Responds in 6 weeks.

Music Mostly **tejano**, **regional Mexican**, **country** (Spanish or English), and **pop**. Released "Chica Bonita" (single), recorded by Albert Zamora and D.J. Cubanito, released 2001 on Hacienda Records; "Si Quieres Verme Llorar" (single) from *Lisa Lopez con Mariachi* (album), recorded by Lisa Lopez (mariachi), released 2002 on Hacienda; "Tartamudo" (single) from *Una Vez Mas* (album), recorded by Peligro (norteno); and "Miento" (single) from *Si Tu Te Vas* (album), recorded by Traizion (tejano), both released 2001 on Hacienda. Other artists include Ricky Naramzo, Gary Hobbs, Steve Jordan, Grammy Award nominees Mingo Saldivar and David Lee Garza, Michelle, Victoria Y Sus Chikos, La Traizion.

◖ HEADS UP INT., LTD.

23309 Commerce Park Dr., Cleveland OH 44122. (216)765-7381. Fax: (216)464-6037. E-mail: dave@headsup.com. Web site: www.headsup.com. **Contact:** Dave Love, president. Record company, music publisher (Heads Up Int., Buntz Music, Musica de Amor), and record producer (Dave Love). Estab. 1980. Staff size: 57. Releases 13 LPs/year. Pays negotiable royalty to artists on contract.

Distributed by Universal Fontana (domestically).

How to Contact Submit demo by mail. Unsolicited submissions are OK. Prefers CD. Does not return material. Responds to all submissions.

Music Mostly **jazz**, **R&B**, **pop** and **world**. Does not want anything else. Released *Long Walk to Freedom* (album), recorded by Ladysmith Black Mambazo (world); *Pilgrimage* (album), recorded by Michael Brecker (contemporary jazz); *Rizing Sun* (album), recorded by Najee (contemporary jazz). Other artists include Diane Schuur, Mateo Parker, Victor Wooten, Esperanza Spalding, Incognito, George Doke, Take 6, Fourplay.

◙ HEART MUSIC, INC.

P.O. Box 160326, Austin TX 78716-0326. (512)795-2375. E-mail: info@heartmusic.com. Web site: www.heartmusic.com. **Contact:** Tab Bartling, president. Record company and music publisher (Coolhot Music). "Studio available for artists." Estab. 1989. Staff size: 2. Releases 1-2 CDs/year. Pays statutory rate to publisher per song on record.

How to Contact *Not interested in new material at this time.* Does not return material. Responds only if interested.

Music Mostly **Folk-rock, pop**, and **jazz**; also **blues** and **contemporary folk**. Coming in 2009, new cd by The Sure coming in 2008, new Libby Kirkpatrick; Released *The Fisherman* (album), recorded by Darin Layne; In the City of Lost Things (jazz), recorded by Joe LoCascio, both released in 2007; *Collaborations* (album), recorded by Will Taylor and Strings Attached (folk rock), featuring Eliza Gilkyson, Shawn Colvin, Patrice Pike, Ian Moore, Guy Forsyth, Ruthie Foster, Libby Kirkpatrick, Jimmy LaFave, Slaid Cleaves, and Barbara K., released 2006; *Goodnight Venus* (album), recorded by Libby Kirkpatrick, released in 2003, and *Be Cool Be Kind* (album), recorded by Carla Helmbrecht (jazz), released January 2001. Prior releases from Monte Montgomery: 1st and Repair, Mirror Tony Campise: First Takes, Once in A Blue Moon, Ballads, Blues and Bebop, Ballads, Blues Bebop and Beyond, strange Beauty; Erich avinger Heart Magic, Si and Poets, Misfits, Beggars and Shamans; Carla Helmbrecht One For My baby; Fred Hamilton Looking Back on Tomorrow; Doug Hall Three Wishes and Jihi; Tod Vullo Uh Huh; Elias Haslanger Standards, For The Moment and Kicks Are For Kids; Joe loCascio Close To So Far, Home, Charmed Life and Silent Motion; Jae Sinnett Listen and The Better Half; Beth Ullman and Rich Harney Aren't We The Lucky Ones

⚫ ◯ HI-BIAS RECORDS INC.

Attn: A&R Dept., 20 Hudson Dr. (side entrance), Maple ON L6A 1X3 Canada. (905)303-9611. Fax: (905)303-6611. E-mail: info@hibias.ca. Web site: www.hibias.ca. **Contact:** Nick Fiorucci, director. Record company, music publisher (Bend 60 Music/SOCAN), and record producer (Nick Fiorucci). Estab. 1990. Staff size: 5. Releases 20-30 singles and 2-5 CDs/year. Pays negotiable royalty to artists on contract; statutory rate to publisher per song on record.

Distributed by Koch Entertainment/Select-O-Hits.

How to Contact Submit demo by mail. Unsolicited submissions are OK. Prefers CD with 3 songs and lyric sheet. Does not return material or respond.

Music Mostly **dance, house, club, pop**, and **R&B**. Released "Hands of Time" (single by N. Fiorucci/B. Cosgrove), recorded by Temperance; "Now That I Found You" (single by B. Farrinco/Cleopatra), recorded by YBZ; and "Lift Me Up" (single), written and recorded by Red 5, all on Hi-Bias (dance/pop). Other artists include DJ's Rule.

⚫ ◯ HOTTRAX RECORDS

1957 Kilburn Dr., Atlanta GA 30324. (770)662-6661. E-mail: hotwax@hottrax.com. Web site: www.hottrax.com. **Contact:** George Burdell, vice president, A&R. Labels include Dance-A-Thon and Hardkor. Record company and music publisher (Starfox Publishing). Staff size: 6. Releases 8 singles and 3-4 CDs/year. Pays 5-15% royalty to artists on contract. **Distributed by** Get Hip Inc.

- Also see the listing for Alexander Janoulis Productions/Big Al Jano Productions in the Record Producers section of this book.

How to Contact *Write first and obtain permission to submit.* Prefers CD with 3 songs and lyric sheet. Does not return material. Responds in 6 months. "When submissions get extremely heavy, we do not have the time to respond/return material we pass on. We do notify those sending the most promising work we review, however."

Music Mostly **blues/blues rock**, some **top 40/pop**, **rock**, and **country**; also **hardcore punk** and **jazz-fusion**. Released *Power Pop Deluxe* (album), by Secret Lover featuring Delanna Protas, *Some of My Best Friends Have the Blues* (album), by Big Al Jano, *Hot to Trot* (album), written and recorded by Starfoxx (rock); *Lady That Digs The Blues* (album), recorded by Big Al Jano's Blues Mafia Show (blues rock); and *Vol. III, Psychedelic Era. 1967-1969* (album), released 2002 on Hottrax. Other artists include Big Al Jano, Sammy Blue, and Sheffield & Webb. Releases scheduled in 2009: *Burnin' 88s* (album) by Barrelhouse Bob Page, *So Much Love* (album) by Michael Rozakis & Yorgos, *Yuck! What Kind of Music Is This?* (album) by Schmaltz.

⬛ IDOL RECORDS PUBLISHING

P.O. Box 720043, Dallas TX 75372. (214)321-8890. E-mail: info@idolrecords.com. Web site: www.IdolRecords.com. **Contact:** Erv Karwelis, president. Record company. Estab. 1992. Releases 30 singles, 80 LPs, 20 EPs and 10-15 CDs/year. Pays negotiable royalty to artists on contract; negotiable rate to publisher per song on record.

Distributed by Koch entertainment.

How to Contact See Web site at www.IdolRecords.com for submission policy. No phone calls or e-mail follow-ups.

Music Mostly **rock**, **pop**, and **alternative**; also some **hip-hop**. Released *The Man* (album), recorded by Sponge (alternative); *Movements* (album), recorded by Black Tie Dynasty (alternative); In Between Days (album), recorded by Glen Reynolds (rock), all released 2006/2006 on Idol Records. Other artists include Flickerstick, the Fags, DARYL, Centro-matic, The Deathray Davies, GBH, PPT, The Crash that Took Me, Shibboleth.

▢ IMAGINARY RECORDS

P.O. Box 66, Whites Creek TN 37189-0066. E-mail: jazz@imaginaryrecords.com. Web site: www.imaginaryrecords.com. **Contact:** Lloyd Townsend, proprietor. Labels include Imaginary Records, Imaginary Jazz Records. Record company. Estab. 1981. Staff size: 1. Releases 1-3 CDs/year. Pays negotiable royalty to artists on contract; statutory rate to publisher per song on record.

Distributed by North Country, Gats Production LTD, Tokyo, Japan, and Imaginary Distribution.

How to Contact *Write first to obtain permission to submit.* "We do not act as a publisher placing songs with artists." Prefers CD with 3-5 songs (or full-length album), cover letter, and press clippings. Include SASE. Responds in 4 months if interested.

Music Mostly **mainstream jazz**, **swing jazz**, and **classical**. Does not want country, rap, hip-hop or metal. Released *Fifth House* (album), recorded by New York Trio Project (mainstream jazz), released 2001; *Get Out of Town* by Stevens, Siegel, and Ferguson (Mainstream Jazz), released 2006.

Tips "Be patient, I'm slow. I'm primarily considering mainstream jazz or classical—other genre submissions are much less likely to get a response."

☑ ⊘ INTERSCOPE/GEFFEN/A&M RECORDS

2220 Colorado Ave., Santa Monica CA 90404. (310)865-1000. Fax: (310)865-7908. Web site: www.interscoperecords.com. Labels include Death Row Records, Nothing Records, Rock Land, Almo Sounds, Aftermath Records, and Trauma Records. Record company.
- Interscope/Geffen/A&M is a subsidiary of Universal Music Group, one of the "Big 4" major labels.

How to Contact *Does not accept unsolicited submissions.*

Music Released *Worlds Apart*, recorded by . . . And You Will Know Us By The Trail Of Dead; and *Guero*, recorded by Beck. Other artists include U2, M.I.A, Keane, and Marilyn Manson.

⊘ ISLAND/DEF JAM MUSIC GROUP

825 Eighth Ave., 29th Floor, New York NY 10019. (212)333-8000. Fax: (212)603-7654. Web site: www.islanddefjam.com. **Los Angeles:** 8920 Sunset Blvd, 2nd Floor, Los Angeles CA 90069. (310)276-4500. Fax: (310)242-7023. Executive A&R: Paul Pontius. Labels include Mouth Almighty Records, Worldly/Triloka Records, Blackheart Records, Private Records, Slipdisc Records, Thirsty Ear, Blue Gorilla, Dubbly, Little Dog Records, Rounder, and Capricorn Records. Record company.
- Island/Def Jam is a subsidiary of Universal Music Group, one of the "Big 4" major labels.

How to Contact *Island/Def Jam Music Group does not accept unsolicited submissions. Do not send material unless requested.*

Music Artists include Bon Jovi, Ja Rule, Jay-Z, and Ludacris.

⊘ KAUPP RECORDS

P.O. Box 5474, Stockton CA 95205. (209)948-8186. **Contact:** Melissa Glenn. Record company, music publisher (Kaupps and Robert Publishing Co./BMI), management firm (Merri-Webb Productions) and record producer (Merri-Webb Productions). Estab. 1990. Releases 1 single and 4 LPs/year. Pays standard royalty to artists on contract; statutory rate to publisher per song on record.

Distributed by Merri-Webb Productions and Cal-Centron Distributing Co.

How to Contact *Write first and obtain permission to submit or to arrange personal interview.* Prefers cassette or VHS videocassette with 3 songs. Include SASE. Responds in 3 months.

Music Mostly **country**, **R&B**, and **A/C rock**; also **pop**, **rock**, and **gospel**. Mostly **country**, **R&B** and **A/C rock**; also **pop**, **rock** and **gospel**. Published "Rushin' In" (singles by N. Merrihew/B. Bolin), recorded by Valerie; "Coin Postal" (singles by N. Merrihew/B. Bolin), recorded by Bruce Bolin (country/rock/pop); and "I Gotta Know" (single by N. Merrihew/ B. Bolin), recorded by Cheryl (country/rock/pop), all released on Kaupp Records.

KILL ROCK STARS

120 N.E. State #418, Olympia WA 98501. E-mail: krs@killrockstars.com. Web site: www.kil lrockstars.com. **Contact:** Slim Moon, CEO, or Maggie Vail, VP of A&R. Record company. Estab. 1991. Releases 4 singles, 10 LPs, 4-6 EPs and 35 CDs/year. Pays 50% of net profit to artists on contract; negotiated rate to publisher per song on record.

Distributed by Touch and Go.

How to Contact *Write first and obtain permission to submit.* Prefers link to Web page or EPK. Does not return material.

Music Mostly **punk rock**, **neo-folk** or **anti-folk** and **spoken word**. Artists include Deerhoof, Xiu Xiu, Mary Timony, The Gossip, Erase Errata, and Two Ton Boa.

Tips "Send a self-released CD or link. NEVER EVER send unsolicited MP3s. We will not listen. We will only work with touring acts, so let us know if you are playing Olympia, Seattle or Portland. Particularly interested in young artists with indie-rock background."

KINGSTON RECORDS

15 Exeter Rd., Kingston NH 03848. (603)642-8493. E-mail: kingstonrecords@adelphia.net. Web site: www.kingstonrecords.com. **Contact:** Harry Mann, coordinator. Record company, record producer and music publisher (Strawberry Soda Publishing/ASCAP). Estab. 1988. Releases 10 singels, 12 CDs/year. Pays 3-5% royalty to artists on contract; statutory rate to publisher per song.

How to Contact *E-mail first and obtain permission to submit.* Prefers CD, cassette, DAT, 15 ips reel-to-reel or videocassette with 3 songs and lyric sheet. Does not return material. Responds in 2 months.

Music Mostly **rock**, **country**, and **pop**; "no heavy metal." Released *Two Lane Highway*, *Count the Stars*, and *Leaving Tracks* written and recorded by CMA winner Doug Mitchell, released 1999-2008, all on Kingston Records.

Tips "Working only with N.E. and local talent."

LANDMARK COMMUNICATIONS GROUP

P.O. Box 1444, Hendersonville TN 37077. E-mail: lmarkcom@bellsouth.net. Web site: www .landmarkcommunicationsgroup.com. **Contact:** Bill Anderson, Jr., president (all styles). Professional Manager (western): Dylan Horse. Labels include Jana and Landmark Records. Record company, record producer, music publisher (Newcreature Music/BMI and Mary Megan Music/ASCAP) and management firm (Landmark Entertainment). Releases 6 singles, 8 CDs/year. Pays 5-7% royalty to artists on contract; statutory rate to publisher for each record sold.

How to Contact Submit demo tape by mail. Unsolicited submissions are OK. Prefers MP3 or CD with 2-4 songs and lyric sheet. Responds in 1 month.

Music Mostly **country/crossover**, **Christian**. Recent projects: *Smoky Mountain Campmeeting* by Various Artists; *The Pilgrim & the Road* by Tiffany Turner; *Fallow Ground* by C.J. Hall; *Prince Charming is Dead* by Kecia Burcham.

Tips "Be professional in presenting yourself."

☑ LARK RECORD PRODUCTIONS, INC.

P.O. Box 35726, Tulsa OK 74153. (918)786-8896. Fax: (918)786-8897. E-mail: janajae@janaj ae.com. Web site: www.janajae.com. **Contact:** Kathleen Pixley, vice president. Record company, music publisher (Jana Jae Music/BMI), management firm (Jana Jae Enterprises) and record producer (Lark Talent and Advertising). Estab. 1980. Staff size: 8. Pays negotiable royalty to artists on contract; statutory rate to publisher per song on record.

How to Contact Submit demo by mail. Unsolicited submissions are OK. Prefers CD or VHS videocassette with 3 songs and lead sheets. Does not return material. Responds only if interested.

Music Mostly **country**, **bluegrass**, and **classical**; also **instrumentals**. Released "Fiddlestix" (single by Jana Jae); "Mayonnaise" (single by Steve Upfold); and "Flyin' South" (single by Cindy Walker), all recorded by Jana Jae on Lark Records (country). Other artists include Sydni, Hotwire, and Matt Greif.

☑ MAGNA CARTA RECORDS

208 E. 51st St., PMB 1820, New York NY 10022.(585)381-5224. Fax: (585)381-0658. E-mail: magcart@aol.com. Web site: www.magnacarta.net. **Contact:** Pete Morticelli. Record label.

How to Contact Contact first and obtain permission to submit. No unsolicited material.

Music Mostly **progressive metal**, **progressive rock**, and **progressive jazz**. Released The Ereyn Chronicles, Part 1 (album), recorded by Anthropia (progressive metal); Last Day in Paradise (album), recorded by The Alex Skolnick Trio (progressive jazz); The Journey (album), recorded by Khallice (progressive metal), all released 2007. Other artists include Tony Levin, Ozric Tentacles, Mike Portnoy, Kansas, Steve Morse, Tony Hymas, Billy Sheehan, Bozzio, The Fareed Haque Group, Liquid Tension Experiment, Niacin, World Trade, and Vapourspace.

☑ ☑ MAVERICK RECORDS

9348 Civic Center Dr., Beverly Hills CA 90210. Web site: www.maverick.com. CEO/Head of A&R: Guy Oseary. A&R: Russ Rieger, Jason Bentley, Danny Strick, Berko Weber, Michael Goldberg. Record company.

- Maverick Records is a subsidiary of Warner Music Group, one of the "Big 4" major labels.

Distributed by WEA.

How to Contact *Maverick Records does not accept unsolicited submissions.*

Music Released *Supposed Former Infatuation Junkie* (album) and *Jagged Little Pill* (album), both recorded by Alanis Morissette; *The Spirit Room* (album), recorded by Michelle Branch; *Tantric* (album), recorded by Tantric; and *Ray of Light* (album), recorded by Madonna. Other artists include Deftones, Home Town Hero, Mest, Michael Lee, Me'shell Ndegeocello, Muse, Onesidezero, Prodigy, and Paul Oakenfold.

☑ ☑ MCA NASHVILLE

(formerly MCA Records), 60 Music Square E., Nashville TN 37203. (615)244-8944. Fax: (615)880-7447. Web site: www.mca-nashville.com. Record company and music publisher (MCA Music).

• MCA Nashville is a subsidiary of Universal Music Group, one of the "Big 4" major labels.

How to Contact MCA Nashville cannot accept unsolicited submissions.

Music Artists include Tracy Byrd, George Strait, Vince Gill, The Mavericks, and Trisha Yearwood.

☐ MEGAFORCE RECORDS

P.O. Box 63584, Philadelphia PA 19147. **New York:** P.O. Box 1955, New York NY 10113. (212)741-8861. Fax: (509)757-8602. E-mail: gregaforce@aol.com. Web site: www.megaforc erecords.com. **Contact:** Robert John, President. General Manager: Missi Callazzo. Record company. Estab. 1983. Staff size: 5. Releases 6 CDs/year. Pays various royalties to artists on contract; ³⁄₄ statutory rate to publisher per song on record.

Distributed by Red/Sony Distribution.

How to Contact *Contact first and obtain permission to submit.* Submissions go to the Philadelphia office.

Music Mostly **rock**. Artists include Ministry, Clutch, S.O.D., and Blackfire Revelation.

☑ METAL BLADE RECORDS

2828 Cochran St., Suite 302, Simi Valley CA 93065. (805)522-9111. Fax: (805)522-9380. E-mail: metalblade@metalblade.com. Web site: www.metalblade.com. **Contact:** A&R. Record company. Estab. 1982. Releases 20 LPs, 2 EPs and 20 CDs/year. Pays negotiable royalty to artists on contract.

How to Contact Submit demo by mail. Unsolicited submissions are OK. Prefers CD with 3 songs. Does not return material. Responds in 3 months.

Music Mostly **heavy metal** and **industrial**; also **hardcore**, **gothic** and **noise**. Released "Gallery of Suicide," recorded by Cannibal Corpse; "Voo Doo," recorded by King Diamond; and "A Pleasant Shade of Gray," recorded by Fates Warning, all on Metal Blade Records. Other artists include As I Lay Dying, The Red Chord, The Black Dahlia Murder, and Unearth.

Tips "Metal Blade is known throughout the underground for quality metal-oriented acts."

☑ MINOTAUR RECORDS

P.O. Box 620, Redwood Estates CA 95044. E-mail: dminotaur@hotmail.com. **Contact:** A&R. Record company. Estab. 1987. Staff size: 2. Releases 2 CDs/year. Pays statutory royalty to publishers per song on record. Distributed by CDbaby.com. Member of BMI, ASCAP, NARAS, TAXI.

How to Contact *We only accept material referred to us by a reputable industry source (manager, entertainment attorney, etc.).* Does not return submissions. Responds only if interested.

Music Mostly **adult contemporary, country, dance**. Also **easy rock, pop**. Does not want rap, heavy metal, jazz, hip-hop, hard rock and instrumentals. "Maybe Love" written by D. Baumgartner and Steven Worthy, from the *Dancing in the Dark* (album) recorded by Andrew Ceglio (pop/dance); "That Was A Great Affair" written by Tab Morales and Ron Dean Tomich, from *This Side of Heaven* (album), recorded by Doug Magpiong (adult contemporary); "Baby Blue Eyes and Tight Levis" written by Ron Dean Tomich, from *This Side of Nashville* (album) recorded by Candy Chase (country).

☐ MODAL MUSIC, INC. ™

P.O. Box 6473, Evanston IL 60204-6473. (847)864-1022. E-mail: info@modalmusic.com. Web site: www.modalmusic.com. President: Terran Doehrer. Assistant: J. Distler. Record company and agent. Estab. 1988. Staff size: 2. Releases 1-2 LPs/year. Pays negotiable royalty to artists on contract; negotiable rate to publisher per song on record.

How to Contact Submit demo package by mail. Unsolicited submissions are OK. Prefers CD with bio, PR, brochures, any info about artist and music. Does not return material. Responds in 4 months.

Music Mostly **ethnic** and **world**. Released "St. James Vet Clinic" (single by T. Doehrer/Z. Doehrer) from *Wolfpak Den Recordings* (album), recorded by Wolfpak, released 2005; "Dance The Night Away" (single by T. Doehrer) from *Dance The Night Away* (album), recorded by Balkan Rhythm Band™; "Sid Beckerman's Rumanian" (single by D. Jacobs) from *Meet Your Neighbor's Folk Music™* (album), recorded by Jutta & The Hi-Dukes™; and *Hold Whatcha Got* (album), recorded by Razzemetazz™, all on Modal Music Records. Other artists include Ensemble M'chaiya™, Nordland Band™ and Terran's Greek Band™.

Tips "Please note our focus is primarily traditional and traditionally-based ethnic which is a very limited, non-mainstream market niche. You waste your time and money by sending us any other type of music. If you are unsure of your music fitting our focus, please call us before sending anything. Put your name and contact info on every item you send!"

☐ NBT RECORDS

228 Morgan Lane, Berkeley Springs WV 25411-3475.(304)261-0228. E-mail: nbtoys@verizon.net. **Contact:** John S. Newbraugh, owner. Record company, music publisher (Newbraugh Brothers Music/BMI, NBT Music/ASCAP). Estab. 1967. Staff size: 1. Releases 4 singles and 52 CDs/year. Pays negotiable royalty to artists on contract; statutory royalty to publishers per song on record.

Distributed by "Distribution depends on the genre of the release. Our biggest distributor is perhaps the artists themselves, for the most part, depending on the genre of the release. We do have product in some stores and on the Internet as well."

How to Contact Submit demo package by mail. Unsolicited submissions are OK. Prefers CD or cassette with any amount of songs, lyric sheet and cover letter. Include SASE. Responds in 4-6 weeks. "Please don't call for permission to submit. Your materials are welcomed."

Music Mostly **rockabilly**, **hillbilly**, **folk** and **bluegrass**; also **rock**, **country** and **gospel**. Does not want any music with vulgar lyrics. "We will accept all genres of music except songs that contain vulgar language." Released *Ride the Train Series Vol. 24; Layin' It On the Line* by Night Drive (2008); *Country Like It Ought to Be* by Bobby "Swampgrass" Anderson (2008) and *The Gospel Songbird* Vol. 2 by Wanda Sue Watkins (2008).

Tips "We are best known for our rockabilly releases. Reviews of our records can be found on both the American and European rockabilly Web sites. Our 'registered' trademark is a train. From time to time, we put out a CD with various artists featuring original songs that use trains as part of their theme. We use all genres of music for our train releases. We have received train songs from various parts of the world. All submissions on this topic are welcomed."

ⓝ ⊕ ◻ NERVOUS RECORDS

5 Sussex Crescent, Northolt, Middlesex UB5 4DL England. 44(20)8423 7373. E-mail: nervous@compuserve.com. Web site: www.nervous.co.uk. **Contact:** R. Williams, managing director. Record company (Rage Records), record producer and music publisher (Nervous Publishing and Zorch Music). Member: MCPS, PRS, PPL, ASCAP, NCB. Releases 10 CDs/year. Pays 8-12% royalty to artists on contract; statutory rate to publisher per song on records. Royalties paid directly to US songwriters and artists or through US publishing or recording affiliate.

- Nervous Records' publishing company, Nervous Publishing, is listed in the Music Publishers section.

How to Contact Submit demo tape by mail. Unsolicited submissions are OK. Prefers cassette with 4-15 songs and lyric sheet. SAE and IRC. Responds in 3 weeks.

Music Mostly **psychobilly** and **rockabilly**. "No heavy rock, AOR, stadium rock, disco, soul, pop—only wild rockabilly and psychobilly." Released "Extra Chrome" , written and recorded by Johnny Black; "It's Still Rock 'N' Roll to Me" , written and recorded by The Time. Other artists include Restless Wild and Taggy Tones.

◪ NEURODISC RECORDS, INC.

3801 N. University Dr., Suite 403, Ft. Lauderdale FL 33351. (954)572-0289. Fax: (954)572-2874. E-mail: info@neurodisc.com. Web site: www.neurodisc.com or www.myspace.com/neurodiscrecords. President: Tom O'Keefe. Business Affairs Manager: Emilie Kennedy. New Media Manager: Pasha Love. Record company and music publisher. Estab. 1992. Releases 6 singles and 10 CDs/year. Pays negotiable royalty to artists on contract.

Distributed by Fontana Distribution.

How to Contact Submit demo package by mail. Unsolicited submissions are OK. Prefers CD, MP3 or DVD. Include SASE and contact information. Responds only if interested.

Music Mostly **electronic**, **chillout in lounge**, **down tempo**, **New Age**, and **electro-bass**. Released albums from The Egg, Sleepthief, Blue Stone, Peplab, Etro Anime, Deviations Project, Ryan Farish & Amethystium, as well as Bass Lo-Ryders and Bass Crunk. Other artists include DaKsha, Eric Hansen, Bella Sonus and NuSound.

ⓝ ◻ NORTH STAR MUSIC

338 Compass Circle A1, North Kingstown RI 02852. (401)886-8888 or (800)346-2706. Fax: (401)886-8880. E-mail: info@northstarmusic.com. Web site: www.northstarmusic.com. **Contact:** Richard Waterman, president. Record company. Estab. 1985. Staff size: 15. Releases 12-16 LPs/year. Pays 9% royalty to artists on contract; ¾ statutory rate to publisher per song on record.

Distributed by Goldenrod and in-house distribution.

How to Contact Submit demo CD by mail. Unsolicited submissions are OK. Prefers finished CD. Does not return material. Responds in 2 months.

Music Mostly **instrumental**, **traditional** and **contemporary jazz**, **New Age**, **traditional world (Cuban, Brasilian, singer/songwriter, Hawaiian and Flamenco)** and **classical**. Released *Sacred* (album), written and recorded by David Tolk (inspirational), released 2003; *An Evening In Tuscany* (album), written and recorded by Bruce Foulke/Howard Kleinfeld (contemporary instrumental), released 2004; *Always & Forever* (album), written and recorded by David Osborne (piano), released 2003, all on North Star Music. Other artists include Judith Lynn Stillman, David Osborne, Emilio Kauderer, Gerry Beaudoin, Cheryl Wheeler and Nathaniel Rosen.

⃞ ⬯ OGLIO RECORDS

P.O. Box 404, Redondo Beach CA 90277. Fax: (310)791-8670. E-mail: getinfo4@oglio.com. Web site: www.oglio.com. Record company. Estab. 1992. Releases 20 LPs and 20 CDs/year. Pays negotiable royalty to artist on contract; statutory rate to publisher per song on record.

How to Contact No unsolicited demos.

Music Mostly **alternative rock** and **comedy**. Released *Shine* (album), recorded by Cyndi Lauper (pop); *Live At The Roxy* (album), recorded by Brian Wilson (rock); *Team Leader* (album), recorded by George Lopez (comedy).

⃞ OUTSTANDING RECORDS

P.O. Box 2111, Huntington Beach CA 92647. (714)377-7447 E-mail: beecher@outstandingm usic.com. Web site: www.outstandingmusic.com. **Contact:** Earl Beecher, owner. Labels include Outstanding, Morrhythm (mainstream/commercial), School Band (educational/charity), Church Choir (religious charity), and Empowerment (educational CDs and DVDs). Record company, music publisher (Earl Beecher Publishing/BMI and Beecher Music Publishing/ASCAP) and record producer (Earl Beecher). Estab. 1968. Staff size: 1. Releases 100 CDs/year. Pays $2/CD royalty to artists on contract; statutory rate to publisher per song on record.

Distributed by Sites on the Internet and "through distribution companies who contact me directly, especially from overseas."

How to Contact Submit demo by mail. Unsolicited submissions are OK. Prefers CD (full albums), lyric sheet, photo and cover letter. Include SASE. Responds in 3 weeks.

Music Mostly **jazz**, **rock** and **country**; also **everything else especially Latin**. Does not want music with negative, anti-social or immoral messages. "View our Web site for a listing of all current releases."

Tips "We prefer to receive full CDs, rather than just three numbers. A lot of submitters suggest we release their song in the form of singles, but we just can't bother with singles at the present time. Especially looking for performers who want to release their material on my labels. Some songwriters are pairing up with performers and putting out CDs with a 'Writer Presents the Performer' concept. No dirty language. Do not encourage listeners to use drugs, alcohol or engage in immoral behavior. I'm especially looking for upbeat, happy, danceable music."

⚃ ◯ P. & N. RECORDS

61 Euphrasia Dr., Toronto ON M6B 3V8 Canada. (416)782-5768. Fax: (416)782-7170. E-mail: panfilo@sympatico.ca. **Contact:** Panfilo Di Matteo, president, A&R. Record company, record producer and music publisher (Lilly Music Publishing). Estab. 1993. Staff size: 2. Releases 10 singles, 20 12″ singles, 15 LPs, 20 EPs and 15 CDs/year. Pays 25-35% royalty to artists on contract; statutory rate to publisher per song on record.

How to Contact Submit demo by mail. Unsolicited submissions are OK. Prefers CD or videocassette with 3 songs and lyric or lead sheet. Does not return material. Responds in 1 month only if interested.

Music Mostly **dance**, **ballads** and **rock**. Released *Only This Way* (album), written and recorded by Angelica Castro; *The End of Us* (album), written and recorded by Putz, both on P. & N. Records (dance); and "Lovers" (single by Marc Singer), recorded by Silvana (dance), released 2001 on P. and N. Records.

⊕ ◲ THE PANAMA MUSIC GROUP OF COMPANIES

(formerly Audio-Visual Media Productions), Sovereign House, 12 Trewartha Rd., Praa Sands, Penzance, Cornwall TR20 9ST England. +44 (0)1736 762826. Fax: +44 (0)1736 763328. E-mail: panamus@aol.com. Web site: www.songwriters-guild.co.uk and www.panamamusic.co.uk. **Contact:** Roderick G. Jones, managing director A&R. Labels include Pure Gold Records, Panama Music Library, Rainy Day Records, Panama Records, Mohock Records, Digimax Records (www.digimaxrecords.com). Registered members of Phonographic Performance Ltd. (PPL). Record company, music publisher, production and development company (Panama Music Library, Melody First Music Library, Eventide Music Library, Musik Image Music Library, Promo Sonor International Music Library, Caribbean Music Library, ADN Creation Music Library, Piano Bar Music Library, Corelia Music Library, PSI Music Library, Scamp Music, First Time Music Publishing U.K.), registered members of the Mechanical Copyright Protection Society (MCPS) and the Performing Right Society (PRS) (London, England UK), management firm and record producer (First Time Management & Production Co.). Estab. 1986. Staff size: 6. Pays variable royalty to artists on contract; statutory rate to publisher per song on record subject to deal.

Distributed by Media U.K. Distributors.

How to Contact Submit demo package by mail. Unsolicited submissions are OK. CD only with unlimited number of songs/instrumentals and lyric or lead sheets where necessary. "We do not return material so there is no need to send return postage. We will, due to volume of material received only respond to you if we have any interest. Please note: no MP3 submissions, attachments, downloads, or referrals to Web sites in the first instance via e-mail. Do not send anything by recorded delivery or courier as it will not be signed for. If we are interested, we will follow up for further requests as necessary."

Music All styles. Published by Scamp Music: "Chill Out" written by Richard Hinsley (single), recorded and released by Panama Productions/Panama Music Library (Film & TV library music) used in Ray Mears: "Wild Food" programme/documentary for BBC television networks and published by Scamp Music (mcps/prs) (www.panamamusic.co.uk); "Listen To My Heart" from Pure Hardcore (album/single and digital downloads), recorded by AudioJunkie, DJ Stylus Featuring Scarlet, released 2008 on Digimix Records Ltd (www.di

gimixrecords.com) published by Scamp Music (mcps/prs) (www.panamamusic.co.uk); "Uncontollable" from Pure Hardcore (album/single digital downloads), recorded by D J Chaos (Happy Hardcore), released 2008 on Digimix Records (www.digimixrecords.com); published by Scamp Music (mcps/prs) (ww.panamamusic.co.uk): "News Headline" by Stephen James for BBC light entertainment TV series *One Foot in the Grave*; "Sanskrit" written by Tim Donovan for UK Independent Television (ITV1) documentary *Art Attack* released by Panama Productions/Panama Music Library (Film & TV library music) published by Panama Music Library (mcps/prs); "The Slammer" from Pure Hardcore (album/single digital downloads), recorded by Jel & Fastraxx (remixed by DJ Sy & Chris Unknown (Happy Hardcore), released 2008 on Digimix Records (www.digimixrecords.com); published by Scamp Music (mcps/prs) (www.panamamusic.co.uk); "Mysterious East" written by Tim Donovan and "Mystic Lands written by David Cherrett" recorded by Panama productions and published by Panama Music Library (mcps/prs) used in ITV network television productions of John Wilson's Dream Fishing programmes and documentaries; "Gospel Lane" and "La Pologne" written by Rodney Payne and Robin Ashmore published by Panama Music Library (mcps/prs) used in the film La France directed by Serge Boson for screening at the Cannes Film festival (2007) and for Worldwide release(2007/2008). The soundtrack of the film was released on CD and DVD by Third Side Records (France)

◙ PARLIAMENT RECORDS
357 S. Fairfax Avenue #430, Los Angeles CA 90036. (323)653-0693. E-mail: parlirec@aol.com. Web site: www.parlirec.com. **Contact:** Ben Weisman, owner. Record company, record producer (Weisman Production Group) and music publisher (Audio Music Publishers, Queen Esther Music Publishing). Estab. 1965. Produces 30 singles/year. Fee derived from sales royalty when song or artist is recorded.
   • Also see the listings for Audio Music Publishers and Queen Esther Music Publishing in the Music Publishers section and Weisman Production Group in the Record Producer section.
How to Contact Submit demo package by mail. Unsolicited submissions are OK. Prefers CD with 3-10 songs and lyric sheet. Include SASE. "Mention Songwriter's Market. Please make return envelope the same size as the envelopes you send material in, otherwise we cannot send everything back." Responds in 6 weeks.
Music Mostly **R&B**, **soul**, **dance**, and **top 40/pop**; also **gospel** and **blues**. Arists include Rapture 7 (gospel), Wisdom (male gospel singers), and Chosen Recovery Ministry (female gospel group).
Tips "Parliament Records will also listen to 'tracks' only. If you send tracks, please include a letter stating what equipment you record on—ADAT, Protools or Roland VS recorders."

◙ QUARK RECORDS
P.O. Box 452, Newtown CT 06470. (917)687-9988. E-mail: quarkent@aol.com. **Contact:** Curtis Urbina. Record company and music publisher (Quarkette Music/BMI and Freedurb Music/ASCAP). Estab. 1984. Releases 3 singles and 3 LPs/year. Pays negotiable royalty to artists on contract; ¾ statutory rate to publisher per song on record.

How to Contact Prefers CD with 2 songs (max). Include SASE. "Must be an absolute 'hit' song!" Responds in 6 weeks.

Music Pop and dance music only.

N ⊘ RAVE RECORDS, INC.

Attn: Production Dept., 13400 W. Seven Mile Rd., Detroit MI 48235. E-mail: info@raverecor ds.com. Web site: www.raverecords.com. **Contact:** Carolyn and Derrick, production managers. Record company and music publisher (Magic Brain Music/ASCAP). Estab. 1992. Staff size: 2. Releases 2-4 singles and 2 CDs/year. Pays various royalty to artists on contract; statutory rate to publisher per song on record.

Distributed by Action Music Sales.

How to Contact *"We do not accept unsolicited submissions."* Submit demo package by mail. Prefers CD with 3 songs, lyric sheet. "Include any bios, fact sheets, and press you may have. We will contact you if we need any further information." Does not return materials.

Music Mostly **alternative rock** and **dance**. Artists include Cyber Cryst, Dorothy, Nicole, and Bukimi 3.

⊘ RAZOR & TIE ENTERTAINMENT

214 Sullivan St., Suite 4A, New York NY 10012. (212)473-9173. E-mail: info@razorandtie.c om. Web site: www.razorandtie.com. Record company.

How to Contact *Does not accept unsolicited material.*

Music Released *The Beauty of the Rain* (album) by Dar Williams; *The Sweetheart Collection* by Frankie & The Knockouts; *Everybody's Normal But Me* by Stuttering John; and *Marigold* (album) by Marty Lloyd, all on Razor & Tie Entertainment. Other artists include Graham Parker, Marshall Crenshaw, Sam Champion and Toshi Reagon.

⊠ ⊘ RCA RECORDS

1540 Broadway, 36th Floor, New York NY 10036. (212)930-4936. Fax: (212)930-4447. E-mail: info@rcarecords.com. Web site: www.rcarecords.com. A&R: Donna Pearce. Beverly Hills: 8750 Wilshire Blvd., Beverly Hills CA 90211. (310)358-4105 Fax: (310)358-4127. Senior Vice President of A&R: Jeff Blue. Nashville: 1400 18th Ave. S., Nashville TN 37212. A&R Director: Jim Catino. Labels include Loud Records, Deconstruction Records and Judgment/RCA Records. Record company.

• RCA Records is a subsidiary of Sony BMG, one of the "Big 4" major labels.

Distributed by BMG.

How to Contact *RCA Records does not accept unsolicited submissions.*

Music Artists include The Strokes, Dave Matthews Band, Anti-Flag, Christina Aguilera, and Foo Fighters.

N ⊕ RED ADMIRAL RECORDS LLP

The Cedars, Elvington Lane, Folkestone Kent CT18 7AD United Kingdom. Estab. 1979. (01)(303)893-472. Fax: (01)(303)893-833. E-mail: info@redadmiralrecords.com. Web site:

www.redadmiralrecords.com. **Contact:** Chris Ashman. Registered members of MCPS, PRS, and PPL. Record company and music publisher (Cringe Music (MCPS/PRS)). Estab. 1979. **How to Contact** Submit demo package by mail. Unsolicited submissions are OK. Submit CD only with unlimited number of songs. Submission materials are not returned. Responds if interested.
Music All styles. Artists include Elliott Frisby, Wim Hautekiet, The Silent Kingdom, Zoo, Keith Harwood, Peter Dinsley, Carmen Wiltshire, Hardly Mozart.

⊘ RED ONION RECORDS

8377 Westview, Houston TX 77055. (713)464-4653. Fax: (713)464-2622. E-mail: jeffwells@ soundartsrecording.com. Web site: www.soundartsrecording.com. **Contact:** Jeff Wells, president. A&R: Peter Verkerk. Record company, music publisher (Reach for the Sky Music Publishing/ASCAP; Earthscream Music Publishing Co./BMI) and record producer (Jeff Wells). Estab. 2007. Releases 4 CDs/year. Pays negotiable royalty to artists on contract; statutory rate to publisher per song on record.
Distributed by Earth Records.
How to Contact Submit demo by mail. Unsolicited submissions are OK. Prefers CD with 4 songs and lyric sheet. Does not return material. Responds in 6 weeks.
Music Mostly **country**, **blues** and **pop/rock**. Released *Glory Baby* (album), recorded by Tony Vega Band (blues); *Two For Tuesday* (album), recorded by Dr. Jeff and the Painkilllers (blues), all released 2007 on Red Onion Records.

Ⓝ ⊕ ⊘ RED SKY RECORDS

P.O. Box 27, Stroud, Glos. GL6 0YQ United Kingdom. 01453-836877. Fax: 01453-836877. Web site: www.redskyrecords.co.uk. **Contact:** Johnny Coppin, producer. Record company and record producer (Johnny Coppin). Estab. 1985. Staff size: 1. Releases 1 album/year. Pays 8-10% to artists on contract; statutory rate to publisher per song on record.
Distributed by Proper Music Distribution.
How to Contact *Write first and obtain permission to submit.* Does not return material. Responds in 6 months.
Music Mostly **singer-songwriters**, **folk** and **roots music**. Released *Keep the Flame* (album) and *The Winding Stair* (album), written and recorded by Johnny Coppin (singer/song-writer); *Breaking the Silence* (album), written and recorded by Mike Silver and Johnny Coppin. Other artists include Paul Burgess.

◖ REDEMPTION RECORDS

P.O. Box 10238, Beverly Hills CA 90213. E-mail: info@redemption.net. Web site: www.rede mption.net. A&R Czar: Ryan D. Kuper (indie rock, power pop, rock, etc.). Record company. Estab. 1990. Staff size: varies. Releases 2-3 (various)/year. "We typically engage in profit splits with signed artists.
Distributed by IRIS Distribution (digital).
How to Contact Submit digital linky by e-mail. "Include band's or artist's goals." Responds only if interested.

Music Mostly **indie rock** and **power pop**. Artists include Vicious Vicious, The Working Title, Race For Titles, Schatzi, Motion City Soundtrack, Nolan, and the Redemption Versus Series featuring indie rock bands from different geographical locations.

Tips "Be prepared to tour to support the release. Make sure the current line-up is secure."

⊘ REPRISE RECORDS

3300 Warner Blvd., 4th Floor, Burbank CA 91505. (818)846-9090. Fax: (818)840-2389. Web site: www.repriserecords.com. Labels include Duck and Sire. Record company.

- Reprise Records is a subsidiary of Warner Music Group, one of the "Big 4" major labels.

Distributed by WEA.

How to Contact *Reprise Records does not accept unsolicited submissions.*

Music Artists include Eric Clapton, My Chemical Romance, Guster, Josh Groban, The Distillers, and Neil Young.

◖ ROBBINS ENTERTAINMENT LLC

159 W. 25th St., 4th Floor, New York NY 10001. (212)675-4321. Fax: (212)675-4441. E-mail: info@robbinsent.com. Web site: www.robbinsent.com. **Contact:** John Parker, vice president, A&R/dance promotion. Record company and music publisher (Rocks, No Salt). Estab. 1996. Staff size: 10. Releases 25 singles and 12-14 CDs/year. Pays negotiable royalty to artists on contract; statutory rate to publisher per song on record.

Distributed by Sony/BMG.

How to Contact Accepts unsolicited radio edit demos as long as it's dance music. Prefers CD with 2 songs or less. "Make sure everything is labeled with the song title information and your contact information. This is important in case the CD and the jewel case get separated. Do not call us and ask if you can send your package. The answer is yes."

Music Commercial **dance** only. Released top 10 pop smashes, "Heaven" (single), recorded by DJ Sammy; "Everytime We Touch" (single), recorded by Cascada; "Listen To Your Heart" (single), recored by DHT; as well as Hot 100 records from Rockell, Lasgo, Reina and K5. Other artists include Ian Van Dahl, September, Andain, Judy Torres, Jenna Drey, Marly, Dee Dee, Milky, Kreo and many others.

Tips "Do not send your package 'Supreme-Overnight-Before-You-Wake-Up' delivery. Save yourself some money. Do not send material if you are going to state in your letter that, 'If I had more (fill in the blank) it would sound better.' We are interested in hearing your best and only your best. Do not call us and ask if you can send your package. The answer is yes. We are looking for dance music with crossover potential."

◌ ROLL ON RECORDS

112 Widmar Pl., Clayton CA 94517. (925)833-4680. E-mail: rollonrecords@aol.com. **Contact:** Edgar J. Brincat, owner. Record company and music publisher (California Country Music). Estab. 1985. Pays 10% royalty to artists on contract; statutory rate to publisher per song on record. Member of Harry Fox Agency.

Distributed by Tower.

How to Contact Submit demo package by mail. Unsolicited submissions are OK. "Do not call or write for permission to submit, if you do you will be rejected." Prefers CD or cassette with 3 songs and lyric sheet. Include SASE and phone number. Responds in 6 weeks.

Music Mostly **contemporary/country** and **modern gospel**. Released "Broken Record" (single by Horace Linsley/Dianne Baumgartner), recorded by Edee Gordon on Roll On Records; Maddy and For Realities Sake (albums both by F.L. Pittman/Madonna Weeks), recorded by Ron Banks/L.J. Reynolds on Life Records/Bellmark Records.

Tips "Be patient and prepare to be in it for the long haul. A successful songwriter does not happen overnight. It's rare to write a song today and have a hit tomorrow. If you give us your song and want it back, then don't give it to us to begin with."

▧ ◯ ROTTEN RECORDS

Attn: A&R Dept., P.O. Box 56, Upland CA 91786. E-mail: rotten@rottenrecords.com. Web site: www.rottenrecords.com. President: Ron Peterson. Promotions/Radio/Video: Andi Jones. Record company. Estab. 1988. Releases 3 LPs, 3 EPs and 3 CDs/year.

Distributed by RIOT (Australia), Sonic Rendezvous (NL), RED (US) and PHD (Canada).

How to Contact Submit demo package by mail. Unsolicited submissions are OK. Prefers CD or MySpace link. Does not return material.

Music Mostly **rock**, **alternative** and **commercial**; also **punk** and **heavy metal**. Released *Paegan Terrorism* (album), written and recorded by Acid Bath; *Kiss the Clown* (album by K. Donivon), recorded by Kiss the Clown; and *Full Speed Ahead* (album by Cassidy/Brecht), recorded by D.R.T., all on Rotten Records.

Tips "Be patient."

◯ ROWENA RECORDS

195 S. 26th St., San Jose CA 95116. (408)286-9840. E-mail: gradie@sbcglobal.net. Web site: www.onealprod.com. Owner/A&R (country, Mexican, gospel): Gradie O'Neal. A&R (all styles): Jeannine O'Neal. Record company and music publisher (Tiki Enterprises). Estab. 1967. Staff size: 3. Releases 8-12 LPs and 8-12 CDs/year. Pays negotiable royalty to artists on contract; pays statutory rate to publisher per song on record.

- Also see the listing for Tiki Enterprises Inc. in the Music Publishers section of this book.

How to Contact Submit demo by mail. Unsolicited submissions are OK. Prefers CD with 2 songs and lyric sheet. Include SASE. Responds in 2 weeks.

Music Mostly **gospel**, **country** and **pop**; also **Mexican** and **R&B**. Released "It Amazes Me" (single by David Davis/Jeannine O'Neal) from *Forgiven* (album), recorded by Amber Littlefield/David Davis (Christian), released 2003-2004; "I'm Healed" (single by Jeannine O'Neal) from *Faith On the Front Lines* (album), recorded by Jeannine O'Neal, released 2004; and "You're Looking Good to Me" (single by Warren R. Spalding) from *A Rock 'N' Roll Love Story* (album), recorded by Warren R. Spalding, released 2003-2004, all on Rowena Records.

Tips "For up-to-date releases, view our Web site."

◪ RUSTIC RECORDS

6337 Murray Lane, Brentwood TN 37027. (615)371-0646. Fax: (615)370-0353. E-mail: rustic recordsinc@aol.com. Web site: www.rusticrecordsinc.com. President: Jack Schneider. Executive VP & Operations Manager: Nell Schneider. VP Publishing, Catalog Manager, and In-house Engineer: Amanda Mark. VP Marketing, Promotions, and Artist Development: Carol-Lynn Daigle. Independent traditional country music record label and music publisher (Iron Skillet Music/ASCAP, Covered Bridge/ BMI, Town Square/SESAC). Estab. 1979. Staff size: 4. Releases 2-3 albums/year. Pays negotiable royalty to artists on contract; statutory royalty to publisher per song on record.

Distributed by CDBaby.com, BathtubMusic.com and available on iTunes, MSN Music, Rhapsody, and more.

How to Contact Submit professional demo package by mail. Unsolicited submissions are OK. CD only; no MP3s or e-mails. Include no more than 4 songs with corresponding lyric sheets and cover letter. Include appropriately-sized SASE. Responds in 4 weeks.

Music Mostly **traditional country**, **redneck novelty**, and **country gospel**. Released *Takin' it South* (debut album), recorded by Lloyd Knight (country), released 2006; ''Drankin' Business'' (single), recorded by Colte Bradley; ''Love Don't Even Know My Name'' (single), recorded by Beckey Burr, both released 2005.

Tips ''Professional demo preferred.''

▨ ◪ SAHARA RECORDS AND FILMWORKS ENTERTAINMENT

10573 W. Pico Blvd., #352, Los Angeles CA 90064-2348. Phone: (310)948-9652. Fax: (310)474-7705. E-mail: info@edmsahara.com. Web site: www.edmsahara.com. **Contact:** Edward De Miles, president. Record company, music publisher (EDM Music/BMI, Edward De Miles Music Company) and record producer (Edward De Miles). Estab. 1981. Releases 15-20 CD singles and 5-10 CDs/year. Pays $9\frac{1}{2}$-11% royalty to artists on contract; statutory rate to publishers per song on record.

How to Contact *Does not accept unsolicited submissions.*

Music Mostly **R&B/dance**, **top 40 pop/rock** and **contemporary jazz**; also **TV-film themes, musical scores and jingles**. Released ''Hooked on U,'' ''Dance Wit Me'' and ''Moments'' (singles), written and recorded by Steve Lynn (R&B) on Sahara Records. Other artists include Lost in Wonder, Devon Edwards and Multiple Choice.

Tips ''We're looking for strong mainstream material. Lyrics and melodies with good hooks that grab people's attention.''

◪ SALEXO MUSIC

P.O. Box 1513, Hillsborough NC 27278. (919)245-0681. E-mail: salexo@bellsouth.net. **Contact:** Samuel OBie, president. Record company. Estab. 1992. Releases 1 CD/year.

How to Contact *Write first and obtain permission to submit.*

Music Mostly **contemporary gospel** and **jazz**. Released *A Joyful Noise* (album), recorded by Samuel Obie with J.H. Walker Unity Choir (gospel), released 2003, Macedonia Baptist Church; ''Favor'' (single) from *Favor* (album), written and recorded by Samuel Obie (contemporary gospel), released 2004 on Salexo Music; ''Hillsborough (NC) USA'' (single), from

TRAGEDY (album), written recorded by Samuel OBie (R&B), released 2006 ("Samuel's new solo project that covers 9/11 subject matter to R&B sounds, including "Hillsborough (NC) USA," a country-sounding story of Samuel's early family life in the '70s. Definitely the one to listen to."
Tips "Make initial investment in the best production."

☐ SANDALPHON RECORDS

P.O. Box 29110, Portland OR 97296. (503)957-3929. E-mail: jackrabbit01@sprintpcs.com. **Contact:** Ruth Otey, president. Record company, music publisher (Sandalphon Music/ BMI), and management agency (Sandalphon Management). Estab. 2005. Staff size: 2. Pays negotiable royalty to artists on contract; statutory royalty to publisher per song on record. **Distributed by** "We are currently negotiating for distribution."
How to Contact Submit demo packageby mail. Unsolicited submissions are OK. Prefers cassette or CD with 1-5 songs with lyric sheet and cover letter. Returns submissions if accompanied by a SASE or SAE and IRC for outside the United States. Responds in 1 month. **Music** Mostly **rock**, **country**, and **alternative**; also **pop**, **gospel**, and **blues**.

☑ SHERIDAN SQUARE ENTERTAINMENT INC.

(formerly Compendia Music), 210 25th Ave. N., Suite 1200, Nashville TN 37203. (615)277-1800. Web site: www.SheridanSquareMusic.com. Vice President/General Manager, Compendia Label & Intersound: Mick Lloyd (country/rock; contemporary jazz); Vice President/ General Manager, Light Records: Phillip White (black gospel). Record company. Labels include Sheridan Square Records, Light, V2, and Intersound. Pays negotiable royalty to artists on contract; negotiable rate to publisher per song on record.
How to Contact *Write or call first and obtain permission to submit.* Prefers CD with 3 songs. "We will contact the songwriter when we are interested in the material." Does not return material. Responds only if interested.
Music Mostly **country**, **rock**, **gospel**, and **classical**. Artists include Joan Osborne, Mighty Clouds of Joy, Moby, and Susan Tedeschi.

☑ SMALL STONE RECORDS

P.O. Box 02007, Detroit MI 48202. (248)219-2613. Fax: (248) 541-6536 E-mail: sstone@smal lstone.com. Web site: www.smallstone.com. Owner: Scott Hamilton. Record company. Estab. 1995. Staff size: 1. Releases 2 singles, 2 EPs and 10 CDs/year. Pays negotiable royalty to artists on contract; statutory rate to publisher per song on record.
Distributed by A EC, Allegro/Nail , Carrot Top.
How to Contact Submit CD/CD Rom by mail. Unsolicited submissions are OK. Does not return material. Responds in 2 months.
Music Mostly **alternative**, **rock** and **blues**; also **funk (not R&B)**. Released *Fat Black Pussy Cat*, written and recorded by Five Horse Johnson (rock/blues); *Wrecked & Remixed*, written and recorded by Morsel (indie rock, electronica); and *Only One Division*, written and recorded by Soul Clique (electronica), all on Small Stone Records. Other artists include Acid King, Perplexa, and Novadriver.

Tips "Looking for esoteric music along the lines of Bill Laswell to Touch & Go/Thrill Jockey records material. Only send along material if it makes sense with what we do. Perhaps owning some of our records would help."

◙ SONY BMG

550 Madison Ave., New York NY 10022. Web site: www.sonymusic.com.

• Sony BMG is one of the primary "Big 4" major labels.

How to Contact For specific contact information see the listings in this section for Sony subsidiaries Columbia Records, Epic Records, Sony Nashville, RCA Records, Arista Records, and American Recordings.

◙ SONY MUSIC NASHVILLE

1400 18th Ave. South, Nashville TN 37212-2809. Labels include Columbia, Epic, Lucky Dog Records, Monument.

• Sony Music Nashville is a subsidiary of Sony BMG, one of the "Big 4" major labels.

How to Contact *Sony Music Nashville does not accept unsolicited submissions.*

◙ SPOONFED MUZIK/HELAPHAT ENTERTAINMENT

(formerly CKB Records/Helaphat Entertainment), 527 Larry Court, Irving TX 75060. E-mail: spoonfedmuzik@yahoo.com. **Contact:** Tony Briggs, CEO. Record company, production company, artist management, and record distribution. Estab. 1999. Staff size: 6. Pays negotiable royalty to artists on contract.

Distributed by CKB Records.

How to Contact Submit demo package by mail. Unsolicited submissions are OK. Prefers CD with 4 songs, cover letter and press clippings. Does not return materials. Responds only if interested.

Music Exclusively **rap**, **hip-hop**, and **R&B**. Released "Dirrty 3rd" (single), recorded by T-SPOON aka NAP (rap/hip-hop), released 2003 on CKB Records; "Sippin' & Creepin' (featuring Squeekie Loc)" (single) from *OZAPHIdE—Tha 40 Oz. CliQue Vol. 1 compilation* (album), written and recorded by Tha 40 Clique and various artists (rap), released 2007 on Ozaphide Musik/Spoonfed Muzik. Other artists include Baby Tek, Lil' Droop, royal Jonez, Deuce Loc, Tre Loc, and Daylight and Forty.

Tips "Be professional and be about your business."

◙ SUGAR HILL RECORDS

P.O. Box 55300, Durham NC 27717-5300. E-mail: info@sugarhillrecords.com. Web site: www.sugarhillrecords.com. Record company. Estab. 1978.

• Welk Music Group acquired Sugar Hill Records in 1998.

How to Contact *No unsolicited submissions.* "If you are interested in having your music heard by Sugar Hill Records or the Welk Music Group, we suggest you establish a relationship with a manager, publisher, or attorney that has an ongoing relationship with our company. We do not have a list of such entities."

Music Mostly **Americana**, **bluegrass**, and **country**. Artists include Nickel Creek, Allison

Moorer, The Duhks, Sonny Landreth, Scott Miller, Reckless Kelly, Tim O'Brien, The Gibson Brothers, and more.

◙ SURFACE RECORDS

8377 Westview, Houston TX 77055. (713)464-4653. Fax: (713)464-2622. E-mail: jeffwells@ soundartsrecording.com. Web site: www.soundartsrecording.com. **Contact:** Jeff Wells, president. A&R: Peter Verkerk. Record company, music publisher (Earthscream Music Publishing Co./BMI) and record producer (Jeff Wells). Estab. 1996. Releases 4 CDs/year. Pays negotiable royalty to artists on contract; statutory rate to publisher per song on record. **Distributed by** Earth Records.

How to Contact Submit demo by mail. Unsolicited submissions are OK. Prefers CD with 4 songs and lyric sheet. Does not return material. Responds in 6 weeks.

Music Mostly **country**, **blues** and **pop/rock**. Released *Everest* (album), recorded by The Jinkies; *Joe "King" Carrasco* (album), recorded by Joe "King" Carrasco; *Perfect Strangers* (album), recorded by Perfect Strangers, all on Surface Records (pop); and "Sheryl Crow" (single) recorded by Dr. Jeff and the Painkillers. Other artists include Rosebud.

☐ TANGENT® RECORDS

P.O. Box 383, Reynoldsburg OH 43068-0383. (614)751-1962. Fax: (614)751-6414. E-mail: info@tangentrecords.com. Web site: www.tangentrecords.com. **Contact:** Andrew Batchelor, president. Director of Marketing: Elisa Batchelor. Record company and music publisher (ArcTangent Music/BMI). Estab. 1986. Staff size: 3. Releases 10-12 CDs/year. Pays negotiable royalty to artists on contract; statutory rate to publisher per song on record.

How to Contact Submit demo package by mail. Unsolicited submissions are OK. Prefers CD, with minimum of 3 songs and lead sheet if available. "Please include a brief biography/ history of artist(s) and/or band, including musical training/education, performance experience, recording studio experience, discography and photos (if available)." Does not return material. Responds if interested.

Music Mostly **artrock** and **contemporary instrumental/rock instrumental**; also **contemporary classical**, **world beat**, **jazz/rock**, **ambient**, **electronic**, and **New Age**.

Tips "Take the time to pull together a quality CD or cassette demo with package/portfolio, including such relevant information as experience (on stage and in studio, etc.), education/ training, biography, career goals, discography, photos, etc. Should be typed. We are not interested in generic sounding or 'straight ahead' music. We are seeking music that is innovative, pioneering and eclectic with a fresh, unique sound."

▧ ◙ TEXAS MUSIC CAFE

3801 Campus Dr., Waco TX 76705. (254)867-3372. E-mail: info@texasmusiccafe.com. Web site: www.texasmusiccafe.com. **Contact:** Paula Unger, booking. Labels include E-Cleff Records Inc. Television show. Estab. 1987. Staff size: 3. Releases 26 CDs/year. Pays negotiable royalty to artists on contract. *ORIGINAL MUSIC ONLY!*

Distributed by PBS, Hastings, Sony.

How to Contact Submit demo by mail. Unsolicited submissions are OK. Prefers CD, videocassette (VHS/DVD) with sample songs. Does not return material. Responds only if interested.

Music Released *Live At the Texas Music Cafe, Vol 1 and 2,* written and recorded by various (eclectic).

Tips "Must be willing to travel to Texas at your expense to be taped."

☑ TEXAS ROSE RECORDS

2002 Platinum St., Garland TX 75042. (972)272-3131. Fax: (972)272-3155. E-mail: txrr1@aol.com. Web site: www.texasroserecords.com. **Contact:** Nancy Baxendale, president. Record company, music publisher (Yellow Rose of Texas Publishing) and record producer (Nancy Baxendale). Estab. 1994. Staff size: 3. Releases 3 CDs/year. Pays negotiable royalty to artists on contract; statutory rate to publisher per song on record.

Distributed by Self distribution.

How to Contact *Call, write or e-mail first for permission to submit.* Submit maximum of 2 songs on CD and lyrics. Does not return material. Responds only if interested.

Music Mostly **country**, **soft rock** and **blues**; also **pop** and **gospel**. Does not want hip-hop, rap, heavy metal. Released *Flyin' High Over Texas* (album), recorded by Dusty Martin (country); *High On The Hog* (album), recorded by Steve Harr (country); *Time For Time to Pay* (album), recorded by Jeff Elliot (country); and *Pendulum Dream* (album), written and recorded by Maureen Kelly (alternative/americana), and "Cowboy Super Hero" (single) written and recorded by Robert Mauldin.

Tips "We are interested in songs written for today's market with a strong hook. Always use a good vocalist."

⊘ TOMMY BOY ENTERTAINMENT LLC

120 Fifth Avenue, 7th Floor, New York NY 10011. (212)388-8300. Fax: (212)388-8431. E-mail: info@tommyboy.com. Web site: www.tommyboy.com. Record company. Labels include Penalty Recordings, Outcaste Records, Timber and Tommy Boy Gospel.

Distributed by WEA.

How to Contact E-mail to obtain current demo submission policy.

Music Artists include Chavela Vargas, Afrika Bambaataa, Biz Markie, Kool Keith, and INXS.

☐ TON RECORDS

4474 Rosewood Ave., Los Angeles CA 90004. E-mail: tonmusic@earthlink.net. Web site: www.tonrecords.com or www.myspace.com/tonrecords. Vice President: Jay Vasquez. Labels include 7″ collectors series and Ton Special Projects. Record company and record producer (RJ Vasquez). Estab. 1992. Releases 6-9 LPs, 1-2 EPs and 10-11 CDs/year. Pays negotiable royalty to artists on contract; statutory rate to publisher per song on record.

Distributed by MS, Com Four, Rotz, Subterranean, Revelation, Get Hip, Impact, Page Canada and Disco Dial.

How to Contact Not signing at present time. Responds in 1 month.

Music Mostly **new music**; also **hard new music**. Released *Intoxicated Birthday Lies* (album), recorded by shoegazer (punk rock); *The Good Times R Killing Me* (album), recorded by Top Jimmy (blues); and *Beyond Repair* (album), recorded by Vasoline Tuner (space rock), all on Ton Records. Other artists include Why? Things Burn, Hungry 5, and the Ramblers.

Tips "Work as hard as we do."

TOPCAT RECORDS

P.O. Box 670234, Dallas TX 75367. (972)484-4141. Fax: (972)620-8333. E-mail: info@topcat records.com. Web site: www.topcatrecords.com or www.myspace.com/topcatrecords. President: Richard Chalk. Record company and record producer. Estab. 1991. Staff size: 3. Releases 4-6 CDs/year. Pays 10-15% royalty to artists on contract; statutory rate to publisher per song on record.

Distributed by City Hall.

How to Contact *Call first and obtain permission to submit.* Prefers CD. Does not return material. Responds in 1 month.

Music Mostly **blues**, **swing**, **rockabilly**, **Americana**, **Texana** and **R&B**. Released *If You Need Me* (album), written and recorded by Robert Ealey (blues); *Texas Blueswomen* (album by 3 Female Singers), recorded by various (blues/R&B); and *Jungle Jane* (album), written and recorded by Holland K. Smith (blues/swing), all on Topcat. Released CDs: *Jim Suhler & Alan Haynes—Live*; Bob Kirkpatrick *Drive Across Texas*; *Rock My Blues to Sleep* by Johnny Nicholas; *Walking Heart Attack*, by Holland K. Smith; *Dirt Road* (album), recorded by Jim Suhler; *Josh Alan Band* (album), recorded by Josh Alan; *Bust Out* (album), recorded by Robin Sylar. Other artists include Grant Cook, Muddy Waters, Big Mama Thornton, Big Joe Turner, Geo. "Harmonica" Smith, J.B. Hutto and Bee Houston. "View our Web site for an up-to-date listing of releases."

Tips "Send me blues (fast, slow, happy, sad, etc.) or good blues oriented R&B. No pop, hip-hop, or rap."

TRANSDREAMER RECORDS

P.O. Box 1955, New York NY 10113. (212)741-8861. Web site: www.transdreamer.com. **Contact:** Greg Caputo, marketing savant. President: Robert John. Record company. Estab. 2002. Staff size: 5. Released 4 CDs/year. Pays negotiable rate to artists on contract; 3/4 statutory rate to publisher per song on record.

 • Also see the listing for Megaforce in this section of the book.

Distributed by Red/Sony.

How to Contact *Contact first and obtain permission to submit.*

Music Mostly **alternative/rock**. Artists include The Delgados, Arab Strap, Dressy Bessy, Bill Richini, and Wellwater Conspiracy.

28 RECORDS

P.O. Box 88456, Los Angeles CA 90009-8456. E-mail: rec28@aol.com. Web site: www.28rec ords.com. **Contact:** Eric Diaz, president/CEO/A&R. Record company. Estab. 1994. Staff size: 1. Releases 2 LPs and 4 CDs/year. Pays 12% royalty to artists on contract; statutory rate to publisher per song on record.

Distributed by Rock Bottom-USA.

How to Contact *Contact first and obtain permission to submit.* Submit demo package by mail. Unsolicited submissions are OK. Prefers cassette, VHS videocassette or CD (if already released on own label for possible distribution or licensing deals). If possible send promo pack and photo. "Please put ATTN: A&R on packages." Does not return material. Responds in 6 weeks.

Music Mostly **hard rock/modern rock**, **metal** and **alternative**; also **punk** and **death metal**. Released *Julian Day* (album), recorded by Helltown's Infamous Vandal (modern/hard rock); *Fractured Fairy Tales* (album), written and recorded by Eric Knight (modern/hard rock); and *Mantra* (album), recorded by Derek Cintron (modern rock), all on 28 Records.

Tips "Be patient and ready for the long haul. We strongly believe in nurturing you, the artist/songwriter. If you're willing to do what it takes, and have what it takes, we will do whatever it takes to get you to the next level. We are looking for artists to develop. We are a very small label but we are giving the attention that is a must for a new band as well as developed and established acts. Give us a call."

Ⓝ ◯ UAR RECORDS (Universal-Athena Records)

Box 1264, 6020 W. Pottstown Rd., Peoria IL 61654-1264. (309)673-5755. Fax: (309)673-7636. E-mail: uarltd@A5.com. Web site: www.unitedcyber.com. Contact: Jerry Hanlon, A&R director. Record company and music publisher (Jerjoy Music/BMI and Katysarah Music/ASCAP). Estab. 1978. Staff size: 1. Releases 3 or more CDs/year.

• Also see the listings for Kaysarah Music (ASCAP) and Jerjoy Music (BMI) in the Music Publishers section of this book.

How to Contact "If you are an artist seeking a record deal, please send a sample of your vocal and/or songwriting work-guitar and vocal is fine, no more than 4 songs. Fully produced demos are NOT necessary. Also send brief information on your background in the business, your goals, etc. If you are NOT a songwriter, please send 4 songs maximum of cover tunes that we can use to evaluate your vocal ability. If you wish a reply, please send a SASE, otherwise, you will not receive an answer. If you want a critique of your vocal abilities, please so state as we do not routinely offer critiques. Unsolicited submissions are OK. If you wish all of your material returned to you, be sure to include mailing materials and postage. WE DO NOT RETURN PHONE CALLS."

Music Mostly **American** and **Irish country**. Released "The Calling Home," "I Thought That You'd Be Mine," "Streets of Keady Town," "Lisa Dance With Me," "Philomena From Ireland," "Rainbow," "I'd Better Stand Up"; all recorded by the Heggarty Twins from Northern Ireland and Jerry Hanlon.

Tips "We are a small independent company, but our belief is that every good voice deserves a chance to be heard and our door is always open to new and aspiring artists."

∅ UNIVERSAL RECORDS

1755 Broadway, 7th Floor, New York NY 10019. (212)841-8000. Fax: (212)331-2580. Web site: www.universalrecords.com. **Universal City office:** 70 Universal City Plaza, 3rd Floor, Universal City CA 91608. (818)777-1000. Vice Presidents A&R: Bruce Carbone, Tse Williams. Labels include Uptown Records, Mojo Records, Republic Records, Bystorm Records and Gut Reaction Records. Record company.

- Universal Records is a subsidiary of Universal Music Group, one of the "Big 4" major labels.

How to Contact *Universal Records in California does not accept unsolicited submissions. The New York office only allows you to call first and obtain permission to submit.*

Music Artists include India Arie, Erykah Bad, Godsmack, Kaiser Chiefs, and Lindsey Lohan.

☒ ☑ THE VERVE MUSIC GROUP

1755 Broadway, 3rd Floor, New York NY 10019. (212)331-2000. Fax: (212)331-2064. Web site: www.vervemusicgroup.com. A&R Director: Dahlia Ambach. A&R Coordinator: Heather Buchanan. **Los Angeles:** 100 N. First St., Burbank CA 91502. (818)729-4804 Fax: (818)845-2564. Vice President A&R: Bud Harner. A&R Assistant: Heather Buchanan. Record company. Labels include Verve, GRP, Blue Thumb and Impulse! Records.

- Verve Music Group is a subsidiary of Universal Music Group, one of the "Big 4" major labels.

How to Contact *The Verve Music Group does not accept unsolicited submissions.*

Music Artists include Roy Hargrove, Diana Krall, George Benson, Al Jarreau, John Scofield, Natalie Cole, and David Sanborn.

☑ VIRGIN RECORDS

1750 Vine St., Los Angeles CA 90028. (323)692-1100. Fax: (310)278-6231. Web site: www.virginrecords.com. **New York office:** 150 5th Ave., 3rd Floor, New York NY 10016. (212)786-8200 Fax:(212)786-8343. Labels include Rap-A-Lot Records, Pointblank Records, Soul-Power Records, AWOL Records, Astralwerks Records, Cheeba Sounds and Noo Trybe Records. Record company.

- Virgin Records is a subsidiary of the EMI Group, one of the "Big 4" major labels.

Distributed by EMD.

How to Contact *Virgin Records does not accept recorded material or lyrics unless submitted by a reputable industry source.* "If your act has received positive press or airplay on prior independent releases, we welcome your written query. Send a letter of introduction accompanied by all pertinent artist information. Do not send a tape until requested. All unsolicited materials will be returned unopened."

Music Mostly **rock** and **pop.** Artists include Lenny Kravitz, Placebo, The Rolling Stones, Joss Stone, Ben Harper, Iggy Pop, and Boz Scaggs.

☒ ☑ WARNER BROS. RECORDS

3300 Warner Blvd., 3rd Floor, Burbank CA 91505. (818)846-9090. Fax: (818)953-3423. Web site: www.wbr.com. **New York:** 75 Rockefeller Plaza, New York NY 10019. (212)275-4500 Fax: (212)275-4596. A&R: James Dowdall, Karl Rybacki. **Nashville:** 20 Music Square E., Nashville TN 37203. (615)748-8000 Fax:(615)214-1567. Labels include American Recordings, Eternal Records, Imago Records, Mute Records, Giant Records, Malpaso Records and Maverick Records. Record company.

• Warner Bros. Records is a subsidiary of Warner Music Group, one of the "Big 4" major labels.

Distributed by WEA.

How to Contact *Warner Bros. Records does not accept unsolicited material.* "All unsolicited material will be returned unopened. Those interested in having their tapes heard should establish a relationship with a manager, publisher or attorney that has an ongoing relationship with Warner Bros. Records."

Music Released *Van Halen 3* (album), recorded by Van Halen; *Evita* (soundtrack); and *Dizzy Up the Girl* (album), recorded by Goo Goo Dolls, both on Warner Bros. Records. Other artists include Faith Hill, Tom Petty & the Heartbreakers, Jeff Foxworthy, Porno For Pyros, Travis Tritt, Yellowjackets, Bela Fleck and the Flecktones, Al Jarreau, Joshua Redmond, Little Texas, and Curtis Mayfield.

☑ WATERDOG MUSIC

(a.k.a. Waterdog Records), 329 W. 18th St., #313, Chicago IL 60616-1120. (312)421-7499. Fax: (312)421-1848. E-mail: waterdog@waterdogmusic.com. Web site: www.waterdogmusic.com. **Contact:** Rob Gillis, label manager. Labels include Whitehouse Records. Record company. Estab. 1991. Staff size: 2. Releases 2 CDs/year. Pays negotiable royalty to artists on contract; statutory rate to publisher per song on record.

Distributed by Big Daddy Music.

How to Contact "Not accepting unsolicited materials, demos at this time. If submission policy changes, it will be posted onour Web site."

Music Mostly **rock** and **pop**. Released *Good Examples of Bad Examples: The Best of Ralph Covert & The Bad Examples, Vol. 2* (album), released 2005. Other artists have included Middle 8, Al Rose & The Transcendos, Kat Parsons, Torben Floor (Carey Ott), Mystery-Driver, Joel Frankel, Dean Goldstein & Coin, and Matt Tiegler.

Tips "Ralph Covert's children's music (Ralph's World) is released in Disney Sound. We are not looking for any other children's music performers or composers."

Ⓝ ☑ WINCHESTER RECORDS

25 Troubadour Lane, Berkeley Springs WV 25411. (304)258-8314. E-mail: mccoytroubadour @aol.com. Web site: www.troubadourlounge.com. **Contact:** Jim or Bertha McCoy, owners. Labels include Master Records and Real McCoy Records. Record company, music publisher (Jim McCoy Music, Clear Music, New Edition Music/BMI), record producer (Jim McCoy Productions) and recording studio. Releases 20 singles and 10 LPs/year. Pays standard royalty to artists; statutory rate to publisher for each record sold.

How to Contact *Write first and obtain permission to submit.* Prefers CD with 5-10 songs and lead sheet. Include SASE. Responds in 1 month.

Music Mostly **bluegrass**, **church/religious**, **country**, **folk**, **gospel**, **progressive** and **rock**. Released "Runaway Girl" (single by Earl Howard/Jim McCoy) from *Earl Howard Sings His Heart Out* (album), recorded by Earl Howard (country), released 2002 on Winchester; *Jim McCoy and Friends Remember Ernest Tubb* (album), recorded by Jim McCoy (country), released January 2003 on Winchester; *The Best of Winchester Records* (album), recorded by RileeGray/J.B. Miller/Jim McCoy/Carroll County (country), released 2002 on Winchester.

⊘ WIND-UP ENTERTAINMENT

79 Madison Ave., 7th Floor, New York NY 10016. (212)895-3100. Web site: www.windupre cords.com. **Contact:** A&R. Record company. Estab. 1997. Releases 6-7 CDs/year. Pays negotiable royalty to artists on contract; statutory rate to publisher per song on record.
Distributed by BMG.
How to Contact *Write first and obtain permission to submit.* Prefers CD or DVD. Does not return material or respond to submissions.
Music Mostly **rock**, **folk** and **hard rock**. Artists include Seether, Evanescence, Finger Eleven, and People In Planes.
Tips ''We rarely look for songwriters as opposed to bands, so writing a big hit single would be the rule of the day.''

⊘ XEMU RECORDS

845 Third Avenue 6th Floor, New York NY 10022. (212)807-0290. Fax: (212)807-0583. E-mail: xemu@xemu.com. Web site: www.xemu.com. **Contact:** Dr. Claw, vice president A&R. Record company. Estab. 1992. Staff size: 4. Releases 4 CDs/year. Pays negotiable royalty to artists on contract; statutory rate to publisher per song on record.
Distributed by Redeye Distribution.
How to Contact *Write first and obtain permission to submit.* Prefers CD with 3 songs. Does not return material. Responds in 2 months.
Music Mostly **alternative**. Released *Happy Suicide, Jim!* (album) by The Love Kills Theory (alternative rock); *Howls From The Hills* (album) by Dead Meadow; *The Fall* (album), recorded by Mikki James (alternative rock); *A is for Alpha* (album), recorded by Alpha Bitch (alternative rock); *Hold the Mayo* (album), recorded by Death Sandwich (alternative rock); *Stockholm Syndrome* (album), recorded by Trigger Happy (alternative rock) all released on Xemu Records. Other artists include Malvert P. Redd, The Fifth Dementia, and the Neanderthal Spongecake.

Record Companies

ADDITIONAL RECORD COMPANIES

The following companies are also record companies, but their listings are found in other sections of the book. Read the listings for submission information.

Record Producers

The independent producer can best be described as a creative coordinator. He's often the one with the most creative control over a recording project and is ultimately responsible for the finished product. Some record companies have in-house producers who work with the acts on that label (although, in more recent years, such producer-label relationships are often non-exclusive). Today, most record companies contract out-of-house, independent record producers on a project-by-project basis.

WHAT RECORD PRODUCERS DO

Producers play a large role in deciding what songs will be recorded for a particular project and are always on the lookout for new songs for their clients. They can be valuable contacts for songwriters because they work so closely with the artists whose records they produce. They usually have a lot more freedom than others in executive positions and are known for having a good ear for potential hit songs. Many producers are songwriters and musicians themselves. Since they wield a great deal of influence, a good song in the hands of the right producer at the right time stands a good chance of being cut. And even if a producer is not working on a specific project, he is well-acquainted with record company executives and artists and can often get material through doors not open to you.

SUBMITTING MATERIAL TO PRODUCERS

It can be difficult to get your tapes to the right producer at the right time. Many producers write their own songs and even if they don't write, they may be involved in their own publishing companies so they have instant access to all the songs in their catalogs. Also, some genres are more dependent on finding outside songs than others. A producer working with a rock group or a singer-songwriter will rarely take outside songs.

It's important to understand the intricacies of the producer/publisher situation. If you pitch your song directly to a producer first, before another publishing company publishes the song, the producer may ask you for the publishing rights (or a percentage thereof) to your song. You must decide whether the producer is really an active publisher who will try to get the song recorded again and again or whether he merely wants the publishing because it means extra income for him from the current recording project. You may be able to work out a co-publishing deal, where you and the producer split the publishing of the song. That means he will still receive his percentage of the publishing income, even if you secure a cover recording of the song by other artists in the future. Even though you would be giving up a little bit initially, you may benefit in the future.

Some producers will offer to sign artists and songwriters to "development deals." These can range from a situation where a producer auditions singers and musicians with the intention of building a group from the ground up, to development deals where a producer signs a band or singer-songwriter to his production company with the intention of developing the act and producing an album to shop to labels (sometimes referred to as a "baby record deal").

You must carefully consider whether such a deal is right for you. In some cases, such a deal can open doors and propel an act to the next level. In other worst-case scenarios, such a deal can result in loss of artistic and career control, with some acts held in contractual bondage for years at a time. Before you consider any such deal, be clear about your goals, the producer's reputation, and the sort of compromises you are willing to make to reach those goals. If you have any reservations whatsoever, don't do it.

The listings that follow outline which aspects of the music industry each producer is involved in, what type of music he is looking for, and what records and artists he's recently produced. Study the listings carefully, noting the artists each producer works with, and consider if any of your songs might fit a particular artist's or producer's style. Then determine whether they are open to your level of experience (see the A Sample Listing Decoded on page 8).

Consult the Category Index on page 359 to find producers who work with the type of music you write, and the Geographic Index at the back of the book to locate producers in your area.

Icons

For More Info

For more instructional information on the listings in this book, including explanations of symbols ( ), read the article *How To Use Songwriter's Market* on page 2.

ADDITIONAL RECORD PRODUCERS

There are **more record producers** located in other sections of the book! On page 201 use the list of Additional Record Producers to find listings within other sections who are also record producers.

⚡ ◐ "A" MAJOR SOUND CORPORATION

RR #1, Kensington PE COB 1MO Canada. (902)836-4571. E-mail: info@amajorsound.com. Web site: www.amajorsound.com. **Contact:** Paul C. Milner, producer. Record producer and music publisher. Estab. 1989. Produces 8 CDs/year. Fee derived in part from sales royalty when song or artist is recorded, and/or outright fee from recording artist or record company, or investors.

How to Contact Submit demo package by mail. Unsolicited submissions are OK. Prefers CD with 5 songs and lyric sheet (lead sheet if available). Does not return material. Responds only if interested in 3 months.

Music Mostly **rock, A/C, alternative** and **pop**; also **Christian** and **R&B**. Produced *COLOUR* (album written by J. MacPhee/R. MacPhee/C. Buchanan/D. MacDonald), recorded by The Chucky Danger Band (pop/rock), released 2006; Winner of ECMA award; *Something In Between* (album, written by Matt Andersen), recorded by Matt Andersen and Friends (Blues), released 2008 on Weatherbox/Andersen; *In A Fever In A Dream* (album, written by Pat Deighan), recorded by Pat Deighan and The Orb Weavers (Rock), released in 2008 on Sandbar Music; *Saddle River String Band* (album, written by Saddle River Stringband), recorded by Saddle River Stringband (Blue Grass) released 2007 on Save As Music; Winner of ECMA award.

◐ ACR PRODUCTIONS

P.O. Box 5636, Midland TX 79704. (432)687-2702. E-mail: dwainethomas@sbcglobal.net. **Contact:** Dwaine Thomas, owner. Record producer, music publisher (Joranda Music/BMI) and record company (ACR Records). Estab. 1986. Produces 120 singles, 8-15 12″ singles, 25 LPs, 25 EPs and 25 CDs/year. Fee derived from sales royalty when song or artist is recorded. "We charge for in-house recording only. Remainder is derived from royalties."

How to Contact Submit demo package by mail. Unsolicited submissions are OK. Prefers CD/DVD with 5 songs and lyric sheet. Does not return material. Responds in 6 weeks if interested.

Music Mostly **country swing**, **pop**, and **rock**; also **R&B** and **gospel**. Produced *Bottle's Almost Gone* (album) and "Black Gold" (single), written and recorded by Mike Nelson (country), both released 1999 on ACR Records; and *Nashville Series* (album), written and recorded by various (country), released 1998 on ProJam Music.

Tips "Be professional. No living room tapes!"

◐ ADR STUDIOS

(formerly Stuart J. Allyn), 250 Taxter Rd., Irvington NY 10533. (914)591-5616. Fax: (914)591-5617. E-mail: jackd@adrinc.org. Web site: www.adrinc.org. Associate: Jack Walker. **Contact:** Jack Davis, general manager. President: Stuart J. Allyn. Record producer. Estab. 1972. Produces 6 singles and 3-6 CDs/year. Fee derived from sales royalty and outright fee from recording artist and record company.

How to Contact *Does not accept unsolicited submissions.*

Music Mostly **pop**, **rock**, **jazz**, and **theatrical**; also **R&B** and **country**. Produced *Thad Jones*

Legacy (album), recorded by Vanquard Jazz Orchestra (jazz), released 2000 on New World Records. Other artists include Billy Joel, Aerosmith, Carole Demas, Michael Garin, The Magic Garden, Bob Stewart, The Dixie Peppers, Nora York, Buddy Barnes and various video and film scores.

◙ AUDIO 911

(formerly Steve Wytas Productions), P.O. Box 212, Haddam CT 06438. (860)916-9947. E-mail: contact@audio911.com. Web site: www.audio911.com. **Contact:** Steven J. Wytas. Record producer. Estab. 1984. Produces 4-8 singles, 3 LPs, 3 EPs and 4 CDs/year. Fee derived from outright fee from recording artist or record company.

How to Contact Submit demo by mail. Unsolicited submissions are OK. Prefers CD or VHS videocassette with several songs and lyric or lead sheet. "Include live material if possible." Does not return material. Responds in 3 months.

Music Mostly **rock**, **pop**, **top 40** and **country/acoustic**. Produced *Already Home* (album), recorded by Hannah Cranna on Big Deal Records (rock); *Under the Rose* (album), recorded by Under the Rose on Utter Records (rock); and *Sickness & Health* (album), recorded by Legs Akimbo on Joyful Noise Records (rock). Other artists include King Hop!, The Shells, The Gravel Pit, G'nu Fuz, Tuesday Welders and Toxic Field Mice.

❏ BLUES ALLEY RECORDS

Rt. 1, Box 288, Clarksburg WV 26301. (304)598-2583. E-mail: info@bluesalleymusic.com. Web site: www.bluesalleymusic.com. **Contact:** Joshua Swiger, producer. Record producer, record company and music publisher (Blues Alley Publishing/BMI). New Christian record label (Joshua Tree Records/BMI). Produces 4-6 LPs and 2 EPs/year. Fee derived from sales royalty when song or artist is recorded.

How to Contact Submit demo package by mail. Unsolicited submissions are OK. Prefers CD with 4 songs and lyric and lead sheets. Does not return material. Responds in 6 weeks.

Music Mostly **Christian**, **alternative** and **pop**. Produced *Songs Your Radio Wants to Hear* (album), recorded by The New Relics (acoustic rock), released 2006; *Sons of Sirens* (album), recorded by Amity (rock), released 2004; and *It's No Secret* (album), recorded by Samantha Caley (pop country), released 2004, all on Blues Alley Records.

◖ CACOPHONY PRODUCTIONS

2400 Vasanta Way, Los Angeles CA 90068. (917)856-8532. Producer: Steven Miller. Record producer and music publisher (In Your Face Music). Estab. 1981. Fee derived from sales royalty when song or artist is recorded, or outright fee from recording artist or record company.

How to Contact *Call first and obtain permission to submit.* Prefers 3 songs and lyric sheet. "Send a cover letter of no more than three paragraphs giving some background on yourself and the music. Also explain specifically what you are looking for Cacophony Productions to do." Does not return material. Responds only if interested.

Music Mostly **progressive pop/rock**, **singer/songwriter** and **progressive country**. Produced Dar Williams, Suzanne Vega, John Gorka, Michael Hedges, Juliana Hatfield, Toad the Wet Sprocket, and Medeski-Martin & Wood.

Ⓝ Ⓩ CANDYSPITEFUL PRODUCTIONS

4204 County Rt 4, Oswego NY 13126. E-mail: mandrakerocks@yahoo.com. Web site: www. myspace.com/candyspiteful. **Contact:** William Ferraro, president. Record producer, record company (Candyspiteful Productions), music publisher (Candyspiteful Productions). Estab. 2000. Produces 30 singles, 12 albums per year. Fee derived from outright fee from recording artist.

- Also see the listings for Candyspiteful Productions in the Record Companies section of this book.

How to Contact Submit demo package by mail. Unsolicited submissions are OK. Prefers CD with 3 songs and lyric sheet and cover letter. Does not return material. Responds only if interested.

Music Mostly **hard rock**, **radio-friendly rock** and **hip-hop**. Produced 8 full-length albums in 2008.

Ⓝ ◻ JAN CELT MUSICAL SERVICES

4015 NE 12th Ave., Portland OR 97212. E-mail: flyheart@teleport.com. Web site: http:// home.teleport.com/ ~ flyheart. **Contact:** Jan Celt, owner. Record producer, music producer and publisher (Wiosna Nasza Music/BMI) and record company (Flying Heart Records). Estab. 1982. Produces 3-5 CDs/year.

- Also see the listing for Flying Heart Records in the Record Companies section of this book.

How to Contact Submit demo tape by mail. Unsolicited submissions are OK. Prefers high-quality cassette with 1-10 songs and lyric sheet. "SASE required for any response." Does not return materials. Responds in 4 months.

Music Mostly **R&B**, **rock** and **blues**; also **jazz**. Produced "Vexatious Progressions" (single), written and recorded by Eddie Harris (jazz); "Bong Hit" (single by Chris Newman), re-corded by Snow Bud & the Flower People (rock); and "She Moved Away" (single by Chris Newman), recorded by Napalm Beach, all on Flying Heart Records. Other artists include The Esquires and Janice Scroggins.

Ⓝ Ⓩ CREATIVE SOUL

Nashville TN 37179. (859)492-6403. Web site: www.creativesoulonline.com. **Contact:** Eric Copeland, producer/writer. Record producer. Produces 5-10 singles and 8-15 albums/year. Fee derived from outright fee from recording artist or company. Other services include consulting/critique/review services.

How to Contact *Contact first by e-mail to obtain permission to submit demo.* Prefers CD with 2-3 songs and lyric sheet and cover sheet. Does not return submissions. Responds only if interested.

Music Mostly **contemporary Christian**, **jazz**, and **instrumental**; also **R&B** and **pop/rock**. Does not want country, metal, punk, or hardcore. Produced *The Heavy and the Holy* (al-bum), recorded by Kristyn Leigh (Contemporary Christian); *I Can Live Again* (album), recorded by Gregory Paul Smith (Contemporary Christian); *Inside Things* (album), recorded by Frances Drost (Contemporary Christian), all released on Creative Soul Records. Other artists include Brett Rush, Stephanie Newton, and Tom Dolan.

Tips "Contact us first by e-mail, but please do not send MP3s without e-mailing first. We will delete any unsolicited MP3s without listening. E-mail us and let's start talking about your music and ministry!"

☑ JERRY CUPIT PRODUCTIONS

Box 121904, Nashville TN 37212. (615)731-0100. Fax: (615)731-3005. E-mail: dan@cupitm usic.com. Web site: www.cupitrecords.com. **Contact:** Elizabeth Howe, creative assistant. Record producer and music publisher (Cupit Music). Estab. 1984. Fee derived from sales royalty when song or artist is recorded or outright fee from artist.

• Also see the listing for Cupit Music Group in the Music Publishers section of this book.

How to Contact *Visit Web site for policy.* Prefers CD with bio and photo. Include SASE. Responds in 2 months.

Music Mostly **traditional and contemporary uptempo country, Southern rock, bluegrass,** and **gospel**. Produced "Make A wish" (single) from *Kevin Sharp* (album), recorded by Kevin Sharp (country), released 2007 on Cupit Records; "Working for the Weekend" (single) from *Ken Mellons* (album), recorded by Ken Mellons, released 1994 on Sony. Other artists include Michelle Cupit, Ben Gregg, Mustang Creek, Jerry Burkhart, and Bobby Seals.

Tips "Be prepared to work hard and be able to take constructive/professional criticism."

☒ DAVINCI'S NOTEBOOK RECORDS

10070 Willoughby Dr., Niagara Falls ON L2E 6S6 Canada. E-mail: admin@davincismusic.c om. Web site: www.davincismusic.com. Owner: Kevin Richard. Record producer, record company, music publisher, distributor and recording studio (The Sound Kitchen). Estab. 1992. Produces 1 CD/year. Fee derived from outright fee from artist or commission on sales. "Distribution is on consignment basis. Artist is responsible for all shipping, taxes, and import/export duties."

How to Contact *"E-mail first for postal details then submit demo CD by mail."* Unsolicited submissions are OK. Prefers CD and bio. Does not return material. Responds in 6 weeks.

Music Mostly **rock, instrumental rock**, **New Age** and **progressive-alternative**; also **R&B, pop** and **jazz**. Produced *Windows* (album by Kevin Hotte/Andy Smith), recorded by Musicom on DaVinci's Notebook Records (power New Age); *Inventing Fire, Illumination, A Different Drum* (albums) written and recorded by Kevin Richard on DNR/Independent (instrumental rock); and *The Cunninghams* (album), written and recorded by The Cunninghams on Independent (gospel).

Tips "DNR is an artist-run label. Local bands and performers will receive priority. You should be more interested in getting a-foot-in-the-door exposure as opposed to making a fortune. Be satisfied with conquering the world using 'baby steps.' Indie labels don't have large corporate budgets for artist development. For non-local artists, we are more about online distribution than artist development. Being a local act means that you can perform live to promote your releases. For indie artist, selling from the stage is probably going to bring you the biggest volume of sales."

☒ ⊘ THE EDWARD DE MILES MUSIC COMPANY

10573 W. Pico Blvd., #352, Los Angeles CA 90064-2348. (310)948-9652. Fax: (310)474-7705. E-mail: info@edmsahara.com. Web site: www.edmsahara.com. **Contact:** Edward De Miles, president. Record producer, music publisher (Edward De Miles Music Co./BMI) and record company (Sahara Records and Filmworks Entertainment). Estab. 1981. Produces 5-10 CDs/year. Fee derived from sales royalty when song or artist is recorded.

   • Also see the listing for Edward De Miles in the Music Publishers and Managers & Booking Agents sections, as well as Sahara Records and Filmworks Entertainment in the Record Companies section of this book.

How to Contact Does not accept unsolicited submissions.

Music Mostly **R&B/dance**, **top 40 pop/rock** and **contemporary jazz**; also **country**, **TV and film themes—songs and jingles**. **Produced** "Moments" and "Dance Wit Me" (singles) (dance), both written and recorded by Steve Lynn; and "Games" (single), written and recorded by D'von Edwards (jazz), all on Sahara Records. Other artists include Multiple Choice.

Tips "Copyright all material before submitting. Equipment and showmanship a must."

⊕ ⊘ DEMI MONDE RECORDS & PUBLISHING LTD.

Foel Studio, Llanfair Caereinion, Powys, Wales SY21 ODS United Kingdom. Phone/Fax: (440)(193)881-0758. E-mail: foel.studio@dial.pipex.com. Web site: www.demimonde.co.uk. **Contact:** Dave Anderson, managing director. Record producer, music publisher (PRS & MCPS) and record company (Demi Monde Records). Estab. 1982. Produces 5 singles, 15 12″ singles, 15 LPs and 10 CDs/year. Fee derived from sales royalty or outright fee from record company.

   • Also see the listings for Demi Monde records & Publishing in the Music Publishing and Record Companies sections of this book.

How to Contact Submit demo tape by mail. Unsolicited submissions are OK. Prefers cassette with 3 or 4 songs and lyric sheet. Does not return material. Responds in 6 weeks.

Music Mostly **rock**, **pop** and **blues**. Produced *Average Man*, recorded by Mother Gong (rock); *Frozen Ones*, recorded by Tangle Edge (rock); and *Blue Boar Blues* (by T.S. McPhee), recorded by Groundhogs (rock), all on Demi Monde Records. Other artists include Gong and Hawkwind.

⊘ JOEL DIAMOND ENTERTAINMENT

Dept. SM, 3940 Laurel Canyon Blvd., Suite 441, Studio City CA 91604. (818)980-9588. Fax: (818)980-9422. E-mail: jdiamond20@aol.com. Web site: www.joeldiamond.com. **Contact:** Joel Diamond. Record producer, music publisher and manager. Fee derived from sales royalty when song is recorded or outright fee from recording artist or record company.

   • Also see the listing for Silver Blue Music/Oceans Blue Music in the Music Publishers section of this book.

How to Contact Does not return material. Responds only if interested.

Music Mostly **dance**, **R&B**, **soul** and **top 40/pop**. The 5 Browns—3 number 1 CDs for Sony/BMG, David Hasselhoff; produced "One Night In Bangkok" (single by Robey); "I Think I

Love You," recorded by Katie Cassidy (daughter of David Cassidy) on Artemis Records; "After the Loving" (single), recorded by E. Humperdinck; "Forever Friends," recorded by Vaneza (featured on Nickelodeon's *The Brothers Garcia*); and "Paradise" (single), recorded by Kaci.

◙ FINAL MIX INC.
(formerly Final Mix Music), 2219 W. Olive Ave., Suite 102, Burbank CA 91506. (818)970-8717. E-mail: finalmix@aol.com. **Contact:** Theresa Frank, A&R. Record producer/remixer/mix engineer, independent label (3.6 Music, Inc.) and music publisher (Ximlanif Music Publishing). Estab. 1989. Releases 12 singles and 3-5 LPs and CDs/year. Fee derived from sales royalty when song or artist is recorded.
How to Contact *Does not accept unsolicited submissions.*
Music Mostly **pop**, **rock**, **dance**, **R&B** and **rap**. Produced Hilary Duff, Jesse McCartney, Christina Aguilera, American Idol, Rach Charles, Quincy Jones, Michael Bolton, K-Ci and Jo Jo (of Jodeci), Will Smith, and/or mixer/remixer for Janet Jackson, Ice Cube, Queen Latifah, Jennifer Paige, and The Corrs.

🅽 ◙ HAILING FREQUENCY MUSIC PRODUCTIONS
7438 Shoshone Ave., Van Nuys CA 91406. (818)881-9888. Fax: (818)881-0555. E-mail: blowinsmokeband@ktb.net. Web site: www.blowinsmokeband.com. President: Lawrence Weisberg. Vice President: Larry Knight. Record producer, record company (Blowin' Smoke Records), management firm (Blowin' Smoke Productions) and music publisher (Hailing Frequency Publishing). Estab. 1992. Produces 3 LPs and 3 CDs/year. Fee derived from sales royalty when song or artist is recorded or outright fee from artist.
  • Also see the listing for Blowin' Smoke Productions/Records in the Managers & Booking Agents section of this book.
How to Contact *Write or call first and obtain permission to submit.* Prefers cassette or VHS ½" videocassette. "Write or print legibly with complete contact instructions." Include SASE. Responds in 1 month.
Music Mostly **contemporary R&B**, **blues** and **blues-rock**; also **songs for film**, **jingles for commercials** and **gospel (contemporary)**. Produced "Beyond the Blues Horizon" (single), recorded by Blowin' Smoke Rhythm & Blues Band, released 2004. Other artists include the Fabulous Smokettes. New division creates songs and music tracks for both the mainstream and adult film industries.

◙ HEART CONSORT MUSIC
410 First St. SW., Mt. Vernon IA 52314. E-mail: mail@heartconsortmusic.com. Web site: www.heartconsortmusic.com. **Contact:** Catherine Lawson, manager. Record producer, record company and music publisher. Estab. 1980. Produces 2-3 CDs/year. Fee derived from sales royalty when song or artist is recorded.
How to Contact Submit demo package by mail. Unsolicited submissions are OK. Prefers CD or cassette with 3 songs and 3 lyric sheets. Include SASE. Responds in 3 months.
Music Mostly **jazz**, **New Age** and **contemporary**. Produced *New Faces* (album), written and recorded by James Kennedy on Heart Consort Music (world/jazz).

Tips "We are interested in jazz/New Age artists with quality demos and original ideas. We aim for an international audience."

N ⊘ HESFREE PRODUCTIONS & PUBLISHING COMPANY

P.O. Box 1214, Bryan TX 77806-1214. (979)268-3263. Fax: (979)589-2544. E-mail: hesfreepr odandpubco@yahoo.com. Web site: www.hesfreeproductions.com. President/CEO/ Owner: Brenda M. Freeman-Heslip. Producer of songwriting: Jamie Heslip. Record producer, music publisher and management agency. Estab. 2001. Fee derived from sales royalty when song or artist is recorded, outright fee from recording artist and outright fee from record company.

How to Submit *Only accepts material referred to by a reputable industry source (manager, entertainment attorney, etc.).* Include CD/CDR. Does not return submissions. Responds in 6 weeks only if interested.

Music Gospel only. No other music will be accepted. "We will ensure that each project is complete with professionalism, with the highest technological strategies possible."

N ◻ HUMAN FACTOR PRODUCTIONS

P.O. Box 3742, Washington DC 20027. (202)415-7748. E-mail: info@hfproductions.com. Web site: www.hfproductions.com. **Contact:** Blake Althen or Paula Bellenoit, producers/ owners. Estab. 2001. Record producer. "Human Factor Productions is a full service music production team offering a range of music production services, including composition, arranging, recording, remixing, and more. Human Factor runs the Free Ride Music Contest Annually."

How to Contact *Please call or e-mail to get permission to submit.* Original material only.

Music Mostly **adult contemporary**, **pop**, **singer/songwriter**, **rock (all types)**, **world/ethnic**, **techno/electronica**, **rap** and **soundtrack/film score**. Produced dance remixes of "No Bomb Is Smart" (single), written and recorded by SONiA of disappear fear (contemporary folk); "Fall Down," and "Without Light" (by S. Bitz), recorded by Abby Someone (heartland rock). Other artists include Jennifer Cutting's Ocean Orchestra (contemporary folk rock, celtic), Rachel Panay (dance), Pale Beneath the Blue (adult contemporary/singer/ songwriter), Paul Kawabori (classical crossover), and Michelangelo (adult contemporary), and more.

Tip "Keep your goals clear in your mind and on paper. What do you want a producer to do for you? Know the answer to this question, and it will guide you to the industry professionals who are right for you. And really work hard on your live show. The best-produced recording in the world will not be worth what you paid for it if no one wants to come to your shows and buy it."

⊘ INTEGRATED ENTERTAINMENT

1815 JFK Blvd., #1612, Philadelphia PA 19103. (215)563-7147. E-mail: gelboni@aol.com. **Contact:** Gelboni, president. Record producer. Estab. 1991. Produces 6 EPs and 6 CDs/ year. Fee derived from sales royalty when song or artist is recorded or outright fee from recording artist or record company.

How to Contact Submit demo package by mail. Solicited submissions only. CD only with 3 songs. "Draw a guitar on the outside of envelope so we'll know it's from a songwriter." Will respond if interested.

Music Mostly **rock** and **pop**. Produced *Gold Record* (album), written and recorded by Dash Rip Rock (rock) on Ichiban Records and many others.

🅽 ⊞ ⬭ JUMP PRODUCTIONS

31 Paul Gilsonstraat, 8200 St-Andries Belgium. (050)31-63-80. E-mail: happymelody@skyn et.be. **Contact:** Eddy Van Mouffaert, general manager. Record producer and music publisher (Jump Music). Estab. 1976. Produces 25 singles and 2 CDs/year. Fee derived from sales royalty when song or artist is recorded.

- Also see the listing for Happy Melody in the Music Publishers section of this book.

How to Contact Submit demo CD or tape by mail. Unsolicited submissions are OK. Prefers CD. Does not return material. Responds in 2 weeks.

Music Mostly **ballads**, **up-tempo**, **easy listening**, **disco** and **light pop**; also **instrumentals**. Produced "De Club Is Kampioen" (single by H. Spider/E. Govert), recorded by Benny Scott (light pop), released 2005 on Scorpion; *A Christmas of Hope* (album), recorded by Chris Clark (pop), released 2004 on 5 Stars; and *The Best of Le Grand Julot* (album), recorded by Le Grand Julot (accordion), released 2000 on Happy Melody.

⊞ ⬭ JUNE PRODUCTIONS LTD.

The White House, 6 Beechwood Lane, Warlingham, Surrey CR6 9LT England. Phone: 44(0) 1883 622411 Fax: 44(0)1883 652457. E-mail: david@mackay99.plus.com. **Contact:** David Mackay, producer. Record producer and music producer (Sabre Music). Estab. 1970. Produces singles, CDs, and live stage show recordings. Fee derived from sales royalty.

How to Contact Submit demo CD or MP3 by mail. Unsolicited submissions are OK. Prefers CD or cassette with 1-2 songs and lyric sheet. SAE and IRC. Responds in 2 months.

Music Mostly **MOR**, **rock** and **top 40/pop**. Produced *Web of Love* (by various), recorded by Sarah Jory on Ritz Records (country rock). Other artists include Bonnie Tyler, Cliff Richard, Frankie Miller, Johnny Hallyday, Dusty Springfield, Charlotte Henry and Barry Humphries.

Tips "I am currently producing the music for a proposed musical in America. I am happy to review songs, but on the understanding that I am only producing occasionally because of theatre commitments."

⬭ KAREN KANE PRODUCER/ENGINEER

(910)681-0220. E-mail: mixmama@total.net. Web site: www.mixmama.com. **Contact:** Karen Kane, producer/engineer. Record producer and recording engineer. Estab. 1978. Produces 3-5 CDs/year. Fee derived from sales royalty when song or artist is recorded or outright fee from recording artist or record company.

How to Contact *E-mail first and obtain permission to submit. Unsolicited submissions are not OK.* "Please note: I am not a song publisher. My expertise is in album production." Does not return material. Responds in 1 week.

Music Mostly **acoustic music of any kind**, **rock**, **blues**, **pop**, **alternative**, **R&B/reggae**, **country**, and **bluegrass**. Produced *Independence Meal* (album), recorded by Alix Olson (blues), released on Subtle Sister Records; Topless (Juno-nominated album), recorded by Big Daddy G, released on Reggie's Records; *Mixed Wise and Otherwise* (Juno-nominated album), recorded by Harry Manx (blues). Other artists include Tracy Chapman (her first demo), Chad Mitchell, Ember Swift, Laura Bird, Wishing Chair, Blue Mule, Barenaked Ladies (live recording for a TV special), and Ron Wiseman.

Tips "Get proper funding to be able to make a competitive, marketable product."

☐ L.A. ENTERTAINMENT, INC.

7095 Hollywood Blvd., #826, Hollywood CA 90028. 1-800-579-9157. Fax: (323)924-1095. E-mail: info@warriorrecords.com. Web site: www.WarriorRecords.com. **Contact:** Jim Ervin, A&R. Record producer, record company (Warrior Records) and music publisher (New Entity Music/ASCAP, New Copyright Music/BMI, New Euphonic Music/SESAC). Estab. 1988. Fee derived from sales royalty when song or artist is recorded.

How to Contact Submit demo package by mail. Unsolicited submissions are OK. Prefers CD and/or videocassette with original songs, lyric and lead sheet if available. "We do not review Internet sites. Do not send MP3s, unless requested. All written submitted materials (e.g., lyric sheets, letter, etc.) should be typed." Does not return material unless SASE is included. Responds in 2 months only via e-mail or SASE.

Music All styles. "All genres are utilized with our music supervision company for Film & TV, but our original focus is on **alternative rock** and **urban genres** (e.g., **R&B**, **rap**, **gospel**).

⚞N⚟ ☐ LANDMARK COMMUNICATIONS GROUP

P.O. Box 1444, Hendersonville TN 37077. E-mail: lmarkcom@bellsouth.net. **Contact:** Bill Anderson Jr., producer. Record producer, record company, music publisher (Newcreature Music/BMI) and TV/radio syndication. Produces 6 singles and 6 LPs/year. Fee derived from sales royalty.

- Also see the listings for Landmark Communications Group in the Record Companies section of this book.

How to Contact *Write first and obtain permission to submit.* Prefers CD, MP3 with 4-10 songs and lyric sheet. Include SASE.

Music Positive message and **country crossover**. Recent projects: *Smoky Mountain Campmeeting* by Various Artists; *The Pilgrim & the Road* by Tiffany Turner; *Fallow Ground* by C.J. Hall; *Prince Charming is Dead* by Kecia Burcham.

☐ LARK TALENT & ADVERTISING

P.O. Box 35726, Tulsa OK 74153. (918)786-8896. Fax: (918)786-8897. E-mail: janajae@janajae.com. Web site: www.janajae.com. **Contact:** Kathleen Pixley, vice president. Owner: Jana Jae. Record producer, music publisher (Jana Jae Music/BMI) and record company (Lark Record Productions, Inc.). Estab. 1980. Fee derived from sales royalty when song or artist is recorded.

- Also see the listings for Jana Jae Music in the Music Publishers section, Lark Record

Productions in the Record Companies section, and Jana Jae Enterprises in the Managers & Booking Agents section of this book.

How to Contact Submit demo by mail. Unsolicited submissions are OK. Prefers CD or VHS videocassette with 3 songs and lead sheet. Does not return material. Responds in 1 month only if interested.

Music Mostly **country**, **bluegrass** and **classical**; also **instrumentals**. Produced "Bussin' Ditty" (single by Steve Upfold); "Mayonnaise" (single by Steve Upfold); and "Flyin' South" (single by Cindy Walker), all recorded by Jana Jae on Lark Records (country). Other artists include Sydni, Hotwire and Matt Greif.

ℕ ◻ LINEAR CYCLE PRODUCTIONS

P.O. Box 2608, Sepulveda CA 91393-2608. E-mail: LCP@wgn.net. Web site: www.westworl d.com/lcp/. **Contact:** Manny Pandanceski, producer. Record producer. Estab. 1980. Produces 15-25 singles, 6-10 12″ singles, 15-20 LPs and 10 CDs/year. Fee derived from sales royalty when song or artist is recorded.

How to Contact Submit demo tape by mail. Unsolicited submissions are OK. Prefers cassette, 7³⁄₈ ips reel-to-reel or DVD. Include SASE. Responds in 6 months.

Music Mostly **rock/pop**, **R&B/blues** and **country**; also **gospel** and **comedy**. Produced *"Not of This Lite"* (single by Hitte.), recorded by Gil Gal (pop/dance), released 2008 on Tozic Googh Records. *"If I Flop"* (single by Robert Stiffe) from his self titled album, recorded and released 2008 on "Swip" brand MP3's; and *"Don't Wanna F"* (single by Brite/Warmewar-tre) from *The Fone Rings 2 Much* (album), recorded by Sir Gagolatte, released 2008 on Too Kool Recordings.

Tips "We only listen to songs and other material recorded on quality tapes and CDs. We will not accept anything that sounds distorted, muffled and just plain bad! If you cannot afford to record demos on quality stock, or in some high aspects, shop somewhere else!"

◻ MAC-ATTACK PRODUCTIONS

868 NE 81 St., Miami FL 33138. (305)949-1422. E-mail: GoMacster@aol.com. **Contact:** Michael McNamee, engineer/producer. Record producer and music publisher (Mac-Attack Publishing/ASCAP). Estab. 1986. Fee derived from outright fee from recording artist or record company.

How to Contact Submit demo by mail. Unsolicited submissions are OK. Prefers CD or cassette or VHS videocassette with 3-5 songs, lyric sheet and bio. Does not return material. Responds in up to 3 months.

Music Mostly **pop**, **alternative rock** and **dance**. Engineered Compositions (album), written and recorded by Paul Martin (experimental), released 2006 on PMR Music. Produced and engineered *Tuscan Tongue* (album by Caution Automatic), recorded by Caution Automatic (rock), released 2005 on C.A. Records; Produced and engineered "Never Gonna Let You Go" (single by Bruce Jordan/John Link/Michael McNamee), recorded by Bruce Jordan (pop), released 2002 on H.M.S. Records. Other artists include Blowfly, Tally Tal, Nina Llopis, The Lead, Girl Talk, Tyranny of Shaw, and Jacobs Ladder.

Ⓝ Ⓩ MAKERSMARK GOLD MUSIC PRODUCTIONS

534 W. Queen Lane, Philadelphia PA 19144. (215)849-7633. E-mail: Makers.Mark@verizon
.net. Web site: www.mp3.com/paulhopkins. **Contact:** Paul E. Hopkins, producer/pub-
lisher. Record producer, music publisher and record company (Prolific Records). Estab.
1991. Produces 15 singles, 5 12″ singles and 4 LPs/year. Fee derived from outright fee from
recording artist or record company. "We produce professional music videos in VHS and
DVD format."

- • Also see the listing for Makers Mark Gold in the Music Publishers section of this book.

How to Contact Submit demo tape or CD with bio by mail. Unsolicited submissions are
OK. "No need to call or send SASE. Explain concept of your music and/or style, and your
future direction as an artist or songwriter." Does not return material. No need to call or
send SASE. Responds in 6 weeks if interested. See Prolific Records in label section.

Music Gospel/Christian genres only! **Contemporary, R&B, Christian, traditional, gospel,
dance** and **pop.** Produced Pastor Alyn E. Waller Presents: The Enon Tabernacle Mass Choir
concert album and digital video (Live from the Tabernacle), released on ECDC Records/
Universal Distributors (www.ebontab.org), Enon Mass Choir (from Philadelphia Live at
the Tabernacle), New Jerusalem (drama ministry). Produced Dr. Jeremiah Cummings and
the Amazing Life Orchestra featuring, Nancya Cummings. Featuring the Sound of Philadelphia Strings and Horns of Larry Gold. Producing music for Bunim/Murray productions
network television, MTV's Real World, Road Rules, Rebel Billionaire, Simple Life, and
movie soundtracks worldwide. Also produced deep soul remixes for Brian McKnight, Musiq
Souchild, Jagged Edge, John Legend, and Elaine Monk.

Tips "Children stay in the Light of God"

Ⓩ COOKIE MARENCO

P.O. Box 874, Belmont CA 94002. E-mail: sonic@acousticartsinternational.com. (650)591-
6857. Record producer/engineer. "Over 20 years experience, 5 Grammy nominations, 2
gold records, proprietary surround recording technique. Estab. 1981. Produces 10 CDs/
year. $2,000 per day payable in advance.

How to Contact *Contact only if interested in production. Does not accept unsolicited material.*

Music Mostly **alternative modern rock, country, folk, rap, ethnic** and **avante-garde**; also
classical, pop and **jazz.** Produced *Winter Solstice II* (album), written and recorded by
various artists; *Heresay* (album by Paul McCandless); and *Deep At Night* (album by Alex
DeGrassi), all on Windham Hill Records (instrumental). Other artists include Tony Furtado
Band, Praxis, Oregon, Mary Chapin Carpenter, Max Roach and Charle Haden & Quartet
West.

Tips "If you're looking for Beat Detective and Autotune, please call someone else. We still
believe in analog recording and great musicianship."

Ⓩ PETE MARTIN/VAAM MUSIC PRODUCTIONS

P.O. Box 29550, Hollywood CA 90029-0550. (323)664-7765. E-mail: pmarti3636@aol.com.
Web site: www.VaamMusic.com. **Contact:** Pete Martin, president. Record producer, music

publisher (Vaam Music/BMI and Pete Martin Music/ASCAP) and record company (Blue Gem Records). Estab. 1982.

- Also see the listings for Vaam Music Group in the Music Publishers section of this book and Blue Gem Records in the Record Companies section of this book.

How to Contact Send CD or cassette with 2 songs and a lyric sheet. Send small packages only. Include SASE. Responds in 1 month.

Music Mostly **top 40/pop**, **country** and **R&B**.

Tips "Study the market in the style that you write. Songs must be capable of reaching top 5 on charts."

☑ ◻ SCOTT MATHEWS, D/B/A HIT OR MYTH PRODUCTIONS INC.

246 Almonte Blvd., Mill Valley CA 94941. Fax: (415)389-9682. E-mail: scott@scottmathews. com. Web site: www.ScottMathews.com. Contact: Mary Ezzell, A&R Director. President: Scott Mathews. Assistant: Tom Luekens. Record producer, song doctor, studio owner and music publisher (Hang On to Your Publishing/BMI). Estab. 1990. Produces 6-9 CDs/year. Fee derived from recording artist or record company (with royalty points).

- Scott Mathews has several gold and platinum awards for sales of nearly 15 million records. He has worked with more than 60 Rock & Roll Hall of Fame inductees and on several Grammy and Oscar-winning releases. In 2007, a "Box Set / Best of" package called Everything You Wanted to Know about The Rubinoos was released on Castle Music, featuring production by Scott Mathews. In 2006, he produced tracks for American Music—The Hightone Records Story and Guitar Hot Shots, released on Hightone Records. Also in 2006, he was nominated for another Grammy in the songwriting category for his work with The Robert Cray Band.

How to Contact "No phone calls or publishing submissions, please." Submit demo CD by mail or an MP3 by email. "Unsolicited submissions are often the best ones and readily accepted. Include SASE if e-mail is not an option. Also include your e-mail address on your demo CD." Responds in 2 months.

Music Mostly **rock/pop**, **alternative and singer/songwriters** of all styles. Produced 4 tracks on Anthology (Best of), recorded by John Hiatt (rock/pop), released 2001 on Hip-O. Has produced Elvis Costello, Roy Orbison, Rosanne Cash, Jerry Garcia, Huey Lewis, and many more. Has recorded records with everyone from Barbra Streisand to John Lee Hooker, including Keith Richards, George Harrison, Mick Jagger, Van Morrison, Bonnie Raitt, and Eric Clapton to name but a few.

Tips "These days if you are not independent, you are dependent. The new artists that are coming up and achieving success in the music industry are the ones that prove they have a vision and can make incredible records without the huge financial commitment of a major label. When an emerging artist makes great product for the genre they are in, they are in the driver's seat to be able to make a fair and equitable deal for distribution, be it with a major or independent label. My philosophy is to go where you are loved. The truth is, a smaller label that is completely dedicated to you and shares your vision may help your career far more than a huge label that will not keep you around if you don't sell millions of units. Perhaps no label is needed at all, if you are up for the challenge of wearing a lot of hats. I feel too much pressure is put on the emerging artist when they have to pay huge sums back to the label in order to see their first royalty check. We all know those records can be made for a fraction of that cost without compromising quality or commercial appeal. I still believe in potential and our company is in business to back up that belief. It is up to us as record makers/visionaries to take that potential into the studio and come out with music that can compete with anything else on the market. Discovering, developing and producing artists that can sustain long careers is our main focus at Hit or Myth Productions. We are proud to be associated with so many legendary and timeless artists and our track record speaks for itself. If you love making music, don't let anyone dim that light. We look forward to hearing from you. (Please check out www.ScottMathews.com for more info, and also www.allmusic.com-keyword; Scott Mathews.) Accept no substitutes!''

Ⓝ ☐ MUSICJONES RECORDS

(formerly SOUND WORKS ENTERTAINMENT PRODUCTIONS INC.), P.O. Box 7624, Charlottesville VA 22906. (434)296-7260. E-mail: mike@musicjones.com. Web site: www.music jones.com. **Contact:** Michael E. Jones, president. Record producer, record company (Sound Works Records) and music publisher (Sound Works Music). Estab. 1989. Produces 16 singles, 2 LPs and 20 CDs/year. Fee derived from sales royalty when song or artist is recorded or outright fee from recording artist or record company.

How to Contact Submit demo package by mail. Unsolicited submissions are OK. Prefers cassette with 3-6 songs and lyric sheet. ''Please include short bio and statement of goals and objectives.'' Does not return material. Responds in 6 weeks.

Music Mostly **country**, **folk** and **pop**; also **rock**. Recent album releases: *The Highway* featuring Mike Jones and ''Oops My Bad'' Featuring Ginger Granger. Also produced ''Lonelyville,'' and ''Alabama Slammer'' (singles), both written and recorded by Wake Eastman; and ''Good Looking Loser'' (single), written and recorded by Renee Rubach, all on Sound Works Records (country). Other artists include Matt Dorman, Steve Gilmore, The Tackroom Boys, The Las Vegas Philharmonic, and J.C. Clark.

Tips ''Put your ego on hold. Don't take criticism personally. Advice is meant to help you grow and improve your skills as an artist/songwriter. Be professional and business-like in all your dealings.''

Ⓒ NEW EXPERIENCE RECORDS/FAZE 4 RECORDS

P.O. Box 683, Lima OH 45802. E-mail: just_chilling_2002@yahoo.com. Web site: www.faze 4records.com. **Contact:** A&R Department. Music Publisher: James L. Milligan Jr. Record producer, music publisher (A New Rap Jam Publishing/ASCAP), management firm (Creative Star Management) and record company (New Experience Records, Grand-Slam Records and Pump It Up Records). Estab. 1989. Produces 15-20 12″ singles, 2 LPs, 3 EPs and 2-5 CDs/year. Fee derived from sales royalty when song or artist is recorded or outright fee from record company, ''depending on services required.''

- Also see the listings for A New Rap Jam Publishing in the Music Publishers section of this book.

How to Contact Write first to arrange personal interview. Address material to A&R Dept. or Talent Coordinator. Prefers CD with a minimum of 3 songs and lyric or lead sheet (if available). "If tapes are to be returned, proper postage should be enclosed and all tapes and letters should have SASE for faster reply." Responds in 6-8 weeks.

Music Mostly **pop**, **R&B** and **rap**; also **gospel**, **soul**, **contemporary gospel** and **rock**. Produced "The Son of God" (single by James Milligan/Anthony Milligan/Melvin Milligan) from *The Final Chapter* (album), recorded by T.M.C. Milligan Conection (R&B, Gospel), released 2002 on New Experience/Pump It Up Records. Other artists include Dion Mikel, Paulette Mikel, Melvin Milligan and Venesta Compton.

Tips "Do your homework on the music business. Be aware of all the new sampling laws. There are too many sound alikes. Be yourself. I look for what is different, vocal ability, voice range and sound stage presence, etc. Be on the look out for our new blues label Rough Edge Records/Rough Edge Entertainment. Blues material is now being reviewed. Send your best studio recorded material. Also be aware of the new digital downloading laws. People are being jailed and fined for recording music that has not been paid for. Do your homework. We have also signed Diamond Sound Productions, located in Fresno, CA and Ground Breakers Records. Now we can better serve our customers on the East and West Coast. You can also visit our Web site at www.faze4records.com for further information on our services. We are reviewing hip-hop and rap material that is positive, clean, and commercial; please no Gangsta rap if you want a deal with us as well as airplay. Also reviewing gospel music, gospel rap and anything with commercial appeal."

ℕ ⬚ NIGHTWORKS RECORDS

355 W. Potter Dr., Anchorage AK 99518. (907)562-3754. Fax: (907)561-4367. E-mail: kurt@ nightworks.com. Web site: www.surrealstudios.com. Owner: Kurt Riemann. Record producer. Produces 16 CDs/year. Fees derived from sales royalty when song or artist is recorded.

How to Contact Submit demo package by mail. Unsolicited submissions are OK. Prefers CD with 2-3 songs "produced as fully as possible. Send jingles and songs on separate CDs." Does not return material. Responds in 1 month.

Music Produces a variety of music from **native Alaskan** to **Techno** to **Christmas**.

⬚ PHILLY BREAKDOWN RECORDING CO.

216 W. Hortter St., Philadelphia PA 19119. (215)848-6725. E-mail: mattcozar@juno.com. **Contact:** Matthew Childs, president. Music Director: Charles Nesbit. Record producer, music publisher (Philly Breakdown/BMI) and record company. Estab. 1974. Produces 3 singles and 2 LPs/year. Fee derived from sales royalty when song or artist is recorded.

How to Contact *Contact first and obtain permission to submit.* Prefers CD with 4 songs and lead sheet. Does not return material. Responds in 2 months.

Music Mostly **R&B**, **hip-hop**, and **pop**; also **jazz**, **gospel**, and **ballads**. Produced "Lonely River" (single by Clarence Patterson/M. Childs) from *Lonely River* (album), recorded by Gloria Clark; and *Taps* (album), recorded by H Factor, both released 2001 on Philly Breakdown. Other artists include Leroy Christy, Gloria Clark, Jerry Walker, Nina Bundy, Mark Adam, Emmit King, Betty Carol, The II Factor, and Four Buddies.

Tips "If you fail, just learn from your past experience and keep on trying, until you get it done right. Never give up."

☐ REEL ADVENTURES

9 Peggy Lane, Salem NH 03079. (603)898-7097. E-mail: rickasmega@mediaone.net. Web site: www.reeladventures1.homestead.com. **Contact:** Rick Asmega, chief engineer/producer. Record producer. Estab. 1972. Produces 100 12″ singles, 200 LPs, 5 EPs and 40 CDs/year. Fee derived from sales royalty when song or artist is recorded, or outright fee from recording artist or record company.

How to Contact Submit demo package by mail. Unsolicited submissions are OK. Prefers CD. Include SASE. Responds in 6 weeks.

Music Mostly **pop**, **funk**, and **country**; also **blues**, **Christian reggae**, and **rock**. Produced *Funky Broadway* (album), recorded by Chris Hicks; *Testafye* (album), recorded by Jay Williams; and "Acoustical Climate" (single by John G.). Other artists include Nicole Hajj, The Bolz, Second Sinni, Larry Sterling, Broken Men, Melvin Crockett, Fred Vigeant, Monster Mash, Carl Armand, Cool Blue Sky, Ransome, Backtrax, Push, Too Cool for Humans, and Burn Alley.

⚡☐ SILVER BOW PRODUCTIONS

Box 5, 720 6th St., New Westminster BC V3L 3C5 Canada. (604)523-9309. Fax: (604)523-9310. E-mail: saddlestone@shaw.ca. Web site: www.saddlestone.net. **Contact:** Candice James, Rex Howard, Grant Lucas—A&R. Record producers. Estab. 1986. Produces 16 singles, and 6 CDs/year. Fee derived from outright fee from recording artist.

- Also see the listings for Saddlestone Publishing in the Music Publishers section and Silver Bow Management in the Managers & Booking Agents section of this book.

How to Contact Prefers CD or cassette with 2 songs and lyric sheet. Does not return material. Responds in 6 weeks.

Music Mostly **country**, **pop**, and **rock**; also **gospel**, **blues** and **jazz**. Produced *Fragile-Handle With Care* (album), recorded by Razzy Bailey on SOA Records (country); *High Society* (album), written and recorded by Darrell Meyers (country); and *Man I Am* (album), written and recorded by Stang Giles (country crossover), both released 2000 on Saddlestone Records. Other artists include Rex Howard, Gerry King, Joe Lonsdale, Barb Farrell, Dorrie Alexander, Peter James, Matt Audette and Cordel James.

☑ SOUND ARTS RECORDING STUDIO

8377 Westview Dr., Houston TX 77055. (713)464-GOLD. E-mail: sarsjef@aol.com. Web site: www.soundartsrecording.com. **Contact:** Jeff Wells, president. Record producer and music publisher (Earthscream Music). Estab. 1974. Produces 12 singles and 3 CDs/year. Fee derived from sales royalty when song or artist is recorded.

- Also see the listings for Earthscream Music Publishing in the Music Publishers section and Surface Records in the Record Companies section of this book.

How to Contact Submit demo by mail. Unsolicited submissions are OK. Prefers CD with 2-5 songs and lyric sheet. Does not return material. Responds in 6 weeks.

Music Mostly **pop/rock**, **country** and **blues**. Produced Texas Johnny Brown (album), written and recorded by Texas Johnny Brown on Quality (blues); and "Sheryl Crow" (single), recorded by Dr. Jeff and the Painkillers. Other artists include Tim Nichols, Perfect Strangers,

B.B. Watson, Jinkies, Joe "King" Carasco (on Surface Records), Mark May (on Icehouse Records), The Barbara Pennington Band (on Earth Records), Tempest, Attitcus Finch, Tony Vega Band (on Red Onion Records), Saliva (Island Records), Earl Gillian, Blue October (Universal Records), and The Wiggles.

SPHERE GROUP ONE, LLC

795 Waterside Dr., Marco Island FL 34145. (239)398-6800. Fax: (239)394-9881. E-mail: spheregroupone@att.net. **Contact:** Tony Zarrella, president. Talent Manager: Janice Salvatore. Record producer, artist development and management firm. Produces 5-6 singles and 3 CDs/year. Estab. 1986.

How to Contact Submit CD/video by mail. Unsolicited submissions are OK. Prefers CD or DVD with 3-5 songs and lyric sheets. "Must include: photos, press, résumé, goals and specifics of project submitted, etc." Does not return material.

Music Mostly **pop/rock (mainstream)**, **progressive/rock**, **New Age** and **crossover country/pop**; also **film soundtracks**. Produced "Rock to the Rescue," "Sunset At Night," "Double Trouble," "Take This Heart," "It's Our Love," and "You and I" (singles by T. Zarrella), recorded by 4 of Hearts (pop/rock) on Sphere Records and/or various labels. Other associated artists include Frontier 9, Oona Falcon, Myth, Survivor, and Wicked Lester/Kiss.

Tips "Be you. Take direction, have faith in yourself, producer and manager. Currently seeking artists/groups incorporating various styles into a focused mainstream product. Groups with a following are a plus. Artist development is our expertise and we listen! In the pocket, exceptional songs, experienced performers necessary."

STUART AUDIO SERVICES

134 Mosher Rd., Gorham ME 04038. (207)892-0960. E-mail: js@stuartaudio.com. Web site: www.stuartaudio.com. **Contact:** John A. Stuart, producer/owner. Record producer and music publisher. Estab. 1979. Produces 5-8 CDs/year. Fee derived from sales royalty when song or artist is recorded, outright fee from recording artist or record company, or demo and consulting fees.

How to Contact *Write or call first and obtain permission to submit or to arrange a personal interview.* Prefers CD with 4 songs and lyric sheet. Include SASE. Responds in 2 months.

Music Mostly **alternative folk-rock**, **rock** and **country**; also **contemporary Christian**, **children's** and **unusual**. Produced *One of a Kind* (by various artists), recorded by Elizabeth Boss on Bosco Records (folk); *Toad Motel*, written and recorded by Rick Charrette on Fine Point Records (children's); and *Holiday Portrait*, recorded by USM Chamber Singers on U.S.M. (chorale). Other artists include Noel Paul Stookey, Beavis & Butthead (Mike Judge), Don Campbell, Jim Newton and John Angus.

STUDIO SEVEN

417 N. Virginia, Oklahoma City OK 73106. (405)236-0643. Fax: (405)236-0686. E-mail: copo@okla.net. **Contact:** Dave Copenhaver, producer. Record producer, record company (Lunacy Records) and music publisher (Lunasong Music). Estab. 1990. Produces 10 LPs and CDs/year. Fee is derived from sales royalty when song or artist is recorded or outright

fee from recording artist or record company. "All projects are on a customized basis."

How to Contact *Contact first and obtain permission to submit.* Prefers CD or cassette with lyric sheet. Include SASE. Responds in 6 weeks.

Music Mostly **rock**, **jazz-blues**, **country**, and **Native American**. Produced *Hear Me* (album), recorded by Albert Aguilar, released 2006 on Lunacy Records; *The Shoe* (album), recorded by Curt Shoemaker, released 2006 on Lunacy Records; *The Road Takes the Blame* (album), recorded by Joe Merrick, released 2007 on Lunacy Records; "American Born" (single), recorded by Jeff Fenholt, released 2006; "Divinely Intoxicated" (single), recorded by Stephanie Musser, released 2006 on Passio Productions. Other artists Hinder, Megan Myers, Tessa Newman, Morris McCraven, Natchez, Ronnie & The Imods.

☐ SWIFT RIVER PRODUCTIONS

P.O. Box 231, Gladeville TN 37071. (615)316-9479. E-mail: office@swiftrivermusic.com. Web site: www.swiftrivermusic.com. **Contact:** Andy May, producer/owner. Record producer and record company. Estab. 1979. Produces 40 singles and 4 CDs/year. Fee paid by artist or artist's management. Works with recording client to come up with budget for individual project. Provides world-class backing musicians and thorough pre-studio preparation as needed.

How to Contact *Write or call first and obtain permission to submit.* "Let us know your background, present goals and reason for contacting us so we can tell if we are able to help you. Demo should be clear and well thought out. Vocal plus guitar or piano is fine." Does not return material. Responds in up to 1 month.

Music Mostly **country**, **singer/songwriter**, **Americana** and **roots (folk, acoustic, bluegrass and rock)**; also **instrumental**. Produced *Everett Lilly & Everybody and His Brother* (album), recroded by Everett Lilly (bluegrass/classic country), released 2007; *Sweet Coyote Guitar* (album), recorded by Moe Dixon (singer-songwriter/guitar & vocals), released 2006; *Natick, There's Talk About a Fence and Look What Thoughts Will Do* (albums), by Rick Lee (folk/Americana); *Second Wind* (album), by Bill Mulroney (contemporary folk/Americana); *Dreamin' the Blues* (album), by Henry May (blues guitar); *Flyin' Fast* (album), by Brycen Fast (country), released 2003 on Swift River.

Tips "I'm interested in artists who are accomplished, self-motivated, and able to accept direction. I'm looking for music that is intelligent, creative and in some way contributes something positive. We are a production house; we accept song submissions from our production clients only. Please refer to www.swiftrivermusic.com for more information and to hear our projects."

◪ WESTWIRES RECORDING USA

(formerly Westwires Digital USA), 1042 Club Ave., Allentown PA 18109. (610)435-1924. E-mail: info@westwires.com. Web site: www.westwires.com. **Contact:** Wayne Becker, owner/producer. Record producer and production company. Fee derived from outright fee from record company or artist retainer.

How to Contact *Contact via e-mail for permission to submit.* "No phone calls, please." Submit demo by mail or MP3 by e-mail. Unsolicited submissions are OK. Prefers MP3 with lyrics in MS Word or Adobe PDF file format, or CD, DVD, or VHS videocassette with 3 songs and lyric sheet. Does not return material. Responds in 1 month.

Music Mostly **rock**, **R&B**, **dance**, **alternative**, **folk** and **eclectic**. Produced Ye Ren (Dimala Records), Weston (Universal/Mojo), Zakk Wylde (Spitfire Records). Other artists include Ryan Asher, Paul Rogers, Anne Le Baron, and Gary Hassay

Tips "We are interested in singer/songwriters and alternative artists living in the mid-Atlantic area. Must have steady gig schedule and established fan base."

☑ FRANK WILLSON

P.O. Box 2297, Universal City TX 78148. (210)653-3989. E-mail: bswr@netscape.com. Web site: www.bsw-records.com. **Contact:** Frank Willson, producer. Record producer, management firm (Universal Music Marketing) and record company (BSW Records/Universal Music Records). Estab. 1987. Produces 20-25 albums/year. Fee derived from sales royalty when song or artist is recorded.

- Also see the listings for BSW Records in the Music Publishers and Record Companies sections and Universal Music Marketing in the Managers & Booking Agents section of this book.

How to Contact Submit demo package by mail. Unsolicited submissions are OK. Prefers CD with 3-4 songs and lyric sheets. Include SASE. Responds in 1 month.

Music Mostly **country**, **blues**, **jazz** and **soft rock**. Other artists include Candee Land, Dan Kimmel, Brad Lee, John Wayne, Sonny Marshall, Bobby Mountain and Crea Beal. "Visit our website for an up-to-date listing of artists."

☑ WLM MUSIC/RECORDING

2808 Cammie St., Durham NC 27705-2020. (919)471-3086. Fax: (919)471-4326. E-mail: wlm-musicrecording@nc.rr.com or wlm-band@nc.rr.com. **Contact:** Watts Lee Mangum, owner. Record producer. Estab. 1980. Fee derived from outright fee from recording artist. "In some cases, an advance payment requested for demo production."

How to Contact Submit demo by mail. Unsolicited submissions are OK. Prefers CD with 2-4 songs and lyric or lead sheet (if possible). Include SASE. Responds in 6 months.

Music Mostly **country**, **country/rock** and **blues/rock**; also **pop**, **rock**, **blues**, **gospel** and **bluegrass**. Produced "911," and "Petals of an Orchid" (singles), both written and recorded by Johnny Scoggins (country); and "Renew the Love" (single by Judy Evans), recorded by Bernie Evans (country), all on Independent. Other artists include Southern Breeze Band and Heart Breakers Band.

☑ WORLD RECORDS

5798 Deer Trail Dr., Traverse City MI 49684. E-mail: jack@worldrec.org. Web site: www.worldrec.org. **Contact:** Jack Conners, producer. Record producer, engineer/technician and record company (World Records). Estab. 1984. Produces 1 CD/year. Fee derived from outright fee from recording artist.

How to Contact *Write first and obtain permission to submit.* Prefers CD with 1 or 2 songs. Include SASE. Responds in 6 weeks.

Music Mostly **classical**, **folk**, and **jazz**. Produced *Mahler, Orff, Collins* (album), recorded by Traverse Symphony Orchestra (classical), released 2006; *Reflections on Schubert* (album) recorded by Michael Coonrod (classical), released 2007. Other artists include Jeff Haas and The Camerata Singers.

◖ ZIG PRODUCTIONS

P.O. Box 707, Hermitage TN 37076.(615)889-7105. E-mail: zig@zigworld.com. Web site: www.zigworld.com. **Contact:** Billy Herzig or Wendy Mazur. Record producer. Music publisher (Thistle Hill/BMI). Estab. 1998. ''Occasionally I produce a single that is recorded separate from a full CD project.'' Produces 6-10 albums. Fee derived from sales royalty when song or artist is recorded and/or outright fee from recording artist. ''Sometimes there are investors.''

How to Contact Submit a demo by mail. Unsolicited submissions are OK. We do not return submissions.Responds only if interested.

Music Mostly **country**, **Americana**, and **rock**; also **pop**, **R&B**, and **alternative**. Produced ''Ask Me to Stay'' (single by King Cone/Josh McDaniel) from *Gallery*, recorded by King Cone (Texas country/Americana). released 2007 on King Cone; ''A Cure for Awkward Silence'' (single), recorded by Tyler Stock (acoustic rock), released 2007 on Payday Records; ''Take Me Back'' (single) from *Peace, Love & Crabs*, written and recorded by Deanna Dove (folk-rock), released 2007 on Island Girl. Also produced Robbins & Jones (country), Jordan Mycoskie (country), Carla Rhodes (comedy), Four Higher (alternative), Charis Thorsell (country), Shane Mallory (country), Rachel Rodriguez (blues-rock), Jessy Daumen (country), Frankie Moreno (rock/r&b), Shawna Russell (country), and many others.

ADDITIONAL RECORD PRODUCERS

The following companies are also record producers, but their listings are found in other sections of the book. Read the listings for submission information.

Record Producers

Managers & Booking Agents

Before submitting to a manager or booking agent, be sure you know exactly what you need. If you're looking for someone to help you with performance opportunities, the booking agency is the one to contact. They can help you book shows either in your local area or throughout the country. If you're looking for someone to help guide your career, you need to contact a management firm. Some management firms may also handle booking; however, it may be in your best interest to look for a separate booking agency. A manager should be your manager—not your agent, publisher, lawyer or accountant.

MANAGERS

Of all the music industry players surrounding successful artists, managers are usually the people closest to the artists themselves. The artist manager can be a valuable contact, both for the songwriter trying to get songs to a particular artist and for the songwriter/performer. A manager and his connections can be invaluable in securing the right publishing deal or recording contract if the writer is also an artist. Getting songs to an artist's manager is yet another way to get your songs recorded, since the manager may play a large part in deciding what material his client uses. For the performer seeking management, a successful manager should be thought of as the foundation for a successful career.

The relationship between a manager and his client relies on mutual trust. A manager works as the liaison between you and the rest of the music industry, and he must know exactly what you want out of your career in order to help you achieve your goals. His handling of publicity, promotion and finances, as well as the contacts he has within the industry, can make or break your career. You should never be afraid to ask questions about any aspect of the relationship between you and a prospective manager.

Always remember that a manager works *for the artist*. A good manager is able to communicate his opinions to you without reservation, and should be willing to explain any confusing terminology or discuss plans with you before taking action. A manager needs to be able to communicate successfully with all segments of the music industry in order to get his client the best deals possible. He needs to be able to work with booking agents, publishers, lawyers and record companies.

Keep in mind that you are both working together toward a common goal: success for you and your songs. Talent, originality, professionalism and a drive to succeed are qualities that will attract a manager to an artist—and a songwriter.

BOOKING AGENTS

The function of the booking agent is to find performance venues for their clients. They usually represent many more acts than a manager does, and have less contact with their acts. A booking agent charges a commission for his services, as does a manager. Managers usually ask for a 15-20% commission on an act's earnings; booking agents usually charge around 10%. In the area of managers and booking agents, more successful acts can negotiate lower percentage deals than the ones set forth above.

SUBMITTING MATERIAL TO MANAGERS & BOOKING AGENTS

The firms listed in this section have provided information about the types of music they work with and the types of acts they represent. You'll want to refer to the Category Index on page 359 to find out which companies deal with the type of music you write, and the Geographic Index at the back of the book to help you locate companies near where you live. Then determine whether they are open to your level of experience (see A Sample Listing Decoded on page 8). Each listing also contains submission requirements and information about what items to include in a press kit and will also specify whether the company is a management firm or a booking agency. Remember that your submission represents you as an artist, and should be as organized and professional as possible.

Icons

For More Info

For more instructional information on the listings in this book, including explanations of symbols (![N] ✓ ☷ ☇ ❀ ⊕ ◯ ◑ ◔ ⊘), read the article *How To Use Songwriter's Market* on page 2.

ADDITIONAL MANAGERS & BOOKING AGENTS

There are **more managers & booking agents** located in other sections of the book! On page 230 use the list of Additional Managers & Booking Agents to find listings within other sections who are also managers/booking agents.

AIR TIGHT MANAGEMENT

115 West Rd., P.O. Box 113, Winchester Center CT 06094. (860)738-9139. Fax: (860)738-9135. E-mail: mainoffice@airtightmanagement.com. Web site: www.airtightmanagement.com. **Contact:** Jack Forchette, president. Management firm. Estab. 1969. Represents individual artists, groups or songwriters from anywhere; currently handles 8 acts. Receives 15-20% commission. Reviews material for acts.

How to Contact *Write e-mail first and obtain permission to submit.* Prefers CD or VHS videocassette. If seeking management, press kit should include photos, bio and recorded material. "Follow up with a fax or e-mail, not a phone call." Does not return material. Responds in 1 month.

Music Mostly **rock**, **country** and **jazz**. Current acts include P.J. Loughran (singer/songwriter), Johnny Colla (songwriter/producer, and guitarist/songwriter for Huey Lewis and the News), Jason Scheff (lead singer/songwriter for the group "Chicago"), Gary Burr (Nashville songwriter/producer), Nathan East (singer/songwriter/bassist—Eric Clapton, Michael Jackson, Madonna, 4-Play and others), Rocco Prestia (legendary R&B musician, "Tower of Power" bassist), Steve Oliver (contemporary jazz/pop songwriter/guitarist/vocalist, recording artist), Kal David (blues), Warren Hill (saxophonist/recording artist), and Harvey Mason (percussionist/composer).

ALERT MUSIC INC.

51 Hillsview Ave., Toronto ON M6P 1J4 Canada. (416)364-4200. Fax: (416)364-8632. E-mail: contact@alertmusic.com. Web site: www.alertmusic.com. **Contact:** W. Tom Berry, president. Management firm, record company and recording artist. Represents local and regional individual artists and groups; currently handles 5 acts. Reviews material for acts.

How to Contact *Write first and obtain permission to submit.* Prefers CD. If seeking management, press kit should include finished CD, photo, press clippings and bio. Include SASE.

Music **All types.** Works primarily with bands and singer/songwriters. Current acts include Holly Cole (jazz vocalist), Kim Mitchell (rock singer/songwriter), Michael Kaeshammer (pianist/singer), and Roxanne Potvin (blues, singer/songwriter).

BILL ANGELINI ENTERPRISES/BOOKYOUREVENT.COM

(formerly Management Plus), P.O. Box 132, Seguin TX 78155. (830)401-0061. Fax: (830)401-0069. E-mail: bill@bookyourevent.com. Web site: www.bookyourevent.com. **Contact:** Bill Angelini, owner. Management firm and booking agency. Estab. 1980. Represents individual artists and groups from anywhere; currently handles 6 acts. Receives 10-15% commission. Reviews material for acts.

How to Contact Submit demo package by mail or EPK. Unsolicited submissions are OK. Press kit should include pictures, bio, and discography. Does not return material. Responds in 1 month.

Music Mostly **Latin American**, **Tejano** and **international**; also **Norteno** and **country**. Current acts include Jay Perez (Tejano), Ram Herrera (Tejano), Michael Salgado (Tejano), Flaco Jimenez (Tex-Mex), Electric Cowboys (tex-mex), Los Palominos (Tejano), Grupo Vida (Tejano), and Texmaniacs (Tex-Mex).

◑ APODACA PROMOTIONS INC.

717 E. Tidwell Rd., Houston TX 77022. (713)691-6677. Fax: (713)692-9298. E-mail: houston @apodacapromotions.com. Web site: www.apodacapromotions.com. Manager: Domingo A. Barrera. Management firm, booking agency, music publisher (Huina Publishing, Co. Inc.). Estab. 1991. Represents songwriters and groups from anywhere; currently handles 40 acts. Reviews material for acts.

How to Contact Submit demo package by mail. Unsolicited submissions are OK. Prefers CD and lyric and lead sheet. Include SASE. Responds in 2 months.

Music Mostly **international** and **Hispanic**; also **rock**. Works primarily with bands and songwriters. Current acts include Pedro Fernandez, Kumbia Kings, Alicia Villarreal, Elefante, Kudai, Conjunto Atardecer, Bobby Pulido, Jennifer Pena, and Ninel Conde.

◑ ARTIST REPRESENTATION AND MANAGEMENT

1257 Arcade St., St. Paul MN 55106. (651)483-8754. Fax: (651)776-6338. E-mail: ra@arment ertainment.com. Web site: www.armentertainment.com. **Contact:** Roger Anderson, agent/manager. Management firm and booking agency. Estab. 1983. Represents artists from anywhere; currently handles 10 acts. Receives 15% commission. Reviews material for acts.

How to Contact Submit CD and video by mail. Unsolicited submissions are OK. Please include minimum 3 songs. If seeking management, references, current schedule, bio, photo, press clippings should also be included. "Priority is placed on original artists with product who are currently touring." Does not return material. Responds only if interested within 30 days.

Music Mostly **melodic rock**. Current acts include Warrant, Firehouse, Jesse Lang, Scarlet Haze, Head East, Frank Hannon of Tesla, LA Guns, Dokken, and Bret Michaels of Poison.

◐ BACCHUS GROUP PRODUCTIONS, LTD.

5701 N. Sheridan Rd., Suite 8-U, Chicago IL 60660. (773)334-1532. E-mail: BacchusGrp@gm ail.com. Web site: www.BacchusGroup.com. **Contact:** D. Maximilian, Managing Director and Executive Producer. Director of Marketing: M. Margarida Rainho. Management firm and record producer (D. Maximilian). Estab. 1990. Represents individual artists or groups from anywhere; currently handles 9 acts. Receives 15-25% commission. Reviews material for acts.

How to Contact *Call or e-mail for permission to submit. Does not accept unsolicited submissions.*

Music Mostly **pop**, **R&B/soul**, and **jazz**; also **Latin** and **world beat**. Works primarily with singer/songwriters, composers, arrangers, bands and orchestras. "Visit our Web site for current acts."

◑ BACKSTREET BOOKING

700 West Pete Rose Way, Cincinnati OH 45203. (513)542-9544. Fax: (513)542-9545. E-mail: info@backstreetbooking.com. Web site: www.backstreetbooking.com. **Contact:** James Sfarnas, president. Booking agency. Estab. 1992. Represents individual artists and groups from anywhere; currently handles 30 acts. Receives 10-15% commission. Reviews material for acts.

How to Contact *Call first and obtain permission to submit.* Accepts only signed acts with product available nationally.

Music Mostly **niche-oriented music** and **rock**. Current acts include Acumen (progressive rock group), Niacin (fusion), Mike Keneally Band (progressive rock), Cab (jazz fusion), Alex Skolnick Trio (progressive jazz), Johnny Combs—The Man in Black (Johnny Cash tribute), and The Van Dells (rock).

Tips "Build a base on your own."

☑ BARNARD MANAGEMENT SERVICES (BMS)

1525 S. Sepulveda, Ste. G, Los Angeles CA 90025. (310)399-8886. Fax: (310)450-0470. E-mail: bms@barnardus.com. **Contact:** Russell Barnard, president. Management firm. Estab. 1979. Represents artists, groups and songwriters; currently handles 2 acts. Receives 10-20% commission. Reviews material for acts.

How to Contact *Write first and obtain permission to submit.* Prefers CD with 3-10 songs and lead sheet. Artists may submit DVD (15-30 minutes) by permission only. If seeking management, press kit should include cover letter, bio, photo, demo DVD/CD, lyric sheets, press clippings, video and résumé. Does not return material. Responds in 2 months.

Music Mostly **country crossover**, **blues**, **country**, **R&B**, **rock** and **soul**. Current acts include Mark Shipper (songwriter/author) and Sally Rose (R&B band).

Tips "Semi-produced demos are of little value. Either save the time and money by submitting material 'in the raw,' or do a finished production version."

☑ BLANK & BLANK

116 West Market St., 1st Floor, Rear, West Chester PA 19382. (610)692-9300. Fax: (610)692-9301. **Contact:** E. Robert Blank, manager. Management firm. Represents individual artists and groups. Reviews material for acts.

How to Contact *Contact first and obtain permission to submit.* Prefers CD, DVD, or video-cassette. If seeking management, press kit should include cover letter, demo tape/CD and video. Does not return material.

ⓝ ☑ BLOWIN' SMOKE PRODUCTIONS/RECORDS

7438 Shoshone Ave., Van Nuys CA 91406-2340. (818)881-9888. Fax: (818)881-0555. E-mail: blowinsmokeband@ktb.net. Web site: www.blowinsmokeband.com. **Contact:** Larry Knight, president. Management firm and record producer. Estab. 1990. Represents local and West Coast individual artists and groups; currently handles 6 acts. Receives 15-20% commission. Reviews material for acts.

- Also see the listing for Hailing Frequency Music Productions in the Record Producers section of this book.

How to Contact *Write or call first and obtain permission to submit.* Prefers cassette or CD. If seeking management, press kit should include cover letter, demo tape/CD, lyric sheets, press clippings, video if available, photo, bios, contact telephone numbers and any info on legal commitments already in place. Include SASE. Responds in 1 month.

Music Mostly **R&B**, **blues** and **blues-rock**. Works primarily with single and group vocalists and a few R&B/blues bands. Current acts include Larry "Fuzzy" Knight (blues singer/ songwriter), King Floyd (R&B artist), The Blowin' Smoke Rhythm & Blues Band, The Fabulous Smokettes, Joyce Lawson, Sky King (rock/blues), and Guardians of the Clouds (alternative rock).

◙ THE BLUE CAT AGENCY

E-mail: bluecat_agency@yahoo.com. Web site: www.geocities.com/bluecat_agency. **Contact:** Karen Kindig, owner/agent. Management firm and booking agency. Estab. 1989. Represents established individual artists and/or groups from anywhere; currently handles 5 acts. Receives 10-15% commission. Reviews material for acts.

How to Contact *E-mail only for permission to submit.* Prefers cassette or CD. If seeking management, press kit should include, CD or tape, bio, press clippings and photo. SASE. Responds in 2 months.

Music Mostly **rock/pop "en espanol"** and **jazz/latin jazz**. Works primarily with bands (established performers only). Current acts include Ylonda Nickell, Kai Eckhardt, Alejandro Santos, Ania Paz, Gabriel Rosati.

◯ BREAD & BUTTER PRODUCTIONS

P.O. Box 1539, Wimberley TX 78676. (512)301-7117. E-mail: sgladson@gmail.com. **Contact:** Steve Gladson, managing partner. Management firm and booking agency. Estab. 1969. Represents individual artists, songwriters and groups from anywhere; currently handles 6 acts. Receives 10-20% commission. Reviews material for acts.

How to Contact Submit demo package by mail. Unsolicited submissions OK. Prefers cassette, videocassette or CD and lyric sheet. If seeking management, press kit should include cover letter, demo tape/CD, lyric sheets, press clippings, video, résumé, picture and bio. Does not return material. Responds in 1 month.

Music Mostly **alternative rock**, **country** and **R&B**; also **classic rock**, **folk** and **Americana**. Works primarily with singer/songwriters and original bands. Current acts include Lou Cabaza (songwriter/producer/manager), Duck Soup (band) and Gaylan Ladd (songwriter/ singer).

Tips "Remember why you are in this biz. The art comes first."

◪ BROTHERS MANAGEMENT ASSOCIATES

141 Dunbar Ave., Fords NJ 08863. (732)738-0880. Fax: (732)738-0970. E-mail: bmaent@ya hoo.com. Web site: www.bmaent.com. **Contact:** Allen A. Faucera, president. Management firm and booking agency. Estab. 1972. Represents artists, groups and songwriters; currently handles 25 acts. Receives 15-20% commission. Reviews material for acts.

How to Contact *Write first and obtain permission to submit.* Prefers CD or DVD with 3-6 songs and lyric sheets. Include photographs and résumé. If seeking management, include photo, bio, tape and return envelope in press kit. Include SASE. Responds in 2 months.

Music Mostly **pop**, **rock**, **MOR** and **R&B**. Works primarily with vocalists and established groups. Current acts include Nils Lofgren.

Tips "Submit very commercial material—make demo of high quality."

🌐 ☑ CIRCUIT RIDER TALENT & MANAGEMENT CO.

123 Walton Ferry Rd., Hendersonville TN 37075. (615)824-1947. Fax: (615)264-0462. E-mail: dotwool@bellsouth.net. **Contact:** Linda S. Dotson, president. Consultation and deal negotiation firm, booking agency and music publisher (Channel Music, Cordial Music, Dotson & Dotson Music Publishers, Shalin Music Co.). Represents individual artists, songwriters and actors; currently handles 10 acts. Works with a large number of recording artists, songwriters, actors, and producers. (Includes the late multi-Grammy-winning producer/writer Skip Scarborough.) Receives 10-15% commissionas booking agent (union rates). Reviews material for acts (free of charge) as publisher.

How to Contact *E-mail or call first and obtain permission to submit.* Prefers DVD or CD with 3 songs and lyric sheet. If seeking consultation, press kit should include bio, cover letter, résumé, lyric sheets if original songs, photo and CD or DVD with 3 songs. "Full press kit or EPK to my e-mail address required of artist's submissions." Include SASE. Responds "ASAP, sometimes 8 weeks, but if by EPK or internet, will be more timely."

Music Mostly **Latin blues**, **pop**, **country** and **gospel**; also **R&B** and **comedy**. Works primarily with vocalists, special concerts, movies and TV. Current acts include Razzy Bailey (award winning blues artist/writer), Clint Walker (actor/recording artist), Ben Colder (comedy/novelty), and Freddy Weller (formerly Paul Revere & The Raiders/hit songwriter), and Dickie Lee.

Tips "Artists, have your act together. Have a full press kit, videos and be professional. Attitudes are a big factor in my agreeing to work with you (no egotists). This is a business, and we will be building your career."

☑ CLASS ACT PRODUCTIONS/MANAGEMENT

P.O. Box 55252, Sherman Oaks CA 91413. (818)980-1039. E-mail: pkimmel@gr8gizmo.com. **Contact:** Peter Kimmel, president. Management firm. Estab. 1985. Currently handles 2 acts. Receives 20% commission. Reviews material for acts.

How to Contact Submit demo package by mail. Unsolicited submissions are OK. Include CD, cover letter, bio, and lyric sheets (essential) in press kit. Include SASE. Responds in 1 month.

Music All styles. Current acts include Terpsichore (cyber dance/pop), Don Cameron (pop/rock), The Wonderelles (50s/60s revue).

Tips "We also operate Sound Image Entertainment—recording studios and video production—www.soundimage.us and www.soundimagevideo.com."

☑ CLOUSHER PRODUCTIONS

P.O. Box 1191, Mechanicsburg PA 17055. (717)766-7644. Fax: (717)766-1490. E-mail: cpinfo@msn.com. Web site: www.clousher.com. **Contact:** Fred Clousher, owner. Booking agency and production company. Estab. 1972. Represents groups from anywhere; currently handles over 100 acts.

How to Contact Submit demo package by mail. Please, no electronic press kits. Unsolicited submissions are OK. Prefers CDs or DVD. Press kit should include bio, testimonials, credits, glossies, song list, references, and your contact information. Does not return material. "Performer should check back with us!"

Music Mostly **country**, **old rock** and **ethnic** (German, Hawaiian, etc.); also **dance bands** (regional), **Dixieland**, and **classical musicians**. "We work mostly with country, old time R&R, regional variety dance bands, tribute acts, and all types of variety acts." Current acts include Jasmine Morgan (country/pop vocalist), Robin Right (country vocalist and Tammy Wynette tribute artist) and Royal Hawaiians (ethnic Hawaiian group).

Tips "The songwriters we work with are entertainers themselves, which is the aspect we deal with. They usually have bands or do some sort of show, either with tracks or live music. We engage them for stage shows, concerts, etc. We DO NOT review songs you've written. We do not publish music, or submit performers to recording companies for contracts. We strictly set up live performances for them."

☐ STEPHEN COX PROMOTIONS & MANAGEMENT

6708 Mammoth Ave., Van Nuys CA 91405. (818)377-4530. Fax: (818)782-5305. E-mail: stephencox@earthlink.net. **Contact:** Stephen Cox, president. Management firm. Estab. 1993. Represents individual artists, groups or songwriters from anywhere; currently handles 5 acts. Receives 15% commission. Reviews material for acts.

How to Contact *Call first and obtain permission to submit.* Prefers CD. If seeking management, press kit should include biographies, performance history and radio play. "Include a clear definition of goals in a thoughtful presentation." Include SASE. Responds in 2 weeks.

Music Mostly **rock**, **New Age/world** and **alternative**; also **blues**, **folk** and **progressive**. Works primarily with bands. Current acts include Joe Sherbanee (jazz), Val Ewell & Pulse (blues rock), Paul Micich & Mitch Espe (New Age/jazz), Covet (metal) and Jill Cohn (folk rock).

Tips "Establish goals based on research, experience and keep learning about the music business. Start the business as though it will always be you as an independent. Establish a foundation before considering alternative commitments. We aim to educate and consult to a level that gives an artist the freedom of choice to choose whether to go to the majors etc., or retain independence. Remember, promote, promote and promote some more. Always be nice to people, treat them as you would wish to be treated."

ℕ ☑ CRAWFISH PRODUCTIONS

P.O. Box 5412, Buena Park CA 90620. **Producer:** Leo J. Eiffert, Jr. Management firm, music publisher (Young Country/BMI), record producer (Leo J. Eiffert, Jr.) and record company (Plain Country Records). Estab. 1968. Represents local and international individual artists and songwriters; currently handles 4 acts. Commission received is open. Reviews material for acts.

- Also see the listings for Young Country Records/Plain Country Records in the Record Companies section of this book and Leo J. Eiffert, Jr. in the Record Producers section of this book.

How to Contact Submit demo tape by mail. Unsolicited submissions are OK. Prefers cassette with 2-3 songs and lyric sheet. Include SASE. Responds in 3 weeks.

Music Mostly **country** and **gospel**. Works primarily with vocalists. Current acts include Pigeons, Southern Spirit and Nashville Snakes.

◑ DAS COMMUNICATIONS, LTD.

83 Riverside Dr., New York NY 10024. (212)877-0400. Fax: (212)595-0176. Management firm. Estab. 1975. Represents individual artists, groups and producers from anywhere; currently handles 25 acts. Receives 20% commission.

How to Contact *Does not accept unsolicited submissions.*

Music Mostly **rock**, **pop**, **R&B**, **alternative** and **hip-hop**. Current acts include Joan Osborne (rock), Wyclef Jean (hip-hop), Black Eyed Peas (hip-hop), John Legend (R&B), Spin Doctors (rock), The Bacon Brothers (rock).

◑ THE EDWARD DE MILES MUSIC COMPANY

10573 W. Pico Blvd., #352, Los Angeles CA 90064-2348. (310)948-9652. Fax: (310)474-7705. E-mail: info@edmsahara.com. Web site: www.edmsahara.com. **Contact:** Edward de Miles, president. Management firm, booking agency, entertainment/sports promoter and TV/radio broadcast producer. Estab. 1984. Represents film, television, radio and musical artists; currently handles 15 acts. Receives 10-20% commission. Reviews material for acts. Regional operations in Chicago, Dallas, Houston and Nashville through marketing representatives. Licensed A.F. of M. booking agent.

• Also see listings for Edward De Miles in the Music Publishers and Record Producers sections, and Sahara Records and Filmworks Entertainment in the Record Companies section of this book.

How to Contact *Does not accept unsolicited materials.* Prefers CD with 3-5 songs, 8×10 b&w photo, bio and lyric sheet. "Copyright all material before submitting." If seeking management, include cover letter, bio, demo CD with 3-5 songs, 8×10 b&w photo, lyric sheet, press clippings and video if available in press kit. Include SASE. Does not return material. Responds in 1 month.

Music Mostly **country**, **dance**, **R&B/soul**, **rock**, **top 40/pop** and **urban contemporary**; also looking for material for **television, radio and film** productions. Works primarily with dance bands and vocalists. Current acts include Steve Lynn (R&B/dance), Multiple Choice (rap) and Devon Edwards (jazz).

Tips "Performers need to be well prepared with their presentations (equipment, showmanship a must)."

◙ ◑ DIVINE INDUSTRIES

(formerly Gangland Artists), Unit 191, 101-1001 W. Broadway, Vancouver BC V6H 4E4 Canada. Fax: (604)737-3602. E-mail: divine@divineindustries.com. Web site: www.divinei ndustries.com. **Contact:** Allen Moy. Management firm, production house and music publisher. Estab. 1985. Represents artists and songwriters; currently handles 5 acts. Reviews material for acts.

How to Contact *Write first and obtain permission to submit.* Prefers CD or MP3 with lyric sheet. "Videos are not entirely necessary for our company. It is certainly a nice touch. If you feel your audio cassette is strong—send the video upon later request. Something wildly creative and individual will grab our attention." Does not return material. Responds in 2 months.

Music **Rock**, **pop**, and **roots**. Works primarily with rock/left-of-center folk show bands. Current acts include 54-40 (rock/pop), Tom Wilson (folk rock), Ridley Bent, Barney Bentall, John Mann (of Spirit of the West).

◻ JOHN ECKERT ENTERTAINMENT CONSULTANTS

(formerly Pro Talent Consultants), 7723 Cora Dr., Lucerne CA 95458. (707)349-1809 or (310)367-5448 (Mar Vista/Beverly Hills, CA). E-mail: talentconsultants@gmail.com. **Contact:** John Eckert, coordinator or Rich Clark. MarVista/Santa Monica management firm and booking agency. Estab. 1979. Represents individual artists and groups; currently handles 12 acts. Receives 15% commission. Reviews material for acts.

How to Contact Submit demo package by mail. Unsolicited submissions are OK. "We prefer CD (4 songs). Submit videocassette with live performance only." If seeking management, press kit should include an 8×10 photo, a cassette or CD of at least 4-6 songs, a bio on group/artist, references, cover letter, press clippings, video and business card, or a phone number with address. Does not return material. Responds in 5 weeks.

Music Mostly **country**, **country/pop** and **rock**. Works primarily with vocalists, show bands, dance bands, and bar bands. Current acts include Ronny and the Daytonas (pop/rock-top 40 band), The Royal Guardsmen (pop/rock/top 40), Gary Lewis & the Playboys (top 40), The Chantays (Surf Group), and The Trashmen (Top 40 band).

◻ SCOTT EVANS PRODUCTIONS

P.O. Box 814028, Hollywood FL 33081-4028. (954)963-4449. E-mail: evansprod@aol.com. Web site: www.theentertainmentmall.com. **Contact:** Ted Jones, new artists, or Jeanne K., Internet marketing and sales. Management firm and booking agency. Estab. 1979. Represents local, regional or international individual artists, groups, songwriters, comedians, novelty acts and dancers; currently handles over 200 acts. Receives 10-50% commission. Reviews material for acts.

How to Contact New artists can make submissions through the 'auditions' link located on the Web site. Unsolicited submissions are OK. "Please be sure that all submissions are copyrighted and not your original copy as we do not return material."

Music Mostly **pop**, **R&B** and **Broadway**. Deals with "all types of entertainers; no limitations." Current acts include Scott Evans and Company (variety song and dance), Dorit Zinger (female vocalist), Jeff Geist, Actors Repertory Theatre, Entertainment Express, Perfect Parties, Joy Deco (dance act), Flashback 2000 Revue (musical song and dance), Everybody Salsa (Latin song and dance) and Around the World (international song and dance).

Tips "Submit a neat, well put together, organized press kit."

◻ EXCLESISA BOOKING AGENCY

716 Windward Rd., Jackson MS 39206. (601)366-0220. E-mail: exclesis@bellsouth.net. Web site: www.exclesisa-booking.com. **Contact:** Roy and Esther Wooten, booking managers/owners. Booking agency. Estab. 1989. Represents groups from anywhere; currently handles 9 acts. Receives 15% commission. Reviews material for acts.

How to Contact *Call first and obtain permission to submit.* Submit demo package by mail.

Unsolicited submissions are OK. Prefers CD or videocassette. If seeking management, press kit should include CD or cassette, videocassette, pictures, address and telephone contact, and bio. Does not return material. Responds in 2 months.

Music Gospel only. Current acts include The Canton Spirituals, Darrell McFadden & The Disciples, The Jackson Southernaires, Slim & The Supreme Angels, The Pilgrim Jubilees, Spencer Taylor & the Highway Q'cs, The Annointed Jackson Singers, The Southern Sons, Jewel & Converted, and Ms. B & Tha' Band.

Tips ''Make sure your demo is clear with a good sound so the agent can make a good judgement.''

⊠ ☑ S.L. FELDMAN & ASSOCIATES

1505 W. Second Ave. #200, Vancouver BC V6H 3Y4 Canada. (604)734-5945. Fax: (604)732-0922. E-mail: feldman@slfa.com. Web site: www.slfa.com. Booking agency and artist management firm. Estab. 1970. Agency represents mostly Canadian artists and groups; currently handles over 200 acts.

How to Contact *Write or call first to obtain permission to submit a demo.* Prefers CD, photo and bio. If seeking management, contact Watchdog for consideration and include video in press kit. SAE and IRC. Responds in 2 months.

Music Current acts include Elvis Costello, The Chieftains, Joni Mitchell, Diana Krall, Norah Jones, Susan Tedeschi, Ry Cooder, Sondre Lerche, Pink Martini, Nikki Yanofsky, and Melody Gardot.

⊠ ☑ B.C. FIEDLER MANAGEMENT

53 Seton Park Rd., Toronto ON M3C 3Z8 Canada. (416)421-4421. Fax: (416)421-0442. E-mail: info@bcfiedler.com. **Contact:** B.C. Fiedler. Management firm, music publisher (B.C. Fiedler Publishing) and record company (Sleeping Giant Music Inc.). Estab. 1964. Represents individual artists, groups and songwriters from anywhere; currently handles 3 acts. Receives 20-25% or consultant fees. Reviews material for acts.

How to Contact *Call first and obtain permission to submit.* Prefers CD or VHS videocassette with 3 songs and lyric sheet. If seeking management, press kit should include bio, list of concerts performed in past 2 years including name of venue, repertoire, reviews and photos. Does not return material. Responds in 2 months.

Music Mostly **classical/crossover**, **voice** and **pop**. Works primarily with classical/crossover ensembles, instrumental soloists, operatic voice and pop singer/songwriters. Current acts include Liona Boyd (classical guitar) and Pavlo (instrumental).

Tips ''Invest in demo production using best quality voice and instrumentalists. If you write songs, hire the vocal talent to best represent your work. Submit CD and lyrics. Artists should follow up 6-8 weeks after submission.''

⊕ ☑ FIRST TIME MANAGEMENT

Sovereign House, 12 Trewartha Rd., Praa Sands-Penzance, Cornwall TR20 9ST England (01736)762826. Fax: (01736)763328. E-mail: panamus@aol.com. Web site: www.songwriters-guild.co.uk. **Contact:** Roderick G. Jones, managing director. Management firm, record company (Digimax Records Ltd www.digimaxrecords.com, Rainy Day Records, Mohock Records, Pure Gold Records) and music publisher (Panama Music Library, Melody First Music Library, Eventide Music Library, Musik' Image Music Library, Promo Sonor International Music Library, Caribbean Music Library, ADN Creation Music Library, Piano Bar Music Library, Corelia Music Library, PSI Music Library,Scamp Music Publishing, First Time Music (Publishing) U.K. (www.panamamusic.co.uk)—registered members of The Mechanical Copyright Protection Society (MCPS) and The Performing Right Society (PRS)). Estab. 1986. Represents local, regional and international individual aritsts, groups, composers and songwriters. Receives 15-25% commission. Reviews material for acts.

● Also see the listings for First Time Music (Publishing) in the Music Publishers section of this book.

How to Contact Submit demo package by mail. Unsolicited submissions are OK. Prefers CD with 3 songs and lyric sheets. If seeking management, press kit should include cover letter, bio, photo, demo tape/CD, press clippings and anything relevant to make an impression. Does not return material. Responds in 1 month.

Music All styles. Works primarily with songwriters, composers, DJs, rappers, vocalists, groups and choirs. Current acts include Willow (pop), Bram Stoker (gothic rock group), Kevin Kendle (New Age) Peter Arnold (folk/roots), and David Jones (urban/R&B).

Tips ''Become a member of the Guild of International Songwriters and Composers (www.so ngwriters-guild.co.uk). Keep everything as professional as possible. Be patient and dedicated to your aims and objectives.''

☑ LAURA GROVER

(formerly Kitchen Sync) 8530 Holloway Dr. #328, West Hollywood CA 90069-2475. (310)855-1631. Fax: (310)657-7197. E-mail: ldg@anet.net. **Contact:** Laura Grover. Music production manager. Estab. 1990. Represents individual artists, groups and songwriters from anywhere. Reviews material for acts. General project direction, artist management, and oversight of production.

How to Contact *Write first and obtain permission to submit.* Prefers DVD with 3 songs and lyric sheet. If seeking management, press kit should include cover letter, resume, bio, press clippings, discography and photo. Include SASE. Responds in 1 month.

Music Mostly **pop/rock**, **country** and **R&B**. Works primarily with producers and singer/songwriters.

Tips ''Have a clear artistic mission statement and career goals. I'm mostly interested in overseeing/managing production of material, i.e., creating budgets and mapping out recording plan, booking studios, vendors, etc.''

☑ BILL HALL ENTERTAINMENT & EVENTS

138 Frog Hollow Rd., Churchville PA 18966-1031. (215)357-5189. Fax: (215)357-0320. E-mail: Billhallevents@verizon.net. **Contact:** William B. Hall III, owner/president. Booking agency and production company. Represents individuals and groups; currently handles 20-25 acts. Receives 15% commission. Reviews material for acts.

How to Contact Submit demo package by mail. Unsolicited submissions are OK. Prefers

CD, cassette, or videocassette of performance with 2-3 songs "and photos, promo material, and CD, record, or tape. We need quality material, preferably before a 'live' audience." Does not return material. Responds only if interested.

Music Marching band, **circus** and novelty. Works primarily with "unusual or novelty attractions in musical line, preferably those that appeal to family groups." Current acts include Fralinger and Polish-American Philadelphia Championship Mummers String Bands (marching and concert group), "Mr. Polynesian" Show Band and Hawaiian Revue (ethnic group), the "Phillies Whiz Kids Band" of Philadelphia Phillies Baseball team, Mummermania Musical Quartet, Philadelphia German Brass Band (concert band), Vogelgesang Circus Calliope, Kromer's Carousel Band Organ, Reilly Raiders Drum & Bugle Corps, Hoebel Steam Calliope, Caesar Rodney Brass Band, Rohe Calliope, Philadelphia Police & Fire Pipes Band, Larry Rothbard's Circus Band, Tim Laushey Pep & Dance Band, Larry Stout (show organist/keyboard player), and Jersey Surf Drum & Bugle Corp.

Tips "Please send whatever helps us to most effectively market the attraction and/or artist. Provide something that gives you a clear edge over others in your field!"

◯ HARDISON INTERNATIONAL ENTERTAINMENT CORPORATION

P.O. Box 1732, Knoxville TN 37901-1732. (865)688-8680. E-mail: dennishardinson@bellsouth.net. Web site: www.myspace.com/hardison_music07 and http://www.hardisoninternational.netfirms.com. **Contact:** Dennis K. Hardison, CEO/founder. Dennis K. Hardison II, president; Travis J. Hardison, president, Denlatrin Record, a division of Hardison International Entertainment Corp. Contact: Management firm, booking agency, music publisher (Denlatrin Music) BMI, record label (Denlatrin Records) and record producer. Estab. 1984. Represents individual artists from anywhere; currently handles 3 acts. Receives 20% commission. Reviews material for acts. "We are seeking level-minded and patient individuals. Our primary interests are established recording acts with prior major deals."

* This company has promoted many acts in show business for over 30 years, including New Edition, Freddie Jackson, M.C. Lyte and Kool Moe Dee.

How to Contact Submit demo package by mail. Unsolicited submissions are OK. Prefers CD with 3 songs only. If seeking management, press kit should include bio, promo picture and CD. Does not return materials. Responds in 6 weeks to the best material. Critiques available through MySpace, so enclose your MySpace address.

Music Mostly **R&B**, **hip-hop** and **rap**. Current acts include Dynamo (hip-hop), Shorti (R&B singer/former original member of female group Blaque) and Triniti (record producer, Public Enemy, Dynamo, among others, current engineer for Chuck D).

Tips "We respond to the hottest material, so make it hot! We no longer accept cassette tapes."

▨ ⊘ HESFREE GOSPEL RECORDS AND HESFREE PRODUCTIONS & PUBLISHING COMPANY

P.O. Box 1214, Bryan TX 77806-1214. (979)268-3263. Fax: (979)589-2544. E-mail: hesfreeprodandpubco@yahoo.com. Web site: www.hesfreeproductions.com. President/CEO/Owner: Brenda M. Freeman-Heslip. Producer of songwriting: Jamie Heslip. Record producer, music publisher and management agency. Estab. 2001. Fee derived from sales royalty when song or artist is recorded, outright fee from recording artist and outright fee from record company.

How to Submit *Only accepts material referred to by a reputable industry source (manager, entertainment attorney, etc.).* Include CD/CDR. Does not return submissions. Responds in 6 weeks only if interested.

Music Gospel only. No other music will be accepted. "We will ensure that each project is complete with professionalism, with the highest technological strategies possible."

Ⓝ Ⓨ Ⓩ A HUGE PRODUCTION, INC.

138 Marston St., Lawrence MA 01841. (978)376-6952. E-mail: rippo@comcast.net. Web site: www.rippo.com. **Contact:** Richard M. Gordon, president. Consulting firm, music publisher (Cat Butt Musik/BMI) and record company (2 Funky International Records). Estab. 1996. Represents regional groups from the northeast; currently handles 2 acts. Receives negotiable commission.

• This company manages Rippopotamus, winner of 1996 Boston Music Award.

How to Contact *Write, e-mail, or call first and obtain permission to submit.* Prefers cassette with 3 songs and lyric sheet. If seeking management, press kit should include press, radio tracking, photo and CD. Include SASE. Responds in 1 month.

Music Mostly **pop/rock** and **funk**. Works with bands exclusively. Current acts include Rippopotamus (8 piece funk band—management), Dr. Akward (funk/rock—consulting) and Josh Cole (folk—consulting).

Tips "At this time we have restricted our activities to consulting and project management. Always call first. Promo packages are expensive, and you should always make sure we're actively seeking material, especially since most modern bands do their own songwriting. Being artists ourselves, we strongly recommend that you be very sure of people you work with and that they have same level of faith and confidence in the project that you do. Never give away the store and always make sure that you are aware of what is transpiring with your career, even if you have someone you trust handling it for you. Ultimately, no one has your interests as much at heart as you do, and thus you should always have your finger on your career's pulse."

Ⓩ INTERNATIONAL ENTERTAINMENT BUREAU

3612 N. Washington Blvd., Indianapolis IN 46205-3592. (317)926-7566. E-mail: ieb@prodigy.net. Booking agency. Estab. 1972. Represents individual artists and groups from anywhere; currently handles 151 acts. Receives 20% commission.

How to Contact *No unsolicited submissions.*

Music Mostly **rock**, **country**, and **A/C**; also **jazz**, **nostalgia**, and **ethnic**. Works primarily with bands, comedians and speakers. Current acts include Five Easy Pieces (A/C), Scott Greeson (country), and Cool City Swing Band (variety).

Ⓩ JANA JAE ENTERPRISES

P.O. Box 35726, Tulsa OK 74153. (918)786-8896. Fax: (918)786-8897. E-mail: janajae@janajae.com. Web site: www.janajae.com. **Contact:** Kathleen Pixley, agent. Booking agency, music publisher (Jana Jae Publishing/BMI) and record company (Lark Record Productions, Inc.). Estab. 1979. Represents individual artists and songwriters; currently handles 12 acts. Receives 15% commission. Reviews material for acts.

- Also see the listings for Jana Jae Music in the Music Publishers section, Lark Record Productions in the Record Companies section and Lark Talent & Advertising in the Record Producers section of this book.

How to Contact Submit demo by mail. Unsolicited submissions are OK. Prefers CD or videocassette of performance. If seeking management, press kit should include cover letter, bio, photo, demo tape/CD, lyric sheets and press clippings. Does not return material.

Music Mostly **country**, **classical** and **jazz instrumentals**; also **pop**. Works with vocalists, show and concert bands, solo instrumentalists. Represents Jana Jae (country singer/fiddle player), Matt Greif (classical guitarist), Sydni (solo singer) and Hotwire (country show band).

☑ KENDALL WEST AGENCY

P.O. Box 173776, Arlington TX 76003-3776. (817)468-7800. E-mail: kendallwestagency@ro adrunner.com. **Contact:** Michelle Vellucci. Booking agency and television producer. Estab. 1994. Represents individual artists and groups from anywhere. Receives 20% commission. Reviews material for acts.

How to Contact *Write first and obtain permission to submit or write to arrange personal interview.* Prefers CD with 5 songs and lead sheet. If seeking management, press kit should include bio, photo, cover letter, CD and resume. Include SASE. Responds in 1 month.

Music Mostly **country**, **blues/jazz**, and **rock**; also **trios**, **dance** and **individuals**. Works primarily with bands. Current acts include Chris & the Roughnecks (Texas music), Shawna Russell (southern rock), Ty England (country), and Jaz-Vil (jazz/blues).

☑ BOB KNIGHT AGENCY

185 Clinton Ave., Staten Island NY 10301. (718)448-8420. **Contact:** Bob Knight, president. Management firm, booking agency, music publisher and royalty collection firm. Estab. 1971. Represents artists, groups and songwriters; currently handles 7 acts. Receives 10-20% commission. Reviews material for acts and for submission to record companies and producers.

How to Contact Submit demo by mail. Unsolicited submissions are OK. Prefers cassette, CD, DVD, or videocassette (if available) with 5 songs and lead sheet "with bio and references." If seeking management, press kit should include bio, DVD, videocassette, CD, or audio cassette, as well as photo. Include SASE. Responds in 2 months.

Music Mostly **top 40/pop**; also **easy listening**, **MOR**, **R&B**, **soul**, **rock (nostalgia '50s and '60s)**, **alternative**, **country**, and **country/pop**. Works primarily with recording and name groups and artists—'50s, '60s and '70s acts, bands, high energy dance and show groups. Current acts include Delfonics (R&B nostalgia), B.T. Express (R&B), Brass Construction (R&B), Main Ingredient (R&B), Denny Carmella's Review, Denny Carmella's Booty Shack, Carl Thomas (R&B), Santa Esmeralda starring Leroy Gomez (disco), Motown Magic (R&B/ tribute), and Skyy (funk/R&B).

Tips "We're seeking artists and groups with completed albums/demos. Also seeking male and female solo artists with powerful and dynamic voice—top 40, pop, R&B, and rock, country, and opera for recording and live performances."

☐ KUPER PERSONAL MANAGEMENT/RECOVERY RECORDINGS

1119 Waugh Drive, Ste. #1, Houston TX 77019. (713)520-5791. Fax: (713)527-0202. E-mail: info@recoveryrecordings.com. Web site: www.recoveryrecordings.com. **Contact:** Koop Kuper, owner. Management firm, music publisher (Kuper-Lam Music/BMI, Uvula Music/BMI, and Meauxtown Music/ASCAP) and record label (Recovery Recordings). Estab. 1979/2002. Represents individual artists, groups and songwriters from Texas; currently handles 5 acts. Receives 20% commission. Reviews material for acts.

How to Contact Submit demo package by mail. Unsolicited submissions are OK. Prefers CD. If seeking management, press kit should include cover letter, press clippings, photo, bio (1 page) tearsheets (reviews, etc.) and demo CD. Does not return material. Responds in 2 months.

Music Mostly **singer/songwriters**, **triple AAA**, **roots rock**, and **Americana**. Works primarily with self-contained and self-produced artists. Current acts include Philip Rodriguez (singer/songwriter), David Rodriguez (singer/songwriter), Def Squad Texas (hip-hop). U.S. Representative for the following Dutch groups: The Watchman (Dutch singer/songwriter), and The Very Girls (Dutch vocal duo).

Tips "Create a market value for yourself, produce your own master tapes, and create a cost-effective situation."

☑ RICK LEVY MANAGEMENT

4250 A1AS, D-11, St. Augustine FL 32080. (904)806-0817. Fax: (904)460-1226. E-mail: rick@ricklevy.com. Web site: www.ricklevy.com. **Contact:** Rick Levy, president. Management firm, music publisher (Flying Governor Music/BMI) and record company (Luxury Records). Estab. 1985. Represents local, regional or international individual artists and groups; currently handles 5 acts. Receives 15-20% commission. Reviews material for acts.

How to Contact *Write or call first and obtain permission to submit.* Prefers CD or DVD with 3 songs and lyric sheet. If seeking management, press kit should include cover letter, bio, demo tape/CD, DVD demo, photo and press clippings. Include SASE. Responds in 2 weeks.

Music Mostly **R&B** (no rap), **pop**, **country** and **oldies**; also **children's** and **educational videos** for schools. Current acts include Jay & the Techniques ('60s hit group), The Original Box Tops ('60s), The Limits (pop), Freddy Cannon ('60s), The Fallin Bones (Blues/rock), Tommy Roe ('60s), The Bushwhackers (country).

Tips "If you don't have 200% passion and committment, don't bother. Be sure to contact only companies that deal with your type of music."

☐ LOGGINS PROMOTION

26239 Senator Ave., Harbor City CA 90710. (310)325-2800. Fax: (310)427-7333. E-mail: promo@logginspromotion.com. Web site: www.logginspromotion.com. **Contact:** Paul Loggins, CEO. Management firm and radio promotion. Represents individual artists, groups and songwriters from anywhere; currently handles 6 acts. Receives 20% commission. Reviews material for acts.

How to Contact If seeking management, press kit should include picture, short bio, cover letter, press clippings and CD (preferred). "Mark on CD which cut you, as the artist, feel is the strongest." Does not return material. Responds in 2 weeks.

Music Mostly **adult**, **top 40** and **AAA**; also **urban**, **rap**, **alternative**, **college**, **smooth jazz** and **Americana**. Works primarily with bands and solo artists.

◐ MANAGEMENT BY JAFFE

68 Ridgewood Ave., Glen Ridge NJ 07028. (973)743-1075. Fax: (973)743-1075. E-mail: jerjaf@aol.com. President: Jerry Jaffe. Management firm. Estab. 1987. Represents individual artists and groups from anywhere; currently handles 2 acts. Receives 20% commission. Reviews material for acts "rarely." Reviews for representation "sometimes."

How to Contact *Write or call first to arrange personal interview.* Prefers CD or cassette and videocassette with 3-4 songs and lyric sheet. Does not return material. Responds in 2 months.

Music Mostly **rock/alternative**, **pop** and **Hot AC**. Works primarily with groups and singers/songwriters.

Tips "If you are influenced by Jesus & Mary Chain, please e-mail. Create some kind of 'buzz' first."

☒ ◖ THE MANAGEMENT TRUST LTD.

411 Queen St. W, 3rd Floor, Toronto ON M5V 2A5 Canada. (416)979-7070. Fax: (416)979-0505. E-mail: mail@mgmtrust.ca. Web site: www.mgmtrust.ca. Manager: Jake Gold. Manager: R.J. Guha. General Manager: Shelley Stertz. Management firm. Estab. 1986. Represents individual artists and/or groups; currently handles 8 acts.

How to Contact Submit demo package by mail (Attn: A&R Dept.). Unsolicited submissions are OK. If seeking management, press kit should include CD, bio, cover letter, photo and press clippings. Does not return material. Responds in 2 months.

Music **All types**. Current acts include Sass Jordan (rock), Brian Byrne (folk rock), The Populars (rock), The Salads (rock), onlyforward (rock), Dearly Beloved (rock/alt), Chris Koster (rock), The Cliks (rock), Billy Klippert (rock), Bobnoxious (rock), The Pursuit of Happiness (rock), and Public (rock).

◖ PHIL MAYO & COMPANY

P.O. Box 304, Bomoseen VT 05732. (802)468-2554. Fax: (802)468-2554. E-mail: pmcamgphil@aol.com. **Contact:** Phil Mayo, President. Management firm and record company (AMG Records). Estab. 1981. Represents individual artists, groups and songwriters from anywhere; currently handles 4 acts. Receives 15-20% commission. Reviews material for acts.

How to Contact *Contact first and obtain permission to submit.* Prefers CD with 3 songs (professionally recorded) and lyric or lead sheet. If seeking management, include bio, photo and lyric sheet in press kit. Does not return material. Responds in 2 months.

Music Mostly **contemporary Christian pop**. Current and past acts have included John Hall, Guy Burlage, Jonell Mosser, Pam Buckland, Orleans, Gary Nicholson, and Jon Pousette-Dart.

✒ MEDIA MANAGEMENT

P.O. Box 3773, San Rafael CA 94912-3773. (415)898-7474. Fax: (415)898-9191. E-mail: mediamanagement9@aol.com. **Contact:** Eugene, proprietor. Management firm. Estab. 1990. Represents international individual artists, groups and songwriters; currently handles 5 acts. Receives 15% commission. Reviews material for acts.

How to Contact Submit demo by mail. Unsolicited submissions are OK. Prefers CD or DVD with lyric sheet. If seeking management, include lyric sheets, demo CD, photo and bio. Does not return material.

Music. R&B, blues, rock, country, and **pop**. Works primarily with songwriting performers/bands. Current acts include The John Lee Hooker Estate—management consultant, (blues); Peter Walker—management, (world folk guitar virtuoso); Zakiya Hooker—management, (blues and R*B) Greg Anton/ZERO II (rock).

Tips "Write great radio-friendly songs with great musical and lyrical hooks."

☐ MERRI-WEBB PRODUCTIONS

P.O. Box 5474, Stockton CA 95205. (209)948-8186. Fax: (209)942-2163. Web site: www.ma kingmusic4u.com. **Contact:** Kristy Ledford, A&R coordinator. Management firm, music publisher (Kaupp's & Robert Publishing Co./BMI) and record company (Kaupp Records). Represents regional (California) individual artists, groups and songwriters; currently handles 7 acts. Receives 10-15% commission. Reviews material for acts.

- Also see the listing for Kaupp & Robert Publishing Company in the Music Publishers section and Kaupp Records in the Record Companies section of the book.

How to Contact *Write first and obtain permission to submit or to arrange personal interview.* Prefers CDs with 3 songs maximum and lyric sheet. Include SASE. Responds in 3 months.

Music Mostly **country, A/C rock** and **R&B**; also **pop**, **rock** and **gospel**. Works primarily with vocalists, bands and songwriters. Current acts include Bruce Bolin (rock/pop singer), Nanci Lynn (country/pop singer) and Rick Webb (country/pop singer).

⊕ ☐ MUSIC MARKETING & PROMOTIONS

106 Harding Road Kendenup 6323, Western Australia. (618)9851-4311. Fax: (618)9851-4225. E-mail: mmp@bluemaxx.com.au. Web site: www.robertsonentertainment.com. **Contact:** Eddie Robertson. Booking agency. Estab. 1991. Represents individual artists and/or groups; currently handles 50 acts. Receives 20% commission. Reviews material for acts.

How to Contact *Write first and obtain permission to submit.* Unsolicited submissions are OK. Prefers cassette or videocassette with photo, information on style and bio. If seeking management, press kit should include photos, bio, cover letter, press clippings, video, demo, lyric sheets and any other useful information. Does not return material. Responds in 1 month.

Music Mostly **top 40/pop, jazz** and **'60s-'90s**; also **reggae** and **blues**. Works primarily with show bands and solo performers. Current acts include Faces (dance band), Peace Love & All That Stuff (retro band), and Soul Corporation (soul).

Tips "Send as much information as possible. If you do not receive a call after four to five weeks, follow up with letter or phone call."

☐ PM MUSIC GROUP. INC.

(formerly Precision Management), 957 W. Marietta St. NW, Suite D, Atlanta GA 30318. (800)275-5336, ext. 0381042. E-mail: precisionmanagement@netzero.com. Web site: www .pmmusicgroup.com. **Contact:** St. Paul Williams, operations director. Management firm and music publisher (Mytrell/BMI). Estab. 1990. Represents individual artists and/or groups and songwriters from anywhere; currently handles 3 acts. Receives 20% commission. Reviews material for acts.

How to Contact Submit demo package by mail. Unsolicited submissions are OK. Prefers cassette or VHS videocassette with 3-4 songs and lyric sheet. If seeking management, press kit should include photo, bio, demo tape/CD, lyric sheets, press clippings and all relevant press information. Include SASE. Responds in 6 weeks.

Music Mostly **R&B**, **rap** and **gospel**; also **all types**.

☑ PRIME TIME ENTERTAINMENT

2388 Research Dr., Livermore CA 94550. (925)449-1724. Fax: (925)905-3813. E-mail: artist manager@aol.com. Web site: www.primetimeentertainment.com. Owner: Jim Douglas. Management firm and booking agency. Estab. 1988. Represents individual artists, groups and songwriters from anywhere. Receives 10-20% commission. Reviews material for acts.

How to Contact Submit demo package by mail. Unsolicited submissions are OK. Prefers CD with 3-5 songs. If seeking management, press kit should include 8×10 photo, reviews and CDs/tapes. Include SASE. Responds in 1 month.

Music Mostly **jazz**, **country** and **alternative**; also **ethnic**. Artists include Grant Geissman (fusion/jazz), Jody Watley (R&B), Ray Parker, Jr. (jazz/R&B), and Craig Chaquico (jazz).

Tips "It's all about the song."

☑ RAINBOW TALENT AGENCY

146 Round Pond Lane, Rochester NY 14626. (585)723-3334. Fax: (585)720-6172. E-mail: carl@rainbowtalentagency.com. Web site: www.rainbowtalentagency.com. **Contact:** Carl Labate, President. Management firm and booking agency. Represents artists and groups; currently handles 6 acts. Receives 15-20% commission.

How to Contact Submit demo package by mail. Unsolicited submissions are OK. Prefers CD with minimum 3 songs. May send DVD if available; "a still photo and bio of the act; if you are a performer, it would be advantageous to show yourself or the group performing live. Theme videos are not helpful." If seeking management, include photos, bio, markets established, CD/DVD. Does not return material. Responds in 1 month.

Music Mostly **blues**, **rock**, and **R&B**. Works primarily with touring bands and recording artists. Current acts include Kristin Mainhart (alt light rock); Classic Albums Live (classic rock symphony); Mike Zale (singer-songwriter/recording artist), and Spanky Haschmann Swing Orchestra (high energy swing).

Tips "My main interest is with groups or performers that are currently touring and have some product. And are at least 50% percent original. Strictly songwriters should apply elsewhere."

☐ RASPBERRY JAM MUSIC

(formerly Endangered Species Artist Management), 4 Berachah Ave., South Nyack NY 10960-4202. (845)353-4001. Fax: (845)353-4332. E-mail: muzik@verizon.net. Web site: www.musicandamerica.com or www.anyamusic.com. **President:** Fred Porter. Vice President: Suzanne Buckley. Management firm. Estab. 1979. Represents individual artists, groups and songwriters from anywhere; currently handles 3 acts. Receives 20% commission. Reviews material for acts.

How to Contact *Call first and obtain permission to submit.* Prefers CD with 3 or more songs and lyric sheet. "Please include a demo of your music, a clear, recent photograph as well as any current press, if any. A cover letter indicating at what stage in your career you are and expectations for your future. Please label the cassette and/or CD with your name and address as well as the song titles." If seeking management, press kit should include cover letter, bio, photo, demo/CD, lyric sheet and press clippings. Include SASE. Responds in 6 weeks.

Music Mostly **pop**, **rock** and **world**; also **Latin/heavy metal**, **R&B**, **jazz** and **instrumental**. Current acts include Jason Wilson & Tabarruk (pop/reggae, nominated for Juno award 2001), and Anya (teen singer).

Tips "Listen to everything, classical to country, old to contemporary, to develop an understanding of many writing styles. Write with many other partners to keep the creativity fresh. Don't feel your style will be ruined by taking a class or a writing seminar. We all process moods and images differently. This leads to uniqueness in the music."

☐ REIGN MUSIC AND MEDIA, LLC

(formerly Bassline Entertainment, Inc.), P.O. Box 2394, New York NY 10185. E-mail: talent @reignmm.com. Web site: www.reignmm.com. **Contact:** Talent Relations Dept. Multimedia/Artist Development firm. Estab. 1993 as Bassline Entertainment. Represents local and regional vocalists, producers, and songwriters. Receives 20-25% commission. Reviews material for acts.

How to Contact Submit demo package by mail. Unsolicited submissions are OK. Prefers CD, MP3, or video. If seeking management, press kit should include cover letter, press clippings and/or reviews, bio, demo (in appropriate format), picture and accurate contact telephone number. Include SASE. Responds in 3 weeks.

Music Mostly **pop**, **R&B**, **club/dance** and **hip-hop/rap**; some **Latin**. Works primarily with singer/songwriters, producers, rappers and bands. Current acts include Stress (hip hop), Dre Random (R&B/pop), and Two Way (rap/hip-hop, R&B).

☑ RIOHCAT MUSIC

P.O. Box 764, Hendersonville TN 37077-0764. (615)824-9313. Fax: (615)824-0797. E-mail: tachoir@bellsouth.net. Web site: www.tachoir.com. **Contact:** Robert Kayne, manager. Management firm, booking agency, record company (Avita Records) and music publisher. Estab. 1975. Represents individual artists and groups; currently handles 4 acts. Receives 15-20% commission.

   • Also see the listing for Avita Records in the Record Companies section of this book.

How to Contact *Contact first and obtain permission to submit.* Prefers CD and lead sheet. If seeking management, press kit should include cover letter, bio, photo, demo tape/CD and press clippings. Does not return material. Responds in 6 weeks.

Music Mostly **contemporary jazz** and **fusion**. Works primarily with jazz ensembles. Current acts include Group Tachoir (jazz), Tachoir/Manakas Duo (jazz) and Jerry Tachoir (jazz vibraphone artist).

SA'MALL MANAGEMENT

P.O. Box 261488, Encino CA 91426. (310)317-0322. Fax: (818)506-8534. E-mail: samusa@aol.com. Web site: www.pplentertainmentgroup.com. **Contact:** Ted Steele, vice president of talent. Management firm, music publisher (Pollybyrd Publications) and record company (PPL Entertainment Group). Estab. 1990. Represents individual artists, groups and songwriters worldwide; currently handles 10 acts. Receives 10-25% commission. Reviews material for acts.

> • Also see the listings for Pollybyrd Publications Limited and Zettitalia Music International in the Music Publishers section and PPL Entertainment Group in the Record Companies section of this book.

How to Contact *E-mail first and obtain permission to submit.* "Only professional full-time artists who tour and have a fan base need apply. No weekend warriors, please." Prefers CD or cassette. If seeking management, press kit should include picture, bio and tape. Include SASE. Responds in 2 months.

Music All types. Current acts include Riki Hendrix (rock), Buddy Wright (blues), Fhyne, Suzette Cuseo, The Band AKA, LeJenz, B.D. Fuoco, Juz-cuz, Donato, MoBeatz, and Kapital P.

SAFFYRE MANAGEMENT

1215 S. Lake St., Unit #D, Burbank CA 91502. (818)842-4368. E-mail: ebsaffyre@yahoo.com. Web site: http://www.heupferd-musik.de. **Contact**: Esta G. Bernstein, president. Management firm. Estab. 1990. Represents individual artists, groups and songwriters from anywhere; currently handles 2 acts. Receives 15% commission.

How to Contact *Call first and obtain permission to submit.* If seeking management, press kit should include cover letter, bio, photo, cassette with 3-4 songs and lyric sheets. Does not return material. Responds in 2 weeks only if interested.

Music Alternative/modern rock and **top 40.** "We work only with bands and solo artists who write their own material; our main objective is to obtain recording deals and contracts, while advising our artists on their careers and business relationships."

SANDALPHON MANAGEMENT

P.O. Box 29110, Portland OR 97296. (503)957-3929. E-mail: jackrabbit01@sprintpcs.com. **Contact:** Ruth Otey, president. Management firm, music publisher (Sandalphon Music Publishing/BMI), and record company (Sandalphon Records). Estab. 2005. Represents individual artists, groups, songwriters; works with individual artists and groups from anywhere. Currently handles 0 acts. Receives negotiable commission. Reviews material for acts.

How to Contact Submit demo by mail. Unsolicited submissions are OK. Prefers cassette or CD with 1-5 songs and lyric sheet, cover letter. "Include name, address, and contact information." Include SASE or SAE and IRC for outside the United States. Responds in 1 month.

Music Mostly **rock**, **country**, and **alternative**; also **pop**, **gospel**, and **blues**. "We are looking for singers, bands, and singer/songwriters who are original but would be current in today's music markets. We help singers, bands, and singer-songwriters achieve their personal career goals."

Tips "Submit material you feel best represents you, your voice, your songs, or your band. Fresh and original songs and style are a plus. We are a West Coast management company looking for singers, bands, and singer-songwriters who are ready for the next level. We are looking for those with talent who are capable of being national and international contenders."

⊠ ☺ SERGE ENTERTAINMENT GROUP

P.O. Box 2760, Acworth GA 30102. (678)445-0006. Fax: (678)494-9289. E-mail: sergeent@aol.com. Web site: www.serge.org. **Contact:** Sandy Serge, president. Management and PR firm and song publishers. Estab. 1987. Represents individual artists, groups, songwriters from anywhere; currently handles 20 acts. Receives 20% commission for management. Monthly fee required for PR acts.

How to Contact *E-mail first for permission to submit.* Submit demo package by mail. Unsolicited submissions are OK. Prefers CD or cassette with 4 songs and lyric sheet. If seeking management, press kit should include 8×10 photo, bio, cover letter, lyric sheets, max of 4 press clips, DVD, performance schedule and CD. "All information submitted must include name, address and phone number on each item." Does not return material. Responds in 6 weeks if interested.

Music Mostly **rock**, **pop** and **country**; also **New Age**. Works primarily with singer/songwriters and bands. Current acts include FEFF (rock), ASIA featuring John Payne (classic prog rock), Erik Norlander (prog rock), and Little Memphis (country).

⊠ ▢ SILVER BOW MANAGEMENT

Box 5, 720 6th St., New Westminster BC V3L 3C5 Canada. (604)523-9309. Fax: (604)523-9310. E-mail: saddlestone@shaw.ca. Web site: www.saddlestone.net. President: Grant Lucas. CEO: Candice James. Management firm, music publisher (Saddlestone Publishing, Silver Bow Publishing), record company (Saddlestone Records) and record producer (Silver Bow Productions, Krazy Cat Productions). Estab. 1988. Represents individual artists, groups, songwriters from anywhere; currently handles 8 acts. Receives standard commission. Reviews material for acts.

   ● Also see the listings for Saddlestone Publishing in the Music Publishers section and Silver Bow Productions in the Record Producers section of this book.

How to Contact Submit demo package by mail. Unsolicited submissions are OK. Prefers cassette with 3 songs and lyric sheet. If seeking management, press kit should include 8×10 photo, bio, cover letter, demo tape or CD with lyric sheets, press clippings, video, résumé and current itinerary. "Visuals are everything—submit accordingly." Does not return material. Responds in 2 months.

Music Mostly **country**, **pop** and **rock**; also **R&B, Christian** and **alternative**. Works primarily with bands, vocalists and singer/songwriters. Current acts include Darrell Meyers (country singer/songwriter), Nite Moves (variety band), Mark Vance (country/pop), and Stan Giles (country).

☑ SOUTHEASTERN ATTRACTIONS

1025 23rd St. South, Suite 302, Birmingham AL 35205. (205)307-6790. Fax: (205)942-7700. E-mail: staff@seattractions.com. Web site: www.seattractions.com. **Contact:** Agent. Booking agency. Estab. 1967. Represents groups from anywhere; currently handles 200 acts. Receives 20% commission.

How to Contact Submit demo package by mail. Unsolicited submissions are OK. Prefers CD or DVD. Does not return material. Responds in 2 months.

Music Mostley **rock**, **alternative**, **oldies**, **country** and **dance**. Works primarily with bands. Current acts include Leaderdog (rock), Undergrounders (variety to contemporary), Style Band (Motown/dance), The Connection (Motown/dance), Rollin in the Hay(bluegrass).

☑ SPHERE GROUP ONE, LLC

795 Waterside Drive, Marco Island FL 34145. (239)398-6800. Fax: (239)394-9881. E-mail: spheregroupone@att.net. President: Tony Zarrella. Talent Manager: Janice Salvatore. Management firm and record producer. Estab. 1987. Represents individual artists and groups nationally and internationally; currently handles 5 acts. Receives commission.

How to Contact Submit CD or DVD by mail or e-mail. Unsolicited submissions are OK. Prefers CD or video with 3-5 songs. All submissions must include cover letter, lyric sheets, tape/CD, photo, bio and all press. "Due to large number of submissions we can only respond to those artists which we may consider working with." Does not return material

Music **Crossover**, **pop/rock**, **pop/country**, and **New Age**; also **R&B**. Works primarily with bands and solo singer/songwriters. Current acts include 4 of Hearts (pop/rock), Frontier 9 (pop/rock), Viewpoint (experimental) and Bombay Green (hybrid pop).

Tips "Develop and create your own style and be you, focus on goals and work as a team and maintain good chemistry with all artists and business relationships."

☐ ST. JOHN ARTISTS

P.O. Box 619, Neenah WI 54957-0619. (920)722-2222. Fax: (920)725-2405. E-mail: jon@stjohn-artists.com. Web site: www.stjohn-artists.com/. **Contact:** Jon St. John and Gary Coquoz, agents. Booking agency. Estab. 1968. Represents local and regional individual artists and groups; currently handles 20 acts. Receives 15-20% commission. Reviews material for acts.

How to Contact *Call first and obtain permission to submit.* Prefers CD or DVD. If seeking management, press kit should include cover letter, bio, photo, demo tape/CD, video and résumé. Include SASE.

Music Mostly **rock** and **MOR**. Current acts include Tribute (variety/pop/country), Boogie

& the Yo-Yo's ('60s-2000s), Vic Ferrari (Top 40 80's-2000's), Little Vito and the Torpedoes (variety 50's-2000's), Center Stage Variety Show Band (variety 60's-2000's) and Da Yoopers (musical comedy/novelty).

☑ STARKRAVIN' MANAGEMENT

11135 Weddington St., #424, N. Hollywood CA 91601. (818)587-6801. Fax: (818)587-6802. E-mail: bcmclane@aol.com. Web site: www.benmclane.com. **Contact:** B.C. McLane, Esq. Management and law firm. Estab. 1994. Represents individual artists, groups and songwriters. Receives 20% commission (management); $250/hour as attorney.

How to Contact Submit demo package by mail. Unsolicited submissions are OK. Prefers cassette. Does not return material. Responds in 1 month if interested.

Music Mostly **rock**, **pop** and **R&B**. Works primarily with bands.

☑ T.L.C. BOOKING AGENCY

37311 N. Valley Rd., Chattaroy WA 99003. (509)292-2201. Fax: (509)292-2205. E-mail: tlcagent@ix.netcom.com. Web site: www.tlcagency.com. **Contact:** Tom or Carrie Lapsansky, agent/owners. Booking agency. Estab. 1970. Represents individual artists and groups from anywhere; currently handles 17 acts. Receives 10-15% commission. Reviews material for acts.

How to Contact *Call first and obtain permission to submit.* Prefers CD with 3-4 songs. Does not return material. Responds in 3 weeks.

Music Mostly **rock**, **country** and **variety**; also **comedians** and **magicians**. Works primarily with bands, singles and duos. Current acts include Nobody Famous (variety/classic rock), Mr. Happy (rock), Mad Rush (rock), Dixie Dandies (dixieland), and The Charm (variety/top 40).

Ⓝ ☑ TAS MUSIC CO./DAVE TASSE ENTERTAINMENT

N2467 Knollwood Dr., Lake Geneva WI 53147-9731. E-mail: david@baybreezerecords.com. Web site: www.baybreezerecords.com. **Contact:** David Tasse. Booking agency, record company and music publisher. Represents artists, groups and songwriters; currently handles 21 acts. Receives 10-20% commission. Reviews material for acts.

How to Contact Submit demo tape by mail. Unsolicited submissions are OK. Prefers cassette with 2-4 songs and lyric sheet. Include performance videocassette if available. If seeking management, press kit should include tape, bio and photo. Does not return material. Responds in 3 weeks.

Music Mostly **pop** and **jazz**; also **dance**, **MOR**, **rock**, **soul** and **top 40**. Works primarily with show and dance bands. Current acts include Max Kelly (philosophic rock) and L.J. Young (rap).

☑ UMBRELLA ARTISTS MANAGEMENT, INC.

2612 Erie Ave., P.O. Box 8369, Cincinnati OH 45208. (513)871-1500. Fax: (513)878-2240. E-mail: shertzman@cinci.rr.com. Web site: www.stanhertzman.com. **Contact:** Stan Hertzman, president. Management firm. Represents artists and groups for specific circumstances.

How to Contact *E-mail or phone specific need.*

Music Mostly **contemporary country**, **rock** and **top 40/pop**. Works with contemporary/progressive pop/rock artists and writers on a per project basis.

☐ UNIVERSAL MUSIC MARKETING

P.O. Box 2297, Universal City TX 78148. (210)653-3989. E-mail: bswrl8@wmconnect.net. Web site: www.bsw-records.com. **Contact:** Frank Willson, president. Management firm, record company (BSW Records), booking agency, music publisher and record producer (Frank Wilson). Estab. 1987. Represents individual artists and groups from anywhere; currently handles 12 acts. Receives 15% commission. Reviews material for acts.

- Also see the listings for BSW Records in the Music Publishers and Record Companies sections and Frank Wilson in the Record Producers section of this book.

How to Contact Submit demo package by mail. Unsolicited submissions are OK. Prefers CD or DVD with 3 songs and lyric sheet. If seeking management, include tape/CD, bio, photo and current activities. Include SASE. Responds in 6 weeks.

Music Mostly **country** and **light rock**; also **blues** and **jazz**. Works primarily with vocalists, singer/songwriters and bands. Current acts include Candee Land, Darlene Austin, Larry Butler, John Wayne, Sonny Marshall, Bobby Mountain, Crea Beal and Butch Martin (country). "Visit our Web site for an up-to-date listing of current acts."

Ⓝ ⊕ ◯ HANS VAN POL MANAGEMENT

Utrechtseweg 39B, 1381 GS Weesp, Netherlands (0)294-413-633. Fax: (0)294-480-844. E-mail: hansvanpol@yahoo.com. **Managing Director:** Hans Van Pol. A&R/Producer: Jochem Fluitsma. Management firm, consultant (Hans Van Pol Music Consultancy), record company (J.E.A.H.! Records) and music publisher (Blue & White Music). Estab. 1984. Represents regional (Holland/Belgium) individual artists and groups; currently handles 7 acts. Receives 20% commission. Reviews material for acts.

How to Contact Submit demo tape by mail. Unsolicited submissions are OK. Prefers CD/DVD with 3 songs and lyric sheets. If seeking management, press kit should include demo, possible DVD, bio, press clippings, photo and release information. SAE and IRC. Responds in 1 month.

Music Mostly **MOR, dance: rap/swing beat/hip house/R&B/soul/c.a.r.** Current acts include Fluitsma & Van Tyn (production, commercials, MOR), Tony Scott (rap) and MC Miker "G" (rap/R&B).

◐ WARNER PRODUCTIONS, INC.

P.O. Box 179, Hermitage TN 37076. Phone: (615)429-7849. E-mail: cherylkwarner@comcast.net. Web site: www.cherylkwarner.com. **Contact:** Warner Productions, Inc. Recording and stage production, music consulting, music publisher, record label. Currently works with 2 acts. Reviews material for acts.

How to Contact Submit demo package by mail. Unsolicited submissions are OK. Prefers CD or DVD, but will accept CD with 3 best songs, lyric or lead sheet, bio and picture. Press kit should include CD, DVD with up-to-date bio, cover letter, lyric sheets, press clippings, and picture. Does not return material. Responds in 6 weeks if interested.

Music Mostly **country/traditional and contemporary**, **Christian/gospel** and **A/C/pop**. Works primarily with singer/songwriters and bands with original and versatile style. Current acts include Cheryl K. Warner (recording artist/entertainer) and Cheryl K. Warner Band (support/studio).

✪ WEMUS ENTERTAINMENT

2006 Seaboard, Suite 400, Midland TX 79705. (432)689-3687. Fax: (432)687-0930. E-mail: wemus@aol.com. Web site: www.wemus.com. **Contact:** Dennis Grubb, president. Management firm, booking agency and music publisher (Wemus Music, Inc.). Estab. 1983. Represents local and regional individual artists and groups; currently handles 4 acts. Receives 15-25% commission. Reviews material for acts.

How to Contact Submit demo package by mail. Unsolicited submissions are OK. Prefers CD, cassette, DVD or VHS videocassette with 3-5 songs and lyric sheet. If seeking management, press kit should include glossy head and full body shots and extensive biography. "Make sure address, phone number and possible fax number is included in the packet, or a business card." Does not return material. Responds in 1 month if interested.

Music Mostly **country**. Current acts include The Image (variety), The Big Time (variety), The Pictures (variety) and Pryce Conner.

Tips "We preview and try to place good songs with national artists who are in need of good materials. We have a very tough qualification process and are very selective in forwarding materials to artists and their management."

✪ ✪ ○ WINTERLAND ENTERTAINMENT MANAGEMENT & PUBLISHING

(formerly T.J. Booker Ltd.), P.O. Box 969, Rossland BC V0G 1Y0 Canada. (250)362-7795. E-mail: winterland@netidea.com. **Contact:** Tom Jones, owner. Management firm, booking agency and music publisher. Estab. 1976. Represents individual artists, groups and songwriters from anywhere; currently handles 6 acts. Receives 15% commission. Reviews material for acts.

How to Contact Submit demo package by mail. Unsolicited submissions are OK. Prefers CD, cassette or videocassette with 3 songs. If seeking management, include demo tape or CD, picture, cover letter and bio in press kit. Does not return material. Responds in 1 month.

Music Mostly **MOR**, **crossover**, **rock**, **pop**, and **country**. "Only book on an occasional basis. If you wish to submit, you are welcome. If I can I will review and critique your material. It is a changing world musically, but if it works, it works. There is no replacement for excellence."

✪ WORLDSOUND, LLC

17837 1st Ave. South Suite 3, Seattle WA 98148. (206)444-0300. Fax: (206)244-0066. E-mail: music@worldsound.com. Web site: www.worldsound.com. **Contact:** Warren Wyatt, A&R manager. Management firm. Estab. 1976. Represents individual artists, groups and songwriters from anywhere; currently handles 8 acts. Receives 20% commission. Reviews material for acts.

How to Contact "Online, send us an e-mail containing a link to your Web site where your songs can be heard and the lyrics are available—PLEASE DO NOT E-MAIL SONG FILES! By regular mail, unsolicited submissions are OK." Prefers CD with 2-10 songs and lyric sheet. "If seeking management, please send an e-mail with a link to your Web site—your site should contain song samples, band biography, photos, video (if available), press and demo reviews. By mail, please send the materials listed above and include SASE." Responds in 1 month.

Music Mostly **rock**, **pop**, and **world**; also **heavy metal**, **hard rock**, and **top 40**. Works primarily with pop/rock/world artists. Current acts include Makana (world music), Treble (pop), La Neo (contemporary/Hawaiian), and Keith Olsen (music producer).

Tips "Always submit new songs/material, even if you have sent material that was previously rejected; the music biz is always changing."

☑ ZANE MANAGEMENT, INC.

1650 Market St., One Liberty Place, 56th Floor, Philadelphia PA 19103. (215)575-3803. Fax: (215)575-3801. E-mail: lzr@braverlaw.com. Web site: www.zanemanagement.com. **Contact:** Lloyd Z. Remick, Esq., president. Entertainment/sports consultants and managers. Represents artists, songwriters, producers and athletes; currently handles 7 acts. Receives 10-15% commission.

How to Contact Submit demo tape by mail. Unsolicited submissions are OK. Prefers CD and lyric sheet. If seeking management, press kit should include cover letter, bio, photo, demo tape and video. Does not return material. Responds in 3 weeks.

Music Mostly **dance, easy listening, folk, jazz (fusion), MOR, rock (hard and country), soul** and **top 40/pop**. Current acts include Bunny Sigler (disco/funk), Peter Nero and Philly Pops (conductor), Cast in Bronze (rock group), Pieces of a Dream (jazz/crossover), Don't Look Down (rock/pop), Christian Josi (pop-swing), Bishop David Evans (gospel), Kevin Roth (children's music), and Rosie Carlino (standards/pop).

☐ D. ZIRILLI MANAGEMENT

P.O. Box 255, Cupertino CA 95015-0255. (408)257-2533. Fax: (408)252-8938. E-mail: donzirilli@aol.com. Web site: www.zirilli.com. Owner: Don Zirilli. Management firm. Estab. 1965. Represents groups from anywhere; currently handles 1 act. Receives 20% commission or does fee-based consulting. Varies by project. Reviews material for acts.

How to Contact Submit demo package by mail. Unsolicited submissions are OK. Prefers CD, videocassette or DVD. If seeking management, press kit should include video. Does not return material. Responds in 2 weeks.

Music Mostly **rock, surf** and **MOR**. Current acts include Papa Doo Run Run (band).

Tips "Less is more."

ADDITIONAL MANAGERS & BOOKING AGENTS

The following companies are also managers/booking agents, but their listings are found in other sections of the book. Read the listings for submission information.

Music Firms

Advertising, Audiovisual & Commercial

I t's happened a million times—you hear a jingle on the radio or television and can't get it out of your head. That's the work of a successful jingle writer, writing songs to catch your attention and make you aware of the product being advertised. But the field of commercial music consists of more than just memorable jingles. It also includes background music that many companies use in videos for corporate and educational presentations, as well as films and TV shows.

SUBMITTING MATERIAL

More than any other market listed in this book, the commercial music market expects composers to have made an investment in the recording of their material before submitting. A sparse, piano/vocal demo won't work here; when dealing with commercial music firms, especially audiovisual firms and music libraries, high quality production is important. Your demo may be kept on file at one of these companies until a need for it arises, and it may be used or sold as you sent it. Therefore, your demo tape or reel must be as fully produced as possible.

The presentation package that goes along with your demo must be just as professional. A list of your credits should be a part of your submission, to give the company an idea of your experience in this field. If you have no experience, look to local television and radio stations to get your start. Don't expect to be paid for many of your first jobs in the commercial music field; it's more important to get the credits and exposure that can lead to higher-paying jobs.

Commercial music and jingle writing can be a lucrative field for the composer/songwriter with a gift for writing catchy melodies and the ability to write in many different music styles. It's a very competitive field, so it pays to have a professional presentation package that makes your work stand out.

Three different segments of the commercial music world are listed here: advertising agencies, audiovisual firms and commercial music houses/music libraries. Each looks for a different type of music, so read these descriptions carefully to see where the music you write fits in.

ADVERTISING AGENCIES

Ad agencies work on assignment as their clients' needs arise. Through consultation and input from the creative staff, ad agencies seek jingles and music to stimulate the consumer to identify with a product or service.

When contacting ad agencies, keep in mind they are searching for music that can capture and then hold an audience's attention. Most jingles are short, with a strong, memorable hook. When an ad agency listens to a demo, it is not necessarily looking for a finished product so much as for an indication of creativity and diversity. Many composers put together a reel of excerpts of work from previous projects, or short pieces of music that show they can write in a variety of styles.

AUDIOVISUAL FIRMS

Audiovisual firms create a variety of products, from film and video shows for sales meetings, corporate gatherings and educational markets, to motion pictures and TV shows. With the increase of home video use, how-to videos are a big market for audiovisual firms, as are spoken word educational videos. All of these products need music to accompany them. For your quick reference, companies working to place music in movies and TV shows (excluding commercials) have a ◧ preceding their listing (also see the Film & TV Index on page 388 for a complete list of these companies).

Like ad agencies, audiovisual firms look for versatile, well-rounded songwriters. When submitting demos to these firms, you need to demonstrate your versatility in writing specialized background music and themes. Listings for companies will tell what facet(s) of the audiovisual field they are involved in and what types of clients they serve. Your demo tape should also be as professional and fully produced as possible; audiovisual firms often seek demo tapes that can be put on file for future use when the need arises.

COMMERCIAL MUSIC HOUSES & MUSIC LIBRARIES

Commercial music houses are companies contracted (either by an ad agency or the advertiser) to compose custom jingles. Since they are neither an ad agency nor an audiovisual firm, their main concern is music. They use a lot of it, too—some composed by inhouse songwriters and some contributed by outside, freelance writers.

Music libraries are different in that their music is not custom composed for a specific client. Their job is to provide a collection of instrumental music in many different styles that, for an annual fee or on a per-use basis, the customer can use however he chooses.

In the following listings, commercial music houses and music libraries, which are usually the most open to works by new composers, are identified as such by **bold** typeface.

The commercial music market is similar to most other businesses in one aspect: experience is important. Until you develop a list of credits, pay for your work may not be high. Don't pass up opportunities if a job is non- or low-paying. These assignments will add to your list of credits, make you contacts in the field, and improve your marketability.

Money and rights

Many of the companies listed in this section pay by the job, but there may be some situations where the company asks you to sign a contract that will specify royalty payments. If this happens, research the contract thoroughly, and know exactly what is expected of you and how much you'll be paid.

Depending on the particular job and the company, you may be asked to sell one-time rights or all rights. One-time rights involve using your material for one presentation only. All rights means the buyer can use your work any way he chooses, as many times as he likes. Be sure you know exactly what you're giving up, and how the company may use your music in the future.

In the commercial world, many of the big advertising agencies have their own publishing companies where writers assign their compositions. In these situations, writers sign contracts whereby they do receive performance and mechanical royalties when applicable.

ADDITIONAL LISTINGS

For additional names and addresses of ad agencies that may use jingles and/or commercial music, refer to the *Standard Directory of Advertising Agencies* (National Register Publishing).

For a list of audiovisual firms, check out the latest edition of *AV Marketplace* (R.R. Bowker). Both these books may be found at your local library. To contact companies in your area, see the Geographic Index at the back of this book.

ADVERTEL, INC.

P.O. Box 18053, Pittsburgh PA 15236-0053. (412)344-4700. Fax: (412)344-4712. E-mail: pberan@advertel.com. Web site: www.advertel.com. **Contact:** Paul Beran, president/CEO. **Telephonic/Internet production company.** Clients include small and multi-national companies. Estab. 1983. Uses the services of music houses and independent songwriters/composers for scoring of instrumentals (all varieties) and telephonic production. Commissions 3-4 composers/year. Pay varies. Buys all rights and phone exclusive rights.

How to Contact Submit demo of previous work. Prefers CD. "Most compositions are 2 minutes strung together in 6, 12, 18 minute length productions." Does not return material; prefers to keep on file. Responds "right away if submission fills an immediate need."

Music Uses all varieties, including unusual; mostly subdued music beds. Radio-type production used exclusively in telephone and Internet applications.

Tips "Go for volume. We have continuous need for all varieties of music in 2 minute lengths."

N ◪ ALLEGRO MUSIC

3990 Sunsetridge, Suite 203, Moorpark CA 93021-3756. E-mail: dannymuse@adelphia.net. Web site: www.danielobrien.com. **Owner:** Daniel O'Brien. Scoring service, jingle/commercial music production house. Clients include film-makers, advertisers, network promotions and aerobics. Estab. 1991. Uses the services of independent songwriters/composers and lyricists for scoring of films, TV and broadcast commercials, jingles for ad agencies and promotions, and commercials for radio and TV. Commissions 3 composers and 1 lyricist/year. Pays 50% royalty. Buys one-time rights.

How to Contact Query with résumé of credits or submit demo tape of previous work. Prefers CD, cassette and lyric sheet. Include SASE. Responds in 1 month (if interested).

Music Varied: Contemporary to orchestral.

N ◪ CANTRAX RECORDERS

Dept. CM, 2119 Fidler Ave., Long Beach CA 90815. (562)498-4593. Fax: (562)498-4852. E-mail: cantrax@earthlink.net. **Contact:** Richard Cannata, owner. Recording studio. Clients include anyone needing recording services (i.e., industrial, radio, commercial). Estab. 1980. Uses the services of independent songwriters/composers and lyricists for scoring of independent features and films and background music for radio, industrials and promotions, commercials for radio and TV and jingles for radio. Commissions 10 composers/year. Pays fees set by the artist. "We take 15%."

How to Contact *"No phone calls, please."* Query with résumé of credits or submit demo CD of previous work. Prefers CD—no cassettes. Does not return material. Responds in 2 weeks if SASE is provided.

Music Uses jazz, New Age, rock, easy listening and classical for slide shows, jingles and soundtracks.

Tips "You must have a serious, professional attitude."

[N] [✓] CEDAR CREST STUDIO

#17 CR 830, Henderson AR 72544. Web site: www.cedarcreststudio.com. **Contact:** Bob Ketchum, owner. **Audiovisual firm and jingle/commercial music production house.** Clients include corporate, industrial, sales, music publishing, training, educational, legal, medical, music and Internet. Estab. 1973. Sometimes uses the services of independent songwriters/composers for background music for video productions, jingles for TV spots and commercials for radio and TV. Pays by the job or by royalties. Buys all rights or one-time rights.

How to Contact Query with résumé of credits or submit demo tape of previous work. Prefers CD, cassette, or DVD. Does not return material. "We keep it on file for future reference." Responds in 2 months.

Music Uses up-tempo pop (not too "rocky"), unobtrusive—no solos for commercials and background music for video presentations.

Tips "Hang, hang, hang. Be open to suggestions. Improvise, adapt, overcome."

[✓] COMMUNICATIONS FOR LEARNING

395 Massachusetts Ave., Arlington MA 02474. (781)641-2350. E-mail: comlearn@thecia.net. Web site: www.communicationsforlearning.com. **Contact:** Jonathan L. Barkan, executive producer/director. Video, multimedia, exhibit and graphic design firm. Clients include multi-nationals, industry, government, institutions, local, national and international non-profits. Uses services of music houses and independent songwriters/composers as theme and background music for videos and multimedia. Commissions 1-2 composers/year. Pays $2,000-5,000/job and one-time fees. Rights purchased varies.

How to Contact Submit demo and work available for useage. Prefers CD to Web links. Does not return material; prefers to keep on file. "For each job we consider our entire collection." Responds in 3 months.

Music Uses all styles of music for all sorts of assignments.

Tips "Please don't call. Just send your best material available for library use on CD. We'll be in touch if a piece works and negotiate a price. Make certain your name and contact information are on the CD itself, not only on the cover letter."

[N] DBF A MEDIA COMPANY

P.O. Box 2458, Waldorf MD 20604. (301)843-7110. Fax: (301)843-7148. E-mail: info@dbfmedia.com. Web site: www.dbfmedia.com. **Contact:** Randy Runyon, general manager. Advertising agency, audiovisual and media firm and audio and video production company. Clients include business and industry. Estab. 1981. Uses the services of music houses, independent songwriters/composers and lyricists for background music for industrial, training, educational and promo videos, jingles and commercials for radio and TV. Commissions 5-12 composers and 5-12 lyricists/year. Pays by the job. Buys all rights.

How to Contact Submit demo CD of previous work. Prefers CD or DVD with 5-8 songs and lead sheet. Include SASE, but prefers to keep material on file. Responds in 6 months.

Music Uses up-tempo contemporary for industrial videos, slide presentations and commercials.

Tips "We're looking for commercial music, primarily A/C."

☒ ☒ ○ DISK PRODUCTIONS

1100 Perkins Rd., Baton Rouge LA 70802. Fax: (225)343-0210. E-mail: disk_productions@yahoo.com. **Contact:** Joey Decker, director. **Jingle/production house.** Clients include advertising agencies and film companies. Estab. 1982. Uses the services of music houses, independent songwriters/composers and lyricists for scoring and background music for TV spots, films and jingles for radio and TV. Commissions 7 songwriters/composers and 7 lyricists/year. Pays by the job. Buys all rights.

How to Contact Submit demo of previous work. Prefers DVD, CD, cassette or DAT. Does not return material. Responds in 2 weeks.

Music Needs all types of music for jingles, music beds or background music for TV and radio, etc.

Tips "Advertising techniques change with time. Don't be locked in a certain style of writing. Give me music that I can't get from pay needle-drop."

☒ ☒ ☒ FINE ART PRODUCTIONS/RICHIE SURACI PICTURES, MULTIMEDIA, INTERACTIVE

67 Maple St., Newburgh NY 12550-4034. (914)527-9740. Fax: (845)561-5866. E-mail: rs7fap @bestweb.net. Web site: www.idsi.net/ ~ rs7fap/tentsales.htm. **Contact:** Richard Suraci, owner. Advertising agency, audiovisual firm, scoring service, **jingle/commercial music production house**, motion picture production company (Richie Suraci Pictures) and **music sound effect library**. Clients include corporate, industrial, motion picture and broadcast firms. Estab. 1987. Uses services of independent songwriters/composers for scoring, background music and jingles for various projects and commercials for radio and TV. Commissions 1-2 songwriters or composers and 1-2 lyricists/year. Pays by the job, royalty or by the hours. Buys all rights.

How to Contact Submit demo tape of previous work or tape demonstrating composition skills, query with résumé of credits or write or call first to arrange personal interview. Prefers CD, DVD, cassette (or ½″, ¾″, or 1″ videocassette) with as many songs as possible and lyric or lead sheets. Include SASE, but prefers to keep material on file. Responds in 1 year.

Music Uses all types of music for all types of assignments.

☒ HOME, INC.

165 Brookside Avenue Extension, Jamaica Plain MA 02130. E-mail: alanmichel@homeinc.o rg. Director: Alan Michel. Audiovisual firm and video production company. Clients include cable television, nonprofit organizations, pilot programs, entertainment companies and industrial. Uses the services of music houses and independent songwriters/composers for

scoring of music videos, background music and commercials for TV. Commissions 2-5 songwriters/year. Pays up to $200-600/job. Buys all rights and one-time rights.

How to Contact Submit demo tape of previous work. Prefers CD or Web site URL with 6 pieces. Does not return material; prefers to keep on file. Responds as projects require.

Music Mostly synthesizer. Uses all styles of music for educational videos.

Tips "Have a variety of products available and be willing to match your skills to the project and the budget."

K&R ALL MEDIA PRODUCTIONS LLC

(formerly K&R's Recording Studios), 28533 Greenfield, Southfield MI 48076. (248)557-8276. E-mail: recordav@knr.net. Web site: www.knr.net. **Contact:** Ken Glaza. Scoring service and **jingle/commercial music production house**. Clients include commercial and industrial firms. Services include sound for pictures (music, dialogue). Uses the services of independent songwriters/composers and lyricists for scoring of film and video, commercials and industrials and jingles and commercials for radio and TV. Commissions 1 composer/month. Pays by the job. Buys all rights.

How to Contact Submit demo tape of previous work. Prefers CD or VHS videocassette with 5-7 short pieces. "We rack your tape for client to judge." Does not return material.

Tips "Keep samples short. Show me what you can do in five minutes. Go to knr.net 'free samples' and listen to the sensitivity expressed in emotional music."

N MALLOF, ABRUZINO & NASH MARKETING

765 Kimberly Dr., Carol Stream IL 60188. (630)929-5200. Fax: (630)752-9288. E-mail: emall of@manmarketing.com. Web site: www.manmarketing.com. **Contact:** Edward G. Mallof, president. Advertising agency. Works primarily with auto dealer jingles. Estab. 1980. Uses music houses for jingles for retail clients and auto dealers, and commercials for radio and TV. Commissions 5-6 songwriters/year. Pays $600-2,000/job. Buys all rights.

How to Contact Submit demo tape of previous work. Prefers CD with 4-12 songs. Include SASE. Does not return material. Responds if interested.

Tips "Send us produced jingles we could re-lyric for our customers' needs."

☑ NOVUS

121 E. 24th St., 12 Floor, New York NY 10010. (212)487-1377. Fax: (212)505-3300. E-mail: novuscom@aol.com. **Contact:** Robert Antonik, president/creative director. Marketing and communications company. Clients include corporations and interactive media. Estab. 1986. Uses the services of music houses, independent songwriters/composers and lyricists for scoring, background music for documentaries, commercials, multimedia applications, Web site, film shorts, and commercials for radio and TV. Commissions 2 composers and 4 lyricists/year. Pay varies per job. Buys one-time rights.

How to Contact *Request a submission of demo.* Query with résumé. Submit demo of work. Prefers CD with 2-3 songs. "We prefer to keep submitted material on file, but will return material if SASE is enclosed. Responds in 6 weeks.

Music Uses **all styles** for a variety of different assignments.

Tips "Always present your best and don't add quantity to your demo. Novus is a creative marketing and communications company. We work with various public relations, artists managements and legal advisors. We create multimedia events."

OMNI COMMUNICATIONS

Dept. SM, P.O. Box 302, Carmel IN 46082-0302. (317)846-2345. E-mail: omni@omniproduct ions.com. Web site: www.omniproductions.com. President: W. H. Long. Creative Director: S.M. Long. Production Manager: Jim Mullet. Television, digital media production and audiovisual firm. Estab. 1978. Serves industrial, commercial and educational clients. Uses the services of music houses and songwriters for scoring of films and television productions, DVD's, CD-ROMs and internet streams; background music for voice overs; lyricists for original music and themes. Pays by the job. Buys all rights.

How to Contact Submit demo tape of previous work. Prefers CD or DVD. Does not return material. Responds in 2 weeks.

Music Varies with each and every project; from classical, contemporary to commercial industrial.

Tips "Submit good demo tape with examples of your range to command the attention of our producers."

☑ QUALLY & COMPANY INC.

2 E. Oak, Suite 2903, Chicago IL 60611. (312)280-1898. **Contact:** Michael Iva, creative director. **Advertising agency.** Uses the services of music houses, independent songwriters/composers and lyricists for scoring, background music and jingles for radio and TV commercials. Commissions 2-4 composers and 2-4 lyricists/year. Pays by the job. Buys various rights depending on deal.

How to Contact Submit demo CD of previous work or query with résumé of credits. Include SASE, but prefers to keep material on file. Responds in 2 weeks.

Music Uses all kinds of music for commercials.

☑ ▣ UTOPIAN EMPIRE CREATIVEWORKS

P.O. Box 9, Traverse City MI 49685-0009 or P.O. Box 458, Kapa 'a (Kaua'i) HI 96746-0458. (231)943-5050 or (231)943-4000. E-mail: creativeworks@utopianempire.com. Web site: www.UtopianEmpire.com. **Contact:** Ms. M'Lynn Hartwell, president. Web design, multimedia firm and motion picture/video production company. Primarily serves commercial, industrial and nonprofit clients. We provide the following services: advertising, marketing, design/packaging, distribution and booking. Uses services of music houses, independent songwriters/composers for jingles and scoring of and background music for multi-image/multimedia, film and video. Negotiates pay. Buys all or one-time rights.

How to Contact Submit CD of previous work, demonstrating composition skills or query with resume of credits. Prefers CD. Does not return material; prefers to keep on file. Responds only if interested.

Music Uses mostly industrial/commercial themes.

VIDEO I-D, INC.

Dept. SM, 105 Muller Rd., Washington IL 61571. (309)444-4323. Fax: (309)444-4333. E-mail: videoid@videoid.com. Web site: www.VideoID.com. **Contact:** Gwen Wagner, manager, operations. Post production/teleproductions. Clients include law enforcement, industrial and business. Estab. 1977. Uses the services of music houses and independent songwriters/composers for background music for video productions. Pays per job. Buys one-time rights.

How to Contact Submit demo of previous work. Prefers CD or VHS videocassette with 5 songs and lyric sheet. Does not return material. Responds in 1 month.

Play Producers & Publishers

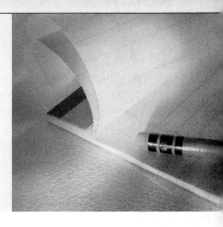

F inding a theater company willing to invest in a new production can be frustrating for an unknown playwright. But whether you write the plays, compose the music or pen the lyrics, it is important to remember not only where to start but how to start. Theater in the U.S. is a hierarchy, with Broadway, Off Broadway and Off Off Broadway being pretty much off limits to all but the Stephen Sondheims of the world.

Aspiring theater writers would do best to train their sights on nonprofit regional and community theaters to get started. The encouraging news is there is a great number of local theater companies throughout the U.S. with experimental artistic directors who are looking for new works to produce, and many are included in this section. This section covers two segments of the industry: theater companies and dinner theaters are listed under Play Producers (beginning on page 240), and publishers of musical theater works are listed under the Play Publishers heading (beginning on page 247). All these markets are actively seeking new works of all types for their stages or publications.

BREAKING IN

Starting locally will allow you to research each company carefully and learn about their past performances, the type of musicals they present, and the kinds of material they're looking for. When you find theaters you think may be interested in your work, attend as many performances as possible, so you know exactly what type of material each theater presents. Or volunteer to work at a theater, whether it be moving sets or selling tickets. This will give you valuable insight into the day-to-day workings of a theater and the creation of a new show. On a national level, you will find prestigious organizations offering workshops and apprenticeships covering every subject from arts administration to directing to costuming. But it could be more helpful to look into professional internships at theaters and attend theater workshops in your area. The more knowledgeable you are about the workings of a particular company or theater, the easier it will be to tailor your work to fit its style and the more responsive they will be to you and your work. (See the Workshops & Conferences section on page 317 for more information.) As a composer for the stage, you need to know as much as possible about a theater and how it works, its history and the different roles played by the people involved in it. Flexibility is the key to successful productions, and knowing how a theater works will only help you in cooperating and collaborating with the director, producer, technical people and actors.

If you're a playwright looking to have his play published in book form or in theater publications, see the listings under the Play Publishers section (page 247). To find play producers and publishers in your area, consult the Geographic Index at the back of this book.

PLAY PRODUCERS

Ⓝ BAILIWICK REPERTORY

Bailiwick Arts Center, 1229 W. Belmont, Chicago IL 60657. (773)883-1090. Fax: (773)883-2017. E-mail: david@bailiwick.org. Web site: www.bailiwick.org. **Director:** David Zak. Producer: Rusty Hernandez. Play producer. Estab. 1982. Produces 5 mainstage, 5 one-act plays and 1-2 new musicals/year. "We do Chicago productions of new works on adaptations that are politically or thematically intriguing and relevant. We also do an annual director's festival which produces 50-75 new short works each year." Pays 5-8% royalty.

How to Contact "Review our manuscript submission guidelines or the professional page of our Web site." Responds in 6 months.

Musical Theater "We want innovative, dangerous, exciting material."

Productions *The Christmas Schooner*, by John Reeger and Julie Shannon (holiday musical); *The Hunchback of Notre Dame* (Dennis DeYoung), *Jerry Springer—The Opera,* American Premiere, *Parade, Dr. Sex* (World Premiere), etc.

Tips "Be creative. Be patient. Be persistent. Make me believe in your dream."

Ⓝ BARTER THEATRE

P.O. Box 867, Abingdon VA 24212. (276)628-3991. Fax: (276)619-3335. E-mail: barterinfo@ bartertheatre.com. Web site: www.bartertheatre.com. **Contact**: Richard Rose, Producing Artistic Director. Play/musical producer. Estab. 1933. Produces app. 10-12 plays and 6-8 musicals (at least 1 new musical)/year. Audience: tourist and local mix, mid-American/ Southern, diverse, all ages. Two spaces: 507-seat proscenium stage, 167-seat thrust stage.

How to Contact Query with synopsis, character breakdown, set description, and CD of the songs. Be sure CDs will play back properly. Include SASE. Responds in 1 year.

Musical Theater We investigate all types. We are not looking for any particular standard. Prefer sellable titles with unique use of music. Prefer small cast musicals, although have done large-scale projects with marketable titles or subject matter. We use original music in many of our plays. Does not wish to see very urban material, or material with very strong language.

Productions 2008 season includes: *Keep on the Sunny Side* by Douglas Pote featuring the music of the original Carter Family; *Evita* by Andrew Lloyd Webber & Tim Rice; *The Who's Tommy; Sweeney Todd* by Stephen Sondheim & Hugh Wheeler; *Disney's Beauty and the Beast*; and *Miracle on 34th Street* by Doug Smith & Vern Stefanic.

Tips "Be patient. Be talented. Be original and make sure subject matter fits our audience. And, please, make sure your CD will play before you send it in."

CIRCA '21 DINNER PLAYHOUSE

Dept. SM, P.O. Box 3784, Rock Island IL 61204-3784. (309)786-2667, ext. 303. Fax: (309)786-4119. E-mail: dpjh@circa21.com. Web site: www.circa21.com. **Contact:** Dennis Hitchcock, producer. Play producer. Estab. 1977. Produces 1-2 plays and 4-5 musicals (1 new musical)/year. Plays produced for a general audience. Three children's works/year, concurrent with major productions. Payment is negotiable.

How to Contact Query with synopsis, character breakdown and set description or submit complete manuscript, score and tape of songs. Include SASE. Responds in 3 months.

Musical Theater "We produce both full length and one act children's musicals. Folk or fairy tale themes. Works that do not condescend to a young audience yet are appropriate for entire family. We're also seeking full-length, small cast musicals suitable for a broad audience." Would also consider original music for use in a play being developed.

Productions *A Closer Walk with Patsy Cline*, *Swingtime Canteen*, *Forever Plaid* and *Lost Highway*.

Tips "Small, upbeat, tourable musicals (like *Pump Boys*) and bright musically-sharp children's productions (like those produced by Prince Street Players) work best. Keep an open mind. Stretch to encompass a musical variety—different keys, rhythms, musical ideas and textures."

THE DIRECTORS COMPANY

311 W. 43rd St., Suite 307, New York NY 10036. (212)246-5877. E-mail: directorscompany @aol.com. Web site: http://mysite.verizon.net/directorscompany. **Contact:** Katherine Heberling, company manager. Artistic/Producing Director: Michael Parva. Play producer. Estab. 1980. Produces 1-2 new musicals/year. Performance space is a 99-seat theatre located in the heart of Manhattan's Theatre District. "It is beautifully equipped with dressing rooms, box office and reception area in the lobby." Pays negotiable rate.

• We are not currently accepting submissions.

How to Contact Query first. Include SASE. Responds in 1 year.

Musical Theater "The Harold Prince Musical Theatre Program develops new musicals by incorporating the director in the early stages of collaboration. The program seeks cutting edge material that works to break boundaries in music theatre. We produce workshops or developmental productions. The emphasis is on the material, not on production values, therefore, we do not limit cast sizes. However, there are limits on props and production values." No children's musicals or reviews.

Productions *Jubilee*, by Kelly Dupuis/Marc Smollin (an absurdly magical exploration of fate, family, and fish); *Tales of Tinseltown* (reading), by Michael Colby/Paul Katz (a sardonic parody of 1930s Hollywood); and *Nightmare Alley* (reading), by Jonathan Brielle (about a drifter in 1932 looking for a way to begin a life in hard times).

ⓝ ENSEMBLE THEATRE OF CINCINNATI

1127 Vine St., Cincinnati OH 45202. (513)421-3555. Fax: (513)562-4104. E-mail: administration@cincyetc.com. Web site: www.cincyetc.com. **Contact:** D. Lynn Meyers, producing artistic director. Play producer. Estab. 1986. Produces 6 plays and at least 1 new musical/ year. Audience is multi-generational and multi-cultural. 191 seats, proscenium stage. Pays 5-8% royalty (negotiable).

How to Contact Please call or write to inquire if ETC is accepting new scripts.

Musical Theater "All types of musicals are acceptable. Cast not over ten, minimum set, please."

Productions *Hedwig & the Angry Inch*, by John Cameron Mitchel (rock star/transgender/

love story); *Alice in Wonderland*, by David Kisor and Joe McDonough (update of the classic tale); and *The Frog Princess*, by Joe McDonough and David Kisor (family retelling of classic tale).

Tips Looking for "creative, inventive, contemporary subjects or classic tales. If we ask you to send your script, please send materials as complete as possible, including a SASE."

FOOLS COMPANY, INC.

P.O. Box 413, Times Square Station, New York NY 10108. E-mail: foolsco@nyc.rr.com. **Contact:** Jill Russell, executive director. Collaborative new and experimental works producer. Estab. 1970. Produces 1 play and 1 musical (1 new musicals) depending on available funding. "Audience is comprised of hip, younger New Yorkers. Plays are performed at various venues in NYC." Pay is negotiable.

How to Contact Query first by e-mail. Include SASE.

Musical Theater "We seek new and unusual, contemporary and experimental material. We would like small, easy-to-tour productions. Nothing classical, folkloric or previously produced." Would also consider working with composers in collaboration or original music for use in plays being developed.

Productions Recent: *Rug Burn*; *Cathleen's Corsage* (alternative performance); and *Blunt Passage* (original drama).

Tips "Come work in NYC!"

⊞ LA JOLLA PLAYHOUSE

P.O. Box 12039, La Jolla CA 92039. (858)550-1070. Fax: (858)550-1075. E-mail: information @ljp.org. Web site: www.lajollaplayhouse.org. **Contact**: Gabriel Greene, literary manager. Play producer. Estab. 1947. Produces 6-show season including 1-2 new musicals/year. Audience is University of California students to senior citizens. Performance spaces include a large proscenium theatre with 492 seats, a ¾ thrust (384 seats), and a black box with up to 400 seats.

How to Contact Query with synopsis, character breakdown, 10-page dialogue sample, demo CD. Include SASE. Responds in 1-2 months.

Musical Theater "We prefer contemporary music but not necessarily a story set in contemporary times. Retellings of classic stories can enlighten us about the times we live in. For budgetary reasons, we'd prefer a smaller cast size."

Productions *Cry-Baby*, book and lyrics by Thomas Meehan and Mark O'Donnell, music by David Javerbaum and Adam Schlesinger; *Dracula, The Musical*, book and lyrics by Don Black and Christopher Hampton, music by Frank Wildhorn (adaptation of Bram Stoker's novel); *Thoroughly Modern Millie*, book by Richard Morris and Dick Scanlan, new music by Jeanine Tesori, new lyrics by Dick Scanlan (based on the 1967 movie); and *Jane Eyre*, book and additional lyrics by John Cairo, music and lyrics by Paul Gordon (adaptation of Charlotte Bronte's novel).

⊞ LOS ANGELES DESIGNERS' THEATRE

P.O. Box 1883, Studio City CA 91614-0883. (323)650-9600. Fax: (323)654-3210. E-mail: ladesigners@juno.com. **Contact:** Richard Niederberg, artistic director. Play producer. Estab. 1970. Produces 20-25 plays and 8-10 new musicals/year. Audience includes Hollywood production executives in film, TV, records and multimedia. Plays are produced at several locations, primarily Studio City, California. Pay is negotiable.

How to Contact Query first. Does not return material. Responds only if interested. *Send proposals only*.

Musical Theater ''We seek out controversial material. Street language OK, nudity is fine, religious themes, social themes, political themes are encouraged. Our audience is very 'jaded' as it consists of TV, motion picture and music publishing executives who have 'seen it all'.'' Does not wish to see bland, 'safe' material. We like first productions. In the cover letter state in great detail the proposed involvement of the songwriter, other than as a writer (i.e., director, actor, singer, publicist, designer, etc.). Also, state if there are any liens on the material or if anything has been promised.''

Productions *St. Tim*, by Fred Grab (historical '60s musical); *Slipper and the Rose* (gang musical); and *1593—The Devils Due* (historical musical).

Tips ''Make it very 'commercial' and inexpensive to produce. Allow for non-traditional casting. Be prepared with ideas as to how to transform your work to film or videotaped entertainment.''

NEW YORK STATE THEATRE INSTITUTE

37 First St., Troy NY 12180. (518)274-3200. E-mail: pbs@capital.net. Web site: www.nysti.o rg. **Contact:** Patricia Di Benedetto Snyder, producing artistic director. Play producer. Produces 5 plays (1 new musical)/year. Plays performed for student audiences grades K-12, family audiences and adult audiences. Theater seats 900 with full stage. Pay negotiable.

How to Contact Query with synopsis, character breakdown, set description and tape of songs. Include SASE. *Do not send ms unless invited*. Responds in 6 weeks for synopsis, 4 months for ms.

Musical Theater Looking for ''intelligent and well-written book with substance, a score that enhances and supplements the book and is musically well-crafted and theatrical.'' Length: up to 2 hours. Could be play with music, musical comedy, musical drama. Excellence and substance in material is essential. Cast could be up to 20; orchestra size up to 8.

Productions *A Tale of Cinderella*, by W.A. Frankonis/Will Severin/George David Weiss (adaptation of fairy tale); *The Silver Skates*, by Lanie Robertson/Byron Janis/George David Weiss (adaptation of book); *The Snow Queen*, by Adrian Mitchell/Richard Peaslee (adaptation of fairy tale); and *Magna Carta*, by Ed Lange/Will Severin/George David Weiss (new musical drama).

Tips ''There is a great need for musicals that are well-written with intelligence and substance which are suitable for family audiences.''

NORTH SHORE MUSIC THEATRE

P.O. Box 62, Beverly MA 01915. (978)232-7200. Fax: (978)921-6351. Web site: www.nsmt.o rg. **Contact:** John La Rock, producer. Play producer. Estab. 1955. Produces 1 Shakespearian play and 7 musicals (1 new musical)/year. General audiences. Performance space is an 1,500-seat arena theatre, 120-seat workshop. Pays royalty (all done via individual commission agreements).

How to Contact Submit synopsis and CD of songs. Include SASE. Responds within 6 months.

Musical Theater Prefers full-length adult pieces not necessarily arena-theatre oriented. Cast sizes from 1-30; orchestra's from 1-16.

Productions *Tom Jones*, by Paul Leigh, George Stiles; *I Sent A Letter to My Love*, by Melissa Manchester and Jeffrey Sweet; *Just So*, by Anthony Drewe & George Stiles (musical based on Rudyard Kipling's fables); *Letters from 'Nam*, by Paris Barclay (Vietnam War experience as told through letters from GI's); and *Friendship of the Sea*, by Michael Wartofsky & Kathleen Cahill (New England maritime adventure musical).

Tips "Keep at it!"

N PLAYWRIGHTS HORIZONS

416 W. 42nd St., New York NY 10036. (212)564-1235. Fax: (212)594-0296. E-mail: literary@ playwrightshorizons.org. Web site: www.playwrightshorizons.org. **Contact:** Christie Evangelista, assistant literary manager. Artistic Director: Christie Evangelisto, director of musical theater. Estab. 1971. Produces about 5 plays and 1 new musical/year. "Adventurous New York City theater-going audience." Pays general Off-Broadway contract.

How to Contact Submit complete manuscript and tape or CD of songs. Attn: Christie Evangelisto. Include SASE. Responds in 8 months.

Musical Theater American writers. "No revivals, one-acts or children's shows; otherwise we're flexible. We have a particular interest in scores with a distinctively contemporary and American flavor. We generally develop work from scratch; we're open to proposals for shows and scripts in early stages of development."

Productions *Grey Gardens, Saved, Floyd and Clea Under the Western Sky, Assassins, Sunday in the Park with George.*

PRINCE MUSIC THEATER

100 S. Broad St., Suite 650, Philadelphia PA 19110. (215)972-1000. Fax: (215)972-1020. E-mail: info@princemusictheater.org. Web site: www.princemusictheater.org. **Contact:** Marjorie Samoff, president and producing director. Play producer. Estab. 1984. Produces 4-5 musicals/year. "Our average audience member is in their mid-40s. We perform to ethnically diverse houses."

How to Contact Submit two-page synopsis with tape or CD of 4 songs. Include SASE. "May include complete script, but be aware that response is at least 10 months."

Music "We seek musicals ranging from the traditional to the experimental. Topics can range. Musical styles can vary from folk pop through opera. Orchestra generally limited to a maximum of 9 pieces; cast size maximum of 10-12."

Tips "We only produce pieces that are music/lyric driven, not merely plays with music."

N THE REPERTORY THEATRE OF ST. LOUIS

P.O. Box 191730, 130 Edgar Road, St. Louis MO 63119. (314)968-7340. E-mail: mail@repstl. org. Web site: www.repstl.org/. **Contact:** Susan Gregg, associate artistic director. Play producer. Estab. 1966. Produces 9 plays and 1 or 2 musicals/year. "Conservative regional theater audience. We produce all our work at the Loretto Hilton Theatre.'' Pays by royalty.

How to Contact Query with synopsis, character breakdown and set description. Does not return material. Responds in 2 years.

Musical Theater "We want plays with a small cast and simple setting. No children's shows or foul language. After a letter of inquiry we would prefer script and demo tape.''

Productions *Almost September* and *Esmeralda*, by David Schechter and Steve Lutvak; *Jack*, by Barbara Field and Hiram Titus; and *Young Rube*, by John Pielmeier and Nattie Selman, *Ace* by Robert Taylor and Richard Oberacker.

SHAKESPEARE SANTA CRUZ

Theater Arts Center, U.C.S.C., 1156 High Street, Santa Cruz CA 95064. (831)459-5810. E-mail: iago@ucsc.edu. Web site: www.shakespearesantacruz.org. **Contact:** Marco Barricelli, artistic director. Play producer. Estab. 1982. Produces 4 plays/year. Performance spaces are an outdoor redwood grove; and an indoor 540-seat thrust. Pay is negotiable.

How to Contact Query first. Include SASE. Responds in 2 months.

Musical Theater "Shakespeare Santa Cruz produces musicals in its Winter Holiday Season (Oct-Dec). We are also interested in composers' original music for pre-existing plays—including songs, for example, for Shakespeare's plays.''

Productions *Cinderella*, by Kate Hawley (book and lyrics) and Gregg Coffin (composer); and *Gretel and Hansel*, by Kate Hawley (book and lyrics) and composer Craig Bohmler; *The Princess and the Pea*, by Kate Hawley (book and lyrics) and composer Adam Wernick; *Sleeping Beauty*, by Kate Hawley (book and lyrics) and composer Adam Wernick.

Tips "Always contact us before sending material.''

THE TEN-MINUTE MUSICALS PROJECT

P.O. Box 461194, West Hollywood CA 90046. E-mail: info@tenminutemusicals.org. Web site: www.tenminutemusicals.org. **Contact:** Michael Koppy, producer. Play producer. Estab. 1987. All pieces are new musicals. Pays $250 advance.

How to Contact Submit complete manuscript, score and tape of songs. Include SASE. Responds in 3 months.

Musical Theater Seeks complete short stage musicals of 8-15 minutes in length. Maximum cast: 9. "No parodies—original music only.''

Productions Away to Pago Pago, by Jack Feldman/Barry Manilow/John PiRoman/Bruce Sussman; The Bottle Imp, by Kenneth Vega (from the story of the same title by Robert Louis Stevenson); and The Furnished Room, by Saragail Katzman (from the story of the same title by O. Henry), and many others.

Tips "Start with a solid story—either an adaptation or an original idea—but with a solid beginning, middle and end (probably with a plot twist at the climax). We caution that it will surely take much time and effort to create a quality work. (Occasionally a clearly talented and capable writer and composer seem to have almost 'dashed' something off, under the misperception that inspiration can carry the day in this format. Works selected in previous rounds all clearly evince that considerable deliberation and craft were invested.) We're seeking short contemporary musical theater material, in the style of what might be found on Broadway, Off-Broadway or the West End. Think of shows like Candide or Little Shop of Horrors, pop operas like Sweeney Todd or Chess, or chamber musicals like Once on this Island or Falsettos. (Even small accessible operas like The Telephone or Trouble in Tahiti are possible models.) All have solid plots, and all rely on sung material to advance them. Of primary importance is to start with a strong story, even if it means postponing work on music and lyrics until the dramatic foundation is complete."

WEST END ARTISTS

% St. Luke's Theatre, 308 West 46th St., New York NY 10036. (212)947-3499. Fax: (212)265-4074. **West Coast:** 18034 Ventura Blvd. #291, Encino CA 91316. (818)623-0040. Fax: (818)623-0202. E-mail: egaynes@aol.com. **Contact:** Pamela Hall, associate artistic director. Artistic Director: Edmund Gaynes. Play producer. Estab. 1983. "We operate St. Luke's Theatre, Actors Temple Theatre, and Theatres at 45 Bleecker St. in New York City, and Whitmore-Lindley Theatre Center in Los Angeles." Produces 5 plays and 3 new musicals/year. Audience "covers a broad spectrum, from general public to heavy theater/film/TV industry crowds. Pays 6% royalty.

How to Contact Submit complete manuscript, score and tape of songs. Include SASE. Responds in 3 months.

Musical Theater "Prefer small-cast musicals and revues. Full length preferred. Interested in children's shows also." Cast size: "Maximum 12; exceptional material with larger casts will be considered."

Productions Off-Broadway: *Picon Pie* - Lambs Theatre (2004-05); *Trolls* - Actors Playhouse, (2005); *The Big Voice: God or Merman?* - Actors Temple Theatre (2006-07)

Tips "If you feel every word or note you have written is sacred and chiseled in stone and are unwilling to work collaboratively with a professional director, don't bother to submit."

WINGS THEATRE CO.

154 Christopher St., New York NY 10014. (212)627-2960. Fax: (212)462-0024. E-mail: jcorrick@wingstheatre.com. Web site: www.wingstheatre.com. **Contact:** Laura Kleeman, literary manager. Artistic Director: Jeffrey Corrick. Play producer. Estab. 1987. Produces 3-5 plays and 3-5 musicals/year. Performance space is a 74-seat O.O.B. proscenium; repertoire includes a New Musicals Series, a gay-play series—we produce musicals in both series. Pays $100 for limited rights to produce against 6% of gross box office receipts.

How to Contact Submit complete manuscript, CD or tape of songs (score is not essential). Include SASE. Responds in 1 year.

Musical Theater "Eclectic. Entertaining. Enlightening. This is an O.O.B. theater. Funds are limited." Does not wish to see "movies posing as plays. Television theater."

Productions *Scott & Zelda*, by Dave Bates (The Fitzgeralds); *Cowboys*, by Clint Jefferies (gay western spoof); and *The Three Musketeers*, by Clint Jefferies (musical adaptation).

Tips "Book needs to have a well-developed plot line and interesting, fully-realized characters. We place emphasis on well-written scripts, as opposed to shows which rely exclusively on the quality of the music to carry the show. Also be patient—we often hold onto plays for a full year before making a final decision."

PLAY PUBLISHERS

BAKER'S PLAYS

45 W. 25th St., New York NY 10010. (617)745-8085. Fax: (212)627-7753. E-mail: info@bake rsplays.com. Web site: www.bakersplays.com. **Contact:** Associate Editor. Play publisher. Estab. 1845. Publishes 15-22 plays and 0-3 new musicals/year. Plays are used by children's theaters, junior and senior high schools, colleges and community theaters. Pays negotiated book and production royalty.

- See the listing for Baker's Plays High School Playwriting Contest in the Contests & Awards section.

How to Contact Submit complete manuscript, score and cassette tape of songs. Include SASE. Responds in 4 months.

Musical Theater "Seeking musicals for teen production and children's theater production. We prefer large cast, contemporary musicals which are easy to stage and produce. Plot your shows strongly, keep your scenery and staging simple, your musical numbers and choreography easily explained and blocked out. Music must be camera-ready." Would consider original music for use in a play being developed or in a pre-existing play.

Productions *Oedipus/A New Magical Comedy*, by Bob Johnson.

Tips "As we publish musicals that can be produced by high school theater departments with high school talent, the writer should know if their play can be done on the high school stage. I recommend that the writer go to performances of original high school musicals whenever possible."

THE DRAMATIC PUBLISHING COMPANY

311 Washington St., Woodstock IL 60098. (815)338-7170. E-mail: plays@dramaticpublishin g.com. Web site: www.dramaticpublishing.com. **Contact:** Music Editor. Play publisher. Publishes 35 plays and 3-5 musicals/year. Estab. 1885. Plays used by professional and community theaters, schools and colleges. Pays negotiable royalty.

How to Contact Submit complete manuscript, score and tape of songs. Include SASE. Responds in 3 months.

Musical Theater Seeking "children's musicals not over $1\frac{1}{4}$ hours, and adult musicals with 2 act format. No adaptations for which the rights to use the original work have not been cleared. If directed toward high school market, large casts with many female roles are preferred. For professional, stock and community theater small casts are better. Cost of producing a play is always a factor to consider in regard to costumes, scenery and special effects." Would also consider original music for use in a pre-existing play, "if we or the composer hold the rights to the non-musical work."

Publications *The Little Prince*, by Rick Cummins/John Scoullar; *Hans Brinker*, by Gayle Hudson/Bobbe Bramson; and *Bubbe Meises, Bubbe Stories*, by Ellen Gould/Holly Gewandter (all are full-length family musicals).

Tips "A complete score, ready to go is highly recommended. Tuneful songs which stand on their own are a must. Good subject matter which has wide appeal is always best but not required."

ELDRIDGE PUBLISHING CO., INC.

P.O. Box 14367, Tallahassee FL 32317. Phone/Fax: (850)385-2463. E-mail: info@histage.c om. Web site: www.histage.com. **Contact:** Susan Shore, musical editor. Play publisher. Estab. 1906. Publishes 50 plays and 1-2 musicals/year. Seeking "large cast musicals which appeal to students. We like variety and originality in the music, easy staging and costuming. Also looking for children's theater musicals which have smaller casts and are easy to tour. We serve the school market (6th grade through 12th); and church market (Christmas musicals)." Pays 50% royalty and 10% copy sales in school market.

How to Contact Submit manuscript, score or lead sheets and CD of songs. Include SASE. Responds in 1 month.

Publications *The Bard is Back*, by Stephen Murray ("a high school's production of Romeo & Juliet is a disaster!"); and *Boogie-Woogie Bugle Girls*, book by Craig Sodaro, music and lyrics by Stephen Murray (WWII themed musical).

Tips "We're always looking for talented composers but not through individual songs. We're only interested in complete school or church musicals. Lead sheets, CDs, and script are best way to submit. Let us see your work!"

THE FREELANCE PRESS

P.O. Box 548, Dover MA 02030. (508)785-8250. E-mail: info@freelancepress.org. Web site: www.freelancepress.org. Managing Editor: Narcissa Campion. Play publisher. Estab. 1979. Publishes up to 3 new musicals/year. "Pieces are primarily to be acted by elementary/ middle school to high school students (9th and 10th grades); large casts (approximately 30); plays are produced by schools and children's theaters." Pays 10% of purchase price of script or score, 50% of collected royalty.

How to Contact Query first. Include SASE. Responds in 6 months.

Musical Theater "We publish previously produced musicals and plays to be acted by children in the primary grades through high school. Plays are for large casts (approximately 30 actors and speaking parts) and run between 45 minutes to 1 hour and 15 minutes. Subject matter should be contemporary issues (sibling rivalry, friendship, etc.) or adaptations of classic literature for children (*Syrano de Bergerac*, *Rip Van Winkle*, *Pied Piper*, *Treasure Island*, etc.). We do not accept any plays written for adults to perform for children."

Publications *Tortoise vs. Hare*, by Stephen Murray (modern version of classic); *Tumbleweed*, by Sebastian Stuart (sleepy time western town turned upside down); and *Mything Links*, by Sam Abel (interweaving of Greek myths with a great pop score).

Tips "We enjoy receiving material that does not condescend to children. They are capable of understanding many current issues, playing complex characters, handling unconventional material, and singing difficult music."

SAMUEL FRENCH, INC.

45 W. 25th St., New York NY 10010. (212)206-8990. Fax: (212)206-1429. Web site: www.sa muelfrench.com. Hollywood office: 7623 Sunset Blvd., Hollywood CA 90046. (323)876-0570. Fax: (323)876-6822. President: Leon Embry. **Contact:** Roxane Heinze-Bradshaw, associate editor. Play publisher. Estab. 1830. Publishes 60-80 plays and 5-10 new musicals/ year. Amateur and professional theaters.

How to Contact *Query first.* Include SASE. Responds in 10 weeks.

Musical Theater "We publish primarily successful musicals from the NYC, London and regional stage."

Publications *Evil Dead: The Musical,* by George Reinblatt—lyrics/book, and Frank Cipolla, Christopher Bond, Melissa Morris, George Reinblatt - music (Horror Movie parody); Gutenberg! The Musical, by Scott Brown and Anthony King - music, lyrics, and book (Musical spoof); *Don't Hug Me,* by Phil Olson—book/lyrics, and Paul Olson—music (love and karaoke in a northern Minnesota bar).

HEUER PUBLISHING CO.

P.O. Box 248, Cedar Rapids IA 52406. Main Office: 211 First Ave., SE Suite 200, Cedar Rapids IA 52401. 1-800-950-7529. E-mail: editor@hitplays.com. Web site: www.hitplays.com. Publisher: C. Emmett McMullen. Play publisher. Estab. 1928. Publishes plays, musicals, operas/operettas and guides (choreography, costume, production/staging) for amateur and professional markets, including junior and senior high schools, college/university and community theatres. Focus includes comedy, drama, fantasy, mystery and holiday. Pays by percentage royalty or outright purchase. Pays by outright purchase or percentage royalty.

How to Contact Query with musical CD/tape or submit complete manuscript and score. Include SASE. Responds in 2 months.

Musical Theater "We prefer one, two or three act comedies or mystery-comedies with a large number of characters."

Publications *Happily Ever After*, by Allen Koepke (musical fairytale); *Brave Buckaroo*, by Renee J. Clark (musical melodrama); and *Pirate Island*, by Martin Follose (musical comedy).

Tips "We are willing to review single-song submissions as cornerstone piece for commissioned works. Special interest focus in multicultural, historic, classic literature, teen issues, and biographies."

PIONEER DRAMA SERVICE

P.O. Box 4267, Englewood CO 80155. 1-800-333-7262. Fax: (303)779-4315. Web site: www. pioneerdrama.com. **Contact:** Lori Conary, assistant editor. Play publisher. Estab. 1963. "Plays are performed by junior high and high school drama departments, church youth groups, college and university theaters, semi-professional and professional children's theaters, parks and recreation departments." Playwrights paid 50% royalty (10% sales).

How to Contact Query with character breakdown, synopsis and set description. Include SASE. Responds in 6 months.

Musical Theater "We seek full length children's musicals, high school musicals and one act children's musicals to be performed by children, secondary school students, and/or adults. We want musicals easy to perform, simple sets, many female roles and very few solos. Must be appropriate for educational market. We are not interested in profanity, themes with exclusively adult interest, sex, drinking, smoking, etc. Several of our full-length plays are being converted to musicals. We edit them, then contract with someone to write the music and lyrics."

Publications *The Stories of Scheherazade*, book by Susan Pargmon, music and lyrics by Bill Francoeur (musical *Arabian Nights*); *Hubba Hubba: The 1940s Hollywood Movie Musical*, by Gene Casey and Jan Casey (tribute to the 1940s Hollywood movie musical); and *Cinderella's Glass Slipper*, book by Vera Morris, music and lyrics by Bill Francoeur (musical fairy tale).

Tips "Research and learn about our company. Our Web site and catalog provide an incredible amount of information."

Classical Performing Arts

F inding an audience is critical to the composer of orchestral music. Fortunately, baby boomers are swelling the ranks of classical music audiences and bringing with them a taste for fresh, innovative music. So the climate is fair for composers seeking their first performance.

Finding a performance venue is particularly important because once a composer has his work performed for an audience and establishes himself as a talented newcomer, it can lead to more performances and commissions for new works.

BEFORE YOU SUBMIT

Be aware that most classical music organizations are nonprofit groups, and don't have a large budget for acquiring new works. It takes a lot of time and money to put together an orchestral performance of a new composition, therefore these groups are quite selective when choosing new works to perform. Don't be disappointed if the payment offered by these groups is small or even non-existent. What you gain is the chance to have your music performed for an appreciative audience. Also realize that many classical groups are understaffed, so it may take longer than expected to hear back on your submission. It pays to be patient, and employ diplomacy, tact and timing in your follow-up.

In this section you will find listings for classical performing arts organizations throughout the U.S. But if you have no prior performances to your credit, it's a good idea to begin with a small chamber orchestra, for example. Smaller symphony and chamber orchestras are usually more inclined to experiment with new works. A local university or conservatory of music, where you may already have contacts, is a great place to start.

All of the groups listed in this section are interested in hearing new works from contemporary classical composers. Pay close attention to the music needs of each group, and when you find one you feel might be interested in your music, follow submission guidelines carefully. To locate classical performing arts groups in your area, consult the Geographic Index at the back of this book.

ACADIANA SYMPHONY ORCHESTRA

412 Travis St., Lafayette LA 70503. (337)232-4277. Fax: (337)237-4712. E-mail: information @acadianasymphony.org. Web site: www.acadianasymphony.org. **Contact**: Geraldine Hubbel, executive director. Symphony orchestra. Estab. 1984. Members are amateurs and professionals. Performs 20 concerts/year, including 1 new work. Commissions 1 new work/ year. Performs in 2,230-seat hall with "wonderful acoustics." Pays "according to the type of composition."

How to Contact Call first. Does not return material. Responds in 2 months.

Music Full orchestra: 10 minutes at most. Reduced orchestra, educational pieces: short, up to 5 minutes.

Performances Quincy Hilliard's *Universal Covenant* (orchestral suite); James Hanna's *In Memoriam* (strings/elegy); and Gregory Danner's *A New Beginning* (full orchestra fanfare).

ADRIAN SYMPHONY ORCHESTRA

110 S. Madison St., Adrian MI 49221. (517)264-3121. Fax: (517)264-3833. E-mail: john@aso .org. Web site: www.aso.org. **Contact:** John Dodson, music director. Symphony orchestra and chamber music ensemble. Estab. 1981. Members are professionals. Performs 25 concerts/year including new works. 1,200 seat hall—"Rural city with remarkably active cultural life." Pays $200-1,000 for performance.

How to Contact Query first. Does not return material. Responds in 6 months.

Music Chamber ensemble to full orchestra. "Limited rehearsal time dictates difficulty of pieces selected." Does not wish to see "rock music or country—not at this time."

Performances Michael Pratt's *Dancing on the Wall* (orchestral—some aleatoric); Sir Peter Maxwell Davies' *Orkney Wedding* (orchestral); and Gwyneth Walker's *Fanfare, Interlude, Finale* (orchestral).

ⓝ THE AMERICAN BOYCHOIR

19 Lambert Dr., Princeton NJ 08540. (609)924-5858. Fax: (609)924-5812. E-mail: jkaltenbac h@americanboychoir.org. Web site: www.americanboychoir.org. General Manager: Janet B. Kaltenbach. Music Director: Fernando Malvar-Ruiz. Professional boychoir. Estab. 1937. Members are musically talented boys in grades 4-8. Performs 150 concerts/year. Commissions 1 new work approximately every 3 years. Actively seeks high quality arrangements. Performs national and international tours, orchestral engagements, church services, workshops, school programs, local concerts, and at corporate and social functions.

How to Contact Submit complete score. Include SASE. Responds in 1 year.

Music Choral works in unison, SA, SSA, SSAA or SATB division; unaccompanied and with piano or organ; occasional chamber orchestra or brass ensemble. Works are usually sung by 28 to 60 boys. Composers must know boychoir sonority.

Performances *Four Seasons*, by Michael Torke (orchestral-choral); *Garden of Light*, by Aaron Kernis (orchestral-choral); *Reasons for Loving the Harmonica*, by Libby Larsen (piano); and *Songs Eternity*, by Steven Paulus (piano).

ANDERSON SYMPHONY ORCHESTRA

1124 Meridian Plaza, Anderson IN 46016. (765)644-2111. Fax: (765)644-7703. E-mail: aso@andersonsymphony.org. Web site: www.andersonsymphony.org. **Contact:** Dr. Richard Sowers, conductor. Executive Director: George W. Vinson. Symphony orchestra. Estab. 1967. Members are professionals. Performs 7 concerts/year. Performs for typical mid-western audience in a 1,500-seat restored Paramount Theatre. Pay negotiable.

How to Contact Query first. Include SASE. Responds in several months.

Music "Shorter lengths better; concerti OK; difficulty level: mod high; limited by typically 3 full service rehearsals."

▣ ARCADY

P.O. Box 955, Simcoe ON N3Y 5B3 Canada. (519)428-3185. E-mail: info@arcady.ca. Web site: www.arcady.ca. **Contact:** Ronald Beckett, director. Professional chorus and orchestra. Members are professionals, university music majors and recent graduates from throughout Ontario. "Arcady forms the bridge between the student and the professional performing career." Performs 12 concerts/year including 1 new works. Pay negotiable.

How to Contact Submit complete score and tape of piece(s). Does not return material. Responds in 3 months.

Music "Compositions appropriate for ensemble accustomed to performance of chamber works, accompanied or unaccompanied, with independence of parts. Specialize in repertoire of 17th, 18th and 20th centuries. Number of singers does not exceed 30. Orchestra is limited to strings, supported by a professional quartet. No popular, commercial or show music."

Performances Ronald Beckett's *I Am . . .* (opera); Ronald Beckett's *John* (opera); and David Lenson's *Prologue to Dido and Aeneas* (masque).

Tips "Arcady is a touring ensemble experienced with both concert and stage performance."

ATLANTA POPS ORCHESTRA

P.O. Box 15037, Atlanta GA 30333. (404)636-0020. E-mail: ladkmusic@aol.com. Web site: www.atlantapops.com. **Contact:** Leonard Altieri, general manager. Pops orchestra. Estab. 1945. Members are professionals. Performs 5-10 concerts/year. Concerts are performed for audiences of 5,000-10,000, "all ages, all types." Composers are not paid; concerts are free to the public.

How to Contact Call to request permission to submit. Then send cassette, and score or music, if requested. Include SASE. Responds "as soon as possible."

Performances Vincent Montana, Jr.'s *Magic Bird of Fire*; Louis Alter's *Manhattan Serenade*; and Nelson Riddle's *It's Alright With Me*.

Tips "My concerts are pops concerts—no deep classics."

▣ THE ATLANTA YOUNG SINGERS OF CALLANWOLDE

980 Briarcliff Rd. N.E., Atlanta GA 30306. (404)873-3365. Fax: (404)873-0756. E-mail: info@aysc.org. Web site: www.aysc.org. **Contact:** Paige F. Mathis, music director. Children's chorus. Estab. 1975. Performs 3 major concerts/year as well as invitational performances

and co-productions with other Atlanta arts organizations. Audience consists of community members, families, alumni, and supporters. Performs most often at churches. Pay is negotiable.

How to Contact Submit complete score and tape of piece(s). Include SASE. Responds in accordance with request.

Music "Subjects and styles appealing to 3rd-12th grade boys and girls. Contemporary concerns of the world of interest. Unusual sacred, folk, classic style. Internationally and ethnically bonding. Medium difficulty preferred, with or without keyboard accompaniment."

Tips "Our mission is to promote service and growth through singing."

Ⓝ AUGSBURG CHOIR

Augsburg College, 731 21st Ave. S., Minneapolis MN 55454. E-mail: hendricp@augsburg.edu. Web site: www.augsburg.edu. **Director of Choral Activities:** Peter A. Hendrickson. Vocal ensemble (SATB choir). Members are amateurs. Performs 25 concerts/year, including 1-6 new works. Commissions 0-2 composers or new works/year. Audience is all ages, "sophisticated and unsophisticated." Concerts are performed in churches, concert halls and schools. Pays for outright purchase.

How to Contact Query first. Include SASE. Responds in 1 month.

Music Seeking "sacred choral pieces, no more than 5-7 minutes long, to be sung a cappella or with obbligato instrument. Can contain vocal solos. We have 50-60 members in our choir."

Performances Carol Barnett's *Spiritual Journey*; Steven Heitzeg's *Litanies for the Living* (choral/orchestral); and Morton Lanriclsen's *O Magnum Mysteries* (a cappella choral).

AUREUS QUARTET

22 Lois Ave., Demarest NJ 07627-2220. (201)767-8704. E-mail: AureusQuartet@aol.com. **Contact:** James J. Seiler, artistic director. Vocal ensemble (a cappella). Estab. 1979. Members are professionals. Performs 75 concerts/year, including 12 new works. Commissions 5 composers or new works/year. Pay varies for outright purchase.

How to Contact Query first. Include SASE. Responds in 2 months.

Music "We perform anything from pop to classic—mixed repertoire so anything goes. Some pieces can be scored for orchestras as we do pops concerts. Up to now, we've only worked with a quartet. Could be expanded if the right piece came along. Level of difficulty—no piece has ever been too hard." Does not wish to see electronic or sacred pieces. "Electronic pieces would be hard to program. Sacred pieces not performed much. Classical/jazz arrangements of old standards are great! Unusual Christmas arrangements are most welcome!"

Tips "We perform for a very diverse audience. Luscious, four part writing that can showcase well-trained voices is a must. Also, clever arrangements of old hits from '50s through '60s are sure bets. (Some pieces could take optional accompaniment)."

BILLINGS SYMPHONY

2721 2nd Ave N., Suite 350, Billings MT 59101-1936. (406)252-3610. Fax: (406)252-3353. E-mail: symphony@billingssymphony.org. Web site: www.billingssymphony.org. **Contact: Dr. Uri Barnea, music director. Symphony orchestra, orchestra and chorale. Estab. 1950. Members are professionals and amateurs. Performs 12-15 concerts/year, including 6-7 new works. Traditional audience. Performs at Alberta Bair Theater (capacity 1,416). Pays by outright purchase (or rental).

How to Contact Query first. Include SASE. Responds in 2 weeks.

Music Any style. Traditional notation preferred.

Performances Jim Cockey's *Symphony No. 2 (Parmly's Dream)* (symphony orchestra with chorus and soloists); Ilse-Mari Lee's *Cello Concerto* (concerto for cello solo and orchestra); and Jim Beckel's *Christmas Fanfare* (brass and percussion).

Tips "Write what you feel (be honest) and sharpen your compositional and craftsmanship skills."

BIRMINGHAM-BLOOMFIELD SYMPHONY ORCHESTRA

155 Bates, Second Fl., Birmingham MI 48009. (248)645-2276. Fax: (248)645-2276, *51. E-mail: bbso@bbso.org. Web site: www.bbso.org. **Contact:** Charles Greenwell, music director and conductor. Conductor Laureate: Felix Resnick. President and Executive Director: Carla Lamphere. Symphony orchestra. Estab. 1975. Members are professionals. Performs 5 concerts including 1 new work/year. Commissions 1 composer or new work/year "with grants." Performs for middle-to-upper class audience at Temple Beth El's Sanctuary. Pays per performance "depending upon grant received."

How to Contact *Query first.* Does not return material. Responds in 6 months.

Music "We are a symphony orchestra but also play pops. Usually 3 works on program (2 hrs.) Orchestra size 65-75. If pianist is involved, they must rent piano."

Performances Brian Belanger's *Tuskegee Airmen Suite* (symphonic full orchestra); Larry Nazer & Friend's *Music from "Warm" CD* (jazz with full orchestra); and Mark Gottlieb's *Violin Concerto for Orchestra* (new world premiere, 2006).

THE BOSTON PHILHARMONIC

295 Huntington Ave., #210, Boston MA 02115. (617)236-0999. Fax: (617)236-8613. E-mail: info@bostonphil.org. Web site: www.bostonphil.org. **Music Director:** Benjamin Zander. Symphony orchestra. Estab. 1979. Members are professionals, amateurs and students. Performs 2 concerts/year. Audience is ages 30-70. Performs at New England Conservatory's Jordan Hall, Boston's Symphony Hall and Sanders Theatre in Cambridge. Both Jordan Hall and Sanders Theatre are small (approximately 1,100 seats) and very intimate.

How to Contact *Does not accept new music at this time.*

Music Full orchestra only.

Performances Dutilleuxs' *Tout un monde lointain* for cello and orchestra (symphonic); Bernstein's *Fancy Free* (symphonic/jazzy); Copland's *El Salon Mexico* (symphonic); Gershwin's *Rhapsody in Blue*; Shostakovitch's *Symphony No. 10*, Harbison's *Concerto for Oboe*; Holst's *The Planet Suite*; Schwantner's *New Morning for the World*; Berg's *Seven Early Songs*; and Ive's *The Unanswered Question*.

BRAVO! L.A.

16823 Liggett St., North Hills CA 91343. (818)892-8737. Fax: (818)892-1227. E-mail: musical menace@earthlink.net and info@bravo-la.com. Web site: www.bravo-la.com. **Contact:** Cellist Dr. Janice Foy, director. An umbrella organization of recording/touring musicians, formed in 1994. Includes the following musical ensembles: the New American Quartet (string quartet); The Ascending Wave (harp, soprano, cello, or harp/cello duo); Celllissimo! L.A. (cello ensemble); Sierra Chamber Players (piano with strings or mixed ensemble), and the Pralitz/Foy violin and cello Duo. Performs concerts throughout the year. "We take care of PR. There is also grant money the composer can apply for—especially in New York."

How to Contact Submit complete score and tape of piece(s). Include SASE. Responds in a few months. "We are also happy to record DEMOS for those needing entry into music schools or the music business. We would run the DEMO contract through the Musicians Union Local 47 and if you want to expand on the DEMO and make it into a limited pressing agreement, then we would also be able to accomplish that with the appropriate contract."

Music "Classical, Romantic, Baroque, Popular (including new arrangements done by Shelly Cohen, from the 'Tonight Show Band'), ethnic (including gypsy) and contemporary works (commissioned as well). The New American Quartet has a CD called "Nod to Moussorgsky (see Web site for soundclips) along with CDs by the Ascending Wave and the CD Gypsy Gold features Dr. Foy in solo works by Bartok, Bolognini, and Dvorak in arrangements by S. Cohen.

Performances Most recently the New American Quartet was featured in a Canadian PBS documentary "Empire of the World" set to air in Fall of 2009. The Quartet were guest artists with Herbie Hancock and Bennie Maupin for a world peace concert in March 2008. Dr. Foy was cello soloist for the same program with Echo Serenade (flamenco style) by Ennio Bolognini. Her duet with Canadian Brass trumpeter Jens Lindemann was a huge hit under the baton of Angel Romero, Royce Hall, '08. Dr. Foy is now organizing a touring violin/cello duo with violin virtuoso Hubert Pralitz and they are open to new works in all styles.

Tips "Please be open to criticism/suggestions about your music and try to appeal to mixed audiences. We also look for innovative techniques, mixed styles or entertaining approaches, such as classical jazz or Bach and pop, or ethnic mixes. There are four CD's currently available for purchase online for $20 each. There are also sound clips on the Web site."

ℕ ☑ CALGARY BOYS CHOIR

B4 - Building Currie Barracks, 2452 Battleford Avenue SW, Calgary AB T3E 7K9 Canada. (403)217-7790. Fax: (403)217-7796. E-mail: manager@calgaryboyschoir.ab.ca. Web site: www.calgaryboyschoir.ab.ca. **Contact:** Gail Majeski, general manager. Artistic director: Lana Lysogor. Boys choir. Estab. 1973. Members are amateurs age 6 and up. Performs 5-10 concerts/year including 1-2 new works. Pay negotiable.

How to Contact Query first. Submit complete score and tape of piece(s). Include SASE. Responds in 6 weeks. Does not return material.

Music "Style fitting for boys choir. Lengths depending on project. Orchestration preferable a cappella/for piano/sometimes orchestra."

Performances Dr. William Jordan's *City of Peace* (world premiere Wednesday September

11, 2002); Lydia Adam's arrangement of *Mi'kmaq Honour Song* (May 26, 2002); *A Child's Evening Prayer*, Dr. Allan Bevan (May 10, 2008).

◼ CANADIAN OPERA COMPANY

227 Front St. E., Toronto ON M5A 1E8 Canada. (416)363-6671. Fax: (416)363-5584. E-mail: ensemble@coc.ca. Web site: www.coc.ca. **Contact:** Sandra J. Gavinchuk, music administrator. Opera company. Estab. 1950. Members are professionals. 50-55 performances, including a minimum of 1 new work/year. Pays by contract.

How to Contact Submit complete score and tapes of vocal and/or operatic works. "Vocal works please." Include SASE. Responds in 5 weeks.

Music Vocal works, operatic in nature. "Do not submit works which are not for voice. Ask for requirements for the Composers-In-Residence program."

Performances Dean Burry's *Brothers Grimm* (children's opera, 50 minutes long); Paul Ruders' *Handmaid's Tale* (full length opera, 2 acts, epilogue); Dean Burry's Isis and the Seven Scorpions (45-minute opera for children); Berg's *Wozzek*; James Rolfe's *Swoon:* James Rolfe's *Donna* (work title for forthcoming work).

Tips "We have a Composers-In-Residence program which is open to Canadian composers or landed immigrants."

CANTATA ACADEMY CHORALE

P.O. Box 1958, Royal Oak MI 48068-1958. (248)358-9868. **Contact:** Phillip O'Jibway, business manager. Music Director: Maurice Draughn, music director. Vocal ensemble. Estab. 1961. Members are professionals. Performs 10-12 concerts/year including 1-3 new works. "We perform in churches and small auditoriums throughout the Metro Detroit area for audiences of about 500 people." Pays variable rate for outright purchase.

How to Contact Submit complete score. Include SASE. Responds in 3 months.

Music Four-part a cappella and keyboard accompanied works, two and three-part works for men's or women's voices. Some small instrumental ensemble accompaniments acceptable. Work must be suitable for forty voice choir. No works requiring orchestra or large ensemble accompaniment. No pop.

Performances Libby Larsen's *Missa Gaia: Mass for the Earth* (SATB, string quartet, oboe, percussion, 4-hand piano); Dede Duson's *To Those Who See* (SATB, SSA); and Sarah Hopkins' *Past Life Melodies* (SATB with Harmonic Overtone Singing); Eric Whiteacre *Five Hebrew Love Songs*; Robert Convery's *Songs of the Children*.

Tips "Be patient. Would prefer to look at several different samples of work at one time."

CARMEL SYMPHONY ORCHESTRA

P.O. Box 761, Carmel IN 46082-0761. (317)844-9717. Fax: (317)844-9916. E-mail: info@carmelsymphony.org. Web site: www.carmelsymphony.org. **Contact**: Allen Davis, executive director. Symphony orchestra. Estab. 1976. Members are professionals and amateurs. Performs 15 concerts/year, including 1-2 new works. Audience is "40% senior citizens, 85% white." Performs in a 1,500-seat high school performing arts center. Pay is negotiable.

How to Contact *Query first*. Include SASE. Responds in 3 months.

Music "Full orchestra works, 10-20 minutes in length. Can be geared toward 'children's' or 'Masterworks' programs. 65-70 piece orchestra, medium difficulty."

Performances Jim Beckel's *Glass Bead Game* (full orchestra); Percy Grainger's *Molly on the Shore* (full orchestra); and Frank Glover's *Impressions of New England* (full orchestra and jazz quartet).

Ⓝ CARSON CITY SYMPHONY

P.O. Box 2001, 191 Heidi Circle, Carson City NV 89701-6532, Carson City NV 89702-2001. (775)883-4154. Fax: (775)883-4371. E-mail: dcbugli@aol.com. Web site: www.ccsymphon y.com. **Contact:** David C. Bugli, music director/conductor. Amateur community orchestra. Estab. 1984. Members are amateurs. Performs 5 concerts, including 2 new works/year. Audience is largely Carson City/Reno area residents, many of them retirees. "Most concerts are performed in the Carson City Community Center Auditorium, which seats 800." Pay varies for outright purchase.

How to Contact Submit complete score and tape or CD of works. Does not return material. Responds in 2 months.

Music "We want classical, pop orchestrations, orchestrations of early music for modern orchestras, concertos for violin or piano, holiday music for chorus and orchestra (children's choirs and handbell ensemble available), music by women, music for brass choir. Most performers are amateurs, but there are a few professionals who perform with us. Available winds and percussion: 2 flutes and flute/piccolo, 2 oboes (E.H. double sometimes), 2 clarinets, 1 bass clarinet, 2 bassoons, 4 horns, 3 trumpets, 3 trombones, 1 tuba, timpani, and percussion. Harp and piano. Strings: 8-8-5-6-3 (or fewer). Avoid music that lacks melodic appeal. Composers should contact us first. Each concert has a different emphasis. Note: Associated choral group, Carson Chamber Singers, performs several times a year with the orchestra and independently."

Performances Thomas Svoboda's *Overture of the Season* (minimalist overture); Gwyneth Walker's *A Concerto of Hymns and Spirituals for Trumpet and Orchestra;* and Jim Cockey's *A Land of Sage and Sun.*

Tips "It is better to write several short movements well than to write long, unimaginative pieces, especially when starting out. Be willing to revise after submitting the work, even if it was premiered elsewhere."

Ⓝ CHATTANOOGA GIRLS CHOIR

P.O. Box 6036, Chattanooga TN 37401. (423)629-6188. E-mail: office@chattanoogagirlschoi r.com. Web site: http://chattanoogagirlschoir.com. **Contact**: LuAnne Holden, artistic director. Vocal ensemble. Estab. 1986. Members are amateurs. Performs 2 concerts/year including at least 1 new work. Audience consists of cultural and civic organizations and national and international tours. Performance space includes concert halls and churches. Pays for outright purchase or per performance.

How to Contact Query first. Include SASE. Responds in 6 weeks.

Music Seeks renaissance, baroque, classical, romantic, twentieth century, folk and musical theatre for young voices of up to 8 minutes. Performers include 5 treble choices: 4th grade

(2 pts.); 5th grade (2 pts.) (SA); grades 6-9 (3 pts.) (SSA); grades 10-12 (3-4 pts.) (SSAA); and a combined choir: grades 6-12 (3-4 pts.) (SSAA). Medium level of difficulty. "Avoid extremely high Tessitura Sop I and extremely low Tessitura Alto II."

Performances Jan Swafford's *Iphigenia Book: Meagher* (choral drama); Penny Tullock's *How Can I Keep from Singing* (Shaker hymn).

N CHEYENNE SYMPHONY ORCHESTRA

P.O. Box 851, Cheyenne WY 82003. (307)778-8561. Fax: (307)634-7512. E-mail: director@c heyennesymphony.org. Web site: www.cheyennesymphony.org. **Contact:** Chloe Illoway, executive director. Symphony orchestra. Estab. 1955. Members are professionals. Performs 6 concerts/year including 1-3 new works. "Orchestra performs for a conservative, mid-to-upper income audience of 1,200 season members." Pay varies.

How to Contact Query first. Does not return material. Responds in 2 months.

Performances Bill Hill's *Seven Abstract Miniatures* (orchestral).

N CIMARRON CIRCUIT OPERA COMPANY

P.O. Box 1085, Norman OK 73070. (405)364-8962. E-mail: info@ccocopera.org. Web site: www.ccocopera.org. **Contact:** Kevin Smith, music director. Opera company. Estab. 1975. Members are semi professional. Performs 75 concerts/year including 1-2 new works. Commissions 1 or less new work/year. "CCOC performs for children across the state of Oklahoma and for a dedicated audience in central Oklahoma. As a touring company, we adapt to the performance space provided, ranging from a classroom to a full raised stage." Pay is negotiable.

How to Contact Query first. Does not return material. Responds in 6 months.

Music "We are seeking operas or operettas in English only. We would like to begin including new, American works in our repertoire. Children's operas should be no longer than 45 minutes and require no more than a synthesizer for accompaniment. Adult operas should be appropriate for families, and may require either full orchestration or synthesizer. CCOC is a professional company whose members have varying degrees of experience, so any difficulty level is appropriate. There should be a small to moderate number of principals. Children's work should have no more than four principals. Our slogan is 'Opera is a family thing to do.' If we cannot market a work to families, we do not want to see it."

Performances Menotti's *Amahl & the Night Visitors*; and Barab's *La Pizza Con Funghi*.

Tips "45-minute fairy tale-type children's operas with possibly a 'moral' work well for our market. Looking for works appealing to K-8 grade students. No more than four principles."

CONNECTICUT CHORAL ARTISTS/CONCORA

52 Main St., New Britain CT 06051. (860)224-7500. Fax: (860) 827-8890. E-mail: contact@co ncora.org. Web site: www.concora.org. **Contact:** Jane Penfield, executive director. Richard Coffey, artistic director. Professional concert choir, also an 18-voice ensemble dedicated to contemporary a cappella works. Estab. 1974. Members are professionals. Performs 15 concerts/year, including 3-5 new works. "Mixed audience in terms of age and background; performs in various halls and churches in the region." Payment "depends upon underwriting we can obtain for the project."

How to Contact Query first. "No unsolicited submissions accepted." Include SASE. Responds in 1 year.

Music Seeking "works for mixed chorus of 36 singers; unaccompanied or with keyboard and/or small instrumental ensemble; text sacred or secular/any language; prefers suites or cyclical works, total time not exceeding 15 minutes. Performance spaces and budgets prohibit large instrumental ensembles. Works suited for 750-seat halls are preferable. Substantial organ or piano parts acceptable. Scores should be very legible in every way."

Performances Don McCullough's *Holocaust Contata* (choral with narration); Robert Cohen's *Sprig of Lilac: Peter Quince at the Clavier* (choral); Greg Bartholomew's *The 21st Century: A Girl Born in Afghanistan* (choral).

Tips "Use conventional notation and be sure manuscript is legible in every way. Recognize and respect the vocal range of each vocal part. Work should have an identifiable rhythmic structure."

DUO CLASICO

4 Essex St., Clifton NJ 07014. (973)655-4379. E-mail: wittend@mail.montclair.edu. Web site: www.davidwitten.com. **Contact:** David Witten. Chamber music ensemble. Estab. 1986. Members are professionals. Performs 16 concerts/year including 4 new works. Commissions 1 composer or new work/year. Performs in small recital halls. Pays 10% royalty.

How to Contact Query first. Include SASE. Responds in 6 weeks.

Music "We welcome scores for flute solo, piano solo or duo. Particular interest in Latin American composers."

Performances Diego Luzuriaga's *La Muchica* (modern, with extended techniques); Robert Starer's *Yizkor & Anima Aeterna* (rhythmic); and Piazzolla's *Etudes Tanguistiques* (solo flute).

Tips "Extended techniques, or with tape, are fine!"

Ⓝ 🌐 EUROPEAN UNION CHAMBER ORCHESTRA

Hollick, Yarnscombe EX31 3LQ United Kingdom. (44)1271 858249. Fax: (44)1271 858375. E-mail: eucorchl@aol.com. Web site: www.etd.gb.com. **Contact:** Ambrose Miller, general manager. Chamber orchestra. Members are professionals. Performs 70 concerts/year, including 6 new works. Commissions 2 composers or new works/year. Performs regular tours of Europe, Americas and Asia, including major venues. Pays per performance or for outright purchase, depending on work.

How to Contact Query first. Does not return material. Responds in 6 weeks.

Music Seeking compositions for strings, 2 oboes and 2 horns with a duration of about 8 minutes.

Performances Peeter Vahi "Prayer Wheel"; James MacMillan "Kiss on Wood", arr Karkof.

Tips "Keep the work to less than 15 minutes in duration, it should be sufficiently 'modern' to be interesting but not too difficult as this could take up rehearsal time. It should be possible to perform without a conductor."

⚅ FONTANA CONCERT SOCIETY

359 S. Kalamazoo Mall, Suite 200, Kalamazoo MI 49007. (616)382-7774. Fax: (616)382-0812. E-mail: info@fontanachamberarts.org. Web site: www.fontanachamberarts.org/history.html. **Contact:** Ms. Anne Berquist, executive and artistic director. Chamber music ensemble presenter. Estab. 1980. Members are professionals. Fontana Chamber Arts presents over 45 events, including the 6-week Summer Festival of Music and Art, which runs from mid-July to the end of August. Regional and guest artists perform classical, contemporary, jazz and nontraditional music. Commissions and performs new works each year. Fontana Chamber Arts presents 7 classical and 2 jazz concerts during the Fall/Winter season. Audience consists of well-educated individuals who accept challenging new works, but like the traditional as well. Summer—180 seat hall; Fall/winter—various venues, from 400 to 1,500 seats.

How to Contact Submit complete score, resume and tapes of piece(s). Include SASE. Responds in approximately 1 month.

Music Chamber music—any combination of strings, winds, piano. No "pop" music, new age type. Special interest in composers attending premiere and speaking to the audience.

Performances 2007- Billy Child's *The Path Among the Trees* (Billy Childs Jazz-Chamber Ensemble with Ying Quartet); 2007-C. Curtis-Smith's *Tulips* (Mary Bonhag, soprano and chamber ensemble); 2006-Stefon Harris' *Portraits of the Promised* (Stefon Harris, vibraphone/marimba and jazz ensemble); 2006-Bright Sheng's *Tibetan Dance* (Birds and Phoenix Ensemble); 2006-Pamela Chen's *Spring Silk II* (Birds and Phoenix Ensemble); 2006-Victoria Bond's *Bridges* (Birds and Phoenix Ensemble); 2006- Lu Pei's *Birds and Phoenix* (Birds and Phoenix Ensemble).

Tips "Provide a résumé and clearly marked tape of a piece played by live performers."

⚅ FORT WORTH CHILDREN'S OPERA

1300 Gendy St., Fort Worth TX 76107. (817)731-0833, ext. 19. Fax: (817)731-0835. E-mail: kwolfe@fwopera.org or clyde@fwopera.org. Web site: www.fwopera.org. **Contact:** Tony Kostecki, director of education. Opera company. Estab. 1946. Members are professionals. Performs over 180 in-school performances/year." Audience consists of elementary school children; performs in major venues for district-wide groups and individual school auditoriums, cafetoriums and gymnasiums. Pays $40/performance.

How to Contact Submit complete score and tape of piece(s). Include SASE. Responds in 6 months.

Music "Familiar fairy tales or stories adapted to music of opera composers, or newly-composed music of suitable quality. Ideal length: 40-45 minutes. Piano or keyboard accompaniment. Should include moral, safety or school issues. Can be ethnic in subject matter and must speak to pre-K and grade 1-6 children. Prefer pieces with good, memorable melodies. Performed by young, trained professionals on 9-month contract. Requires work for four performers, doubled roles OK, SATB plus accompanist/narrator. Special interest in bilingual (Spanish/English) works."

GREATER GRAND FORKS SYMPHONY ORCHESTRA

3350 Campus Rd., Mail Stop 7084, Grand Forks ND 58202-7084. (701)777-3359. Fax: (701)777-3320. E-mail: ggfso@und.edu. Web site: www.ggfso.org. **Contact:** James Han-

Classical Arts

non, music director. Symphony orchestra. Estab. 1908. Members are professionals and/or amateurs. Performs 6 concerts/year. "New works are presented in 2-4 of our programs." Audience is "a mix of ages and musical experience. In 1997-98 we moved into a renovated, 420-seat theater." Pay is negotiable, depending on licensing agreements.

How to Contact Submit complete score or complete score and tape of pieces. Include SASE. Responds in 6 months.

Music "Style is open, instrumentation the limiting factor. Music can be scored for an ensemble up to but not exceeding: 3,2,3,2/4,3,3,1/3 percussion/strings. Rehearsal time limited to 3 hours for new works."

Performances Michael Harwood's *Amusement Park Suite* (orchestra); Randall Davidson's *Mexico Bolivar Tango* (chamber orchestra); and John Corigliano's *Voyage* (flute and orchestra); Linda Tutas Haugen's *Fable of Old Turtle* (saxophone concerto); Michael Wittgraf's *Landmarks*; Joan Tower's *Made in America*.

HEARTLAND MEN'S CHORUS

P.O. Box 32374, Kansas City MO 64171-5374. (816)931-3338. Fax: (816)531-1367. E-mail: hmc@hmckc.org. Web site: www.hmckc.org. **Contact:** Joseph Nadeau, artistic director. Men's chorus. Estab. 1986. Members are professionals and amateurs. Performs 3 concerts/year; 9-10 are new works. Commissions 1 composer or new works/year. Performs for a diverse audience at the Folly Theater (1,100 seats). Pay is negotiable.

How to Contact Query first. Include SASE. Responds in 2 months.

Music "Interested in works for male chorus (ttbb). Must be suitable for performance by a gay male chorus. We will consider any orchestration, or a cappella."

Performances Mark Hayes' *Two Flutes Playing* (commissioned song cycle); Alan Shorter's *Country Angel Christmas* (commissioned chidren's musical); Kevin Robinson's *Life is a Cabaret: The Music of Kander and Ebb* (commissioned musical).

Tips "Find a text that relates to the contemporary gay experience, something that will touch peoples' lives."

N HELENA SYMPHONY

P.O. Box 1073, Helena MT 59624. (406)442-1860. E-mail: boxoffice@helenasymphony.org. Web site: www.helenasymphony.org. **Contact:** Allan R. Scott, music director and conductor. Symphony orchestra. Estab. 1955. Members are professionals and amateurs. Performs 7-10 concerts/year including new works. Performance space is an 1,800 seat concert hall. Payment varies.

How to Contact Query first. Include SASE. Responds in 3 months.

Music "Imaginative, collaborative, not too atonal. We want to appeal to an audience of all ages. We don't have a huge string complement. Medium to difficult okay—at frontiers of professional ability we cannot do."

Performances Eric Funk's *A Christmas Overture* (orchestra); Donald O. Johnston's *A Christmas Processional* (orchestra/chorale); and Elizabeth Sellers' *Prairie* (orchestra/short ballet piece).

Tips "Try to balance tension and repose in your works. New instrument combinations are appealing."

Ⓝ HENDERSONVILLE SYMPHONY ORCHESTRA

P.O. Box 1811, Hendersonville NC 28739. (828)697-5884. Fax: (828)697-5765. E-mail: hso1 @bellsouth.net. Web site: www.hendersonvillesymphony.org. **Contact:** Sandie Salvaggio-Walker, general manager. Symphony orchestra. Estab. 1971. Members are professionals and amateurs. Performs 6 concerts/year. "We would welcome a new work per year." Audience is a cross-section of retirees, professionals and some children. Performance space is a 857-seat high school audiorium.

How to Contact Query first. Include SASE. Responds in 1 month.

Music "We use a broad spectrum of music (classical concerts and pops)."

Performances Nelson's *Jubilee* (personal expression in a traditional method); Britten's "The Courtly Dances" from Glorina (time-tested); and Chip Davis' arrangement for Mannheim Steamroller's *Deck the Halls* (modern adaptation of traditional melody).

Tips "Submit your work even though we are a community orchestra. We like to be challenged. We have the most heavily patronized fine arts group in the county. Our emphasis is on education."

HERMANN SONS GERMAN BAND

P.O. Box 162, Medina TX 78055. (830)589-2268. E-mail: herbert@festmusik.com. Web site: www.festmusik.com. **Contact:** Herbert Bilhartz, music director. Community band with German instrumentation. Estab. 1990. Members are both professionals and amateurs. Performs 4 concerts/year including 2 new works. Commissions no new composers or new works/year. Performs for "mostly older people who like German polkas, waltzes and marches. We normally play only published arrangements from Germany."

How to Contact Query first; then submit full set of parts and score, condensed or full. Include SASE. Responds in 6 weeks.

Music "We like European-style polkas or waltzes (Viennese or Missouri tempo), either original or arrangements of public domain tunes. Arrangements of traditional American folk tunes in this genre would be especially welcome. Also, polkas or waltzes featuring one or two solo instruments (from instrumentation below) would be great. OK for solo parts to be technically demanding. Although we have no funds to commission works, we will provide you with a cassette recording of our performance. Also, we would assist composers in submitting works to band music publishers in Germany for possible publication. Polkas and waltzes generally follow this format: Intro; 1st strain repeated; 2nd strain repeated; DS to 1 strain; Trio: Intro; 32 bar strain; 'break-up' strain; Trio DS. Much like military march form. Instrumentation: Fl/Picc, 3 clars in Bb, 2 Fluegelhorns in Bb; 3 Tpts in Bb, 2 or 4 Hns in F or Eb, 2 Baritones (melody/countermelody parts; 1 in Bb TC, 1 in BC), 2 Baritones in Bb TC (rhythm parts), 3 Trombones, 2 Tubas (in octaves, mostly), Drum set, Timpani optional. We don't use saxes, but a German publisher would want 4-5 sax parts. Parts should be medium to medium difficult. All brass parts should be considered one player to the part; woodwinds, two to the part. No concert type pieces; no modern popular or rock styles. However, a 'theme and variations' form with contrasting jazz, rock, country, modern variations would be clever, and our fans might go for such a piece (as might a German publisher)."

Performances New music performed in 2005: Stefan Rundel's *Mein Gluecksstern ("My Lucky Star")*.

Tips "German town bands love to play American tunes. There are many thousands of these bands over there and competition among band music publishers in Germany is keen. Few Americans are aware of this potential market, so few American arrangers get published over there. Simple harmony is best for this style, but good counterpoint helps a lot. Make use of the dark quality of the Fluegelhorns and the bright, fanfare quality of the trumpets. Give the two baritones (one in TC and one in BC) plenty of exposed melodic material. Keep them in harmony with each other (3rds and 6ths), unlike American band arrangements, which have only one Baritone line. If you want to write a piece in this style, give me a call, and I will send you some sample scores to give you a better idea."

HERSHEY SYMPHONY ORCHESTRA

P.O. Box 93, Hershey PA 17033. (800)533-3088. E-mail: drdackow@aol.com. **Contact:** Dr. Sandra Dackow, music director. Symphony orchestra. Estab. 1969. Members are professionals and amateurs. Performs 8 concerts/year, including 1-3 new works. Commissions "possibly 1-2" composers or new works/year. Audience is family and friends of community theater. Performance space is a 1,900 seat grand old movie theater. Pays commission fee.

How to Contact Submit complete score and tape of piece(s). Include SASE. Responds in 3 months.

Music "Symphonic works of various lengths and types which can be performed by a non-professional orchestra. We are flexible but like to involve all our players."

Performances Paul W. Whear's *Celtic Christmas Carol* (orchestra/bell choir) and Linda Robbins Coleman's *In Good King Charlie's Golden Days* (overture).

Tips "Please lay out rehearsal numbers/letter and rests according to phrases and other logical musical divisions rather than in groups of ten measures, etc., which is very unmusical and wastes time and causes a surprising number of problems. Also, please do not send a score written in concert pitch; use the usual transpositions so that the conductor sees what the players see; rehearsal is much more effective this way. Cross cue all important solos; this helps in rehearsal where instruments may be missing."

HUDSON VALLEY PHILHARMONIC

35 Market St., Poughkeepise NY 12601. (845)473-5288. Fax: (845)473-4259. E-mail: slamarc a@bardavon.org. Web site: www.bardavon.org. **Contact:** Stephen LaMarca, production manager. Symphony orchestra. Estab. 1969. Members are professionals. Performs 20 concerts/year including 1 new work. "Classical subscription concerts for all ages; Pops concerts for all ages; New Wave concerts—crossover projects with a rock 'n' roll artist performing with an orchestra. HVP performs in three main theatres which are concert auditoriums with stages and professional lighting and sound." Pay is negotiable.

How to Contact Query first. Include SASE. Responds only if interested.

Music "HVP is open to serious classical music, pop music and rock 'n' roll crossover projects. Desired length of work between 10-20 minutes. Orchestrations can be varied by should always include strings. There is no limit to difficulty since our musicians are professional. The ideal number of musicians to write for would include up to a Brahms-size orchestra 2222, 4231, T, 2P, piano, harp, strings.''

Performances Joan Tower's *Island Rhythms* (serious classical work); Bill Vanaver's *P'nai El* (symphony work with dance); and Joseph Bertolozzi's *Serenade* (light classical, pop work).

Tips ''Don't get locked into doing very traditional orchestrations or styles. Our music director is interested in fresh, creative formats. He is an orchestrator as well and can offer good advice on what works well. Songwriters who are into crossover projects should definitely submit works. Over the past four years, HVP has done concerts featuring the works of Natalie Merchant, John Cale, Sterling Morrison, Richie Havens, and R. Carlos Naka (Native American flute player), all reorchestrated by our music director for small orchestra with the artist.''

N INDIANA UNIVERSITY NEW MUSIC ENSEMBLE

Indiana University Bloomington, School of Music, Bloomington IN 47405-2200. E-mail: ddzubay@indiana.edu. Web site: www.indiana.edu/~nme. **Contact**: David Dzubay, director. Performs solo, chamber and large ensemble works. Estab.1974. Members are students. Presents 4 concerts/year.

Music Peter Lieberson's *Free and Easy Wanderer*; Sven-David Sandstrom's *Wind Pieces*; Atar Arad's *Sonata*; and David Dzubay's *Dancesing in a Green Bay*.

KENTUCKY OPERA

101 S. Eighth St. at Main, Louisville KY 40202. (502)584-4500. Fax: (502)584-7484. E-mail: info@kyopera.org. Web site: www.kyopera.org. **Contact:** Alise Oliver, artistic administration. Opera. Estab. 1952. Members are professionals. Performs 3 main stage/year. Performs at Whitney Hall, The Kentucky Center for the Arts, seating is 2,400; Bomhard Theatre, The Kentucky Center for the Arts, 620; Brown Theatre, 1,400. Pays by royalty, outright purchase or per performance.

How to Contact *Write or call first before submitting. No unsolicited submissions.* Submit complete score. Include SASE. Responds in 6 months.

Music Seeks opera—1 to 3 acts with orchestrations. No limitations.

Performances *Othello, Pirates of Penzance, A Showcase of Baroque Opera, Werther, Iolanta.*

N LEXINGTON PHILHARMONIC SOCIETY

161 N. Mill St., Arts Place, Lexington KY 40507. (859)233-4226. Fax: (859)233-7896. Web site: www.lexingtonphilharmonic.org. **Contact:** Dr. George Zack, music director. Symphony orchestra. Estab. 1961. Members are professionals. Series includes ''8 serious, classical subscription concerts (hall seats 1,500); 3 concerts called Pops the Series; 3 Family Concerts; 10 outdoor pops concerts (from 1,500 to 5,000 tickets sold); 5-10 run-out concerts (½ serious/½ pops); and 10 children's concerts.'' Pays via ASCAP and BMI, rental purchase and private arrangements.

How to Contact Submit complete score and tape of piece(s). Include SASE.

Music Seeking ''good current pops material and good serious classical works. No specific restrictions, but overly large orchestra requirements, unusual instruments and extra rentals help limit our interest.''

Performances ''Visit our Web site for complete concert season listing.''

Tips ''When working on large-format arrangement, use cross-cues so orchestra can be cut back if required. Submit good quality copy, scores and parts. Tape is helpful.''

[N] LIMA SYMPHONY ORCHESTRA

133 Elizabeth St., Lima OH 45801. (419)222-5701. Fax: (419)222-6587. Web site: www.lima symphony.com. **Contact:** Crafton Beck, music conductor. Symphony orchestra. Estab. 1953. Members are professionals. Performs 17-18 concerts including at least 1 new work/ year. Commissions at least 1 composer or new work/year. Middle to older audience; also Young People's Series. Mixture for stage and summer productions. Performs in Veterans' Memorial Civic & Convention Center, a beautiful hall seating 1,670; various temporary shells for summer outdoors events; churches; museums and libraries. Pays $2,500 for out-right purchase (Anniversary commission) or grants $1,500-5,000.

How to Contact Submit complete score if not performed; otherwise submit complete score and tape of piece(s). Include SASE. Responds in 3 months.

Music ''Good balance of incisive rhythm, lyricism, dynamic contrast and pacing. Chamber orchestra to full (85-member) symphony orchestra.'' Does not wish to see ''excessive odd meter changes.''

Performances Frank Proto's *American Overture* (some original music and fantasy); Werner Tharichen's *Concerto for Timpani and Orchestra*; and James Oliverio's *Pilgrimage—Concerto for Brass* (interesting, dynamic writing for brass and the orchestra).

Tips ''Know your instruments, be willing to experiment with unconventional textures, be available for in depth analysis with conductor, be at more than one rehearsal. Be sure that individual parts are correctly matching the score and done in good, neat calligraphy.''

LITHOPOLIS AREA FINE ARTS ASSOCIATION

LAFAA, P.O. Box 187, Lithograph OH 43136. (614)837-4765. Web site: http://www.mainstr eetcanalwinchester.org/LAFAA/. **Contact:** Virginia E. Heffner, assistant series director. Performing Arts Series. Estab. 1973. Members are professionals and amateurs. Performs 6-7 concerts/year. ''Our audience consists of couples and families 30-80 in age. Their tastes run from classical, folk, ethnic, big band, pop and jazz. Our hall is acoustically excellent and seats 400. It was designed as a lecture-recital hall in 1925.'' Composers ''may apply for Ohio Arts Council Grant under the New Works category.'' Pays straight fee to ASCAP.

How to Contact *Query first.* Include SASE. Responds in 3 weeks.

Music ''We prefer that a composer is also the performer and works in conjunction with another artist, so they could be one of the performers on our series. Piece should be musically pleasant and not too dissonant. It should be scored for small vocal or instrumental ensemble. Dance ensembles have difficulty with 15' high 15' deep and 27' wide stage. We do not want avant-garde or obscene dance routines. No ballet (space problem). We're interested in something historical—national or Ohio emphasis would be nice. Small ensembles or solo format is fine.''

Performances Patsy Ford Simms' *Holiday Gloria* (Christmas SSA vocal); Andrew Carter's *A Maiden Most Gentle* (Christmas SSA vocal); and Luigi Zaninelli's *Alleluia, Silent Night* (Christmas SSA vocal).

Tips "Call in December of 2007 or January 2008 for queries about our 2007-2008 season. We do a varied program. We don't commission artists. Contemporary music is used by some of our artist or groups. By contacting these artists, you could offer your work for inclusion in their program."

LYRIC OPERA OF CHICAGO

20 N. Wacker Dr., Chicago IL 60606. (312)332-2244 ext. 3500. Fax: (312)419-8345. E-mail: jgriffin@lyricopera.org. Web site: www.lyricopera.org. **Contact:** Julie Griffin-Meadors, music administrator. Opera company. Estab. 1953. Members are professionals. Performs 80 operas/year including 1 new work in some years. Commissions 1 new work every 4 or 5 years. "Performances are held in a 3,563 seat house for a sophisticated opera audience, predominantly 30+ years old." Payment varies.

How to Contact Query first. Does not return material. Responds in 6 months.

Music "Full-length opera suitable for a large house with full orchestra. No musical comedy or Broadway musical style. We rarely perform one-act operas. We are only interested in works by composers and librettists with extensive theatrical experience. We have few openings for new works, so candidates must be of the highest quality. Do not send score or other materials without a prior contact."

Performances William Bolcom's *View from the Bridge*; John Corigliano's *Ghosts of Versailles*; and Leonard Bernstein's *Candide*.

Tips "Have extensive credentials and an international reputation."

MASTER CHORALE OF WASHINGTON

1200 29th St. NW, Suite LL2, Washington DC 20007. (202)471-4050. Fax: (202)471-4051. E-mail: singing@masterchorale.org. Web site: www.masterchorale.org. **Contact:** Donald McCullough, music director. Vocal ensemble. Estab. 1967. Members are professionals and amateurs. Performs 8 concerts/year including 1-3 new works. Commissions one new composer or work every 2 years. "Audience covers a wide range of ages and economic levels drawn from the greater Washington DC metropolitan area. Kennedy Center Concert Hall seats 2,400." Pays by outright purchase.

How to Contact Submit complete score and tape of piece(s). Include SASE. Responds in 9 months.

Music Seeks new works for: 1) large chorus with or without symphony orchestras; 2) chamber choir and small ensemble.

Performances Stephen Paulus' *Mass*; Joonas Kokkonen's *Requiem* (symphonic choral with orchestra); Morton Lauridoen's *Lux Aeterna*; Donald McCullough's *Let My People Go!. A Spiritual Journey*; and Daniel E. Gawthorp's *In Quiet Resting Places*; and Adolphus Hailstork's *Whitman's Journey*.

Ⓝ MILWAUKEE YOUTH SYMPHONY ORCHESTRA

325 West Walnut St., Milwaukee WI 53212. (414)267-2950. Fax: (414)267-2960. E-mail: general@myso.org. Web site: www.myso.org. **Contact:** Frances Richman, executive director. Multiple youth orchestras and other instrumental ensembles. Estab. 1956. Members are students. Performs 12-15 concerts/year including 1-2 new works. "Our groups perform in Uihlein Hall at the Marcus Center for the Performing Arts in Milwaukee plus area sites. The audiences usually consist of parents, music teachers and other interested community members, with periodic reviews in the *Milwaukee Journal Sentinel*." Payment varies.

How to Contact Query first. Include SASE. Does not return material. Responds in 1 month.

Performances James Woodward's *Tuba Concerto*.

Tips "Be sure you realize you are working with *students* (albeit many of the best in southeastern Wisconsin) and not professional musicians. The music needs to be on a technical level students can handle. Our students are 8-18 years of age, in 2 full symphony orchestras, a wind ensemble and 2 string orchestras, plus two flute choirs, advanced chamber orchestra and 15-20 small chamber ensembles."

Ⓝ MOORES OPERA CENTER

Moores School of Music, University of Houston, 120 School of Music Building, Houston TX 77204-4201. (713)743-3009. E-mail: info@www.music.uh.edu. Web site: www.uh.edu/music/Mooresopera/. **Director of Opera:** Buck Ross. Opera/music theater program. Members are professionals, amateurs and students. Performs 12-14 concerts/year including 1 new work. Performs in a proscenium theater which seats 800. Pit seats approximately up to 75 players. Audience covers wide spectrum, from first time opera-goers to very sophisticated. Pays per performance.

How to Contact Submit complete score and tapes of piece(s). Include SASE. Responds in 6 months.

Music "We seek music that is feasible for high graduate level student singers. Chamber orchestras are very useful. No more than two and a half hours. No children's operas."

Performances John Corigliano's *The Ghosts of Versailles*; Carlisle Floyd's *Bilby's Doll*; Robert Nelson's *A Room With a View*; Conrad Susa's *The Dangerous Liaisons*; and Dominick Argento's *Casanova's Homecoming*.

Ⓝ OPERA MEMPHIS

6745 Wolf River Parkway, Memphis TN 38120. (901)257-3100. Fax: (901)257-3109. E-mail: info@operamemphis.org. Web site: www.operamemphis.org. **Contact:** Michael Ching, artistic director. Opera company. Estab. 1955. Members are professionals. Performs 8-12 concerts/year including new works. Occasionally commissions composers. Audience consists of older, wealthier patrons, along with many students and young professionals. Pay is negotiable.

How to Contact Query first. Include SASE. Responds in 1 year or less.

Music Accessible practical pieces for educational or second stage programs. Educational pieces should not exceed 90 minutes or 4-6 performers. We encourage songwriters to contact us with proposals or work samples for theatrical works. We are very interested in crossover work.

Performances Mike Reid's *Different Fields* (one act opera); David Olney's *Light in August* (folk opera); and Sid Selvidge's *Riversongs* (one act blues opera).

Tips "Spend many hours thinking about the synopsis (plot outline)."

ORCHESTRA SEATTLE/SEATTLE CHAMBER SINGERS

P.O. Box 15825, Seattle WA 98115. (206)682-5208. E-mail: osscs@osscs.org. Web site: www.osscs.org. **Contact**: Andrew Danilchik, librarian. Symphony orchestra, chamber music ensemble and community chorus. Estab. 1969. Members are amateurs and professionals. Performs 8 concerts/year including 2-3 new works. Commissions 1-2 composers or new works/year. "Our audience is made up of both experienced and novice classical music patrons. The median age is 45 with an equal number of males and females in the upper income range. Most concerts now held in Benaroya Hall."

How to Contact Query first. Include SASE. Responds in 1 year.

Performances Robert Kechley's *Trumpet Concerto* (classical concerto); Carol Sams's *Earthmakers* (oratorio); and Murl Allen Sanders's *Accordion Concerto* (classical concerto).

Ⓝ PALMETTO MASTERSINGERS

P.O. Box 7441, Columbia SC 29202. (803)765-0777. E-mail: info@palmettomastersingers.org. Web site: www.palmettomastersingers.org. **Contact:** Walter Cuttino, music director. 80 voice male chorus. Estab. 1981 by the late Dr. Arpad Darasz. Members are professionals and amateurs. Performs 8-10 concerts/year. Commissions 1 composer of new works every other year (on average). Audience is generally older adults, "but it's a wide mix." Performance space for the season series is the Koger Center (approximately 2,000 seats) in Columbia, SC. More intimate venues also available. Fee is negotiable for outright purchase.

How to Contact Query first. Include SASE. Or e-mail to info@palmettomastersingers.org.

Music Seeking music of 10-15 minutes in length, "not too far out tonally. Orchestration is negotiable, but chamber size (10-15 players) is normal. We rehearse once a week and probably will not have more than 8-10 rehearsals. These rehearsals (2 hours each) are spent learning a 1½-hour program. Only 1-2 rehearsals (max) are with the orchestra. Piano accompaniments need not be simplified, as our accompanist is exceptional."

Performances Randal Alan Bass' *Te Deum* (12-minute, brass and percussion); Dick Goodwin's *Mark Twain Remarks* (40 minute, full symphony); and Randol Alan Bass' *A Simple Prayer* (a capella 6 minute).

Tips "Contact us as early as possible, given that programs are planned by July. Although this is an amateur chorus, we have performed concert tours of Europe, performed at Carnegie Hall, The National Cathedral and the White House in Washington, DC. We are skilled amateurs."

PICCOLO OPERA COMPANY INC.

24 Del Rio Blvd., Boca Raton FL 33432-4734. (800)282-3161. Fax: (561)394-0520. E-mail: leejon51@msn.com. **Contact:** Lee Merrill, executive assistant. Traveling opera company. Estab. 1962. Members are professionals. Performs 1-50 concerts/year including 1-2 new works. Commissions 0-1 composer or new work/year. Operas are performed for a mixed

audience of children and adults. Pays by performance or outright purchase. Operas in English.

How to Contact *Query first.* Include SASE.

Music "Productions for either children or adults. Musical theater pieces, lasting about one hour, for adults to perform for adults and/or youngsters. Performers are mature singers with experience. The cast should have few performers (up to 10), no chorus or ballet, accompanied by piano or local orchestra. Skeletal scenery. All in English."

Performances Menotti's *The Telephone*; Mozart's *Cosi Fan Tutte*; and Puccini's *La Boheme* (repertoire of more than 22 productions).

⟦N⟧ PRINCETON SYMPHONY ORCHESTRA

P.O. Box 250, Princeton NJ 08542. E-mail: info@princetonsymphony.org. Web site: www.princetonsymphony.org. **Contact:** Mark Laycock, music director. Symphony orchestra. Estab. 1980. Members are professionals. Performs 6-10 concerts/year including some new works. Commissions 1 composer or new work/year. Performs in a "beautiful, intimate 800-seat hall with amazing sound." Pays by arrangement.

Music "Orchestra usually numbers 40-60 individuals."

⟦N⟧ PRISM SAXOPHONE QUARTET

257 Harvey St., Philadelphia PA 19144. (215)438-5282. E-mail: info@prismquartet.com. Web site: www.prismquartet.com. President, New Sounds Music Inc. Prism Quartet: Matthew Levy. Chamber music ensemble. Estab. 1984. Members are professionals. Performs 80 concerts/year including 10-15 new works. Commissions 4 composers or new works/year. "Ours are primarily traditional chamber music audiences." Pays royalty per performance from BMI or ASCAP or commission range from $100 to $15,000.

How to Contact Submit complete score (with parts) and tape of piece(s). Does not return material. Responds in 3 months.

Music "Orchestration—sax quartet, SATB. Lengths—5-25 minutes. Styles—contemporary, classical, jazz, crossover, ethnic, gospel, avant-garde. No limitations on level of difficulty. No more than 4 performers (SATB sax quartet). No transcriptions. The Prism Quartet places special emphasis on crossover works which integrate a variety of musical styles."

Performances David Liebman's *The Gray Convoy* (jazz); Bradford Ellis's *Tooka-Ood Zasch* (ethnic-world music); and William Albright's *Fantasy Etudes* (contemporary classical).

⟦N⟧ SACRAMENTO MASTER SINGERS

P.O. Box 417997, Sacramento CA 95841. (916)971-3159. Fax: (916)788-7464. E-mail: smscbarb@aol.com. Web site: www.mastersingers.org. **Contact:** Ralph Hughes, conductor/artistic director. Vocal ensemble. Estab. 1984. Members are professionals and amateurs. Performs 9 concerts/year including 5-6 new works. Commissions 2 new works/year. Audience is made up of mainly college age and older patrons. Performs mostly in churches with 500-900 seating capacity. Pays $200 for outright purchase.

How to Contact Submit complete score and tape of piece(s). Include SASE. Responds in 5 weeks.

Music "A cappella works; works with small orchestras or few instruments; works based on classical styles with a 'modern' twist; multi-cultural music; shorter works probably preferable, but this is not a requirement. We usually have 38-45 singers capable of a high level of difficulty, but find that often simple works are very pleasing."

Performances Joe Jennings' *An Old Black Woman, Homeless and Indistinct* (SATB, oboe, strings, dramatic).

Tips "Keep in mind we are a chamber ensemble, not a 100-voice choir."

ℕ ☑ SAN FRANCISCO GIRLS CHORUS

44 Page Street, Suite 200, San Francisco CA 94102. (415)863-1752. E-mail: info@sfgirlschor us.org. Web site: www.sfgirlschorus.org. **Contact:** Susan McMane, artistic director. Choral ensemble. Estab. 1978. Advanced choral ensemble of young women's voices. Performs 8-10 concerts/year including 3-4 new works. Commissions 2 composers or new works/year. Concerts are performed for "choral/classical music lovers, plus family audiences and audiences interested in international repertoire. Season concerts are performed in a 800-seat church with excellent acoustics and in San Francisco's Davies Symphony Hall, a 2,800-seat state-of-the-art auditorium." Pay negotiable for outright purchase.

- The San Francisco Girls Chorus has won three Grammy Awards as guest performers on the San Francisco Symphony's recordings.

How to Contact Submit complete score and CD recording, if possible. Does not return material. Responds in 6 months.

Music "Music for treble voices (SSAA); a cappella, piano accompaniment, or small orchestration; 3-10 minutes in length. Wide variety of styles; 45 singers; challenging music is encouraged."

Performances See Web site under "Music/Commissions" for a listing of SFGC commissions. Examples: Jake Heggie's *Patterns* (piano, mezzo-soprano soloist, chorus); and Chen Yi's *Chinese Poems* (a cappella).

Tips "Choose excellent texts and write challenging music. The San Francisco Girls Chorus has pioneered in establishing girls choral music as an art form in the United States. The Girls Chorus is praised for its 'stunning musical standard' (San Francisco Chronicle) in performances in the San Francisco Bay Area and on tour. SFGC's annual concert season showcases the organization's concert/touring ensemble, Chorissima, in performances of choral masterworks from around the world, commissioned works by contemporary composers, and 18th-century music from the Venetian Ospedali and Mexican Baroque which SFGC has brought out of the archives and onto the concert stage. Chorissima tours through California with partial support provided by the California Arts Council Touring Program and have represented the U.S. and the City of San Francisco nationally and abroad. The chorus provides ensemble and solo singers for performances and recordings with the San Francisco Symphony and San Francisco Opera, Women's Philharmonic, and many other music ensembles. The Chorus has produced six solo CD recordings including: Voices of Hope and Peace, a recording that includes "Anne Frank: A Living Voice" by an American composer Linda Tutas Haugen; Christmas, featuring diverse holiday selections; Crossroads, a collection of world folk music; and Music from the Venetian Ospedali, a disc of Italian Baroque music of which the New Yorker described the Chorus as "tremendously accomplished.'' The Chorus can also be heard on several San Francisco Symphony recordings, including three GRAMMY® Award-winners.''

SINGING BOYS OF PENNSYLVANIA

P.O. Box 206, Wind Gap PA 18091. (610)759-6002. Fax: (610)759-6042. Web site: http://www.singingboys.org/. **Contact:** K. Bernard Schade, Ed. D., director. Vocal ensemble. Estab. 1970. Members are professional children. Performs 100 concerts/year including 3-5 new works. "We attract general audiences: family, senior citizens, churches, concert associations, university concert series and schools.'' Pays $300-3,000 for outright purchase.

How to Contact *Query first.* Does not return material. Responds in 3 weeks.

Music "We want music for commercials, voices in the SSA or SSAA ranges, sacred works or arrangements of American folk music with accompaniment. Our range of voices are from G below middle C to A (13th above middle C). Reading ability of choir is good but works which require a lot of work with little possibility of more than one performance are of little value. We sing very few popular songs except for special events. We perform music by composers who are well-known and works by living composers who are writing in traditional choral forms. Works which have a full orchestral score are of interest. The orchestration should be fairly light, so as not to cover the voices. Works for Christmas have more value than some other, since we perform with orchestras on an annual basis.''

Performances Don Locklair's *The Columbus Madrigals* (opera).

Tips "It must be appropriate music and words for children. We do not deal in pop music. Folk music, classics and sacred are acceptable.''

ST. LOUIS CHAMBER CHORUS

P.O. Box 11558, Clayton MO 63105. (636)458-4343. E-mail: maltworm@inlink.com. Web site: www.chamberchorus.org. **Contact:** Philip Barnes, artistic director. Vocal ensemble, chamber music ensemble. Estab. 1956. Members are professionals and amateurs. Performs 6 concerts/year including 5-10 new works. Commissions 3-4 new works/year. Audience is "diverse and interested in unaccompanied choral work and outstanding architectural/acoustic venues.'' Performances take place at various auditoria noted for their excellent acoustics—churches, synagogues, schools and university halls. Pays by arrangement.

How to Contact Query first. Does not return material. "Panel of 'readers' submit report to Artistic Director. Responds in 3 months. 'General Advice' leaflet available on request.''

Music *Only a cappella writing!* No contemporary 'popular' works; historical editions welcomed. No improvisatory works. Our programs are tailored for specific acoustics—composers should indicate their preference.''

Performances Sir Richard Rodney Bennett's *A Contemplation Upon Flowers* (a cappella madrigal); Ned Rorem's *Ode to Man* (a cappella chorus for mixed voices); and Sasha Johnson Manning's *Requiem* (a cappella oratorio).

Tips "We only consider a cappella works which can be produced in five rehearsals. Therefore pieces of great complexity or duration are discouraged. Our seasons are planned 2-3 years ahead, so much lead time is required for programming a new work. We will accept hand-written manuscript, but we prefer typeset music.''

SUSQUEHANNA SYMPHONY ORCHESTRA

P.O. Box 963, Abingdon, MD 21009. (410)838-6465. E-mail: sheldon.bair@ssorchestra.org. Web site: www.ssorchestra.org. **Contact:** Sheldon Bair, music director. Symphony orchestra. Estab. 1978. Members are amateurs. Performs 6 concerts/year including 1-2 new works. Composers paid depending on the circumstances. ''We perform in 1 hall, 600 seats with fine acoustics. Our audience encompasses all ages.''

How to Contact Query first. Include SASE. Responds in 3 or more months.

Music ''We desire works for large orchestra, any length, in a 'conservative 20th and 21st century' style. Seek fine music for large orchestra. We are a community orchestra, so the music must be within our grasp. Violin I to 7th position by step only; Violin II—stay within 5th position; English horn and harp are OK. Full orchestra pieces preferred.''

Performances Derek Bourgeois' *Trombone Concerto*; Gwyneth Walker's *The Magic Oboe*; Johan de Meij's *Symphony No. 1, Lord of the Rings*; Karen Amrhein's *Christmas Mirror*; Deborah Teason's *Steelband Concerto: Trinity*.

N ☑ TORONTO MENDELSSOHN CHOIR

60 Simcoe St., Toronto ON M5J 2H5 Canada. (416)598-0422. Fax: (416)598-2992. E-mail: manager@tmchoir.org or admin@tmchoir.org. Web site: www.tmchoir.org. **Contact:** Eileen Keown, executive director. Vocal ensemble. Members are professionals and amateurs. Performs 25 concerts/year including 1-3 new works. ''Most performances take place in Roy Thomson Hall. The audience is reasonably sophisticated, musically knowledgeable but with moderately conservative tastes.'' Pays by commission and ASCAP/SOCAN.

How to Contact Query first or submit complete score and tapes of pieces. Include SASE. Responds in 6 months.

Music All works must suit a large choir (180 voices) and standard orchestral forces or with some other not-too-exotic accompaniment. Length should be restricted to no longer than $\frac{1}{2}$ of a nocturnal concert. The choir sings at a very professional level and can sight-read almost anything. ''Works should fit naturally with the repertoire of a large choir which performs the standard choral orchestral repertoire.''

Performances Holman's *Jezebel*; Orff's *Catulli Carmina*; and Lambert's *Rio Grande*.

TOURING CONCERT OPERA CO. INC.

228 E. 80th, New York NY 10021. (212)988-2542. Fax: (518)851-6778. E-mail: tcoc@mhonline.net. **Contact:** Anne DeFigols, director. Opera company. Estab. 1971. Members are professionals. Performs 30 concerts/year including 1 new work. Payment varies.

How to Contact Submit complete score and tape of piece(s). Does not return material. Response time varies.

Music ''Operas or similar with small casts.''

Tips ''We are a touring company which travels all over the world. Therefore, operas with casts that are not large and simple but effective sets are the most practical.''

☑ VANCOUVER CHAMBER CHOIR

1254 W. Seventh Ave., Vancouver BC V6H 1B6 Canada. E-mail: info@vancouverchamberchoir.com. Web site: www.vancouverchamberchoir.com. **Contact:** Jon Washburn, artistic director. Vocal ensemble. Members are professionals. Performs 40 concerts/year including 5-8 new works. Commissions 2-4 composers or new works/year. Pays SOCAN royalty or negotiated fee for commissions.

How to Contact Submit complete score and tape of piece(s). Does not return material. Responds in 6 months if possible.

Music Seeks "choral works of all types for small chorus, with or without accompaniment and/or soloists. Concert music only. Choir made up of 20 singers. Large or unusual instrumental accompaniments are less likely to be appropriate. No pop music."

Performances The VCC has commissioned and premiered over 200 new works by Canadian and international composers, including Alice Parker's *That Sturdy Vine* (cantata for chorus, soloists and orchestra); R. Murray Schafer's *Magic Songs* (SATB a cappella); and Jon Washburn's *A Stephen Foster Medley* (SSAATTBB/piano).

Tips "We are looking for choral music that is performable yet innovative, and which has the potential to become 'standard repertoire.' Although we perform much new music, only a small portion of the many scores which are submitted can be utilized."

VANCOUVER YOUTH SYMPHONY ORCHESTRA SOCIETY

3214 West 10th Ave., Vancouver BC V6K 2L2 Canada. (604)737-0714. Fax: (604)737-0739. E-mail: vyso@telus.net. Web site: www.vyso.com. **Music Directors:** Roger Cole (artistic director and senior orchestra conductor), Jim Zhang (intermediate orchestra director), and Margerita Kress (debut and junior string orchestra director). Youth orchestra. "Four divisions consisting of musicians ranging in age from 8-22 years old." Estab. 1930. Members are amateurs. Performs 10-15 concerts/year in various lower mainland venues. Concert admission by donation.

Music "Extensive and varies orchestral repertoire is performed by all divisions. Please contact the VYSO for more information."

VIRGINIA OPERA

P.O. Box 2580, Norfolk VA 23501. (757)627-9545. E-mail: info@vaopera.com. Web site: www.vaopera.org. **Director of Education:** Jeff Corrirean. Artistic Director: Peter Mark. Opera company. Estab. 1974. Members are professionals. Performs more than 560 concerts/year. Commissions vary on number of composers or new works/year. Concerts are performed for school children throughout Virginia, grades K-5, 6-8 and 9-12 at the Harrison Opera House in Norfolk, and at public/private schools in Virginia. Pays on commission.

How to Contact Query first. Include SASE. Response time varies.

Music "Audience accessible style approximately 45 minutes in length. Limit cast list to three vocal artists of any combination. Accompanied by piano and/or keyboard. Works are performed before school children of all ages. Pieces must be age appropriate both aurally and dramatically. Musical styles are encouraged to be diverse, contemporary as well as traditional. Works are produced and presented with sets, costumes, etc." Limitations: "Three vocal performers (any combination). One keyboardist. Medium to difficult acceptable, but prefer easy to medium. Seeking only pieces which are suitable for presentation as part of an opera education program for Virginia Opera's education and outreach department. Subject matter must meet strict guidelines relative to Learning Objectives, etc. Musical idiom must be representative of current trends in opera, musical theater. Extreme dissonance, row systems not applicable to this environment.''

Performances Seymour Barab's *Cinderella*; John David Earnest's *The Legend of Sleepy Hollow*; and Seymour Barab's *The Pied Piper of Hamelin*.

Tips ''Theatricality is very important. New works should stimulate interest in musical theater as a legitimate art form for school children with no prior exposure to live theatrical entertainment. Composer should be willing to create a product which will find success within the educational system.''

WHEATON SYMPHONY ORCHESTRA

344 Spring Ave., Glen Ellyn IL 60137. (630)858-5552. Fax: (630)790-9703. E-mail: dmattob @aol.com. **Contact:** Don Mattison, manager. Symphony orchestra. Estab. 1959. Members are professionals and amateurs. Performs 6 concerts/year including a varying number of new works. ''No pay for performance but can probably record your piece.''

How to Contact Query first. Include SASE. Responds in 1 month.

Music ''This is a good amateur orchestra that wants pieces in a traditional idiom. Large scale works for orchestra only. No avant garde, 12-tone or atonal material. Pieces should be 20 minutes or less and must be prepared in 3 rehearsals. Instrumentation needed for woodwinds in 3s, full brass 4-3-3-1, 4 percussion and strings—full-instrumentation only. Selections for full orchestra only. No pay for reading your piece, but we will record it at our expense.''

Performances Richard Williams's *Symphony in G Minor* (4 movement symphony); Dennis Johnson's *Must Jesus Bear the Cross Alone, Azon* (traditional); and Michael Diemer's *Skating* (traditional style).

Contests & Awards

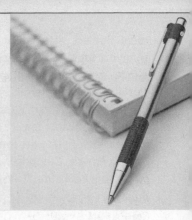

Participating in contests is a great way to gain exposure for your music. Prizes vary from contest to contest, from cash to musical merchandise to studio time, and even publishing and recording deals. For musical theater and classical composers, the prize may be a performance of your work. Even if you don't win, valuable contacts can be made through contests. Many times, contests are judged by music publishers and other industry professionals, so your music may find its way into the hands of key industry people who can help further your career.

HOW TO SELECT A CONTEST

It's important to remember when entering any contest to do proper research before signing anything or sending any money. We have confidence in the contests listed in *Songwriter's Market*, but it pays to read the fine print. First, be sure you understand the contest rules and stipulations once you receive the entry forms and guidelines. Then you need to weigh what you will gain against what they're asking you to give up. If a publishing or recording contract is the only prize a contest is offering, you may want to think twice before entering. Basically, the company sponsoring the contest is asking you to pay a fee for them to listen to your song under the guise of a contest, something a legitimate publisher or record company would not do. For those contests offering studio time, musical equipment or cash prizes, you need to decide if the entry fee you're paying is worth the chance to win such prizes.

Be wary of exorbitant entry fees, and if you have any doubts whatsoever as to the legitimacy of a contest, it's best to stay away. Songwriters need to approach a contest, award or grant in the same manner as they would a record or publishing company. Make your submission as professional as possible; follow directions and submit material exactly as stated on the entry form.

Contests in this section encompass all types of music and levels of competition. Read each listing carefully and contact them if the contest interests you. Many contests now have Web sites that offer additional information and even entry forms you can print. Be sure to read the rules carefully and be sure you understand exactly what a contest is offering before entering.

⊞ AGO AWARD IN ORGAN COMPOSITION

American Guild of Organists, 475 Riverside Dr., Suite 1260, New York NY 10115. (212)870-2310. Fax: (212)870-2163. E-mail: info@agohq.org. Web site: www.agohq.org. **Contact:** Harold Calhoun, competitions administrator. For composers and performing artists. Biennial award.

Requirements Organ solo, no longer than 8 minutes in duration. Specifics vary from year to year. Deadline: TBA, but usually early spring of odd-numbered year. Go to the Web site for application.

Award $2,000; publication by Hinshaw Music Inc.; performance at the biennial National Convention of the American Guild of Organists.

AGO/ECS PUBLISHING AWARD IN CHORAL COMPOSITION

American Guild of Organists, 475 Riverside Dr., Suite 1260, New York NY 10115. (212)870-2310. Fax: (212)870-2163. E-mail: info@agohq.org. Web site: www.agohq.org. **Contact:** Harold Calhoun, competitions administrator. Biannual award.

Requirements Composers are invited to submit a work for SATB choir and organ in which the organ plays a significant and independent role. Work submitted must be unpublished and are usually 3.5 to 5 minutes in length. There is no age restriction. Deadline: TBA, "but usually late fall in even numbered years." Application information on the website.

Awards $2,000 cash prize, publication by ECS Publishing and premier performance at the AGO National Convention.

ALEA III INTERNATIONAL COMPOSITION PRIZE

855 Commonwealth Ave., Boston MA 02215. (617)353-3340. E-mail: kalogeras@earthlink.com. Web site: www.aleaiii.com. For composers. Annual award.

Purpose To promote and encourage young composers in the composition of new music.

Requirements Composers born after January 1, 1979 may participate; 1 composition per composer. Works may be for solo voice or instrument or for chamber ensemble up to 15 members lasting between 6 and 15 minutes. Available instruments are: one flute (doubling piccolo or alto), one oboe (doubling English horn), one clarinet (doubling bass clarinet), one bassoon, one horn, one trumpet, one trombone, one tuba, two percussion players, one harp, one keyboard player, one guitar, two violins, one viola, one cello, one bass, tape and one voice. "One of the 15 performers could play an unusual, exotic or rare instrument, or be a specialized vocalist. For more info and guidelines, please refer to our Web site." All works must be unpublished and must not have been publicly performed or broadcast, in whole or in part or in any other version before the announcement of the prize in late September or early October of 2009. Works that have won other awards are not eligible. Deadline: March 15 2009. Send for application. Submitted work required with application. "Real name should not appear on score; a nom de plume should be signed instead. Sealed envelope with entry form should be attached to each score."

Awards ALEA III International Composition Prize: $2,500. Awarded once annually. Between 6-8 finalists are chosen and their works are performed in a competition concert by the ALEA III contemporary music ensemble. At the end of the concert, one piece will be selected to receive the prize. One grand prize winner is selected by a panel of judges.

Tips "Emphasis placed on works written in 20th century compositional idioms."

AMERICAN SONGWRITER LYRIC CONTEST

1303 16th Avenue S., 2nd Floor, Nashville TN 37212. (615)321-6096. Fax: (615)321-6097. E-mail: info@americansongwriter.com. Web site: www.americansongwriter.com. **Contact:** Matt Shearon. Estab. 1984. For songwriters and composers. Award for each bimonthly issue of American Songwriter magazine, plus grand prize winner at year-end.

Purpose To promote and encourage the craft of lyric writing.

Requirements Lyrics must be typed and a check for $10 (per entry) must be enclosed. Deadlines: January 22, March 23, May 23, July 24, September 25, November 16. Send along with official entry form found on our Web site, or submit online through sonicbids.com. Lyrics only, no cassettes. "If you enter two or more lyrics, you automatically receive a 1-year subscription to *American Songwriter* magazine (Canada: 3 or more; Other Countries: 4 or more)."

Awards A DX1 Martin guitar valued at $700 to bi-monthly contest winner. Grand prize winner receives airfare to Nashville and a demo session; and top 5 winning lyrics reprinted in each magazine, and 12 Honorable Mentions. One entrant interviewed each issue. Also: Grand Prize Winner gets to choose his/her "Dream Co-Writing Session" with either Bobby Braddock ("He Stopped Loving Her Today") or Kent Blazy ("If Tomorrow Never Comes"). Lyrics judged by independent A&R, PRO representatives, songwriters, publishers, and *American Songwriter* staff.

Tips "You do not have to be a subscriber to enter or win. You may submit as many entries as you like. All genres of music accepted."

ℕ ANNUAL ONE-ACT PLAYWRIGHTING COMPETITION

15 W. 28th St., 3rd Floor, New York NY 10001. (212)252-1619. Fax: (212)252-8763. E-mail: info@tadatheater.com. Web site: www.tadatheater.com. **Contact:** Playwrighting Contest. Estab. 1984. The contest is on hiatus during the 2009 season."

ARTISTS' FELLOWSHIPS

New York Foundation for the Arts, 155 Avenue of Americas, 14th Floor, New York NY 10013. (212)366-6900. Fax: (212)366-1778. E-mail: nyfaafp@nyfa.org. Web site: www.nyfa.org. To receive an application, or contact the fellowship's department, call: (212)366-6900, ext. 219. **Contact:** Margie Lempert, senior officer. For songwriters, composers and musical playwrights. Annual award, but each category funded biennially. Estab. 1984.

Purpose "Artists' Fellowships are $7,000 grants awarded by the New York Foundation for the Arts to individual originating artists living in New York State. The Foundation is committed to supporting artists from all over New York State at all stages of their professional careers. Fellows may use the grant according to their own needs; it should not be confused with project support."

Requirements Must be 18 years of age or older; resident of New York State for 2 years prior to application; and cannot be enrolled in any graduate or undergraduate degree program. Applications will be available in July. Deadline: October. Samples of work are required with application. 1 or 2 original compositions on separate audiotapes or audio CDs and at least 2 copies of corresponding scores or fully harmonized lead sheets.

Awards All Artists' Fellowships awards are for $7,000. Payment of $6,300 upon verification of NY State residency, and remainder upon completion of a mutually agreed upon public service activity. Nonrenewable. "Fellowships are awarded on the basis of the quality of work submitted. Applications are reviewed by a panel of 5 composers representing the aesthetic, ethnic, sexual and geographic diversity within New York State. The panelists change each year and review all allowable material submitted."

Tips "Please note that musical playwrights may submit only if they write the music for their plays—librettists must submit in our playwriting category."

BILLBOARD SONG CONTEST

P.O. Box 1000, Mounds OK 74047. (918)827-6529. Fax: (918)827-6533. E-mail: mark@jimhalsey.com. Web site: www.billboardsongcontest.com. **Contact:** Mark Furnas, Director. Estab. 1988. For songwriters, composers and performing artists. Annual international contest.

Purpose "To reward deserving songwriters and performers for their talent."

Requirements Entry fee: $30.

Awards To be announced. For entry forms and additional information send SASE to the above address or visit website.

Tips "Participants should understand popular music structure."

THE BLANK THEATRE COMPANY YOUNG PLAYWRIGHTS FESTIVAL

1301 Lucile Ave., Los Angeles CA 90026. (323)662-7734. Fax: (323)661-3903. E-mail: submissions@youngplaywrights.com. Web site: www.youngplaywrights.com. Estab. 1993. For both musical and non-musical playwrights. Annual award.

Purpose "To give young playwrights an opportunity to learn more about playwriting and to give them a chance to have their work mentored, developed, and presented by professional artists."

Requirements Playwrights must be 19 years old or younger on March 15, 2008. Send legible, original plays of any length and on any subject (co-written plays are acceptable provided all co-writers meet eligibility requirements). Submissions must be postmarked by March 15 and must include a cover sheet with the playwright's name, date of birth, school (if any), home address, home phone number, e-mail address and production history. Pages must be numbered and submitted unbound (unstapled). For musicals, a tape or CD of a selection from the score should be submitted with the script. Manuscripts will not be returned. Please do not send originals. Semi-finalists and winners will be contacted in May.

Awards Winning playwrights receive a workshop presentation of their work.

BUSH ARTIST FELLOWS PROGRAM

E-900 First National Bank Bldg., 332 Minnesota St., St. Paul MN 55101. (651)227-0891. Fax: (651)297-6485. E-mail: info@bushfoundation.org. Web site: www.bushfoundation.o

rg. Estab. 1976. For songwriters, composers and musical playwrights. Applications in music composition are accepted in even-numbered years.

Purpose "To provide artists with significant financial support that enables them to further their work and their contribution to their communities."

Requirements Applicant must be U.S. Citizens or Permanent Residents AND a Minnesota, North Dakota, South Dakota or western Wisconsin resident for 12 of preceeding 36 months, 25 years or older, not a student. Deadline: late October. Send for application. Audio work samples required with application. "Music composition applications will not be taken again until the fall of 2006. Applications will be taken in the fall of 2006 in the following areas: music composition, scriptworks (screenwriting and playwriting), literature (creative non-fiction, fiction, poetry) and film/video.

Awards Fellowships: $48,000 stipend for a period of 12-24 months. "Five years after completion of preceding fellowship, one may apply again." Applications are judged by peer review panels.

CMT/NSAI ANNUAL SONG CONTEST

1710 Roy Acuff Place, Nashville TN 37203. (615)256-3354. Fax: (615)256-0034. E-mail: songcontest@nashvillesongwriters.com. Web site: www.nashvillesongwriters.com. **Contact:** Deanie Williams, director. Annual award for songwriters.

Purpose "A chance for aspiring songwriters to be heard by music industry decision makers. Winners are flown to Nashville for a recording session and an appointment with Music Row executives."

Requirements Entry fee: $45 for one entry; $60 for 2. In order to be eligible contestants must not be receiving income from any work submitted—original material only. Submissions must include both lyrics and melody. Deadline is different each year; check website or send for application. Samples are required with application in the format of cassette or CD.

Awards Varies from year to year; check Web site.

CRS NATIONAL COMPOSERS COMPETITION

724 Winchester Rd., Broomall PA 19008. (610)544-5920. E-mail: crsnews@verizon.net. Web site: www.crsnews.org. **Contact:** Caroline Hunt, administrative assistant. Senior Representative: Jack Shusterman. Estab. 1981. For songwriters, composers and performing artists. College faculty and gifted artists. Annual award.

Requirements For composers, songwriters, performing artists and ensembles. The work submitted must be non-published (prior to acceptance) and not commercially recorded on any label. The work submitted must not exceed nine performers. Each composer may submit one work for each application submitted. (Taped performances are additionally encouraged.) Composition must not exceed twenty-five minutes in length. CRS reserves the right not to accept a First Prize Winner. Write with SASE for application or visit website. Add $3.50 for postage and handling. Deadline: December 10. Must send a detailed résumé with application form available on our Web page under "Events" category. Samples of work required with application. Send score and parts with optional CD or DAT. Application fee: $50.

Awards 1st Prize: Commercial recording grant. Applications are judged by panel of judges determined each year.

CUNNINGHAM COMMISSION FOR YOUTH THEATRE

(formerly Cunningham Prize for Playwriting), The Theatre School at DePaul University, 2135 N. Kenmore Ave., Chicago IL 60614. (773)325-7938. Fax: (773)325-7920. E-mail: aable s@depaul.edu. Web site: http://theatreschool.depaul.edu. **Contact:** Anna Ables. Estab. 1990. For playwrights. Annual award.

Purpose "The purpose of the Commission is to encourage the writing of dramatic works for young audiences that affirm the centrality of religion, broadly defined, and the human quest for meaning, truth, and community. The Theatre School intends to produce the plays created through this commission in its award-winning Chicago Playworks for Families and Young Audiences series at the historic Merle Reskin Theatre. Each year Chicago Playworks productions are seen by 35,000 students and families from throughout the Chicago area."

Requirements "Candidates for the commission must be writers whose residence is in the Chicago area, defined as within 100 miles of the Loop. Playwrights who have won the award within the last five years are not eligible. Deadline: annually by December 1. Candidates should submit a resumé, a 20 page sample of their work, and a brief statement about their interest in the commission. The submission should not include a proposal for a project the playwright would complete if awarded the commission. The writing sample may be from a play of any genre for any audience."

Awards $6,000. "Winners will be notified by May 1. The Selection Committee is chaired by the Dean of The Theatre School and is composed of members of the Cunningham Commission advisory committee and faculty of The Theatre School."

EUROPEAN INTERNATIONAL COMPETITION FOR COMPOSERS/IBLA FOUNDATION

226 East 2nd St., Loft 1B, New York NY 10009. (212)387-0111. E-mail: iblanyc@aol.com. Web site: www.ibla.org. **Contact:** Mr. Michael Yasenak, executive director. Chairman: Dr. S. Moltisanti. Estab. 1995. For songwriters and composers. Annual award.

Purpose "To promote the winners' career through exposure, publicity, recordings with Athena Records and nationwide distribution with the Empire Group."

Requirements Deadline: April 30. Send for application. Music score and/or recording of one work are required with application. Application fee is refunded if not admitted into the program.

Awards Winners are presented in concerts in Europe-Japan, USA.

FULBRIGHT SCHOLAR PROGRAM, COUNCIL FOR INTERNATIONAL EXCHANGE OF SCHOLARS

3007 Tilden St. NW, Suite 5L, Washington DC 20008-3009. (202)686-7877. E-mail: scholars @cies.iie.org. Web site: www.cies.org. Estab. 1946. For composers and academics. Annual award.

Purpose "Awards for university lecturing and advanced research abroad are offered annually in virtually all academic disciplines including musical composition."

Requirements "U.S. citizenship at time of application; M.F.A., Ph.D. or equivalent professional qualifications; for lecturing awards, university teaching experience (some awards are for professionals non-academic)." Applications become available in March each year, for grants to be taken up $1\frac{1}{2}$ years later. Application deadlines: August 1, all world areas. Write or call for application. Samples of work are required with application.

Awards "Benefits vary by country, but generally include round-trip travel for the grantee and for most full academic-year awards, one dependent; stipend in U.S. dollars and/or local currency; in many countries, tuition allowance for school age children; and book and baggage allowance. Grant duration ranges from 3 months-1 academic year."

GRASSY HILL KERRVILLE NEW FOLK COMPETITION

(formerly New Folk Concerts For Emerging Songwriters), P.O. Box 291466, Kerrville TX 78029. (830)257-3600. Fax: (830)257-8680. E-mail: info@kerrville-music.com. Web site: www.kerrvillefolkfestival.com. Contact: Dalis Allen, producer. For songwriters. Annual award.

- Also see the listing for Kerrville Folk Festival in the Workshops section of this book.

Purpose "To provide an opportunity for emerging songwriters to be heard and rewarded for excellence."

Requirements Songwriter enters 2 original songs burned to CD (cassettes no longer accepted), or uploaded to SonicBids, with entry fee; no more than one submission may be entered; 6-8 minutes total for 2 songs. Application online, no lyric sheets or press material needed. Submissions accepted between December 1-March 15 or first 800 entries received prior to that date. Call or e-mail to request rules. Entry fee: $25.

Awards New Folk Award Winner. 32 finalists invited to sing the 2 songs entered during The Kerrville Folk Festival in May. 6 writers are chosen as award winners. Each of the 6 receives a cash award of $450 or more and performs at a winner's concert during the Kerrville Folk Festival in June. Initial round of entries judged by the Festival Producer. 32 finalists judged by panel of 3 performer/songwriters.

Tips "Do not allow instrumental accompaniment to drown out lyric content. Don't enter without complete copy of the rules. Former winners and finalists include Lyle Lovett, Nanci Griffith, Hal Ketchum, John Gorka, David Wilcox, Lucinda Williams and Robert Earl Keen, Tish Hinojosa, Carrie Newcomer, Jimmy Lafave, etc."

GREAT AMERICAN SONG CONTEST

PMB 135, 6327-C SW Capitol Hill Hwy., Portland OR 97239-1937. E-mail: info@GreatAmeri canSong.com. Web site: www.GreatAmericanSong.com. **Contact:** Carla Starrett, event coordinator. Estab. 1998. For songwriters, composers and lyricists. Annual award.

- Also see the listing for Songwriters Resource Network in the Organizations section of this book.

Purpose To help songwriters get their songs heard by music-industry professionals; to generate educational and networking opportunities for participating songwriters; to help songwriters open doors in the music business.

Requirements Entry fee: $25. "Annual deadline. Check our website for details or send SASE along with your mailed request for information."

Awards Winners receive a mix of cash awards and prizes. The focus of the contest is on networking and educational opportunities. (All participants receive detailed evaluations of their songs by industry professionals.) Songs are judged by knowledgeable music-industry professionals, including prominent hit songwriters, producers and publishers.

Tips "Focus should be on the song. The quality of the demo isn't important. Judges will be looking for good songwriting talent. They will base their evaluations on the song—not the quality of the recording or the voice performance."

HENRICO THEATRE COMPANY ONE-ACT PLAYWRITING COMPETITION

P.O. Box 27032, Richmond VA 23273. (804)501-5115. Fax: (804)501-5284. E-mail: per22@c o.henrico.va.us. **Contact:** Amy A. Perdue, cultural arts senior coordinator. For musical playwrights, songwriters, composers and performing artists. Annual award.

Purpose Original one-act musicals for a community theater organization.

Requirements "Only one-act plays or musicals will be considered. The manuscript should be a one-act original (not an adaptation), unpublished, and unproduced, free of royalty and copyright restrictions. Scripts with smaller casts and simpler sets may be given preference. Controversial themes and excessive language should be avoided. Standard play script form should be used. All plays will be judged anonymously; therefore, there should be two title pages; the first must contain the play's title and the author's complete address and telephone number. The second title page must contain only the play's title. The playwright must submit two excellent quality copies. Receipt of all scripts will be acknowledged by mail. Scripts will be returned if SASE is included. No scripts will be returned until after the winner is announced. The HTC does not assume responsibility for loss, damage or return of scripts. All reasonable care will be taken." Deadline: July 1st.

Awards 1st Prize $300; 2nd Prize $200; 3rd Prize $200.

IAMA (INTERNATIONAL ACOUSTIC MUSIC AWARDS)

2881 E. Oakland Park Blvd, Suite 414, Fort Lauderdale FL 33306. (954)537-3127. **Contact:** Jessica Brandon, artist relations. Established 2004. E-mail: info@inacoustic.com. Web site: www.inacoustic.com. For singer-songwriters, musicians, performing musicians in the acoustic genre.

Purpose "The purpose is to promote the excellence in Acoustic music performance and songwriting." Genres include: Folk, Alternative, Bluegrass, etc.

Requirements Visit Web site for entry form and details. "All songs submitted must be original. There must be at least an acoustic instrument (voice) in any song. Electric and Electronic instruments, along with loops is allowed but acoustic instruments (or voice) must be clearly heard in all songs submitted. Contestants may enter as many songs in as many categories as desired but each entry requires a separate CD, entry form, lyric sheet and entry fee. CDs and lyrics will not be returned. Winners will be chosen by a Blue Ribbon Judging Committee comprised of music industry professionals including A&R managers from record labels, publishers and producers. Entries are judged equally on music perform-ance, production, originality, lyrics, melody and composition. Songs may be in any lan-guage. Winners will be notified by e-mail and must sign and return an affidavit confirming that winner's song is original and he/she holds rights to the song. Entry fee: $35/entry.

Awards Prizes: Overall Grand Prize receives $11,000.00 worth of merchandise, First Prizes in all categories win $900.00 worth of merchandise and services, Runner-Up prizes in all categories receive $600.00 worth of merchandise and services. All first prizes and runner-up winners will receive a track on IAMA compilation CD which goes out to radio stations.

Tips "Judging is based on music performance, music production, songwriting and originality/artistry."

L.A. DESIGNERS' THEATRE MUSIC AWARDS

P.O. Box 1883, Studio City CA 91614-0883. (323)650-9600. Fax: (323)654-3210. E-mail: ladesigners@juno.com. Artistic Director: Richard Niederberg. For songwriters, composers, performing artists, musical playwrights and rights holders of music.

Purpose To produce new musicals, operettas, opera-boufes and plays with music, as well as new dance pieces with new music scores.

Requirements Submit nonreturnable cassette, tape, CD or any other medium by first or 4th class mail. "We prefer proposals to scripts." Acceptance: continuous. Submit nonreturnable materials with cover letter. No application form or fee is necessary.

Awards Music is commissioned for a particular project. Amounts are negotiable. Applications judged by our artistic staff.

Tips "Make the material 'classic, yet commercial' and easy to record/re-record/edit. Make sure rights are totally free of all 'strings,' 'understandings,' 'promises,' etc. ASCAP/BMI/SESAC registration is OK, as long as 'grand' or 'performing rights' are available."

THE JOHN LENNON SONGWRITING CONTEST

180 Brighton Rd., Suite 801, Clifton NJ 07012. E-mail: info@jlsc.com. Web site: www.jlsc.com. Estab. 1996. For songwriters. Open year-round.

Purpose "The purpose of the John Lennon Songwriting Contest is to promote the art of songwriting by assisting in the discovery of new talent as well as providing more established songwriters with an opportunity to advance their careers."

Requirements Each entry must consist of the following: completed and signed application; audio cassette, CD or MP3 containing one song only, 5 minutes or less in length; lyric sheet typed or printed legibly (English translation is required when applicable); $30 entry fee. Deadline: December 15, 2006. Applications can be found in various music-oriented magazines and on our website. Prospective entrants can send for an application or contact the contest via e-mail at info@jlsc.com.

Awards Entries are accepted in the following 12 categories: rock, country, jazz, pop, world, gospel/inspirational, R&B, hip-hop, Latin, electronic, folk and children's music. Winners will receive EMI Publishing Contracts, Studio Equipment from Brian Moore Guitars, Roland, Edirol and Audio Technica, 1,000 CDs in full color with premium 6-panel Digipaks courtesy of Discmakers, and gift certificates from Musiciansfriend.com. One entrant wil be chosen to TOUR and PERFORM for one week on Warped Tour '06. One Lennon Award winning song will be named "Maxell Song of the Year" and take home an additional $20,000 in cash courtesy of the Maxell Corporation.

MAXIM MAZUMDAR NEW PLAY COMPETITION

One Curtain Up Alley, Buffalo NY 14202-1911. (716)852-2600. Fax: (716)852-2266. E-mail: newplays@alleyway.com. Web site: www.alleyway.com. **Contact:** Literary Manager. For musical playwrights. Annual award.

Purpose Alleyway Theatre is dedicated to the development and production of new works. Winners of the competition will receive production and royalties.

Requirements Unproduced full-length work not less than 90 minutes long with cast limit of 10 and unit or simple set, or unproduced one-act work less than 15 minutes long with cast limit of 6 and simple set; prefers work with unconventional setting that explores the boundaries of theatricality; limit of 1 submission in each category; guidelines available online, no entry form. $25 playwright entry fee. Script, resume, SASE optional. CD or cassette mandatory. Deadline: July 1.

Awards Production for full-length play or musical with royalty and production for one-act play or musical.

Tips "Entries may be of any style, but preference will be given to those scripts which take place in unconventional settings and explore the boundaries of theatricality. No more than ten performers is a definite, unchangeable requirement."

MID-ATLANTIC SONG CONTEST

Songwriters' Association of Washington, PMB 106-137, 4200 Wisconsin Ave., NW, Washington DC 20016. (301)654-8434. E-mail: masc@saw.org. Web site: www.saw.org. For songwriters and composers. Estab. 1982. Annual award.

- Also see the listing for Songwriters Association of Washington in the Organizations section.

Purpose This is one of the longest-running contests in the nation; SAW has organized twenty contests since 1982. The competition is designed to afford rising songwriters in a wide variety of genres the opportunity to receive awards and exposure in an environment of peer competition.

Requirements Amateur status is important. Applicants should request a brochure/application using the contact information above. Rules and procedures are clearly explained in that brochure. Cassette or CD and 3 copies of the lyrics are to be submitted with an application form and fee for each entry. Beginning this year, online entries will also be accepted. Reduced entry fees are offered to members of Songwriters' Association of Washington; membership can be arranged simultaneously with entering. Multie-song discounts are also offered. Applications are mailed out and posted on their website around June 1; the submission deadline is usually sometime in mid-August; awards are typically announced late in the fall.

Awards The two best songs in each of ten categories win prize packages donated by the contest's corporate sponsors: Writer's Digest Books, BMI, Oasis CD Manufacturing, Omega Recording Studios, TAXI, Mary Cliff and Sonic Bids. Winning songwriters are invited to perform in Washington, DC at the Awards Ceremony Gala, and the twenty winning songs are included on a compilation CD. The best song in each category is eligible for three grand cash prizes. Certificates are awarded to other entries meriting honorable mention.

Tips "Enter the song in the most appropriate category. Make the sound recording the best it can be (even though judges are asked to focus on melody and lyric and not on production.) Avoid clichés, extended introductions, and long instrumental solos.''

THELONIOUS MONK INTERNATIONAL JAZZ COMPOSERS COMPETITION

(Sponsored by BMI) Thelonious Monk Institute of Jazz, 5225 Wisconsin Ave. NW, #605, Washington DC 20015. (202)364-7272. Fax: (202)364-0176. E-mail: lebrown@tmonkinst.org. Web site: www.monkinstitute.org. **Contact:** Leonard Brown, program director. Estab. 1993. For songwriters and composers. Annual award.

Purpose The award is given to an aspiring jazz composer who best demonstrates originality, creativity and excellence in jazz composition.

Requirements Deadline: July 17. Send for application. Submission must include application form, resume of musical experience, CD or cassette, entry, four copies of the full score, and a photo. The composition features a different instrument each year. Entry fee: $35.

Awards $10,000. Applications are judged by panel of jazz musicians. ''The Institute will provide piano, bass, guitar, drum set, tenor saxophone, and trumpet for the final performance. The winner will be responsible for the costs of any different instrumentation included in the composition.''

PORTLAND SONGWRITERS ASSOCIATION ANNUAL SONGWRITING COMPETITION

P.O. Box 42389, Portland OR 97242. (503)914-1000. E-mail: info@portlandsongwriters.org. Web site: www.portlandsongwriters.org. Estab. 1991. For songwriters and composers. Annual award.

Purpose To provide opportunities for songwriters to improve their skills in the art and craft of songwriting, to connect our performing songwriters with the public through PSA sponsored venues and to create a presence and an avenue of approach for members' songs to be heard by industry professionals.

Requirements For information, send SASE. All amateur songwriters may enter. Deadline: December 1, 2007 postmark. Entry fee: $15 members; $20 nonmembers.

Awards Multiple awards totaling $1,000 in prizes. All songs will be reviewed by at least three qualified judges, including industry pros. Finalists may have their songs reviewed by celebrity judges.

PULITZER PRIZE IN MUSIC

709 Journalism Building, Columbia University, New York NY 10027. (212)854-3841. Fax: (212)854-3342. E-mail: pulitzer@www.pulitzer.org. Web site: www.pulitzer.org. **Contact:** Music Secretary. For composers and musical playwrights. Annual award.

Requirements ''For distinguished musical composition by an American that has had its first performance or recording in the United States during the year.'' Entries should reflect current creative activity. Works that receive their American premiere between January 16, 2006 and January 15, 2007 are eligible. A public performance or the public release of a recording shall constitute a premiere. Deadline: January 15. Samples of work are required with application, biography and photograph of composer, date and place of performance, score or manuscript and recording of the work, entry form and $50 entry fee.

Awards "One award: $10,000. Applications are judged first by a nominating jury, then by the Pulitzer Prize Board."

ROCKY MOUNTAIN FOLKS FESTIVAL SONGWRITER SHOWCASE

Planet Bluegrass, ATTN: Songwriter Showcase, P.O. Box 769, Lyons CO 80540. (800)624-2422 or (303)823-0848. Fax: (303)823-0849. E-mail: emily@bluegrass.com. Web site: www.bluegrass.com. **Contact:** Steve Szymanski, director. Estab. 1993. For songwriters, composers and performers. Annual award.

Purpose Award based on having the best song and performance.

Requirements Deadline: June 30. Finalists notified by July 14. Rules available on Web site. Samples of work are required with application. Send CD or cassette with $10/song entry fee. Can now submit online: www.sonicbids.com/rockymountainfolk06. Contestants cannot be signed to a major label or publishing deal. No backup musicians allowed.

Awards 1st Place is a 2006 Festival Main Stage set, custom Hayes Guitar, $100, and a free one song drumoverdubs (http://www.drumoverdubs.com) certificate (valued at $300); 2nd Place is $500 and a Baby Taylor Guitar; 3rd Place is $400 and a Baby Taylor Guitar; 4th Place is $300; 5th Place is $200; 6th to 10th Place is $100 each. Each finalist will also receive a complimentary three-day Folks Festival pass that includes onsite camping, and a Songwriter In The Round slot during the Festival on our workshop stage.

RICHARD RODGERS AWARDS

American Academy of Arts and Letters, 633 W. 155th St., New York NY 10032. (212)368-5900. **Contact:** Jane Bolster, coordinator. Estab. 1978. Deadline: November 1, 2007. "The Richard Rodgers Awards subsidize staged reading, studio productions, and full productions by nonprofit theaters in New York City of works by composers and writers who are not already established in the field of musical theater. The awards are only for musicals—songs by themselves are not eligible. The authors must be citizens or permanent residents of the United States." Guidelines for this award may be obtained by sending a SASE to above address or download from www.artsandletters.org.

ROME PRIZE COMPETITION FELLOWSHIP

American Academy in Rome, 7 E. 60th St., New York NY 10022-1001. (212)751-7200. Fax: (212)751-7220. E-mail: info@aarome.org. Web site: www.aarome.org. **Contact:** Programs Department. For composers. Annual award.

Purpose "Through its annual Rome Prize Competition, the academy awards up to thirty fellowships in eleven disciplines, including musical composition. Winners of the Rome Prize pursue independent projects while residing at the Academy's eleven acre center in Rome."

Requirements "Applicants for 11-month fellowships must be US citizens and hold a bachelor's degree in music, musical composition or its equivalent." Deadline: November 1. Entry fee: $25. Application guidelines are available through the Academy's Web site.

Awards "Up to two fellowships are awarded annually in musical composition. Fellowship consists of room, board, and a studio at the Academy facilities in Rome as well as a stipend of $25,000. In all cases, excellence is the primary criterion for selection, based on the quality of the materials submitted. Winners are announced in mid-April and fellowships generally begin in early September."

TELLURIDE TROUBADOUR CONTEST

Planet Bluegrass, ATTN: Troubadour Competition, P.O. Box 769, Lyons CO 80540. (303)823-0848 or (800)624-2422. Fax: (303)823-0849. E-mail: emily@bluegrass.com. Web site: www.bluegrass.com. **Contact:** Steve Szymanski, director. Estab. 1991. For songwriters, composers and performers. Annual award.

Purpose Award based on having best song and performance.

Requirements Deadline: must be postmarked by April 28; notified May 12, if selected. Rules available on website. Send cassette or CD and $10/song entry fee (limit of 2 songs). Can now submit music online at www.sonicbids.com/telluride2006. Contestants cannot be signed to a major label or publishing deal. No backup musicians allowed.

Awards 1st: custom Shanti Guitar, $200 and Festival Main Stage Set; 2nd: $400, "Limo" portable amplifier, and Little Martin guitar; 3rd: $300 and Little Martin guitar; 4th: $200 and Little Martin guitar; 5th: $100 and Baby Taylor guitar. Applications judged by panel of judges.

THE TEN-MINUTE MUSICALS PROJECT

P.O. Box 461194, West Hollywood CA 90046. Web site: www.tenminutemusicals.org. **Contact:** Michael Koppy, producer. For songwriters, composers and musical playwrights. Annual award.

Purpose "We are building a full-length stage musical comprised of complete short musicals, each of which play for between 8-14 minutes. Award is $250 for each work chosen for development towards inclusion in the project, plus a share of royalties when produced."

Requirements Deadline: August 31. See Web site for guidelines. Final submission should include script, cassette or CD, and lead sheets.

Awards $250 for each work selected. "Works should have complete stories, with a definite beginning, middle and end."

U.S.-JAPAN CREATIVE ARTISTS EXCHANGE FELLOWSHIP PROGRAM

Japan-U.S. Friendship Commission, 1201 15th St. NW, Suite 330, Washington DC 20005. (202)653-9800. Fax: (202)653-9802. E-mail: jusfc@jusfc.gov. Web site: www.jusfc.gov. **Contact:** Margaret Mihori, assistant executive director. Estab. 1980. For all creative artists. Annual award.

Purpose "For artists to go as seekers, as cultural visionaries, and as living liaisons to the traditional and contemporary life of Japan."

Requirements "Artists' works must exemplify the best in U.S. arts." Deadline: Feb. 1, 2008. Send for application and guidelines. Applications available via Internet. Samples of work are required with application. Requires 2 pieces on CD or DVD.

Awards Five artists are awarded a 5 month residency anywhere in Japan. Awards monthly stipend for living expenses, housing and professional support services; up to $6,000 for pre-departure costs, including such items as language training and economy class roundtrip airfare, plus 600,000 yen for monthly living expenses, housing allowance, and professional support services, as well as other arts professionals with expertise in Japanese culture.

Tips "Applicants should anticipate a highly rigorous review of their artistry and should have compelling reasons for wanting to work in Japan."

U.S.A. SONGWRITING COMPETITION

2881 E. Oakland Park Blvd., Suite 414, Ft. Lauderdale FL 33306. (954)537-3127. Fax: (954)537-9690. E-mail: info@songwriting.net. Web site: www.songwriting.net. **Contact:** Contest Manager. Estab. 1994. For songwriters, composers, performing artists and lyricists. Annual award.

Purpose "To honor good songwriters/composers all over the world, especially the unknown ones."

Requirements Open to professional and beginner songwriters. No limit on entries. Each entry must include an entry fee, a cassette tape of song(s) and lyric sheet(s). Judged by music industry representatives. Past judges have included record label representatives and publishers from Arista Records, EMI and Warner/Chappell. Deadline: To be announced. Entry fee: To be announced. Send SASE with request or e-mail for entry forms at any time. Samples of work are not required.

Awards Prizes include cash and merchandise in 15 different categories: pop, rock, country, Latin, R&B, gospel, folk, jazz, "lyrics only" category, instrumental and many others.

Tips "Judging is based on lyrics, originality, melody and overall composition. CD-quality production is great but not a consideration in judging."

UNISONG INTERNATIONAL SONG CONTEST

6520 Platt Ave., #729, West Hills CA 91307-3218. (213)673-4067. E-mail: info@unisong.com. Web site: www.unisong.com. Founders: Alan Roy Scott and David Stark. Estab. 1997. For songwriters (composers and lyricists) and performers. Annual songwriting contest.

Purpose "Unisong . . . created by songwriters for songwriters."

Requirements Open for entries from June 1st until November 1st. Categories cover most song genres, including Lyrics Only and a Performance category. Professional critiques available. Download entry form from Web site or enter directly online. You may also request an entry form by phone or e-mail. CDs or cassettes are accepted by mail. Entries also accepted via MP3.

Awards Over $70,000 in cash and prizes. Grand Prize winner receives an all expenses paid writing and performing retreat to their choice of Ireland, Crete, Sweden, Denmark, Spain, Faroe Islands, or Big Sur to collaborate with other writers & artists from around the world. There's also an additional "Winner of the Month" contest-within-the-contest, "People's Choice" Award, and Discmakers Winners Compilation CD. Songs judged on song quality above all, not just demo.

Tips "Please make sure your song is professionally presented. Make sure lyrics are typed or printed clearly. Print your personal information clearly. Enter your song in the most appropriate categories, or we can choose them for you for an additional fee."

Y.E.S. FESTIVAL OF NEW PLAYS

Northern Kentucky University Dept. of Theatre, FA-205, Highland Heights KY 41099-1007. (859)572-6303. Fax: (859)572-6057. E-mail: forman@nku.edu. **Contact:** Sandra Forman, project director. Estab. 1983. For musical playwrights. Biennial award (odd numbered years).

Purpose "The festival seeks to encourage new playwrights and develop new plays and musicals. Three plays or musicals are given full productions."

Requirements "No entry fee. Submit a script with a completed entry form. Musicals should be submitted with a piano/conductor's score and/or a vocal parts score. Scripts may be submitted May 1 through Sept. 30, 2008, for the New Play Festival occuring April 2009. Send SASE for application."

Awards Three awards of $500. "The winners are brought to NKU at our expense to view late rehearsals and opening night." Submissions are judged by a panel of readers.

Tips "Plays/musicals which have heavy demands for mature actors are not as likely to be selected as an equally good script with roles for 18-30 year olds."

Organizations

One of the first places a beginning songwriter should look for guidance and support is a songwriting organization. Offering encouragement, instruction, contacts and feedback, these groups of professional and amateur songwriters can help an aspiring songwriter hone the skills needed to compete in the ever-changing music industry.

The type of organization you choose to join depends on what you want to get out of it. Local groups can offer a friendly, supportive environment where you can work on your songs and have them critiqued in a constructive way by other songwriters. They're also great places to meet collaborators. Larger, national organizations can give you access to music business professionals and other songwriters across the country.

Most of the organizations listed in this book are non-profit groups with membership open to specific groups of people—songwriters, musicians, classical composers, etc. They can be local groups with a membership of less than 100 people, or large national organizations with thousands of members from all over the country. In addition to regular meetings, most organizations occasionally sponsor events such as seminars and workshops to which music industry personnel are invited to talk about the business, and perhaps listen to and critique demo tapes.

Check the following listings, bulletin boards at local music stores and your local newspapers for area organizations. If you are unable to locate an organization within an easy distance of your home, you may want to consider joining one of the national groups. These groups, based in New York, Los Angeles and Nashville, keep their members involved and informed through newsletters, regional workshops and large yearly conferences. They can help a writer who feels isolated in his hometown get his music heard by professionals in the major music centers.

In the following listings, organizations describe their purpose and activities, as well as how much it costs to join. Before joining any organization, consider what they have to offer and how becoming a member will benefit you. To locate organizations close to home, see the Geographic Index at the back of this book.

ACADEMY OF COUNTRY MUSIC

5500 Balboa Blvd., #200, Encino CA 91316. (818)788-8000. Fax: (818)877-0999. E-mail: info@acmcountry.com. Web site: www.acmcountry.com. **Contact:** Bob Romeo, executive director. Estab. 1964. Serves country music industry professionals. Eligibility for professional members is limited to those individuals who derive some portion of their income directly from country music. Each member is classified by one of the following categories: artist/entertainer, club/venue operator, musician, on-air personality, manager, talent agent, composer, music publisher, public relations, publications, radio, TV/motion picture, record company, talent buyer or affiliated (general). The purpose of ACM is to promote and enhance the image of country music. The Academy is involved year-round in activities important to the country music community. Some of these activities include charity fundraisers, participation in country music seminars, talent contests, artist showcases, assistance to producers in placing country music on television and in motion pictures and backing legislation that benefits the interests of the country music community. The ACM is governed by directors and run by officers elected annually. Applications are accepted throughout the year. Membership is $75/year.

AMERICAN COMPOSERS FORUM

332 Minnesota St., Suite E-145, St. Paul MN 55101. (651)251-2824. Fax: (651)291-7978. Web site: www.composersforum.org. **Contact:** Wendy Collins, member services manager. Estab. 1973. "The American Composers Forum links communities with composers and performers, encouraging the making, playing and enjoyment of new music. Building two-way relationships between artists and the public, the Forum develops programs that educate today's and tomorrow's audiences, energize composers' and performers' careers, stimulate entrepreneurship and collaboration, promote musical creativity, and serve as models of effective support for the arts. Programs include residencies, fellowships, commissions, producing and performance opportunities, a recording assistance program and a widely-distributed recording label. The Forum's members, more than 1,200 strong, live in 49 states and 16 countries; membership is open to all." Membership dues: Regular (U.S.): $55; Student/Senior (U.S.): $35; Regular (Outside U.S.): $65; Student/Senior (Outside U.S.): $45.

AMERICAN MUSIC CENTER, INC.

30 W. 26th St., Suite 1001, New York NY 10010-2011. (212)366-5260. Fax: (212)366-5265. E-mail: amcinfo@amc.net. Web site: www.amc.net. **Contact:** Membership Department. The American Music Center, founded by a consortium led by Aaron Copland in 1939, is the first-ever national service and information center for new classical music and jazz by American composers. The Center has a variety of innovative new programs and services, including a montly Internet magazine (www.newmusicbox.org) for new American music, online databases of contemporary ensembles and ongoing opportunities for composers, an online catalog of new music for educators specifically targeted to young audiences, a series of professional development workshops, and an online listening library (www.newmusicju kebox.org). Each month, AMC provides its over 2,500 members with a listing of opportuni-

ties including calls for scores, competitions, and other new music performance information. Each year, AMC's Information Services Department fields thousands of requests concerning composers, performers, data, funding, and support programs. The AMC Collection at the New York Public Library for the Performing Arts presently includes over 60,000 scores and recordings, many unavailable elsewhere. "AMC also continues to administer several grant programs: the Aaron Copland Fund for Music; the Henry Cowell Performance Incentive Fund; and its own programs Live Music for Dance and the Composer Assistance Program." Members also receive a link their Web sites on www.amc.net. The American Music Center is not-for-profit and has an annual membership fee.

AMERICAN SOCIETY OF COMPOSERS, AUTHORS AND PUBLISHERS (ASCAP)

One Lincoln Plaza, New York NY 10023. (212)621-6000 (administration); (212)621-6240 (membership). E-mail: info@ascap.com. Web site: www.ascap.com. President and Chairman of the Board: Marilyn Bergman. CEO: John LoFrumento. Executive Vice President/ Membership: Todd Brabec. **Contact:** Member Services at (800)95-ASCAP. **Regional offices—West Coast:** 7920 Sunset Blvd., 3rd Floor, Los Angeles CA 90046, (323)883-1000; **Nashville:** 2 Music Square W., Nashville TN 37203, (615)742-5000; **Chicago:** 1608 N. Milwaukee Ave., Suite 1007, Chicago IL 60647, (773)394-4286; **Atlanta:** PMB 400-541 10th St. NW, Atlanta GA 30318, (404)351-1224; **Florida:** 420 Lincoln Rd., Suite 385, Miami Beach FL 33139, (305)673-3446; **United Kingdom:** 8 Cork St., London W1S 3LJ England, 011-44-207-439-0909; **Puerto Rico:** 654 Ave. Munoz Rivera, IBM Plaza Suite 1101 B, Hato Rey, Puerto Rico 00918, (787)281-0782. ASCAP is a membership association of over 240,000 composers, lyricists, songwriters, and music publishers, whose function is to protect the rights of its members by licensing and collecting royalties for the nondramatic public performance of their copyrighted works. ASCAP licensees include radio, television, cable, live concert promoters, bars, restaurants, symphony orchestras, new media, and other users of music. ASCAP is the leading performing rights society in the world. All revenues, less operating expenses, are distributed to members (about 86 cents of each dollar). ASCAP was the first US performing rights organization to distribute royalties from the Internet. Founded in 1914, ASCAP is the only society created and owned by writers and publishers. The ASCAP Board of Directors consists of 12 writers and 12 publishers, elected by the membership. ASCAP's Member Card provides exclusive benefits geared towards working music professionals. Among the benefits are health, musical instrument and equipment, tour and studio liability, term life and long term care insurance, discounts on musical instruments, equipment and supplies, access to a credit union, and much more. ASCAP hosts a wide array of showcases and workshops throughout the year, and offers grants, special awards, and networking opportunities in a variety of genres. Visit their Web site listed above for more information.

⚏ ARIZONA SONGWRITERS ASSOCIATION

420 E. Thunderbird Rd., #737, Phoenix AZ 85022. (602)973-1988. E-mail: azsongwriters@cox.net. **Contact:** Jon Iger, president. Estab. 1977. Members are all ages; all styles of music, novice to pro; many make money placing their songs in film and TV. Most members are

residents of Arizona. Purpose is to educate about the craft and business of songwriting and to facilitate networking with business professionals and other songwriters, musicians, singers and studios. Offers instruction, e-newsletter, workshops, performance, and song pitching opportunities. Applications accepted year-round. Membership fee: $25/year.

⚄ ASSOCIATION DES PROFESSIONEL.LE.S DE LA CHANSON ET DE LA MUSIQUE

292 Montreal Rd, Suite 200, ON K1L 6B7 Canada. (613)745-5642. Fax: (613)745-9715. E-mail: info-apcm@rogers.com. Web site: www.apcm.ca. **Contact:** Jean-Emmanuel Simiand, agent de communication. Director: Lucie Mailloux. Estab. 1989. Members are French Canadian singers and musicians. Members must be French singing and may have a CD to be distributed. Purpose is to gather French speaking artists (outside of Quebec, mainly in Ontario) to distribute their material, other workshops, instructions, lectures, etc. Offers instruction, newsletter, lectures, workshops, and distribution. Applications accepted year-round. Membership fee: $60 (Canadian).

ASSOCIATION OF INDEPENDENT MUSIC PUBLISHERS

Los Angeles Chapter: P.O. Box 69473, Los Angeles CA 90069. (818)771-7301. New York line: (212)391-2532. E-mail: LAinfo@aimp.org or NYinfo@aimp.org. Web site: www.aimp.org. Estab. 1977. Purpose is to educate members on new developments in the music publishing industry and to provide networking opportunities. Offers monthly panels and networking events. Applications accepted year-round. Membership fee: NY: $75/year; LA: $65/year.

AUSTIN SONGWRITERS GROUP

P.O. Box 2578, Austin TX 78768. (512)203-1972. E-mail: info@austinsongwritersgroup.com. Web site: www.austinsongwritersgroup.com. **Contact:** Lee Duffy, president. Vice President: Brent Allen. Estab. 1986. Serves all ages and all levels, from just beginning to advanced. Perspective members should have an interest in the field of songwriting, whether it be for profit or hobby. The main purpose of this organization is "to educate members in the craft and business of songwriting; to provide resources for growth and advancement in the area of songwriting; and to provide opportunities for performance and contact with the music industry." The primary benefit of membership to a songwriter is "exposure to music industry professionals, which increases contacts and furthers the songwriter's education in both craft and business aspects." Offers competitions, instruction, lectures, library, newsletter, performance opportunities, evaluation services, workshops and "contact with music industry professionals through special guest speakers at meetings, plus our yearly 'Austin Songwriters Conference,' which includes instruction, song evaluations, and song pitching direct to those pros currently seeking material for their artists, publishing companies, etc." Applications accepted year-round. Membership fee: $40/year.

Tips "Our newsletter is top-quality—packed with helpful information on all aspects of songwriting—craft, business, recording and producing tips, and industry networking opportunities."

BALTIMORE SONGWRITERS ASSOCIATION

P.O. Box 22496, Baltimore MD 21203. (410)669-1075. E-mail: info@baltimoresongwriters.o rg. Web site: www.baltimoresongwriters.org. **Contact:** Ken Gutberlet, president. Estab. 1997. ''The BSA is an inclusive organization with all ages, skill levels and genres of music welcome.'' Offers instruction, newsletter, lectures, workshops, performance opportunities. Applications accepted year-round; membership not limited to location or musical status. Membership fee: $25.

Tips ''We are trying to build a musical community that is more supportive and less competitive. We are dedicated to helping songwriters grow and become better in their craft.''

THE BLACK ROCK COALITION

P.O. Box 1054, Cooper Station, New York NY 10276. (212)713-5097. E-mail: ldavis@blackro ckcoalition.org. Web site: www.blackrockcoalition.org. **Contact**: LaRonda Davis, president. Estab. 1985. Serves musicians, songwriters—male and female ages 18-40 (average). Also engineers, entertainment attorneys and producers. Looking for members who are ''mature and serious about music as an artist or activist willing to help fellow musicians. The BRC independently produces, promotes and distributes Black alternative music acts as a collective and supportive voice for such musicians within the music and record business. The main purpose of this organization is to produce, promote and distribute the full spectrum of black music along with educating the public on what black music is. The BRC is now soliciting recorded music by bands and individuals for Black Rock Coalition Records. Please send copyrighted and original material only.'' Offers instruction, newsletter, lectures, free seminars and workshops, monthly membership meeting, quarterly magazine, performing opportunities, evaluation services, business advice, full roster of all members. Applications accepted year-round. Bands must submit a tape, bio with picture and a self-addressed, stamped envelope before sending their membership fee. Membership fee: $25 per individual/$100 per band.

BROADCAST MUSIC, INC. (BMI)

320 W. 57th St., New York NY 10019. (212)586-2000. E-mail: newyork@bmi.com. Web site: www.bmi.com. **Los Angeles:** 8730 Sunset Blvd., Los Angeles CA 90069. (310)659-9109. E-mail: losangeles@bmi.com. **Nashville:** 10 Music Square East, Nashville TN 37203. (615)401-2000. E-mail: nashville@bmi.com. **Miami:** 5201 Blue Lagoon Dr., Suite 310, Miami FL 33126. (305)266-3636. E-mail: miami@bmi.com. **Atlanta:** Tower Place 100, 3340 Peachtree Rd., NE, Suite 570, Atlanta GA 30326. (404)261-5151. E-mail: atlanta@bmi.com. **Puerto Rico:** MCS Plaza, Suite 206, 255 Ponce De Leon Ave., San Juan PR 00917. (787)754-6490. **United Kingdom:** 84 Harley House, Marylebone Rd., London NW1 5HN United Kingdom. 011-44-207-486-2036. E-mail: london@bmi.com. President and CEO: Del R. Bryant. Senior Vice Presidents, New York: Phillip Graham, Writer/Publisher Relations; Alison Smith, Performing Rights. Vice Presidents: New York: Charlie Feldman; Los Angeles: Barbara Cane and Doreen Ringer Ross, Nashville: Paul Corbin; Miami: Diane J. Almodovar; Atlanta: Catherine Brewton. Senior Executive, London: Brandon Bakshi. BMI is a performing rights organization representing approximately 300,000 songwriters, composers and

music publishers in all genres of music, including pop, rock, country, R&B, rap, jazz, Latin, gospel and contemporary classical. "Applicants must have written a musical composition, alone or in collaboration with other writers, which is commercially published, recorded or otherwise likely to be performed." Purpose: BMI acts on behalf of its songwriters, composers and music publishers by insuring payment for performance of their works through the collection of licensing fees from radio stations, Internet outlets, broadcast and cable TV stations, hotels, nightclubs, aerobics centers and other users of music. This income is distributed to the writers and publishers in the form of royalty payments, based on how the music is used. BMI also undertakes intensive lobbying efforts in Washington D.C. on behalf of its affiliates, seeking to protect their performing rights through the enactment of new legislation and enforcement of current copyright law. In addition, BMI helps aspiring songwriters develop their skills through various workshops, seminars and competitions it sponsors throughout the country. Applications accepted year-round. There is no membership fee for songwriters; a one-time fee of $150 is required to affiliate an individually-owned publishing company; $250 for partnerships, corporations and limited-liability companies. "Visit our Web site for specific contacts, e-mail addresses and additional membership information."

CALIFORNIA LAWYERS FOR THE ARTS

Fort Mason Center, Building C, Room 255, San Francisco CA 94123. (415)775-7200. Fax: (415)775-1143. E-mail: cla@calawyersforthearts.org. Web site: www.calawyersforthearts. org. **Southern California:** 1641 18th St., Santa Monica CA 90404. (310)998-5590. Fax: (310)998-5594. E-mail: usercla@aol.com. **Sacramento Office:** 1127 11th St., Suite 214, Sacramento CA 95814. (916)442-6210. Fax: (916)442-6281. E-mail: clasacto@aol.com. **Oakland Office:** 1212 Broadway St., Suite 834, Oakland CA 94612. (510)444-6351. Fax: (510)444-6352. E-mail: oakcla@there.net. **Contact:** Alma Robinson, executive director. Systems Coordinator: Josie Porter. Estab. 1974. "For artists of all disciplines, skill levels, and ages, supporting individuals and organizations, and arts organizations. Artists of all disciplines are welcome, whether professionals or amateurs. We also welcome groups and individuals who support the arts. We work most closely with the California arts community. Our mission is to establish a bridge between the legal and arts communities so that artists and art groups may handle their creative activities with greater business and legal competence; the legal profession will be more aware of issues affecting the arts community; and the law will become more responsive to the arts community." Offers newsletter, lectures, library, workshops, mediation service, attorney referral service, housing referrals, publications and advocacy. Membership fee: $20 for senior citizens and full-time students; $25 for working artists; $40 for general individual; $60 for panel attorney; $100 to $1,000 for patrons. Organizations: $50 for small organizations (budget under $100,000); $90 for large organizations (budget of $100,000 or more); $100 to $1,000 for corporate sponsors.

⚂ CANADA COUNCIL FOR THE ARTS/CONSEIL DES ARTS DU CANADA

350 Albert St., P.O. Box 1047, Ottawa ON K1P 5V8 Canada. (613)566-4414, ext. 5060. E-mail: info@canadacouncil.ca. Web site: www.canadacouncil.ca. **Contact:** Lise Rochon,

information officers. Estab. 1957. An independent agency that fosters and promotes the arts in Canada by providing grants and services to professional artists including songwriters and musicians. "Individual artists must be Canadian citizens or permanent residents of Canada, and must have completed basic training and/or have the recognition as professionals within their fields. The Canada Council offers grants to professional musicians to pursue their individual artistic development and creation. There are specific deadline dates for the various programs of assistance. Visit our Web site at www.canadacouncil.ca/music for more details."

✪ CANADIAN ACADEMY OF RECORDING ARTS & SCIENCES (CARAS)

345 Adelaide Street West, 2nd Floor, Toronto ON M5V 1R5 Canada. (416)485-3135. Fax: (416)485-4978. E-mail: info@carasonline.ca. Web site: www.junoawards.ca. **Contact:** Meghan McCabe, office coordinator. President: Melanie Berry. Manager, Awards and Events: Leisa Peacock. Manager, Marketing and Communications: Tammy Kitchener. Membership is open to all employees (including support staff) in broadcasting and record companies, as well as producers, personal managers, recording artists, recording engineers, arrangers, composers, music publishers, album designers, promoters, talent and booking agents, record retailers, rack jobbers, distributors, recording studios and other music industry related professions (on approval). Applicants must be affiliated with the Canadian recording industry. Offers newsletter, nomination and voting privileges for Juno Awards and discount tickets to Juno Awards show. "CARAS strives to foster the development of the Canadian music and recording industries and to contribute toward higher artistic standards." Applications accepted year-round. Membership fee is $50/year (Canadian) + GST = $53.00. Applications accepted from individuals only, not from companies or organizations.

✪ CANADIAN COUNTRY MUSIC ASSOCIATION (CCMA)

626 King Street West, Suite 203, Toronto ON MV5 1M7 Canada. (416)947-1331. Fax: (416)947-5924. E-mail: country@ccma.org. Web site: www.ccma.org. **Contact:** Brandi Mills, communications & marketing. Estab. 1976. Members are artists, songwriters, musicians, producers, radio station personnel, managers, booking agents and others. Offers newsletter, workshops, performance opportunities and the CCMA awards every September. "Through our newsletters and conventions we offer a means of meeting and associating with artists and others in the industry. The CCMA is a federally chartered, nonprofit organization, dedicated to the promotion and development of Canadian country music throughout Canada and the world and to providing a unity of purpose for the Canadian country music industry." See website for membership information and benefits.

✪ CANADIAN MUSICAL REPRODUCTION RIGHTS AGENCY LTD.

56 Wellesley St. W, #320, Toronto ON M5S 2S3 Canada. (416)926-1966. Fax: (416)926-7521. E-mail: inquiries@cmrra.ca. Web site: www.cmrra.ca. **Contact:** Michael Mackie, membership services. Estab. 1975. Members are music copyright owners, music publishers, sub-publishers and administrators. Representation by CMRRA is open to any person, firm

or corporation anywhere in the world, which owns and/or administers one or more copyrighted musical works. CMRRA is a music licensing agency—Canada's largest—which represents music copyright owners, publishers and administrators for the purpose of mechanical and synchronization licensing in Canada. Offers mechanical and synchronization licensing. Applications accepted year-round.

CENTRAL CAROLINA SONGWRITERS ASSOCIATION (CCSA)

131 Henry Baker Road, Zebulon NC 27597. (919) 269-6240. E-mail: ccsa_raleigh@yahoo.com. Web site: www.ccsa-raleigh.com. **Contact:** Tony Dickens, president, or vice president Diana Dimsdale. Established in 1997, CCSA welcomes songwriters of all experience levels from beginner to professional within the local RDU/Triad/Eastern area of North Carolina to join our group. Our members' musical background varies, covering a wide array of musical genres. CCSA meets monthly in Raleigh, NC. We are unable to accept applications from incarcerated persons or those who do not reside in the local area as our group's primary focus is on songwriters who are able to attend the monthly meetings-to ensure members get the best value for their yearly dues. CCSA strives to provide each songwriter and musician a resourceful organization where members grow musically by networking and sharing with one another. Offers yearly newsletter, some workshops, critiques at the monthly meetings, and ability to network with fellow members. Applications are accepted year round. Dues are $24/year (pro-rated for new members at $2/month by date of application) with annual renewal each January.

CENTRAL OREGON SONGWRITERS ASSOCIATION

782 SW Rimrock Way, Redmond OR 97756. (541)548-6306. E-mail: administrator@centraloregonmusic.com. Web site: www.centraloregonmusic.com. President: Claudia Valiquet. Estab. 1993. "Our members range in age from their 20s into their 80s. Membership includes aspiring beginners, accomplished singer/songwriter performing artists and all in between. Anyone with an interest in songwriting (any style) is invited to and welcome at COSA. COSA is a nonprofit organization to promote, educate and motivate members in the skills of writing, marketing and improving their craft." Offers competitions, instruction, newsletter, lectures, library, workshops, performance opportunities, songwriters round, awards, evaluation services and collaboration. Applications accepted year-round. Membership fee is $25.

THE COLLEGE MUSIC SOCIETY

312 E. Pine St., Missoula MT 59802. (406)721-9616. Fax: (406)721-9419. E-mail: cms@music.org. Web site: www.music.org. Estab. 1959. Serves college, university and conservatory professors, as well as independent musicians. "The College Music Society is a consortium of college, conservatory, university and independent musicians and scholars interested in all disciplines of music. Its mission is to promote music teaching and learning, musical creativity and expression, research and dialogue, and diversity and interdisciplinary interaction." Offers journal, newsletter, lectures, workshops, performance opportunities, job listing service, databases of organizations and institutions, music faculty and mailing lists. Applications accepted year-round. Membership fee: $65 (regular dues), $35 (student dues), $35 (retiree dues).

CONNECTICUT SONGWRITERS ASSOCIATION

P.O. Box 511, Mystic CT 06355. E-mail: info@ctsongs.com. Web site: www.ctsongs.com. **Contact:** Bill Pere, Executive Director. Associate Director: Kay Pere. "We are an educational, nonprofit organization dedicated to improving the art and craft of original music. Founded in 1979, CSA has had almost 2,000 active members and has become one of the best known and respected songwriters' associations in the country. Membership in the CSA admits you to 12-18 seminars/workshops/song critique sessions per year at multiple locations in Connecticut. Out-of-state members may mail in songs for free critiques at our meetings. Noted professionals deal with all aspects of the craft and business of music including lyric writing, music theory, music technology, arrangement and production, legal and business aspects, performance techniques, song analysis and recording techniques. CSA offers song screening sessions for members and songs that pass are then eligible for inclusion on the CSA sampler anthology through various retail and online outlets and are brought to national music conferences. CSA is well connected in both the independent music scene and the traditional music industry. CSA also offers showcases and concerts which are open to the public and designed to give artists a venue for performing their original material for an attentive, listening audience. CSA benefits help local soup kitchens, group homes, hospice, world hunger, libraries, nature centers, community centers and more. CSA shows encompass ballads to bluegrass and Bach to rock. Our monthly newsletter, *Connecticut Songsmith*, offers free classified advertising for members, and has been edited and published by Bill Pere since 1980. Annual dues: $40; senior citizen and full time students $30; organizations $80. Memberships are tax-deductible as business expenses or as charitable contributions to the extent allowed by law."

DALLAS SONGWRITERS ASSOCIATION

Sammons Center for the Arts, 3630 Harry Hines, Box 20, Dallas TX 75219. (214)750-0916. E-mail: info@dallassongwriters.org. Web site: www.dallassongwriters.org. **Contact:** Charles Sterling, membership director. President: Steve Sullivan. Founding President Emeritis: Barbara McMillen. Estab. 1986. Serves songwriters and lyricists of Dallas/Ft. Worth metroplex. Members are adults ages 18-65, Dallas/Ft. Worth area songwriters/lyricists who are or aspire to be professionals. Purpose is to provide songwriters an opportunity to meet other songwriters, share information, find co-writers and support each other through group discussions at monthly meetings; to provide songwriters an opportunity to have their songs heard and critiqued by peers and professionals by playing cassettes and providing an open mike at monthly meetings and open mics, showcases, and festival stages, and by offering contests judged by publishers; to provide songwriters opportunities to meet other music business professionals by inviting guest speakers to monthly meetings and workshops; and to provide songwriters opportunities to learn more about the craft of songwriting and the business of music by presenting mini-workshops at each monthly meeting. "We offer a chance for the songwriter to learn from peers and industry professionals and an opportunity to belong to a supportive group environment to encourage the individual to continue his/her songwriting endeavors." Offers competitions (including the Annual Song Contest with over $5,000 in prizes, and the Quarterly Lyric Contest), field trips, instruction, lectures, newsletter, performance opportunities, social outings, workshops and seminars. "Our members are eligible for discounts at several local music stores and seminars.'' Applications accepted year-round. Membership fee: $55. ''When inquiring by phone, please leave complete mailing address and phone number where you can be reached day and night.''

THE DRAMATISTS GUILD OF AMERICA, INC.

(formerly The Dramatists Guild, Inc.), 1501 Broadway, Suite 701, New York NY 10036. (212)398-9366. Fax: (212)944-0420. E-mail: membership@dramatistsguild.com. Web site: www.dramatistsguild.com. **Contact:** Joshua Levine, director of membership. ''For over three-quarters of a century, The Dramatists Guild has been the professional association of playwrights, composers and lyricists, with more than 6,000 members across the country. All theater writers, whether produced or not, are eligible for Associate membership ($95/ year); those who are engaged in a drama-related field but are not a playwright are eligible for Subscribing membership ($25/year); students enrolled in writing degree programs at colleges or universities are eligible for Student membership ($35/year); writers who have been produced on Broadway, Off-Broadway or on the main stage of a LORT theater are eligible for Active membership ($150/year). The Guild offers its members the following activities and services: use of the Guild's contracts (including the Approved Production Contract for Broadway, the Off-Broadway contract, the LORT contract, the collaboration agreements for both musicals and drama, the 99 Seat Theatre Plan contract, the Small Theatre contract, commissioning agreements, and the Underlying Rights Agreements contract; advice on all theatrical contracts including Broadway, Off-Broadway, regional, showcase, Equity-waiver, dinner theater and collaboration contracts); a nationwide toll-free number for all members with business or contract questions or problems; advice and information on a wide spectrum of issues affecting writers; free and/or discounted ticket service; symposia led by experienced professionals in major cities nationwide; access to health insurance programs; and a spacious meeting room which can accommodate up to 50 people for readings and auditions on a rental basis. The Guild's publications are: *The Dramatist*, a bimonthly journal containing articles on all aspects of the theater (which includes *The Dramatists Guild Newsletter*, with announcements of all Guild activities and current information of interest to dramatists); and an annual resource directory with up-to-date information on agents, publishers, grants, producers, playwriting contests, conferences and workshops, and an interactive Web site that brings our community of writers together to exchange ideas and share information.

THE FIELD

161 Sixth Ave., New York NY 10013. (212)691-6969. Fax: (212)255-2053. E-mail: info@thefi eld.org. Web site: www.thefield.org. **Contact:** any staff member. Estab. 1986. ''The Field gives independent performing artists the tools to develop and sustain their creative and professional lives, while allowing the public to have immediate, direct access to a remarkable range of contemporary artwork. The organization was started by eight emerging artists who shared common roots in contemporary dance and theater. Meeting regularly, these artists created a structure to help each other improve their artwork, and counter the isolation that often comes with the territory of an artistic career. The Field offers a comprehensive

series of edcuational programs, resources, and services. Artists can participate in a broad array of programs and services including art development workshops, performance opportunities, career management training and development, fundraising consultations, fiscal sponsorship, a Resource Center, and artist residencies. The Field's goal is to help artists develop their best artwork by deepening the artistic process and finding effective ways to bring that art into the marketplace. Most Field programs cost between $35 and $150, and tickets to our performance events are $10. In addition, since 1992, The Field has coordinated a network of satellite sites in Atlanta, Chicago, Houston, Miami, Philadelphia, Phoenix, Rochester (NY), Salt Lake City, San Francisco, Seattle, Tucson, Richmond (VA), and Washington. The Field is the only organization in New York that provides comprehensive programming for independent performing artists on a completely non-exclusive basis. Programs are open to artists from all disciplines, aesthetic viewpoints, and levels of development." Offers workshops and performance opportunities on a seasonal basis. Applications accepted year-round. Membership fee: $100/year.

Tips "The Field's resource center is an artist-focused library/computer lab where artists can access office equipment and work in a quiet and supportive environment. Located at The Field's office, the Resource Center offers fund-raising resources and hands-on assistance, including databases such as the Foundation Directory Online, computer workstations, and a library of books, journals, and information directories. One-on-one assistance and consultations are also available to guide users through grant writing and other fundraising endeavors. GoTour (www.gotour.org) is a free Web site offering independent artists the resources they need to take their show on the road. Visitors log on for free and access a national arts network where they can search for venues, network with artists nationwide, find media contacts, read advice from other artists and arts professionals, add information on their local arts community, post tour anecdotes, and list concert information and classified ads."

FORT WORTH SONGWRITERS ASSOCIATION

P.O. Box 162443, Fort Worth TX 76161. (817)654-5400. E-mail: info@fwsa.com. Web site: www.fwsa.com. President: Judy Boots. Vice-Presidents: Rick Tate and John Terry. Secretary: Lynda Timmons Elvington. Treasurer: Rick Tate. Estab. 1992. Members are ages 18-83, beginners up to and including published writers. Interests cover gospel, country, western swing, rock, pop, bluegrass and blues. Purpose is to allow songwriters to become more proficient at songwriting; to provide an opportunity for their efforts to be performed before a live audience; to provide songwriters an opportunity to meet co-writers. "We provide our members free critiques of their efforts. We provide a monthly newsletter outlining current happenings in the business of songwriting. We offer competitions and mini workshops with guest speakers from the music industry. We promote a weekly open 'mic' for singers of original material, and hold invitational songwriter showcase events a various times throughout the year. Each year, we hold a Christmas Song Contest, judged by independent music industry professionals. We also offer free web pages for members or links to member Web sites." Applications accepted year-round. Membership fee: $35.

⊕ THE GUILD OF INTERNATIONAL SONGWRITERS & COMPOSERS

Sovereign House, 12 Trewartha Road, Praa Sands, Penzance, Cornwall TR20 9ST England. (01736)762826. Fax: (01736)763328. E-mail: songmag@aol.com. Web site: www.songwriters-guild.com. General Secretary: Carole Jones. The Guild of international songwriters & Composers is an international music industry organization based in England in the United Kingdom. Guild members are songwriters, composers, lyricists, poets, performing songwriters, musicians, music publishers, studio owners, managers, independent record companies, music industry personnel, etc., from many countries throughout the world. The Guild of International Songwriters & Composers has been publishing *Songwriting and Composing Magazine* since 1986, which is issued free to all Guild members throughout their membership. The Guild of International Songwriters and Composers offers advice, guidance, assistance, copyright protection service, information, encouragement, contact information, Intellectual property/copyright protection of members works through the Guild's Copyright Registration Centre along with other free services and more to Guild members with regard to helping members achieve their aims, ambitions, progression and advancement in respect to the many different aspects of the music industry. Information, advice and services available to Guild members throughout their membership includes assistance, advice and help on many matters and issues relating to the music industry in general. Annual membership fees: are £50. For further information please visit the Guild's Web site at: www.songwriters-guild.co.uk.

HAWAI'I SONGWRITERS ASSOCIATION

P.O. Box 231325, Las Vegas NV 89105. (702)897-9066. E-mail: stanrubens@aol.com. Web site: www.stanrubens.com. **Contact:** Stan Rubens, secretary. Estab. 1972. "We have two classes of membership: Professional (must have had at least one song commercially published and for sale to general public) and Regular (any one who wants to join and share in our activities). Both classes can vote equally, but only Professional members can hold office. Must be 18 years old to join. Our members include musicians, entertainers and record producers. Membership is world-wide and open to all varieties of music, not just ethnic Hawaiian. President, Stan Rubens, has published 4 albums." Offers competitions, instruction, monthly newsletter, lectures, workshops, performance opportunities and evaluation services. Applications accepted year-round. Membership fee: $24. Stan Rubens teaches songwriting either privately or in group or school sessions.

INTERNATIONAL BLUEGRASS MUSIC ASSOCIATION (IBMA)

2 Music Circle South, Suite 100, Nashville TN 37203. 1(888)GET-IBMA. Fax: (615)256-0450. E-mail: info@ibma.org. Web site: www.ibma.org. Member Services: Jill Snider. Estab. 1985. Serves songwriters, musicians and professionals in bluegrass music. "IBMA is a trade association composed of people and organizations involved professionally and semi-professionally in the bluegrass music industry, including performers, agents, songwriters, music publishers, promoters, print and broadcast media, local associations, recording manufacturers and distributors. Voting members must be currently or formerly involved in the bluegrass industry as full or part-time professionals. A songwriter attempting to become

professionally involved in our field would be eligible. Our mission statement reads: "IBMA: Working together for high standards of professionalism, a greater appreciation for our music, and the success of the world-wide bluegrass music community." IBMA publishes a bimonthly International Bluegrass, holds an annual trade show/convention with a songwriters showcase in the fall, represents our field outside the bluegrass music community, and compiles and disseminates databases of bluegrass related resources and organizations. Market research on the bluegrass consumer is available and we offer Bluegrass in the Schools information and matching grants. The primary value in this organization for a songwriter is having current information about the bluegrass music field and contacts with other songwriters, publishers, musicians and record companies." Offers workshops, liability insurance, rental car discounts, consultation and databases of record companies, radio stations, press, organizations and gigs. Applications accepted year-round. Membership fee: for a non-voting patron $40/year; for an individual voting professional $70/year; for an organizational voting professional $200/year.

⊕ INTERNATIONAL SONGWRITERS ASSOCIATION LTD.

P.O. Box 46, Limerick City, Ireland. E-mail: jliddane@songwriter.iol.ie. Web site: www.son gwriter.co.uk. Contact: Anna M. Sinden, membership department. Serves songwriters and music publishers. "The ISA headquarters is in Limerick City, Ireland, and from there it provides its members with assessment services, copyright services, legal and other advisory services and an investigations service, plus a magazine for one yearly fee. Our members are songwriters in more than 50 countries worldwide, of all ages. There are no qualifications, but applicants under 18 are not accepted. We provide information and assistance to professional or semi-professional songwriters. Our publication, *Songwriter*, which was founded in 1967, features detailed exclusive interviews with songwriters and music publishers, as well as directory information of value to writers." Offers competitions, instruction, library, newsletter and a weekly e-mail newsletter *Songwriter Newswire*. Applications accepted year-round. Membership fee for European writers is £19.95; for non-European writers, US $30.

JUST PLAIN FOLKS MUSIC ORGANIZATION

5327 Kit Dr., Indianapolis IN 46237. (317)513-6557. E-mail: info@jpfolks.com. Web site: www.jpfolks.com. **Contact:** Brian Austin Whitney (brian@jpfolks.com), founder or Linda Berger (linda@jpfolks.com), projects director. Estab. 1998. "Just Plain Folks is among the world's largest Music Organizations. Our members cover nearly every musical style and professional field, from songwriters, artists, publishers, producers, record labels, entertainment attorneys, publicists and PR experts, performing rights organization staffers, live and recording engineers, educators, music students, musical instrument manufacturers, TV, Radio and Print Media and almost every major Internet Music entity. Representing all 50 US States and over 100 countries worldwide, we have members of all ages, musical styles and levels of success, including winners and nominees of every major music industry award, as well as those just starting out. A complete demographics listing of our group is available on our website. Whether you are a #1 hit songwriter or artist, or the newest kid

on the block, you are welcome to join. Membership does require an active e-mail account."
The purpose of this organization is "to share wisdom, ideas and experiences with others
who have been there, and to help educate those who have yet to make the journey. Just
Plain Folks provides its members with a friendly networking and support community that
uses the power of the Internet and combines it with good old-fashioned human interaction.
We help promote our members ready for success and educate those still learning." Offers
special programs to members, including:

- *Just Plain Notes Newsletter:* Members receive our frequent e-mail newsletters full of
expert info on how to succeed in the music business, profiles of members successes and
advice, opportunities to develop your career and tons of first-person networking contacts
to help you along the way. (Note: we send this out 2-3 times/month via e-mail only.)
- *Just Plain Mentors:* We have some of the friendliest expert educators, writers, artists
and industry folks in the business who volunteer their time as part of our Mentor Staff.
Included are John and JoAnn Braheny, Jason Blume, Harriet Schock, Pat and Pete Luboff,
Derek Sivers, Jodi Krangle, Steve Seskin, Alan O'Day, Walter Egan, Sara Light, Danny
Arena, Barbara Cloyd, Michael Laskow, Anne Leighton, Mark Keefner, Valerie DeLa-
Cruz, Karen Angela Moore, Ben McLane, Jack Perricone, Pat Pattison, Mark Baxter,
Harold Payne, Joey Arreguin, John Beland, Susan Gibson, Art Twain, Diane Rapaport,
Nancy Moran, Fett, Mike Dunbar, R. Chris Murphy, Bobby Borg, Paul Reisler, and many
others.
- *JPFolks.com Web site:* Our home page serves as your pathway to the resources and
members of the group worldwide. With message boards, lyric feedback forums, featured
members music, member profiles, member contact listings, member links pages, chapter
homepages, demographics information, our Internet radio station and all the back issues
of our newsletter, "Just Plain Notes."
- *Roadtrips:* We regularly tour the US and Canada, hosting showcases, workshops and
friendly member gatherings in each city we visit. We provide opportunities for all our
members, at all levels and welcome everyone to our events. Most events are free of
charge.
- *Chapters:* Just Plain Folks has over 100 active local chapters around the world run by
local member volunteer coordinators. Each chapter is unique but many host monthly
networking gatherings, showcases, educational workshops and community service
events. To join a chapter, or start one in your city, please visit the chapter section of the
jpfolks.com Web site for a current list of chapters and guidelines.
- *Music Awards:* Just Plain Folks has one of the largest and most diverse Member Music
Awards programs in the world. The most recent awards involved over 25,000 albums and
350,000 songs in over 50 genres. Music Award nominees and winners receive featured
performance slots at showcases around the world throughout the year. Current submission instructions can be found on the website in the Awards section.

Membership requests are accepted year-round. "To become a member, simply send an e-
mail to join@jpfolks.com with the words 'I Want To Join Just Plain Folks.' In the e-mail,
include your name, address, Web site (if applicable) and phone number for our files."
There are currently no membership fees.

Tips "Our motto is 'We're All In This Together!'"

THE LAS VEGAS SONGWRITERS ASSOCIATION

P.O. Box 42683, Las Vegas NV 89116-0683. (702)223-7255. E-mail: writeon4011@earthlink. net. Web site: www.lasvegassongwriters.com. **Contact:** Betty Kay Miller, president. Estab. 1980. "We are an educational, nonprofit organization dedicated to improving the art and craft of the songwriter. We want members who are serious about their craft. We want our members to respect their craft and to treat it as a business. Members must be at least 18 years of age. We offer quarterly newsletters, monthly information meetings, workshops three times a month and quarterly seminars with professionals in the music business. We provide support and encouragement to both new and more experienced songwriters. We critique each song or lyric that's presented during workshops, we make suggestions on changes—if needed. We help turn amateur writers into professionals. Several of our song-writers have had their songs recorded on both independent and major labels." Dues: $30/ year.

LOS ANGELES MUSIC NETWORK

P.O. Box 2446, Toluca Lake CA 91610-2446. (818)769-6095. E-mail: info@lamn.com. Web site: www.lamn.com. **Contact:** Tess Taylor, president. Estab. 1988. "Connections. Perform-ance opportunities. Facts. Career advancement. All that is available with your membership in the Los Angeles Music Network (LAMN). Our emphasis is on sharing knowledge and information, giving you access to top professionals and promoting career development. LAMN is an association of music industry professionals, i.e., artists, singers, songwriters, and people who work in various aspects of the music industry with an emphasis on the creative. Members are ambitious and interested in advancing their careers. LAMN promotes career advancement, communication and education among artists and creatives. LAMN sponsors industry events and educational panels held at venues in the Los Angeles area and now in other major music hubs around the country (New York, Las Vegas, Phoenix, and San Francisco). LAMN Jams are popular among our members. Experience LAMN Jams in L.A. or N.Y. by performing your original music in front of industry experts who can advance your career by getting your music in the hands of hard-to-reach music supervisors. the 'anti-American Idol' singer-songwriter contest gives artists an opportunity to perform in front of industry experts and receive instant feedback to their music, lyrics and perform-ance. As a result of the exposure, Tim Fagan won the John Mayer Songwriting Contest and was invited to tour with the Goo Goo Dolls, Lifehouse, and recently, the platinum recording artist Colbie Caillat. This paired him with multi-platinum songwriter and recording artist John Mayer, with whom Fagan co-wrote 'Deeper.' Publisher Robert Walls has pitched music from LAMN Jam performers to hit TV shows like *The OC* and *Gray's Anatomy*, and the upcoming flick *The Devil Wears Prada*. Other performers have received offers including publishing and production deals and studio gigs. Offers performance opportunities, instruc-tion, newsletter, lectures, seminars, music industry job listings, career counseling, resume publishing, mentor network, and many professional networking opportunities. See our Web site for current job listings and a calendar of upcoming events. Applications accepted year-round. Annual membership fee is $115.

LOUISIANA SONGWRITERS ASSOCIATION

P.O. Box 80425, Baton Rouge LA 70898-0425. (504)443-5390. E-mail: zimshah@aol.com. Web site: www.lasongwriters.org. **Contact:** Connie Zimmermann, membership coordinator. Serves songwriters. "LSA was organized to educate songwriters in all areas of their trade, and promote the art of songwriting in Louisiana. LSA is honored to have a growing number of songwriters from other states join LSA and fellowship with us. LSA membership is open to people interested in songwriting, regardless of age, musical ability, musical preference, ethnic background, etc. At this time we are operating as an Internet-only Yahoo Group where we share info, gigs, opportunities, etc. At this time we are not holding regular meetings, although we do meet for various functions periodically. Please visit our group at http://launch.groups.yahoo.com/group/louisianasongwriters/. We do not at this time require any dues for membership participation."

◙ MANITOBA AUDIO RECORDING INDUSTRY ASSOCIATION (MARIA)

1-376 Donald St., Winnipeg MB R3B 2J2 Canada. (204)942-8650. Fax: (204)942-6083. E-mail: info@manitobamusic.com. Web site: www.manitobamusic.com. **Contact:** Rachel Stone, associate coordinator. Estab. 1987. Organization consists of "songwriters, producers, agents, musicians, managers, retailers, publicists, radio, talent buyers, media, record labels, etc. (no age limit, no skill level minimum). Must have interest in the future of Manitoba's sound recording industry." The main purpose of MARIA is to foster growth in all areas of the Manitoba music industry primarily through education, promotion and lobbying. Offers newsletter, lectures, directory of Manitoba's music industry, workshops and performance opportunities; also presents demo critiquing sessions and comprehensive member discount program featuring a host of participating Manitoba businesses. MARIA is also involved with the Prairie Music Weekend festival, conference and awards show. Applications accepted year-round. Membership fee: $50 (Canadian funds).

MEET THE COMPOSER

90 John St., Suite 312, New York NY 10038. (212)645-6949. Fax: (212)645-9669. E-mail: mtc@meetthecomposer.org. Web site: www.meetthecomposer.org. Estab. 1974. "Meet The Composer serves composers working in all styles of music, at every career stage, through a variety of grant programs and information resources. A nonprofit organization, Meet The Composer raises money from foundations, corporations, individual patrons and government sources and designs programs that support all genres of music—from folk, ethnic, jazz, electronic, symphonic, and chamber to choral, music theater, opera and dance. Meet The Composer awards grants for composer fees to non-profit organizations that perform, present, or commission original works. This is not a membership organization; all composers are eligible for support. Meet The Composer was founded in 1974 to increase artistic and financial opportunities for composers by fostering the creation, performance, dissemination, and appreciation of their music." Offers grant programs and information services. Deadlines vary for each grant program.

MEMPHIS SONGWRITERS' ASSOCIATION

4728 Spottswood, #191, Memphis TN 38117-4815. (901)577-0906. E-mail: admin@memphissongwriters.org. Web site: www.memphissongwriters.org and www.myspace.com/memp

hissongwriters. **Contact:** Phillip Beasley, MSA president. Estab. 1973. "MSA is a nonprofit songwriters organization serving songwriters nationally. Our mission is to dedicate our services to promote, advance, and help songwriters in the composition of music, lyrics and songs; to work for better conditions in our profession; and to secure and protect the rights of MSA songwriters. The Memphis Songwriters Association are organizational members of the Folk Alliance (FA.org). We also supply copyright forms. We offer critique sessions for writers at our monthly meetings. We also have monthly open mic songwriters night to encourage creativity, networking and co-writing. We host an annual songwriter's seminar and an annual songwriter's showcase, as well as a bi-monthly guest speaker series, which provide education, competition and entertainment for the songwriter. In addition, our members receive a bimonthly newsletter to keep them informed of MSA activities, demo services and opportunities in the songwriting field." Annual fee: $50; Student/Senior: $35.

MINNESOTA ASSOCIATION OF SONGWRITERS

P.O. Box 4262, Saint Paul MN 55104. E-mail: info@mnsongwriters.org. Web site: www.mns ongwriters.org. "Includes a wide variety of members, ranging in age from 18 to 80; type of music is very diverse ranging from alternative rock to contemporary Christian; skill levels range from beginning songwriters to writers with recorded and published material. Main requirement is an interest in songwriting. Although most members come from the Minneapolis-St. Paul area, others come in from surrounding cities, nearby Wisconsin, and other parts of the country. Some members are fulltime musicians, but most represent a wide variety of occupations. MAS is a nonprofit community of songwriters which informs, educates, inspires and assists its members in the art and business of songwriting." Offers instruction, newsletter, lectures, workshops, performance opportunities and evaluation services. Applications accepted year-round. Membership fee: Individual: $25; Business: $65. **Tips** "Members are kept current on resources and opportunities. Original works are played at meetings and are critiqued by involved members. Through this process, writers hone their skills and gain experience and confidence in submitting their works to others."

◪ MUSIC BC—PACIFIC MUSIC INDUSTRY ASSOCIATION

#530-425 Carrall St., Vancouver BC V6B 6E3 Canada. (604)873-1914. 1-888-866-8570 (Toll Free in BC). Fax: (604)873-9686. E-mail: info@musicbc.org. Web site: www.musicbc.org. Estab. 1990. Music BC(formerly PMIA) is a non-profit society that supports and promotes the spirit, development, and growth of the BC music community provincially, nationally, and internationally. Music BC provides education, resources, advocacy, opportunities for funding, and a forum for communication. Visit Web site for membership benefits.

MUSICIANS CONTACT

P.O. Box 788, Woodland Hills CA 91365. (818)888-7879. E-mail: information@musiciansco ntact.com. Web site: www.musicianscontact.com. **Contact:** Sterling Howard, president. Estab. 1969. "The primary source of paying jobs for musicians and vocalists nationwide. Job opportunities are posted daily on the Internet. Also offers exposure to the music industry for solo artists and complete acts seeking representation."

NASHVILLE SONGWRITERS ASSOCIATION INTERNATIONAL (NSAI)

1710 Roy Acuff Place, Nashville TN 37203. (615)256-3354 or (800)321-6008. Fax: (615)256-0034. E-mail: nsai@nashvillesongwriters.com. Web site: www.nashvillesongwriters.com. Executive Director: Barton Herbison. Purpose: a not-for-profit service organization for both aspiring and professional songwriters in all fields of music. Membership: Spans the United States and several foreign countries. Songwriters may apply in one of four annual categories: Active ($150 U.S/$100 International—for songwriters who have at least one song contractually signed to a publisher affiliated with ASCAP, BMI or SESAC); Associate ($150 U.S/$100 International—for songwriters who are not yet published or for anyone wishing to support songwriters); Student ($100 U.S/$100 International—for full-time college students or for students of an accredited senior high school); Professional ($100—for songwriters who derive their primary source of income from songwriting or who are generally recognized as such by the professional songwriting community). Membership benefits: music industry information and advice, song evaluations by mail, quarterly newsletter, access to industry professionals through weekly Nashville workshop and several annual events, regional workshops, use of office facilities, discounts on books and discounts on NSAI's three annual events. There are also "branch" workshops of NSAI. Workshops must meet certain standards and are accountable to NSAI. Interested coordinators may apply to NSAI.

- Also see the listing for NSAI Songwriters Symposium (formerly NSAI Spring Symposium) in the Workshops section of this book.

THE NATIONAL ASSOCIATION OF COMPOSERS/USA (NACUSA)

P.O. Box 49256, Barrington Station, Los Angeles CA 90049. E-mail: nacusa@music-usa.org. Web site: www.music-usa.org/nacusa. **Contact**: Daniel Kessner, president. Estab. 1932. Serves songwriters, musicians and classical composers. "We are of most value to the concert hall composer. Members are serious music composers of all ages and from all parts of the country, who have a real interest in composing, performing, and listening to modern concert hall music. The main purpose of our organization is to perform, publish, broadcast and write news about composers of serious concert hall music—mostly chamber and solo pieces. Composers may achieve national notice of their work through our newsletter and concerts, and the fairly rare feeling of supporting a non-commercial music enterprise dedicated to raising the musical and social position of the serious composer." Offers competitions, lectures, performance opportunities, library and newsletter. Applications accepted year-round. Membership fee: National (regular): $25; National (students/seniors): $15.

- Also see the listing for NACUSA Young Composers' Competition in the Contests section of this book.

Tips "99% of the money earned in music is earned, or so it seems, by popular songwriters who might feel they owe the art of music something, and this is one way they might help support that art. It's a chance to foster fraternal solidarity with their less prosperous, but wonderfully interesting classical colleagues at a time when the very existence of serious art seems to be questioned by the general populace."

OKLAHOMA SONGWRITERS & COMPOSERS ASSOCIATION

105 S. Glenn English, Cordell OK 73632. Web site: www.oksongwriters.com. **Contact:** Ann Wilson Hardin, treasurer/membership. Estab. 1983. Serves songwriters, musicians, profes-

sional writers and amateur writers. "A nonprofit, all-volunteer organization providing educational and networking opportunities for songwriters, lyricists, composers and performing musicians. All styles of music. We sponsor major workshops, open-mic nights, demo critiques and the OSCA Newsletter. Throughout the year we sponsor contests and original music showcases." Applications accepted year-round. Membership fee: $20 for new members, $10 for renewal. Applications may be made through our website.

OPERA AMERICA

330 Seventh Ave., 16th Floor, New York NY 10001. (212)796-8620. Fax: (212)796-8631. E-mail: frontdesk@operaamerica.org. Web site: www.operaamerica.org. **Contact:** Rebecca Ackerman, membership manager. Estab. 1970. Members are composers, librettists, musicians, singers, and opera/music theater producers. Offers conferences, workshops, and seminars for artists. Publishes online database of opera/music theater companies in the US and Canada, database of opportunities for performing and creative artists, online directory of opera and musical performances world-wide and US, and an online directory of new works created and being developed by current-day composers and librettists, to encourage the performance of new works. Applications accepted year-round. Publishes quarterly magazine and a variety of electronic newsletters. Membership fee is on a sliding scale by membership level.

OUTMUSIC

P.O. Box 376, Old Chelsea Station, New York NY 10113-0376. (212)330-9197. E-mail: feedback@outmusic.com. Web site: www.outmusic.com. **Contact:** Ed Mannix, communications director. Estab. 1990. "OUTMUSIC is comprised of gay men, lesbians, bisexuals and transgenders. They represent all different musical styles from rock to classical. Many are writers of original material. We are open to all levels of accomplishment—professional, amateur, and interested industry people. The only requirement for membership is an interest in the growth and visibility of music and lyrics created by the LGBT community. We supply our members with support and networking opportunities. In addition, we help to encourage artists to bring their work 'OUT' into the world." Offers newsletter, lectures, workshops, performance opportunities, networking, industry leads and monthly open mics. Sponsors Outmusic Awards. Applications accepted year-round. For membership information go to www.outmusic.com.
Tips "OUTMUSIC has spawned *The Gay Music Guide*, The Gay and Lesbian American Music Awards (GLAMA), several compilation albums and many independent recording projects."

PACIFIC NORTHWEST SONGWRITERS ASSOCIATION

P.O. Box 98564, Seattle WA 98198. (206)824-1568. E-mail: pnsapals@hotmail.com. "PNSA is a nonprofit organization, serving the songwriters of the Puget Sound area since 1977. Members have had songs recorded by national artists on singles, albums, videos and network television specials. Several have released their own albums and the group has done an album together. For only $45 per year, PNSA offers monthly workshops, a quarterly newsletter and direct contact with national artists, publishers, producers and record companies. New members are welcome and good times are guaranteed. And remember, the world always needs another great song!''

SAN DIEGO SONGWRITERS GUILD

3368 Governor Dr., Suite F-326, San Diego CA 92122. E-mail: sdsongwriters@hotmail.com. Web site: www.sdsongwriters.org. **Contact:** Joseph Carmel, membership/correspondence. Estab. 1982. ''Members range from their early 20s to senior citizens with a variety of skill levels. Several members perform and work full time in music. Many are published and have songs recorded. Some are getting major artist record cuts. Most members are from San Diego county. New writers are encouraged to participate and meet others. All musical styles are represented.'' The purpose of this organization is to ''serve the needs of songwriters and artists, especially helping them in the business and craft of songwriting through industry guest appearances.'' Offers competitions, newsletter, workshops, performance opportunities, discounts on services offered by fellow members, in-person song pitches and evaluations by publishers, producers and A&R executives. Applications accepted year-round. Membership dues: $55 full; $30 student; $125 corporate sponsorship. Meeting admission for non-members: $20 (may be applied toward membership if joining within 30 days).

Tips ''Members benefit most from participation in meetings and concerts. Generally, one major meeting held monthly on a Monday evening, at the Doubletree Hotel, Hazard Center, San Diego. E-mail for meeting details. Can join at meetings.''

SESAC INC.

55 Music Square East, Nashville TN 37203. (615)320-0055. Fax: (615) 329-9627 or 152 W. 57th St., 57th Floor, New York NY 10019. (212)586-3450. Fax: (212)489-5699. Web site: www.sesac.com. **Los Angeles:** 501 Santa Monica Blvd., Suite 450, Santa Monica CA 90401. (310)393-9671. Fax: (310)393-6497; **Atlanta**: 981 Joseph E. Lowery Blvd NW, Ste 111, Atlanta GA 30318. (404)867-1330. Fax: (404)897-1306; **Miami:** 420 Lincoln Rd, Ste 502, Miami FL 33139, (305)534-7500. Fax: (305)534-7578; **London:** 67 Upper Berkeley St., London WIH 7QX United Kingdom. (020)76169284. **Contact:** Tim Fink, associate vice president writer/publisher relations. Chief Operating Officer: Pat Collins. Coordinator-Writer/Publisher Relations: Diana Akin. SESAC is a selective organization taking pride in having a repertory based on quality rather than quantity. Serves writers and publishers in all types of music who have their works performed by radio, television, nightclubs, cable TV, etc. Purpose of organization is to collect and distribute performance royalties to all active affiliates. As a SESAC affiliate, the individual may obtain equipment insurance at competitive rates. Music is reviewed upon invitation by the Writer/Publisher Relations dept.

⊡ SOCAN (SOCIETY OF COMPOSERS, AUTHORS AND MUSIC PUBLISHERS OF CANADA)

Head Office: 41 Valleybrook Dr., Toronto ON M3B 2S6 Canada. English Information Center: (866)(307)6226. French Information Center: (866) (800)55-SOCAN. Fax: (416)445-7108. Web site: www.socan.ca. CEO: Andre LeBel. Vice President Member Relations & General Manager, West Coast Division: Kent Sturgeon. Vice President Member Services: Jeff King.

Director, Member Relations: Lynne Foster. "SOCAN is the Canadian copyright collective for the communication and performance of musical works. We administer these rights on behalf of our members (composers, lyricists, songwriters, and their publishers) and those of affiliated international organizations by licensing this use of their music in Canada. The fees collected are distributed as royalties to our members and to affiliated organizations throughout the world. We also distribute royalties received from those organizations to our members for the use of their music worldwide. SOCAN has offices in Toronto, Montreal, Vancouver, Edmonton, and Dartmouth."

SOCIETY OF COMPOSERS & LYRICISTS

8447 Wilshire Blvd., Suite 401, Beverly Hills CA 90211. (310)281-2812. Fax: (310)284-4861. E-mail: execdir@thescl.com. Web site: www.thescl.com. The professional nonprofit trade organization for members actively engaged in writing music/lyrics for films, TV, and/or video games, or are students of film composition or songwriting for film. Primary mission is to advance the interests of the film and TV music community. Offers an award-winning quarterly publication, educational seminars, screenings, special member-only events, and other member benefits. Applications accepted year-round. Membership fee: $135 Full Membership (composers, lyricists, songwriters—film/TV music credits must be submitted); $85 Associate/Student Membership for composers, lyricists, songwriters without credits only; $135 Sponsor/Special Friend Membership (music editors, music supervisors, music attorneys, agents, etc.).

◪ ◻ SODRAC INC.

759 Square Victoria, Suite 420, Montreal QC H2Y 2J7 Canada. (514)845-3268. Fax: (514)845-3401. E-mail: sodrac@sodrac.ca. Web site: www.sodrac.ca. **Contact:** Jean-Francois Marquis, membership department (author, composer and publisher) or François Dell' Aniello, visual arts and crafts department (visual artist and rights owner). Estab. 1985. "SODRAC is a reproduction rights collective society facilitating since 1985 the clearing of rights on musical and artistic works based on the Copyright Board of Canada tariffs or through collective agreements concluded with any users and is responsible for the distribution of royalties to its national and international members. The Society counts over 5,000 Canadian members and represents musical repertoire originating from nearly 100 foreign countries and manages the right of over 25,000 Canadian and foreign visual artists. SODRAC is the only reproduction rights society in Canada where both songwriters and music publishers are represented, equally and directly." Serves those with an interest in songwriting and music publishing no matter what their age or skill level is. "Members must have written or published at least one musical work that has been reproduced on an audio (CD, cassette, or LP) or audio-visual support (TV, DVD, video), or published five musical works that have been recorded and used for commercial purposes. The new member will benefit from a society working to secure his reproduction rights (mechanicals) and broadcast mechanicals." Applications accepted year-round.

SONGWRITERS & LYRICISTS CLUB

E-mail: makinsonrobert@hotmail.com. Contact: Robert Makinson, founder/director. Estab. 1984.

• **The Songwriters & Lyricists Club is not currently taking on new members.** Offers booklet titled *Songwriters & Lyricists Handbook*, available on Amazon.com.

Tips "Plan and achieve realistic goals. We specialize in classical, folk, country, inspirational, and humorous novelty songs and lyrics."

SONGWRITERS AND POETS CRITIQUE

Attn: Steve Kreis, 23870 North Darby Rd., Milford Center OH 43045. (937)537-1248. Web site: www.songwriterscritique.com. **Contact:** LeeAnn Pretzman, secretary. Estab. 1985. Serves songwriters, musicians, poets, lyricists and performers. Meets second and fourth Friday of every month to discuss club events and critique one another's work. Offers seminars and workshops with professionals in the music industry. "We critique mail-in submissions from long-distance members. Our goal is to provide support and opportunity to anyone interested in creating songs or poetry." Applications are accepted year-round. Annual dues: $30.

SONGWRITERS ASSOCIATION OF WASHINGTON

PMB 106-137, 4200 Wisconsin Ave. NW, Washington DC 20016. (301)654-8434. E-mail: membership@SAW.org. Web site: www.saw.org. Estab. 1979. "SAW is a nonprofit organization operated by a volunteer board of directors. It is committed to providing its members opportunities to learn more about the art of songwriting, learn more about the music business, perform in public, and connect with fellow songwriters. SAW sponsors various events to achieve these goals: workshops, open mics, songwriter exchanges, and showcases. In addition, SAW organizes the Mid-Atlantic Song Contest open to entrants nationwide each year; "the competition in 2008 will be the 25th contest SAW has adjudicated since 1982, making it one of the longest-running song contests in the nation." (Contest information masc@saw.org). As well as maintaining a Web site, SAW publishes a monthly e-newsletter for members containing information on upcoming local events, member news, contest information, and articles of interest, as well as a member directory, a valuable tool for networking. Joint membership with the Washington Area Music Association as well as a two-year membership are available at a savings. Use the contact information above for membership inquiries.

THE SONGWRITERS GUILD OF AMERICA (SGA)

1560 Broadway, Suite #1306, New York NY 10036. (212)768-7902. Fax: (212)768-9048. E-mail: ny@songwritersguild.com. Web site: www.songwritersguild.com. **New York Office:** 1560 Broadway, Suite #408, New York NY 10036. (212)768-7902. Fax: (212)768-9048; **Los Angeles Office:** New address to be announced. (323)462-1108. Fax: (323)462-5430. E-mail: la@songwritersguild.com. **Nashville Office:** 209 10th Ave. S., Suite 321, Nashville TN 37203. (615)742-9945. Fax: (615)742-9948. E-mail: nash@songwritersguild.com. **SGA Administration:** 1500 Harbor Blvd., Wechawken NJ 07086. (201)867-7603. Fax:(201)867-7535. E-mail: corporate@songwritersguild.com.

• Also see the listings for The Songwriters Guild Foundation in the Workshops & Conferences section.

President: Rick Carnes. Executive Director: Lewis M. Bachman. East Coast Project Manager: Mark Saxon. Central Project Manager: Kimberly Maiers Shaw. Estab. 1931. "The Songwriters Guild of America Foundation offers a series of workshops with discounts to SGA members, including online classes and song critique opportunities. There is a charge for many songwriting classes and seminars; however, online classes and some monthly events are included with an SGA membership. Charges vary depending on the class or event. Current class offerings and workshops vary. Visit Web site to sign up for the monthly newsletter and for more information on current events and workshops. Also see the Songwriters Guild of America listing in the Organizations section. Some regular events in Nashville are the Ask-a-Pro and ProCritique sessions that give SGA members the opportunity to present their songs and receive constructive feedback from industry professionals. Various performance opportunities are also available to members, including Tunesmithing @ Borders Books, SGA Showcase at the Bluebird Café and Chick Singer Night. The New York office hosts a Pro-Shop, which is coordinated by producer/musician/award winning singer Ann Johns Ruckert. For each of six sessions an active publisher, producer or A&R person is invited to personally screen material from SGA writers. Participation is limited to 10 writers and an audit of one session. Audition of material is required. Various performance opportunities and critique sessions also available to members. SGA Week is held each year and is a week of scheduled events and seminars of interest to songwriters at each of SGA's regional offices. Includes workshops, seminars and showcases. The Write Key is a weekend songwriting seminar held in Orange Beach, Alabama each November in conjunction with the Frank Brown International Songwriters' Festival. This is an opportunity to expand your songwriting skills and learn from professional songwriters and music industry professionals in an intense, intimate weekend. Hands-on writing sessions and showcase opportunities available to all attendees."

N SONGWRITERS HALL OF FAME (SONGHALL)

330 W. 58th St., Suite 411, New York NY 10019-1827. (212)957-9230. Fax: (212)957-9227. E-mail: info@songhall.org. Web site: www.songhall.org. **Contact**: Managing Director: April Anderson. Estab. 1969. "SongHall membership consists of songwriters of all levels, music publishers, producers, record company executives, music attorneys, and lovers of popular music of all ages. There are different levels of membership, all able to vote in the election for inductees, except Associates who pay only $25 in dues, but are unable to vote. SongHall's mission is to honor the popular songwriters who write the soundtrack for the world, as well as providing educational and networking opportunities to our members through our workshop and showcase programs." Offers: newsletter, workshops, performance opportunities, networking meetings with industry pros and scholarships for excellence in songwriting. Applications accepted year-round. Membership fees: $25 and up.

SONGWRITERS OF WISCONSIN INTERNATIONAL

P.O. Box 1027, Neenah WI 54957-1027. (920)725-5129. E-mail: sowi@new.rr.com. Web site: www.SongwritersOfWisconsin.org. **Contact:** Tony Ansems, president. Workshops Coordinator: Mike Heath. Estab. 1983. Serves songwriters. "Membership is open to songwriters writing all styles of music. Residency in Wisconsin is recommended but not required. Members are encouraged to bring tapes and lyric sheets of their songs to the meetings, but it is not required. We are striving to improve the craft of songwriting in Wisconsin. Living in Wisconsin, a songwriter would be close to any of the workshops and showcases offered each month at different towns. The primary value of membership for a songwriter is in sharing ideas with other songwriters, being critiqued and helping other songwriters." Offers competitions (contest entry deadline: May 15), field trips, instruction, lectures, newsletter, performance opportunities, social outings, workshops and critique sessions. Applications accepted year-round. Membership dues: $30/year.

Tips "Critique meetings every last Thursday of each month, January through October, 7 p.m.-10 p.m. at The Country Inn & Suites, 355 N. Fox River Dr., Appleton WI."

Ⓝ SONGWRITERS RESOURCE NETWORK

PMB 135, 6327-C SW Capitol Hill Hwy, Portland OR 97239-1937. E-mail: info@Songwriters ResourceNetwork.com. Web site: www.SongwritersResourceNetwork.com. **Contact:** Steve Cahill, president. Estab. 1998. "For songwriters and lyricists of every kind, from beginners to advanced." No eligibility requirements. "Purpose is to provide free information to help songwriters develop their craft, market their songs, and learn about songwriting opportunities." Sponsors the annual Great American Song Contest, offers marketing tips and website access to music industry contacts. "We provide leads to publishers, producers and other music industry professionals." Visit website or send SASE for more information.

- Also see the listing for Great American Song Contest in the Contests and Awards section of this book.

Ⓝ SOUTHWEST VIRGINIA SONGWRITERS ASSOCIATION

P.O. Box 698, Salem VA 24153. Web site: www.svsa.info. **Contact:** Greg Trafidlo. Estab. 1981. 80 members of all ages and skill all levels, mainly country, folk, gospel, contemporary and rock but other musical interests too. "The purpose of SVSA is to increase, broaden and expand the knowledge of each member and to support, better and further the progress and success of each member in songwriting and related fields of endeavor." Offers performance opportunities, evaluation services, instruction, newsletter, workshops, monthly meetings and monthly newsletter. Application accepted year-round. Membership fee: $20/year.

🌐 SPNM—PROMOTING NEW MUSIC

St. Margarets House, 4th Floor, 18-20 Southwark St., London SE1 1TJ United Kingdom. 020 7407 1640. Fax: 020 7403 7652. E-mail: spnm@spnm.org.uk. Web site: www.spnm.org.uk. Executive Director: Abigail Pogson. Administrator: Katy Kirk. Estab. 1943. "All ages and backgrounds are welcome, with a common interest in the innovative and unexplored. We enable new composers to hear their works performed by top-class professionals in quality venues." Offers magazine, lectures, workshops, special offers and concerts. Annual selection procedure, deadline September 30. "From contemporary jazz, classical and popular music to that written for film, dance and other creative media, spnm is one of the main advocates of new music in Britain today. Through its eclectic program of concerts, workshops, education projects and collaborations and through its publications, new notes, spnm brings new music in all guises to many, many people." Other calls for specific events throughout year. Membership fee: Ordinary: £25; Concessions: £10; Friend: £35.

Tips "Most calls for pieces are restricted to those living and/or studying in UK/Ireland, or to British composers living overseas."

TEXAS MUSIC OFFICE

P.O. Box 13246, Austin TX 78711. (512)463-6666. Fax: (512)463-4114. E-mail: music@gove rnor.state.tx.us. Web site: www.enjoytexasmusic.com. **Contact:** Casey Monahan, director. Estab. 1990. "The main purpose of the Texas Music Office is to promote the Texas music industry and Texas music, and to assist music professionals around the world with information about the Texas market. The Texas Music Office serves as a clearinghouse for Texas music industry information using their seven databases: Texas Music Industry (7,150 Texas music businesses in 94 music business categories); Texas Music Events (915 Texas music events); Texas Talent Register (7,050 Texas recording artists); Texas Radio Stations (837 Texas stations); U.S. Record Labels; Classical Texas (detailed information for all classical music organizations in Texas); and International (450 foreign businesses interested in Texas music). Provides referrals to Texas music businesses, talent and events in order to attract new business to Texas and/or to encourage Texas businesses and individuals to keep music business in-state. Serves as a liaison between music businesses and other government offices and agencies. Publicizes significant developments within the Texas music industry." Publishes the Texas Music Industry Directory (see the Publications of Interest section for more information).

☒ TORONTO MUSICIANS' ASSOCIATION

15 Gervais Dr., Suite 500, Toronto ON M3C 1Y8 Canada. (416)421-1020. Fax: (416)421-7011. E-mail: info@torontomusicians.org. Web site: www.torontomusicians.org. Executive Director: Bill Skolnick. Estab. 1887. Serves musicians—*All* musical styles, background, areas of the industry. "Must be a Canadian citizen, show proof of immigration status, or have a valid work permit for an extended period of time." The purpose of this organization is "to unite musicians into one organization, in order that they may, individually and collectively, secure, maintain and profit from improved economic, working and artistic conditions." Offers newsletter. Applications accepted year-round. Joining fee: $225 (Canadian); student fee: $100 (Canadian). Student must have proof of school enrollment.

VOLUNTEER LAWYERS FOR THE ARTS

1 E. 53rd St., 6th Floor, New York NY 10022. (212)319-ARTS (2787), ext. 1 (Monday-Friday 9:30-12 and 1-4 EST). Fax: (212)752-6575. E-mail: epaul@vlany.org. Web site: www.vlany.org. **Contact:** Elena M. Paul, esq., executive director. Estab. 1969. Serves songwriters, musicians and all performing, visual, literary and fine arts artists and groups. Offers legal assistance and representation to eligible individual artists and arts organizations who cannot afford private counsel and a mediation service. VLA sells publications on arts-related issues and offers educational conferences, lectures, seminars

and workshops. In addition, there are affiliates nationwide who assist local arts organizations and artists. Call for information.

WASHINGTON AREA MUSIC ASSOCIATION

6263 Occoquan Forest Drive, Manassas VA 20112. (202)338-1134. Fax: (703)393-1028. E-mail: dcmusic@wamadc.com. Web site: www.wamadc.com. **Contact:** Mike Schreibman, president. Estab. 1985. Serves songwriters, musicians and performers, managers, club owners and entertainment lawyers; "all those with an interest in the Washington music scene." The organization is designed to promote the Washington music scene and increase its visibility. Its primary value to members is its seminars and networking opportunities. Offers lectures, newsletter, performance opportunities and workshops. WAMA sponsors the annual Washington Music Awards (The Wammies) and The Crosstown Jam or annual showcase of artists in the DC area. Applications accepted year-round. Annual dues: $35 for one year; $60 for two years.

WEST COAST SONGWRITERS

(formerly Northern California Songwriters Association), 1724 Laurel St., Suite 120, San Carlos CA 94070. (650)654-3966. E-mail: ian@westcoastsongwriters.org. Web site: www.westcoastsongwriters.org. **Contact:** Ian Crombie, executive director. Serves songwriters and musicians. Estab. 1979. "Our 1,200 members are lyricists and composers from ages 16-80, from beginners to professional songwriters. No eligibility requirements. Our purpose is to provide the education and opportunities that will support our writers in creating and marketing outstanding songs. WCS provides support and direction through local networking and input from Los Angeles and Nashville music industry leaders, as well as valuable marketing opportunities. Most songwriters need some form of collaboration, and by being a member they are exposed to other writers, ideas, critiquing, etc." Offers annual West Coast Songwriters Conference, "the largest event of its kind in northern California. This 2-day event held the second hand in September features 16 seminars, 50 screening sessions (over 1,200 songs listened to by industry professionals) and a sunset concert with hit songwriters performing their songs." Also offers monthly visits from major publishers, songwriting classes, competitions, seminars conducted by hit songwriters ("we sell audio tapes of our seminars—list of tapes available on request"), mail-in song-screening service for members who cannot attend due to time or location, a monthly e-newsletter, monthly performance opportunities and workshops. Applications accepted year-round. Dues: $40/year, student; $75/year, regular membership; $150/year, pro-membership; $250/year, contributing membership.

Tips "WCS's functions draw local talent and nationally recognized names together. This is of a tremendous value to writers outside a major music center. We are developing a strong songwriting community in Northern and Southern California. We serve the San Jose, Monterey Bay, East Bay, San Francisco, Los Angeles, and Sacramento areas and we have the support of some outstanding writers and publishers from both Los Angeles and Nashville. They provide us with invaluable direction and inspiration."

Workshops & Conferences

For a songwriter just starting out, conferences and workshops can provide valuable learning opportunities. At conferences, songwriters can have their songs evaluated, hear suggestions for further improvement and receive feedback from music business experts. They are also excellent places to make valuable industry contacts. Workshops can help a songwriter improve his craft and learn more about the business of songwriting. They may involve classes on songwriting and the business, as well as lectures and seminars by industry professionals.

Each year, hundreds of workshops and conferences take place all over the country. Songwriters can choose from small regional workshops held in someone's living room to large national conferences such as South by Southwest in Austin, Texas, which hosts more than 6,000 industry people, songwriters and performers. Many songwriting organizations—national and local—host workshops that offer instruction on just about every songwriting topic imaginable, from lyric writing and marketing strategy to contract negotiation. Conferences provide songwriters the chance to meet one on one with publishing and record company professionals and give performers the chance to showcase their work for a live audience (usually consisting of industry people) during the conference. There are conferences and workshops that address almost every type of music, offering programs for songwriters, performers, musical playwrights and much more.

This section includes national and local workshops and conferences with a brief description of what they offer, when they are held and how much they cost to attend. Write or call any that interest you for further information. To find out what workshops or conferences take place in specific parts of the country, see the Geographic Index at the end of this book.

Get the Most From a Conference

BEFORE YOU GO:

- **Save money.** Sign up early for a conference and take advantage of the early registration fee. Don't put off making hotel reservations either—the conference will usually have a block of rooms reserved at a discounted price.

- **Become familiar with all the pre-conference literature.** Study the maps of the area, especially the locations of the rooms in which your meetings/events are scheduled.

- **Make a list of three to five objectives you'd like to obtain,** e.g., what you want to learn more about, what you want to improve on, how many new contacts you want to make.

AT THE CONFERENCE

- **Budget your time.** Label a map so you know where, when and how to get to each session. Note what you want to do most. Then, schedule time for demo critiques if they are offered.

- **Don't be afraid to explore new areas.** You are there to learn. Pick one or two sessions you wouldn't typically attend. Keep your mind open to new ideas and advice.

- **Allow time for mingling.** Some of the best information is given after the sessions. Find out "frank truths" and inside scoops. Asking people what they've learned at the conference will trigger a conversation that may branch into areas you want to know more about, but won't hear from the speakers.

- **Attend panels.** Panels consist of a group of industry professionals who have the capability to further your career. If you're new to the business you can learn so much straight from the horse's mouth. Even if you're a veteran, you can brush up on your knowledge or even learn something new. Whatever your experience, the panelist's presence is an open invitation to approach him with a question during the panel or with a handshake afterwards.

- **Collect everything:** especially informational materials and business cards. Make notes about the personalities of the people you meet to later remind you who to contact and who to avoid.

AFTER THE CONFERENCE:

- **Evaluate.** Write down the answers to these questions: Would I attend again? What were the pluses and minuses, e.g., speakers, location, food, topics, cost, lodging? What do I want to remember for next year? What should I try to do next time? Who would I like to meet?

- **Write a thank-you letter** to someone who has been particularly helpful. They'll remember you when you later solicit a submission.

Resources

APPEL FARM ARTS AND MUSIC FESTIVAL

P.O. Box 888, Elmer NJ 08318. (856)358-2472. Fax: (856)358-6513. E-mail: perform@appelf arm.org. Web site: www.appelfarm.org. **Contact:** Sean Timmons, artistic director. Estab Festival: 1989; Series: 1970. "Our annual open air festival is the highlight of our year-round Performing Arts Series which was established to bring high quality arts programs to the people of South Jersey. Festival includes acoustic and folk music, blues, etc." Past perform-ers have included Indigo Girls, John Prine, Ani DiFranco, Randy Newman, Jackson Browne, Mary Chapin Carpenter, David Gray, Nanci Griffith and Shawn Colvin. In addition, our Country Music concerts have featured Toby Keith, Joe Diffie, Ricky Van Shelton, Doug Stone and others. Programs for songwriters and musicians include performance opportuni-ties as part of Festival and Performing Arts Series. Programs for musical playwrights also include performance opportunities as part of Performing Arts Series. Festival is a one-day event held in June, and Performing Arts Series is held year-round. Both are held at the Appel Farm Arts and Music Center, a 176-acre farm in Southern New Jersey. Up to 20 songwriters/musicians participate in each event. Participants are songwriters, individual vocalists, bands, ensembles, vocal groups, composers, individual instrumentalists and dance/mime/movement. Participants are selected by CD submissions. Applicants should send a press packet, CD and biographical information. Application materials accepted year round. Faculty opportunities are available as part of residential Summer Arts Program for children, July/August.

ASCAP MUSICAL THEATRE WORKSHOP

1 Lincoln Plaza, New York NY 10023. (212)621-6234. Fax: (212)621-6558. E-mail: mkerker @ascap.com. Web site: www.ascap.com. **Contact:** Michael A. Kerker, director of musical theatre. Estab. 1981. Workshop is for musical theatre composers and lyricists only. Its purpose is to nurture and develop new musicals for the theatre. Offers programs for song-writers. Offers programs annually, usually April through May. Event took place in New York City. Four musical works are selected. Others are invited to audit the workshop. Participants are amateur and professional songwriters, composers and musical playwrights. Participants are selected by demo CD submission. Deadline: mid-March. Also available: the annual ASCAP/Disney Musical Theatre Workshop in Los Angeles. It takes place in January and February. Deadline is late November. Details similar to New York workshop as above.

ASCAP WEST COAST/LESTER SILL SONGWRITER'S WORKSHOP

7920 Sunset Blvd., 3rd Floor, Los Angeles CA 90046. (323)883-1000. Fax: (323)883-1049. E-mail: info@ascap.com. Web site: www.ascap.com. Estab. 1963. Annual workshop for advanced songwriters sponsored by the ASCAP Foundation. Re-named in 1995 to honor ASCAP's late Board member and industry pioneer Lester Sill, the workshop takes place over a four-week period and features prominent guest speakers from various facets of the music business. Workshop dates and deadlines vary from year to year; refer to www.ascap. com for updated info. Applicants must submit two songs on a CD (cassette tapes not accepted), lyrics, brief bio and short explanation as to why they would like to participate. Limited number of participants are selected each year.

BMI-LEHMAN ENGEL MUSICAL THEATRE WORKSHOP

320 W. 57th St., New York NY 10019. (212)586-2000. E-mail: musicaltheatre@bmi.com. Web site: www.bmi.com. **Contact:** Jean Banks, senior director of musical theatre. Estab. 1961. "BMI is a music licensing company which collects royalties for affiliated writers. We have departments to help writers in jazz, concert, Latin, pop and musical theater writing." Offers programs "to musical theater composers, lyricists and librettists. The BMI-Lehman Engel Musical Theatre Workshops were formed in an effort to refresh and stimulate professional writers, as well as to encourage and develop new creative talent for the musical theater." Each workshop meets 1 afternoon a week for 2 hours at BMI, New York. Participants are professional songwriters, composers and playwrights. "BMI-Lehman Engel Musical Theatre Workshop Showcase presents the best of the workshop to producers, agents, record and publishing company execs, press and directors for possible option and production." Call for application. Tape and lyrics of 3 compositions required with application. "BMI also sponsors a jazz composers workshop. For more information call Raette Johnson at (212)830-8337."

N BROADWAY TOMORROW PREVIEWS

% Science of Light, Inc., 191 Claremont Ave., Suite 53, New York NY 10027. E-mail: solministry@juno.com. Web site: www.solministry.com/bway_tom.html. **Contact:** Elyse Curtis, artistic director. Estab. 1983. Purpose is the enrichment of American theater by nurturing new musicals. Offers series in which composers living in New York city area present self-contained scores of their new musicals in concert. Submission is by audio cassette or CD of music, synopsis, cast breakdown, résumé, reviews, if any, acknowledgement postcard and SASE. Participants selected by screening of submissions. Programs are presented in fall and spring with possibility of full production of works presented in concert.

☒ CANADIAN MUSIC WEEK

5355 Vail Court, Mississauga ON L5M 6G9 Canada. (905)858-4747. Fax: (905)858-4848. E-mail: festival@cmw.net. Web site: www.cmw.net. Contact: Phil Klygo, festival coordinator. Estab. 1985. Offers annual programs for songwriters, composers and performers. Event takes place mid-March in Toronto. 100,000 public, 300 bands and 1,200 delegates participate in each event. Participants are amateur and professional songwriters, vocalists, composers, bands and instrumentalists. Participants are selected by submitting demonstration tape. Send for application and more information. Concerts take place in 25 clubs and 5 concert halls, and 3 days of seminars and exhibits are provided. Fee: $375 (Canadian).

N CMJ MUSIC MARATHON, MUSICFEST & FILMFEST

151 W. 25th St., 12th Floor, New York NY 10001. (917)606-1908. Fax: (917)606-1914. Web site: http://www.cmj.com/marathon/. **Contact:** Operations Manager. Estab. 1981. Premier annual alternative music gathering of more than 9,000 music business and film professionals. Fall, NYC. Features 4 days and nights of more than 50 panels and workshops focusing on every facet of the industry; exclusive film screenings; keynote speeches by the world's most intriguing and controversial voices; exhibition area featuring live performance stage;

over 1,000 of music's brightest and most visionary talents (from the unsigned to the legendary) performing over 4 evenings at more than 50 of NYC's most important music venues. Participants are selected by submitting demonstration tape. Go to website for application.

CUTTING EDGE MUSIC BUSINESS CONFERENCE

1524 N. Claiborne Ave., New Orleans LA 70116. (504)945-1800. Fax: (504)945-1873. E-mail: cut_edge@bellsouth.net. Web site: www.jass.com/cuttingedge. Executive Producer: Eric L. Cager. Showcase Producer: Nathaniel Franklin. Estab. 1993. "The conference is a five-day international conference which covers the business and educational aspects of the music industry. As part of the conference, the New Works showcase features over 200 bands and artists from around the country and Canada in showcases of original music. All music genres are represented." Offers programs for songwriters and performers. "Bands and artists should submit material for consideration of entry into the New Works showcase." Event takes place during August in New Orleans. 1,000 songwriters/musicians participate in each event. Participants are songwriters, vocalists and bands. Send for application. Deadline: June 1. "The Music Business Institute offers a month-long series of free educational workshops for those involved in the music industry. The workshops take place each October. Further information is available via our Web site."

FOLK ALLIANCE ANNUAL CONFERENCE

962 Wayne Ave., Suite 902, Silver Spring MD 20910. (301)588-8185. Fax: (301)588-8186. E-mail: fa@folk.org. Web site: www.folk.org. **Contact:** Tony Ziselberger, membership services director. Estab. 1989. Conference/workshop topics change each year. Conference takes place mid-February and lasts 4 days at a different location each year. 2,000 attendees include artists, agents, arts administrators, print/broadcast media, folklorists, folk societies, merchandisers, presenters, festivals, recording companies, etc. Artists wishing to showcase should contact the office for a showcase application form. Closing date for application is May 31. Application fee is $20 for 2005 conference. Additional costs vary from year to year. Housing is separate for the event, scheduled for Feb. 16-19, 2006 in Austin, TX.

• Also see the listing for The Folk Alliance in the Organizations section of this book.

ⓝ HOLLYWOOD REPORTER/BILLBOARD FILM & TV MUSIC CONFERENCE

Sofitel LA, 8555 Beverly Blvd., Los Angeles CA 90048. (646)654-4626. E-mail: bbevents@billboard.com. Web site: www.billboardevents.com/. **Contact**: Special Events Coordinator. Estab. 1995. Promotes all music for film and television. Offers programs for songwriters and composers. Held at the Directors Guild of America. More than 350 songwriters/musicians participate in each event. Participants are professional songwriters, composers, plus producers, directors, etc. Conference panelists are selected by invitation. For registration information, call the Special Events Dept. at Hollywood Reporter. Fee: $349-499/person.

INDEPENDENT MUSIC CONFERENCE

InterMixx.com, Inc., 304 Main Ave., PMB 287, Norwalk CT 06851. (203)606-4649. E-mail: imc08@intermixx.com. Web site: www.gopmc.com. Executive Director: Noel Ramos. Estab. 1992. "The purpose of the IMC is to bring together rock, hip hop and acoustic music for of panels and showcases. Offers programs for songwriters, composers and performers. 250 showcases at 20 clubs around the city. Also offer a DJ cutting contest." Held annually at the Sheraton Society Hill Hotel in Philadelphia in September. 3,000 amateur and professional songwriters, composers, individual vocalists, bands, individual instrumentalists, attorneys, managers, agents, publishers, A&R, promotions, club owners, etc. participate each year. Send for application.

KERRVILLE FOLK FESTIVAL

Kerrville Festivals, Inc., P.O. Box 291466, Kerrville TX 78029. (830)257-3600. E-mail: info@kerrville-music.com. Web site: www.kerrvillefolkfestival.com. **Contact:** Dalis Allen, producer. Estab. 1972. Hosts 3-day songwriters' school, a 4-day music business school and New Folk concert competition sponsored by *Performing Songwriter* magazine. Festival produced in late spring and late summer. Spring festival lasts 18 days and is held outdoors at Quiet Valley Ranch. 110 or more songwriters participate. Performers are professional songwriters and bands. Participants selected by submitting demo, by invitation only. Send cassette, or CD, promotional material and list of upcoming appearances. "Songwriter and music schools include lunch, experienced professional instructors, camping on ranch and concerts. Rustic facilities. Food available at reasonable cost. Audition materials accepted at above address. These three-day and four-day seminars include noon meals, handouts and camping on the ranch. Usually held during Kerrville Folk Festival, first and second week in June. Write or check the Web site for contest rules, schools and seminars information, and festival schedules. Also establishing a Phoenix Fund to provide assistance to ill or injured singer/songwriters who find themselves in distress."

- Also see the listing for New Folk Concerts For Emerging Songwriters in the Contests & Awards section of this book.

LAMB'S RETREAT FOR SONGWRITERS

Presented by SPRINGFED ARTS, a nonprofit organization, P.O. Box 304, Royal Oak MI 48068-0304. (248)589-1594. Fax: (248)589-3913. E-mail: johndlamb@ameritech.net. Web site: www.springfed.org. **Contact:** John D. Lamb, director. Estab. 1995. Offers programs for songwriters on annual basis; November 6-9, 2008 and November 13-16, 2008 at The Birchwood Inn, Harbor Springs, MI. 60 songwriters/musicians participate in each event. Participants are amateur and professional songwriters. Anyone can participate. Send for registration or e-mail. Deadline: two weeks before event begins. Fee: $275-495, includes all meals. Facilities are single/double occupancy lodging with private baths; 2 conference rooms and hospitality lodge. Offers song assignments, songwriting workshops, song swaps, open mic and one-on-one mentoring. Faculty are noted songwriters, such as Michael Smith, Chuck Brodsky, Tom Prasada Rao, and Corinne West. Partial scholarships may be available by writing: Blissfest Music Organization, % Jim Gillespie, P.O. Box 441, Harbor Springs, MI 49740. Deadline: 2 weeks before event.

MANCHESTER MUSIC FESTIVAL

P.O. Box 33, Manchester VT 05254. (802)362-1956 or (800)639-5868. Fax: (802)362-0711. E-mail: mmfvt@comcast.net. Web site: www.manchestermusicfestival.org. **Contact:** Robyn

Madison, managing director. Estab. 1974. Offers classical music education and perform-ances. Summer program for young professional musicians offered in tandem with a profes-sional concert series in the mountains of Manchester VT. Up to 23 young professionals, age 19 and up, are selected by audition for the Young Artists Program, which provides instruction, performance and teaching opportunities, with full scholarship for all partici-pants. Commissioning opportunities for new music, and performance opportunities for professional chamber ensembles and soloists for both summer and fall/winter concert se-ries. "Celebrating 34 years of fine music."

MUSIC BUSINESS SOLUTIONS/CAREER BUILDING WORKSHOPS

P.O. Box 230266, Boston MA 02123-0266. (888)655-8335. E-mail: peter@mbsolutions.com. Web site: www.mbsolutions.com. **Contact:** Peter Spellman, director. Estab. 1991. Work-shop titles include "Discovering Your Music Career Niche," "How to Release an Indepen-dent Record" and "Promoting and Marketing Music in the 21st Century." Offers programs for music entrepreneurs, songwriters, musical playwrights, composers and performers. Offers programs year-round, annually and bi-annually. Event takes place at various col-leges, recording studios, hotels, conferences. 10-100 songwriters/musicians participate in each event. Participants are both amateur and professional songwriters, vocalists, music business professionals, composers, bands, musical playwrights and instrumentalists. Any-one can participate. Fee: varies. "Music Business Solutions offers a number of other services and programs for both songwriters and musicians including: private music career counsel-ing, business plan development and internet marketing; publication of *Music Biz Insight: Power Reading for Busy Music Professionals*, a bimonthly e-zine chock full of music manage-ment and marketing tips and resources. Free subscription with e-mail address."

⊠ THE NEW HARMONY PROJECT

P.O. Box 441062, Indianapolis IN 46244-1062. (317)464-1103. E-mail: newharmony@newh armonyproject.org. Web site: www.newharmonyproject.org. **Contact:** Joel Grynheim, con-ference director. Estab. 1986. Selected scripts receive various levels of development with rehearsals and readings, both public and private. "Our mission is to nurture writers and their life-affirming scripts. This includes plays, screenplays, musicals and TV scripts." Of-fers programs for musical playwrights. Event takes place in May/June in southwest Indiana. Participants are amateur and professional writers and media professionals. Send for applica-tion.

⊠ ⊠ NEW MUSIC WEST

1062 Homer St., #301, Vancouver BC V6B 2W9 Canada. (604)689-2910. Fax: (604)689-2912. Web site: www.newmusicwest.com. Estab. 1990. A four day music festival and con-ference held May each year in Vancouver BC. The conference offers songwriter intensive workshops; demo critique sessions with A&R and publishers; information on the business of publishing; master producer workshops: "We invite established hit record producers to conduct three-hour intensive hands-on workshops with 30 young producers/musicians in studio environments." The festival offers songwriters in the round and 250 original music showcases. Largest music industry event in the North Pacific Rim. Entry fee: Full Pass: $150; Student: $50; Registered Artists (not selected for showcase): $70. Check website for most recent festival dates.

N NORFOLK CHAMBER MUSIC FESTIVAL

September-May address: Woolsey Hall, 500 College St., Suite 301, New Haven CT 06520. (203)432-1966. Fax: (203)432-2136. E-mail: norfolk@yale.edu. Web site: www.yale.edu/norfolk. June-August address: Ellen Battell, Stoeckel Estate, Routes 44 and 272, Norfolk CT 06058. (860)542-3000. Fax: (860)542-3004. **Contact**: Deanne E. Chin, operations manager. Estab. 1941. Festival season of chamber music. Offers programs for composers and performers. Offers programs summer only. Approximately 45 fellows participate. Participants are up-and-coming composers and instrumentalists. Participants are selected by following a screening round. Auditions are held in New Haven, CT. Send for application. Deadline: January 16. Fee: $50. Held at the Ellen Battell Stoeckel Estate, the Festival offers a magnificent Music Shed with seating for 1,000, practice facilities, music library, dining hall, laundry and art gallery. Nearby are hiking, bicycling and swimming.

N NORTH BY NORTHEAST MUSIC FESTIVAL AND CONFERENCE (NXNE)

189 Church St., Lower Level, Toronto ON M5B 1Y7 Canada. (416)863-6963. Fax: (416)863-0828. E-mail: info@nxne.com. Web site: www.nxne.com. **Contact:** Gillian Zulauf, conference and panel coordinator. Estab. 1995. "Our festival takes place mid-June at over 30 venues across downtown Toronto, drawing over 2,000 conference delegates, 500 bands and 50,000 music fans. Musical genres include everything from folk to funk, roots to rock, polka to punk and all points in between, bringing exceptional new talent, media frontrunners, music business heavies and music fans from all over the world to Toronto." Participants include emerging and established songwriters, vocalists, composers, bands and instrumentalists. Festival performers are selected by submitting a CD and accompanying press kit or applying through sonicbids.com. Application forms are available by website or by calling the office. Submission period each year is from November 1 to the third weekend in January. Submissions "early bird" fee: $25. Conference registration fee: $149-249. "Our conference is held at the deluxe Holiday Inn on King and the program includes mentor sessions—15-minute one-on-one opportunities for songwriters and composers to ask questions of industry experts, roundtables, panel discussions, keynote speakers, etc. North By Northeast 2008 will be held June 12-15."

NSAI SONG CAMPS

1710 Roy Acuff Place, Nashville TN 37023. 1-800-321-6008 or (615)256-3354. Fax: (615)256-0034. E-mail: songcamps@nashvillesongwriters.com. Web site: www.nashvillesongwriters.com. **Contact:** Deanie Williams, NSAI Events Director. Estab. 1992. Offers programs strictly for songwriters. Event held 4 times/year in Nashville. "We provide most meals and lodging is available. We also present an amazing evening of music presented by the faculty." Camps are 3 days long, with 36-112 participants, depending on the camp. "There are different levels of camps, some having preferred prerequisites. Each camp varies. Please call, e-mail or refer to Web site. It really isn't about the genre of music, but the quality of the song itself. Song Camp strives to strengthen the writer's vision and skills, therefore producing the better song. Song Camp is known as 'boot camp' for songwriters. It is guaranteed to catapult you forward in your writing! Participants are all aspiring songwriters led by a pro faculty. We do accept lyricists only and composers only with the hopes of expanding their scope." Participants are selected through submission of 2 songs with lyric sheet. Song Camp is open to NSAI members, although anyone can apply and upon acceptance join the organization. There is no formal application form. See Web site for membership and event information.

- Also see the listing for Nashville Songwriters Association International (NSAI) in the Organizations section of this book.

NSAI SONGWRITERS SONGPOSIUM

1710 Roy Acuff Place, Nashville TN 37203. (615)256-3354 OR 1-800-321-6008. Fax: (615)256-0034. E-mail: events@NashvilleSongwriters.com. Web site: www.nashvillesong writers.com. Covers "all types of music. Participants take part in publisher evaluations, as well as large group sessions with different guest speakers." Offers annual programs for songwriters. Event takes place in April in downtown Nashville. 300 amateur songwriters/ musicians participate in each event. Send for application.

⚏ ORFORD FESTIVAL

Orford Arts Centre, 3165 Chemim DuParc, Orford QC J1X 7A2 Canada. (819)843-9871 or 1-800-567-6155. Fax: (819)843-7274. E-mail: centre@arts-orford.org. Web site: www.arts-orford.org. **Contact:** Anne-Marie Dubois, registrar/information manager. Artistic Coordinator: Nicolas Bélanger. Estab. 1951. "Each year, the Orford Arts Centre produces up to 35 concerts in the context of its Music Festival. It receives artists from all over the world in classical and chamber music." Offers master classes for music students, young professional classical musicians and chamber music ensembles. New offerings include master classes for all instruments,voice, and opera. Master classes last 2 months and take place at Orford Arts Centre from the end of June to the middle of August. 350 students participate each year. Participants are selected by demo tape submissions. Send for application. Closing date for application is mid to late March. Check our website for specific dates and deadlines. Scholarships for qualified students.

⚏ SONGWRITERS PLAYGROUND®

75-A Lake Rd., #366, Congers NY 10920. (845)267-0001. E-mail: heavyhitters@earthlink.n et. **Contact:** Barbara Jordan, director. Estab. 1990. "To help songwriters, performers and composers develop creative and business skills through the critically acclaimed programs *Songwriters Playground®, The 'Reel' Deal on Getting Songs Placed in Film and Television*, and the *Mind Your Own Business* Seminars. We offer programs year-round. Workshops last anywhere from 2-15 hours. Workshops are held at various venues throughout the United States. Prices vary according to the length of the workshop." Participants are amateur and professionals. Anyone can participate. Send or call for application.

SOUTH BY SOUTHWEST MUSIC CONFERENCE (SXSW)

SXSW Headquarters, P.O. Box 4999, Austin TX 78765. (512)467-7979. Fax: (512)451-0754. E-mail: sxsw@sxsw.com. Web site: www.sxsw.com. **Contact:** Conference Organizer. **Europe:** Cill Ruan, 7 Ard na Croise, Thurles, Co. Tipperary Ireland. Phone: 353-504-26488. Fax: 353-504-26787. E-mail: una@sxsw.com. **Contact:** Una Johnston. **Asia:** Meijidori Bldg. 403, 2-3-21 Kabuki-cho Shinjuku-ku, Tokyo 160-0021 Japan. Phone: +82 3-5292-5551. Fax: +82 3-5292-5552. E-mail: info@sxsw-asia.com. **Contact:** Hiroshi Asada. **Australia/New Zealand/Hawaii:** 20 Hordern St., Newtown NSW 2042 Australia. Phone: 61-2-9557-7766. Fax: 61-2-9557-7788. E-mail: tripp@sxsw.om. **Contact:** Phil Tripp. Estab. 1987. South by Southwest (SXSW) is a private company based in Austin, Texas, with a year-round staff of professionals dedicated to building and delivering conference and festival events for entertainment and related media industry professionals. Since 1987, SXSW has produced the internationally-recognized music and media conference and festival (SXSW). As the entertainment business adjusted to issues of future growth and development, in 1993, SXSW added conferences and festivals for the film industry (SXSW Film) as well as for the blossoming interactive media (SXSW Interactive Festival). Now three industry events converge in Austin during a Texas-sized week, mirroring the ever increasing convergence of entertainment/media outlets. The next SXSW Music Conference and Festival will be held March 18-22, 2009 at the Austin Convention Center in Austin, TX. Offers panel discussions, "Crash Course" educational seminars and nighttime showcases. SXSW Music seeks out speakers who have developed unique ways to create and sell music. With our Wednesday Crash Courses and introductory panels, the basics will be covered in plain English. From Thursday through Saturday, the conference includes over fifty sessions including a panel of label heads discussing strategy, interviews with notable artists, topical discussions, demo listening sessions and the mentor program. And when the sun goes down, a multitude of performances by musicians and songwriters from across the country and around the world populate the SXSW Music Festival, held in venues in central Austin." Write, e-mail or visit Web site for dates and registration instructions.

Tips "Go to the Web site in early-September to apply for showcase consideraton. SXSW is also involved in North by Northeast (NXNE), held in Toronto, Canada in late Spring."

THE SWANNANOA GATHERING—CONTEMPORARY FOLK WEEK

Warren Wilson College, P.O. Box 9000, Asheville NC 28815-9000. E-mail: gathering@warren-wilson.edu. Web site: www.swangathering.com. Director: Jim Magill. "For anyone who ever wanted to make music for an audience, we offer a comprehensive week in artist development, including classes in Songwriting—with a special concentration in melody writing and commercial songwriting—Performance, Sound & Recording, and Vocal Coaching, along with daily panel discussions of other business matters such as promotion, agents and managers, logistics of touring, etc." 2007 staff include Ellis Paul, Tom Paxton, Cliff Eberhardt, Christine Kane, Brooks Williams, Tom Kimmel, Kate Campbell, Billy Jonas, Andrea Stolpe, Alan Rowoth, Siobhan Quinn, and Ray Chesna. For a brochure or other info contact The Swannanoa Gathering at the phone number/address above. Tuition: $417. Takes place last week in July. Housing (including all meals): $317. Annual program of The Swannanoa Gathering Folk Arts Workshops.

THE TEN-MINUTE MUSICALS PROJECT

P.O. Box 461194, West Hollywood CA 90046. E-mail: info@tenminutemusicals.org. Web site: www.tenminutemusicals.org. **Contact:** Michael Koppy, producer. Estab. 1986. Promotes short complete stage musicals. Offers programs for songwriters, composers and musical playwrights. "Works selected are generally included in full-length 'anthology musical'— 11 of the first 16 selected works are now in the show Stories 1.0, for instance." Awards a $250 royalty advance for each work selected. Participants are amateur and professional songwriters, composers and musical playwrights. Participants are selected by demonstration tape or CD, script, lead sheets. Send Web site for submission guidelines. Deadline: August 31st annually.

TUNESMITH PRO—The Next Step . . .

E-mail: info@tunesmith.net. Web site: www.tunesmith.net. **Contact:** Nancy Cassidy, Tune smith.net and Tunesmith PRO owner. Estab. 2001. "Tunesmith Pro offers serious songwriters the opportunity to get their music heard in Nashville. We offer songwriting competitions annually at writer's venues in Nashville the first week in March. A new "Best of Tunesmith" compilation CD is released each quarter listing the best songs from our pro members. For more information, e-mail at info@tunesmith.net."

UNDERCURRENTS

P.O. Box 94040, Cleveland OH 44101-6040. (440)331-0700. E-mail: music@undercurrents.com. Web site: www.undercurrents.com. **Contact:** John Latimer, president. Estab. 1989. A music, event and art marketing and promotion network with online and offline exposure featuring music showcases, seminars, trade shows, networking forums. Ongoing programs and performances for songwriters, composers, and performers. Participants are selected by EPK, demo, biography and photo. Register at www.undercurrents.com.

WEST COAST SONGWRITERS CONFERENCE

(formerly Northern California Songwriters Association Conference), 1724 Laurel St., Suite 120, San Carlos CA 94070. (650)654-3966 or (800)FOR-SONG. Fax: (650)654-2156. E-mail: info@westcoastsongwriters.org. Web site: www.westcoastsongwriters.org. **Contact:** Ian Crombie, executive director. Estab. 1980. "Conference offers opportunity and education. 16 seminars, 50 song screening sessions (1,500 songs reviewed), performance showcases, one on one sessions and concerts." Offers programs for lyricists, songwriters, composers and performers. "During the year we have competitive live Songwriter competitions. Winners go into the playoffs. Winners of the playoffs perform at the sunset concert at the conference." Event takes place second weekend in September at Foothill College, Los Altos Hills CA. Over 500 songwriters/musicians participate in this event. Participants are songwriters, composers, musical playwrights, vocalists, bands, instrumentalists and those interested in a career in the music business. Send for application. Deadline: September 1. Fee: $150-275. "See our listing in the Organizations section."

☒ WESTERN WIND WORKSHOP IN ENSEMBLE SINGING

263 W. 86 St., New York NY 10024. (212)873-2848 or (800)788-2187. Fax: (212)873-2849. E-mail: workshops@westernwind.org. Web site: www.westernwind.org. **Contact**: William Zukoff, executive producer. Estab. 1981. Participants learn the art of ensemble singing—no conductor, one on-a-part. Workshop focuses on blend, diction, phrasing and production. Offers programs for performers. Limited talent-based scholarship available. Offers programs annually. Takes place June, July and August in the music department at Smith College, Northampton MA. 70-80 songwriters/musicians participate in each event. Participants are amateur and professional vocalists. Anyone can participate. Send for application or register at their website. Workshop takes place in the Smith College music department. Arrangers' works are frequently studied and performed. Also offers additional workshops President's Day weekend in Brattleboro VT and Columbus Day weekend in Woodstock VT.

WINTER MUSIC CONFERENCE INC.

3450 NE 12 Terrace, Ft. Lauderdale FL 33334. (954)563-4444. Fax: (954)563-1599. E-mail: info@wintermusicconference.com. Web site: www.wintermusicconference.com. President: Margo Possenti. Estab. 1985. Features educational seminars and showcases for dance, hip hop, alternative and rap. Offers programs for songwriters and performers. Offers programs annually. Event takes place March of each year in Miami FL. 3,000 songwriters/musicians participate in each event. Participants are amateur and professional songwriters, composers, musical playwrights, vocalists, bands and instrumentalists. Participants are selected by submitting demo tape. Send SASE, visit website or call for application. Deadline: February. Event held at either nightclubs or hotel with complete staging, lights and sound.

Retreats & Colonies

This section provides information on retreats and artists' colonies. These are places for creatives, including songwriters, to find solitude and spend concentrated time focusing on their work. While a residency at a colony may offer participation in seminars, critiques or performances, the atmosphere of a colony or retreat is much more relaxed than that of a conference or workshop. Also, a songwriter's stay at a colony is typically anywhere from one to twelve weeks (sometimes longer), while time spent at a conference may only run from one to fourteen days.

Like conferences and workshops, however, artists' colonies and retreats span a wide range. Yaddo, perhaps the most well-known colony, limits its residencies to artists "working at a professional level in their field, as determined by a judging panel of professionals in the field." The Brevard Music Center offers residencies only to those involved in classical music. Despite different focuses, all artists' colonies and retreats have one thing in common: They are places where you may work undisturbed, usually in nature-oriented, secluded settings.

SELECTING A COLONY OR RETREAT

When selecting a colony or retreat, the primary consideration for many songwriters is cost, and you'll discover that arrangements vary greatly. Some colonies provide residencies as well as stipends for personal expenses. Some suggest donations of a certain amount. Still others offer residencies for substantial sums but have financial assistance available.

When investigating the various options, consider meal and housing arrangements and your family obligations. Some colonies provide meals for residents, while others require residents to pay for meals. Some colonies house artists in one main building; others provide separate cottages. A few have provisions for spouses and families. Others prohibit families altogether.

Overall, residencies at colonies and retreats are competitive. Since only a handful of spots are available at each place, you often must apply months in advance for the time period you desire. A number of locations are open year-round, and you may find planning to go during the "off-season" lessens your competition. Other colonies, however, are only available during certain months. In any case, be prepared to include a sample of your best work with your application. Also, know what project you'll work on while in residence and have alternative projects in mind in case the first one doesn't work out once you're there.

Each listing in this section details fee requirements, meal and housing arrangements, and space and time availability, as well as the retreat's surroundings, facilities and special activities. Of course, before making a final decision, send a SASE to the colonies or retreats that interest you to receive their most up-to-date details. Costs, application requirements and deadlines are particularly subject to change.

MUSICIAN'S RESOURCE

For other listings of songwriter-friendly colonies, see *Musician's Resource* (available from Watson-Guptill Publications, 770 Broadway, New York NY 10003, 1-800-278-8477, info@watsonguptill.com), which not only provides information about conferences, workshops and academic programs but also residencies and retreats. Also check the Publications of Interest section in this book for newsletters and other periodicals providing this information.

BREVARD MUSIC CENTER

P.O. Box 312, 349 Andante Ln., Brevard NC 28712. (828)862-2140. Fax: (828)884-2036. E-mail: bmc@brevardmusic.org. Web site: www.brevardmusic.org. **Contact:** Dorothy Knowles, admissions coordinator. Estab. 1936. Offers 6-week residencies from June through the first week of August. Open to professional and student composers, pianists, vocalists, collaborative pianists and instrumentalists of classical music. A 2-week jazz workshop is offered in June. Accommodates 400 at one time. Personal living quarters include cabins. Offers rehearsal, teaching and practice cabins.

Costs $4,100 for tuition, room and board. Scholarships are available.

Requirements Call for application forms and guidelines. $50 application fee. Participants are selected by audition or demonstration tape and then by invitation. There are 80 different audition sites throughout the US.

BYRDCLIFFE ARTS COLONY

34 Tinker St., Woodstock NY 12498. (845)679-2079. Fax: (845)679-4529. E-mail: wguild@ulster.net. Web site: www.woodstockguild.org. **Contact:** Carla T. Smith, executive director. Estab. 1991. Offers 1-month residencies June-September. Open to composers, writers and visual artists. Accommodates 10 at one time. Personal living quarters include single rooms, shared baths and kitchen facilities. Offers separate private studio space. Composers must provide their own keyboard with headphone. Activities include open studio, readings, followed by pot luck dinner once a month. The Woodstock Guild, parent organization, offers music and dance performances, gallery exhibits and book signings.

Costs $300/month. Residents are responsible for own meals and transportation.

Requirements Deadline: March 1. Send SASE for application forms and guidelines. Accepts inquiries via fax or e-mail. $35 application fee. Submit a score of at least 10 minutes with 2 references, résumé and application.

DORSET COLONY HOUSE

P.O. Box 221, Dorset VT 05251-0510. (802)867-2223. Fax: (802)867-5937. E-mail: dorsetcolony@hotmail.com. Web site: www.dorsetcolony.org. **Contact:** John Nassivera, executive director. Estab. 1980. Offers up to 1-month residencies September-November and April-May. Open to writers, composers, directors, designers and collaborators of the theatre. Accommodates 9 at one time. Personal living quarters include single rooms with desks with shared bath and shared kitchen facilities.

Costs $230/week and $800/month. Meals not included. Transportation is residents' responsibility.

Requirements Send SASE for application forms and guidelines. Accepts inquiries via fax or e-mail. Submit letter with requested dates, description of project and résumé of productions.

THE TYRONE GUTHRIE CENTRE

Annaghmakerrig, Newbliss, County Monaghan, Ireland. (353)(047)54003. Fax: (353)(047)54380. E-mail: info@tyroneguthrie.ie. Web site: www.tyroneguthrie.ie. **Contact**: Program Director. Estab. 1981. Offers year-round residencies. Artists may stay for anything from 1 week to 3 months in the Big House, or for up to 6 months at a time in one of the 5 self-catering houses in the old farmyard. Open to artists of all disciplines. Accommodates 15 at one time. Personal living quarters include bedroom with bathroom en suite. Offers a variety of workspaces. There is a music room for composers and musicians, a photographic darkroom and a number of studios for visual artists. At certain times of the year it is possible, by special arrangement, to accommodate groups of artists, symposiums, master classes, workshops and other collaborations.

Costs Artists who are not Irish residents must pay €650 per week, all found, for a residency in the Big House and €325 per week (plus gas and electricity costs) for one of the self-catering farmyard houses. To qualify for a residency, it is necessary to show evidence of a significant level of achievement in the relevant field.

Requirements Send SAE and IRC for application forms and guidelines. Accepts inquiries via fax or e-mail. Fill in application form with cv to be reviewed by the board members at regular meetings.

THE HAMBIDGE CENTER

Attn: Residency Director, P.O. Box 339, Rabun Gap GA 30568. (706)746-5718. Fax: (706)746-9933 E-mail: center@hambidge.org. Web site: www.hambidge.org. **Contact**: Rosemary Magee, residency chair. Estab. 1934 (Center); 1988 (residency). Offers 2-week to 2-month residencies year round. Open to all artists. Accommodates 8 at one time. Personal living quarters include a private cottage with kitchen, bath, and living/studio space. Offers composer/musical studio equipped with piano. Activities include communal dinners February through December and nightly or periodic sharing of works-in-progress.

Costs $150/week.

Requirements Send SASE for application forms and guidelines, or available on Web site. Accepts inquiries via fax and e-mail. Application fee: $30. Deadlines: January 15, April 15, and September 15.

ISLE ROYALE NATIONAL PARK ARTIST-IN-RESIDENCE PROGRAM

800 E. Lakeshore Dr., Houghton MI 49931. (906)482-0984. Fax: (906)482-8753. E-mail: ISRO_Parkinfo@nps.gov. Web site: www.nps.gov/ISRO/. **Contact:** Greg Blust, coordinator. Estab. 1991. Offers 2-3 week residencies from mid-June to mid-September. Open to all art forms. Accommodates 1 artist with 1 companion at one time. Personal living quarters include cabin with shared outhouse. A canoe is provided for transportation. Offers a guest house at the site that can be used as a studio. The artist is asked to contribute a piece of work representative of their stay at Isle Royale, to be used by the park in an appropriate

manner. During their residency, artists will be asked to share their experience (1 presentation per week of residency, about 1 hour/week) with the public by demonstration, talk, or other means.

Requirements Deadline: postmarked February 16, 2009. Send for application forms and guidelines. Accepts inquiries via fax or e-mail. A panel of professionals from various disciplines, and park representatives will choose the finalists. The selection is based on artistic integrity, ability to reside in a wilderness environment, a willingness to donate a finished piece of work inspired on the island, and the artist's ability to relate and interpret the park through their work.

KALANI OCEANSIDE RETREAT

RR 2 Box 4500, Pahoa-Beach Road HI 96778-9724. (808)965-7828. Fax: (808)965-0527. E-mail: kalani@kalani.com. Web site: www.kalani.com. **Contact:** Richard Koob, director. Estab. 1980. Offers 2-week to 2-month residencies. Open to all artists who can verify professional accomplishments. Accommodates 120 at one time. Personal living quarters include private cottage or lodge room with private or shared bath. Full (3 meals/day) dining service. Offers shared studio/library spaces. Activities include opportunity to share works in progress, ongoing yoga, hula and other classes; beach, thermal springs, Volcanos National Park nearby; olympic pool/spa on 120-acre facility.

Cost $58-230/night lodging with stipend, including 3 meals/day. Transportation by rental car from $35/day, Kalani service $55/trip, or taxi $80/trip.

Requirements Accepts inquiries via fax or e-mail.

THE MACDOWELL COLONY

100 High St., Peterborough NH 03458. (603)924-3886. Fax: (603)924-9142. E-mail: admissions@macdowellcolony.org. Web site: www.macdowellcolony.org. **Contact:** Admissions Director. Estab. 1907. Offers year-round residencies of up to 8 weeks. Open to writers and playwrights, composers, film/video makers, visual artists, architects and interdisciplinary artists. Personal living quarters include single rooms with shared baths. Offers private studios on 450-acre grounds. Travel assistance and artist grants awarded based on need.

Cost None (contributions accepted).

Requirements Visit Web site for application forms and guidelines (which include work sample requirements). Application deadline: January 15, April 15 and September 15.

NORTHWOOD UNIVERSITY ALDEN B. DOW CREATIVITY CENTER

4000 Whiting Dr., Midland MI 48640. (989)837-4478. E-mail: creativity@northwood.edu. Web site: www.northwood.edu/abd. **Contact** Nancy Barker, executive director. Estab. 1979. Offers 10-week summer residencies (mid-June through mid-August). Fellowship Residency is open to individuals in all fields (the arts, humanities or sciences, etc.) who have innovative, creative projects to pursue. Accommodates 3 at one time. Each Fellow is given a furnished apartment on campus, kitchen, bath and large living room. Fellows' apartments serve as their work space as well as their living quarters unless special needs are requested.

Cost $10 application fee. Room and board is provided plus a $750 stipend to be used toward project costs or personal needs. "We look for projects which are innovative, creative, unique. We ask the applicant to set accomplishable goals for the 10-week residency."

Requirements Send for application information and guidelines. Accepts inquiries via e-mail. Applicants submit 2-page typed description of their project; cover page with name, address, phone numbers plus summary (30 words or less) of project; support materials must be submitted via e-mail—will not accept tapes, CDs, or slides by postal mail; personal résumé; facilities or equipment needed; and $10 application fee. Application deadline: December 31 (postmarked).

SITKA CENTER FOR ART & ECOLOGY

P.O. Box 65, Otis OR 97368-0065. (541)994-5485. Fax: (541)994-8024. E-mail: info@sitkacenter.org. Web site: www.sitkacenter.org. **Contact:** Eric Vines, executive director. Estab. 1971. Offers 4-month residencies in October through January or February through May; shorter residencies are available upon arrangement. Open to emerging, mid-career, or professional artists and naturalists. Residences include 3 living quarters, each self-contained with a sleeping area, kitchen and bathroom. Offers 4 studios. Workshops or presentations are encouraged; an exhibition/presentation to share residents' works is held in January and May.

Cost Residency and housing provided. The resident is asked to provide some form of community service on behalf of Sitka.

Requirements *Applications due by April 21 for a Fall or Spring residency.* Send completed application with résumé, 2 letters of recommendation, work samples and SASE.

VIRGINIA CENTER FOR THE CREATIVE ARTS

154 San Angelo Dr., Amherst VA 24521. (434)946-7236. Fax: (434)946-7239. E-mail: vcca@vcca.com. Web site: www.vcca.com. **Contact:** Sheila Gulley Pleasants, director of artists' services. Estab. 1971. Offers residencies year-round, typical residency lasts 2 weeks to 2 months. Open to originating artists: composers, writers and visual artists. Accommodates 25 at one time. Personal living quarters include 21 single rooms, 2 double rooms, bathrooms shared with one other person. All meals are served. Kitchens for fellows' use available at studios and residence. Activities include trips in the VCCA van twice a week into town. Fellows share their work regularly. Four studios have pianos.

Cost No transportation costs are covered. There is no fee to attend the VCCA. Artists are accepted at the VCCA without consideration for their financial situation. The actual cost of a residency at the Virginia Center is $120 per day per Fellow. "We ask Fellows to contribute according to their ability. Suggested daily contribution is $30."

Requirements Send SASE for application form or download from Web site. Applications are reviewed by a panel of judges. Application fee: $25. Deadline: May 15 for October-January residency; September 15 for February-May residency; January 15 for June-September residency.

State & Provincial Grants

Arts councils in the United States and Canada provide assistance to artists (including poets) in the form of fellowships or grants. These grants can be substantial and confer prestige upon recipients; however, **only state or province residents are eligible**. Because deadlines and available support vary annually, query first (with a SASE) or check Web sites for guidelines.

UNITED STATES ARTS AGENCIES

Alabama State Council on the Arts, 201 Monroe St., Montgomery AL 36130-1800. (334)242-4076. E-mail: staff@arts.alabama.gov. Web site: www.arts.state.al.us.

Alaska State Council on the Arts, 411 W. Fourth Ave., Suite 1-E, Anchorage AK 99501-2343. (907)269-6610 or (888)278-7424. E-mail: aksca_info@eed.state.ak.us. Web site: www.eed. state.ak.us/aksca.

Arizona Commission on the Arts, 417 W. Roosevelt St., Phoenix AZ 85003-1326. (602)771-6501. E-mail: info@azarts.gov. Web site: www.azarts.gov.

Arkansas Arts Council, 1500 Tower Bldg., 323 Center St., Little Rock AR 72201. (501)324-9766. E-mail: info@arkansasarts.com. Web site: www.arkansasarts.com.

California Arts Council, 1300 I St., Suite 930, Sacramento CA 95814. (916)322-6555. E-mail: info@caartscouncil.com. Web site: www.cac.ca.gov.

Colorado Council on the Arts, 1625 Broadway, Suite 2700, Denver CO 80202. (303)892-3802. E-mail: online form. Web site: www.coloarts.state.co.us.

Connecticut Commission on Culture & Tourism, Arts Division, One Financial Plaza, 755 Main St., Hartford CT 06103. (860)256-2800. Web site: www.cultureandtourism.org.

Delaware Division of the Arts, Carvel State Office Bldg., 4th Floor, 820 N. French St., Wilmington DE 19801. (302)577-8278 (New Castle Co.) or (302)739-5304 (Kent or Sussex Counties). E-mail: delarts@state.de.us. Web site: www.artsdel.org.

District of Columbia Commission on the Arts & Humanities, 410 Eighth St. NW, 5th Floor, Washington DC 20004. (202)724-5613. E-mail: cah@dc.gov. Web site: http://dcarts .dc.gov.

Florida Arts Council, Division of Cultural Affairs, R.A. Gray Building, Third Floor, 500 S. Bronough St., Tallahassee FL 32399-0250. (850)245-6470. E-mail: info@florida-arts.org. Web site: http://dcarts.dc.gov.

Georgia Council for the Arts, 260 14th St., Suite 401, Atlanta GA 30318. (404)685-2787. E-mail: gaarts@gaarts.org. Web site: www.gaarts.org.

Guam Council on the Arts & Humanities Agency, P.O. Box 2950, Hagatna GU 96932. (671)646-2781. Web site: www.guam.net.

Hawaii State Foundation on Culture & the Arts, 2500 S. Hotel St., 2nd Floor, Honolulu HI 96813. (808)586-0300. E-mail: ken.hamilton@hawaii.gov. Web site: http.state.hi.us/sfca.

Idaho Commission on the Arts, 2410 N. Old Penitentiary Rd., Boise ID 83712. (208)334-2119 or (800)278-3863. E-mail: info@arts.idaho.gov. Web site: www.arts.idaho.gov.

Illinois Arts Council, James R. Thompson Center, 100 W. Randolph, Suite 10-500, Chicago IL 60601. (312)814-6750. E-mail: iac.info@illinois.gov. Web site: www.state.il.us/agency/iac.

Indiana Arts Commission, 150 W. Market St., Suite 618, Indianapolis IN 46204. (317)232-1268. E-mail: IndianaArtsCommission@iac.in.gov. Web site: www.in.gov/arts.

Iowa Arts Council, 600 E. Locust, Des Moines IA 50319-0290. (515)281-6412. Web site: www.iowaartscouncil.org.

Kansas Arts Commission, 700 SW Jackson, Suite 1004, Topeka KS 66603-3761. (785)296-3335. E-mail: KAC@arts.state.ks.us. Web site: http://arts.state.ks.us.

Kentucky Arts Council, 21st Floor, Capital Plaza Tower, 500 Mero St., Frankfort KY 40601-1987. (502)564-3757 or (888)833-2787. E-mail: kyarts@ky.gov. Web site: http://artscouncil.ky.gov.

Louisiana Division of the Arts, Capitol Annex Bldg., 1051 N. 3rd St., 4th Floor, Room #420, Baton Rouge LA 70804. (225)342-8180. Web site: www.crt.state.la.us/arts.

Maine Arts Commission, 193 State St., 25 State House Station, Augusta ME 04333-0025. (207)287-2724. E-mail: MaineArts.info@maine.gov. Web site: www.mainearts.com.

Maryland State Arts Council, 175 W. Ostend St., Suite E, Baltimore MD 21230. (410)767-6555. E-mail: msac@msac.org. Web site: www.msac.org.

Massachusetts Cultural Council, 10 St. James Ave., 3rd Floor, Boston MA 02116-3803. (617)727-3668. E-mail: mcc@art.state.ma.us. Web site: www.massculturalcouncil.org.

Michigan Council of History, Arts, and Libraries, 702 W. Kalamazoo St., P.O. Box 30705, Lansing MI 48909-8205. (517)241-4011. E-mail: artsinfo@michigan.gov. Web site: www.michigan.gov/hal/0,1607,7-160-17445_19272---,00.html.

Minnesota State Arts Board, Park Square Court, 400 Sibley St., Suite 200, St. Paul MN 55101-1928. (651)215-1600 or (800)866-2787. E-mail: msab@arts.state.mn.us. Web site: www.arts.state.mn.us.

Mississippi Arts Commission, 501 N. West St., Suite 701B, Woolfolk Bldg., Jackson MS 39201. (601)359-6030. Web site: www.arts.state.ms.us.

Missouri Arts Council, 815 Olive St., Suite 16, St. Louis MO 63101-1503. (314)340-6845 or (866)407-4752. E-mail: moarts@ded.mo.gov. Web site: www.missouriartscouncil.org.

Montana Arts Council, 316 N. Park Ave., Suite 252, Helena MT 59620-2201. (406)444-6430. E-mail: mac@mt.gov. Web site: www.art.state.mt.us.

Resources

National Assembly of State Arts Agencies, 1029 Vermont Ave. NW, 2nd Floor, Washington DC 20005. (202)347-6352. E-mail: nasaa@nasaa-arts.org. Web site: www.nasaa-arts.org.

Nebraska Arts Council, 1004 Farnam St., Plaza Level, Omaha NE 68102. (402)595-2122 or (800)341-4067. Web site: www.nebraskaartscouncil.org.

Nevada Arts Council, 716 N. Carson St., Suite A, Carson City NV 89701. (775)687-6680. E-mail: online form. Web site: http://dmla.clan.lib.nv.us/docs/arts.

New Hampshire State Council on the Arts, 2½ Beacon St., 2nd Floor, Concord NH 03301-4974. (603)271-2789. Web site: www.nh.gov/nharts.

New Jersey State Council on the Arts, 225 W. State St., P.O. Box 306, Trenton NJ 08625. (609)292-6130. Web site: www.njartscouncil.org.

New Mexico Arts, Dept. of Cultural Affairs, P.O. Box 1450, Santa Fe NM 87504-1450. (505)827-6490 or (800)879-4278. Web site: www.nmarts.org.

New York State Council on the Arts, 175 Varick St., New York NY 10014. (212)627-4455. Web site: www.nysca.org.

North Carolina Arts Council, 109 East Jones St., Cultural Resources Building, Raleigh NC 27601. (919)807-6500. E-mail: ncarts@ncmail.net. Web site: www.ncarts.org.

North Dakota Council on the Arts, 1600 E. Century Ave., Suite 6, Bismarck ND 58503. (701)328-7590. E-mail: comserv@state.nd.us. Web site: www.state.nd.us/arts.

Commonwealth Council for Arts and Culture (Northern Mariana Islands), P.O. Box 5553, CHRB, Saipan MP 96950. (670)322-9982 or (670)322-9983. E-mail: galaidi@vzpacifica.net. Web site: www.geocities.com/ccacarts/ccacwebsite.html.

Ohio Arts Council, 727 E. Main St., Columbus OH 43205-1796. (614)466-2613. Web site: www.oac.state.oh.us.

Oklahoma Arts Council, Jim Thorpe Building, 2101 N. Lincoln Blvd., Suite 640, Oklahoma City OK 73105. (405)521-2931. E-mail: okarts@arts.ok.gov. Web site: www.arts.state.ok.us.

Oregon Arts Commission, 775 Summer St. NE, Suite 200, Salem OR 97301-1280. (503)986-0082. E-mail: oregon.artscomm@state.or.us. Web site: www.oregonartscommission.org.

Pennsylvania Council on the Arts, 216 Finance Bldg., Harrisburg PA 17120. (717)787-6883. Web site: www.pacouncilonthearts.org.

Institute of Puerto Rican Culture, P.O. Box 9024184, San Juan PR 00902-4184. (787)724-0700. E-mail: www@icp.gobierno.pr. Web site: www.icp.gobierno.pr.

Rhode Island State Council on the Arts, One Capitol Hill, Third Floor, Providence RI 02908. (401)222-3880. E-mail: info@arts.ri.gov. Web site: www.arts.ri.gov.

South Carolina Arts Commission, 1800 Gervais St., Columbia SC 29201. (803)734-8696. E-mail: info@arts.state.sc.us. Web site: www.southcarolinaarts.com.

South Dakota Arts Council, 711 E. Wells Ave., Pierre SD 57501-3369. (605)773-3301. E-mail: sdac@state.sd.us. Web site: www.artscouncil.sd.gov.

Tennessee Arts Commission, 401 Charlotte Ave., Nashville TN 37243-0780. (615)741-1701. Web site: www.arts.state.tn.us.

Texas Commission on the Arts, E.O. Thompson Office Building, 920 Colorado, Suite 501,

Austin TX 78701. (512)463-5535. E-mail: front.desk@arts.state.tx.us. Web site: www.arts.state.tx.us.

Utah Arts Council, 617 E. South Temple, Salt Lake City UT 84102-1177. (801)236-7555. Web site: http://arts.utah.gov.

Vermont Arts Council, 136 State St., Drawer 33, Montpelier VT 05633-6001. (802)828-3291. E-mail: online form. Web site: www.vermontartscouncil.org.

Virgin Islands Council on the Arts, 5070 Norre Gade, St. Thomas VI 00802-6872. (340)774-5984. Web site: http://vicouncilonarts.org.

Virginia Commission for the Arts, Lewis House, 223 Governor St., 2nd Floor, Richmond VA 23219. (804)225-3132. E-mail: arts@arts.virginia.gov. Web site: www.arts.state.va.us.

Washington State Arts Commission, 711 Capitol Way S., Suite 600, P.O. Box 42675, Olympia WA 98504-2675. (360)753-3860. E-mail: info@arts.wa.gov. Web site: www.arts.wa.gov.

West Virginia Commission on the Arts, The Cultural Center, Capitol Complex, 1900 Kanawha Blvd. E., Charleston WV 25305-0300. (304)558-0220. Web site: www.wvculture.org/arts.

Wisconsin Arts Board, 101 E. Wilson St., 1st Floor, Madison WI 53702. (608)266-0190. E-mail: artsboard@arts.state.wi.us. Web site: www.arts.state.wi.us.

Wyoming Arts Council, 2320 Capitol Ave., Cheyenne WY 82002. (307)777-7742. E-mail: ebratt@state.wy.us. Web site: http://wyoarts.state.wy.us.

CANADIAN PROVINCES ARTS AGENCIES

Alberta Foundation for the Arts, 10708-105 Ave., Edmonton AB T5H 0A1. (780)427-9968. Web site: www.affta.ab.ca/index.shtml.

British Columbia Arts Council, P.O. Box 9819, Stn. Prov. Govt., Victoria BC V8W 9W3. (250)356-1718. E-mail: BCArtsCouncil@gov.bc.ca. Web site: www.bcartscouncil.ca.

The Canada Council for the Arts, 350 Albert St., P.O. Box 1047, Ottawa ON K1P 5V8. (613)566-4414 or (800)263-5588 (within Canada). Web site: www.canadacouncil.ca.

Manitoba Arts Council, 525-93 Lombard Ave., Winnipeg MB R3B 3B1. (204)945-2237 or (866)994-2787 (in Manitoba). E-mail: info@artscouncil.mb.ca. Web site: www.artscouncil.mb.ca.

New Brunswick Arts Board (NBAB), 634 Queen St., Suite 300, Fredericton NB E3B 1C2. (506)444-4444 or (866)460-2787. Web site: www.artsnb.ca.

Newfoundland & Labrador Arts Council, P.O. Box 98, St. John's NL A1C 5H5. (709)726-2212 or (866)726-2212. E-mail: nlacmail@nfld.net. Web site: www.nlac.nf.ca.

Nova Scotia Department of Tourism, Culture, and Heritage, Culture Division, 1800 Argyle St., Suite 601, P.O. Box 456, Halifax NS B3J 2R5. (902)424-4510. E-mail: cultaffs@gov.ns.ca. Web site: www.gov.ns.ca/dtc/culture.

Ontario Arts Council, 151 Bloor St. W., 5th Floor, Toronto ON M5S 1T6. (416)961-1660 or (800)387-0058 (in Ontario). E-mail: info@arts.on.ca. Web site: www.arts.on.ca.

Prince Edward Island Council of the Arts, 115 Richmond St., Charlottetown PE C1A 1H7.

(902)368-4410 or (888)734-2784. E-mail: info@peiartscouncil.com. Web site: www.peiart scouncil.com.

Québec Council for Arts & Literature, 79 boul. René-Lévesque Est, 3e étage, Québec QC G1R 5N5. (418)643-1707 or (800)897-1707. E-mail: info@calq.gouv.qc.ca. Web site: www.calq. gouv.qc.ca.

The Saskatchewan Arts Board, 2135 Broad St., Regina SK S4P 1Y6. (306)787-4056 or (800)667-7526 (Saskatchewan only). E-mail: sab@artsboard.sk.ca. Web site: www.artsbo ard.sk.ca.

Yukon Arts Funding Program, Cultural Services Branch, Dept. of Tourism & Culture, Government of Yukon, Box 2703 (L-3), Whitehorse YT Y1A 2C6. (867)667-8589 or (800)661-0408 (in Yukon). E-mail: arts@gov.yk.ca. Web site: www.tc.gov.yk.ca/216.html.

Publications of Interest

Knowledge about the music industry is essential for both creative and business success. Staying informed requires keeping up with constantly changing information. Updates on the evolving trends in the music business are available to you in the form of music magazines, music trade papers and books. There is a publication aimed at almost every type of musician, songwriter and music fan, from the most technical knowledge of amplification systems to gossip about your favorite singer. These publications can enlighten and inspire you and provide information vital in helping you become a more well-rounded, educated, and, ultimately, successful musical artist.

This section lists all types of magazines and books you may find interesting. From songwriters' newsletters and glossy music magazines to tip sheets and how-to books, there should be something listed here that you'll enjoy and benefit from.

PERIODICALS

The Album Network, 110 West Spazier, Burbank CA 91502. (818)842-2600. Web site: www.musicbiz.com. *Weekly music industry trade magazine.*

American Songwriter Magazine, 50 Music Square W., Suite 604, Nashville TN 37203-3227. (615)321-6096. E-mail: info@americansongwriter.com. Web site: www.americansongwriter.com. *Bimonthly publication for and about songwriters.*

Back Stage East, 770 Broadway, 4th Floor, New York NY 10003. (646)654-5700.

Back Stage West, 5055 Wilshire Blvd., Los Angeles CA 90036. (323)525-2358 or (800)745-8922. Web site: www.backstage.com. *Weekly East and West Coast performing artist trade papers.*

Bass Player, P.O. Box 57324, Boulder CO 80323-7324. (800)234-1831. E-mail: bassplayer@neodata.com. Web site: www.bassplayer.com. *Monthly magazine for bass players with lessons, interviews, articles, and transcriptions.*

Billboard, 1515 Broadway, New York NY 10036. (800)745-8922. E-mail: bbstore@billboard.com. Web site: www.billboard.com. *Weekly industry trade magazine.*

Canadian Musician, 23 Hannover Dr., Suite 7, St. Catharines ON L2W 1A3 Canada. (877)746-4692. Web site: www.canadianmusician.com. *Bimonthly publication for amateur and professional Canadian musicians.*

Chart, 200-41 Britain St., Toronto ON M5A 1R7 Canada. (416)363-3101. E-mail: chart@chart net.com. Web site: www.chartattack.com. *Monthly magazine covering the Canadian and international music scenes.*

CMJ New Music Report/CMJ New Music Monthly, 151 W. 25th St., 12 Floor, New York NY 10001. (917)606-1908. Web site: www.cmj.com. *Weekly college radio and alternative music tip sheet.*

Country Line Magazine, 16150 S. IH-35, Buda TX 78610. (512)295-8400. E-mail: editor@cou ntrylinemagazine.com. Web site: www.countrylinemagazine.com. *Monthly Texas-only country music cowboy and lifestyle magazine.*

Daily Variety, 5700 Wilshire Blvd., Suite 120, Los Angeles CA 90036. (323)857-6600. Web site: www.variety.com. *Daily entertainment trade newspaper.*

Dramalogue, 1456 N. Gordon, Hollywood CA 90028. Web site: www.dramalogue.com. *L.A.-based entertainment newspaper with an emphasis on theatre and cabaret.*

The Dramatist, 1501 Broadway, Suite 701, New York NY 10036. (212)398-9366. Fax: (212)944-0420. Web site: www.dramaguild.com. *The quarterly journal of the Dramatists Guild, the professional association of playwrights, composers and lyricists.*

Entertainment Law & Finance, New York Law Publishing Co., 345 Park Ave. S., 8th Floor, New York NY 10010. (212)545-6174. *Monthly newsletter covering music industry contracts, lawsuit filings, court rulings and legislation.*

Exclaim!, 7-B Pleasant Blvd., Suite 966, Toronto ON M4T 1K2 Canada. (416)535-9735. E-mail: exclaim@exclaim.ca. Web site: http://exclaim.ca. *Canadian music monthly covering all genres of non-mainstream music.*

Fast Forward, Disc Makers, 7905 N. Rt. 130, Pennsauken NJ 08110-1402. (800)468-9353. Web site: www.discmakers.com/music/ffwd. *Quarterly newsletter featuring companies and products for performing and recording artists in the independent music industry.*

Guitar Player, 1601 W. 23rd St., Suite 200, Lawrence KS 60046-0127. (800)289-9839. Web site: www.guitarplayer.com. *Monthly guitar magazine with transcriptions, columns, and interviews, including occasional articles on songwriting.*

Hits Magazine, 14958 Ventura Blvd., Sherman Oaks CA 91403. (818)501-7900. Web site: www.hitsmagazine.com. *Weekly music industry trade publication.*

Jazztimes, 8737 Colesville Rd., 9th Floor, Silver Spring MD 20910-3921. (301)588-4114. Web site: www.jazztimes.com. *10 issues/year magazine covering the American jazz scene.*

The Leads Sheet, Allegheny Music Works, 1611 Menoher Blvd., Johnstown PA 15905. (814)255-4007. Web site: www.alleghenymusicworks.com. *Monthly tip sheet.*

Music Business International Magazine, 460 Park Ave., S. of 9th, New York NY 10116. (212)378-0406. *Bimonthly magazine for senior executives in the music industry.*

Music Connection Magazine, 16130 Ventura Blvd., Suite 540, Encino CA 91436. (818)795-0101. E-mail: contactMC@musicconnection.com. Web site: www.musicconnection.com. *Biweekly music industry trade publication.*

Music Morsels, P.O. Box 2760, Acworth GA 30102. (678)445-0006. Fax: (678)494-9269. E-mail: SergeEnt@aol.com. Web site: www.serge.org/musicmorsels.htm. *Monthly songwriting publication.*

Music Row Magazine, 1231 17th Ave. S, Nashville TN 37212. (615)321-3617. E-mail: info@ musicrow.com. Web site: www.musicrow.com. *Biweekly Nashville industry publication.*

Offbeat Magazine, OffBeat Publications, 421 Frenchman St., Suite 200, New Orleans LA 70116. (504)944-4300. E-mail: offbeat@offbeat.com. Web site: www.offbeat.com. *Monthly magazine covering Louisiana music and artists.*

The Performing Songwriter, P.O. Box 40931, Nashville TN 37204. (800)883-7664. E-mail: order @performingsongwriter.com. Web site: www.performingsongwriter.com. *Bimonthly songwriters' magazine.*

Radio and Records, 2049 Century Park East, 41st Floor, Los Angeles CA 90067. (310)553-4330. Fax: (310)203-9763. E-mail: subscribe@radioandrecords.com. Web site: www.radio andrecords.com. *Weekly newspaper covering the radio and record industries.*

Radir, Radio Mall, 2412 Unity Ave. N., Dept. WEB, Minneapolis MN 55422. (800)759-4561. E-mail: info@bbhsoftware.com. Web site: www.bbhsoftware.com. *Quarterly radio station database on disk.*

Sing Out!, P.O. Box 5460, Bethlehem PA 18015. (888)SING-OUT. Fax: (610)865-5129. E-mail: info@singout.org. Web site: www.singout.org. *Quarterly folk music magazine.*

Songcasting, 15445 Ventura Blvd. #260, Sherman Oaks CA 91403. (818)377-4084. *Monthly tip sheet.*

Songlink International, 23 Belsize Crescent, London NW3 5QY England. Web site: www.son glink.com. *10 issues/year newsletter including details of recording artists looking for songs; contact details for industry sources; also news and features on the music business.*

Variety, 5700 Wilshire Blvd., Suite 120, Los Angeles CA 90036. (323)857-6600. Fax: (323)857-0494. Web site: www.variety.com. *Weekly entertainment trade newspaper.*

Words and Music, 41 Valleybrook Dr., Don Mills ON M3B 2S6 Canada. (416)445-8700. Web site: www.socan.ca. *Monthly songwriters' magazine.*

BOOKS & DIRECTORIES

101 Songwriting Wrongs & How to Right Them, by Pat & Pete Luboff, Writer's Digest Books, 4700 E. Galbraith Rd., Cincinnati OH 45236. (800)448-0915. Web site: www.writers digest.com.

The A&R Registry, by Ritch Esra, SRS Publishing, 7510 Sunset Blvd. #1041, Los Angeles CA 90046-3418. (800)377-7411 or (800)552-7411. E-mail: musicregistry@compuserve.com.

Attention: A&R, by Teri Muench and Susan Pomerantz, Alfred Publishing Co. Inc., P.O. Box 10003, Van Nuys CA 91410-0003. (818)892-2452. Web site: www.alfredpub.com.

The Billboard Guide to Music Publicity, revised edition, by Jim Pettigrew, Jr., Billboard Books, 1695 Oak St., Lakewood NJ 08701. (800)344-7119.

Breakin' Into Nashville, by Jennifer Ember Pierce, Madison Books, University Press of America, 4501 Forbes Rd., Suite 200, Lanham MD 20706. (800)462-6420.

CMJ Directory, 151 W. 25th St., 12th Floor, New York NY 10001. (917)606-1908. Web site: www.cmj.com.

Contracts for the Music Industry, P.O. Box 952063, Lake Mary FL 32795-2063. (407)834-8555. E-mail: info@songwriterproducts.com. Web site: www.songwriterproducts.com. *Book and computer software of a variety of music contracts.*

The Craft and Business of Songwriting, by John Braheny, Writer's Digest Books, 4700 E. Galbraith Rd., Cincinnati OH 45236. (800)448-0915. Web site: www.writersdigest.com.

The Craft of Lyric Writing, by Sheila Davis, Writer's Digest Books, 4700 E. Galbraith Rd., Cincinnati OH 45236. (800)448-0915. Web site: www.writersdigest.com.

Creating Melodies, by Dick Weissman, Writer's Digest Books, 4700 E. Galbraith Rd., Cincinnati OH 45236. (800)448-0915. Web site: www.writersdigest.com.

Directory of Independent Music Distributors, by Jason Ojalvo, Disc Makers, 7905 N. Rt. 130, Pennsauken NJ 08110. (800)468-9353. E-mail: discman@discmakers.com. Web site: www.discmakers.com.

Easy Tools for Composing, by Charles Segal, Segal's Publications, 16 Grace Rd., Newton MA 02159. (617)969-6196.

FILM/TV MUSIC GUIDE, by Ritch Esra, SRS Publishing, 7510 Sunset Blvd. #1041, Los Angeles CA 90046-3418. (800)552-7411. E-mail: musicregistry@compuserve.com or srspubl@aol.com. Web site: www.musicregistry.com.

Finding Fans & Selling CDs, by Veronique Berry and Jason Ojalvo, Disk Makers, 7905 N. Rt. 130, Pennsauken NJ 08110-1402. (800)468-9353. E-mail: discman@diskmakers.com. Web site: www.discmakers.com.

Guide to Independent Music Publicity, by Veronique Berry, Disc Makers, 7905 N. Rt. 130, Pennsauken NJ 08110-1402. (800)468-9353. E-mail: discman@discmakers.com.

Guide to Master Tape Preparation, by Dave Moyssiadis, Disk Makers, 7905 N. Rt. 130, Pennsauken NJ 08110-1402. (800)468-9353. E-mail: discman@discmakers.com.

Hollywood Creative Directory, 3000 W. Olympic Blvd. #2525, Santa Monica CA 90404. (800)815-0503. Web site: www.hcdonline.com. *Lists producers in film and TV.*

The Hollywood Reporter Blu-Book Production Directory, 5055 Wilshire Blvd., Los Angeles CA 90036. (323)525-2150. Web site: www.hollywoodreporter.com.

Hot Tips for the Home Recording Studio, by Hank Linderman, Writer's Digest Books, 4700 E. Galbraith Rd., Cincinnati OH 45236. (800)448-0915. Web site: www.writersdigest.com.

How to Get Somewhere in the Music Business from Nowhere with Nothing, by Mary Dawson, CQK Books, % CQK Music Group, 2221 Justin Rd., Suite 119-142, Flower Mound TX 75028. (972)317-2720. Fax: (972)317-4737. Web site: www.FromNowhereWithNothing.com.

How to Promote Your Music Successfully on the Internet, by David Nevue, Midnight Rain Productions, P.O. Box 21831, Eugene OR 97402. Web site: www.rainmusic.com.

How to Write Songs on Guitar: A Guitar-Playing and Songwriting Course, by Rikky Rooksby, Backbeat Books, 600 Harrison St., San Francisco CA 94107. (415)947-6615. E-mail: books@musicplayer.com. Web site: www.backbeatbooks.com.

How You Can Break Into the Music Business, by Marty Garrett, Lonesome Wind Corporation, P.O. Box 2143, Broken Arrow OK 74013-2143. (800)210-4416.

Louisiana Music Directory, OffBeat, Inc., 421 Frenchmen St., Suite 200, New Orleans LA 70116. (504)944-4300. Web site: www.offbeat.com.

Lydian Chromatic Concept of Tonal Organization, Volume One: The Art and Science of Tonal Gravity, by George Russell, Concept Publishing Company, 258 Harvard St., #296,

Brookline MA 02446-2904. E-mail: lydconcept@aol.com. Web site: www.lydianchromatic concept.com

Melody in Songwriting, by Jack Perricone, Berklee Press, 1140 Boylston St., Boston MA 02215. (617)747-2146. E-mail: info@berkleepress.com. Web site: www.berkleepress.com.

Melody: How to Write Great Tunes, by Rikky Rooksby, Backbeat Books, 600 Harrison St., San Francisco CA 94107. (415)947-6115. E-mail: books@musicplayer.com. Web site: www.backbeatbooks.com.

Music Attorney Legal & Business Affairs Registry, by Ritch Esra and Steve Trumbull, SRS Publishing, 7510 Sunset Blvd. #1041, Los Angeles CA 90046-3418. (800)552-7411. E-mail: musicregistry@compuserve.com or srspubl@aol.com.

Music Directory Canada, seventh edition, Norris-Whitney Communications Inc., 23 Hanno-ver Dr., Suite 7, St. Catherines ON L2W 1A3 Canada. (877)RING-NWC. E-mail: mail@nor.com. Web site: http://nor.com.

Music Law: How to Run Your Band's Business, by Richard Stin, Nolo Press, 950 Parker St., Berkeley CA 94710-9867. (510)549-1976. Web site: www.nolo.com.

Music, Money and Success: The Insider's Guide to the Music Industry, by Jeffrey Brabec and Todd Brabec, Schirmer Books, 1633 Broadway, New York NY 10019.

The Music Publisher Registry, by Ritch Esra, SRS Publishing, 7510 Sunset Blvd. #1041, Los Angeles CA 90046-3418. (800)552-7411. E-mail: musicregistry@compuserve.com or srspubl@aol.com.

Music Publishing: A Songwriter's Guide, revised edition, by Randy Poe, Writer's Digest Books, 4700 E. Galbraith Rd., Cincinnati OH 45236. (800)448-0915. Web site: www.writers digest.com.

The Musician's Guide to Making & Selling Your Own CDs & Cassettes, by Jana Stanfield, Writer's Digest Books, 4700 E. Galbraith Rd., Cincinnati OH 45236. (800)448-0915. Web site: www.writersdigest.com.

Musicians' Phone Book, The Los Angeles Music Industry Directory, Get Yourself Some Publishing, 28336 Simsalido Ave., Canyon Country CA 91351. (805)299-2405. E-mail: mpb@earthlink.net. Web site: www.musiciansphonebook.com.

Nashville Music Business Directory, by Mark Dreyer, NMBD Publishing, 9 Music Square S., Suite 210, Nashville TN 37203. (615)826-4141. E-mail: nmbd@nashvilleconnection.com. Web site: www.nashvilleconnection.com.

Nashville's Unwritten Rules: Inside the Business of the Country Music Machine, by Dan Daley, Overlook Press, One Overlook Dr., Woodstock NY 12498. (845)679-6838. E-mail: overlook@netstep.net.

National Directory of Independent Record Distributors, P.O. Box 452063, Lake Mary FL 32795-2063. (407)834-8555. E-mail: info@songwriterproducts.com. Web site: www.song writerproducts.com.

The Official Country Music Directory, ICMA Music Directory, P.O. Box 271238, Nashville TN 37227.

Performance Magazine Guides, 1203 Lake St., Suite 200, Fort Worth TX 76102-4504. (817)338-9444. E-mail: sales@performancemagazine.com. Web site: www.performance magazine.com.

Resources

Radio Stations of America: A National Directory, P.O. Box 452063, Lake Mary FL 32795-2063. (407)834-8555. E-mail: info@songwriterproducts.com. Web site: www.songwriterproducts.com.

The Real Deal—How to Get Signed to a Record Label from A to Z, by Daylle Deanna Schwartz, Billboard Books, 1695 Oak St., Lakewood NJ 08701. (800)344-7119.

Recording Industry Sourcebook, Music Books Plus, P.O. Box 670, 240 Portage Rd., Lewiston NY 14092. (800)265-8481. Web site: www.musicbooksplus.com.

Reharmonization Techniques, by Randy Felts, Berklee Press, 1140 Boylston St., Boston MA 02215. (617)747-2146. E-mail: info@berkleepress.com. Web site: www.berkleepress.com.

The Songwriters Idea Book, by Sheila Davis, Writer's Digest Books, 4700 E. Galbraith Rd., Cincinnati OH 45236. (800)448-0915. Web site: www.writersdigest.com.

Songwriter's Market Guide to Song & Demo Submission Formats, Writer's Digest Books, 4700 E. Galbraith Rd., Cincinnati OH 45236. (800)448-0915. Web site: www.writersdigest.com.

Songwriter's Playground—Innovative Exercises in Creative Songwriting, by Barbara L. Jordan, Creative Music Marketing, 1085 Commonwealth Ave., Suite 323, Boston MA 02215. (617)926-8766.

The Songwriter's Workshop: Harmony, by Jimmy Kachulis, Berklee Press, 1140 Boylston St., Boston MA 02215. (617)747-2146. E-mail: info@berkleepress.com. Web site: www.berkleepress.com.

The Songwriter's Workshop: Melody, by Jimmy Kachulis, Berklee Press, 1140 Boylston St., Boston MA 02215. (617)747-2146. E-mail: info@berkleepress.com. Web site: www.berkleepress.com.

Songwriting and the Creative Process, by Steve Gillette, Sing Out! Publications, P.O. Box 5640, Bethlehem PA 18015-0253. (888)SING-OUT. E-mail: singout@libertynet.org. Web site: www.singout.org/sopubs.html.

Songwriting: Essential Guide to Lyric Form and Structure, by Pat Pattison, Berklee Press, 1140 Boylston St., Boston MA 02215. (617)747-2146. E-mail: info@berkleepress.com. Web site: www.www.berkleepress.com.

Songwriting: Essential Guide to Rhyming, by Pat Pattison, Berklee Press, 1140 Boylston St., Boston MA 02215. (617)747-2146. E-mail: info@berkleepress.com. Web site: www.berkleepress.com.

The Songwriting Sourcebook: How to Turn Chords Into Great Songs, by Rikky Rooksby, Backbeat Books, 600 Harrison St., San Francisco CA 94107. (415)947-6615. E-mail: books@musicplayer.com. Web site: www.backbeatbooks.com.

The Soul of the Writer, by Susan Tucker with Linda Lee Strother, Journey Publishing, P.O. Box 92411, Nashville TN 37209. (615)952-4894. Web site: www.journeypublishing.com.

Successful Lyric Writing, by Sheila Davis, Writer's Digest Books, 4700 E. Galbraith Rd., Cincinnati OH 45236. (800)448-0915. Web site: www.writersdigest.com.

This Business of Music Marketing and Promotion, by Tad Lathrop and Jim Pettigrew, Jr., Billboard Books, Watson-Guptill Publications, 770 Broadway, New York NY 10003. E-mail: info@watsonguptill.com.

Tim Sweeney's Guide to Releasing Independent Records, by Tim Sweeney, TSA Books, 31805 Highway 79 S., Temecula CA 92592. (909)303-9506. E-mail: info@tsamusic.com. Web site: www.tsamusic.com.

Tim Sweeney's Guide to Succeeding at Music Conventions, by Tim Sweeney, TSA Books, 31805 Highway 79 S., Temecula CA 92592. (909)303-9506. Web site: www.tsamusic.com.

Texas Music Industry Directory, Texas Music Office, Office of the Governor, P.O. Box 13246, Austin TX 78711. (512)463-6666. E-mail: music@governor.state.tx.us. Web site: www.governor.state.tx.us/music.

Tunesmith: Inside the Art of Songwriting, by Jimmy Webb, Hyperion, 77 W. 66th St., 11th Floor, New York NY 10023. (800)759-0190.

Volunteer Lawyers for the Arts Guide to Copyright for Musicians and Composers, One E. 53rd St., 6th Floor, New York NY 10022. (212)319-2787.

Writing Better Lyrics, by Pat Pattison, Writer's Digest Books, 4700 E. Galbraith Rd., Cincinnati OH 45236. (800)448-0915. Web site: www.writersdigest.com.

Writing Music for Hit Songs, by Jai Josefs, Schirmer Trade Books, 257 Park Ave. S., New York NY 10010. (212)254-2100.

The Yellow Pages of Rock, The Album Network, 120 N. Victory Blvd., Burbank CA 91502. (800)222-4382. Fax: (818)955-9048. E-mail: ypinfo@yprock.com.

Web Sites of Interest

The Internet provides a wealth of information for songwriters and performers, and the number of sites devoted to music grows each day. Below is a list of some Web sites that can offer you information, links to other music sites, contact with other songwriters and places to showcase your songs. Since the online world is changing and expanding at such a rapid pace, this is hardly a comprehensive list. But it gives you a place to start on your journey through the Internet to search for opportunities to get your music heard.

About.com Musicians' Exchange: http://musicians.about.com
Site featuring headlines and articles of interest to independent musicians, as well as numerous links.

American Music Center: www.amc.net
Classical/jazz archives, includes a list of composer organizations and contacts.

American Society of Composers, Authors and Publishers (ASCAP): www.ascap.com
Database of performed works in ASCAP's repertoire. Also includes songwriter, performer and publisher information, ASCAP membership information and industry news.

American Songwriter Magazine Homepage: www.americansongwriter.com
This is the official homepage for *American Songwriter Magazine,* featuring an online article archive, e-mail newsletter, and links.

Backstage Commerce: www.backstagecommerce.com
Offers secure online ordering support to artist Web sites for a commission.

The Bandit A&R Newsletter: www.banditnewsletter.com
Offers newsletter to help musicians target demos and press kits to labels, publishers, managers and production companies actively looking for new talent.

Bandname.com: www.bandname.com
Online band name registry and archive, as well as digital storefront services and classifieds.

Bathtubmusic.com: www.bathtubmusic.com
Online distributor of independent music.

Beaird Music Group Demos: www.beairdmusicgroup.com
Nashville demo service with samples and testimonial by *6 Steps to Songwriting Success* author Jason Blume.

Berklee School of Music: www.berkleemusic.com
Offers online instruction, including a certificate program in songwriting.

Billboard.com: www.billboard.com
Music industry news and searchable online database of music companies by subscription.

The Blues Foundation: www.blues.org
Information on the foundation, its membership and events.

Jason Blume Hompage: www.jasonblume.com
This is the official homepage for *6 Steps to Songwriting Success* and *This Business of Songwriting* author Jason Blume. Offers articles and song critique services.

John Braheny Homepage: www.johnbraheny.com
John Braheny is the author of *The Craft and Business of Songwriting*, and his site features articles, interviews, and a blog with commentary on business and creative issues.

Broadcast Music, Inc. (BMI): www.bmi.com
Offers lists of song titles, songwriters and publishers of the BMI repertoire. Also includes BMI membership information, and general information on songwriting and licensing.

The Buzz Factor: www.thebuzzfactor.com
Offers press kit evaluation, press release writing, guerrilla music marketing, tips and weekly newsletter.

CDBABY: www.cdbaby.com
An online CD store dedicated solely to independent music.

CDFreedom: www.cdfreedom.com
Online CD store for independent musicians.

Center for the Promotion of Contemporary Composers (CPCC): www.under.org/cpcc
Web site for the Center for the Promotion of Contemporary Composers.

Chorus America: www.chorusamerica.org
The Web site of Chorus America, a national service organization for professional and volunteer choruses, including job listings and professional development information.

Cat Cohen's Homepage: www.catcohen.com
Homepage for singer-songwriter/producer Cat Cohen, author of *Songwriting for your Original Act* and contributor to John Braheny's *Craft & Business of Songwriting*. Offers "Anatomy of a Hit" hit song analysis columns, as well as songwriters' workshops.

Creative Musicians Coalition (CMC): www.aimcmc.com
Web site of the CMC, an international organization dedicated to the advancement of independent musicians, links to artists, and tips and techniques for musicians.

Custom Drum Tracks: www.realdrumstudio.com
Demo services by drummer/producer Pat Bautz, featuring custom drum tracks recorded and delivered online.

Dino's Demos: www.dinosdemos.com
Nashville song demo service with samples available online.

Film Music Network: www.filmmusicworld.com or www.filmmusic.net
Offers new about the fim music world, as well as educational and networking opportunities and an e-mail newsletter.

Resources

Fourfront Media and Music: www.knab.com
This site by music industry consultant Christopher Knab offers in-depth information on product development, promotion, publicity and performance.

Frank's Nashville Demos: www.nashville-songdemo.com
Nashville song demo service with sample demos available online.

Robin Frederick Homepage: www.robinfrederick.com
Official Web site for songwriting instructor Robin Frederick, offering articles and information on courses.

FromNowhereWithNothing.com: www.fromnowherewithnothing.com
Web site for Mary Dawson's new book about breaking into the music business, *How to Get Somewhere in the Music Business from Nowhere with Nothing.*

Garageband.com: www.garageband.com
Online music hosting site where bands can post music and profiles, and then be critiqued by online listeners and industry insiders.

Getsigned.com: www.getsigned.com
Interviews with industry executives, how-to business information and more.

Government Liaison Services: www.trademarkinfo.com
An intellectual property research firm. Offers a variety of trademark searches.

Guitar Nine Records: www.guitar9.com
Offers articles on songwriting, music theory, guitar techniques, etc.

Guitar Principles: www.guitarprinciples.com
Homepage for guitar teacher Jamie Andreas, offering instructional books, free newsletter, and message boards.

Harmony Central: www.harmony-central.com
Online musicians community with in-depth reviews of just about every piece of music equipment imaginable.

Harry Fox Agency: www.harryfox.com
Offers a comprehensive FAQ about licensing songs for use in recording, performance and film.

Independent Distribution Network: www.idnmusic.com/
Web site of independent bands distributing their music, with advice on everything from starting a band to finding labels.

Independent Songwriter Web Magazine: www.independentsongwriter.com
Independent music reviews, classifieds, message board and chat sessions.

Indie-Music.com: http://indie-music.com
Full of how-to articles, record label directory, radio links and venue listing.

International Songwriters Association (ISA): www.songwriter.co.uk
Homepage for *Songwriter Magazine*, offering articles and newsletter.

Jazz Composers Collective: www.jazzcollective.com
Industry information on composers, projects, recordings, concerts and events.

Jazz Corner: www.jazzcorner.com
Web site for musicians and organizations featuring links to 70 Web sites for jazz musicians and organizations, and the Speakeasy, an interactive conference area.

Resources

Just Plain Folks: www.jpfolks.com or www.justplainfolks.org
Online songwriting organization featuring messageboards, lyric feedback forums, member profiles, featured members' music, contact listings, chapter homepages, and an Internet radio station. (See the Just Plain Folks listing in the Organizations section).

Kathode Ray Music: www.kathoderaymusic.com
Specializes in marketing and promotion consultation.

Li'l Hank's Guide for Songwriters in L.A.: www.halsguide.com
Web site for songwriters with information on clubs, publishers, books, etc. as well as links to other songwriting sites.

Los Angeles Goes Underground: http://lagu.somaweb.org
Web site dedicated to underground rock bands from Los Angeles and Hollywood.

Pat & Pete Luboff Homepage: www.writesongs.com
This is the official Web site for *101 Songwriting Wrongs & How to Right Them* authors Pat & Pete Luboff. Offers information on workshops, consultation services, articles, useful links, and a collaboration agreement template for songwriters to download and use.

Lyrical Line: www.lyricalline.com
Offers places to market your songs, critique service, industry news and more.

LyricIdeas.com: www.lyricideas.com
Offers songwriting prompts, themes, and creative techniques for songwriting.

Lyricist.com: www.lyricist.com
Jeff Mallet's songwriter site offering contests, tips and job opportunities in the music industry.

MI2N (THE MUSIC INDUSTRY NEWS NETWORK): www.mi2n.com
Offers news on happenings in the music industry and career postings.

The Muse's Muse: www.musesmuse.com
Classifieds, catalog of lyric samples, songwriting articles, organizations, and chat room.

Music Books Plus: www.musicbooksplus.com
Online bookstore dedicated to music books on every imaginable music-related topic. Offers a free e-mail newsletter.

Music Publishers Association: www.mpa.org
Provides a copyright resource center, directory of member publishers and information on the organization.

Music Yellow Pages: www.musicyellowpages.com
Phone book listings of music-related businesses.

The Musicians Guide Through the Legal Jungle: www.legaljungleguide.com/resource.htm
Offers articles on copyright law, music publishing and talent agents.

MySpace.com: www.myspace.com
Social networking site featuring music Web pages for musicians and songwriters.

Nashville Songwriters Association International (NSAI): www.nashvillesongwriters.com
Official NSAI homepage offers news, links, online membership registration, and message board for members.

National Association of Composers USA (NACUSA): www.music-usa.org/nacusa
Web site of the organization dedicated to promotion and performance of new music by Americans, featuring a young composers' competition, concert schedule, job opportunities and more.

National Music Publishers Association: www.nmpa.org
The organization's online site with information about copyright, legislation and other concerns of the music publishing world.

Online Rock: www.onlinerock.com
Offers e-mail, marketing and free webpage services. Also features articles, chat rooms, links, etc.

Opera America: www.operaamerica.org
Web site of Opera America, featuring information on advocacy and awareness programs, publications, conference schedules and more.

Outersound: www.outersound.com
Information on finding a recording studio, educating yourself in the music industry, and a list of music magazines to advertise in or get reviewed by.

PerformerMag: www.performermag.com
Offers articles, music industry news, classifieds, and reviews.

***Performing Songwriter Magazine* Homepage:** www.performingsongwriter.com
This is the official homepage for *Performing Songwriter Magazine*, featuring articles and links.

Pamela Philips-Oland Homepage: www.pamoland.com
This the official site for *The Art of Writing Great Lyrics* and *The Art of Writing Love Songs* author Pamela Philips-Oland. Offers lyric critique service and a blog on various topics of interest to songwriters.

Pollack's Beatles Analysis: www.icce.rug.nl/~soundscapes/DATABASES/AWP/awp-notes_on.shtml
In their time, the Beatles rewrote the book on pop songwriting, and this Web site is a treasure trove of insights into how the Beatles' songwriting worked.

Public Domain Music: www.pdinfo.com
Articles on public domain works and copyright, including public domain song lists, research resources, tips and a FAQ.

PUMP AUDIO: www.pumpaudio.com
License music for film and TV on a non-exclusive basis.

RecordingProject.com: www.recordingproject.com
Site dedicated to recording enthusiasts, both professional and beginning/amateur. Features discussion boards and extensive articles on tracking, mixing, effects, etc.

Record-Producer.com: www.record-producer.com
Extensive site dedicated to audio engineering and record production. Offers a free newsletter, online instruction, and e-books on various aspects of record production and audio engineering.

Rhythm Net: www.rhythmnet.com
Online CD store for independent musicians.

SESAC Inc.: www.sesac.com
Includes SESAC performing rights organization information, songwriter profiles, organization news, licensing information and links to other sites.

Soma FM: www.somafm.com
Internet underground/alterative radio with nine stations broadcasting from San Francisco.

Song Shark: www.geocities.com/songshark
Web site of information on known song sharks.

Songcatalog.com: www.songcatalog.com
Online song catalog database for licensing.

SongConsultant.com: www.songconsultant.com
Song consultations by Nashville songwriter/producer/publisher Dude McLean.

Songlink: www.songlink.com
Offers opportunities to pitch songs to music publishers for specific recording projects, also industry news.

SongRamp.com: www.songramp.com
Online songwriting organization with message boards, blogs, news, and streaming music channels.

Songsalive!: www.songsalive.org
Online songwriters organization and community.

Songscope.com: www.songscope.com
Online song catalog database for pitching and licensing.

Songwriter101.com: www.songwriter101.com
Offers articles, music industry news, and message boards.

SongwriterDemo.com: www.songwriterdemo.com
Song demo studio based in Nashville.

The Songwriters Connection: www.songwritersconnection.com
Offers articles, song critiques, workshops, seminars, and one-on-one consultations with *The Secrets of Songwriting* author Sarah Tucker.

Songwriter's Guild of America (SGA): www.songwritersguild.com
Offers industry news, member services information, newsletters, contract reviews and more.

Songwriter's Resource Network: www.songwritersresourcenetwork.com
Online information and services designed especially for songwriters.

The Songwriters Studio: www.thesongwritersstudio.com
Nashville demo service operated by producer Steven Cooper.

SongwriterUniverse.com: www.songwriteruniverse.com
Features articles, interviews, song evaluations, consultations, streaming music channels, a monthly contest, message boards, and links.

The Songwriting Education Resource: www.craftofsongwriting.com
An educational site for Nashville songwriters offering discussion boards, articles, and links.

SongU.com: www.songu.com
Offers online songwriting courses, networking opportunities, e-mail newsletter, and opportunities to pitch songs to industry professionals.

Sonic Bids: www.sonicbids.com
Features an online press kit template with photos, bio, music samples, and a date calendar.

StarPolish: www.starpolish.com
Features articles and interviews on the music industry.

SummerSongs Songwriting Camps: www.summersongs.com
Offers songwriting camp information and online registration.

Tagworld.com: www.tagworld.com
Social networking site similar to MySpace where bands and singer-songwriters can post songs, build a fanbase, and network.

TAXI: www.taxi.com
Independent A&R vehicle that shops demos to A&R professionals.

United States Copyright Office: http://www.copyright.gov
The homepage for the U.S. copyright office, offering information on registering songs.

The Velvet Rope: www.velvetrope.com
Famous/infamous online music industry message board.

Weirdomusic.com: www.weirdomusic.com
Online music magazine with articles, reviews, downloads, and links to Internet radio shows.

Yahoo!: www.yahoo.com/Entertainment/Music/
Use this search engine to retrieve over 20,000 music listings.

Glossary

A cappella. Choral singing without accompaniment.

AAA form. A song form in which every verse has the same melody; often used for songs that tell a story.

AABA, ABAB. A commonly used song pattern consisting of two verses, a bridge and a verse, or a repeated pattern of verse and bridge, where the verses are musically the same.

A&R Director. Record company executive in charge of the Artists and Repertoire Department who is responsible for finding and developing new artists and matching songs with artists.

A/C. Adult contemporary music.

Advance. Money paid to the songwriter or recording artist, which is then recouped before regular royalty payment begins. Sometimes called ''up front'' money, advances are deducted from royalties.

AFIM. Association for Independent Music (formerly NAIRD). Organization for independent record companies, distributors, retailers, manufacturers, etc.

AFM. American Federation of Musicians. A union for musicians and arrangers.

AFTRA. American Federation of Television and Radio Artists. A union for performers.

AIMP. Association of Independent Music Publishers.

Airplay. The radio broadcast of a recording.

AOR. Album-Oriented Rock. A radio format that primarily plays selections from rock albums as opposed to hit singles.

Arrangement. An adaptation of a composition for a recording or performance, with consideration for the melody, harmony, instrumentation, tempo, style, etc.

ASCAP. American Society of Composers, Authors and Publishers. A performing rights society. (See the Organizations section.)

Assignment. Transfer of rights of a song from writer to publisher.

Audio Visual Index (AVI). A database containing title and production information for cue sheets which are available from a performing rights organization. Currently, BMI, ASCAP, SOCAN, PRS, APRA and SACEM contribute their cue sheet listings to the AVI.

Audiovisual. Refers to presentations that use audio backup for visual material.

Background music. Music used that creates mood and supports the spoken dialogue of a radio program or visual action of an audiovisual work. Not feature or theme music.

b&w. Black and white.

Bed. Prerecorded music used as background material in commercials. In rap music, often refers to the sampled and looped drums and music over which the rapper performs.

Black box. Theater without fixed stage or seating arrangements, capable of a variety of formations. Usually a small space, often attached to a major theater complex, used for workshops or experimental works calling for small casts and limited sets.

BMI. Broadcast Music, Inc. A performing rights society. (See the Organizations section.)

Booking agent. Person who schedules performances for entertainers.

Bootlegging. Unauthorized recording and selling of a song.

Business manager. Person who handles the financial aspects of artistic careers.

Buzz. Attention an act generates through the media and word of mouth.

b/w. Backed with. Usually refers to the B-side of a single.

C&W. Country and western.

Catalog. The collected songs of one writer, or all songs handled by one publisher.

CD. Compact Disc (see below).

CD-R. A recordable CD.

CD-ROM. Compact Disc-Read Only Memory. A computer information storage medium capable of holding enormous amounts of data. Information on a CD-ROM cannot be deleted. A computer user must have a CD-ROM drive to access a CD-ROM.

Chamber music. Any music suitable for performance in a small audience area or chamber.

Chamber orchestra. A miniature orchestra usually containing one instrument per part.

Chart. The written arrangement of a song.

Charts. The trade magazines' lists of the best-selling records.

CHR. Comtemporary Hit Radio. Top 40 pop music.

Collaboration. Two or more artists, writers, etc., working together on a single project; for instance, a playwright and a songwriter creating a musical together.

Compact disc. A small disc (about 4.7 inches in diameter) holding digitally encoded music that is read by a laser beam in a CD player.

Composers. The men and women who create musical compositions for motion pictures and other audio visual works, or the creators of classical music composition.

Co-publish. Two or more parties own publishing rights to the same song.

Copyright. The exclusive legal right giving the creator of a work the power to control the publishing, reproduction and selling of the work. Although a song is technically copyrighted at the time it is written, the best legal protection of that copyright comes through registering the copyright with the Library of Congress.

Copyright infringement. Unauthorized use of a copyrighted song or portions thereof.

Cover recording. A new version of a previously recorded song.

Crossover. A song that becomes popular in two or more musical categories (e.g., country and pop).

Cut. Any finished recording; a selection from a LP. Also to record.

DAT. Digital Audio Tape. A professional and consumer audio cassette format for recording and playing back digitally-encoded material. DAT cassettes are approximately one-third smaller than conventional audio cassettes.

DCC. Digital Compact Cassette. A consumer audio cassette format for recording and playing back digitally-encoded tape. DCC tapes are the same size as analog cassettes.

Demo. A recording of a song submitted as a demonstration of a writer's or artist's skills.

Derivative work. A work derived from another work, such as a translation, musical arrangement, sound recording, or motion picture version.

Distributor. Wholesale marketing agent responsible for getting records from manufacturers to retailers.

Donut. A jingle with singing at the beginning and end and instrumental background in the middle. Ad copy is recorded over the middle section.

E-mail. Electronic mail. Computer address where a company or individual can be reached via modem.

Engineer. A specially-trained individual who operates recording studio equipment.

Enhanced CD. General term for an audio CD that also contains multimedia computer information. It is playable in both standard CD players and CD-ROM drives.

EP. Extended play record or cassette containing more selections than a standard single, but fewer than a standard album.

EPK. Electronic press kit. Usually contains photos, sound files, bio information, reviews, tour dates, etc. posted online. Sonicbids.com is a popular EPK hosting Web site.

Final mix. The art of combining all the various sounds that take place during the recording session into a two-track stereo or mono tape. Reflects the total product and all of the energies and talents the artist, producer and engineer have put into the project.

Fly space. The area above a stage from which set pieces are lowered and raised during a performance.

Folio. A softcover collection of printed music prepared for sale.

Following. A fan base committed to going to gigs and buying albums.

Foreign rights societies. Performing rights societies other than domestic which have reciprocal agreements with ASCAP and BMI for the collection of royalties accrued by foreign radio and television airplay and other public performance of the writer members of the above groups.

Harry Fox Agency. Organization that collects mechanical royalties.

Grammy. Music industry awards presented by the National Academy of Recording Arts and Sciences.

Hip-hop. A dance oriented musical style derived from a combination of disco, rap and R&B.

Hit. A song or record that achieves top 40 status.

Hook. A memorable ''catch'' phrase or melody line that is repeated in a song.

House. Dance music created by remixing samples from other songs.

Hypertext. Words or groups of words in an electronic document that are linked to other text, such as a definition or a related document. Hypertext can also be linked to illustrations.

Indie. An independent record label, music publisher or producer.

Infringement. A violation of the exclusive rights granted by the copyright law to a copyright owner.

Internet. A worldwide network of computers that offers access to a wide variety of electronic resources.

ips. Inches per second; a speed designation for tape recording.

IRC. International reply coupon, necessary for the return of materials sent out of the country. Available at most post offices.

Jingle. Usually a short verse set to music designed as a commercial message.

Lead sheet. Written version (melody, chord symbols and lyric) of a song.

Leader. Plastic (non-recordable) tape at the beginning and between songs for ease in selection.

Libretto. The text of an opera or any long choral work. The booklet containing such text.

Listing. Block of information in this book about a specific company.

LP. Designation for long-playing record played at $33\frac{1}{3}$ rpm.

Lyric sheet. A typed or written copy of a song's lyrics.

Market. A potential song or music buyer; also a demographic division of the record-buying public.

Master. Edited and mixed tape used in the production of records; the best or original copy of a recording from which copies are made.

MD. MiniDisc. A 2.5 inch disk for recording and playing back digitally-encoded music.

Mechanical right. The right to profit from the physical reproduction of a song.

Mechanical royalty. Money earned from record, tape and CD sales.

MIDI. Musical instrument digital interface. Universal standard interface that allows musical instruments to communicate with each other and computers.

Mini Disc. (See MD above.)

Mix. To blend a multi-track recording into the desired balance of sound, usually to a 2-track stereo master.

Modem. MOdulator/DEModulator. A computer device used to send data from one computer to another via telephone line.

MOR. Middle of the road. Easy-listening popular music.

MP3. File format of a relatively small size that stores audio files on a computer. Music saved in a MP3 format can be played only with a MP3 player (which can be downloaded onto a computer).

Ms. Manuscript.

Multimedia. Computers and software capable of integrating text, sound, photographic-quality images, animation and video.

Music bed. (See **Bed** above.)

Music jobber. A wholesale distributor of printed music.

Music library. A business that purchases canned music, which can then be bought by producers of radio and TV commercials, films, videos and audiovisual productions to use however they wish.

Music publisher. A company that evaluates songs for commercial potential, finds artists to record them, finds other uses (such as TV or film) for the songs, collects income generated by the songs and protects copyrights from infringement.

Music Row. An area of Nashville, TN, encompassing Sixteenth, Seventeeth and Eighteenth avenues where most of the major publishing houses, recording studios, mastering labs, songwriters, singers, promoters, etc. practice their trade.

NARAS. National Academy of Recording Arts and Sciences.

The National Academy of Songwriters (NAS). The largest U.S. songwriters' association. (See the Organizations section.)

Needle-drop. Refers to a type of music library. A needledrop music library is a licensed library that allows producers to borrow music on a rate schedule. The price depends on how the music will be used.

Network. A group of computers electronically linked to share information and resources.

NMPA. National Music Publishers Association.

One-off. A deal between songwriter and publisher which includes only one song or project at a time. No future involvement is implicated. Many times a single song contract accompanies a one-off deal.

One-stop. A wholesale distributor of who sells small quantities of records to ''mom and pop'' record stores, retailers and jukebox operators.

Operetta. Light, humorous, satiric plot or poem, set to cheerful light music with occasional spoken dialogue.

Overdub. To record an additional part (vocal or instrumental) onto a basic multi-track recording.

Parody. A satirical imitation of a literary or musical work. Permission from the owner of the copyright is generally required before commercial exploitation of a parody.

Payola. Dishonest payment to broadcasters in exchange for airplay.

Performing rights. A specific right granted by U.S. copyright law protecting a composition from being publicly performed without the owner's permission.

Performing rights organization. An organization that collects income from the public performance of songs written by its members and then proportionally distributes this income to the individual copyright holder based on the number of performances of each song.

Personal manager. A person who represents artists to develop and enhance their careers. Personal managers may negotiate contracts, hire and dismiss other agencies and personnel relating to the artist's career, review material, help with artist promotions and perform many services.

Piracy. The unauthorized reproduction and selling of printed or recorded music.

Pitch. To attempt to solicit interest for a song by audition.

Playlist. List of songs a radio station will play.

Points. A negotiable percentage paid to producers and artists for records sold.

Producer. Person who supervises every aspect of a recording project.

Production company. Company specializing in producing jingle packages for advertising agencies. May also refer to companies specializing in audiovisual programs.

Professional manager. Member of a music publisher's staff who screens submitted material and tries to get the company's catalog of songs recorded.

Proscenium. Permanent architectural arch in a theater that separates the stage from the audience.

Public domain. Any composition with an expired, lapsed or invalid copyright, and therefore belonging to everyone.

Purchase license. Fee paid for music used from a stock music library.

Query. A letter of inquiry to an industry professional soliciting his interest.

R&B. Rhythm and blues.

Rack Jobber. Distributors who lease floor space from department stores and put in racks of albums.

Rate. The percentage of royalty as specified by contract.

Release. Any record issued by a record company.

Residuals. In advertising or television, payments to singers and musicians for use of a performance.

RIAA. Recording Industry Association of America.

Royalty. Percentage of money earned from the sale of records or use of a song.

RPM. Revolutions per minute. Refers to phonograph turntable speed.

SAE. Self-addressed envelope (with no postage attached).

SASE. Self-addressed stamped envelope.

SATB. The abbreviation for parts in choral music, meaning Soprano, Alto, Tenor and Bass.

Score. A complete arrangement of all the notes and parts of a composition (vocal or instrumental) written out on staves. A full score, or orchestral score, depicts every orchestral part on a separate staff and is used by a conductor.

Self-contained. A band or recording act that writes all their own material.

SESAC. A performing rights organization, originally the Society of European Stage Authors and Composers. (See the Organizations section.)

SFX. Sound effects.

Shop. To pitch songs to a number of companies or publishers.

Single. 45 rpm record with only one song per side. A 12" single refers to a long version of one song on a 12" disc, usually used for dance music.

Ska. Fast tempo dance music influenced primarily by reggae and punk, usually featuring horns, saxophone and bass.

SOCAN. Society of Composers, Authors and Music Publishers of Canada. A Canadian performing rights organization. (See the Organizations section.)

Solicited. Songs or materials that have been requested.

Song plugger. A songwriter representative whose main responsibility is promoting uncut songs to music publishers, record companies, artists and producers.

Song shark. Person who deals with songwriters deceptively for his own profit.

SoundScan. A company that collates the register tapes of reporting stores to track the actual number of albums sold at the retail level.

Soundtrack. The audio, including music and narration, of a film, videotape or audiovisual program.

Space stage. Open stage that features lighting and, perhaps, projected scenery.

Split publishing. To divide publishing rights between two or more publishers.

Staff songwriter. A songwriter who has an exclusive agreement with a publisher.

Statutory royalty rate. The maximum payment for mechanical rights guaranteed by law that a record company may pay the songwriter and his publisher for each record or tape sold.

Subpublishing. Certain rights granted by a U.S. publisher to a foreign publisher in exchange for promoting the U.S. catalog in his territory.

Synchronization. Technique of timing a musical soundtrack to action on film or video.

Take. Either an attempt to record a vocal or instrument part, or an acceptable recording of a performance.

Tejano. A musical form begun in the late 1970s by regional bands in south Texas, its style reflects a blended Mexican-American culture. Incorporates elements of rock, country, R&B and jazz, and often features accordion and 12-string guitar.

Thrust stage. Stage with audience on three sides and a stagehouse or wall on the fourth side.

Top 40. The first 40 songs on the pop music charts at any given time. Also refers to a style of music which emulates that heard on the current top 40.

Track. Divisions of a recording tape (e.g., 24-track tape) that can be individually recorded in the studio, then mixed into a finished master.

Trades. Publications covering the music industry.

12″ Single. A 12-inch record containing one or more remixes of a song, originally intended for dance club play.

Unsolicited. Songs or materials that were not requested and are not expected.

VHS. $\frac{1}{2}$″ videocassette format.

Vocal score. An arrangement of vocal music detailing all vocal parts, and condensing all accompanying instrumental music into one piano part.

Web site. An address on the World Wide Web that can be accessed by computer modem. It may contain text, graphics and sound.

Wing space. The offstage area surrounding the playing stage in a theater, unseen by the audience, where sets and props are hidden, actors wait for cues, and stagehands prepare to chance sets.

World music. A general music category which includes most musical forms originating outside the U.S. and Europe, including reggae and calypso. World music finds its roots primarily in the Caribbean, Latin America, Africa and the south Pacific.

World Wide Web (WWW). An Internet resource that utilizes hypertext to access information. It also supports formatted text, illustrations and sounds, depending on the user's computer capabilities.

Category
Indexes

The Category Indexes are a good place to begin searching for a markets. They break down the listings by section (music publishers, record companies, etc.) and by the type of music they are interested in. For example, if you write country songs, and are looking for a publisher to pitch them, go to the Music Publishers heading and then check the companies listed under the Country subheading. The music categories cover a wide range of variations within each genre, so be sure to read each listing thoroughly to make sure your own unique take on that genre is a good match. Some listings do not appear in these indexes because they did not cite a specific preference. Listings that were very specific, or whose music descriptions don't quite fit into these categories also do not appear. (Category listings for **Music Publishers** begin on this page, **Record Companies** on page 367, **Record Producers** on page 372 and **Managers & Booking Agents** begin on page 375.)

MUSIC PUBLISHERS
Adult Contemporary (also easy listening, middle of the road, AAA, ballads, etc.)

Alpha Music Inc. 93
AVI 39563 Music 94
Big Fish Music Publishing Group 95
Bug Music, Inc. 97
California Country Music 98
Come Alive Communications, Inc. 99
Corelli Music Group 100
Cringe Music 101
Define Something in Nothing Music 102
Emstone Music Publishing 104

First Time Music (Publishing) U.K. 105
Hammel Associates, Inc., R L 108
Happy Melody 108
Ivory Pen Entertainment 110
Kaupps & Robert Publishing Co. 111
Lilly Music Publishing 112
Many Lives Music Publishers 114
MIDI Track Publishing 116
Must Have Music 117
New Rap Jam Publishing, A 118
Pegasus Music 120
Tourmaline Music, Inc. 127
Transition Music Corporation 129
Walkerbout Music Group 130

Category Index

Alternative (also modern rock, punk, college rock, new wave, hardcore, new music, industrial, ska, indie rock, garage, etc.)

Alias John Henry Tunes 92

Alpha Music Inc. 93

Bug Music, Inc. 97

Burnsongs 97

Cornelius Companies/Gateway Entertainment, Inc., The 100

Cringe Music 101

Define Something in Nothing Music 102

Emstone Music Publishing 104

First Time Music (Publishing) U.K. 105

Many Lives Music Publishers 114

McJames Music Inc./37 Songs 116

Sandalphon Music Publishing 124

Tourmaline Music, Inc. 127

Transition Music Corporation 129

Unknown Source Music 129

Blues

Alpha Music Inc. 93

AVI 39563 Music 94

Bearsongs 94

Brandon Hills Music, LLC/Heath Brown Music/Steven Lynn Music 97

Bug Music, Inc. 97

Cringe Music 101

Cupit Music Group 101

Define Something in Nothing Music 102

Earthscream Music Publishing Co. 103

Emstone Music Publishing 104

First Time Music (Publishing) U.K. 105

Good Publishing, L.J. 107

Many Lives Music Publishers 114

Nervous Publishing 117

New Rap Jam Publishing, A 118

Sandalphon Music Publishing 124

Sound Cellar Music 126

Tower Music Group 128

Transition Music Corporation 129

Children's

Alpha Music Inc. 93

Brandon Hills Music, LLC/Heath Brown Music/Steven Lynn Music 97

Bug Music, Inc. 97

Cringe Music 101

Define Something in Nothing Music 102

Emstone Music Publishing 104

First Time Music (Publishing) U.K. 105

Many Lives Music Publishers 114

Piano Press 120

Ren Zone Music 123

Transition Music Corporation 129

Classical (also opera, chamber music, serious music, choral, etc.)

Alpha Music Inc. 93

Bug Music, Inc. 97

Cringe Music 101

Define Something in Nothing Music 102

First Time Music (Publishing) U.K. 105

Jae Music, Jana 110

Many Lives Music Publishers 114

Silver Blue Music/Oceans Blue Music 125

Transition Music Corporation 129

Rap (also hip-hop, bass, etc.)

Religious (also gospel, sacred, Christian, church, hymns, praise, inspirational, worship, etc.)

Rock (also rockabilly, AOR, rock 'n' roll, etc.)

World Music (also reggae, ethnic, calypso, international, world beat, etc.)

RECORD COMPANIES
Adult Contemporary (also easy
listening, middle of the road, AAA, ballads, etc.)

Alternative (also modern rock, punk, college rock, new wave, hardcore, new music, industrial, ska, indie rock, garage, etc.)

Blues

Children's

Classical (also opera, chamber music, serious music, choral, etc.)

Category Index

Pop (also top 40, top 100, popular, chart hits, etc.)

R&B (also soul, black, urban, etc.)

Rap (also hip-hop, bass, etc.)

Religious (also gospel, sacred, Christian, church, hymns, praise, inspirational, worship, etc.)

Rock (also rockabilly, AOR, rock 'n' roll, etc.)

World Music (also reggae, ethnic, calypso, international, world beat, etc.)

RECORD PRODUCERS
Adult Contemporary (also easy listening, middle of the road, AAA, ballads, etc.)

Alternative (also modern rock, punk, college rock, new wave, hardcore, new music, industrial, ska, indie rock, garage, etc.)

Blues

Children's

Classical (also opera, chamber music, serious music, choral, etc.)

Country (also western, C&W, bluegrass, cowboy songs, western swing, honky-tonk, etc.)

Rock (also rockabilly, AOR, rock 'n' roll, etc.)

World Music (also reggae, ethnic, calypso, international, world beat, etc.)

MANAGERS & BOOKING AGENTS
Adult Contemporary (also easy listening, middle of the road, AAA, ballads, etc.)

Alternative (also modern rock, punk, college rock, new wave, hardcore, new music, industrial, ska, indie rock, garage, etc.)

Blues

Children's

Classical (also opera, chamber music, serious music, choral, etc.)

Alert Music, Inc. 205
Class Act Productions/Management 209
Fiedler Management, B.C. 213
First Time Management 213
Jae Enterprises, Jana 216
Management Trust Ltd., The 219
Sa'Mall Management 223

Country (also western, C&W, bluegrass, cowboy songs, western swing, honky-tonk, etc.)

Air Tight Management 205
Alert Music, Inc. 205
Angelini Enterprises, Bill/ BookYourEvent.com 205
Barnard Management Services 207
Bread & Butter Productions 208
Circuit Rider Talent & Management Co. 209
Class Act Productions/Management 209
Crawfish Productions 210
De Miles Music Company, The Edward 211
Eckert Entertainment Consultants, John 212
First Time Management 213
Grover, Laura 214
International Entertainment Bureau 216
Jae Enterprises, Jana 216
Kendall West Agency 217
Knight Agency, Bob 217
Levy Management, Rick 218
Management Trust Ltd., The 219
Media Management 220

Merri-Webb Productions 220
Prime Time Entertainment 221
Sa'Mall Management 223
Sandalphon Management 223
Serge Entertainment Group 224
Silver Bow Management 224
Southeastern Attractions 225
Sphere Group One, LLC 225
T.L.C. Booking Agency 226
Umbrella Artists Management, Inc. 226
Universal Music Marketing 227
Warner Productions, Inc. 227
Wemus Entertainment 228
Winterland Entertainment Management & Publishing 228

Dance (also house, hi-NRG, disco, club, rave, techno, trip-hop, trance, etc.)

Alert Music, Inc. 205
Class Act Productions/Management 209
De Miles Music Company, The Edward 211
First Time Management 213
Kendall West Agency 217
Management Trust Ltd., The 219
Reign Music and Media, LLC 222
Sa'Mall Management 223
Southeastern Attractions 225
Tas Music Co./Dave Tasse Entertainment 226
Van Pol Management, Hans 227
Zane Management, Inc. 229

Folk (also acoustic, Celtic, etc.)

Alert Music, Inc. 205
Bread & Butter Productions 208

Openness to Submissions Index

Use this index to find companies open to your level of experience. It is recommended to use this index in conjunction with the Category Indexes found on page 359. Once you have compiled a list of companies open to your experience and music, read the information in these listings, paying close attention to the **How to Contact** subhead. (Also see A Sample Listing Decoded on page 8.)

◪ PREFERS EXPERIENCED, BUT OPEN TO BEGINNERS
Music Publishers

Record Companies

Openness Index

☑ OPEN TO PREVIOUSLY PUBLISHED/WELL-ESTABLISHED
Music Publishers
Pegasus Music 120

Record Companies
Alligator Records 138
Ariana Records 139
Arkadia Entertainment Corp. 140
Astralwerks 140
Cambria Records & Publishing 143
Cantilena Records 144
Heads Up Int., Ltd. 152
Kingston Records 156
Oglio Records 161
Robbins Entertainment LLC 166

Record Producers
Cacophony Productions 183
Final Mix Inc. 187

Managers & Booking Agents
Blue Cat Agency, The 208
DAS Communications, Ltd. 211
De Miles Music Company, The Edward 211
Levy Management, Rick 218
Management by Jaffe 219
Serge Entertainment Group 224
Van Pol Management, Hans 227

☒ DOES NOT ACCEPT UNSOLICITED MATERIAL
Music Publishers
Bixio Music Group & Associates/ IDM Music 96
BMG Music Publishing 96
Bug Music, Inc. 97
Chrysalis Music Group 99

Copperfield Music Group/Penny Annie Music/Top Brass Music/ Biddy Baby Music 99
Delev Music Company 102
Disney Music Publishing 103
EMI Music Publishing 104
Hesfree Productions & Publishing Company 108
Intoxygene Sarl 109
Maverick Music 114
McJames Music Inc./37 Songs 116
MIDI Track Publishing 116
Old Slowpoke Music 119
Perla Music 120
Rainbow Music Corp. 122
Ren Zone Music 123
SDB Music Group 124
Silver Blue Music/Oceans Blue Music 125
Sony/ATV Music Publishing 126
Universal Music Publishing 129
Warner/Chappell Music, Inc. 130

Record Companies
Angel Records 139
Arista Records 140
Atlantic Records 141
Avita Records 141
Aware Records 142
Capitol Records 144
Columbia Records 146
Cosmotone Records 147
Curb Records 148
DreamWorks Records 149
Elektra Records 149
Epic Records 149
Heart Music, Inc. 152
Interscope/Geffen/A&M Records 155
Island/Def Jam Music Group 155
Maverick Records 157

Record Producers

Managers & Booking Agents

Film & TV Index

This index lists companies who place music in motion pictures and TV shows (excluding commercials). To learn more about their film/TV experience, read the information under **Film & TV** in their listings. It is recommended to use this index in conjunction with the Openness to Submissions Index beginning on page 382.

Geographic Index

This Geographic Index will help you locate companies by state, as well as those in countries outside of the U.S. It is recommended to use this index in conjunction with the Openness to Submissions Index on page 382. Once you find the names of companies in this index you are interested in, check the listings within each section for addresses, phone numbers, contact names and submission details.

Geographic Index

CONNECTICUT
Music Publishers
Quark, Inc. 122

Record Companies
Generic Records, Inc. 151
Quark Records 163

Record Producers
Audio 911 183

Managers & Booking Agents
Air Tight Management 205

Classical Performing Arts
Connecticut Choral Artists/Concora 259

Organizations
Connecticut Songwriters Association 299

Workshops & Conferences
Independent Music Conference 321
Norfolk Chamber Music Festival 324

DISTRICT OF COLUMBIA
Record Producers
Human Factor Productions 188

Classical Performing Arts
Master Chorale of Washington 267

Contests & Awards
Fulbright Scholar Program, Council for International Exchange of Scholars 281
Mid-Atlantic Song Contest 285
Monk International Jazz Composers Competition, Thelonious 286

U.S.-Japan Creative Artists Exchange Fellowship Program 288

Organizations
Songwriters Association of Washington 312
Washington Area Music Association 316

FLORIDA
Music Publishers
Emstone Music Publishing 104
Encore Performance Publishing 105

Record Companies
Neurodisc Records, Inc. 160

Record Producers
Mac-Attack Productions 191
Sphere Group One, LLC 197

Managers & Booking Agents
Evans Productions, Scott 212
Levy Management, Rick 218
Sphere Group One, LLC 225

Play Producers & Publishers
Eldridge Publishing Co., Inc. 248

Classical Performing Arts
Piccolo Opera Company Inc. 269

Contests & Awards
IAMA (International Acoustic Music Awards) 283
U.S.A. Songwriting Competition 289

Organizations
American Society of Composers, Authors and Publishers (ASCAP) 293

INDIANA
Music Publishers
Hammel Associates, Inc., R L 108

Managers & Booking Agents
International Entertainment Bureau
216

Music Firms—Advertising, Audiovisual & Commercial
Omni Communications 237

Classical Performing Arts
Anderson Symphony Orchestra 253
Carmel Symphony Orchestra 257
Indiana University New Music
Ensemble 265

Organizations
Just Plain Folks Music Organization
303

Workshops & Conferences
New Harmony Project, The 323

IOWA
Record Producers
Heart Consort Music 187

Play Producers & Publishers
Heuer Publishing Co. 249

KENTUCKY
Classical Performing Arts
Kentucky Opera 265
Lexington Philharmonic Society 265

Contests & Awards
Y.E.S. Festival of New Plays 290

LOUISIANA
Music Publishers
EMF Productions 104

Music Firms—Advertising, Audiovisual & Commercial
Disk Productions 235

Classical Performing Arts
Acadiana Symphony Orchestra 252

Organizations
Louisiana Songwriters Association
306

Workshops & Conferences
Cutting Edge Music Business
Conference 321

MAINE
Record Producers
Stuart Audio Services 197

MARYLAND
Music Publishers
Ivory Pen Entertainment 110

Music Firms—Advertising, Audiovisual & Commercial
dbF A Media Company 234

Classical Performing Arts
Susquehanna Symphony Orchestra
273

Workshops & Conferences
Baltimore Songwriters Association
295
Folk Alliance Annual Conference
321

General Index

Songwriter's Market
Feedback

If you have a suggestion for improving *Songwriter's Market,* or would like to take part in a reader survey we conduct from time to time, please make a photocopy of this form (or cut it out of the book), fill it out, and return it to:

Songwriter's Market Feedback
4700 East Galbraith Road
Cincinnati, OH 45236
Fax: (513) 531-2686

○ **Yes!** I'm willing to fill out a short survey by mail or online to provide feedback on *Songwriter's Market* or other books on songwriting.

○ **Yes!** I have a suggestion to improve *Songwriter's Market* (attach a second sheet if more room is necessary):

_____
_____
_____
_____
_____
_____
_____
_____

Name: _____
Address: _____
City: _____ State: _____ Zip: _____
Phone: _____ Fax: _____
E-mail: _____ Web site: _____

I am a

○ songwriter
○ performing songwriter
○ musician
○ other: _____

NOTES

NOTES

NOTES

NOTES

NOTES

NOTES

NOTES

NOTES